Experimental and Quasi-Experimental Designs for Generalized Causal Inference

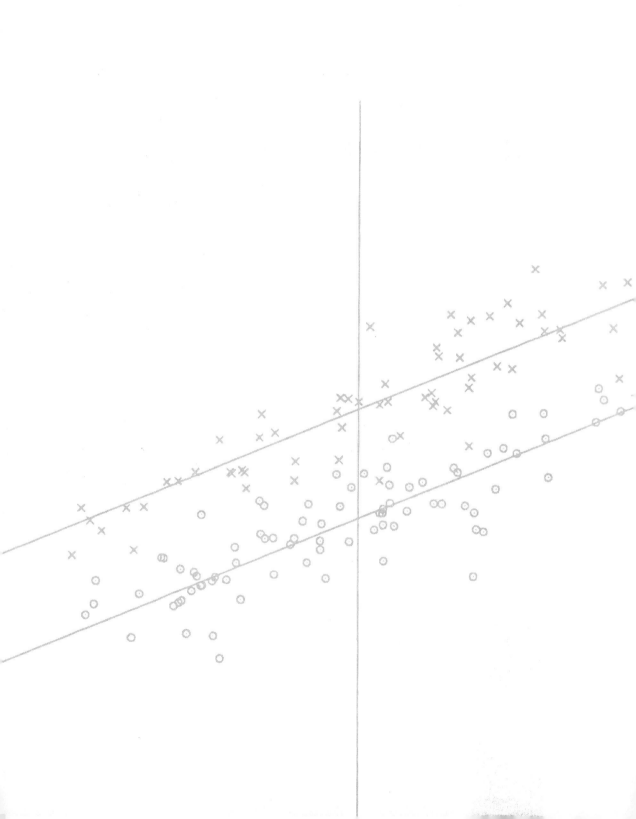

EXPERIMENTAL AND QUASI-EXPERIMENTAL DESIGNS FOR GENERALIZED CAUSAL INFERENCE

William R. Shadish
THE UNIVERSITY OF MEMPHIS

Thomas D. Cook
NORTHWESTERN UNIVERSITY

Donald T. Campbell

HOUGHTON MIFFLIN COMPANY   Boston   New York

To Donald T. Campbell and Lee J. Cronbach,
who helped us to understand science,
and to our wives, Betty, Fay, and Barbara,
who helped us to understand life.

Editor-in-Chief: *Kathi Prancan*
Senior Sponsoring Editor: *Kerry Baruth*
Associate Editor: *Sara Wise*
Associate Project Editor: *Jane Lee*
Editorial Assistant: *Martha Rogers*
Production Design Coordinator: *Lisa Jelly*
Senior Manufacturing Coordinator: *Marie Barnes*
Executive Marketing Manager: *Ros Kane*
Marketing Associate: *Caroline Guy*

Printed in Canada

Library of Congress Catalog Card Number: 2001131551

ISBN: 0-395-61556-9

23456789-BBS-05 04 03 02

Contents

Preface

THIS IS a book for those who have already decided that identifying a dependable relationship between a cause and its effects is a high priority and who wish to consider experimental methods for doing so. Such causal relationships are of great importance in human affairs. The rewards associated with being correct in identifying causal relationships can be high, and the costs of misidentification can be tremendous. To know whether increased schooling pays off in later life happiness or in increased lifetime earnings is a boon to individuals facing the decision about whether to spend more time in school, and it also helps policymakers determine how much financial support to give educational institutions. In health, from the earliest years of human existence, causation has helped to identify which strategies are effective in dealing with disease. In pharmacology, divinations and reflections on experience in the remote past sometimes led to the development of many useful treatments, but other judgments about effective plants and ways of placating gods were certainly more incorrect than correct and presumably contributed to many unnecessary deaths. The utility of finding such causal connections is so widely understood that much effort goes to locating them in both human affairs in general and in science in particular.

However, history also teaches us that it is rare for those causes to be so universally true that they hold under all conditions with all types of people and at all historical time periods. All causal statements are inevitably contingent. Thus, although threat from an out-group often causes in-group cohesion, this is not always the case. For instance, in 1492 the king of Granada had to watch as his Moorish subjects left the city to go to their ancestral homes in North Africa, being unwilling to fight against the numerically superior troops of the Catholic kings of Spain who were lodged in Santa Fe de la Frontera nearby. Here, the external threat from the out-group of Christian Spaniards led not to increased social cohesion among the Moslem Spaniards but rather to the latter's disintegration as a defensive force. Still, some causal hypotheses are more contingent than others. It is of obvious utility to learn as much as one can about those contingencies and to identify those relationships that hold more consistently. For instance, aspirin is such a wonderful drug because it reduces the symptoms associated with many different kinds of illness, including head colds, colon cancer, and cardiovascular disease; it works whether taken at low or high altitudes, in warm or cold climes, in capsule or liquid form, by children or adults; and it is effective in people who suffer from many types of secondary infirmity other than stomach ulcers. However, other drugs are more limited in their range of application, able to alleviate only one type of cancer, say, and then only in patients with a certain degree of physical strength, only when the dose is strictly adhered to, or only if antibodies have not already developed to counteract the drug. Although the lay use of causal language is often general, it is important to identify the most important conditions that limit the applicability of causal connections.

This book has two major purposes that parallel this dual interest in identifying causal connections and in understanding their generality. The first is to describe ways in which testing causal propositions can be improved in specific research projects. To achieve this we prefer to use what we call structural design features from the theory of experimentation rather than to use statistical modeling procedures. Recent statistical developments concerning causal inference in observational data (e.g., Holland, 1986; Rosenbaum, 1995a; Rubin, 1986) have advanced understanding enormously. However, to judge from our experience in consulting to field experiments, those developments may have also created an unrealistic expectation among some readers that new statistics, such as propensity score matching or stratification, selection bias models, and hidden bias sensitivity analyses, can by themselves suffice to warrant valid causal inference. Although such adjustments are sometimes necessary and frequently useful *after* good experimental design features are in place, they may work poorly without such features. Too few economists and statisticians who are associated with these new developments have emphasized the importance of such design features—though we are pleased to see more recent emphasis on these design features in, for example, Heckman, Ichimura, and Todd (1997) on the use of common measurement frameworks and local controls, Winship and Morgan (1999) on the usefulness of multiple pretests and posttests, and Rosenbaum (1999b) on the importance of many design choices in observational data. We want this book to complement such statistical work by emphasizing that, in the interplay between design and statistics, design rules (Shadish & Cook, 1999)!

The second purpose of this book is to describe ways to improve generalizations about causal propositions. Although formal sampling procedures are the best warranted means of generalizing, they rarely apply to generalizing about causal relationships. So we turn instead to improving causal generalization through a grounded theory of causal generalization. This theory reflects the principles that scientists use in their daily work to make generalizations in such diverse areas as animal modeling of human disease, deciding if a specimen belongs to a more general category, identifying general trends in literature reviews, and deciding whether epidemiological studies support a general connection between secondhand smoke and cancer. The result is, we hope, a more practical theory of causal generalization than sampling theory but one that incorporates sampling theory as a special case.

In these dual purposes, this book is a successor to Campbell and Stanley (1963) and Cook and Campbell (1979). However, it differs from them in several important ways. The most obvious is the emphasis now placed on the generalization of causal connections. Though this past work clearly acknowledged the importance of such generalization and even coined the phrase "external validity" to refer to it, much more emphasis was placed on examining the plausibility of conclusions about whether a particular relationship was likely to be causal in the unique research context in which it was tested. In this book, methods for studying external validity now receive the extensive attention that our past work gave to internal validity.

A second difference is that we have had to grapple with recent philosophy of science that questions some of the most important pillars on which our received scientific logic stands, especially as concerns the possibility of objectivity and the fallibility of both induction *and* deduction as ways of acquiring certain knowledge. Also relevant are the implications of many descriptive findings from meta-science (the systematic study of the history, sociology, psychology, and philosophy of science) that illustrate the high frequency with which scientific practice deviates from the preferred scientific logic of the day. Science is conducted by humans and is validated by a collectivity of scientists who have cognitive and economic interests to define, defend, and promote. So even more than its predecessors, this book assumes panfallibility, the total and inevitable absence of certain knowledge from the methods social scientists use. But we do not throw in the towel because of this belief, nor do we counsel that "anything goes." The fallible nature of knowledge need not entail either worthlessness (i.e., if it's not perfect, it's worthless) or strong methodological relativism (that no method ever has any privileged status over any other for any purpose). Rather, we defend the beliefs that some causal statements are better warranted than others and that logic and craft experience in science indicate that some practices are often (but not always) superior to others *for causal purposes*, though not necessarily for other purposes.

A third difference concerns the emphasis placed on design elements rather than on designs, especially when considering experimental studies without random assignment to treatment conditions. The scientific practice most often associated with causal research is the experiment, which in all its many forms is the main focus of this book. Today, experimentation refers to a systematic study designed to examine the consequences of deliberately varying a potential causal agent. Experiments require (1) variation in the treatment, (2) posttreatment measures of outcomes, (3) at least one unit on which observation is made, and (4) a mechanism for inferring what the outcome would have been without treatment—the so-called "counterfactual inference" against which we infer that the treatment produced an effect that otherwise would not have occurred. We shall see that there are many other structural features of experimentation, most of which serve the purpose of improving the quality of this counterfactual inference. But as popular as experiments are in the natural sciences, mathematical statistics, medicine, psychology, education, and labor economics, they are not the only form of research that claims to justify causal conclusions. Many correlational studies in sociology, political science, developmental science, and certain branches of economics rely on causal ideas for theory development but do not knowingly use the structures or the formal language of experimentation. Yet we contend that all nonexperimental methods can be analyzed for the structural design elements that are or are not present in them, clarifying the likely strengths and weaknesses they have for inferring cause. In describing the structural elements that characterize experimentation and in showing how they can be combined to create experimental designs that have not been used before, we claim a general utility for thinking in terms of structural design elements rather than in terms of a finite series of designs. Such designs were the centerpiece of the predecessors to this book (Campbell & Stanley, 1963; Cook & Campbell, 1979). By focusing on design elements instead, we hope to help readers acquire a set of tools that is flexible enough so that some of them will be relevant for improving causal claims in almost any research context.

A fourth difference is that this book, unlike Cook and Campbell (1979), does not deal so much with the statistical analysis of data. Rather than full chapters of statistical detail, we present brief paragraphs or occasional chapter appendices about data analysis, couched more at a conceptual level, with infrequent equations, often placed in footnotes—just enough, we hope, to clarify some of the essential issues and to refer the reader to more detailed sources. In part, the reason for this change is practical. Twenty years ago, accessible descriptions of statistical procedures for such methods as time series or nonequivalent control group designs were so rare that extended treatment was warranted. Today, however, statistical treatments of these matters are widespread at an array of technical levels, so our space is better devoted to developments concerning design and generalization. However, our reduced attention to statistics also reflects our preference for design solutions over statistical solutions for causal inference, for all the reasons previously cited.

A fifth difference is that this book includes extended treatment of randomized experiments, with three chapters devoted to their logic and design and to practical problems and solutions in their implementation. Especially in the latter area, the past few decades have seen many new developments addressing a host of problems such as poor treatment implementation, preventing and analyzing attrition, ensuring the integrity of the assignment process, and conducting experiments that better address certain ethical and legal matters. These developments promise to improve the practicality of randomized experiments. As an added benefit, many of them will improve nonrandomized experiments as well.

A sixth difference is that this book introduces some emendations to the general conceptual scheme that has always been the central hallmark of Campbell's work over the years, the validity typology. The changes are minor in most respects, for we still retain the overall emphasis on four validity types (internal, statistical conclusion, construct, and external) and on the centrality of identifying plausible threats to validity in practical causal inference. But we have changed the scheme in a number of ways. For example, with statistical conclusion validity, we have tried to display a greater sensitivity to the magnitude of an effect than to its statistical significance. Our thinking on generalization (both external and construct validity) now reflects the influence of Cronbach's (e.g., 1982) cogent writings on the problems of causal generalization. And we have made minor changes to lists of threats to validity. Although many of these changes may be of interest only to fellow theorists of experimental methodology, we hope that some of them (for example, the increased emphasis on magnitude of effects) will have an impact on the practice of experimentation as well.

Despite these changes, this book retains an overall emphasis on field experimentation, on human behavior in nonlaboratory settings (although much of the book will apply to laboratory experiments). In such settings as schools, businesses, clinics, hospitals, welfare agencies, and homes, researchers have far from perfect control, are typically guests and not royalty, have to negotiate and not command, and often must compromise rather than get everything they would like. Some compromises cause more worry than others. In particular, field experimenters are reluctant to give up all control over the measurement, selection, and treatment scheduling process and, especially, over treatment assignment, for causal inference is most difficult when individuals completely self-select themselves into groups that vary in treatment exposure. However, it is clear that such control is usually a subject for negotiation rather than unilateral decision.

As with all books, the authors owe debts to many people who have helped to shape its ideas. Colleagues who gave us raw data with which to create graphs and figures include Xavier Ballart (Figure 6.4), Dick Berk (7.5), Robert Gebotys (6.2), Janet Hankin (6.3), Lynn McClannahan (6.14), Dick McCleary (6.1, 6.10), Jack McKillip (6.13), Steve Mellor (7.3), Mel Mark (7.3), and Clara Riba (6.4). Others helped us by reading and criticizing parts or all of the book, by providing examples to use in it, or by stimulating us to think more about key problems, including Mary Battle, Joseph Cappelleri, Laura Dreuth, Peter Grant (and his students), John Hetherington, Paul Holland, Karen Kirkhart, Dan Lewis, Ken Lichstein, Sue Marcus, Mel Mark, Dick McCleary, Jack McKillip, David Murray, Jennifer Owens, Dave Rindskopf, Virgil Sheets, William Trochim, Alan Vaux, Steve West (and his students), and Chris Winship. We single out Laura Leviton, Scott Maxwell, and Chip Reichardt for providing exceptionally detailed and helpful reviews. However, because the book has been in the writing for a decade, memory for these contributions and influences undoubtedly fails us, and so we apologize to all those whose names we have inadvertently omitted.

We acknowledge several organizations for their support of the research and preparation of this book. William Shadish's contribution was partially supported by a sabbatical award from the Institute for Policy Research at Northwestern University, by a Supplemental Sabbatical Award from the James McKeen Cattell Foundation, by a Professional Development Assignment Award from the University of Memphis, and by both the Center for Applied Psychological Research and the psychology department at the University of Memphis. Thomas Cook's contribution was partially funded by fellowships from the Institute for Advanced Study in the Behavioral Sciences at Stanford University and from the Max Planck Institute for Human Development in Berlin.

Finally, we want to acknowledge the contributions of the third author of this book, Donald Thomas Campbell, who passed away in May 1996 when this book was only half done. Acknowledging those contributions is no easy task. Clearly, they go far beyond the particular writing he did for this book, given how profoundly and broadly his ideas influenced both his colleagues and his students. He was the founder of the entire tradition of field experimentation and quasi-experimentation represented in this book, a tradition that is so closely associated with him that we and others often call it Campbellian. Many of the most important concepts in this book, such as internal and external validity, threats to validity and their logic, and quasi-experimentation, were originated and developed by him. Many others of his ideas—about the fallibility of knowledge constructions ("We are cousins to the amoeba, and have received no direct revelations not shared with it. How then, indeed, could we know for certain?"), about the fitful and haphazard nature of scientific progress ("The fish-scale model of collective omniscience"), and about the social nature of the scientific enterprise ("A tribal model of the social system vehicle carrying scientific knowledge")—are so much a part of our thinking that they appear implicitly throughout the book. Our debt to Campbell, both as his colleagues and as his students, is undoubtedly greater than we recognize.

Campbell (e.g., 1988) was fond of a metaphor often used by the philosopher and mathematician W. V. Quine, that scientists are like sailors who must repair a rotting ship at sea. They trust the great bulk of timbers while they replace a particularly weak plank. Each of the timbers that they now trust they may, in its turn, replace. The proportion of the planks they are replacing to those they treat as sound must always be small. Campbell used this metaphor to illustrate the pervasive role of trust in science, and the lack of truly firm foundations in science. In the spirit of this metaphor, then, the following four lines from Seamus Heaney's (1991) poem "The Settle Bed" are an apt summary not only of Campbell's love of Quine's metaphor, but also of Campbell's own contribution to one of the ships of science:

> And now this is 'an inheritance'—
> Upright, rudimentary, unshiftably planked
> In the long ago, yet willable forward
> Again and again and again.[1]

Alternatively, for those readers whose preferences are more folksy, we close with words that Woody Guthrie wrote in the song *Another Man's Done Gone*, written as he anticipated his own death: "I don't know, I may go down or up or anywhere,

---

[1]Excerpt from "The Settle Bed," from *Opened Ground: Selected Poems 1966–1998* by Seamus Heaney. Copyright © 1998 by Seamus Heaney. Reprinted by permission of Farrar, Straus and Giroux, LLC.

but I feel like this scribbling might stay." We hope this book helps keep Don's seminal contributions to field experimentation alive for generations to come.

William R. Shadish
Memphis, Tennessee

Thomas D. Cook
Evanston, Illinois

Experimental and Quasi-Experimental Designs for Generalized Causal Inference

1

Experiments and Generalized Causal Inference

TO MANY historians and philosophers, the increased emphasis on experimentation in the 16th and 17th centuries marked the emergence of modern science from its roots in natural philosophy (Hacking, 1983). Drake (1981) cites Galileo's 1612 treatise *Bodies That Stay Atop Water, or Move in It* as ushering in modern experimental science, but earlier claims can be made favoring William Gilbert's 1600 study *On the Loadstone and Magnetic Bodies,* Leonardo da Vinci's (1452–1519) many investigations, and perhaps even the 5th-century B.C. philosopher Empedocles, who used various empirical demonstrations to argue against Parmenides (Jones, 1969a, 1969b). In the everyday sense of the term, humans have been experimenting with different ways of doing things from the earliest moments of their history. Such experimenting is as natural a part of our life as trying a new recipe or a different way of starting campfires.

However, the scientific revolution of the 17th century departed in three ways from the common use of observation in natural philosophy at that time. First, it increasingly used observation to correct errors in theory. Throughout history, natural philosophers often used observation *in* their theories, usually to win philosophical arguments by finding observations that supported their theories. However, they still subordinated the use of observation to the practice of deriving theories from "first principles," starting points that humans know to be true by our nature or by divine revelation (e.g., the assumed properties of the four basic elements of fire, water, earth, and air in Aristotelian natural philosophy). According to some accounts, this subordination of evidence to theory degenerated in the 17th century: "The Aristotelian principle of appealing to experience had degenerated among philosophers into dependence on reasoning supported by casual examples and the refutation of opponents by pointing to apparent exceptions not carefully examined" (Drake, 1981, p. xxi). When some 17th-century scholars then began to use observation to *correct* apparent errors in theoretical and religious first principles, they came into conflict with religious or philosophical authorities, as in the case of the Inquisition's demands that Galileo recant his account of the earth revolving around the sun. Given such hazards, the fact that the new experimental science tipped the balance toward observation and away from dogma is remarkable. By the time Galileo died, the role of systematic observation was firmly entrenched as a central feature of science, and it has remained so ever since (Harré, 1981).

Second, before the 17th century, appeals to experience were usually based on passive observation of ongoing systems rather than on observation of what happens after a system is deliberately changed. After the scientific revolution in the 17th century, the word **experiment** (terms in **boldface** in this book are defined in the Glossary) came to connote taking a deliberate action followed by systematic observation of what occurred afterward. As Hacking (1983) noted of Francis Bacon: "He taught that not only must we observe nature in the raw, but that we must also 'twist the lion's tale', that is, manipulate our world in order to learn its secrets" (p. 149). Although passive observation reveals much about the world, active manipulation is required to discover some of the world's regularities and possibilities (Greenwood, 1989). As a mundane example, stainless steel does not occur naturally; humans must manipulate it into existence. Experimental science came to be concerned with observing the effects of such manipulations.

Third, early experimenters realized the desirability of controlling extraneous influences that might limit or bias observation. So telescopes were carried to higher points at which the air was clearer, the glass for microscopes was ground ever more accurately, and scientists constructed laboratories in which it was possible to use walls to keep out potentially biasing ether waves and to use (eventually sterilized) test tubes to keep out dust or bacteria. At first, these controls were developed for astronomy, chemistry, and physics, the natural sciences in which interest in science first bloomed. But when scientists started to use experiments in areas such as public health or education, in which extraneous influences are harder to control (e.g., Lind, 1753), they found that the controls used in natural science in the laboratory worked poorly in these new applications. So they developed new methods of dealing with extraneous influence, such as **random assignment** (Fisher, 1925) or adding a nonrandomized **control group** (Coover & Angell, 1907). As theoretical and observational experience accumulated across these settings and topics, more sources of **bias** were identified and more methods were developed to cope with them (Dehue, 2000).

Today, the key feature common to all experiments is still to deliberately vary something so as to discover what happens to something else later—to discover the effects of presumed causes. As laypersons we do this, for example, to assess what happens to our blood pressure if we exercise more, to our weight if we diet less, or to our behavior if we read a self-help book. However, *scientific* experimentation has developed increasingly specialized substance, language, and tools, including the practice of field experimentation in the social sciences that is the primary focus of this book. This chapter begins to explore these matters by (1) discussing the nature of causation that experiments test, (2) explaining the specialized terminology (e.g., randomized experiments, quasi-experiments) that describes social experiments, (3) introducing the problem of how to generalize causal connections from individual experiments, and (4) briefly situating the experiment within a larger literature on the nature of science.

EXPERIMENTS AND CAUSATION

A sensible discussion of experiments requires both a vocabulary for talking about causation and an understanding of key concepts that underlie that vocabulary.

Defining Cause, Effect, and Causal Relationships

Most people intuitively recognize causal relationships in their daily lives. For instance, you may say that another automobile's hitting yours was a **cause** of the damage to your car; that the number of hours you spent studying was a cause of your test grades; or that the amount of food a friend eats was a cause of his weight. You may even point to more complicated causal relationships, noting that a low test grade was demoralizing, which reduced subsequent studying, which caused even lower grades. Here the same variable (low grade) can be both a cause and an effect, and there can be a **reciprocal relationship** between two variables (low grades and not studying) that cause each other.

Despite this intuitive familiarity with causal relationships, a precise definition of cause and effect has eluded philosophers for centuries.[1] Indeed, the definitions

---

1. Our analysis reflects the use of the word *causation* in ordinary language, not the more detailed discussions of cause by philosophers. Readers interested in such detail may consult a host of works that we reference in this chapter, including Cook and Campbell (1979).

of terms such as *cause* and *effect* depend partly on each other and on the causal relationship in which both are embedded. So the 17th-century philosopher John Locke said: "That which produces any simple or complex idea, we denote by the general name *cause,* and that which is produced, *effect*" (1975, p. 324) and also: "A *cause* is that which makes any other thing, either simple *idea,* substance, or mode, begin to be; and an *effect* is that, which had its beginning from some other thing" (p. 325). Since then, other philosophers and scientists have given us useful definitions of the three key ideas—cause, effect, and causal relationship—that are more specific and that better illuminate how experiments work. We would not defend any of these as the true or correct definition, given that the latter has eluded philosophers for millennia; but we do claim that these ideas help to clarify the scientific practice of probing causes.

Cause

Consider the cause of a forest fire. We know that fires start in different ways—a match tossed from a car, a lightning strike, or a smoldering campfire, for example. None of these causes is necessary because a forest fire can start even when, say, a match is not present. Also, none of them is sufficient to start the fire. After all, a match must stay "hot" long enough to start combustion; it must contact combustible material such as dry leaves; there must be oxygen for combustion to occur; and the weather must be dry enough so that the leaves are dry and the match is not doused by rain. So the match is part of a constellation of conditions without which a fire will not result, although some of these conditions can be usually taken for granted, such as the availability of oxygen. A lighted match is, therefore, what Mackie (1974) called an **inus condition**—"an *insufficient* but *nonredundant* part of an *unnecessary* but *sufficient* condition" (p. 62; italics in original). It is insufficient because a match cannot start a fire without the other conditions. It is nonredundant only if it adds something fire-promoting that is uniquely different from what the other factors in the constellation (e.g., oxygen, dry leaves) contribute to starting a fire; after all, it would be harder to say whether the match caused the fire if someone else simultaneously tried starting it with a cigarette lighter. It is part of a sufficient condition to start a fire in combination with the full constellation of factors. But that condition is not necessary because there are other sets of conditions that can also start fires.

A research example of an inus condition concerns a new potential treatment for cancer. In the late 1990s, a team of researchers in Boston headed by Dr. Judah Folkman reported that a new drug called Endostatin shrank tumors by limiting their blood supply (Folkman, 1996). Other respected researchers could not replicate the effect even when using drugs shipped to them from Folkman's lab. Scientists eventually replicated the results after they had traveled to Folkman's lab to learn how to properly manufacture, transport, store, and handle the drug and how to inject it in the right location at the right depth and angle. One observer labeled these contingencies the "in-our-hands" phenomenon, meaning "even we don't know which details are important, so it might take you some time to work it out" (Rowe, 1999, p. 732). Endostatin was an inus condition. It was insufficient cause by itself, and its effectiveness required it to be embedded in a larger set of conditions that were not even fully understood by the original investigators.

Most causes are more accurately called inus conditions. Many factors are usually required for an effect to occur, but we rarely know all of them and how they relate to each other. This is one reason that the causal relationships we discuss in this book are not deterministic but only increase the probability that an effect will occur (Eells, 1991; Holland, 1994). It also explains why a given causal relationship will occur under some conditions but not universally across time, space, human populations, or other kinds of treatments and outcomes that are more or less related to those studied. To different degrees, all causal relationships are context dependent, so the generalization of experimental effects is always at issue. That is why we return to such generalizations throughout this book.

Effect

We can better understand what an effect is through a **counterfactual** model that goes back at least to the 18th-century philosopher David Hume (Lewis, 1973, p. 556). A counterfactual is something that is contrary to fact. In an experiment, we observe what *did happen* when people received a treatment. The counterfactual is knowledge of what *would have happened* to those same people if they simultaneously had not received treatment. An **effect** is the difference between what did happen and what would have happened.

We cannot actually observe a counterfactual. Consider phenylketonuria (PKU), a genetically-based metabolic disease that causes mental retardation unless treated during the first few weeks of life. PKU is the absence of an enzyme that would otherwise prevent a buildup of phenylalanine, a substance toxic to the nervous system. When a restricted phenylalanine diet is begun early and maintained, retardation is prevented. In this example, the cause could be thought of as the underlying genetic defect, as the enzymatic disorder, or as the diet. Each implies a different counterfactual. For example, if we say that a restricted phenylalanine diet caused a decrease in PKU-based mental retardation in infants who are phenylketonuric at birth, the counterfactual is whatever would have happened had these same infants not received a restricted phenylalanine diet. The same logic applies to the genetic or enzymatic version of the cause. But it is impossible for these very same infants *simultaneously* to both have and not have the diet, the genetic disorder, or the enzyme deficiency.

So a central task for all cause-probing research is to create reasonable approximations to this physically impossible counterfactual. For instance, if it were ethical to do so, we might contrast phenylketonuric infants who were given the diet with other phenylketonuric infants who were not given the diet but who were similar in many ways to those who were (e.g., similar race, gender, age, socioeconomic status, health status). Or we might (if it were ethical) contrast infants who were not on the diet for the first 3 months of their lives with those same infants after they were put on the diet starting in the 4th month. Neither of these approximations is a true counterfactual. In the first case, the individual infants in the treatment condition are different from those in the comparison condition; in the second case, the identities are the same, but time has passed and many changes other than the treatment have occurred to the infants (including permanent damage done by phenylalanine during the first 3 months of life). So two central tasks in experimental design are creating a high-quality but necessarily imperfect source of counterfactual inference and understanding how this source differs from the treatment condition.

This counterfactual reasoning is fundamentally qualitative because causal inference, even in experiments, is fundamentally qualitative (Campbell, 1975; Shadish, 1995a; Shadish & Cook, 1999). However, some of these points have been formalized by statisticians into a special case that is sometimes called Rubin's Causal Model (Holland, 1986; Rubin, 1974, 1977, 1978, 1986). This book is not about statistics, so we do not describe that model in detail (West, Biesanz, & Pitts [2000] do so and relate it to the Campbell tradition). A primary emphasis of Rubin's model is the analysis of cause in experiments, and its basic premises are consistent with those of this book.[2] Rubin's model has also been widely used to analyze causal inference in **case-control studies** in public health and medicine (Holland & Rubin, 1988), in path analysis in sociology (Holland, 1986), and in a paradox that Lord (1967) introduced into psychology (Holland & Rubin, 1983); and it has generated many statistical innovations that we cover later in this book. It is new enough that critiques of it are just now beginning to appear (e.g., Dawid, 2000; Pearl, 2000). What is clear, however, is that Rubin's is a very general model with obvious and subtle implications. Both it and the critiques of it are required material for advanced students and scholars of cause-probing methods.

Causal Relationship

How do we know if cause and effect are related? In a classic analysis formalized by the 19th-century philosopher John Stuart Mill, a causal relationship exists if (1) the cause preceded the effect, (2) the cause was related to the effect, and (3) we can find no plausible alternative explanation for the effect other than the cause. These three characteristics mirror what happens in experiments in which (1) we manipulate the presumed cause and observe an outcome afterward; (2) we see whether variation in the cause is related to variation in the effect; and (3) we use various methods during the experiment to reduce the plausibility of other explanations for the effect, along with ancillary methods to explore the plausibility of those we cannot rule out (most of this book is about methods for doing this).

---

2. However, Rubin's model is not intended to say much about the matters of causal generalization that we address in this book.

Hence experiments are well-suited to studying causal relationships. No other scientific method regularly matches the characteristics of causal relationships so well. Mill's analysis also points to the weakness of other methods. In many correlational studies, for example, it is impossible to know which of two variables came first, so defending a causal relationship between them is precarious. Understanding this **logic of causal relationships** and how its key terms, such as cause and effect, are defined helps researchers to critique cause-probing studies.

Causation, Correlation, and Confounds

A well-known maxim in research is: *Correlation does not prove causation.* This is so because we may not know which variable came first nor whether alternative explanations for the presumed effect exist. For example, suppose income and education are correlated. Do you have to have a high income before you can afford to pay for education, or do you first have to get a good education before you can get a better paying job? Each possibility may be true, and so both need investigation. But until those investigations are completed and evaluated by the scholarly community, a simple **correlation** does not indicate which variable came first. Correlations also do little to rule out alternative explanations for a relationship between two variables such as education and income. That relationship may not be causal at all but rather due to a third variable (often called a **confound**), such as intelligence or family socioeconomic status, that causes both high education and high income. For example, if high intelligence causes success in education and on the job, then intelligent people would have correlated education and incomes, not because education causes income (or vice versa) but because both would be caused by intelligence. Thus a central task in the study of experiments is identifying the different kinds of confounds that can operate in a particular research area and understanding the strengths and weaknesses associated with various ways of dealing with them.

Manipulable and Nonmanipulable Causes

In the intuitive understanding of experimentation that most people have, it makes sense to say, "Let's see what happens if we require welfare recipients to work"; but it makes no sense to say, "Let's see what happens if I change this adult male into a three-year-old girl." And so it is also in scientific experiments. Experiments explore the effects of things that can be *manipulated,* such as the dose of a medicine, the amount of a welfare check, the kind or amount of psychotherapy, or the number of children in a classroom. Nonmanipulable events (e.g., the explosion of a supernova) or attributes (e.g., people's ages, their raw genetic material, or their biological sex) cannot be causes in experiments because we cannot deliberately vary them to see what then happens. Consequently, most scientists and philosophers agree that it is much harder to discover the effects of nonmanipulable causes.

To be clear, we are not arguing that *all* causes must be manipulable—only that *experimental* causes must be so. Many variables that we correctly think of as causes are not directly manipulable. Thus it is well established that a genetic defect causes PKU even though that defect is not directly manipulable. We can investigate such causes indirectly in nonexperimental studies or even in experiments by manipulating biological processes that prevent the gene from exerting its influence, as through the use of diet to inhibit the gene's biological consequences. Both the nonmanipulable gene and the manipulable diet can be viewed as causes—both covary with PKU-based retardation, both precede the retardation, and it is possible to explore other explanations for the gene's and the diet's effects on cognitive functioning. However, investigating the manipulable diet as a cause has two important advantages over considering the nonmanipulable genetic problem as a cause. First, only the diet provides a direct action to solve the problem; and second, we will see that studying manipulable agents allows a higher quality source of counterfactual inference through such methods as random assignment. When individuals with the nonmanipulable genetic problem are compared with persons without it, the latter are likely to be different from the former in many ways other than the genetic defect. So the counterfactual inference about what would have happened to those with the PKU genetic defect is much more difficult to make.

Nonetheless, nonmanipulable causes should be studied using whatever means are available and seem useful. This is true because such causes eventually help us to find manipulable agents that can then be used to ameliorate the problem at hand. The PKU example illustrates this. Medical researchers did not discover how to treat PKU effectively by first trying different diets with retarded children. They first discovered the nonmanipulable biological features of retarded children affected with PKU, finding abnormally high levels of phenylalanine and its associated metabolic and genetic problems in those children. Those findings pointed in certain ameliorative directions and away from others, leading scientists to experiment with treatments they thought might be effective and practical. Thus the new diet resulted from a sequence of studies with different immediate purposes, with different forms, and with varying degrees of uncertainty reduction. Some were experimental, but others were not.

Further, **analogue experiments** can sometimes be done on nonmanipulable causes, that is, experiments that manipulate an agent that is similar to the cause of interest. Thus we cannot change a person's race, but we can chemically induce skin pigmentation changes in volunteer individuals—though such analogues do not match the reality of being Black every day and everywhere for an entire life. Similarly, past events, which are normally nonmanipulable, sometimes constitute a **natural experiment** that may even have been randomized, as when the 1970 Vietnam-era draft lottery was used to investigate a variety of outcomes (e.g., Angrist, Imbens, & Rubin, 1996a; Notz, Staw, & Cook, 1971).

Although experimenting on manipulable causes makes the job of discovering their effects easier, experiments are far from perfect means of investigating causes.

Sometimes experiments modify the conditions in which testing occurs in a way that reduces the fit between those conditions and the situation to which the results are to be generalized. Also, knowledge of the effects of manipulable causes tells nothing about how and why those effects occur. Nor do experiments answer many other questions relevant to the real world—for example, which questions are worth asking, how strong the need for treatment is, how a cause is distributed through society, whether the treatment is implemented with theoretical fidelity, and what value should be attached to the experimental results.

In addition, in experiments, we first manipulate a treatment and only then observe its effects; but in some other studies we first observe an effect, such as AIDS, and then search for its cause, whether manipulable or not. Experiments cannot help us with that search. Scriven (1976) likens such searches to detective work in which a crime has been committed (e.g., a robbery), the detectives observe a particular pattern of evidence surrounding the crime (e.g., the robber wore a baseball cap and a distinct jacket and used a certain kind of gun), and then the detectives search for criminals whose known method of operating (their **modus operandi** or **m.o.**) includes this pattern. A criminal whose m.o. fits that pattern of evidence then becomes a suspect to be investigated further. Epidemiologists use a similar method, the case-control design (Ahlbom & Norell, 1990), in which they observe a particular health outcome (e.g., an increase in brain tumors) that is not seen in another group and then attempt to identify associated causes (e.g., increased cell phone use). Experiments do not aspire to answer all the kinds of questions, not even all the types of causal questions, that social scientists ask.

Causal Description and Causal Explanation

The unique strength of experimentation is in describing the consequences attributable to deliberately varying a treatment. We call this **causal description.** In contrast, experiments do less well in clarifying the mechanisms through which and the conditions under which that causal relationship holds—what we call **causal explanation.** For example, most children very quickly learn the descriptive causal relationship between flicking a light switch and obtaining illumination in a room. However, few children (or even adults) can fully explain *why* that light goes on. To do so, they would have to decompose the treatment (the act of flicking a light switch) into its causally efficacious features (e.g., closing an insulated circuit) and its nonessential features (e.g., whether the switch is thrown by hand or a motion detector). They would have to do the same for the effect (either incandescent or fluorescent light can be produced, but light will still be produced whether the light fixture is recessed or not). For full explanation, they would then have to show how the causally efficacious parts of the treatment influence the causally affected parts of the outcome through identified mediating processes (e.g., the passage of electricity through the circuit, the excitation of photons).[3] Clearly, the cause of the light going on is a complex cluster of many factors. For those philosophers who equate cause with identifying that constellation of variables that necessarily, inevitably, and infallibly results in the effect (Beauchamp, 1974), talk of cause is not warranted until everything of relevance is known. For them, there is no causal description without causal explanation. Whatever the philosophic merits of their position, though, it is not practical to expect much current social science to achieve such complete explanation.

The practical importance of causal explanation is brought home when the switch fails to make the light go on and when replacing the light bulb (another easily learned manipulation) fails to solve the problem. Explanatory knowledge then offers clues about how to fix the problem—for example, by detecting and repairing a short circuit. Or if we wanted to create illumination in a place without lights and we had explanatory knowledge, we would know exactly which features of the cause-and-effect relationship are essential to create light and which are irrelevant. Our explanation might tell us that there must be a source of electricity but that that source could take several different molar forms, such as a battery, a generator, a windmill, or a solar array. There must also be a switch mechanism to close a circuit, but this could also take many forms, including the touching of two bare wires or even a motion detector that trips the switch when someone enters the room. So causal explanation is an important route to the generalization of causal descriptions because it tells us which features of the causal relationship are essential to transfer to other situations.

This benefit of causal explanation helps elucidate its priority and prestige in all sciences and helps explain why, once a novel and important causal relationship is discovered, the bulk of basic scientific effort turns toward explaining why and how it happens. Usually, this involves decomposing the cause into its causally effective parts, decomposing the effects into its causally affected parts, and identifying the processes through which the effective causal parts influence the causally affected outcome parts.

These examples also show the close parallel between descriptive and explanatory causation and **molar** and **molecular** causation.[4] Descriptive causation usually concerns simple bivariate relationships between molar treatments and molar outcomes, molar here referring to a package that consists of many different parts. For instance, we may find that psychotherapy decreases depression, a simple descriptive causal relationship between a molar treatment package and a molar outcome. However, psychotherapy consists of such parts as verbal interactions, **placebo-**

---

3. However, the full explanation a physicist would offer might be quite different from this electrician's explanation, perhaps invoking the behavior of subparticles. This difference indicates just how complicated is the notion of explanation and how it can quickly become quite complex once one shifts levels of analysis.

4. By *molar*, we mean something taken as a whole rather than in parts. An analogy is to physics, in which molar might refer to the properties or motions of masses, as distinguished from those of molecules or atoms that make up those masses.

generating procedures, setting characteristics, time constraints, and payment for services. Similarly, many depression measures consist of items pertaining to the physiological, cognitive, and affective aspects of depression. Explanatory causation breaks these molar causes and effects into their molecular parts so as to learn, say, that the verbal interactions and the placebo features of therapy both cause changes in the cognitive symptoms of depression, but that payment for services does not do so even though it is part of the molar treatment package.

If experiments are less able to provide this highly-prized explanatory causal knowledge, why are experiments so central to science, especially to basic social science, in which theory and explanation are often the coin of the realm? The answer is that the dichotomy between descriptive and explanatory causation is less clear in scientific practice than in abstract discussions about causation. First, many causal explanations consist of chains of descriptive causal links in which one event causes the next. Experiments help to test the links in each chain. Second, experiments help distinguish between the validity of competing explanatory theories, for example, by testing competing mediating links proposed by those theories. Third, some experiments test whether a descriptive causal relationship varies in strength or direction under Condition A versus Condition B (then the condition is a **moderator** variable that explains the conditions under which the effect holds). Fourth, some experiments add quantitative or qualitative observations of the links in the explanatory chain (**mediator** variables) to generate and study explanations for the descriptive causal effect.

Experiments are also prized in applied areas of social science, in which the identification of practical solutions to social problems has as great or even greater priority than explanations of those solutions. After all, explanation is not always required for identifying practical solutions. Lewontin (1997) makes this point about the Human Genome Project, a coordinated multibillion-dollar research program to map the human genome that it is hoped eventually will clarify the genetic causes of diseases. Lewontin is skeptical about aspects of this search:

> What is involved here is the difference between explanation and intervention. Many disorders can be *explained* by the failure of the organism to make a normal protein, a failure that is the consequence of a gene mutation. But *intervention* requires that the normal protein be provided at the right place in the right cells, at the right time and in the right amount, or else that an alternative way be found to provide normal cellular function. What is worse, it might even be necessary to keep the abnormal protein away from the cells at critical moments. None of these objectives is served by knowing the DNA sequence of the defective gene. (Lewontin, 1997, p. 29)

Practical applications are not immediately revealed by theoretical advance. Instead, to reveal them may take decades of follow-up work, including tests of simple descriptive causal relationships. The same point is illustrated by the cancer drug Endostatin, discussed earlier. Scientists knew the action of the drug occurred through cutting off tumor blood supplies; but to successfully use the drug to treat cancers in mice required administering it at the right place, angle, and depth, and those details were not part of the usual scientific explanation of the drug's effects.

In the end, then, causal descriptions and causal explanations are in delicate balance in experiments. What experiments do best is to improve causal descriptions; they do less well at explaining causal relationships. But most experiments can be designed to provide better explanations than is typically the case today. Further, in focusing on causal descriptions, experiments often investigate molar events that may be less strongly related to outcomes than are more molecular mediating processes, especially those processes that are closer to the outcome in the explanatory chain. However, many causal descriptions are still dependable and strong enough to be useful, to be worth making the building blocks around which important policies and theories are created. Just consider the dependability of such causal statements as that school desegregation causes white flight, or that outgroup threat causes ingroup cohesion, or that psychotherapy improves mental health, or that diet reduces the retardation due to PKU. Such dependable causal relationships are useful to policymakers, practitioners, and scientists alike.

MODERN DESCRIPTIONS OF EXPERIMENTS

Some of the terms used in describing modern experimentation (see Table 1.1) are unique, clearly defined, and consistently used; others are blurred and inconsistently used. The common attribute in all experiments is control of treatment (though control can take many different forms). So Mosteller (1990, p. 225) writes, "In an experiment the investigator controls the application of the treatment"; and Yaremko, Harari, Harrison, and Lynn (1986, p. 72) write, "one or more independent variables are manipulated to observe their effects on one or more dependent variables." However, over time many different experimental subtypes have developed in response to the needs and histories of different sciences (Winston, 1990; Winston & Blais, 1996).

TABLE 1.1 The Vocabulary of Experiments

Experiment: A study in which an intervention is deliberately introduced to observe its effects.

Randomized Experiment: An experiment in which units are assigned to receive the treatment or an alternative condition by a random process such as the toss of a coin or a table of random numbers.

Quasi-Experiment: An experiment in which units are not assigned to conditions randomly.

Natural Experiment: Not really an experiment because the cause usually cannot be manipulated; a study that contrasts a naturally occurring event such as an earthquake with a comparison condition.

Correlational Study: Usually synonymous with nonexperimental or observational study; a study that simply observes the size and direction of a relationship among variables.

Randomized Experiment

The most clearly described variant is the **randomized experiment,** widely credited to Sir Ronald Fisher (1925, 1926). It was first used in agriculture but later spread to other topic areas because it promised control over extraneous sources of variation without requiring the physical isolation of the laboratory. Its distinguishing feature is clear and important—that the various treatments being contrasted (including no treatment at all) are assigned to experimental **units**[5] by chance, for example, by coin toss or use of a table of random numbers. If implemented correctly, random assignment creates two or more groups of units that are probabilistically similar to each other on the average.[6] Hence, any outcome differences that are observed between those groups at the end of a study are likely to be due to treatment, not to differences between the groups that already existed at the start of the study. Further, when certain assumptions are met, the randomized experiment yields an estimate of the size of a treatment effect that has desirable statistical properties, along with estimates of the probability that the true effect falls within a defined confidence interval. These features of experiments are so highly prized that in a research area such as medicine the randomized experiment is often referred to as the gold standard for treatment outcome research.[7]

Closely related to the randomized experiment is a more ambiguous and inconsistently used term, **true experiment.** Some authors use it synonymously with randomized experiment (Rosenthal & Rosnow, 1991). Others use it more generally to refer to any study in which an **independent variable** is deliberately manipulated (Yaremko et al., 1986) and a **dependent variable** is assessed. We shall not use the term at all given its ambiguity and given that the modifier *true* seems to imply restricted claims to a single correct experimental method.

Quasi-Experiment

Much of this book focuses on a class of designs that Campbell and Stanley (1963) popularized as **quasi-experiments.**[8] Quasi-experiments share with all other

---

5. Units can be people, animals, time periods, institutions, or almost anything else. Typically in field experimentation they are people or some aggregate of people, such as classrooms or work sites. In addition, a little thought shows that random assignment of units to treatments is the same as assignment of treatments to units, so these phrases are frequently used interchangeably.

6. The word *probabilistically* is crucial, as is explained in more detail in Chapter 8.

7. Although the term *randomized experiment* is used this way consistently across many fields and in this book, statisticians sometimes use the closely related term *random experiment* in a different way to indicate experiments for which the outcome cannot be predicted with certainty (e.g., Hogg & Tanis, 1988).

8. Campbell (1957) first called these **compromise designs** but changed terminology very quickly; Rosenbaum (1995a) and Cochran (1965) refer to these as **observational studies,** a term we avoid because many people use it to refer to correlational or nonexperimental studies, as well. Greenberg and Shroder (1997) use *quasi-experiment* to refer to studies that randomly assign groups (e.g., communities) to conditions, but we would consider these group-randomized experiments (Murray, 1998).

experiments a similar purpose—to test descriptive causal hypotheses about manipulable causes—as well as many structural details, such as the frequent presence of control groups and pretest measures, to support a counterfactual inference about what would have happened in the absence of treatment. But, by definition, quasi-experiments lack random assignment. Assignment to conditions is by means of **self-selection,** by which units choose treatment for themselves, or by means of administrator **selection,** by which teachers, bureaucrats, legislators, therapists, physicians, or others decide which persons should get which treatment. However, researchers who use quasi-experiments may still have considerable control over selecting and scheduling measures, over how nonrandom assignment is executed, over the kinds of **comparison groups** with which treatment groups are compared, and over some aspects of how treatment is scheduled. As Campbell and Stanley note:

> There are many natural social settings in which the research person can introduce something like experimental design into his scheduling of data collection procedures (e.g., the *when* and *to whom* of measurement), even though he lacks the full control over the scheduling of experimental stimuli (the *when* and *to whom* of exposure and the ability to randomize exposures) which makes a true experiment possible. Collectively, such situations can be regarded as quasi-experimental designs. (Campbell & Stanley, 1963, p. 34)

In quasi-experiments, the cause is manipulable and occurs before the effect is measured. However, quasi-experimental design features usually create less compelling support for counterfactual inferences. For example, quasi-experimental control groups may differ from the treatment condition in many systematic (nonrandom) ways other than the presence of the treatment. Many of these ways could be alternative explanations for the observed effect, and so researchers have to worry about ruling them out in order to get a more valid estimate of the treatment effect. By contrast, with random assignment the researcher does not have to think *as much* about all these alternative explanations. If correctly done, random assignment makes most of the alternatives less likely as causes of the observed treatment effect at the start of the study.

In quasi-experiments, the researcher has to enumerate alternative explanations one by one, decide which are plausible, and then use logic, design, and measurement to assess whether each one is operating in a way that might explain any observed effect. The difficulties are that these alternative explanations are never completely enumerable in advance, that some of them are particular to the context being studied, and that the methods needed to eliminate them from contention will vary from alternative to alternative and from study to study. For example, suppose two nonrandomly formed groups of children are studied, a volunteer **treatment group** that gets a new reading program and a control group of nonvolunteers who do not get it. If the treatment group does better, is it because of treatment or because the cognitive development of the volunteers was increasing more rapidly even before treatment began? (In a randomized experiment, maturation rates would have been probabilistically equal in both groups.) To assess this alternative, the researcher might add multiple pretests to reveal maturational trend before the treatment, and then compare that trend with the trend after treatment.

Another alternative explanation might be that the nonrandom control group included more disadvantaged children who had less access to books in their homes or who had parents who read to them less often. (In a randomized experiment, both groups would have had similar proportions of such children.) To assess this alternative, the experimenter may measure the number of books at home, parental time spent reading to children, and perhaps trips to libraries. Then the researcher would see if these variables differed across treatment and control groups in the hypothesized direction that could explain the observed treatment effect. Obviously, as the number of plausible alternative explanations increases, the design of the quasi-experiment becomes more intellectually demanding and complex—especially because we are never certain we have identified all the alternative explanations. The efforts of the quasi-experimenter start to look like attempts to bandage a wound that would have been less severe if random assignment had been used initially.

The ruling out of alternative hypotheses is closely related to a falsificationist logic popularized by Popper (1959). Popper noted how hard it is to be sure that a general conclusion (e.g., all swans are white) is correct based on a limited set of observations (e.g., all the swans I've seen were white). After all, future observations may change (e.g., someday I may see a black swan). So **confirmation** is logically difficult. By contrast, observing a disconfirming instance (e.g., a black swan) is sufficient, in Popper's view, to falsify the general conclusion that all swans are white. Accordingly, Popper urged scientists to try deliberately to falsify the conclusions they wish to draw rather than only to seek information corroborating them. Conclusions that withstand **falsification** are retained in scientific books or journals and treated as plausible until better evidence comes along. Quasi-experimentation is falsificationist in that it requires experimenters to identify a causal claim and then to generate and examine plausible alternative explanations that might falsify the claim.

However, such falsification can never be as definitive as Popper hoped. Kuhn (1962) pointed out that falsification depends on two assumptions that can never be fully tested. The first is that the causal claim is perfectly specified. But that is never the case. So many features of both the claim and the test of the claim are debatable—for example, which outcome is of interest, how it is measured, the conditions of treatment, who needs treatment, and all the many other decisions that researchers must make in testing causal relationships. As a result, disconfirmation often leads theorists to respecify part of their causal theories. For example, they might now specify novel conditions that must hold for their theory to be true and that were derived from the apparently disconfirming observations. Second, falsification requires measures that are perfectly valid reflections of the theory being tested. However, most philosophers maintain that all observation is theory-laden. It is laden both with intellectual nuances specific to the partially unique scientific understandings of the theory held by the individual or group devising the test and also with the experimenters' extrascientific wishes, hopes, aspirations, and broadly shared cultural assumptions and understandings. If measures are not independent of theories, how can they provide independent theory tests, including tests of causal theories? If the possibility of theory-neutral observations is denied, with them disappears the possibility of definitive knowledge both of what seems to confirm a causal claim and of what seems to disconfirm it.

Nonetheless, a fallibilist version of falsification is possible. It argues that studies of causal hypotheses can still usefully improve understanding of general trends despite ignorance of all the contingencies that might pertain to those trends. It argues that causal studies are useful even if we have to respecify the initial hypothesis repeatedly to accommodate new contingencies and new understandings. After all, those respecifications are usually minor in scope; they rarely involve wholesale overthrowing of general trends in favor of completely opposite trends. Fallibilist falsification also assumes that theory-neutral observation is impossible but that observations can approach a more factlike status when they have been repeatedly made across different theoretical conceptions of a **construct,** across multiple kinds of measurements, and at multiple times. It also assumes that observations are imbued with multiple theories, not just one, and that different operational procedures do not share the same multiple theories. As a result, observations that repeatedly occur despite different theories being built into them have a special factlike status even if they can never be fully justified as completely theory-neutral facts. In summary, then, fallible falsification is more than just seeing whether observations disconfirm a prediction. It involves discovering and judging the worth of ancillary assumptions about the restricted specificity of the causal hypothesis under test and also about the heterogeneity of theories, viewpoints, settings, and times built into the measures of the cause and effect and of any contingencies modifying their relationship.

It is neither feasible nor desirable to rule out all *possible* alternative interpretations of a causal relationship. Instead, only *plausible* alternatives constitute the major focus. This serves partly to keep matters tractable because the number of possible alternatives is endless. It also recognizes that many alternatives have no serious empirical or experiential support and so do not warrant special attention. However, the lack of support can sometimes be deceiving. For example, the cause of stomach ulcers was long thought to be a combination of lifestyle (e.g., stress) and excess acid production. Few scientists seriously thought that ulcers were caused by a pathogen (e.g., virus, germ, bacteria) because it was assumed that an acid-filled stomach would destroy all living organisms. However, in 1982 Australian researchers Barry Marshall and Robin Warren discovered spiral-shaped bacteria, later named *Helicobacter pylori* (*H. pylori*), in ulcer patients' stomachs. With this discovery, the previously possible but implausible became plausible. By 1994, a U.S. National Institutes of Health Consensus Development Conference concluded that *H. pylori* was the major cause of most peptic ulcers. So labeling rival hypotheses as plausible depends not just on what is logically possible but on social consensus, shared experience and, empirical data.

Because such factors are often context specific, different substantive areas develop their own lore about which alternatives are important enough to need to be controlled, even developing their own methods for doing so. In early psychology, for example, a control group with pretest observations was invented to control for the plausible alternative explanation that, by giving practice in answering test content, pretests would produce gains in performance even in the absence of a treatment effect (Coover & Angell, 1907). Thus the focus on plausibility is a two-edged sword: it reduces the range of alternatives to be considered in quasi-experimental work, yet it also leaves the resulting causal inference vulnerable to the discovery that an implausible-seeming alternative may later emerge as a likely causal agent.

Natural Experiment

The term *natural experiment* describes a naturally-occurring contrast between a treatment and a comparison condition (Fagan, 1990; Meyer, 1995; Zeisel, 1973). Often the treatments are not even potentially manipulable, as when researchers retrospectively examined whether earthquakes in California caused drops in property values (Brunette, 1995; Murdoch, Singh, & Thayer, 1993). Yet plausible causal inferences about the effects of earthquakes are easy to construct and defend. After all, the earthquakes occurred before the observations on property values, and it is easy to see whether earthquakes are related to property values. A useful source of counterfactual inference can be constructed by examining property values in the same locale before the earthquake or by studying similar locales that did not experience an earthquake during the same time. If property values dropped right after the earthquake in the earthquake condition but not in the comparison condition, it is difficult to find an alternative explanation for that drop.

Natural experiments have recently gained a high profile in economics. Before the 1990s economists had great faith in their ability to produce valid causal inferences through statistical adjustments for initial nonequivalence between treatment and control groups. But two studies on the effects of job training programs showed that those adjustments produced estimates that were not close to those generated from a randomized experiment and were unstable across tests of the model's sensitivity (Fraker & Maynard, 1987; LaLonde, 1986). Hence, in their search for alternative methods, many economists came to do natural experiments, such as the economic study of the effects that occurred in the Miami job market when many prisoners were released from Cuban jails and allowed to come to the United States (Card, 1990). They assume that the release of prisoners (or the timing of an earthquake) is independent of the ongoing processes that usually affect unemployment rates (or housing values). Later we explore the validity of this assumption—of its desirability there can be little question.

Nonexperimental Designs

The terms **correlational design, passive observational design,** and **nonexperimental design** refer to situations in which a presumed cause and effect are identified and measured but in which other structural features of experiments are missing. Random assignment is not part of the design, nor are such **design elements** as pretests and control groups from which researchers might construct a useful counterfactual inference. Instead, reliance is placed on measuring alternative explanations individually and then statistically controlling for them. In cross-sectional studies in which all the data are gathered on the respondents at one time, the researcher may not even know if the cause precedes the effect. When these studies are used for causal purposes, the missing design features can be problematic unless much is already known about which alternative interpretations are plausible, unless those that are plausible can be validly measured, and unless the substantive model used for statistical adjustment is well-specified. These are difficult conditions to meet in the real world of research practice, and therefore many commentators doubt the potential of such designs to support strong causal inferences in most cases.

EXPERIMENTS AND THE GENERALIZATION OF CAUSAL CONNECTIONS

The strength of experimentation is its ability to illuminate causal inference. The weakness of experimentation is doubt about the extent to which that causal relationship generalizes. We hope that an innovative feature of this book is its focus on generalization. Here we introduce the general issues that are expanded in later chapters.

Most Experiments Are Highly Local But Have General Aspirations

Most experiments are highly localized and particularistic. They are almost always conducted in a restricted range of settings, often just one, with a particular version of one type of treatment rather than, say, a sample of all possible versions. Usually, they have several measures—each with theoretical assumptions that are different from those present in other measures—but far from a complete set of all possible measures. Each experiment nearly always uses a convenient sample of people rather than one that reflects a well-described population; and it will inevitably be conducted at a particular point in time that rapidly becomes history.

Yet readers of experimental results are rarely concerned with what happened in that particular, past, local study. Rather, they usually aim to learn either about theoretical constructs of interest or about a larger policy. Theorists often want to connect experimental results to theories with broad conceptual applicability, which requires generalization at the linguistic level of **constructs** rather than at the level of the **operations** used to represent these constructs in a given experiment. They nearly always want to generalize to more people and settings than are represented in a single experiment. Indeed, the value assigned to a substantive theory usually depends on how broad a range of phenomena the theory covers. Similarly, policymakers may be interested in whether a causal relationship would hold (probabilistically) across the many sites at which it would be implemented as a policy, an inference that requires generalization beyond the original experimental study context. Indeed, all human beings probably value the perceptual and cognitive stability that is fostered by generalizations. Otherwise, the world might appear as a buzzing cacophony of isolated instances requiring constant cognitive processing that would overwhelm our limited capacities.

In defining generalization as a problem, we do not assume that more broadly applicable results are always more desirable (Greenwood, 1989). For example, physicists who use particle accelerators to discover new elements may not expect that it would be desirable to introduce such elements into the world. Similarly, social scientists sometimes aim to demonstrate that an effect is possible and to understand its mechanisms without expecting that the effect can be produced more generally. For instance, when a "sleeper effect" occurs in an attitude change study involving persuasive communications, the implication is that change is manifest after a time delay but not immediately so. The circumstances under which this effect occurs turn out to be quite limited and unlikely to be of any general interest other than to show that the theory predicting it (and many other ancillary theories) may not be wrong (Cook, Gruder, Hennigan & Flay, 1979). Experiments that demonstrate limited generalization may be just as valuable as those that demonstrate broad generalization.

Nonetheless, a conflict seems to exist between the localized nature of the causal knowledge that individual experiments provide and the more generalized causal goals that research aspires to attain. Cronbach and his colleagues (Cronbach et al., 1980; Cronbach, 1982) have made this argument most forcefully, and their works have contributed much to our thinking about **causal generalization.** Cronbach noted that each experiment consists of *units* that receive the experiences being contrasted, of the *treatments* themselves, of *observations* made on the units, and of the *settings* in which the study is conducted. Taking the first letter from each of these four words, he defined the acronym *utos* to refer to the "instances on which data are collected" (Cronbach, 1982, p. 78)—to the actual people, treatments, measures, and settings that were sampled in the experiment. He then defined two problems of generalization: (1) generalizing to the "domain about which [the] question is asked" (p. 79), which he called *UTOS;* and (2) generalizing to "units, treatments, variables, and settings not directly observed" (p. 83), which he called **UTOS.*[9]

9. We oversimplify Cronbach's presentation here for pedagogical reasons. For example, Cronbach only used capital *S*, not small *s*, so that his system referred only to *utoS,* not *utos.* He offered diverse and not always consistent definitions of *UTOS* and **UTOS,* in particular. And he does not use the word *generalization* in the same broad way we do here.

Our theory of causal generalization, outlined below and presented in more detail in Chapters 11 through 13, melds Cronbach's thinking with our own ideas about generalization from previous works (Cook, 1990, 1991; Cook & Campbell, 1979), creating a theory that is different in modest ways from both of these predecessors. Our theory is influenced by Cronbach's work in two ways. First, we follow him by describing experiments consistently throughout this book as consisting of the elements of units, treatments, observations, and settings,[10] though we frequently substitute *persons* for *units* given that most field experimentation is conducted with humans as participants. We also often substitute *outcome* for *observations* given the centrality of observations about outcome when examining causal relationships. Second, we acknowledge that researchers are often interested in two kinds of generalization about each of these five elements, and that these two types are inspired by, but not identical to, the two kinds of generalization that Cronbach defined. We call these **construct validity** generalizations (inferences about the constructs that research operations represent) and **external validity** generalizations (inferences about whether the causal relationship holds over variation in persons, settings, treatment, and measurement variables).

Construct Validity: Causal Generalization as Representation

The first causal generalization problem concerns how to go from the particular units, treatments, observations, and settings on which data are collected to the higher order constructs these instances represent. These constructs are almost always couched in terms that are more abstract than the particular instances sampled in an experiment. The labels may pertain to the individual elements of the experiment (e.g., is the outcome measured by a given test best described as intelligence or as achievement?). Or the labels may pertain to the nature of relationships among elements, including causal relationships, as when cancer treatments are classified as cytotoxic or cytostatic depending on whether they kill tumor cells directly or delay tumor growth by modulating their environment. Consider a randomized experiment by Fortin and Kirouac (1976). The treatment was a brief educational course administered by several nurses, who gave a tour of their hospital and covered some basic facts about surgery with individuals who were to have elective abdominal or thoracic surgery 15 to 20 days later in a single Montreal hospital. Ten specific outcome measures were used after the surgery, such as an activities of daily living scale and a count of the analgesics used to control pain. Now compare this study with its likely target constructs—whether

---

10. We occasionally refer to time as a separate feature of experiments, following Campbell (1957) and Cook and Campbell (1979), because time can cut across the other factors independently. Cronbach did not include time in his notational system, instead incorporating time into treatment (e.g., the scheduling of treatment), observations (e.g., when measures are administered), or setting (e.g., the historical context of the experiment).

patient education (the target cause) promotes physical recovery (the target effect) among surgical patients (the target population of units) in hospitals (the target universe of settings). Another example occurs in basic research, in which the question frequently arises as to whether the actual manipulations and measures used in an experiment really tap into the specific cause and effect constructs specified by the theory. One way to dismiss an empirical challenge to a theory is simply to make the case that the data do not really represent the concepts as they are specified in the theory.

Empirical results often force researchers to change their initial understanding of what the domain under study is. Sometimes the reconceptualization leads to a more restricted inference about what has been studied. Thus the planned causal agent in the Fortin and Kirouac (1976) study—*patient education*—might need to be respecified as *informational patient education* if the information component of the treatment proved to be causally related to recovery from surgery but the tour of the hospital did not. Conversely, data can sometimes lead researchers to think in terms of target constructs and categories that are more general than those with which they began a research program. Thus the creative analyst of patient education studies might surmise that the treatment is a subclass of interventions that function by increasing "perceived control" or that recovery from surgery can be treated as a subclass of "personal coping." Subsequent readers of the study can even add their own interpretations, perhaps claiming that perceived control is really just a special case of the even more general self-efficacy construct. There is a subtle interplay over time among the original categories the researcher intended to represent, the study as it was actually conducted, the study results, and subsequent interpretations. This interplay can change the researcher's thinking about what the study particulars actually achieved at a more conceptual level, as can feedback from readers. But whatever reconceptualizations occur, the first problem of causal generalization is always the same: How can we generalize from a sample of instances and the data patterns associated with them to the particular target constructs they represent?

External Validity: Causal Generalization as Extrapolation

The second problem of generalization is to infer whether a causal relationship holds over variations in persons, settings, treatments, and outcomes. For example, someone reading the results of an experiment on the effects of a kindergarten Head Start program on the subsequent grammar school reading test scores of poor African American children in Memphis during the 1980s may want to know if a program with partially overlapping cognitive and social development goals would be as effective in improving the mathematics test scores of poor Hispanic children in Dallas if this program were to be implemented tomorrow.

This example again reminds us that generalization is not a synonym for *broader* application. Here, generalization is from one city to another city and from one kind of clientele to another kind, but there is no presumption that Dallas is somehow broader than Memphis or that Hispanic children constitute a broader population than African American children. Of course, some generalizations are from narrow to broad. For example, a researcher who **randomly samples** experimental participants from a national population may generalize (probabilistically) from the sample to all the other unstudied members of that same population. Indeed, that is the rationale for choosing **random selection** in the first place. Similarly, when policymakers consider whether Head Start should be continued on a national basis, they are not so interested in what happened in Memphis. They are more interested in what would happen on the average across the United States, as its many local programs still differ from each other despite efforts in the 1990s to standardize much of what happens to Head Start children and parents. But generalization can also go from the broad to the narrow. Cronbach (1982) gives the example of an experiment that studied differences between the performances of groups of students attending private and public schools. In this case, the concern of individual parents is to know which type of school is better for their particular child, not for the whole group. Whether from narrow to broad, broad to narrow, or across units at about the same level of aggregation, all these examples of external validity questions share the same need—to infer the extent to which the effect holds over variations in persons, settings, treatments, or outcomes.

Approaches to Making Causal Generalizations

Whichever way the causal generalization issue is framed, experiments do not seem at first glance to be very useful. Almost invariably, a given experiment uses a limited set of operations to represent units, treatments, outcomes, and settings. This high degree of localization is not unique to the experiment; it also characterizes case studies, performance monitoring systems, and opportunistically-administered marketing questionnaires given to, say, a haphazard sample of respondents at local shopping centers (Shadish, 1995b). Even when questionnaires are administered to nationally representative samples, they are ideal for representing that particular population of persons but have little relevance to citizens outside of that nation. Moreover, responses may also vary by the setting in which the interview took place (a doorstep, a living room, or a work site), by the time of day at which it was administered, by how each question was framed, or by the particular race, age, and gender combination of interviewers. But the fact that the experiment is not alone in its vulnerability to generalization issues does not make it any less a problem. So what is it that justifies any belief that an experiment can achieve a better fit between the sampling particulars of a study and more general inferences to constructs or over variations in persons, settings, treatments, and outcomes?

Sampling and Causal Generalization

The method most often recommended for achieving this close fit is the use of formal probability sampling of instances of units, treatments, observations, or settings (Rossi, Wright, & Anderson, 1983). This presupposes that we have clearly delineated populations of each and that we can sample with known probability from within each of these populations. In effect, this entails the random selection of instances, to be carefully distinguished from random assignment discussed earlier in this chapter. Random selection involves selecting cases by chance to represent that population, whereas random assignment involves assigning cases to multiple conditions.

In cause-probing research that is *not* experimental, random samples of individuals are often used. Large-scale longitudinal surveys such as the Panel Study of Income Dynamics or the National Longitudinal Survey are used to represent the population of the United States—or certain age brackets within it—and measures of potential causes and effects are then related to each other using time lags in measurement and statistical controls for group nonequivalence. All this is done in hopes of approximating what a randomized experiment achieves. However, cases of random selection from a broad population followed by random assignment from within this population are much rarer (see Chapter 12 for examples). Also rare are studies of random selection followed by a quality quasi-experiment. Such experiments require a high level of resources and a degree of logistical control that is rarely feasible, so many researchers prefer to rely on an implicit set of nonstatistical heuristics for generalization that we hope to make more explicit and systematic in this book.

Random selection occurs even more rarely with treatments, outcomes, and settings than with people. Consider the outcomes observed in an experiment. How often are they randomly sampled? We grant that the domain sampling model of classical test theory (Nunnally & Bernstein, 1994) assumes that the items used to measure a construct have been randomly sampled from a domain of all possible items. However, in actual experimental practice few researchers ever randomly sample items when constructing measures. Nor do they do so when choosing manipulations or settings. For instance, many settings will not agree to be sampled, and some of the settings that agree to be randomly sampled will almost certainly not agree to be randomly assigned to conditions. For treatments, no definitive list of possible treatments usually exists, as is most obvious in areas in which treatments are being discovered and developed rapidly, such as in AIDS research. In general, then, random sampling is always desirable, but it is only rarely and contingently feasible.

However, formal sampling methods are not the only option. Two informal, purposive sampling methods are sometimes useful—purposive sampling of heterogeneous instances and purposive sampling of typical instances. In the former case, the aim is to include instances chosen deliberately to reflect diversity on presumptively important dimensions, even though the sample is not formally random. In the latter case, the aim is to explicate the kinds of units, treatments, observations, and settings to which one most wants to generalize and then to select at least one instance of each class that is impressionistically similar to the class mode. Although these purposive sampling methods are more practical than formal probability sampling, they are not backed by a statistical logic that justifies formal generalizations. Nonetheless, they are probably the most commonly used of all sampling methods for facilitating generalizations. A task we set ourselves in this book is to explicate such methods and to describe how they can be used more often than is the case today.

However, sampling methods of any kind are insufficient to solve either problem of generalization. Formal probability sampling requires specifying a target population from which sampling then takes place, but defining such populations is difficult for some targets of generalization such as treatments. Purposive sampling of heterogeneous instances is differentially feasible for different elements in a study; it is often more feasible to make measures diverse than it is to obtain diverse settings, for example. Purposive sampling of typical instances is often feasible when target modes, medians, or means are known, but it leaves questions about generalizations to a wider range than is typical. Besides, as Cronbach points out, most challenges to the causal generalization of an experiment typically emerge *after* a study is done. In such cases, sampling is relevant only if the instances in the original study were sampled diversely enough to promote responsible reanalyses of the data to see if a treatment effect holds across most or all of the targets about which generalization has been challenged. But packing so many sources of variation into a single experimental study is rarely practical and will almost certainly conflict with other goals of the experiment. Formal sampling methods usually offer only a limited solution to causal generalization problems. A theory of generalized causal inference needs additional tools.

A Grounded Theory of Causal Generalization

Practicing scientists routinely make causal generalizations in their research, and they almost never use formal probability sampling when they do. In this book, we present a theory of causal generalization that is grounded in the actual practice of science (Matt, Cook, & Shadish, 2000). Although this theory was originally developed from ideas that were grounded in the construct and external validity literatures (Cook, 1990, 1991), we have since found that these ideas are common in a diverse literature about scientific generalizations (e.g., Abelson, 1995; Campbell & Fiske, 1959; Cronbach & Meehl, 1955; Davis, 1994; Locke, 1986; Medin, 1989; Messick, 1989, 1995; Rubins, 1994; Willner, 1991; Wilson, Hayward, Tunis, Bass, & Guyatt, 1995). We provide more details about this grounded theory in Chapters 11 through 13, but in brief it suggests that scientists make causal generalizations in their work by using five closely related principles:

1. *Surface Similarity.* They assess the apparent similarities between study operations and the prototypical characteristics of the target of generalization.

2. *Ruling Out Irrelevancies.* They identify those things that are irrelevant because they do not change a generalization.
3. *Making Discriminations.* They clarify key discriminations that limit generalization.
4. *Interpolation and Extrapolation.* They make interpolations to unsampled values within the range of the sampled instances and, much more difficult, they explore extrapolations beyond the sampled range.
5. *Causal Explanation.* They develop and test explanatory theories about the pattern of effects, causes, and mediational processes that are essential to the transfer of a causal relationship.

In this book, we want to show how scientists can and do use these five principles to draw generalized conclusions about a causal connection. Sometimes the conclusion is about the higher order constructs to use in describing an obtained connection at the sample level. In this sense, these five principles have analogues or parallels both in the construct validity literature (e.g., with construct content, with convergent and discriminant validity, and with the need for theoretical rationales for constructs) and in the cognitive science and philosophy literatures that study how people decide whether instances fall into a category (e.g., concerning the roles that prototypical characteristics and surface versus deep similarity play in determining category membership). But at other times, the conclusion about generalization refers to whether a connection holds broadly or narrowly over variations in persons, settings, treatments, or outcomes. Here, too, the principles have analogues or parallels that we can recognize from scientific theory and practice, as in the study of dose-response relationships (a form of interpolation-extrapolation) or the appeal to explanatory mechanisms in generalizing from animals to humans (a form of causal explanation).

Scientists use these five principles almost constantly during all phases of research. For example, when they read a published study and wonder if some variation on the study's particulars would work in their lab, they think about similarities of the published study to what they propose to do. When they conceptualize the new study, they anticipate how the instances they plan to study will match the prototypical features of the constructs about which they are curious. They may design their study on the assumption that certain variations will be irrelevant to it but that others will point to key discriminations over which the causal relationship does not hold or the very character of the constructs changes. They may include measures of key theoretical mechanisms to clarify how the intervention works. During data analysis, they test all these hypotheses and adjust their construct descriptions to match better what the data suggest happened in the study. The introduction section of their articles tries to convince the reader that the study bears on specific constructs, and the discussion sometimes speculates about how results might extrapolate to different units, treatments, outcomes, and settings.

Further, practicing scientists do all this not just with single studies that they read or conduct but also with multiple studies. They nearly always think about how their own studies fit into a larger literature about both the constructs being measured and the variables that may or may not bound or explain a causal connection, often documenting this fit in the introduction to their study. And they apply all five principles when they conduct reviews of the literature, in which they make inferences about the kinds of generalizations that a body of research can support.

Throughout this book, and especially in Chapters 11 to 13, we provide more details about this grounded theory of causal generalization and about the scientific practices that it suggests. Adopting this grounded theory of generalization does not imply a rejection of formal probability sampling. Indeed, we recommend such sampling unambiguously when it is feasible, along with purposive sampling schemes to aid generalization when formal random selection methods cannot be implemented. But we also show that sampling is just one method that practicing scientists use to make causal generalizations, along with practical logic, application of diverse statistical methods, and use of features of design other than sampling.

EXPERIMENTS AND METASCIENCE

Extensive philosophical debate sometimes surrounds experimentation. Here we briefly summarize some key features of these debates, and then we discuss some implications of these debates for experimentation. However, there is a sense in which all this philosophical debate is incidental to the practice of experimentation. Experimentation is as old as humanity itself, so it preceded humanity's philosophical efforts to understand causation and generalization by thousands of years. Even over just the past 400 years of scientific experimentation, we can see some constancy of experimental concept and method, whereas diverse philosophical conceptions of the experiment have come and gone. As Hacking (1983) said, "Experimentation has a life of its own" (p. 150). It has been one of science's most powerful methods for discovering descriptive causal relationships, and it has done so well in so many ways that its place in science is probably assured forever. To justify its practice today, a scientist need not resort to sophisticated philosophical reasoning about experimentation.

Nonetheless, it does help scientists to understand these philosophical debates. For example, previous distinctions in this chapter between molar and molecular causation, descriptive and explanatory cause, or probabilistic and deterministic causal inferences all help both philosophers and scientists to understand better both the purpose and the results of experiments (e.g., Bunge, 1959; Eells, 1991; Hart & Honore, 1985; Humphreys, 1989; Mackie, 1974; Salmon, 1984, 1989; Sobel, 1993; P. A. White, 1990). Here we focus on a different and broader set of critiques of science itself, not only from philosophy but also from the history, sociology, and psychology of science (see useful general reviews by Bechtel, 1988; H. I. Brown, 1977; Oldroyd, 1986). Some of these works have been explicitly about the nature of experimentation, seeking to create a justified role for it (e.g.,

Bhaskar, 1975; Campbell, 1982, 1988; Danziger, 1990; S. Drake, 1981; Gergen, 1973; Gholson, Shadish, Neimeyer, & Houts, 1989; Gooding, Pinch, & Schaffer, 1989b; Greenwood, 1989; Hacking, 1983; Latour, 1987; Latour & Woolgar, 1979; Morawski, 1988; Orne, 1962; R. Rosenthal, 1966; Shadish & Fuller, 1994; Shapin, 1994). These critiques help scientists to see some limits of experimentation in both science and society.

The Kuhnian Critique

Kuhn (1962) described scientific revolutions as different and partly incommensurable paradigms that abruptly succeeded each other in time and in which the gradual accumulation of scientific knowledge was a chimera. Hanson (1958), Polanyi (1958), Popper (1959), Toulmin (1961), Feyerabend (1975), and Quine (1951, 1969) contributed to the critical momentum, in part by exposing the gross mistakes in logical positivism's attempt to build a philosophy of science based on reconstructing a successful science such as physics. All these critiques denied any firm foundations for scientific knowledge (so, by extension, experiments do not provide firm causal knowledge). The logical positivists hoped to achieve foundations on which to build knowledge by tying all theory tightly to theory-free observation through predicate logic. But this left out important scientific concepts that could not be tied tightly to observation; and it failed to recognize that all observations are impregnated with substantive and methodological theory, making it impossible to conduct theory-free tests.[11]

The impossibility of theory-neutral observation (often referred to as the Quine-Duhem thesis) implies that the results of any single test (and so any single experiment) are inevitably ambiguous. They could be disputed, for example, on grounds that the theoretical assumptions built into the outcome measure were wrong or that the study made a faulty assumption about how high a treatment dose was required to be effective. Some of these assumptions are small, easily detected, and correctable, such as when a voltmeter gives the wrong reading because the impedance of the voltage source was much higher than that of the meter (Wilson, 1952). But other assumptions are more paradigmlike, impregnating a theory so completely that other parts of the theory make no sense without them (e.g., the assumption that the earth is the center of the universe in pre-Galilean astronomy). Because the number of assumptions involved in any scientific test is very large, researchers can easily find some assumptions to fault or can even posit new

---

11. However, Holton (1986) reminds us not to overstate the reliance of positivists on empirical data: "Even the father of positivism, Auguste Comte, had written . . . that without a theory of some sort by which to link phenomena to some principles 'it would not only be impossible to combine the isolated observations and draw any useful conclusions, we would not even be able to remember them, and, for the most part, the fact would not be noticed by our eyes'" (p. 32). Similarly, Uebel (1992) provides a more detailed historical analysis of the protocol sentence debate in logical positivism, showing some surprisingly nonstereotypical positions held by key players such as Carnap.

assumptions (Mitroff & Fitzgerald, 1977). In this way, substantive theories are less testable than their authors originally conceived. How can a theory be tested if it is made of clay rather than granite?

For reasons we clarify later, this critique is more true of single studies and less true of programs of research. But even in the latter case, undetected constant biases can result in flawed inferences about cause and its generalization. As a result, no experiment is ever fully certain, and extrascientific beliefs and preferences always have room to influence the many discretionary judgments involved in all scientific belief.

Modern Social Psychological Critiques

Sociologists working within traditions variously called social constructivism, epistemological relativism, and the strong program (e.g., Barnes, 1974; Bloor, 1976; Collins, 1981; Knorr-Cetina, 1981; Latour & Woolgar, 1979; Mulkay, 1979) have shown those extrascientific processes at work in science. Their empirical studies show that scientists often fail to adhere to norms commonly proposed as part of good science (e.g., objectivity, neutrality, sharing of information). They have also shown how that which comes to be reported as scientific knowledge is partly determined by social and psychological forces and partly by issues of economic and political power both within science and in the larger society—issues that are rarely mentioned in published research reports. The most extreme among these sociologists attributes *all* scientific knowledge to such extrascientific processes, claiming that "the natural world has a small or nonexistent role in the construction of scientific knowledge" (Collins, 1981, p. 3).

Collins does not deny *ontological realism*, that real entities exist in the world. Rather, he denies *epistemological (scientific) realism,* that whatever external reality may exist can constrain our scientific theories. For example, if atoms really exist, do they affect our scientific theories at all? If our theory postulates an atom, is it describing a real entity that exists roughly as we describe it? *Epistemological relativists* such as Collins respond negatively to both questions, believing that the most important influences in science are social, psychological, economic, and political, and that these might even be the only influences on scientific theories. This view is not widely endorsed outside a small group of sociologists, but it is a useful counterweight to naïve assumptions that scientific studies somehow directly reveal nature to us (an assumption we call *naïve realism*). The results of all studies, including experiments, are profoundly subject to these extrascientific influences, from their conception to reports of their results.

Science and Trust

A standard image of the scientist is as a skeptic, a person who only trusts results that have been personally verified. Indeed, the scientific revolution of the 17th century claimed that trust, particularly trust in authority and dogma, was antithetical to good science. Every authoritative assertion, every dogma, was to be open to question, and the job of science was to do that questioning.

That image is partly wrong. Any single scientific study is an exercise in trust (Pinch, 1986; Shapin, 1994). Studies trust the vast majority of already developed methods, findings, and concepts that they use when they test a new hypothesis. For example, statistical theories and methods are usually taken on faith rather than personally verified, as are measurement instruments. The ratio of trust to skepticism in any given study is more like 99% trust to 1% skepticism than the opposite. Even in lifelong programs of research, the single scientist trusts much more than he or she ever doubts. Indeed, thoroughgoing skepticism is probably impossible for the individual scientist, to judge from what we know of the psychology of science (Gholson et al., 1989; Shadish & Fuller, 1994). Finally, skepticism is not even an accurate characterization of past scientific revolutions; Shapin (1994) shows that the role of "gentlemanly trust" in 17th-century England was central to the establishment of experimental science. Trust pervades science, despite its rhetoric of skepticism.

Implications for Experiments

The net result of these criticisms is a greater appreciation for the equivocality of all scientific knowledge. The experiment is not a clear window that reveals nature directly to us. To the contrary, experiments yield hypothetical and fallible knowledge that is often dependent on context and imbued with many unstated theoretical assumptions. Consequently, experimental results are partly relative to those assumptions and contexts and might well change with new assumptions or contexts. In this sense, all scientists are epistemological constructivists and relativists. The difference is whether they are strong or weak relativists. Strong relativists share Collins's position that only extrascientific factors influence our theories. Weak relativists believe that both the ontological world and the worlds of ideology, interests, values, hopes, and wishes play a role in the construction of scientific knowledge. Most practicing scientists, including ourselves, would probably describe themselves as ontological realists but weak epistemological relativists.[12] To the extent that experiments reveal nature to us, it is through a very clouded windowpane (Campbell, 1988).

Such counterweights to naïve views of experiments were badly needed. As recently as 30 years ago, the central role of the experiment in science was probably

---

12. If space permitted, we could extend this discussion to a host of other philosophical issues that have been raised about the experiment, such as its role in discovery versus confirmation, incorrect assertions that the experiment is tied to some specific philosophy such as logical positivism or pragmatism, and the various mistakes that are frequently made in such discussions (e.g., Campbell, 1982, 1988; Cook, 1991; Cook & Campbell, 1986; Shadish, 1995a).

taken more for granted than is the case today. For example, Campbell and Stanley (1963) described themselves as:

> committed to the experiment: as the only means for settling disputes regarding educational practice, as the only way of verifying educational improvements, and as the only way of establishing a cumulative tradition in which improvements can be introduced without the danger of a faddish discard of old wisdom in favor of inferior novelties. (p. 2)

Indeed, Hacking (1983) points out that "'experimental method' used to be just another name for scientific method" (p. 149); and experimentation was then a more fertile ground for examples illustrating basic philosophical issues than it was a source of contention itself.

Not so today. We now understand better that the experiment is a profoundly human endeavor, affected by all the same human foibles as any other human endeavor, though with well-developed procedures for partial control of some of the limitations that have been identified to date. Some of these limitations are common to all science, of course. For example, scientists tend to notice evidence that confirms their preferred hypotheses and to overlook contradictory evidence. They make routine cognitive errors of judgment and have limited capacity to process large amounts of information. They react to peer pressures to agree with accepted dogma and to social role pressures in their relationships to students, participants, and other scientists. They are partly motivated by sociological and economic rewards for their work (sadly, sometimes to the point of fraud), and they display all-too-human psychological needs and irrationalities about their work. Other limitations have unique relevance to experimentation. For example, if causal results are ambiguous, as in many weaker quasi-experiments, experimenters may attribute causation or causal generalization based on study features that have little to do with orthodox logic or method. They may fail to pursue all the alternative causal explanations because of a lack of energy, a need to achieve closure, or a bias toward accepting evidence that confirms their preferred hypothesis. Each experiment is also a social situation, full of social roles (e.g., participant, experimenter, assistant) and social expectations (e.g., that people should provide true information) but with a uniqueness (e.g., that the experimenter does not always tell the truth) that can lead to problems when social cues are misread or deliberately thwarted by either party. Fortunately, these limits are not insurmountable, as formal training can help overcome some of them (Lehman, Lempert, & Nisbett, 1988). Still, the relationship between scientific results and the world that science studies is neither simple nor fully trustworthy.

These social and psychological analyses have taken some of the luster from the experiment as a centerpiece of science. The experiment may have a life of its own, but it is no longer life on a pedestal. Among scientists, belief in the experiment as the *only* means to settle disputes about causation is gone, though it is still the preferred method in many circumstances. Gone, too, is the belief that the power experimental methods often displayed in the laboratory would transfer easily to applications in field settings. As a result of highly publicized science-related events such as the tragic results of the Chernobyl nuclear disaster, the disputes over certainty levels of DNA testing in the O.J. Simpson trials, and the failure to find a cure for most cancers after decades of highly publicized and funded effort, the general public now better understands the limits of science.

Yet we should not take these critiques too far. Those who argue against theory-free tests often seem to suggest that every experiment will come out just as the experimenter wishes. This expectation is totally contrary to the experience of researchers, who find instead that experimentation is often frustrating and disappointing for the theories they loved so much. Laboratory results may not speak for themselves, but they certainly do not speak only for one's hopes and wishes. We find much to value in the laboratory scientist's belief in "stubborn facts" with a life span that is greater than the fluctuating theories with which one tries to explain them. Thus many basic results about gravity are the same, whether they are contained within a framework developed by Newton or by Einstein; and no successor theory to Einstein's would be plausible unless it could account for most of the stubborn factlike findings about falling bodies. There may not be pure facts, but some observations are clearly worth treating as if they were facts.

Some theorists of science—Hanson, Polanyi, Kuhn, and Feyerabend included—have so exaggerated the role of theory in science as to make experimental evidence seem almost irrelevant. But exploratory experiments that were unguided by formal theory and unexpected experimental discoveries tangential to the initial research motivations have repeatedly been the source of great scientific advances. Experiments have provided many stubborn, dependable, replicable results that then become the subject of theory. Experimental physicists feel that their laboratory data help keep their more speculative theoretical counterparts honest, giving experiments an indispensable role in science. Of course, these stubborn facts often involve both commonsense presumptions and trust in many well-established theories that make up the shared core of belief of the science in question. And of course, these stubborn facts sometimes prove to be undependable, are reinterpreted as experimental artifacts, or are so laden with a dominant focal theory that they disappear once that theory is replaced. But this is not the case with the great bulk of the factual base, which remains reasonably dependable over relatively long periods of time.

A WORLD WITHOUT EXPERIMENTS OR CAUSES?

To borrow a thought experiment from MacIntyre (1981), imagine that the slates of science and philosophy were wiped clean and that we had to construct our understanding of the world anew. As part of that reconstruction, would we reinvent the notion of a manipulable cause? We think so, largely because of the practical utility that dependable manipulanda have for our ability to survive and prosper. Would we reinvent the experiment as a method for investigating such causes?

Again yes, because humans will always be trying to better know how well these manipulable causes work. Over time, they will refine how they conduct those experiments and so will again be drawn to problems of counterfactual inference, of cause preceding effect, of alternative explanations, and of all of the other features of causation that we have discussed in this chapter. In the end, we would probably end up with the experiment or something very much like it. This book is one more step in that ongoing process of refining experiments. It is about improving the yield from experiments that take place in complex field settings, both the quality of causal inferences they yield and our ability to generalize these inferences to constructs and over variations in persons, settings, treatments, and outcomes.

2

Statistical Conclusion Validity and Internal Validity

Val·id (văl´ĭd): [French *valide*, from Old French from Latin *validus*, strong, from *valre*, to be strong; see *wal-* in Indo-European Roots.] adj. 1. Well grounded; just: *a valid objection.* 2. Producing the desired results; efficacious: *valid methods.* 3. Having legal force; effective or binding: *a valid title.* 4. Logic. a. Containing premises from which the conclusion may logically be derived: *a valid argument.* b. Correctly inferred or deduced from a premise: *a valid conclusion.*

Ty·pol·o·gy (tī-pŏl´ə-jē): n., pl. ty·pol·o·gies. 1. The study or systematic classification of types that have characteristics or traits in common. 2. A theory or doctrine of types, as in scriptural studies.

Threat (thrĕt): [Middle English from Old English *thrat*, oppression; see *treud-* in Indo-European Roots.] n. 1. An expression of an intention to inflict pain, injury, evil, or punishment. 2. An indication of impending danger or harm. 3. One that is regarded as a possible danger; a menace.

A FAMOUS STUDY in early psychology concerned a horse named Clever Hans who seemed to solve mathematics problems, tapping out the answer with his hoof. A psychologist, Oskar Pfungst, critically examined the performance of Clever Hans and concluded that he was really responding to subtly conveyed researcher expectations about when to start and stop tapping (Pfungst, 1911). In short, Pfungst questioned the **validity** of the initial inference that Clever Hans solved math problems. All science and all experiments rely on making such inferences validly. This chapter presents the theory of validity that underlies the approach to generalized causal inference taken in this book. It begins by discussing the meaning ascribed to validity both in theory and in social science practice and then describes a validity typology that introduces the twin ideas of validity types and **threats to validity.** This chapter and the next provide an extended description of these types of validity and of threats that go with them.

VALIDITY

We use the term *validity* to refer to the approximate truth of an inference.[1] When we say something is valid, we make a judgment about the extent to which relevant evidence supports that inference as being true or correct. Usually, that evidence comes from both empirical findings and the consistency of these findings with other sources of knowledge, including past findings and theories. Assessing validity always entails fallible human judgments. We can never be certain that all of the many inferences drawn from a single experiment are true or even that other inferences have been conclusively falsified. That is why validity judgments are not absolute; various degrees of validity can be invoked. As a result, when we use terms such as *valid* or *invalid* or *true* or *false* in this book, they should always be understood as prefaced by "approximately" or "tentatively." For reasons of style we usually omit these modifiers.

Validity is a property of inferences. It is *not* a property of designs or methods, for the same design may contribute to more or less valid inferences under different circumstances. For example, using a randomized experiment does not guarantee that one will make a valid inference about the existence of a descriptive causal relationship. After all, differential attrition may vitiate randomization, **power** may be too low to detect the effect, improper statistics may be used to analyze the data, and **sampling error** might even lead us to misestimate the direction of the effect. So it is wrong to say that a randomized experiment is internally valid or has internal validity—although we may occasionally speak that way for convenience. The same criticism is, of course, true of *any* other method used in science, from the case study to the random sample survey. No method guarantees the validity of an inference.

As a corollary, because methods do not have a one-to-one correspondence with any one type of validity, the use of a method may affect more than one type of validity simultaneously. The best-known example is the decision to use a randomized experiment, which often helps internal validity but hampers external validity. But there are many other examples, such as the case in which diversifying participants improves external validity but decreases statistical conclusion validity or in which treatment standardization clarifies construct validity of the treatment but reduces external validity to practical settings in which such standardi-

---

1. We might use the terms *knowledge claim* or *proposition* in place of *inference* here, the former being observable embodiments of inferences. There are differences implied by each of these terms, but we treat them interchangeably for present purposes.

zation is not common. This is the nature of practical action: our design choices have multiple consequences for validity, not always ones we anticipate. Put differently, every solution to a problem tends to create new problems. This is not unique to science but is true of human action generally (Sarason, 1978).

Still, in our theory, validity is intimately tied to the idea of truth. In philosophy, three theories of truth have traditionally dominated (Schmitt, 1995). **Correspondence theory** says that a knowledge claim is true if it corresponds to the world—for example, the claim that it is raining is true if we look out and see rain falling. **Coherence theory** says that a claim is true if it belongs to a coherent set of claims—for example, the claim that smoking marijuana causes cancer is true if it is consistent with what we know about the results of marijuana smoking on animal systems much like human ones, if cancer has resulted from other forms of smoking, if the causes of cancer include some elements that are known to follow from marijuana smoking, and if the physiological mechanisms that relate smoking tobacco to cancer are also activated by smoking marijuana. **Pragmatism** says that a claim is true if it is useful to believe that claim—for example, we say that "electrons exist" if inferring such entities brings meaning or predictability into a set of observations that are otherwise more difficult to understand. To play this role, electrons need not actually exist; rather, postulating them provides intellectual order, and following the practices associated with them in theory provides practical utility.[2]

Unfortunately, philosophers do not agree on which of these three theories of truth is correct and have successfully criticized aspects of all of them. Fortunately, we need not endorse any one of these as the single *correct definition* of truth in order to endorse each of them as part of a complete description of the *practical strategies* scientists actually use to construct, revise, and justify knowledge claims. Correspondence theory is apparent in the nearly universal scientific concern of gathering data to assess how well knowledge claims match the world. Scientists also judge how well a given knowledge claim coheres with other knowledge claims built into accepted current theories and past findings. Thus Eisenhart and Howe (1992) suggest that a case study's conclusions must cohere with existing theoretical, substantive, and practical knowledge in order to be valid, and scientists traditionally view with skepticism any knowledge claim that flatly contradicts what is already thought to be well established (Cook et al., 1979). On the pragmatic front, Latour (1987) claims that what comes to be accepted as true in science is what scientists can convince others to use, for it is by use that knowledge claims gain currency and that practical accomplishments accrue. This view is apparent in

---

2. A fourth theory, **deflationism** (sometimes called the redundancy or minimalist theory of truth; Horowich, 1990), denies that truth involves correspondence to the world, coherence, or usefulness. Instead, it postulates that the word *truth* is a trivial linguistic device "for assenting to propositions expressed by sentences too numerous, lengthy, or cumbersome to utter" (Schmitt, 1995, p. 128). For example, the claim that "Euclidean geometry is true" is said instead of repeating one's assent to all the axioms of Euclidean geometry, and the claim means no more than that list of axioms.

Mishler's (1990) assertion that qualitative methods are validated by "a functional criterion—whether findings are relied upon for further work" (p. 419) and in a recent response to a statistical-philosophical debate that "in the interest of science, performance counts for more than rigid adherence to philosophical principles" (Casella & Schwartz, 2000, p. 427).

Our theory of validity similarly makes some use of each of these approaches to truth—as we believe all practical theories of validity must do. Our theory clearly appeals to the correspondence between empirical evidence and abstract inferences. It is sensitive to the degree to which an inference coheres with relevant theory and findings. And it has a pragmatic emphasis in emphasizing the utility of ruling out the alternative explanations that practicing scientists in a given research area believe could compromise knowledge claims, even though such threats are, in logic, just a subset of all possible alternatives to the claim. Thus a mix of strategies characterizes how we will proceed, reluctantly eschewing a single, royal road to truth, for each of these single roads is compromised. Correspondence theory is compromised because the data to which a claim is compared are themselves theory laden and so cannot provide a theory-free test of that claim (Kuhn, 1962). Coherence theory is vulnerable to the criticism that coherent stories need not bear any exact relationship to the world. After all, effective swindlers' tales are often highly coherent, even though they are, in fact, false in some crucial ways. Finally, pragmatism is vulnerable because many beliefs known to be true by other criteria have little utility—for example, knowledge of the precise temperature of small regions in the interior of some distant star. Because philosophers do not agree among themselves about which theory of truth is best, practicing scientists should not have to choose among them in justifying a viable approach to the validity of inferences about causation and its generalization.

Social and psychological forces also profoundly influence what is accepted as true in science (Bloor, 1997; Latour, 1987; Pinch, 1986; Shapin, 1994). This is illustrated by Galileo's famous tribulations with the Inquisition and by the history of the causes of ulcers that we covered in Chapter 1. But following Shapin's (1994) distinction between an evaluative and a social theory of truth, we

> want to preserve . . . the loose equation between truth, knowledge and the facts of the matter, while defending the practical interest and legitimacy of a more liberal notion of truth, a notion in which there is indeed a socio-historical story to be told about truth. (Shapin, 1994, p. 4)

As Bloor (1997) points out, science is not a zero-sum game whose social and cognitive-evaluative influences detract from each other; instead, they complement each other. Evaluative theories deal with factors influencing what we *should* accept as true and, for the limited realm of causal inferences and their generality, our theory of validity tries to be evaluative in this normative sense. The social theory tells about external factors influencing what we *do* accept as true, including how we come to believe that one thing causes another (Heider, 1944)—so a social theory of truth might be based on insight, on findings from psychology, or on features in the social, political, and economic environment (e.g., Cordray, 1986). Social theory about truth is not a central topic of this book, though we touch on it in several places. However, truth is manifestly a social construction, and it depends on more than evaluative theories of truth such as correspondence, coherence, and pragmatism. But we believe that truth *does* depend on these in part, and it is this part we develop most thoroughly.

A Validity Typology

A little history will place the current typology in context. Campbell (1957) first defined **internal validity** as the question, "did in fact the experimental stimulus make some significant difference in this specific instance?" (p. 297) and **external validity** as the question, "to what populations, settings, and variables can this effect be generalized?" (p. 297).[3] Campbell and Stanley (1963) followed this lead closely. Internal validity referred to inferences about whether "the experimental treatments make a difference in this specific experimental instance" (Campbell & Stanley, 1963, p. 5). External validity asked "to what populations, settings, treatment variables, and measurement variables can this effect be generalized" (Campbell & Stanley, 1963, p. 5).[4]

Cook and Campbell (1979) elaborated this validity typology into four related components: **statistical conclusion validity,** internal validity, construct validity, and external validity. Statistical conclusion validity referred to the appropriate use of statistics to infer whether the presumed independent and dependent variables covary. Internal validity referred to whether their covariation resulted from a causal relationship. Both construct and external validity referred to generalizations—the former from operations to constructs (with particular emphasis on cause and effect constructs) and the latter from the samples of persons,

3. Campbell (1986) suggests that the distinction was partly motivated by the emphasis in the 1950s on Fisherian randomized experiments, leaving students with the erroneous impression that randomization took care of all threats to validity. He said that the concept of external validity was originated to call attention to those threats that randomization did not reduce and that therefore "backhandedly, threats to internal validity were, initially and implicitly, those for which random assignment did control" (p. 68). Though this cannot be literally true—attrition was among his internal validity threats, but it is not controlled by random assignment—this quote does provide useful insight into the thinking that initiated the distinction.

4. External validity is sometimes confused with ecological validity. The latter is used in many different ways (e.g., Bronfenbrenner, 1979; Brunswick, 1943, 1956). However, in its original meaning it is not a validity type but a method that calls for research with samples of settings and participants that reflect the ecology of application (although Bronfenbrenner understood it slightly differently; 1979, p. 29). The internal-external validity distinction is also sometimes confused with the laboratory-field distinction. Although the latter distinction did help motivate Campbell's (1957) thinking, the two are logically orthogonal. In principle, the causal inference from a field experiment can have high internal validity, and one can ask whether a finding first identified in the field would generalize to the laboratory setting.

TABLE 2.1 Four Types of Validity

Statistical Conclusion Validity: The validity of inferences about the correlation (covariation) between treatment and outcome.

Internal Validity: The validity of inferences about whether observed covariation between A (the presumed treatment) and B (the presumed outcome) reflects a causal relationship from A to B as those variables were manipulated or measured.

Construct Validity: The validity of inferences about the higher order constructs that represent sampling particulars.

External Validity: The validity of inferences about whether the cause-effect relationship holds over variation in persons, settings, treatment variables, and measurement variables.

settings, and times achieved in a study to and across populations about which questions of generalization might be raised.

In this book, the definitions of statistical conclusion and internal validity remain essentially unchanged from Cook and Campbell (1979), extending the former only to consider the role of effect sizes in experiments. However, we modify construct and external validity to accommodate Cronbach's (1982) points that both kinds of causal generalizations (representations and extrapolations) apply to all elements of a study (units, treatments, observations and settings; see Table 2.1). Hence construct validity is now defined as the degree to which inferences are warranted from the observed persons, settings, and cause and effect operations included in a study to the constructs that these instances might represent. External validity is now defined as the validity of inferences about whether the causal relationship holds over variation in persons, settings, treatment variables, and measurement variables.

In Cook and Campbell (1979), construct validity was mostly limited to inferences about higher order constructs that represent the treatments and observations actually studied;[5] in our current usage, we extend this definition of construct validity to cover persons and settings, as well. In Cook and Campbell (1979), external validity referred only to inferences about how a causal relationship would generalize to and across populations of persons and settings; here we extend their definition of external validity to include treatments and observations, as well. Creating a separate construct validity label only for cause and effect issues was justi-

---

5. However, Cook and Campbell (1979) explicitly recognized the possibility of inferences about constructs regarding other study features such as persons and settings: "In the discussion that follows we shall restrict ourselves to the construct validity of presumed causes and effects, since these play an especially crucial role in experiments whose raison d'etre is to test causal propositions. But it should be clearly noted that construct validity concerns are not limited to cause and effect constructs. All aspects of the research require naming samples in generalizable terms, including samples of peoples and settings as well as samples of measures or manipulations" (p. 59).

fied pragmatically in Cook and Campbell because of the attention it focused on a central issue in causation: how the cause and effect should be characterized theoretically. But this salience was sometimes interpreted to imply that characterizing populations of units and settings is trivial. Because it is not, construct validity should refer to them also. Similarly, we should not limit external generalizations to persons and settings, for it is worth assessing whether a particular cause-and-effect relationship would hold if different variants of the causes or effects were used—those differences are often small variations but can sometimes be substantial. We will provide examples of these inferences in Chapter 3.

Our justification for discussing these four slightly reformulated validity types remains pragmatic, however, based on their correspondence to four major questions that practicing researchers face when interpreting causal studies: (1) How large and reliable is the covariation between the presumed cause and effect? (2) Is the covariation causal, or would the same covariation have been obtained without the treatment? (3) Which general constructs are involved in the persons, settings, treatments, and observations used in the experiment? and (4) How generalizable is the locally embedded causal relationship over varied persons, treatments, observations, and settings? Although these questions are often highly interrelated, it is worth treating them separately because the inferences drawn about them often occur independently and because the reasoning we use to construct each type of inference differs in important ways. In the end, however, readers should always remember that "A validity typology can greatly aid . . . design, but it does not substitute for critical analysis of the particular case or for logic" (Mark, 1986 p. 63).

Threats to Validity

Threats to validity are specific reasons why we can be partly or completely wrong when we make an inference about covariance, about causation, about constructs, or about whether the causal relationship holds over variations in persons, settings, treatments, and outcomes. In this chapter we describe threats to statistical conclusion validity and internal validity; in the following chapter we do the same for construct and external validity. The threats we present to each of the four validity types have been identified through a process that is partly conceptual and partly empirical. In the former case, for example, many of the threats to internal validity are tied to the nature of reasoning about descriptive causal inferences outlined in Chapter 1. In the latter case, Campbell (1957) identified many threats from critical commentary on past experiments, most of those threats being theoretically mundane. The empirically based threats can, should, and do change over time as experience indicates both the need for new threats and the obsolescence of former ones. Thus we add a new threat to the traditional statistical conclusion validity threats. We call it "Inaccurate Effect Size Estimation" in order to reflect the reality that social scientists now emphasize estimating the size of causal effects, in addition to running the usual statistical significance tests. Conversely, although each of the threats we describe do indeed occur in experiments, the likelihood that they will occur varies across contexts. Lists of validity threats are heuristic aids; they are not etched in stone, and they are not universally relevant across all research areas in the social sciences.

These threats serve a valuable function: they help experimenters to anticipate the likely criticisms of inferences from experiments that experience has shown occur frequently, so that the experimenter can try to rule them out.[6] The primary method we advocate for ruling them out is to use design controls that minimize the number and plausibility of those threats that remain by the end of a study. This book is primarily about how to conduct such studies, particularly with the help of design rather than statistical adjustment controls. The latter are highlighted in presentations of causal inference in much of economics, say, but less so in statistics itself, in which the design controls we prefer also tend to be preferred. Random assignment is a salient example of good design control. This book describes the experimental design elements that generally increase the quality of causal inferences by ruling out more alternative interpretations to a causal claim. Chapter 8 shows how and when random assignment to treatment and comparison conditions can enhance causal inference, whereas Chapters 4 through 7 show what design controls can be used when random assignment is not possible or has broken down.

However, many threats to validity cannot be ruled out by design controls, either because the logic of design control does not apply (e.g., with some threats to construct validity such as inadequate construct explication) or because practical constraints prevent available controls from being used. In these cases, the appropriate method is to identify and explore the role and influence of the threat in the study. In doing this, three questions are critical: (1) How would the threat apply in this case? (2) Is there evidence that the threat is plausible rather than just possible? (3) Does the threat operate in the same direction as the observed effect, so that it could partially or totally explain the observed findings? For example, suppose a critic claims that history (other events occurring at the same time as treatment that could have caused the same outcome) is a threat to the internal validity of a quasi-experiment you have conducted on the effects of the federal Women, Infants, and Children (WIC) Program to improve pregnancy outcome among eligible low-income women compared with a control group of ineligible women. First, we need to know how "history" applies in this case, for example, whether other social programs are available and whether women who are eligible for WIC are also eligible for these other programs. A little thought shows that the food stamps program might be such a threat. Second, we need to know if there is evi-

---

6. We agree with Reichardt (2000) that it would be better to speak of "taking account of threats to validity" than to say "ruling out threats to validity," for the latter implies a finality that can rarely be achieved in either theory or practice. Talking about "ruling out" threats implies an all-or-none quality in which threats either do or do not apply; but in many cases threats are a matter of degree rather than being absolute. However, we also agree with Reichardt that the term "ruling out" has such a strong foothold in this literature that we can continue to use the term for stylistic reasons.

dence—or at least a reasonable expectation given past findings or background knowledge—that more women who are eligible for WIC are getting food stamps than women who are ineligible for WIC. If not, then although this particular history threat is possible, it may not be plausible. In this case, background knowledge suggests that the threat is plausible because both the WIC Program and the food stamps program use similar eligibility criteria. Third, if the threat is plausible, we need to know if the effects of food stamps on pregnancy outcome would be similar to the effects of the WIC Program. If not, then this history threat could not explain the observed effect, and so it does not threaten it. In this case, the threat would be real, for food stamps could lead to better nutrition, which could also improve pregnancy outcome. Throughout this book, we will emphasize these three crucial questions about threats in the examples we use.

The previous example concerns a threat identified by a critic after a study was done. Given the difficulties all researchers have in criticizing their own work, such post hoc criticisms are probably the most common source of identified threats to studies. However, it is better if the experimenter can anticipate such a threat before the study has begun. If he or she can anticipate it but cannot institute design controls to prevent the threat, the best alternative is to measure the threat directly to see if it actually operated in a given study and, if so, to conduct statistical analyses to examine whether it can plausibly account for the obtained cause-effect relationship. We heartily endorse the direct assessment of possible threats, whether done using quantitative or qualitative observations. It will sometimes reveal that a specific threat that might have operated did not in fact do so or that the threat operated in a way opposite to the observed effect and so could not account for the effect (e.g., Gastwirth, Krieger, & Rosenbaum, 1994). However, we are cautious about using such direct measures of threats in statistical analyses that claim to rule out the threat. The technical reasons for this caution are explained in subsequent chapters, but they have to do with the need for full knowledge of how a threat operates and for perfect measurement of the threat. The frequent absence of such knowledge is why we usually prefer design over statistical control, though in practice most studies will achieve a mix of both. We want to tilt the mix more in the design direction, and to this end this book features a large variety of practical design elements that, in different real-world circumstances, can aid in causal inference while limiting the need for statistical adjustment.

In doing all this, the experimenter must remember that ruling out threats to validity is a falsificationist enterprise, subject to all the criticisms of falsificationism that we outlined in Chapter 1. For example, ruling out plausible threats to validity in experiments depends on knowing the relevant threats. However, this knowledge depends on the quality of the relevant methodological and substantive theories available and on the extent of background information available from experience with the topic on hand. It also depends on the existence of a widely accepted theory of "plausibility," so that we know which of the many possible threats are plausible in this particular context. Without such a theory, most researchers rely on their own all-too-fallible judgment (Mark, 1986; Rindskopf, 2000). And it depends on measuring the threats in unbiased ways that do not include the theories, wishes, expectations, hopes, or category systems of the observers. So the process of ruling out threats to validity exemplifies the fallible falsificationism that we described in Chapter 1.

STATISTICAL CONCLUSION VALIDITY

Statistical conclusion validity concerns two related statistical inferences that affect the covariation component of causal inferences:[7] (1) whether the presumed cause and effect covary and (2) how strongly they covary. For the first of these inferences, we can incorrectly conclude that cause and effect covary when they do not (a **Type I error**) or incorrectly conclude that they do not covary when they do (a **Type II error**). For the second inference, we can overestimate or underestimate the magnitude of covariation, as well as the degree of confidence that magnitude estimate warrants. In this chapter, we restrict ourselves to classical statistical conceptions of covariation and its magnitude, even though qualitative analyses of covariation are both plausible and important.[8] We begin with a brief description of the nature of covariation statistics and then discuss the specific threats to those inferences.

Reporting Results of Statistical Tests of Covariation

The most widely used way of addressing whether cause and effect covary is **null hypothesis significance testing** (NHST). An example is that of an experimenter who computes a *t*-test on treatment and comparison group means at posttest, with the usual **null hypothesis** being that the difference between the population means from which these samples were drawn is zero.[9] A test of this hypothesis is typically accompanied by a statement of the probability that a difference of the size obtained (or larger) would have occurred by chance (e.g., $p = .036$) in a popula-

---

7. We use covariation and correlation interchangeably, the latter being a standardized version of the former. The distinction can be important for other purposes, however, such as when we model explanatory processes in Chapter 12.

8. Qualitative researchers often make inferences about covariation based on their observations, as when they talk about how one thing seems related to another. We can think about threats to the validity of those inferences, too. Psychological theory about biases in covariation judgments might have much to offer to this program (e.g., Crocker, 1981; Faust, 1984), as with the "illusory correlation" bias in clinical psychology (Chapman & Chapman, 1969). But we do not know all or most of these threats to qualitative inferences about covariation; and some we know have been seriously criticized (e.g., Gigerenzer, 1996) because they seem to operate mostly with individuals' first reactions. Outlining threats to qualitative covariation inferences is a task best left to qualitative researchers whose contextual familiarity with such work makes them better suited to the task than we are.

9. Cohen (1994) suggests calling this zero-difference hypothesis the "nil" hypothesis to emphasize that the hypothesis of zero difference is not the only possible hypothesis to be nullified. We discuss other possible null hypotheses shortly. Traditionally, the opposite of the null hypothesis has been called the **alternative hypothesis,** for example, that the difference between group means is not zero.

tion in which no between-group difference exists. Following a tradition first suggested by Fisher (1926, p. 504), it has unfortunately become customary to describe this result dichotomously—as statistically significant if $p < .05$ or as nonsignificant otherwise. Because the implication of nonsignificance is that a cause and effect do not covary—a conclusion that can be wrong and have serious consequences—threats to statistical conclusion validity are partly about why a researcher might be wrong in claiming not to find a significant effect using NHST.

However, problems with this kind of NHST have been known for decades (Meehl, 1967, 1978; Rozeboom, 1960), and the debate has intensified recently (Abelson, 1997; Cohen, 1994; Estes, 1997; Frick, 1996; Harlow, Mulaik, & Steiger, 1997; Harris, 1997; Hunter, 1977; Nickerson, 2000; Scarr, 1997; Schmidt, 1996; Shrout, 1997; Thompson, 1993). Some critics even want to replace NHST totally with other options (Hunter, 1997; Schmidt, 1996). The arguments are beyond the scope of this text, but primarily they reduce to two: (1) scientists routinely misunderstand NHST, believing that p describes the chances that the null hypothesis is true or that the experiment would replicate (Greenwald, Gonzalez, Harris, & Guthrie, 1996); and (2) NHST tells us little about the size of an effect. Indeed, some scientists wrongly think that nonsignificance implies a zero effect when it is more often true that such **effect sizes** are different from zero (e.g., Lipsey & Wilson, 1993).

This is why most parties to the debate about statistical significance tests prefer reporting results as effect sizes bounded by confidence intervals, and even the advocates of NHST believe it should play a less prominent role in describing experimental results. But few parties to the debate believe that NHST should be banned outright (e.g., Howard, Maxwell, & Fleming, 2000; Kirk, 1996). It can still be useful for understanding the role that chance may play in our findings (Krantz, 1999; Nickerson, 2000). So we prefer to see results reported first as effect size estimates accompanied by 95% confidence intervals, followed by the exact probability level of a Type I error from a NHST.[10] This is feasible for any focused comparison between two conditions (e.g., treatment versus control); Rosenthal and Rubin (1994) suggest methods for contrasts involving more than two conditions.

The effect size and 95% confidence interval contain all the information provided by traditional NHST but focus attention on the magnitude of covariation and the precision of the effect size estimate; for example, "the 95% confidence interval of 6 ± 2 shows more precision than the 95% confidence interval of 6 ± 5"

---

10. The American Psychological Association's Task Force on Statistical Inference concluded, *"It is hard to imagine a situation in which a dichotomous accept-reject decision is better than reporting an actual p value or, better still, a confidence interval. . . . Always provide some effect-size estimate when reporting a p value. . . . Interval estimates should be given for any effect sizes involving principal outcomes"* (Wilkinson and the Task Force on Statistical Inference, 1999, p. 599). Cohen (1994) suggests reporting "confidence curves" (Birnbaum, 1961) from which can be read all confidence intervals from 50% to 100% so that just one confidence interval need not be chosen; a computer program for generating these curves is available (Borenstein, Cohen, & Rothstein, in press).

(Frick, 1996, p. 383). Confidence intervals also help to distinguish between situations of low statistical power, and hence wide confidence intervals, and situations with precise but small effect sizes—situations that have quite different implications. Reporting the preceding statistics would also decrease current dependence on speciously precise point estimates, replacing them with more realistic ranges that better reflect uncertainty even though they may complicate public communication. Thus the statement "the average increase in income was $1,000 per year" would be complemented by "the likely outcome is an average increase ranging between $400 and $1600 per year."

In the classic interpretation, exact Type I probability levels tell us the probability that the results that were observed in the experiment could have been obtained by chance from a population in which the null hypothesis is true (Cohen, 1994). In this sense, NHST provides some information that the results could have arisen due to chance—perhaps not the most interesting hypothesis but one about which it has become customary to provide the reader with information. A more interesting interpretation (Frick, 1996; Harris, 1997; Tukey, 1991) is that the probability level tells us about the confidence we can have in deciding among three claims: (1) the sign of the effect in the population is positive (Treatment A did better than Treatment B); (2) the sign is negative (Treatment B did better than Treatment A); or (3) the sign is uncertain. The smaller the p value, the less likely it is that our conclusion about the sign of the population effect is wrong; and if $p >$ .05 (or, equivalently, if the confidence interval contains zero), then our conclusion about the sign of the effect is too close to call.

In any case, whatever interpretation of the p value from NHST one prefers, all this discourages the overly simplistic conclusion that either "there is an effect" or "there is no effect." We believe that traditional NHST will play an increasingly small role in social science, though no new approach will be perfect.[11] As Abelson recently said:

> Whatever else is done about null-hypothesis tests, let us stop viewing statistical analysis as a sanctification process. We are awash in a sea of uncertainty, caused by a flood tide of sampling and measurement errors, and there are no objective procedures that avoid human judgment and guarantee correct interpretations of results. (1997, p. 13)

---

11. An alternative (more accurately, a complement) to both NHST and reporting effect sizes with confidence intervals is the use of Bayesian statistics (Etzioni & Kadane, 1995; Howard et al., 2000). Rather than simply accept or reject the null hypothesis, Bayesian approaches use the results from a study to update existing knowledge on an ongoing basis, either prospectively by specifying expectations about study outcomes before the study begins (called prior probabilities) or retrospectively by adding results from an experiment to an existing corpus of experiments that has already been analyzed with Bayesian methods to update results. The latter is very close to random effects meta-analytic procedures (Hedges, 1998) that we cover in Chapter 13. Until recently, Bayesian statistics have been used sparingly, partly because of ambiguity about how prior probabilities should be obtained and partly because Bayesian methods were computationally intensive with few computer programs to implement them. The latter objection is rapidly dissipating as more powerful computers and acceptable programs are developed (Thomas, Spiegelhalter, & Gilks, 1992), and the former is beginning to be addressed in useful ways (Howard et al., 2000). We expect to see increasing use of Bayesian statistics in the next few decades, and as their use becomes more frequent, we will undoubtedly find threats to the validity of them that we do not yet include here.

TABLE 2.2 Threats to Statistical Conclusion Validity: Reasons Why Inferences About Covariation Between Two Variables May Be Incorrect

1. *Low Statistical Power:* An insufficiently powered experiment may incorrectly conclude that the relationship between treatment and outcome is not significant.

2. *Violated Assumptions of Statistical Tests:* Violations of statistical test assumptions can lead to either overestimating or underestimating the size and significance of an effect.

3. *Fishing and the Error Rate Problem:* Repeated tests for significant relationships, if uncorrected for the number of tests, can artifactually inflate statistical significance.

4. *Unreliability of Measures:* Measurement error weakens the relationship between two variables and strengthens or weakens the relationships among three or more variables.

5. *Restriction of Range:* Reduced range on a variable usually weakens the relationship between it and another variable.

6. *Unreliability of Treatment Implementation:* If a treatment that is intended to be implemented in a standardized manner is implemented only partially for some respondents, effects may be underestimated compared with full implementation.

7. *Extraneous Variance in the Experimental Setting:* Some features of an experimental setting may inflate error, making detection of an effect more difficult.

8. *Heterogeneity of Units:* Increased variability on the outcome variable within conditions increases error variance, making detection of a relationship more difficult.

9. *Inaccurate Effect Size Estimation:* Some statistics systematically overestimate or underestimate the size of an effect.

Threats to Statistical Conclusion Validity

Table 2.2 presents a list of threats to statistical conclusion validity, that is, reasons why researchers may be wrong in drawing valid inferences about the existence and size of covariation between two variables.

Low Statistical Power

Power refers to the ability of a test to detect relationships that exist in the population, and it is conventionally defined as the probability that a statistical test will reject the null hypothesis when it is false (Cohen, 1988; Lipsey, 1990; Maxwell & Delaney, 1990). When a study has low power, effect size estimates will be less precise (have wider confidence intervals), and traditional NHST may incorrectly conclude that cause and effect do not covary. Simple computer programs can calculate power if we know or can estimate the sample size, the Type I and Type II error rates, and the effect sizes (Borenstein & Cohen, 1988; Dennis, Lennox, & Foss, 1997; Hintze, 1996; Thomas & Krebs, 1997). In social science practice, Type I error rates are usually set at $\alpha = .05$, although good reasons often exist to deviate from this

(Makuch & Simon, 1978)—for example, when testing a new drug for harmful side effects, a higher Type I error rate might be fitting (e.g., $\alpha = .20$). It is also common to set the Type II error rate (β) at .20, and power is then $1 - \beta = .80$. The target effect size is often inferred from what is judged to be a practically important or theoretically meaningful effect (Cohen, 1996; Lipsey, 1990), and the standard deviation needed to compute effect sizes is usually taken from past research or pilot work. If the power is too low for detecting an effect of the specified size, steps can be taken to increase power. Given the central importance of power in practical experimental design, Table 2.3 summarizes the many factors that affect power that will be discussed in this book and provides comments about such matters as their feasibility, application, exceptions to their use, and disadvantages.

TABLE 2.3 Methods to Increase Power

Method	Comments
Use matching, stratifying, blocking	1. Be sure the variable used for matching, stratifying, or blocking is correlated with outcome (Maxwell, 1993), or use a variable on which subanalyses are planned. 2. If the number of units is small, power can decrease when matching is used (Gail et al., 1996).
Measure and correct for covariates	1. Measure covariates correlated with outcome and adjust for them in statistical analysis (Maxwell, 1993). 2. Consider cost and power tradeoffs between adding covariates and increasing sample size (Allison, 1995; Allison et al., 1997). 3. Choose covariates that are nonredundant with other covariates (McClelland, 2000). 4. Use covariance to analyze variables used for blocking, matching, or stratifying.
Use larger sample sizes	1. If the number of treatment participants is fixed, increase the number of control participants. 2. If the budget is fixed and treatment is more expensive than control, compute optimal distribution of resources for power (Orr, 1999). 3. With a fixed total sample size in which aggregates are assigned to conditions, increase the number of aggregates and decrease the number of units within aggregates.
Use equal cell sample sizes	1. Unequal cell splits do not affect power greatly until they exceed 2:1 splits (Pocock, 1983). 2. For some effects, unequal sample size splits can be more powerful (McClelland, 1997).

TABLE 2.3 Continued

Method	Comments
Improve measurement	1. Increase measurement reliability or use latent variable modeling.
	2. Eliminate unnecessary restriction of range (e.g., rarely dichotomize continuous variables).
	3. Allocate more resources to posttest than to pretest measurement (Maxwell, 1994).
	4. Add additional waves of measurement (Maxwell, 1998).
	5. Avoid floor or ceiling effects.
Increase the strength of treatment	1. Increase dose differential between conditions.
	2. Reduce diffusion over conditions.
	3. Ensure reliable treatment delivery, receipt, and adherence.
Increase the variability of treatment	1. Extend the range of levels of treatment that are tested (McClelland, 2000).
	2. In some cases, oversample from extreme levels of treatment (McClelland, 1997).
Use a within-participants design	1. Less feasible outside laboratory settings.
	2. Subject to fatigue, practice, contamination effects.
Use homogenous participants selected to be responsive to treatment	1. Can compromise generalizability.
Reduce random setting irrelevancies	1. Can compromise some kinds of generalizability.
Ensure that powerful statistical tests are used and their assumptions are met	1. Failure to meet test assumptions sometimes increases power (e.g., treating dependent units as independent), so you must know the relationship between assumption and power.
	2. Transforming data to meet normality assumptions can improve power even though it may not affect Type I error rates much (McClelland, 2000).
	3. Consider alternative statistical methods (e.g., Wilcox, 1996).

To judge from reviews, low power occurs frequently in experiments. For instance, Kazdin and Bass (1989) found that most psychotherapy outcome studies comparing two treatments had very low power (see also Freiman, Chalmers, Smith, & Kuebler, 1978; Lipsey, 1990; Sedlmeier & Gigerenzer, 1989). So low power is a major cause of false null conclusions in individual studies. But when effects are small, it is frequently impossible to increase power sufficiently using the methods in Table 2.3. This is one reason why the synthesis of many studies (see Chapter 13) is now so routinely advocated as a path to more powerful tests of small effects.

Violated Assumptions of the Test Statistics

Inferences about covariation may be inaccurate if the assumptions of a statistical test are violated. Some assumptions can be violated with relative impunity. For instance, a two-tailed t-test is reasonably robust to violations of normality if group sample sizes are large and about equal and only Type I error is at issue (Judd, McClelland, & Culhane, 1995; but for Type II error, see Wilcox, 1995). However, violations of other assumptions are more serious. For instance, inferences about covariation may be inaccurate if observations are not independent—for example, children in the same classroom may be more related to each other than randomly selected children are; patients in the same physician's practice or workers in the same workplace may be more similar to each other than randomly selected individuals are.[12] This threat occurs often and violates the assumption of independently distributed errors. It can introduce severe bias to the estimation of standard errors, the exact effects of which depend on the design and the kind of dependence (Judd et al., 1995). In the most common case of units **nested** within aggregates (e.g., children in some schools get one treatment and children in other schools get the comparison condition), the bias is to increase the Type I error rate dramatically so that researchers will conclude that there is a "significant" treatment difference far more often than they should. Fortunately, recent years have seen the development of relevant statistical remedies and accompanying computer programs (Bryk & Raudenbush, 1992; Bryk, Raudenbush, & Congdon, 1996; DeLeeuw & Kreft, 1986; Goldstein, 1987).

Fishing and the Error Rate Problem

An inference about covariation may be inaccurate if it results from fishing through the data set to find a "significant" effect under NHST or to pursue leads suggested by the data themselves, and this inaccuracy can also occur when multiple investigators reanalyze the same data set (Denton, 1985). When the Type I error rate for a single test is $\alpha = .05$, the error rate for a set of tests is quite different and increases with more tests. If three tests are done with a nominal $\alpha = .05$, then the actual alpha (or the probability of making a Type I error over all three tests) is .143; with twenty tests it is .642; and with fifty tests it is .923 (Maxwell & Delaney, 1990). Especially if only a subset of results are reported (e.g., only the significant ones), the research conclusions can be misleading.

---

12. Violations of this assumption used to be called the "**unit of analysis**" problem; we discuss this problem in far more detail in Chapter 8.

The simplest corrective procedure is the very conservative Bonferroni correction, which divides the overall target Type I error rate for a set (e.g., $\alpha = .05$) by the number of tests in the set and then uses the resulting Bonferroni-corrected α in all individual tests. This ensures that the error rate over all tests will not exceed the nominal $\alpha = .05$. Other corrections include the use of conservative multiple comparison follow-up tests in analysis of variance (ANOVA) or the use of a multivariate ANOVA if multiple dependent variables are tested (Maxwell & Delaney, 1990). Some critics of NHST discourage such corrections, arguing that we already tend to overlook small effects and that conservative corrections make this even more likely. They argue that reporting effect sizes, confidence intervals, and exact p values shifts the emphasis from "significant-nonsignificant" decisions toward confidence about the likely sign and size of the effect. Other critics argue that if results are reported for all statistical tests, then readers can assess for themselves the chances of spuriously "significant" results by inspection (Greenwald et al., 1996). However, it is unlikely that complete reporting will occur because of limited publication space and the tendency of authors to limit reports to the subset of results that tell an interesting story. So in most applications, fishing will still lead researchers to have more confidence in associations between variables than they should.

Unreliability of Measures

A conclusion about covariation may be inaccurate if either variable is measured unreliably (Nunnally & Bernstein, 1994). **Unreliability** always attenuates bivariate relationships. When relationships involve three or more variables, the effects of unreliability are less predictable. Maxwell and Delaney (1990) showed that unreliability of a covariate in an analysis of covariance can produce significant treatment effects when the true effect is zero or produce zero effects in the presence of true effects. Similarly, Rogosa (1980) showed that the effects of unreliability in certain correlational designs depended on the pattern of relationships among variables and the differential **reliability** of the variables, so that nearly any effect or null effect could be found no matter what the true effect might be. Special reliability issues arise in longitudinal studies that assess rates of change, acceleration, or other features of development (Willett, 1988). So reliability should be assessed and reported for each measure. Remedies for unreliability include increasing the number of measurements (e.g., using more items or more raters), improving the quality of measures (e.g., better items, better training of raters), using special kinds of growth curve analyses (Willett, 1988), and using techniques like **latent variable** modeling of several observed measures to parcel out true score from error variance (Bentler, 1995).

Restriction of Range

Sometimes variables are restricted to a narrow range; for instance, in experiments two highly similar treatments might be compared or the outcome may have only two values or be subject to floor or ceiling effects. This restriction also lowers power and attenuates bivariate relations. Restriction on the independent variable can be decreased by, for example, studying distinctly different treatment doses or even full-dose treatment versus no treatment. This is especially valuable early in a research program when it is important to test whether large effects can be found under circumstances most favorable to its emergence. Dependent variables are restricted by **floor effects** when all respondents cluster near the lowest possible score, as when most respondents score normally on a scale measuring pathological levels of depression, and by **ceiling effects** when all respondents cluster near the highest score, as when a study is limited to the most talented students. When continuous measures are dichotomized (or trichotomized, etc.), range is again restricted, as when a researcher uses the median weight of a sample to create high- and low-weight groups. In general, such splits should be avoided.[13] Pilot testing measures and selection procedures help detect range restriction, and item response theory analyses can help to correct the problem if a suitable calibration sample is available (Hambleton, Swaminathan, & Rogers, 1991; Lord, 1980).

Unreliability of Treatment Implementation

Conclusions about covariation will be affected if treatment is implemented inconsistently from site to site or from person to person within sites (Boruch & Gomez, 1977; Cook, Habib, Philips, Settersten, Shagle, & Degirmencioglu, 1999; Lipsey, 1990). This threat is pervasive in field experiments, in which controlling the treatment is less feasible than in the laboratory. Lack of standardized implementation is commonly thought to decrease an effect size, requiring more attention to other design features that increase power, such as sample size. However, some authors note that variable implementation may reflect a tailoring of the intervention to the recipient in order to increase its effects (Scott & Sechrest, 1989; Sechrest, West, Phillips, Redner, & Yeaton, 1979; Yeaton & Sechrest, 1981). Further, lack of standardization is also not a problem if the desired inference is to a treatment that is supposed to differ widely across units. Indeed, a lack of standardization is intrinsic to some real-world interventions. Thus, in studies of the Comprehensive Child Development Program (Goodson, Layzer, St. Pierre, Bernstein & Lopez, 2000) and Early Head Start (Kisker & Love, 1999), poor parents of young children were provided with different packages of services depending on the varying nature of their needs. Thus some combinations of job training, formal education, parent training, counseling, or emergency housing might be needed, creating a very heterogeneous treatment across the families studied. In all these cases, however, efforts should be made to measure the components of the treatment package and to explore how the various components are related to changes

---

13. Counterintuitively, Maxwell and Delaney (1990) showed that dichotomizing two continuous independent variables to create a factorial ANOVA design can sometimes increase power (by increasing Type I error rate).

in outcomes. Because this issue is so important, in Chapters 10 and 12 we discuss methods for improving, measuring, and analyzing treatment implementation that help reduce this threat.

Extraneous Variance in the Experimental Setting

Conclusions about covariation can be inaccurate if features of an experimental setting artifactually inflate error. Examples include distracting noises, fluctuations in temperature due to faulty heating/cooling systems, or frequent fiscal or administrative changes that distract practitioners. A solution is to control these factors or to choose experimental procedures that force respondents' attention on the treatment or that lower environmental salience. But in many field settings, these suggestions are impossible to implement fully. This situation entails the need to measure those sources of extraneous variance that cannot otherwise be reduced, using them later in the statistical analysis. Early qualitative monitoring of the experiment will help suggest what these variables might be.

Heterogeneity of Units (Respondents)

The more the units in a study are heterogeneous within conditions on an outcome variable, the greater will be the standard deviations on that variable (and on any others correlated with it). Other things being equal, this heterogeneity will obscure systematic covariation between treatment and outcome. Error also increases when researchers fail to specify respondent characteristics that interact with a cause-and-effect relationship, as in the case of some forms of depression that respond better to a psychotherapeutic treatment than others. Unless they are specifically measured and modeled, these **interactions** will be part of error, obscuring systematic covariation. A solution is to sample respondents who are homogenous on characteristics correlated with major outcomes. However, such selection may reduce external validity and can cause restriction of range if it is not carefully monitored. Sometimes a better solution is to measure relevant respondent characteristics and use them for **blocking** or as covariates. Also, within-participant designs can be used in which the extent of the advantage depends on the size of the correlation between pre- and posttest scores.

Inaccurate Effect Size Estimation

Covariance estimates can be inaccurate when the size of the effect is measured poorly. For example, when outliers cause a distribution to depart even a little from normality, this can dramatically decrease effect sizes (Wilcox, 1995). Wilcox (in press) suggests alternative effect size estimation methods for such data (along with Minitab computer programs), though they may not fit well with standard statistical techniques. Also, analyzing dichotomous outcomes with effect size measures designed for continuous variables (i.e., the correlation coefficient or standardized mean difference statistic) will usually underestimate effect size; **odds ratios** are usually a better choice (Fleiss, 1981, p. 60). Effect size estimates are also implicit in common statistical tests. For example, if an ordinary *t*-test is computed on a dichotomous outcome, it implicitly uses the standardized mean difference **statistic** and will have lower power. As researchers increasingly report effect size and confidence intervals, more causes of inaccurate effect size estimation will undoubtedly be found.

The Problem of Accepting the Null Hypothesis

Although we hope to discourage researchers from describing a failure to reject the null hypothesis as "no effect," there are circumstances in which they must consider such a conclusion. One circumstance is that in which the true hypothesis of interest is a no-effect one, for example, that a new treatment does as well as the accepted standard, that a feared side effect does not occur (Makuch & Simon, 1978), that extrasensory perception experiments have no effect (Rosenthal, 1986), or that the result of a first coin toss has no relationship to the result of a second if the coin is fair (Frick, 1996). Another is that in which a series of experiments yields results that are all "too close to call," leading the experimenter to wonder whether to continue to investigate the treatment. A third is the case in which the analyst wants to show that groups do not differ on various threats to validity, as when group equivalence on pretests is examined for **selection bias** (Yeaton & Sechrest, 1986). Each of these situations requires testing whether the obtained covariation can be reliably distinguished from zero. However, it is very hard to prove that covariation is exactly zero because power theory suggests that, even when an effect is very small, larger sample sizes, more reliable measures, better treatment implementation, or more accurate statistics might distinguish it from zero. From this emerges the maxim that we cannot prove the null hypothesis (Frick, 1995).

To cope with situations such as these, the first thing to do is to maximize power so as to avoid "too close to call" conclusions. Table 2.3 listed many ways in which this can be done, though each differs in its feasibility for any given study and some may not be desirable if they conflict with other goals of the experiment. Nonetheless, examining studies against these power criteria will often reveal whether it is desirable and practical to conduct new experiments with more powerful designs.

A second thing to do is to pay particular attention to identifying the size of an effect worth pursuing, for example, the maximum acceptable harm or the smallest effect that makes a practical difference (Fowler, 1985; Prentice & Miller, 1992; Rouanet, 1996; Serlin & Lapsley, 1993). Aschenfelter's (1978) study of the effects of manpower training programs on subsequent earnings estimated that an increase in earnings of $200 would be adequate for declaring the program a success. He could then use power analysis to ensure a sufficient sample to detect this effect. However, specifying such an effect size is a political act, because a reference point is then created against which an innovation can be evaluated. Thus, even if an innovation has a partial effect, it may not be given credit for this if the promised effect size has not been achieved. Hence managers of educational programs learn to assert, "We want to increase achievement" rather than stating, "We want to increase achievement by two years for every year of teaching." However, even when such factors mitigate against specifying a minimally acceptable effect size, presenting the absolute magnitude of an obtained treatment effect allows readers to infer for themselves whether an effect is so small as to be practically unimportant or whether a nonsignificant effect is so large as to merit further research with more powerful analyses.

Third, if the hypothesis concerns the equivalency of two treatments, biostatisticians have developed equivalency testing techniques that could be used in place of traditional NHST. These methods test whether an observed effect falls into a range that the researcher judges to be equivalent for practical purposes, even if the difference between treatments is not zero (Erbland, Deupree, & Niewoehner, 1999; Rogers, Howard, & Vessey, 1993; Westlake, 1988).

A fourth option is to use quasi-experimental analyses to see if larger effects can be located under some important conditions—for example, subtypes of participants who respond to treatment more strongly or naturally occurring dosage variations that are larger than average in an experiment. Caution is required in interpreting such results because of the risk of capitalizing on chance and because individuals will often have self-selected themselves into treatments differentially. Nonetheless, if sophisticated quasi-experimental analyses fail to show minimally interesting covariation between treatment and outcome measures, then the analyst's confidence that the effect is too small to pursue increases.

INTERNAL VALIDITY

We use the term *internal validity* to refer to inferences about whether observed covariation between A and B reflects a causal relationship from A to B in the form in which the variables were manipulated or measured. To support such an inference, the researcher must show that A preceded B in time, that A covaries with B (already covered under statistical conclusion validity) and that no other explanations for the relationship are plausible. The first problem is easily solved in experiments because they force the manipulation of A to come before the measurement of B. However, causal order is a real problem in nonexperimental research, especially in cross-sectional work.

Although the term *internal validity* has been widely adopted in the social sciences, some of its uses are not faithful to the concept as first described by Campbell (1957). Internal validity was not about reproducibility (Cronbach, 1982), nor inferences to the target population (Kleinbaum, Kupper, & Morgenstern, 1982), nor measurement validity (Menard, 1991), nor whether researchers measure what they think they measure (Goetz & LeCompte, 1984). To reduce such misunderstandings, Campbell (1986) proposed relabeling internal validity as **local molar causal validity,** a relabeling that is instructive to explicate even though it is so cumbersome that we will not use it, sticking with the older but more memorable and widely accepted term (internal validity).

The word *causal* in *local molar causal validity* emphasizes that internal validity is about causal inferences, not about other types of inference that social scientists make. The word *local* emphasizes that causal conclusions are limited to the context of the particular treatments, outcomes, times, settings, and persons studied. The word *molar* recognizes that experiments test treatments that are a complex package consisting of many components, all of which are tested as a whole within the treatment condition. Psychotherapy, for example, consists of different verbal interventions used at different times for different purposes. There are also nonverbal cues both common to human interactions and specific to provider-client relationships. Then there is the professional placebo provided by prominently displayed graduate degrees and office suites modeled on medical precedents, financial arrangements for reimbursing therapists privately or through insurance, and the physical condition of the psychotherapy room (to name just some parts of the package). A client assigned to psychotherapy is assigned to all parts of this molar package and others, not just to the part that the researcher may intend to test. Thus the causal inference from an experiment is about the effects of being assigned to the whole molar package. Of course, experiments can and should break down such molar packages into molecular parts that can be tested individually or against each other. But even those molecular parts are packages consisting of many components. Understood as local molar causal validity, internal validity is about whether a complex and inevitably multivariate treatment package caused a difference in some variable-as-it-was-measured within the particular setting, time frames, and kinds of units that were sampled in a study.

Threats to Internal Validity

In what may be the most widely accepted analysis of causation in philosophy, Mackie (1974) stated: "Typically, we infer from an effect to a cause (inus condition) by eliminating other possible causes" (p. 67). Threats to internal validity are those other possible causes—reasons to think that the relationship between A and B is not causal, that it could have occurred even in the absence of the treatment, and that it could have led to the same outcomes that were observed for the treatment. We present these threats (Table 2.4) separately even though they are not totally independent. Enough experience with this list has accumulated to suggest that it applies to any descriptive molar causal inference, whether generated from experiments, correlational studies, observational studies, or case studies. After all, validity is not the property of a method; it is a characteristic of knowledge claims (Shadish, 1995b)—in this case, claims about causal knowledge.

TABLE 2.4 Threats to Internal Validity: Reasons Why Inferences That the Relationship Between Two Variables Is Causal May Be Incorrect

1. *Ambiguous Temporal Precedence:* Lack of clarity about which variable occurred first may yield confusion about which variable is the cause and which is the effect.

2. *Selection:* Systematic differences over conditions in respondent characteristics that could also cause the observed effect.

3. *History:* Events occurring concurrently with treatment could cause the observed effect.

4. *Maturation:* Naturally occurring changes over time could be confused with a treatment effect.

5. *Regression:* When units are selected for their extreme scores, they will often have less extreme scores on other variables, an occurrence that can be confused with a treatment effect.

6. *Attrition:* Loss of respondents to treatment or to measurement can produce artifactual effects if that loss is systematically correlated with conditions.

7. *Testing:* Exposure to a test can affect scores on subsequent exposures to that test, an occurrence that can be confused with a treatment effect.

8. *Instrumentation:* The nature of a measure may change over time or conditions in a way that could be confused with a treatment effect.

9. *Additive and Interactive Effects of Threats to Internal Validity:* The impact of a threat can be added to that of another threat or may depend on the level of another threat.

Ambiguous Temporal Precedence

Cause must precede effect, but sometimes it is unclear whether A precedes B or vice versa, especially in correlational studies. But even in correlational studies, one direction of causal influence is sometimes implausible (e.g., an increase in heating fuel consumption does not cause a decrease in outside temperature). Also, some correlational studies are longitudinal and involve data collection at more than one time. This permits analyzing as potential causes only those variables that occurred before their possible effects. However, the fact that A occurs before B does not justify claiming that A causes B; other conditions of causation must also be met.

Some causation is bidirectional (reciprocal), as with the criminal behavior that causes incarceration that causes criminal behavior that causes incarceration, or with high levels of school performance that generate self-efficacy in a student that generates even higher school performance. Most of this book is about testing unidirectional causation in experiments. Experiments were created for this purpose precisely because it is known which factor was deliberately manipulated before another was measured. However, separate experiments can test first whether A causes B and second whether B causes A. So experiments are not irrelevant to causal reciprocation, though simple experiments are. Other methods for testing reciprocal causation are discussed briefly in Chapter 12.

Selection

Sometimes, at the start of an experiment, the average person receiving one experimental condition already differs from the average person receiving another condition. This difference might account for any result after the experiment ends that the analysts might want to attribute to treatment. Suppose that a compensatory education program is given to children whose parents volunteer them and that the comparison condition includes only children who were not so volunteered. The volunteering parents might also read to their children more, have more books at home, or otherwise differ from nonvolunteers in ways that might affect their child's achievement. So children in the compensatory education program might do better even without the program.[14] When properly implemented, random assignment definitionally eliminates such selection bias because randomly formed groups differ only by chance. Of course, faulty randomization can introduce selection bias, as can a successfully implemented randomized experiment in which subsequent attrition differs by treatment group. Selection is presumed to be pervasive in quasi-experiments, given that they are defined as using the structural attributes of experiments but without random assignment. The key feature of selection bias is a confounding of treatment effects with population differences. Much of this book will be concerned with selection, both when individuals select themselves into treatments and when administrators place them in different treatments.

History

History refers to all events that occur between the beginning of the treatment and the posttest that could have produced the observed outcome in the absence of that treatment. We discussed an example of a history threat earlier in this chapter regarding the evaluation of programs to improve pregnancy outcome in which receipt of food stamps was that threat (Shadish & Reis, 1984). In laboratory research, history is controlled by isolating respondents from outside events (e.g., in a quiet laboratory) or by choosing dependent variables that could rarely be affected by the world outside (e.g., learning nonsense syllables). However, experimental isolation is rarely available in field research—we cannot and would not stop pregnant mothers from receiving food stamps and other external events that might improve pregnancy outcomes. Even in field research, though, the plausibility of history can be reduced; for example, by selecting groups from the same general location and by ensuring that the schedule for testing is the same in both groups (i.e., that one group is not being tested at a very different time than another, such as testing all control participants prior to testing treatment participants; Murray, 1998).

---

14. Though it is common to discuss selection in two-group designs, such selection biases can also occur in single-group designs when the composition of the group changes over time.

Maturation

Participants in research projects experience many natural changes that would occur even in the absence of treatment, such as growing older, hungrier, wiser, stronger, or more experienced. Those changes threaten internal validity if they could have produced the outcome attributed to the treatment. For example, one problem in studying the effects of compensatory education programs such as Head Start is that normal cognitive development ensures that children improve their cognitive performance over time, a major goal of Head Start. Even in short studies such processes are a problem; for example, fatigue can occur quickly in a verbal learning experiment and cause a performance decrement. At the community level or higher, maturation includes secular trends (Rossi & Freeman, 1989), changes that are occurring over time in a community that may affect the outcome. For example, if the local economy is growing, employment levels may rise even if a program to increase employment has no specific effect. Maturation threats can often be reduced by ensuring that all groups are roughly of the same age so that their individual maturational status is about the same and by ensuring that they are from the same location so that local secular trends are not differentially affecting them (Murray, 1998).

Regression Artifacts

Sometimes respondents are selected to receive a treatment because their scores were high (or low) on some measure. This often happens in quasi-experiments in which treatments are made available either to those with special merits (who are often then compared with people with lesser merits) or to those with special needs (who are then compared with those with lesser needs). When such extreme scorers are selected, there will be a tendency for them to score less extremely on other measures, including a retest on the original measure (Campbell & Kenny, 1999). For example, the person who scores highest on the first test in a class is not likely to score highest on the second test; and people who come to psychotherapy when they are extremely distressed are likely to be less distressed on subsequent occasions, even if psychotherapy had no effect. This phenomenon is often called regression to the mean (Campbell & Stanley, 1963; Furby, 1973; Lord, 1963; Galton, 1886, called it regression toward mediocrity) and is easily mistaken for a treatment effect. The prototypical case is selection of people to receive a treatment because they have extreme pretest scores, in which case those scores will tend to be less extreme at posttest. However, regression also occurs "backward" in time. That is, when units are selected because of extreme posttest scores, their pretest scores will tend to be less extreme; and it occurs on simultaneous measures, as when extreme observations on one posttest entail less extreme observations on a correlated posttest. As a general rule, readers should explore the plausibility of this threat in detail *whenever respondents are selected (or select themselves) because they had scores that were higher or lower than average.*

Regression to the mean occurs because measures are not perfectly correlated with each other (Campbell & Kenny, 1999; Nesselroade, Stigler, & Baltes, 1980; Rogosa, 1988). **Random measurement error** is part of the explanation for this imperfect correlation. Test theory assumes that every measure has a true score component reflecting a true ability, such as depression or capacity to work, *plus* a random error component that is normally and randomly distributed around the mean of the measure. On any given occasion, high scores will tend to have more positive random error pushing them up, whereas low scores will tend to have more negative random error pulling them down. On the same measure at a later time, or on other measures at the same time, the random error is less likely to be so extreme, so the observed score (the same true score plus less extreme random error) will be less extreme. So using more reliable measures can help reduce regression.

However, it will not prevent it, because most variables are imperfectly correlated with each other by their very nature and would be imperfectly correlated even if they were perfectly measured (Campbell & Kenny, 1999). For instance, both height and weight are nearly perfectly measured; yet in any given sample, the tallest person is not always the heaviest, nor is the lightest person always the shortest. This, too, is regression to the mean. Even when the same variable is measured perfectly at two different times, a real set of forces can cause an extreme score at one of those times; but these forces are unlikely to be maintained over time. For example, an adult's weight is usually measured with very little error. However, adults who first attend a weight-control clinic are likely to have done so because their weight surged after an eating binge on a long business trip exacerbated by marital stress; their weight will regress to a lower level as those causal factors dissipate even if the weight-control treatment has no effect. But notice that in all these cases, the key clue to the possibility of regression artifacts is always present—selection based on an extreme score, whether it be the person who scored highest on the first test, the person who comes to psychotherapy when most distressed, the tallest person, or the person whose weight just reached a new high.

What should researchers do to detect or reduce statistical regression? If selection of extreme scorers is a necessary part of the question, the best solution is to create a large group of extreme scorers from within which random assignment to different treatments then occurs. This unconfounds regression and receipt of treatment so that regression occurs equally for each group. By contrast, the worst situation occurs when participants are selected into a group based on extreme scores on some unreliable variable and that group is then compared with a group selected differently. This builds in the very strong likelihood of group differences in regression that can masquerade as a treatment effect (Campbell & Erlebacher, 1970). In such cases, because regression is most apparent when inspecting standardized rather than raw scores, diagnostic tests for regression (e.g., Galton squeeze diagrams; Campbell & Kenny, 1999) should be done on standardized scores. Researchers should also increase the reliability of any selection measure by increasing the number of items on it, by averaging it over several time points, or by using a multivariate function of several variables instead of a single variable for selection. Another procedure is working with three or more time points; for example, making the selection into groups based on the Time 1 measure, implementing the treatment after the Time 2 measure, and then examining change between Time 2 and Time 3 rather than between Time 1 and Time 3 (Nesselroade et al., 1980).

Regression does not require quantitative analysis to occur. Psychologists have identified it as an illusion that occurs in ordinary cognition (Fischhoff, 1975; Gilovich, 1991; G. Smith, 1997; Tversky & Kahneman, 1974). Psychotherapists have long noted that clients come to therapy when they are more distressed than usual and tend to improve over time even without therapy. They call this spontaneous remission rather than statistical regression, but it is the same phenomenon. The clients' measured progress is partly a movement back toward their stable individual mean as the temporary shock that led them to therapy (a death, a job loss, a shift in the marriage) grows less acute. Similar examples are those alcoholics who appear for treatment when they have "hit bottom" or those schools and businesses that call for outside professional help when things are suddenly worse. Many business consultants earn their living by capitalizing on regression, avoiding institutions that are stably bad but manage to stay in business and concentrating instead on those that have recently had a downturn for reasons that are unclear.

Attrition

Attrition (sometimes called experimental **mortality**) refers to the fact that participants in an experiment sometimes fail to complete the outcome measures. If different kinds of people remain to be measured in one condition versus another, then such differences could produce posttest outcome differences even in the absence of treatment. Thus, in a randomized experiment comparing family therapy with discussion groups for treatment of drug addicts, addicts with the worst prognosis tend to drop out of the discussion group more often than out of family therapy. If the results of the experiment suggest that family therapy does less well than discussion groups, this might just reflect differential attrition, by which the worst addicts stayed in family therapy (Stanton & Shadish, 1997). Similarly, in a longitudinal study of a study-skills treatment, the group of college seniors that eventually graduates is only a subset of the incoming freshmen and might be systematically different from the initial population, perhaps because they are more persistent or more affluent or higher achieving. This then raises the question: Was the final grade point average of the senior class higher than that of the freshman class because of the effects of a treatment or because those who dropped out had lower scores initially? Attrition is therefore a special subset of selection bias occurring after the treatment is in place. But unlike selection, differential attrition is not controlled by random assignment to conditions.

Testing

Sometimes taking a test once will influence scores when the test is taken again. Practice, familiarity, or other forms of reactivity are the relevant mechanisms and could be mistaken for treatment effects. For example, weighing someone may cause the person to try to lose weight when they otherwise might not have done so, or taking a vocabulary pretest may cause someone to look up a novel word and so perform better at posttest. On the other hand, many measures are not reactive in this way. For example, a person could not change his or her height (see Webb, Campbell, Schwartz, & Sechrest, 1966, and Webb, Campbell, Schwartz, Sechrest, & Grove, 1981, for other examples). Techniques such as item response theory sometimes help reduce **testing effects** by allowing use of different tests that are calibrated to yield equivalent ability estimates (Lord, 1980). Sometimes testing effects can be assessed using a Solomon Four Group Design (Braver & Braver, 1988; Dukes, Ullman, & Stein, 1995; Solomon, 1949), in which some units receive a pretest and others do not, to see if the pretest causes different treatment effects. Empirical research suggests that testing effects are sufficiently prevalent to be of concern (Willson & Putnam, 1982), although less so in designs in which the interval between tests is quite large (Menard, 1991).

Instrumentation

A change in a measuring instrument can occur over time even in the absence of treatment, mimicking a treatment effect. For example, the spring on a bar press might become weaker and easier to push over time, artifactually increasing reaction times; the component stocks of the Dow Jones Industrial Average might have changed so that the new index reflects technology more than the old one; and human observers may become more experienced between pretest and posttest and so report more accurate scores at later time points. Instrumentation problems are especially prevalent in studies of child development, in which the measurement unit or scale may not have constant meaning over the age range of interest (Shonkoff & Phillips, 2000). Instrumentation differs from testing because the former involves a change in the instrument, the latter a change in the participant. Instrumentation changes are particularly important in longitudinal designs, in which the way measures are taken may change over time (see Figure 6.7 in Chapter 6) or in which the meaning of a variable may change over life stages (Menard, 1991).[15] Methods for investigating these changes are discussed by Cunningham (1991) and Horn (1991). Researchers should avoid switching instruments during a study; but

---

15. Epidemiologists sometimes call instrumentation changes surveillance bias.

if switches are required, the researcher should retain both the old and new items (if feasible) to calibrate one against the other (Murray, 1998).

Additive and Interactive Effects of Threats to Internal Validity

Validity threats need not operate singly. Several can operate simultaneously. If they do, the net bias depends on the direction and magnitude of each individual bias plus whether they combine additively or multiplicatively (interactively). In the real world of social science practice, it is difficult to estimate the size of such net bias. We presume that inaccurate causal inferences are more likely the more numerous and powerful are the simultaneously operating validity threats and the more homogeneous their direction. For example, a **selection-maturation** additive effect may result when nonequivalent experimental groups formed at the start of treatment are also maturing at different rates over time. An illustration might be that higher achieving students are more likely to be given National Merit Scholarships and also likely to be improving their academic skills at a more rapid rate. Both initial high achievement and more rapid achievement growth serve to doubly inflate the perceived effects of National Merit Scholarships. Similarly, a **selection-history** additive effect may result if nonequivalent groups also come from different settings and each group experiences a unique local history. A **selection-instrumentation** additive effect might occur if nonequivalent groups have different means on a test with unequal intervals along its distribution, as would occur if there is a ceiling or floor effect for one group but not for another.[16]

Estimating Internal Validity in Randomized Experiments and Quasi-Experiments

Random assignment eliminates selection bias definitionally, leaving a role only to chance differences. It also reduces the plausibility of other threats to internal validity. Because groups are randomly formed, any initial group differences in maturational rates, in the experience of simultaneous historical events, and in regression artifacts ought to be due to chance. And so long as the researcher administers the same tests in each condition, pretesting effects and instrumentation changes should be experienced equally over conditions within the limits of chance. So random assignment and treating groups equivalently in such matters as pretesting and instrumentation improve internal validity.

---

16. Cook and Campbell (1979) previously called these interactive effects; but they are more accurately described as additive. Interactions among threats are also possible, including higher order interactions, but describing examples of these accurately can be more complex than needed here.

Given random assignment, inferential problems about causation arise in only two situations. In the first, attrition from the experiment is differential by treatment group, in which case the outcome differences between groups might be due to differential attrition rather than to treatment. Techniques have recently been advanced for dealing with this problem (e.g., Angrist et al., 1996a), and we review them in Chapter 10. In the second circumstance, testing must be different in each group, as when the expense or **response burden** of testing on participants is so high that the experimenter decides to administer pretests only to a treatment group that is more likely to be cooperative if they are getting, say, a desirable treatment. Experimenters should monitor a study to detect any differential attrition early and to try to correct it before it goes too far, and they should strive to make testing procedures as similar as possible across various groups.

With quasi-experiments, the causal situation is more murky, because differences between groups will be more systematic than random. So the investigator must rely on other options to reduce internal validity threats. The main option is to modify a study's design features. For example, regression artifacts can be reduced by not selecting treatment units on the basis of extreme and partially unreliable scores, provided that this restriction does not trivialize the research question. History can be made less plausible to the extent that experimental isolation is feasible. Attrition can be reduced using many methods to be detailed in Chapter 10. But it is not always feasible to implement these design features, and doing so sometimes subtly changes the nature of the research question. This is why the omnibus character of random assignment is so desirable.

Another option is to make all the threats explicit and then try to rule them out one by one. Identifying each threat is always context specific; for example, what may count as history in one context (e.g., the introduction of *Sesame Street* during an experiment on compensatory education in the 1970s) may not count as a threat at all in another context (e.g., watching *Sesame Street* is an implausible means of reducing unwanted pregnancies). Once identified, the presence of a threat can be assessed either quantitatively by measurement or qualitatively by observation or interview. In both cases, the presumed effect of the threat can then be compared with the outcome to see if the *direction* of the threat's bias is the same as that of the observed outcome. If so, the threat may be plausible, as with the example of the introduction of *Sesame Street* helping to improve reading rather than a contemporary education program helping to improve it. If not, the threat may still be implausible, as in the discovery that the healthiest mothers are more likely to drop out of a treatment but that the treatment group still performs better than the controls. When the threat is measured quantitatively, it might be addressed by state-of-the-art statistical adjustments, though this is problematic because those adjustments have not always proven very accurate and because it is not easy to be confident that all the context-specific threats to internal validity have been identified. Thus the task of individually assessing the plausibility of internal validity threats is definitely more laborious and less certain than relying on experimental design, randomization in particular but also the many design elements we introduce throughout this book.

THE RELATIONSHIP BETWEEN INTERNAL VALIDITY AND STATISTICAL CONCLUSION VALIDITY

These two validity types are closely related. Both are primarily concerned with study operations (rather than with the constructs those operations reflect) and with the relationship between treatment and outcome. Statistical conclusion validity is concerned with errors in assessing statistical covariation, whereas internal validity is concerned with causal-reasoning errors. Even when all the statistical analyses in a study are impeccable, errors of causal reasoning may still lead to the wrong causal conclusion. So statistical covariation does not prove causation. Conversely, when a study is properly implemented as a randomized experiment, statistical errors can still occur and lead to incorrect judgments about statistical significance and misestimated effect sizes. Thus, in quantitative experiments, internal validity depends substantially on statistical conclusion validity.

However, experiments need not be quantitative in how either the intervention or the outcome are conceived and measured (Lewin, 1935; Lieberson, 1985; Mishler, 1990), and some scholars have even argued that the statistical analysis of quantitative data is detrimental (e.g., Skinner, 1961). Moreover, examples of qualitative experiments abound in the physical sciences (e.g., Drake, 1981; Hacking, 1983; Naylor, 1989; Schaffer, 1989), and there are even some in the social sciences. For instance, Sherif's famous Robber's Cave Experiment (Sherif, Harvey, White, Hood, & Sherif, 1961) was mostly qualitative. In that study, boys at a summer camp were divided into two groups of eleven each. Within-group cohesion was fostered for each group separately, and then intergroup conflict was introduced. Finally, conflict was reduced using an intervention to facilitate equal status cooperation and contact while working on common goals. Much of the data in this experiment was qualitative, including the highly cited effects on the reduction of intergroup conflict. In such cases, internal validity no longer depends directly on statistical conclusion validity, though clearly an assessment that treatment covaried with the effect is still necessary, albeit a qualitative assessment.

Indeed, given such logic, Campbell (1975) recanted his previous rejection (Campbell & Stanley, 1963) of using case studies to investigate causal inferences because the reasoning of causal inference *is* qualitative and because all the logical requirements for inferring cause apply as much to qualitative as to quantitative work. Scriven (1976) has made a similar argument. Although each makes clear that causal inferences from case studies are likely to be valid only under limited circumstances (e.g., when isolation of the cause from other confounds is feasible), neither believes that causation requires quantitatively scaled treatments or outcomes. We agree.

3

Construct Validity and External Validity

Re·la·tion·ship (rĭ-lā´shən-shĭp´): n. 1. The condition or fact of being related; connection or association. 2. Connection by blood or marriage; kinship.

Trade·off or **Trade-off** (trād´ôf´, -ŏf´): n. An exchange of one thing in return for another, especially relinquishment of one benefit or advantage for another regarded as more desirable: *"a fundamental trade-off between capitalist prosperity and economic security"* (David A. Stockman).

Pri·or·i·ty (prī-ôr´ĭ-tē, -ŏr´-): [Middle English *priorite*, from Old French from Medieval Latin *pririts*, from Latin *prior*, first; see prior.] n., pl. pri·or·i·ties. 1. Precedence, especially established by order of importance or urgency. 2. a. An established right to precedence. b. An authoritative rating that establishes such precedence. 3. A preceding or coming earlier in time. 4. Something afforded or deserving prior attention.

I N THIS chapter, we continue the consideration of validity by discussing both construct and external validity, including threats to each of them. We then end with a more general discussion of relationships, tradeoffs, and priorities among validity types.

CONSTRUCT VALIDITY

A recent report by the National Academy of Sciences on research in early childhood development succinctly captured the problems of construct validity:

> In measuring human height (or weight or lung capacity, for example), there is little disagreement about the meaning of the construct being measured, or about the units of measurement (e.g., centimeters, grams, cubic centimeters). . . . Measuring growth in psychological domains (e.g., vocabulary, quantitative reasoning, verbal memory, hand–eye coordination, self-regulation) is more problematic. Disagreement is more

likely to arise about the definition of the constructs to be assessed. This occurs, in part, because there are often no natural units of measurement (i.e., nothing comparable to the use of inches when measuring height). (Shonkoff & Phillips, 2000, pp. 82–83)

Here we see the twin problems of construct validity—understanding constructs and assessing them. In this chapter, we elaborate on how these problems occur in characterizing and measuring the persons, settings, treatments, and outcomes used in an experiment.

Scientists do empirical studies with specific instances of units, treatments, observations, and settings; but these instances are often of interest only because they can be defended as measures of general constructs. Construct validity involves making inferences from the sampling particulars of a study to the higher-order constructs they represent. Regarding the persons studied, for example, an economist may be interested in the construct of unemployed, disadvantaged workers; but the sample of persons actually studied may be those who have had family income below the poverty level for 6 months before the experiment begins or who participate in government welfare or food stamp programs. The economist intends the match between construct and operations to be close, but sometimes discrepancies occur—in one study, some highly skilled workers who only recently lost their jobs met the preceding criteria and so were included in the study, despite not really being disadvantaged in the intended sense (Heckman, Ichimura, & Todd, 1997). Similar examples apply to the treatments, outcomes, and settings studied. Psychotherapists are rarely concerned only with answers to the 21 items on the Beck Depression Inventory; rather, they want to know if their clients are depressed. When agricultural economists study farming methods in the foothills of the Atlas Mountains in Morocco, they are frequently interested in arid agriculture in poor countries. When physicians study 5-year mortality rates among cancer patients, they are interested in the more general concept of survival.

As these examples show, research cannot be done without using constructs. As Albert Einstein once said, "Thinking without the positing of categories and concepts in general would be as impossible as breathing in a vacuum" (Einstein, 1949, pp. 673–674). Construct validity is important for three other reasons, as well. First, constructs are the central means we have for connecting the operations used in an experiment to pertinent theory and to the language communities that will use the results to inform practical action. To the extent that experiments contain construct errors, they risk misleading both theory and practice. Second, construct labels often carry social, political, and economic implications (Hopson, 2000). They shape perceptions, frame debates, and elicit support and criticism. Consider, for example, the radical disagreements that stakeholders have about the label of a "hostile work environment" in sexual or racial harassment litigation, disagreements about what that construct means, how it should be measured, and whether it applies in any given setting. Third, the creation and defense of basic constructs is a fundamental task of all science. Examples from the physical sciences include "the development of the periodic table of elements, the identification of the composition of water, the laying out of different genera and species of plants and animals, and the discovery of the structure of genes" (Mark, 2000, p. 150)—though such taxonomic work is considerably more difficult in the social sciences, for reasons which we now discuss.

Why Construct Inferences Are a Problem

The naming of things is a key problem in all science, for names reflect category memberships that themselves have implications about relationships to other concepts, theories, and uses. This is true even for seemingly simple labeling problems. For example, a recent newspaper article reported a debate among astronomers over what to call 18 newly discovered celestial objects ("Scientists Quibble," 2000). The Spanish astronomers who discovered the bodies called them planets, a choice immediately criticized by some other astronomers: "I think this is probably an inappropriate use of the 'p' word," said one of them. At issue was the lack of a match between some characteristics of the 18 objects (they are drifting freely through space and are only about 5 million years old) and some characteristics that are prototypical of planets (they orbit a star and require tens of millions of years to form). Critics said these objects were more reasonably called brown dwarfs, objects that are too massive to be planets but not massive enough to sustain the thermonuclear processes in a star. Brown dwarfs would drift freely and be young, like these 18 objects. The Spanish astronomers responded that these objects are too small to be brown dwarfs and are so cool that they could not be that young. All this is more than just a quibble: If these objects really are planets, then current theories of how planets form by condensing around a star are wrong! And this is a simple case, for the category of planets is so broadly defined that, as the article pointed out, "Gassy monsters like Jupiter are in, and so are icy little spitwads like Pluto." Construct validity is a much more difficult problem in the field experiments that are the topic of this book.

Construct validity is fostered by (1) starting with a clear explication of the person, setting, treatment, and outcome constructs of interest; (2) carefully selecting instances that match those constructs; (3) assessing the match between instances and constructs to see if any slippage between the two occurred; and (4) revising construct descriptions accordingly. In this chapter, we primarily deal with construct explication and some prototypical ways in which researchers tend to pick instances that fail to represent those constructs well. However, throughout this book, we discuss methods that bear on construct validity. Chapter 9, for example, devotes a section to ensuring that enough of the intended participants exist to be recruited into an experiment and randomized to conditions; and Chapter 10 devotes a section to ensuring that the intended treatment is well conceptualized, induced, and assessed.

There is a considerable literature in philosophy and the social sciences about the problems of construct explication (Lakoff, 1985; Medin, 1989; Rosch, 1978; Smith & Medin, 1981; Zadeh, 1987). In what is probably the most common theory, each construct has multiple features, some of which are more central than others and so are called prototypical. To take a simple example, the prototypical features of a tree are that it is a tall, woody plant with a distinct main stem or trunk that lives for at least 3 years (a perennial). However, each of these attributes is associated with some degree of fuzziness in application. For example, their height and distinct trunk distinguish trees from shrubs, which tend to be shorter and have multiple stems. But some trees have more than one main trunk, and others are shorter than some tall shrubs, such as rhododendrons. No attributes are foundational. Rather, we use a **pattern-matching** logic to decide whether a given instance sufficiently matches the prototypical features to warrant using the category label, especially given alternative category labels that could be used.

But these are only surface similarities. Scientists are often more concerned with deep similarities, prototypical features of particular scientific importance that may be visually peripheral to the layperson. To the layperson, for example, the difference between deciduous (leaf-shedding) and coniferous (evergreen) trees is visually salient; but scientists prefer to classify trees as angiosperms (flowering trees in which the seed is encased in a protective ovary) or gymnosperms (trees that do not bear flowers and whose seeds lie exposed in structures such as cones). Scientists value this discrimination because it clarifies the processes by which trees reproduce, more crucial to understanding forestation and survival than is the lay distinction between deciduous and coniferous. It is thus difficult to decide which features of a thing are more peripheral or more prototypical, but practicing researchers always make this decision, either explicitly or implicitly, when selecting participants, settings, measures, and treatment manipulations.

This difficulty arises in part because deciding which features are prototypical depends on the context in which the construct is to be used. For example, it is not that scientists are right and laypersons wrong about how they classify trees. To a layperson who is considering buying a house on a large lot with many trees, the fact that the trees are deciduous means that substantial annual fall leaf cleanup expenses will be incurred. Medin (1989) gives a similar example, asking what label should be applied to the category that comprises children, money, photo albums, and pets. These are not items we normally see as sharing prototypical construct features, but in one context they do—when deciding what to rescue from a fire.

Deciding which features are prototypical also depends on the particular language community doing the choosing. Consider the provocative title of Lakoff's (1985) book *Women, Fire, and Dangerous Things*. Most of us would rarely think of women, fire, and dangerous things as belonging to the same category. The title provokes us to think of what these things have in common: Are women fiery and dangerous? Are both women and fires dangerous? It provokes us partly because we do not have a natural category that would incorporate all these elements. In the language community of natural scientists, fire might belong to a category having to do with oxidation processes, but women are not in that category. In the language community of ancient philosophy, fire might belong to a category of basic elements along with air, water, and earth, but dangerous things are not among those elements. But in the Australian aboriginal language called Dyirbal, women, fire, and dangerous things are all part of one category.[1]

All these difficulties in deciding which features are prototypical are exacerbated in the social sciences. In part, this is because so many important constructs are still being discovered and developed, so that strong consensus about prototypical construct features is as much the exception as the rule. In the face of only weak consensus, slippage between instance and construct is even greater than otherwise. And in part, it is because of the abstract nature of the entities with which social scientists typically work, such as violence, incentive, decision, plan, and intention. This renders largely irrelevant a theory of categorization that is widely used in some areas—the theory of natural kinds. This theory postulates that nature cuts things at the joint, and so we evolve names and shared understandings for the entities separated by joints. Thus we have separate words for a tree's trunk and its branches, but no word for the bottom left section of a tree. Likewise, we have words for a twig and leaf, but no word for the entity formed by the bottom half of a twig and the attached top third of a leaf. There are many fewer "joints" (or equivalents thereof) in the social sciences—what would they be for intentions or aggression, for instance?

By virtue of all these difficulties, it is never possible to establish a one-to-one relationship between the operations of a study and corresponding constructs. Logical positivists mistakenly assumed that it would be possible to do this, creating a subtheory around the notion of definitional operationalism—that a thing is only what its measure captures, so that each measure is a perfect representation of its own construct. Definitional operationalism failed for many reasons (Bechtel, 1988; H. I. Brown, 1977). Indeed, various kinds of definitional operationalism are threats to construct validity in our list below. Therefore, a theory of constructs must emphasize (1) operationalizing each construct several ways within and across studies; (2) probing the pattern match between the multivariate characteristics of instances and the characteristics of the target construct, and (3) acknowledging legitimate debate about the quality of that match given the socially constructed nature of both operations and constructs. Doing all this is facilitated by detailed description of the studied instances, clear explication of the prototypical elements of the target construct, and valid observation of relationships among the instances, the target construct, and any other pertinent constructs.[2]

---

1. The explanation is complex, occupying a score of pages in Lakoff (1985), but a brief summary follows. The Dyirbal language classifies words into four categories (much as the French language classifies nouns as masculine or feminine): (1) Bayi: (human) males; animals; (2) Balan: (human) females; water; fire; fighting; (3) Balam: nonflesh food; (4) Bala: everything not in the other three classes. The moon is thought to be husband to the sun, and so is included in the first category as male; hence the sun is female and in the second category. Fire reflects the same domain of experience as the sun, and so is also in the second category. Because fire is associated with danger, dangerousness in general is also part of the second category.

2. Cronbach and Meehl (1955) called this set of theoretical relationships a nomological net. We avoid this phrase because its dictionary definition (nomological: the science of physical and logical laws) fosters an image of lawful relationships that is incompatible with field experimentation as we understand it.

Assessment of Sampling Particulars

Good construct explication is essential to construct validity, but it is only half the job. The other half is good assessment of the sampling particulars in a study, so that the researcher can assess the match between those assessments and the constructs. For example, the quibble among astronomers about whether to call 18 newly discovered celestial objects "planets" required *both* a set of prototypical characteristics of planets versus brown dwarfs *and* measurements of the 18 objects on these characteristics—their mass, position, trajectory, radiated heat, and likely age. Because the prototypical characteristics of planets are well-established and accepted among astronomers, critics tend first to target the accuracy of the measurements in such debates, for example, speculating that the Spanish astronomers measured the mass or radiated heat of these objects incorrectly. Consequently, other astronomers try to replicate these measurements, some using the same methods and others using different ones. If the measurements prove correct, then the prototypical characteristics of the construct called planets will have to be changed, or perhaps a new category of celestial object will be invented to account for the anomalous measurements.

Not surprisingly, this attention to measurement was fundamental to the origins of construct validity (Cronbach & Meehl, 1955), which grew out of concern with the quality of psychological tests. The American Psychological Association's (1954) Committee on Psychological Tests had as its job to specify the qualities that should be investigated before a test is published. They concluded that one of those qualities was construct validity. For example, Cronbach and Meehl (1955) said that the question addressed by construct validity is, "What constructs account for variance in test performance?" (p. 282) and also that construct validity involved "how one is to defend a proposed interpretation of a test" (p. 284). The measurement and the construct are two sides of the same construct validity coin.

Of course, Cronbach and Meehl (1955) were not writing about experiments. Rather, their concern was with the practice of psychological testing of such matters as intelligence, personality, educational achievement, or psychological pathology, a practice that blossomed in the aftermath of World War II with the establishment of the profession of clinical psychology. However, those psychological tests were used frequently in experiments, especially as outcome measures in, say, experiments on the effects of educational interventions. So it was only natural that critics of particular experimental findings might question the construct validity of inferences about what is being measured by those outcome measurements. In adding construct validity to the D. T. Campbell and Stanley (1963) validity typology, Cook and Campbell (1979) recognized this usage; and they extended this usage from outcomes to treatments, recognizing that it is just as important to characterize accurately the nature of the treatments that are applied in an experiment. In this book, we extend this usage two steps further to cover persons and settings, as well. Of course, our categorization of experiments as consisting of units (persons), settings, treatments, and outcomes is partly arbitrary, and we could have chosen to treat, say, time as a separate feature of each experiment, as we occasionally have in some of our past work. Such additions would not change the key point. Construct validity involves making inferences from assessments of *any* of the sampling particulars in a study to the higher-order constructs they represent.

Most researchers probably understand and accept the rationale for construct validity of outcome measures. It may help, however, to give examples of construct validity of persons, settings, and treatments. A few of the simplest person constructs that we use require no sophisticated measurement procedures, as when we classify persons as males or females, usually done with no controversy on the basis of either self-report or direct observation. But many other constructs that we use to characterize people are less consensually agreed upon or more controversial. For example, consider the superficially simple problem of racial and ethnic identity for descendants of the indigenous peoples of North America. The labels have changed over the years (Indians, Native Americans, First Peoples), and the ways researchers have measured whether someone merits any one of these labels have varied from self-report (e.g., on basic U.S. Census forms) to formal assessments of the percentage of appropriate ancestry (e.g., by various tribal registries). Similarly, persons labeled schizophrenic will differ considerably depending on whether their diagnosis was measured by criteria of the American Psychiatric Association's *Diagnostic and Statistical Manual of Mental Disorders* (1994), by one of the earlier editions of that manual, by the recorded diagnosis in a nursing home chart, or by the Schizophrenia subscale of the Minnesota Multiphasic Personality Inventory-2 (Hathaway & McKinley, 1989). When one then turns to common but very loosely applied terms such as *the disadvantaged* (as with the Heckman et al., 1996, example earlier in this chapter), it is not surprising to find dramatically different kinds of persons represented under the same label, especially across studies, but often within studies, too.

Regarding settings, the constructs we use again range from simple to complex and controversial. Frequently the settings investigated in a study are a sample of convenience, described as, say, "the Psychology Department Psychological Services Center" based on the researcher's personal experience with the setting, a label that conveys virtually no information about the size of the setting, its funding, client flow, staff, or the range of diagnoses that are encountered. Such clinics, in fact, vary considerably—from small centers with few nonpaying clients who are almost entirely college students and who are seen by graduate students under the supervision of a single staff member to large centers with a large staff of full-time professionals, who themselves see a wide array of diagnostic problems from local communities, in addition to supervising such cases. But settings are often assessed more formally, as with the measures of setting environment developed by Moos (e.g., Moos, 1997) or with descriptors that are inferred from empirical data, as when profile analysis of the characteristics of nursing homes is used to identify different types of nursing homes (e.g., Shadish, Straw, McSweeny, Koller, & Bootzin, 1981).

Regarding treatments, many areas have well-developed traditions of assessing the characteristics of treatments they administer. In laboratory social psychology experiments by Festinger (e.g., 1953) on cognitive dissonance, for example, detailed scripts were prepared to ensure that the prototypical features of cognitive dissonance were included in the study operations; then those scripts were meticulously rehearsed; and finally manipulation checks were used to see whether the participants perceived the study operations to reflect the constructs that were intended. These measurements increase our confidence that the treatment construct was, in fact, delivered. They are, however, difficult to do for complex social programs such as psychotherapy or whole-school reform. In psychotherapy experiments, for example, primary experimenters usually provide only simple labels about the kind of therapy performed (e.g., behavioral, systemic, psychodynamic). Sometimes these labels are accompanied by one- or two-page descriptions of what was done in therapy, and some quantitative measurements such as the number of sessions are usually provided. More sophisticated systems for measuring therapy content are the exception rather than the rule (e.g., Hill, O'Grady, & Elkin, 1992), in part because of their expense and in part because of a paucity of consensually accepted measures of most therapies.

Construct mislabelings often have serious implications for either theory or practice. For example, some persons who score low on intelligence tests have been given labels such as "retarded," though it turned out that their low performance may have been due to language barriers or to insufficient exposure to those aspects of U.S. culture referenced in intelligence tests. The impact on them for school placement and the stigmatization were often enormous. Similarly, the move on the part of some psychotherapy researchers to call a narrow subset of treatments "empirically supported psychological therapies" (Chambless & Hollon, 1998; Kendall, 1998) implies to both researchers and funders that other psychological therapies are not empirically supported, despite several decades of psychotherapy experiments that confirm their effectiveness. When these mislabelings occur in a description of an experiment, they may lead the reader to err in how they apply experimental results to their theory or practice. Indeed, this is one reason that qualitative researchers so much value the "thick description" of study instances (Emerson, 1981; Geertz, 1973; Ryle, 1971)—so that readers of a study can rely more on their own "naturalistic generalizations" than on one researcher's labels (Stake & Trumbull, 1982). We entirely support this aspiration, at least within the limits of reporting conventions that usually apply to experiments; and so we also support the addition of qualitative methodologies to experiments to provide this capacity.

These examples make clear that assessments of study particulars need not be done using formal multi-item scales—though the information obtained would often be better if such scales were used. Rather, assessments include any method for generating data about sampling particulars. They would include archival records, such as patient charts in psychiatric hospitals in which data on diagnosis and symptoms are often recorded by hand or U.S. Census Bureau records in which respondents indicated their racial and ethnic identities by checking a box. They would include qualitative observations, sometimes formal ones such as participant observation or unstructured interviews conducted by a trained anthropologist but often simply the report of the research team who, say, describe a setting as a "poverty neighborhood" based on their personal observations of it as they drive to and from work each day. Assessments may even include some experimental manipulations that are designed to shed light on the nature of study operations, as when a treatment is compared with a placebo control to clarify the extent to which treatment *is* a placebo.

Of course, the attention paid to construct validity in experiments has historically been uneven across persons, treatments, observations, and settings. Concern with construct representations of settings has probably been a low priority, except for researchers interested in the role of environment and culture. Similarly, in most applied experimental research, greater care may go into the construct validity of outcomes, for unless the experimenter uses a measure of recidivism or of employment or of academic achievement that most competent language community members find reasonable, the research is likely to be seen as irrelevant. In basic research, greater attention may be paid to construct validity of the cause so that its link to theory is strong. Such differentiation of priorities is partly functional and may well have evolved to meet needs in a given research field; but it is probably also partly accidental. If so, increased attention to construct validity across persons and settings would probably be beneficial.

The preceding discussion treated persons, treatments, settings, and outcomes separately. But as we mentioned in Chapter 1, construct labels are appropriately applied to relationships among the elements of a study, as well. Labeling the causal relationship between treatment and outcome is a frequent construct validity concern, as when we categorize certain treatments for cancer as cytotoxic or cytostatic to refer to whether they kill tumor cells directly or delay tumor growth by modulating tumor environment. Some other labels have taken on consensual meanings that include more than one feature; the label Medicare in the United States, for example, is nearly universally understood to refer both to the intervention (health care) and to the persons targeted (the elderly).

Threats to Construct Validity

Threats to construct validity (Table 3.1) concern the match between study operations and the constructs used to describe those operations. Sometimes the problem is the explication of constructs, and sometimes it is the sampling or measurement design. A study's operations might not incorporate all the characteristics of the relevant construct (construct underrepresentation), or they may contain extraneous construct content. The threats that follow are specific versions of these more general errors, versions that research or experience have shown tend to occur frequently. The first five threats clearly apply to persons, settings, treatments, and outcomes. The remaining threats primarily concern construct validity of outcomes and especially treatments, mostly carried forward by us from Cook and

TABLE 3.1 Threats to Construct Validity: Reasons Why Inferences About the Constructs That Characterize Study Operations May Be Incorrect

1. *Inadequate Explication of Constructs:* Failure to adequately explicate a construct may lead to incorrect inferences about the relationship between operation and construct.

2. *Construct Confounding:* Operations usually involve more than one construct, and failure to describe all the constructs may result in incomplete construct inferences.

3. *Mono-Operation Bias:* Any one operationalization of a construct both underrepresents the construct of interest and measures irrelevant constructs, complicating inference.

4. *Mono-Method Bias:* When all operationalizations use the same method (e.g., self-report), that method is part of the construct actually studied.

5. *Confounding Constructs with Levels of Constructs:* Inferences about the constructs that best represent study operations may fail to describe the limited levels of the construct that were actually studied.

6. *Treatment Sensitive Factorial Structure:* The structure of a measure may change as a result of treatment, change that may be hidden if the same scoring is always used.

7. *Reactive Self-Report Changes:* Self-reports can be affected by participant motivation to be in a treatment condition, motivation that can change after assignment is made.

8. *Reactivity to the Experimental Situation:* Participant responses reflect not just treatments and measures but also participants' perceptions of the experimental situation, and those perceptions are part of the treatment construct actually tested.

9. *Experimenter Expectancies:* The experimenter can influence participant responses by conveying expectations about desirable responses, and those expectations are part of the treatment construct as actually tested.

10. *Novelty and Disruption Effects:* Participants may respond unusually well to a novel innovation or unusually poorly to one that disrupts their routine, a response that must then be included as part of the treatment construct description.

11. *Compensatory Equalization:* When treatment provides desirable goods or services, administrators, staff, or constituents may provide compensatory goods or services to those not receiving treatment, and this action must then be included as part of the treatment construct description.

12. *Compensatory Rivalry:* Participants not receiving treatment may be motivated to show they can do as well as those receiving treatment, and this compensatory rivalry must then be included as part of the treatment construct description.

13. *Resentful Demoralization:* Participants not receiving a desirable treatment may be so resentful or demoralized that they may respond more negatively than otherwise, and this resentful demoralization must then be included as part of the treatment construct description.

14. *Treatment Diffusion:* Participants may receive services from a condition to which they were not assigned, making construct descriptions of both conditions more difficult.

Campbell's (1979) list. We could have added a host of new threats particular to the construct validity of persons and settings. For example, Table 4.3 in the next chapter lists threats to validity that have been identified by epidemiologists for case-control studies. The threats in that list under the heading "Specifying and selecting the study sample" are particularly relevant to construct validity of persons (i.e., 2d, e, h, k, l, m, q, s, t, u, v) and settings (i.e., 2a, b, c, j). We do not add them here to keep the length of this list tractable. Conceptually, these biases always occur as one of the first five threats listed in Table 3.1; but specific instances of them in Table 4.3 often shed light on common errors that we make in describing people and settings in health contexts.

Inadequate Explication of Constructs

A mismatch between operations and constructs can arise from inadequate analysis of a construct under study. For instance, many definitions of aggression require both intent to harm others and a harmful result. This is to distinguish between (1) the black eye one boy gives another as they collide coming around a blind bend, (2) the black eye that one boy gives another to get his candy (instrumental aggression) or to harm him (noninstrumental aggression), and (3) the verbal threat by one child to another that he will give him a black eye unless the other boy gives him the candy. If both intent and physical harm are part of the definition, only (2) is an instance of aggression. A precise explication of constructs permits tailoring the study instances to whichever definitions emerge from the explication and allows future readers to critique the operations of past studies. When several definitions are reasonable, resources and the extent to which one definition is preferred in the relevant language community play an important role in shaping the research.

Poststudy criticism of construct explications is always called for, however careful the initial explication, because results themselves sometimes suggest the need to reformulate the construct. For example, many researchers have studied the deterrent effects of jail sentences on drunk drivers compared with less severe sanctions such as monetary fines. After many studies showed that jail time did not reduce instances of recidivism, researchers began to question whether jail is experienced as "more severe" than fines (e.g., Martin, Annan, & Forst, 1993). Notice that the finding of no effect is not at issue here (that is an internal validity question), only whether that finding is best characterized as comparing more severe with less severe treatments.

Mark (2000) suggests that researchers make four common errors in explicating constructs: (1) the construct may be identified at too general a level, for example, calling the treatment in a study psychotherapy even though its characteristics make it better described as research psychotherapy (Weisz, Weiss & Donenberg, 1992); (2) the construct may be identified at too specific a level, such as arguing that the levels of unhappiness characteristic of mental patients in nursing homes are really characteristic of mental patients in *any* poverty setting

(Shadish, Silber, Orwin, & Bootzin, 1985); (3) the wrong construct may be identified, as in the case of immigrants to the United States who are labeled retarded because of low scores on intelligence tests when the meaning of their test scores might be better described as lack of familiarity with U.S. language and culture; and (4) a study operation that really reflects two or more constructs may be described using only one construct; for instance, outcome measures that are typically referred to by the names of the traits they measure should also be named for the methods used to measure them (e.g., self-reports of depression). As these examples illustrate, each of these errors occurs in characterizing all four study features—persons, settings, treatments, and outcomes.

Construct Confounding

The operations in an experiment are rarely pure representations of constructs. Consider the example given at the start of this chapter about a study of persons called "unemployed." The researcher may have applied that label as the best representation of the persons actually studied—those whose family income has been below the poverty level for 6 months before the experiment begins or who participate in government welfare or food stamp programs. However, it may also have been the case that these men were disproportionately African-American and victims of racial prejudice. These latter characteristics were not part of the intended construct of the unemployed but were nonetheless confounded with it in the study operations.

Mono-Operation Bias

Many experiments use only one **operationalization** of each construct. Because single operations both underrepresent constructs and may contain irrelevancies, construct validity will be lower in single-operation research than in research in which each construct is multiply operationalized. It is usually inexpensive to use several measures of a given outcome, and this procedure tends to be most prevalent in social science research. Multiple kinds of units and occasionally many different times can be used, too. But most experiments often have only one or two manipulations of an intervention per study and only one setting, because multisite studies are expensive; and increasing the total number of treatments can entail very large sample sizes (or sizes that are too small within each cell in a study with a fixed total sample size). Still, there is no substitute for deliberately varying several exemplars of a treatment. Hence, if one were studying the effects of communicator expertise, one might use, say, three fictitious sources: a distinguished male professor from a well-known university, a distinguished female scientist from a prestigious research center, and a famous science journalist from Germany. The variance due to source differences can then be examined to see if the sources differentially affected responses. If they did, the assumption that communicator expertise is a single construct might be worth revisiting. But even if sample size does not permit analyzing results by each of these sources, the data can still be combined from all three. Then the investigator can test if expertise is effective despite whatever sources of heterogeneity are contained within the three particular operations.

Monomethod Bias

Having more than one operational representation of a construct is helpful, but if all treatments are presented to respondents in the same way, the method itself may influence results. The same is true if all the outcome measures use the same means of recording responses, if all the descriptions of settings rely on an interview with a manager, or if all the person characteristics are taken from hospital charts. Thus, in the previous hypothetical example, if the respondents had been presented with written statements from all the experts, it would be more accurate to label the treatment as *experts presented in writing,* to make clearer that we do not know if the results would hold with experts who are seen or heard. Similarly, attitude scales are often presented to respondents without much thought to (1) using methods of recording other than paper and pencil or (2) varying whether statements are positively or negatively worded. Yet in the first case, different results might occur for physiological measures or for observer ratings, and in the second case, response biases might be fostered when all items are worded in one direction.

Confounding Constructs with Levels of Constructs

Sometimes an experimenter will draw a general conclusion about constructs that fails to recognize that only some levels of each facet of that construct were actually studied and that the results might have been different if different levels were studied (Cooper & Richardson, 1986). In treatment-control comparisons, for example, the treatment may be implemented at such low levels that no effects are observed, leading to an incorrect characterization of the study as showing that treatment had no effect when the correct characterization is that treatment-implemented-at-low-level had no effect. One way to address this threat is to use several levels of treatment. This confounding can be even more complex when comparing two treatments that are operationalized in procedurally nonequivalent ways. The researcher might erroneously conclude that Treatment A works better than Treatment B when the conclusion should have been that Treatment-A-at-Level-1 works better than Treatment-B-at-Level-0. Similar confounding occurs for persons, outcomes, and settings, for example, when restricted person characteristics (e.g., restricted age) or setting characteristics (e.g., using only public schools) were used but this fact was not made clear in the report of the study.

Treatment-Sensitive Factorial Structure

When discussing internal validity previously, we mentioned instrumentation changes that occur even in the absence of treatment. However, instrumentation changes can sometimes occur because of treatment, as when those exposed to an educational treatment learn to see a test in a different way from those not so exposed. For instance, those not getting treatment might respond to an attitude test about people of another race on a largely uniform basis that yields a one-factor test of racial prejudice. Those exposed to treatment might make responses with a more complex factor structure (e.g., "I don't engage in physical harassment or verbal denigration in conversation, but I now see that racial jokes constitute a class of discrimination I did not previously appreciate"). This changed factor structure is itself part of the outcome of the treatment, but few researchers look for different factor structures over groups as an outcome. When all items are summed to a total for both groups, such a summation could mischaracterize the construct being measured, assuming it to be comparable across groups.

Reactive Self-Report Changes

Aiken and West (1990) describe related measurement problems with self-report observations by which both the factorial structure and the level of responses can be affected by whether a person is or is not accepted into the treatment or control group—even before they receive treatment. For example, applicants wanting treatment may make themselves look either more needy or more meritorious (depending on which one they think will get them access to their preferred condition). Once assignment is made, this motivation may end for those who receive treatment but continue for those who do not. Posttest differences then reflect both symptom changes and differential motivation, but the researcher is likely to mistakenly characterize the outcome as only symptom changes. In a similar vein, Bracht and Glass (1968) suggest that posttest (as opposed to pretest) sensitization can occur if the posttest sensitizes participants to the previous intervention they received and so prompts a response that would otherwise not have occurred. Remedies include using external (not self-report) measures that may be less reactive (Webb et al., 1966, 1981); techniques that encourage accurate responding, such as the bogus pipeline, in which participants are monitored by a physiological device they are (falsely) told can detect the correct answer (Jones & Sigall, 1971; Roese & Jamieson, 1993); preventing pretest scores from being available to those allocating treatment; and using explicit reference groups or behavioral criteria to anchor responding.

Reactivity to the Experimental Situation

Humans actively interpret the situations they enter, including experimental treatment conditions, so that the meaning of the molar treatment package includes those reactions. This reactivity takes many forms.[3] Rosenzweig (1933) suggested

---

3. See Rosnow and Rosenthal (1997) for a far more extended treatment of this and the next threat, including an analysis of ethical issues and **informed consent** raised by these threats.

that research participants might try to guess what the experimenter is studying and then try to provide results the researcher wants to see. Orne (1959, 1962, 1969) showed that "demand characteristics" in the experimental situation might provide cues to the participant about expected behavior and that the participant might be motivated (e.g., by altruism or obedience) to comply. Reactivity includes placebo effects due to features of treatment not thought to be "active ingredients" (Shapiro & Shapiro, 1997; L. White, Tursky, & Schwartz, 1985). In drug research, for example, the mere act of being given a pill may cause improvement even if the pill contains only sugar. Rosenberg (1969) provided evidence that respondents are apprehensive about being evaluated by persons who are experts in the outcome and so may respond in ways they think will be seen as competent and psychologically healthy.

Rosenthal and Rosnow (1991) suggest many ways to reduce these problems, including many of those discussed previously with reactive self-report changes, but also by (1) making the dependent variable less obvious by measuring it outside the experimental setting, (2) measuring the outcome at a point much later in time, (3) avoiding pretests that provide cues about expected outcomes, (4) using the Solomon Four-Group Design to assess the presence of the problem, (5) standardizing or reducing experimenter interactions with participants, (6) using masking procedures that prevent participants and experimenters from knowing hypotheses,[4] (7) using deception when ethical by providing false hypotheses, (8) using quasi-control participants who are told about procedures and asked how they think they should respond, (9) finding a preexperimental way of satisfying the participant's desire to please the experimenter that satiates their motivation, and (10) making the conditions less threatening to reduce evaluation apprehension, including ensuring anonymity and confidentiality. These solutions are at best partial because it is impossible to prevent respondents from generating their own treatment-related hypotheses and because in field settings it is often impossible, impractical, or unethical to do some of them.

Experimenter Expectancies

A similar class of problems was suggested by Rosenthal (1956): that the *experimenter's* expectancies are also a part of the molar treatment package and can influence outcomes. Rosenthal first took note of the problem in clinical psychology in his own dissertation on the experimental induction of defense mechanisms. He developed the idea extensively in laboratory research, especially in social psychology. But it has also been demonstrated in field research. In education, for example, the problem includes the Pygmalion effect, whereby teachers' expectancies

---

4. These procedures were called "blinding" in the past, as with double-blind designs; but we follow the recommendation of the American Psychological Association's (1994) Publication Manual in referring to masking rather than blinding.

about student achievements become self-fulfilling prophecies (Rosenthal, 1973a, 1973b). Those parts of the placebo effect from the previous threat that are induced by experimenter expectancies—such as a nurse telling a patient that a pill will help, even if the pill is an inert placebo—fall under this category as well. To reduce the problem, Rosenthal and Rosnow (1991) suggest (1) using more experimenters, especially if their expectancies can be manipulated or studied, (2) observing experimenters to detect and reduce expectancy-inducing behavior, (3) using masking procedures in which those who administer treatments do not know the hypotheses, (4) minimizing contacts between experimenter and participant, and (5) using control groups to assess the presence of these problems, such as placebo controls.

Novelty and Disruption Effects

Bracht and Glass (1968) suggested that when an innovation is introduced, it can breed excitement, energy, and enthusiasm that contribute to success, especially if little innovation previously occurred.[5] After many years of innovation, however, introducing another one may not elicit welcoming reactions, making treatment less effective. Conversely, introducing an innovation may also be quite disruptive, especially if it impedes implementation of current effective services. The innovation may then be less effective. Novelty and disruption are both part of the molar treatment package.

Compensatory Equalization

When treatment provides desirable goods or services, administrators, staff, or constituents may resist the focused inequality that results (Stevens, 1994).[6] For example, Schumacher and colleagues (1994) describe a study in which usual day care for homeless persons with substance abuse problems was compared with an enhanced day treatment condition. Service providers complained about the inequity and provided some enhanced services to clients receiving usual care. Thus the planned contrast broke down. Equalization can also involve taking benefits away from treatment recipients rather than adding them for control group members. In one study,

---

5. One instance of this threat is frequently called the "Hawthorne effect" after studies at Western Electric Company's Hawthorne site (Roethlisberger & Dickson, 1939). In an early interpretation of this research, it was thought that participants responded to the attention being given to them by increasing their productivity, whatever the treatment was. This interpretation has been called into question (e.g., Adair, 1973; Bramel & Friend, 1981; Gillespie, 1988); but the label "Hawthorne effect" is likely to continue to be used to describe it.

6. Cook and Campbell's (1979) previous discussion of this threat and the next three (resentful demoralization, compensatory rivalry, diffusion) may have misled some readers (e.g., Conrad & Conrad, 1994) into thinking that they occur only with random assignment. To the contrary, they result from a comparison process that can occur in any study in which participants are aware of discrepancies between what they received and what they might have received. Such comparison processes occur in quasi-experiments and are not even limited to research studies (see J. Z. Shapiro, 1984, for an example in a regression discontinuity design).

lawyers in a district attorney's office thought the treatment condition was too favorable to defendants and so refused to plea bargain with them at all (compensatory deprivation), as the treatment required them to do (Wallace, 1987). Such focused inequities may explain some administrators' reluctance to employ random assignment when they believe their constituencies want one treatment more than another. To assess this problem, interviews with administrators, staff, and participants are invaluable.

Compensatory Rivalry

Public assignment of units to experimental and control conditions may cause social competition, whereby the control group tries to show it can do as well as the treatment group despite not getting treatment benefits. Saretsky (1972) called this a "John Henry effect" after the steel driver who, when he knew his output was to be compared with that of a steam drill, worked so hard that he outperformed the drill and died of overexertion. Saretsky gave the example of an education experiment in which the success of treatment-group performance contractors (commercial contractors paid according to the size of learning gains made by students) would threaten the job security of control teachers who might be replaced by those contractors. Hence teachers in the control groups may have performed much better than usual to avoid this possibility. Saretsky (1972), Fetterman (1982), and Walther and Ross (1982) describe other examples. Qualitative methods such as unstructured interviews and direct observation can help discover such effects. Saretsky (1972) tried to detect the effects by comparing performance in current control classes to the performance in the same classes in the years before the experiment began.

Resentful Demoralization

Conversely, members of a group receiving a less desirable treatment or no treatment can be resentful and demoralized, changing their responses to the outcome measures (Bishop & Hill, 1971; Hand & Slocum, 1972; J. Z. Shapiro, 1984; Walther & Ross, 1982). Fetterman (1982) describes an evaluation of an educational program that solicited unemployed high school dropouts to give them a second chance at a career orientation and a high school diploma. Although the design called for assigning only one fourth of applicants to the control group so as to maximize participation, those assigned to the control group were often profoundly demoralized. Many had low academic confidence and had to muster up courage just to take one more chance, a chance that may really have been their last chance rather than a second chance. Resentful demoralization is not always this serious, but the example highlights the ethical problems it can cause. Of course, it is wrong to think that participant reactions are uniform. Lam, Hartwell, and Jekel (1994) show that those denied treatment report diverse reactions. Finally, Schumacher et al. (1994) show how resentful demoralization can occur in a group assigned to a *more* desirable treatment—client expectations for enhanced services were raised but then dashed when funds were cut and community resistance to proposed housing arrangements emerged. Reactivity problems can occur not just in reaction to other groups but also to one's own hopes for the future.

Treatment Diffusion

Sometimes the participants in one condition receive some or all of the treatment in the other condition. For example, in Florida's Trade Welfare for Work experiment, about one fourth of all control group participants crossed over to receive the job-training treatment (D. Greenberg & Shroder, 1997). Although these crossovers were discovered by the researchers, participants who cross over often do it surreptitiously for fear that the researcher would stop the diffusion, so the researcher is frequently unaware of it. The problem is most acute in cases in which experimental and control units are in physical proximity or can communicate. For example, if Massachusetts is used as a control group to study the effects of changes in a New York abortion law, the true effects of the law would be obscured if those from Massachusetts went freely to New York for abortions. Diffusion can occur when both conditions are exposed to the same treatment providers, as in a study comparing behavior therapy with eclectic psychotherapy. The same therapists administered both treatments, and one therapist used extensive behavioral techniques in the eclectic condition (Kazdin, 1992). Preventing diffusion is best achieved by minimizing common influences over conditions (e.g., using different therapists for each condition) and by isolating participants in each condition from those in other conditions (e.g., using geographically separate units). When this is not practical, measurement of treatment implementation in both groups helps, for a small or nonexistent experimental contrast on implementation measures suggests that diffusion may have occurred (see Chapter 10).

Construct Validity, Preexperimental Tailoring, and Postexperimental Specification

The process of assessing and understanding constructs is never fully done. The preceding treatment of construct validity emphasizes that, before the experiment begins, the researcher should critically (1) think through how constructs should be defined, (2) differentiate them from cognate constructs, and (3) decide how to index each construct of interest. We might call this the domain of intended application. Then we emphasized (4) the need to use multiple operations to index each construct when possible (e.g., multiple measures, manipulations, settings, and units) and when no single way is clearly best. We also indicated (5) the need to ensure that each of the multiple operations reflects multiple methods so that single-method confounds (e.g., self-report biases) can be better assessed.

After the data have been collected and provisionally analyzed, researchers may reconsider the extent to which the initially conceptualized construct has or has not been achieved (the domain of achieved application), perhaps because the planned operations were not implemented as intended or because evidence suggests that constructs other than the intended ones may better represent what the study actually did. Some postexperimental respecification of constructs is almost inevitable, particularly in programs of research. Imagine an experiment intended to compare more credible with less credible communicators in which a difference on the outcome measure is found. If a reliable measure of communicator credibility suggests that a communicator was not perceived to be more credible in one experimental group than in another, the investigator is forced to use whatever means are available to specify what might have caused the observed effects if credibility did not. Or suppose that a manipulation affected two reliably measured exemplars of a particular construct but not three other reliable measures of the same construct. R. Feldman's (1968) experiment in Boston, Athens, and Paris used five measures of cooperation (the construct as conceived at the start of the study) to test whether compatriots receive greater cooperation than foreigners. The measures were: giving street directions; doing a favor by mailing a lost letter; giving back money that one could easily, but falsely, claim as one's own; giving correct change when one did not have to; and charging the correct amount to passengers in taxis. The data suggested that giving street directions and mailing the lost letter were differently related to the experimental manipulations than were forgoing chances to cheat in ways that would be to one's advantage. This forced Feldman to specify two kinds of cooperation (low-cost favors versus forgoing one's own financial advantage). However, the process of hypothesizing constructs and testing how well operations fit these constructs is similar both before the research begins and after the data are received.

Once a study has been completed, disagreements about how well a given study represents various constructs are common, with critics frequently leveling the charge that different constructs were sampled or operationalized from those the researcher claims was the case. Because construct validity entails socially creating *and recreating* the meanings of research operations, lasting resolutions are rare, and constructs are often revisited. Fortunately, these disagreements about the composition of constructs and about the best way to measure them make for better inferences about constructs because they can be successfully tested, not only across overlapping operational representations of the same definition but also across different (but overlapping) definitions of the same construct. For example, various language communities disagree about whether to include intent to harm as part of the construct of aggression. It is only when we have learned that such intent makes little difference to actual study outcomes that we can safely omit it from our description of the concept of aggression. Disagreements about construct definitions are potentially of great utility, therefore.

EXTERNAL VALIDITY

External validity concerns inferences about the extent to which a causal relationship holds over variations in persons, settings, treatments, and outcomes. For example, the Transitional Employment Training Demonstration experiment randomly assigned 18- to 40-year-old adults with mental retardation to either a control condition receiving usual services or a treatment condition that received job training along with unsubsidized and potentially permanent jobs (Greenberg & Shroder, 1997). Results showed that the treatment improved both job placement and earnings. Yet the researchers noted serious remaining questions about the external validity of these effects. For example, their own data suggested that results were larger for participants with higher IQs and that participants with IQs less than 40 showed little or no gain; and their between-site analyses showed that success rates depended greatly on the kind of job in which the site tried to place the participant. The researchers also raised other external validity questions that their data did not allow them to explore. For example, the program was implemented in 12 sites in the United States, but no sites were in the South. In addition, only 5% of those who were sent invitation letters volunteered to participate; and of these, two thirds were screened out because they did not meet study eligibility criteria that included lack of severe emotional problems and likelihood of benefiting from treatment. Whether results would also be found in more severely disturbed, nonvolunteer retarded adults remains at issue. Further, the researchers noted that successful program participants were more adventuresome and willing to move from the well-established and comparatively safe confines of traditional sheltered employment into the real world of employment; they questioned whether less adventuresome retarded adults would show the same benefits.

As this example shows, external validity questions can be about whether a causal relationship holds (1) over variations in persons, settings, treatments, and outcomes that *were* in the experiment and (2) for persons, settings, treatments, and outcomes that *were not* in the experiment. Targets of generalization can be quite diverse:

- *Narrow to Broad:* For instance, from the persons, settings, treatments, and outcomes in an experiment to a larger population, as when a policymaker asks if the findings from the income maintenance experiments in New Jersey, Seattle, and Denver would generalize to the U.S. population if adopted as national policy.
- *Broad to Narrow:* From the experimental sample to a smaller group or even to a single person, as when an advanced breast cancer patient asks whether a newly-developed treatment that improves survival in general would improve her survival in particular, given her pathology, her clinical stage, and her prior treatments.
- *At a Similar Level:* From the experimental sample to another sample at about the same level of aggregation, as when a state governor considers adapting a new welfare reform based on experimental findings supporting that reform in a nearby state of similar size.

- *To a Similar or Different Kind:* In all three of the preceding cases, the targets of generalization might be similar to the experimental samples (e.g., from male job applicants in Seattle to male job applicants in the United States) or very different (e.g., from African American males in New Jersey to Hispanic females in Houston).
- *Random Sample to Population Members:* In those rare cases with random sampling, a generalization can be made from the random sample to other members of the population from which the sample was drawn.

Cronbach and his colleagues (Cronbach et al., 1980; Cronbach, 1982) argue that most external validity questions are about persons, settings, treatments, and outcomes that *were not* studied in the experiment—because they arise only after a study is done, too late to include the instances in question in the study. Some scientists reject this version of the external validity question (except when random sampling is used). They argue that scientists should be held responsible only for answering the questions they pose and study, not questions that others might pose later about conditions of application that might be different from the original ones. They argue that inferences to as-yet-unstudied applications are no business of science until they can be answered by reanalyses of an existing study or by a new study.

On this disagreement, we side with Cronbach. Inferences from completed studies to as-yet-unstudied applications are necessary to both science and society. During the last two decades of the 20th century, for example, researchers at the U.S. General Accounting Office's Program Evaluation and Methodology Division frequently advised Congress about policy based on reviews of past studies that overlap only partially with the exact application that Congress has in mind (e.g., Droitcour, 1997). In a very real sense, in fact, the essence of creative science is to move a program of research forward by incremental extensions of both theory and experiment into untested realms that the scientist believes are likely to have fruitful yields given past knowledge (e.g., McGuire, 1997). Usually, such extrapolations are justified because they are incremental variations in some rather than all study features, making these extrapolations to things not yet studied more plausible. For example, questions may arise about whether the effects of a worksite smoking prevention program that was studied in the private sector would generalize to public sector settings. Even though the public sector setting may never have been studied before, it is still a work site, the treatment and observations are likely to remain substantially the same, and the people studied tend to share many key characteristics, such as being smokers. External validity questions about what would happen if *all* features of a study were different are possible but are so rare in practice that we cannot even construct a plausible example.

On the other hand, it is also wrong to limit external validity to questions about as-yet-unstudied instances. Campbell and Stanley (1963) made no such distinction in their original formulation of external validity as asking the question, "to what populations, settings, treatment variables, and measurement variables can this effect be generalized?" (p. 5). Indeed, one of the goals of their theory was to point out "numerous ways in which experiments can be made more valid externally" (p. 17). For example, they said that external validity was enhanced in single studies "if in the initial experiment we have demonstrated the phenomenon over a wide variety of conditions" (p. 19) and also enhanced by inducing "maximum similarity of experiments to the conditions of application" (p. 18). This goal of designing experiments to yield inferences that are "more valid externally" is not a novel concept. To the contrary, most experiments already test whether treatment effects hold over several different outcomes. Many also report whether the effect holds over different kinds of persons, although power is reduced as a sample is subdivided. Tests of effect stability over variations in treatments are limited to studies having multiple treatments, but these do occur regularly in the scientific literature (e.g., Wampold et al., 1997). And tests of how well causal relationships hold over settings also occur regularly, for example, in education (Raudenbush & Willms, 1995) and in large multisite medical and public health trials (Ioannidis et al., 1999).

Yet there are clear limits to this strategy. Few investigators are omniscient enough to anticipate all the conditions that might affect a causal relationship. Even if they were that omniscient, a full solution requires the experiment to include a fully heterogeneous range of units, treatments, observations, and settings. Diversifying outcomes is usually feasible. But in using multiple sites *or* many operationalizations of treatments *or* tests of causal relationships broken down by various participant characteristics, each becomes increasingly difficult; and doing all of them at once is impossibly expensive and logistically complex. Even if an experiment had the requisite diversity, detecting such interactions is more difficult than detecting treatment main effects. Although power to detect interactions can be increased by using certain designs (e.g., West, Aiken, & Todd, 1993), these designs must be implemented before the study starts, which makes their use irrelevant to the majority of questions about external validity that arise after a study is completed. Moreover, researchers often have an excellent reason *not* to diversify all these characteristics—after all, extraneous variation in settings and respondents is a threat to statistical conclusion validity. So when heterogeneous sampling is done because interactions are expected, the total sample size must be increased to obtain adequate power. This, too, costs money that could be used to improve other design characteristics. In a world of limited resources, designing studies to anticipate external validity questions will often conflict with other design priorities that may require precedence.

Sometimes, when the original study included the pertinent variable but did not analyze or report it, then the original investigator or others (in the latter case, called **secondary analysis**; Kiecolt & Nathan, 1990) can reanalyze data from the experiment to see what happens to the causal relationship as the variable in question is varied. For example, a study on the effects of a weight-loss program may have found it to be effective in a sample composed of both men and women. Later, a question may arise about whether the results would have held separately for both men and women. If the original data can be accessed, and if they were coded and stored in such a way that the analysis is possible, the question can be addressed by reanalyzing the data to test this interaction.

Usually, however, the original data set is either no longer available or does not contain the required data. In such cases, reviews of published results from many studies on the same question are often excellent sources for answering external validity questions. As Campbell and Stanley (1963) noted, we usually "learn how far we can generalize an internally valid finding only piece by piece through trial and error" (p. 19), typically over multiple studies that contain different kinds of persons, settings, treatments, and outcomes. Scientists do this by conducting programs of research during their research careers, a time-consuming process that gives maximum control over the particular generalizations at issue. Scientists also do this by combining their own work with that of other scientists, combining basic and applied research or laboratory and field studies, as Dwyer and Flesch-Janys (1995) did in their review of the effects of Agent Orange in Vietnam. Finally, scientists do this by conducting quantitative reviews of many experiments that addressed a common question. Such **meta-analysis** is more feasible than secondary analysis because it does not require the original data. However, meta-analysis has problems of its own, such as poor quality of reporting or statistical analysis in some studies. Chapter 13 of this book discusses all these methods.

Threats to External Validity

Estimates of the extent to which a causal relationship holds over variations in persons, settings, treatments, and outcomes are conceptually similar to tests of statistical interactions. If an interaction exists between, say, an educational treatment and the social class of children, then we cannot say that the same result holds across social classes. We know that it does not, for the significant interaction shows that the effect size is different in different social classes. Consequently, we have chosen to list threats to external validity in terms of interactions (Table 3.2) of the causal relationship (including mediators of that relationship) with (1) units, (2) treatments, (3) outcomes, and (4) settings.

However, our use of the word *interaction* in naming these threats is not intended to limit them to statistical interactions. Rather, it is the concept behind the interaction that is important—the search for ways in which a causal relationship might or might not change over persons, settings, treatments, and outcomes. If that question can be answered using an interaction that can be quantified and tested statistically, well and good. But the inability to do so should not stop the search for these threats. For example, in the case of generalizations to persons, settings, treatments, and outcomes that were not studied, no statistical test of interactions is possible. But this does not stop researchers from generating plausible hypotheses about likely interactions, sometimes based on professional experience and sometimes on related studies, with which to criticize the generalizability of

TABLE 3.2 Threats to External Validity: Reasons Why Inferences About How Study Results Would Hold Over Variations in Persons, Settings, Treatments, and Outcomes May Be Incorrect

1. *Interaction of the Causal Relationship with Units:* An effect found with certain kinds of units might not hold if other kinds of units had been studied.

2. *Interaction of the Causal Relationship Over Treatment Variations:* An effect found with one treatment variation might not hold with other variations of that treatment, or when that treatment is combined with other treatments, or when only part of that treatment is used.

3. *Interaction of the Causal Relationship with Outcomes:* An effect found on one kind of outcome observation may not hold if other outcome observations were used.

4. *Interactions of the Causal Relationship with Settings:* An effect found in one kind of setting may not hold if other kinds of settings were to be used.

5. *Context-Dependent Mediation:* An explanatory mediator of a causal relationship in one context may not mediate in another context.

experimental results and around which to design new studies. Nor should we be slaves to the statistical significance of interactions. Nonsignificant interactions may reflect low power, yet the result may still be of sufficient practical importance to be grounds for further research. Conversely, significant interactions may be demonstrably trivial for practice or theory. At issue, then, is not just the statistical significance of interactions but also their practical and theoretical significance; not just their demonstration in a data set but also their potential fruitfulness in generating compelling lines of research about the limits of causal relationships.

Interaction of Causal Relationship with Units

In which units does a cause-effect relationship hold? For example, common belief in the 1980s in the United States was that health research was disproportionately conducted on white males—to the point where the quip became, "Even the rats were white males," because the most commonly used rats were white in color and because to facilitate homogeneity only male rats were studied.[7] Researchers became concerned that effects observed with human white males might not hold equally well for females and for more diverse ethnic groups, so the U.S. National

7. Regarding gender, this problem may not have been as prevalent as feared. Meinart, Gilpin, Unalp, and Dawson (2000) reviewed 724 clinical trials appearing between 1966 and 1998 in *Annals of Internal Medicine, British Medical Journal, Journal of the American Medical Association, Lancet,* and *New England Journal of Medicine.* They found in the U.S. journals that 55.2% of those trials contained both males and females, 12.2% contained males only, 11.2% females only, and 21.4% did not specify gender. Over all journals, 355,624 males and 550,743 females were included in these trials.

Institutes of Health (National Institutes of Health, 1994) launched formal initiatives to ensure that such variability is systematically examined in the future (Hohmann & Parron, 1996). Even when participants in an experiment belong to the target class of interest (e.g., African American females), those who are successfully recruited into an experiment may differ systematically from those who are not. They may be volunteers, exhibitionists, hypochondriacs, scientific do-gooders, those who need the proffered cash, those who need course credit, those who are desperate for help, or those who have nothing else to do. In the Arkansas Work Program experiment, for example, the program intentionally selected the most job-ready applicants to treat, and such "creaming" may result in effect estimates that are higher than those that would have been obtained for less job-ready applicants (Greenberg & Shroder, 1997). Similarly, when the unit is an aggregate such as a school, the volunteering organizations may be the most progressive, proud, or self-confident. For example, Campbell (1956), although working with the Office of Naval Research, could not get access to destroyer crews and had to use high-morale submarine crews. Can we generalize from such situations to those in which morale is lower?

Interaction of Causal Relationship Over Treatment Variations

Here, the size or direction of a causal relationship varies over different treatment variations. For example, reducing class size may work well when it is accompanied by substantial new funding to build new classrooms and hire skilled teachers, but it may work poorly if that funding is lacking, so that the new small classes are taught in temporary trailers by inexperienced teachers. Similarly, because of the limited duration of most experimental treatments, people may react differently than they would if the treatment were extended. Thus, in the New Jersey Income Maintenance Experiment, respondents reacted to an income that was guaranteed to them for 3 years only. Because of suspicion that the respondents would react differently if the treatment lasted longer, the later Seattle-Denver Income Maintenance Experiment contained some families whose benefits were guaranteed for 20 years, more like a permanent program (Orr, 1999). Similarly, the effects in a small-scale experimental test might be quite different from those in a full-scale implementation of the same treatment (Garfinkel, Manski, & Michalopoulos, 1992; Manski & Garfinkel, 1992). For example, this could happen if a social intervention is intended to cause changes in community attitudes and norms that could occur only when the intervention is widely implemented. In such cases, social experiments that are implemented on a smaller scale than that of the intended policy implementation might not cause these community changes. Finally, this threat also includes interaction effects that occur when treatments are administered jointly. Drug interaction effects are a well-known example. A drug may have a very positive effect by itself, but when used in combination with other drugs may be either deadly (the interaction of Viagra with certain blood pressure medications) or totally ineffective (the interaction of some antibiotics with dairy products). Conversely, a combination of drugs to treat AIDS may dramatically reduce death, but each drug by itself might be ineffective.

Interaction of Causal Relationship with Outcomes

Can a cause-effect relationship be generalized over different outcomes? In cancer research, for example, treatments vary in effectiveness depending on whether the outcome is quality of life, 5-year metastasis-free survival, or overall survival; yet only the latter is what laypersons understand as a "cure." Similarly, when social science results are presented to audiences, it is very common to hear comments such as: "Yes, I accept that the youth job-training program increases the likelihood of being employed immediately after graduation. But what does it do to adaptive job skills such as punctuality or the ability to follow orders?" Answers to such questions give a fuller picture of a treatment's total impact. Sometimes treatments will have a positive effect on one outcome, no effect on a second, and a negative effect on a third. In the New Jersey Income Maintenance Experiment, for example, income maintenance payments reduced the number of hours worked by wives in experimental families, had no effect on home ownership or major appliance purchases, and increased the likelihood that teenagers in experimental families would complete high school (Kershaw & Fair, 1977; Watts & Rees, 1976). Fortunately, this is the easiest study feature to vary. Consultation with **stakeholders** prior to study design is an excellent method for ensuring that likely questions about generalizability over outcomes are anticipated in the study design.

Interaction of Causal Relationship with Settings

In which settings does a cause-effect relationship hold? For example, Kazdin (1992) described a program for drug abusers that was effective in rural areas but did not work in urban areas, perhaps because drugs are more easily available in the latter settings. In principle, answers to such questions can be obtained by varying settings and analyzing for a causal relationship within each. But this is often costly, so that such options are rarely feasible. Sometimes, though, a single large site (e.g., a university) has some subsettings (e.g., different departments) that vary naturally along dimensions that might affect outcome, allowing some study of generalizability. Large multisite studies also have the capacity to address such issues (Turpin & Sinacore, 1991), and they are doing an increasingly sophisticated job of exploring the reasons why sites differ (Raudenbush & Willms, 1991).

Context-Dependent Mediation

Causal explanation is one of the five principles of causal generalization in the grounded theory we outlined in Chapter 1. Though we discuss this principle in more detail in Chapter 12, one part of explanation is identification of mediating processes. The idea is that studies of causal mediation identify the essential processes that must occur in order to transfer an effect. However, even if a correct mediator is identified in one context, that variable may not mediate the effect in another context. For example, a study of the effects of a new health care insurance program in nonprofit hospitals might show that the program reduces costs through a reduction in the number of middle management positions. But this explanation might not generalize to for-profit hospitals in which, even if the cost reduction does occur, it may occur through reduction in patient services instead. In this example, the contextual change is settings, but it could also be a change in the persons studied or in the nature of the treatment or the outcome variables used. Context dependencies in any of these are also interactions—in this case an interaction of the mediator in the causal relationship with whatever feature of the context was varied. When such mediator variables can be identified and studied over multiple contexts, their consistency as mediators can be tested using multigroup structural equation models.

Constancy of Effect Size Versus Constancy of Causal Direction

We have phrased threats to external validity as interactions. How large must these interactions be to threaten generalization? Does just a tiny change in effect size count as a failure to generalize? These questions are important statistically because a study with high power can detect even small variations in effect sizes over levels of a potential moderator. They are important philosophically because many theorists believe that the world is full of interactions by its very nature, so that statistical main effects will rarely describe the world with perfect accuracy (Mackie, 1974). And they are important practically because some scientists claim that complex statistical interactions are the norm, including Cronbach and Snow (1977) in education, Magnusson (2000) in developmental science, and McGuire (1984) in social psychology. It is entirely possible, then, that if robustness were specified as *constancy of effect sizes*, few causal relationships in the social world would be generalizable.

However, we believe that generalization often is appropriately conceptualized as *constancy of causal direction*, that the sign of the causal relationship is constant across levels of a moderator. Several factors argue for this. First, casual examination of many meta-analyses convinces us that, for at least some topics in which treatments are compared with control groups, causal signs often tend to be similar across individual studies even when the effect sizes vary considerably (e.g., Shadish, 1992a). Second, in the social policy world it is difficult to shape legislation or regulations to suit local contingencies. Instead, the same plan has to be promulgated across an entire nation or state to avoid focused inequities between individual places or groups. Policymakers hope for positive effects overall, despite the inevitable variability in effect sizes from site to site or person to person or over different kinds of outcomes or different ways of delivering the treatment. Their fear is of different causal signs over these variations. Third, substantive theories are usually built around causal relationships whose occurrence is particularly dependable, not just those that are obviously novel. The former reduces the risk of theorizing about unstable phenomena—an unfortunate commonplace in much of today's social science! Fourth, the very nature of scientific theory is that it reduces complex phenomena to simpler terms, and minor fluctuations in effect size are often irrelevant to basic theoretical points. Because defining robustness in terms of constant effect sizes loses all these advantages, we favor a looser criterion based on the stability of causal signs, especially when research that some might call applied is involved.

Nonetheless, we would not abandon constancy of effect size entirely, for sometimes small differences in effect size have large practical or theoretical importance. An example is the case in which the outcome of interest is a harm, such as death. For instance, if the addition of an angiogenesis inhibitor to chemotherapy increases life expectancy in prostate cancer patients by only 6 months but the cost of the drug is low and it has no significant side effects, then many patients and their physicians would want that addition because of the value they place on having even just a little more time to live. Such judgments take into account individual differences in the value placed on small differences in effects, estimates of the contextual costs and benefits of the intervention, and knowledge of possible side effects of treatment. Again, judgments about the external validity of a causal relationship cannot be reduced to statistical terms.

Random Sampling and External Validity

We have not put much emphasis on random sampling for external validity, primarily because it is so rarely feasible in experiments. When it is feasible, however, we strongly recommend it, for just as random assignment simplifies internal validity inferences, so random sampling simplifies external validity inferences (assuming little or no attrition, as with random assignment). For example, if an experimenter randomly samples persons before randomly assigning them to conditions, then random sampling guarantees—within the limits of sampling error—that the average causal relationship observed in the sample will be the same as (1) the average causal relationship that would have been observed in any other random sample of persons of the same size from the same population and (2) the average causal relationship that would have been observed across *all* other persons in that population who were not in the original random sample. That is, random sampling eliminates possible interactions between the causal relationship and the class of persons who are studied versus the class of persons who are not studied within the same population. We cite examples of such experiments in Chapter 11, though they are rare. Further, suppose the researcher also tests the interaction of treatment with a characteristic of persons (e.g., gender). Random sampling also guarantees that interaction will be the same in the groups defined in (1) and (2)—although power decreases as samples are subdivided. So, although we argue in Chapters 1 and 11 that random sampling has major practical limitations when combined with experiments, its benefits for external validity are so great that it should be used on those rare occasions when it is feasible.

These benefits hold for random samples of settings, too. For example, Puma, Burstein, Merrell, and Silverstein (1990) randomly sampled food stamp agencies in one randomized experiment about the Food Stamp Employment and Training Program. But random samples of settings are even more rare in experiments than are random samples of persons. Although defined populations of settings are fairly common—for example, Head Start Centers, mental health centers, or hospitals—the rarity of random sampling from these populations is probably due to the logistical costs of successfully randomly sampling from them, costs that must be added to the already high costs of multisite experiments.

Finally, these benefits also would hold for treatments and outcomes. But lists of treatments (e.g., Steiner & Gingrich, 2000) and outcomes (e.g., American Psychiatric Association, 2000) are rare, and efforts to defend random sampling from them are probably nonexistent. In the former case, this rarity exists because the motivation to experiment in any given study stems from questions about the effects of a particular treatment, and in the latter case it exists because most researchers probably believe diversity in outcome measures is better achieved by more deliberate methods such as the following.

Purposive Sampling and External Validity

Purposive sampling of heterogeneous instances is much more frequently used in single experiments than is random sampling; that is, persons, settings, treatments, or outcomes are deliberately chosen to be diverse on variables that are presumed to be important to the causal relationship. For instance, if there is reason to be concerned that gender might moderate an effect, then both males and females are deliberately included. Doing so has two benefits for external validity. Most obviously, it allows tests of the interaction between the causal relationship and gender in the study data. If an interaction is detected, this is prima facie evidence of limited external validity. However, sometimes sample sizes are so small that responsible tests of interactions cannot be done, and in any case there will be many potential moderators that the experimenter does not think to test. In these cases, heterogeneous sampling still has the benefit of demonstrating that a main effect for treatment occurs *despite* the heterogeneity in the sample. Of course, random sampling demonstrates this even more effectively, for it makes the sample heterogeneous on every possible moderator variable; but deliberately heterogeneous sampling makes up for its weakness by being practical.

The same benefits ensue from purposive sampling of heterogeneous settings, so that it is common in multisite research to ensure some diversity in including, say, both public and private schools or both nonprofit and proprietary hospitals. Purposive sampling of heterogeneous outcome measures is so common in most areas of field experimentation that its value for exploring the generalizability of the effect is taken for granted, though there is surprisingly little theory trying to explain or predict such variability (e.g., Shadish & Sweeney, 1991). Purposive sampling of heterogeneous treatments in single experiments is again probably nonexistent, for the same reasons for which random sampling of treatments is not done. However, over a program of research or over a set of studies conducted by many different researchers, heterogeneity is frequently high for persons, settings, treatments, and outcomes. This is one reason that our grounded theory of causal generalization relies so heavily on methods for multiple studies.

MORE ON RELATIONSHIPS, TRADEOFFS, AND PRIORITIES

At the end of Chapter 2, we discussed the relationship between internal and statistical conclusion validity. We now extend that discussion to other relationships between validity types and to priorities and tradeoffs among them.

The Relationship Between Construct Validity and External Validity

Construct validity and external validity are related to each other in two ways. First, both are generalizations. Consequently, the grounded theory of generalization that we briefly described in Chapter 1 and that we extend significantly in Chapters 11 through 13 helps enhance both kinds of validities. Second, valid knowledge of the constructs that are involved in a study can shed light on external validity questions, especially if a well-developed theory exists that describes how various constructs and instances are related to each other. Medicine, for example, has well-developed theories for categorizing certain therapies (say, the class of drugs we call chemotherapies for cancer) and for knowing how these therapies affect patients (how they affect blood tests and survival and what their side effects are). Consequently, when a new drug meets the criteria for being called a chemotherapy, we can predict much of its likely performance before actually testing it (e.g., we can say it is likely to cause hair loss and nausea and to increase survival in patients with low tumor burdens but not advanced cases). This knowledge makes the design of new experiments easier by narrowing the scope of pertinent patients and outcomes, and it makes extrapolations about treatment effects likely to be more accurate. But once we move from these cases to most topics of field experimentation in this book, such well-developed theories are mostly lacking. In these common cases, knowledge of construct validity provides only weak evidence about external validity. We provide some examples of how this occurs in Chapters 11 through 13.

However, construct and external validity are different from each other in more ways than they are similar. First, they differ in the kinds of inferences being made. The inference of construct validity is, by definition, always a *construct* that is applied to study instances. For external validity generalizations, the inference concerns whether the size or direction of a causal relationship changes over persons, treatments, settings, or outcomes. A challenge to construct validity might be that we have mischaracterized the settings in a health care study as private sector hospitals and that it would have been more accurate to call them private nonprofit hospitals to distinguish them from the for-profit hospitals that were not in the study. In raising this challenge, the size or direction of the causal relationship need never be mentioned.

Second, external validity generalizations cannot be divorced from the causal relationship under study, but questions about construct validity can be. This point is most clear in the phrasing of threats to external validity, which are always interactions of the *causal relationship* with some other real or potential persons, treatments, settings, or outcomes. There is no external validity threat about, say, the interaction of persons and settings without reference to the causal relationship. It is not that such interactions could not happen—it is well known, for example, that the number of persons with different psychiatric diagnoses that one finds in state mental hospitals is quite different from the number generally found in the outpatient offices of a private sector clinical psychologist. We can even raise construct validity questions about all these labels (e.g., did we properly label the setting as a state mental hospital? Or might it have been better characterized as a state psychiatric long-term-care facility to distinguish it from those state-run facilities that treat only short-term cases?). But because this particular interaction did not involve a causal relationship, it cannot be about external validity.

Of course, in practice we use abstract labels when we raise external validity questions. In the real world of science, no one would say, "I think this causal relationship holds for units on List A but not for units on List B." Rather, they might say, "I think that gene therapies for cancer are likely to work for patients with low tumor burden rather than with high tumor burden." But the use of construct labels in this latter sentence does not make external validity the same as, or even dependent on, construct validity. The parallel with internal validity is instructive here. No one in the real world of science ever talks about whether A caused B. Rather, they always talk about descriptive causal relationships in terms of constructs, say, that gene therapy increased 5-year survival rates. Yet we have phrased internal validity as concerning whether A caused B *without* construct labels in order to highlight the fact that the logical issues involved in validating a descriptive causal inference (i.e., whether cause precedes effect, whether alternative causes can be ruled out, and so forth) are orthogonal to the accuracy of those construct labels. The same point holds for external validity—the logical issues involved in knowing whether a causal relationship holds over variations in persons, settings, treatments, and outcomes are orthogonal to those involved in naming the constructs.

Third, external and construct validity differ in that we may be wrong about one and right about the other. Imagine two sets of units for which we have well-justified construct labels, say, males versus females or U.S. cities versus Canadian cities or self-report measures versus observer ratings. In these cases, the construct validity of those labels is not at issue. Imagine further that we have done an experiment with one of the two sets, say, using only self-report measures. The fact that we correctly know the label for the other set that we did not use (observer ratings) rarely makes it easier for us to answer the external validity question of whether the causal effect on self-reported outcomes would be the same as for observer-rated outcomes (the exception being those rare cases in which strong theory exists to help make the prediction). And the converse is also true: that I may have the labels for these two sets of units incorrect, but if I have done the same experiment with both sets of units, I still can provide helpful answers to external validity questions about whether the effect holds over the two kinds of outcomes despite using the wrong labels for them.

Finally, external and construct validity differ in the methods emphasized to improve them. Construct validity relies more on clear construct explication and on good assessment of study particulars, so that the match between construct and particulars can be judged. External validity relies more on tests of changes in the size and direction of a causal relationship. Of course, those tests cannot be done without some assessments; but that is also true of statistical conclusion and internal validity, both of which depend in practice on having assessments to work with.

The Relationship Between Internal Validity and Construct Validity

Both internal and construct validity share in common the notion of confounds. The relationship between internal validity and construct validity is best illustrated by the four threats listed under internal validity in Cook and Campbell (1979) that are now listed under construct validity: resentful demoralization, compensatory equalization, compensatory rivalry, and treatment diffusion. The problem of whether these threats should count under internal or construct validity hinges on exactly what kinds of confounds they are. Internal validity confounds are forces that could have occurred in the absence of the treatment and could have caused some or all of the outcome observed. By contrast, these four threats would not have occurred had a treatment not been introduced; indeed, they occurred because the treatment was introduced, and so are part of the treatment condition (or perhaps more exactly, part of the treatment contrast). They threaten construct validity to the extent that they are usually not part of the intended conceptual structure of the treatment, and so are often omitted from the description of the treatment construct.

Tradeoffs and Priorities

In the last two chapters, we have presented a daunting list of threats to the validity of generalized causal inferences. This might lead the reader to wonder if any single experiment can successfully avoid all of them. The answer is no. We cannot reasonably expect one study to deal with all of them simultaneously, primarily because of logistical and practical tradeoffs among them that we describe in this section. Rather, the threats to validity are heuristic devices that are intended to raise consciousness about priorities and tradeoffs, not to be a source of skepticism or despair. Some are much more important than others in terms of both prevalence and consequences for quality of inference, and experience helps the researcher to identify those that are more prevalent and important for any given context. It *is* more realistic to expect a program of research to deal with most or all of these threats over time. Knowledge growth is more cumulative than episodic, both with experiments and with other types of research. However, we do not mean all this to say that single experiments are useless or all equally full of uncertainty in the results. A good experiment does not have to deal with all threats but only with the subset of threats that a particular field considers most serious at the time. Nor is dealing with threats the only mark of a good experiment; for example, the best experiments influence a field by testing truly novel ideas (Eysenck & Eysenck, 1983; Harré, 1981).

In a world of limited resources, researchers always make tradeoffs among validity types in any single study. For example, if a researcher increases sample size in order to improve statistical conclusion validity, he or she is reducing resources that could be used to prevent treatment-correlated attrition and so improve internal validity. Similarly, random assignment can help greatly in improving internal validity, but the organizations willing to tolerate this are probably less representative than organizations willing to tolerate passive measurement, so external validity may be compromised. Also, increasing the construct validity of effects by operationalizing each of them in multiple ways is likely to increase the response burden and so cause attrition from the experiment; or, if the measurement budget is fixed, then increasing the number of measures may lower reliability for individual measures that must then be shorter.

Such countervailing relationships suggest how crucial it is in planning any experiment to be explicit about the priority ordering among validity types. Unnecessary tradeoffs between one kind of validity and another have to be avoided, and the loss entailed by necessary tradeoffs has to be estimated and minimized. Scholars differ in their estimate of which tradeoffs are more desirable. Cronbach (1982) maintains that timely, representative, but less rigorous studies can lead to reasonable causal inferences that have greater external validity, even if the studies are nonexperimental. Campbell and Boruch (1975), on the other hand, maintain that causal inference is problematic outside of experiments because many threats to internal validity remain unexamined or must be ruled out by fiat rather than through direct design or measurement. This is an example of the major and most discussed tradeoff—that between internal and external validity.

Internal Validity: A Sine Qua Non?

Noting that internal validity and external validity often conflict in any given experiment, Campbell and Stanley (1963) said that "*internal validity* is the *sine qua non*" (p. 5).[8] This one statement gave internal validity priority for a generation of field experimenters. Eventually, Cronbach took issue with this priority, claiming that internal validity is "trivial, past-tense, and local" (1982, p. 137), whereas external validity is more important because it is forward looking and asks general questions. Because Cronbach was not alone in his concerns about the original validity typology, we discuss here the priorities among internal validity and other validities, particularly external validity.

Campbell and Stanley's (1963) assertion that internal validity is the sine qua non of experimentation is one of the most quoted lines in research methodology. It appeared in a book on experimental and quasi-experimental design, and the text makes clear that the remark was meant to apply *only* to experiments, not to other forms of research:

> *Internal validity* is the basic minimum without which any experiment is uninterpretable: Did in fact the experimental treatments make a difference in this specific experimental instance? *External validity* asks the question of *generalizability:* To what populations, settings, treatment variables, and measurement variables can this effect be generalized? Both types of criteria are obviously important, even though they are frequently at odds in that features increasing one may jeopardize the other. While *internal validity* is the *sine qua non,* and while the question of *external validity,* like the question of inductive inference, is never completely answerable, the selection of designs strong in both types of validity is obviously our ideal. This is particularly the case for research on teaching, in which generalization to applied settings of known character is the desideratum. (Campbell & Stanley, 1963, p. 5)

Thus Campbell and Stanley claimed that internal validity was necessary for experimental and quasi-experimental designs probing causal hypotheses, not for research generally. Moreover, the final sentence of this quote is almost always overlooked. Yet it states that external validity is a *desideratum* (purpose, objective, requirement, aim, goal) in educational research. This is nearly as strong a claim as the sine qua non claim about internal validity.

As Cook and Campbell (1979) further clarified, the sine qua non statement is, to a certain degree, a tautology:

> There is also a circular justification for the primacy of internal validity that pertains in any book dealing with experiments. The unique purpose of experiments is to provide stronger tests of *causal* hypotheses than is permitted by other forms of research, most of which were developed for other purposes. For instance, surveys were developed to describe population attitudes and reported behaviors while participant observation

---

8. *Sine qua non* is Latin for "without which not" and describes something that is essential or necessary. So this phrase describes internal validity as necessary.

methods were developed to describe and generate new hypotheses about ongoing behaviors *in situ*. Given that the unique original purpose of experiments is cause-related, internal validity has to assume a special importance in experimentation since it is concerned with how confident one can be that an observed relationship between variables is *causal* or that the absence of a relationship implies *no cause*. (p. 84)

Despite all these disclaimers, many readers still misinterpret our position on internal validity. To discourage such misinterpretation, let us be clear: *Internal validity is not the sine qua non of all research. It does have a special (but not inviolate) place in cause-probing research, and especially in experimental research, by encouraging critical thinking about descriptive causal claims*. Next we examine some issues that must be examined before knowing exactly how high a priority internal validity should be.

Is Descriptive Causation a Priority?

Internal validity can have high priority only if a researcher is self-consciously interested in a descriptive causal question from among the many competing questions on a topic that might be asked. Such competing questions could be about how the problem is formulated, what needs the treatment might address, how well a treatment is implemented, how best to measure something, how mediating causal processes should be understood, how meanings should be attached to findings, and how costs and fiscal benefits should be measured. Experiments rarely provide helpful information about these questions, for which other methods are to be preferred. Even when descriptive causation is a high priority, these other questions might also need to be answered, all within the same resource constraints. Then a method such as a survey might be preferred because it has a wider **bandwidth**[9] that permits answering a broader array of questions even if the causal question is answered less well than it would be with an experiment (Cronbach, 1982). The decision to prioritize on descriptive causal questions or some alternative goes far beyond the scope of this book (Shadish, Cook, & Leviton, 1991). Our presumption is that the researcher has already justified such a question before he or she begins work within the experimental framework being elaborated in this book.

Can Nonexperimental Methods Give a Satisfactory Answer?

Even if a descriptive causal inference has been well justified as a high priority, experimental methods are still not the only choice. Descriptive causal questions can be studied nonexperimentally. This happens with correlational path analysis in sociology (e.g., Wright, 1921, 1934), with case-control studies in epidemiology (e.g.,

---

9. Cronbach's analogy is to radios that can have high bandwidth or high fidelity, there being a tradeoff between the two. **Bandwidth** means a method can answer many questions but with less accuracy, and **fidelity** describes methods that answer one or a few questions but with more accuracy.

Ahlbom & Norell, 1990), or with qualitative methods such as case studies (e.g., Campbell, 1975). The decision to investigate a descriptive causal question using such methods depends on many factors. Partly these reflect disciplinary traditions that developed for either good or poor reasons. Some phenomena are simply not amenable to the manipulation that experimental work requires, and at other times manipulation may be undesirable for ethical reasons or for fear of changing the phenomenon being studied in undesirable ways. Sometimes the cause of interest is not yet sufficiently clear, so that interest is more in exploring a range of possible causes than in zeroing in on one or two of them. Sometimes the investment of time and resources that experiments may require is premature, perhaps because insufficient pilot work has been done to develop a treatment in terms of its theoretical fidelity and practical implementability, because crucial aspects of experimental procedures such as outcome measurement are underdeveloped, or because results are needed more quickly than an experiment can provide. Premature experimental work is a common research sin.

However, the nature of nonexperimental methods can often prevent them from making internal validity the highest priority. The reason is that experimental methods match the requirements of causal reasoning more closely than do other methods, particularly in ensuring that cause precedes effect, that there is a credible source of counterfactual inference, and that the number of plausible alternative explanations is reduced. In their favor, however, the data generally used with nonexperimental causal methods often entail more representative samples of constructs than in an experiment and a broader sampling scheme that facilitates external validity. So nonexperimental methods will usually be less able to facilitate internal validity but equally or more able to promote external or construct validity. But these tendencies are not universal. Nonexperimental methods can sometimes yield descriptive causal inferences that are fully as plausible as those yielded by experiments, as in some epidemiological studies. As we said at the start of Chapter 2, validity is an attribute of knowledge claims, not methods. Internal validity depends on meeting the demands of causal reasoning rather than on using a particular method. No method, including the experiment, guarantees an internally valid causal inference, even if the experiment is often superior.

The Weak and Strong Senses of Sine Qua Non

However, suppose the researcher has worked through all these matters and has decided to use an experiment to study a descriptive causal inference. Then internal validity can be a sine qua non in two senses. The weak sense is the tautological one from Campbell and Stanley (1963): "*internal validity* is the basic minimum without which any experiment is uninterpretable" (p. 5). That is, to do an experiment and have no interest in internal validity is an oxymoron. Doing an experiment makes sense only if the researcher has an interest in a descriptive causal question, and to have this interest without a concomitant interest in the validity of the causal answer seems hard to justify.

The strong sense in which internal validity can have priority occurs when the experimenter can exercise choice within an experiment about how much priority to give to each validity type. Unfortunately, any attempt to answer this question is complicated by the fact that we have no accepted measures of the amount of each kind of validity, and so it is difficult to tell how much of each validity is present. One option would be to use methodological indices, for example, claiming that randomized studies with low attrition yield inferences that are likely to be higher in internal validity. But such an index fails to measure the internal validity of other cause-probing studies. Another option would be to use measures based on the number of identified threats to validity that still remain to be ruled out. But the conceptual obstacles to such measures are daunting; and even if it were possible to construct them for all the validity types, we can think of no way to put them on the common metric that would be needed for making comparative priorities.

A feasible option is to use the amount of resources devoted to a particular validity type as an indirect index of its priority. After all, it is possible to reduce the resources given, say, to fostering internal validity and to redistribute them to fostering some other validity type. For example, a researcher might take resources that would otherwise be devoted to random assignment, to measuring selection bias, or to reducing attrition and use them either (1) to study a larger number of units (in order to facilitate statistical conclusion validity), (2) to implement several quasi-experiments on existing treatments at a larger number of representatively sampled sites (in order to facilitate external validity), or (3) to increase the quality of outcome measurement (in order to facilitate construct validity). Such resource allocations effectively reduce the priority of internal validity.

These allocation decisions vary as a function of many variables. One is the basic versus applied research distinction. Basic researchers have high interest in construct validity because of the key role that constructs play in theory construction and testing. Applied researchers tend to have more interest in external validity because of the particular value that accrues to knowledge about the reach of a causal relationship in applied contexts. For example, Festinger's (e.g., 1953) basic social psychology experiments were justly famous for the care they put into ensuring that the variable being manipulated was indeed cognitive dissonance. Similarly, regarding units, Piagetian developmental psychologists often devote extra resources to assessing whether children are at preoperational or concrete operational stages of development. By contrast, the construct validity of settings tends to be of less concern in basic research because few theories specify crucial target settings. Finally, external validity is frequently of the lowest interest in basic research. Much basic psychological research is conducted using college sophomores for the greater statistical power that comes through having large numbers of homogeneous respondent populations. The tradeoff is defended by the hope that the results achieved with such students will be general because they tap into general psychological processes—an assumption that needs frequent empirical testing. However, assuming (as we are) that these examples occurred in the context of an experiment, it is still unlikely that the basic researcher would let the resources given to internal validity fall below a minimally acceptable level.

By contrast, much applied experimentation has different priorities. Applied experiments are often concerned with testing whether a particular problem is alleviated by an intervention, so many readers are concerned with the construct validity of effects. Consider, for example, debates about which cost-of-living adjustment based on the Consumer Price Index (CPI) most accurately reflects the actual rise in living costs—or indeed, whether the CPI should be considered a cost-of-living measure at all. Similarly, psychotherapy researchers have debated whether traditional therapy outcome measures accurately reflect the notion of clinically significant improvement among therapy clients (Jacobson, Follette, & Revenstorf, 1984). Applied research also has great stake in plausible generalization to the specific external validity targets in which the applied community is interested. Weisz, Weiss, and Donenberg (1992), for example, suggested that most psychotherapy experiments were done with units, treatments, observations, and settings that are so far removed from those used in clinical practice as to jeopardize external validity inferences about how well psychotherapy works in those contexts.

It is clear from these examples that decisions about the relative priority of different validities in a given experiment cannot be made in a vacuum. They must take into account the status of knowledge in the relevant research literature generally. For example, in the "phase model" of cancer research at the National Institutes of Health (Greenwald & Cullen, 1984), causal inferences about treatment effects are always an issue, but at different phases different validity types have priority. Early on, the search for possibly effective treatments tolerates weaker experimental designs and allows for many false positives so as not to overlook a potentially effective treatment. As more knowledge accrues, internal validity gets higher priority to sort out those treatments that really do work under at least some ideal circumstances (efficacy studies). By the last phase of research, external validity is the priority, especially exploring how well the treatment works under conditions of actual application (effectiveness studies).

Relatively few programs of research are this systematic. However, one might view the four validity types as a loose guide to programmatic experimentation, instructing the researcher to iterate back and forth among them as comparative weaknesses in generalized causal knowledge of one kind or another become apparent. For example, many researchers start a program of research by noticing an interesting relationship between two variables (e.g., McGuire, 1997). They may do further studies to confirm the size and dependability of the relationship (statistical conclusion validity), then study whether the relationship is causal (internal validity), then try to characterize it more precisely (construct validity) and to specify its boundaries (external validity). Sometimes, the phenomenon that piques an experimenter's curiosity already has considerable external validity; for instance, the covariation between smoking and lung cancer across different kinds of people in different settings and at different times led to a program of research designed to determine if the relationship was causal, to characterize its size and dependability, and then to explain it. Other times, the construct validity of the variables has already been subject to much attention, but the question of a causal relationship between them suddenly attracts notice. For instance, the construct validity of both race and intelligence had already been extensively studied when a controversy arose in the 1990s over the possibility of a causal relationship between them (Devlin, 1997; Herrnstein & Murray, 1994). Programs of experimental research can start at many different points, with existing knowledge lending strength to different kinds of inferences and with need to repair knowledge weaknesses of many different kinds. Across a program of research, all validity types are a high priority. By the end of a program of research, each validity type should have had its turn in the spotlight.

SUMMARY

In Chapters 2 and 3, we have explicated the theory of validity that drives the rest of this book. It is a heavily pragmatic theory, rooted as much or more in the needs and experiences of experimental practice as in any particular philosophy of science. Chapter 2 presented a validity typology consisting of statistical conclusion validity, internal validity, construct validity, and external validity that retains the central ideas of Campbell and Stanley (1963) and Cook and Campbell (1979) but that does so in slightly expanded terms that extend the logic of generalizations to more parts of the experiment. With a few minor exceptions, the threats to validity outlined in previous volumes remain largely unchanged in this book.

However, the presentation to this point has been abstract, as any such theory must partly be. If the theory is to retain the pragmatic utility that it achieved in the past, we have to show how this theory is used to design and criticize cause-probing studies. We begin doing so in the next chapter, in which we start with the simplest quasi-experimental designs that have sometimes been used for investigating causal relationships, showing how each can be analyzed in terms of threats to validity and how those threats can be better diagnosed or sometimes reduced in plausibility by improving those designs in various ways. Each subsequent chapter in the book presents a new class of designs, each of which is in turn subject to a similar validity analysis—quasi-experimental designs with comparison groups and pretests, **interrupted time series designs, regression discontinuity designs,** and randomized designs. In all these chapters, the focus is primarily but not exclusively on internal validity. Finally, following the presentation of these designs, the emphasis is reversed as the book moves to a discussion of methods and designs for improving construct and external validity.

4

Quasi-Experimental Designs That Either Lack a Control Group or Lack Pretest Observations on the Outcome

Qua·si (kwā´zī´, sī´, kwä´zī, sī´): [Middle English as if, from Old French from Latin *quasi: quam,* as; see *kwo-* in Indo-European Roots + *s,* if; see *swo-* in Indo-European Roots.] adj. Having a likeness to something; resembling: *a quasi success.*

W̶E BEGIN this chapter (and subsequent ones) with a brief example that illustrates the kind of design being discussed. In 1966, the Canadian Province of Ontario began a program to screen and treat infants born with phenylketonuria (PKU) in order to prevent PKU-based retardation. An evaluation found that, after the program was completed, 44 infants born with PKU experienced no retardation, whereas only 3 infants showed evidence of retardation—and of these three, two had been missed by the screening program (Webb et al., 1973). Statistics from prior years showed a higher rate of retardation due to PKU. Although the methodology in this study was quite primitive, particularly because it lacked a control group[1] that did not receive treatment, the authors concluded that the program successfully prevented PKU-based retardation. Subsequently, such programs were widely adopted in Canada and the United States and are still seen as extremely effective. How did this study achieve such a clear, correct, and useful conclusion when it used neither a control group nor random assignment? That is the topic of this chapter.

---

1. The term *control group* usually refers to a group that does not receive treatment; the more general term *comparison group* may include both control groups and alternative treatment groups.

In this chapter, we describe quasi-experimental designs that either lack a control group or that lack pretest observations on the outcome. Although few such studies achieve causal conclusions as clear as this PKU example, it is sometimes possible. More importantly, researchers often have good reasons for using such designs, such as a need to devote more resources to construct validity or external validity; practical necessities imposed by funding, ethics, or administrators; or logistical constraints that occur when an intervention has already been fielded before the evaluation of that intervention is designed. Indeed, given such contingencies, sometimes one of these designs will be the *best* design for a given study, even if the causal inference itself may be weaker than might otherwise be possible. Consequently, in this chapter we present such designs and the conditions that make them more likely to be successful for descriptive causal inference. But we use this chapter to make three more points. First, these designs are used quite frequently in field research; for example, in a recent review of the Even Start Literacy Program (St. Pierre, Ricciuti & Creps, 1998), the vast majority (76%) of studies used a one group pretest-posttest design, and most of the rest used the same design without a pretest. Sometimes such uses reflect a mistaken belief that design elements such as control groups or pretests are undesirable or unnecessary—even when descriptive causal inference is the highest priority. We want to cast doubt on such beliefs by showing the costs to internal validity that such designs can incur so that researchers can choose whether to incur these costs given their other research priorities. Second, we use these designs to illustrate how various validity threats operate with actual examples, for it is more important to learn how to think critically about these threats than it is to learn a list of designs. Successive exposure to these threats here and in later chapters will make it easier to detect them in studies one reads or designs. Finally, we use these designs to introduce the structural elements common to all experimental designs, out of which researchers build designs that are stronger for internal validity to suit the circumstances of their work, elements that are used again and again in the designs we describe in later chapters.

THE LOGIC OF QUASI-EXPERIMENTATION IN BRIEF

The designs in this chapter are **quasi-experiments**—experiments that lack random assignment of units to conditions but that otherwise have similar purposes and structural attributes to randomized experiments. Quasi-experiments have been used for many years. Lind (1753) described a quasi-experimental comparison of six medical treatments for scurvy, and Galton (1872) described a quasi-experimental thought experiment he never actually implemented on the effects of prayer. Hartmann (1936) studied the effects of emotionally versus rationally based political leaflets on election results in Pennsylvania. He matched three voting wards that received the emotional leaflets with four others that received the rational leaflets, matching on size of ward, density of population, assessed real-estate values, previous voting patterns, and socioeconomic status.

A causal inference from any quasi-experiment must meet the basic requirements for all causal relationships: that cause precede effect, that cause covary with effect, and that alternative explanations for the causal relationship are implausible. Both randomized and quasi-experiments manipulate the treatment to force it to occur before the effect. Assessing covariation between cause and effect is easily accomplished in all experiments, usually during statistical analysis. To meet the third requirement, randomized experiments make alternative explanations implausible by ensuring that they are randomly distributed over the experimental conditions. Because quasi-experiments do not use random assignment, they rely on other principles to show that alternative explanations are implausible. We emphasize three closely related principles to address this requirement in quasi-experimentation.

- The first principle is the *identification and study of plausible threats to internal validity.* Once identified, those threats can be studied to probe how likely it is that they explain treatment–outcome covariation (Reichardt, 2000). This chapter provides numerous examples of how to criticize inferences from quasi-experiments using the threats to validity presented in the previous chapters.
- A second principle is the *primacy of control by design.* By adding design elements (e.g., observation at more pretest time points, additional control groups), quasi-experimentation aims either to prevent the confounding of a threat to validity with treatment effects or to provide evidence about the plausibility of those threats. The usual alternative to design controls are statistical controls that attempt to remove confounds from effect estimates using statistical adjustments after the study is done. Design controls and statistics can and should be used together, of course. But we encourage as much prior use of design controls as possible, leaving statistical control to deal with any smaller differences that remain after design controls have been used.
- A third principle for reducing the plausibility of alternative causal explanations in quasi-experiments is *coherent pattern matching.* That is, a complex prediction is made about a given causal hypothesis that few alternative explanations can match. Examples in this chapter include the use of **nonequivalent dependent variables** and of predicted interactions. The more complex the pattern that is successfully predicted, the less likely it is that alternative explanations could generate the same pattern, and so the more likely it is that the treatment had a real effect.

None of these three principles provide the ease of causal inference or the elegant statistical rationale associated with random assignment. Instead, the logic of causal inference in quasi-experimentation requires careful and detailed attention to identifying and reducing the plausibility of alternative causal explanations.

TABLE 4.1 Quasi-Experimental Designs Without Control Groups

The One-Group Posttest-Only Design

$$X \qquad O_1$$

The One-Group Posttest-Only Design With Multiple Substantive Posttests

$$X_1 \qquad \{O_{1A}\ O_{1B}...O_{1N}\}$$

The One-Group Pretest–Posttest Design

$$O_1 \qquad X \qquad O_2$$

The One-Group Pretest–Posttest Design Using a Double Pretest

$$O_1 \qquad O_2 \qquad X \qquad O_3$$

The One-Group Pretest–Posttest Design Using a Nonequivalent Dependent Variable

$$\{O_{1A},\ O_{1B}\} \quad X \qquad \{O_{2A},\ O_{2B}\}$$

The Removed-Treatment Design

$$O_1 \qquad X \qquad O_2 \qquad\qquad O_3 \qquad \not{X} \qquad O_4$$

The Repeated-Treatment Design

$$O_1 \qquad X \qquad O_2 \qquad \not{X} \qquad O_3 \qquad X \qquad O_4$$

DESIGNS WITHOUT CONTROL GROUPS

In this section, we discuss designs without a control group (Table 4.1). Designs without control groups can yield strong causal inferences only by reducing the plausibility of alternative explanations for the treatment effect. Some designs do a poor job of that, and others do better. Progressing from the former to the latter demonstrates how to build designs that render more threats to internal validity implausible.

The One-Group Posttest-Only Design

This design obtains one posttest observation on respondents who experienced a treatment, but there are neither control groups nor pretests. This design is diagrammed as:

$$X \qquad O_1$$

where X is the treatment, O_1 is the posttest, and position from left to right indicates temporal order. The absence of a pretest makes it difficult to know if a change has occurred, and the absence of a no-treatment control group makes it difficult to know what would have happened without treatment. Nearly all the threats to internal validity except ambiguity about temporal precedence usually apply to this design. For example, a history threat is nearly always present because other events might have occurred at the same time as treatment to produce the observed effect.

However, the design has merit in rare cases in which much specific background knowledge exists about how the dependent variable behaves. For example, background knowledge of calculus is very low and stable in the average high school population in the United States. So if students pass a calculus test at levels substantially above chance after taking a calculus course, this effect is likely to be due to the course. Students simply do not learn much calculus from their homes, friends, television sets, recreational activities, or even other academic courses. But for valid descriptive causal inferences to result, the effect must be large enough to stand out clearly, and either the possible alternative causes must be known and be clearly implausible or there should be no known alternatives that could operate in the study context (Campbell, 1975). These conditions are rarely met in the social sciences, and so this design is rarely useful in this simple form.

Improving the One-Group Posttest-Only Design Using Multiple Substantive Posttests

The one-group design without pretests can be more interpretable under theory-linked conditions variously called pattern matching (Campbell, 1966a; Trochim, 1985) or coherence (Rosenbaum, 1995a). Consider the analogy of a crime such as murder. Noting that detectives can be successful in discovering the cause of such crimes (the murderer), Scriven (1976) attributes their success to the saliency of the effect (a dead body), to the availability of a pattern of clues that specify the time and manner of death (multiple posttests), and to the ability to link these clues to the modus operandi of criminals (potential alternative explanations) who are known to commit their crimes in distinctive ways that might overlap with the details found at the crime scene. If more than one person has a particular *modus operandi*, then the known suspects can be questioned to probe their alibis (Abelson, 1995, calls this the method of signatures).

Pathologists use this detective-like approach to investigate why someone died (the effect), using evidence from the corpse, the setting, and the time of death (a pattern of data). They identify possible causes of the death by matching that pattern of data to the descriptions in the scientific literature that differentiate one disease from another. Epidemiologists do something similar. To learn how AIDS arrived in the United States, they used available clues (early prevalence in the homosexual community, high prevalence among Africans living in Europe, and the military involvement of Cuba in equatorial Africa) to tentatively trace the disease's origin to a homosexual Air Canada steward who was very sexually active in the United States and who had visited Cuba and had consorted there with soldiers who had served in equatorial Africa, where AIDS was already endemic.

These clues serve as multiple, unique, and substantive posttests to the design:

$$X_1 \qquad \{O_{1A} \; O_{1B} ... O_{1N}\}$$

where $\{O_{1A}\ O_{1B}...O_{1N}\}$ refers to measures of different posttreatment constructs *A* through *N* that are matched to the pattern of effects (the modus operandi) left by the possible causes that are known (i.e., the suspects). This is very different from a design in which only one posttest construct (O_{1A}) is assessed so that a pattern-matching logic cannot be used.

However, in all these examples, the effect is known, but the cause is unknown and is searched for retrospectively. In most quasi-experimentation, the situation is the opposite: the potential cause is known (e.g., a new calculus course) but the effect is unknown and is searched for prospectively (e.g., what happens to student achievement). In this latter case, the pattern-matching logic is less compelling because the cause is often an innovation with an unknown pattern of effects. So adding multiple posttests under a prospective design can increase Type I errors, doubly risky because humans are adept at finding and interpreting patterns even in random data (Fischhoff, 1975; Paulos, 1988; Wood, 1978). Careful *prior* specification of patterns that support a causal relationship is crucial and sometimes occurs in fields with well-developed theory. But even then it is crucial that the predicted pattern be unique. If pathology textbooks show similar changes associated with three different diseases, we cannot discriminate among those diseases based on those changes.

The One-Group Pretest–Posttest Design

Adding a pretest measure of the outcome construct to the preceding design yields a one-group pretest–posttest design. A single pretest observation is taken on a group of respondents (O_1), treatment (X) then occurs, and a single posttest observation on the same measure (O_2) follows:

$$O_1 \quad X \quad O_2$$

Adding the pretest provides weak information about the counterfactual inference concerning what might have happened to participants had the treatment not occurred. However, because O_1 occurs before O_2, the two may differ for reasons unrelated to treatment, such as maturation or history. For example, Jason, McCoy, Blanco, and Zolik (1981) studied the effects of a campaign to reduce dog litter in Chicago by distributing to residents both educational material and "pooper-scoopers" with plastic bags. The subsequent reduction in dog litter was dramatic. The outcome can be causally tied to the intervention to the extent to which one can assume that other possible alternative hypotheses are implausible—for example, that the weather had turned worse and dogs were on the street less often or that a citywide campaign to reduce litter had begun at the same time or that there had been a dramatic increase in local crimes that kept residents indoors.

The design can be implemented either with the same units or different units receiving both pretest and posttest. When the same units are used, this is often called a within-participants design.[2] Duckart (1998) used the within-participants version of this design to evaluate the effects of a program to reduce environmental lead in low-income urban housing units in Baltimore. The program used both education and physical changes to reduce sources of lead in each home. Using lead wipe samples, lead levels were measured at various locations in each home at pretest, immediately after the intervention (posttest), and 6 months later (follow-up). Significant reductions occurred in lead levels between pretest and posttest and to a lesser extent at follow-up. Because lead levels are stable over short periods of time, spontaneous changes that a control group might detect are unlikely to occur, so this topic lends itself to this design better than most other topics.

Even so, Duckart (1998) identifies several threats to validity for this design. Regarding internal validity, maturation may affect changes from pretest to follow-up because lead dust levels are lower in winter than in summer; and most of the follow-ups were conducted in winter. History is a threat because another Baltimore agency concurrently provided services that could have affected lead levels at some homes in the sample. Testing is a threat because pretest feedback to residents about lead levels may have caused them to clean more diligently, which would reduce lead levels even if the intervention were ineffective. Regarding attrition, about one third of participants did not continue beyond pretest, and it may have been the least motivated or cooperative residents who dropped out. Statistical conclusion validity may have been reduced by low sample sizes and consequent low power for those tests that were not significant, and power could have been further reduced because treatment **implementation** varied considerably from site to site. Construct validity of the outcome measures may have been hampered because the same persons who administered the intervention in the homes also administered the outcome measures, and they may have done so in a way that inadvertently made the results look favorable to the intervention.

This example is particularly instructive about the logic of applying threats to the validity of a causal inference. Duckart (1998) did two key things. First, he showed that the threats were more than just possible but were plausible. He did this by providing data to show that a threat was likely to have occurred in his study—past research shows that lead dust levels are indeed lower in winter than in summer. Second, he showed that this threat would produce an effect like the

---

2. Here the within-participants factor is time: repeated measures at pretest and posttest within each unit. In other within-participant designs, more than one condition can be administered to the same units. By contrast, an experiment having multiple conditions and different units in each condition is often called a **between-participants design** (S. E. Maxwell & Delaney, 1990). Within-participants designs can increase statistical power by controlling individual differences between units within conditions, and so they can use fewer units to test the same number of treatments. However, within-participants designs can cause **fatigue effects, practice effects, carryover effects,** and **order effects.** To avoid confounding such effects with treatment, the order of treatments in a within-participants design is often either randomized for each unit or deliberately **counterbalanced** so that some units get treatments in one order (e.g., A then B) but others get a second order (B then A) so that order effects can be assessed.

one he wanted to attribute to the cause—he found lower lead levels after treatment, which also happened to be in winter. So those lower lead levels could have been due to seasonality effects. Both these conditions are necessary to weaken the inference that the program caused the observed effects. Imagine, for example, that past research showed that lead dust levels were lower in summer than in winter. This could not possibly explain his finding of lowered levels in winter and so could not threaten internal validity. For a threat to validity to be plausible, it must produce an effect that is similar in size to the one observed, not of a magnitude that is too small to explain a large observed effect and not an effect in the opposite direction (e.g., not an increase in dust when a decrease was observed).

However, social scientists in field settings will rarely be able to construct confident causal knowledge with the simple pretest–posttest design unless the outcomes are particularly well behaved and the interval between pretest and posttest is short. Persons considering this design should consider adding even more design elements.

Improving the One-Group Pretest–Posttest Design Using a Double Pretest

The plausibility of maturation and regression threats is reduced by adding a second pretest prior to the first pretest:

$$O_1 \qquad O_2 \quad X \quad O_3$$

The two pretests function as a "dry run" to clarify the biases that might exist in estimating the effects of treatment from O_2 to O_3. For example, Marin, Marin, Perez-Stable, Sabogal, and Ostero-Sabogal (1990) tested the effects of a culturally appropriate smoking cessation information campaign for Hispanics. The first pretest occurred in the fall of 1986, the second pretest in the summer of 1987, and the posttest in the summer of 1988. Results showed that information levels after the campaign (O_3) were far higher than before it (O_2) and also far higher than the maturational trend from O_1 to O_2 would yield. Of course, a nonlinear change in maturation trend before treatment could be detected only with even more pretests.

Improving the One-Group Pretest–Posttest Design Using a Nonequivalent Dependent Variable

The addition of a nonequivalent dependent variable is diagrammed below, where A and B represent different measures collected from a single group at times 1 and 2:

$$\{O_{1A}, O_{1B}\} \quad X \quad \{O_{2A}, O_{2B}\}$$

Measures A and B assess similar constructs. Measure A (the outcome) is expected to change because of treatment. Measure B (the nonequivalent dependent variable) is not; however, Measure B is expected to respond to salient internal validity threats in the same way as Measure A.[3] For example, a nonequivalent dependent variable was used by Robertson and Rossiter (1976) to study children's preferences for advertised toys during the Christmas marketing period. They showed that toys advertised in November and December increased in desirability (the outcome) more than nonadvertised toys (the nonequivalent dependent variable). This design reduces the plausibility of many threats to internal validity. For example, history is a threat, given the frequent references to gifts and toys at that time of year in American culture. However, this should affect preferences for all toys, not just advertised toys. A different history problem arises, though, if toys advertised on television are supported by ads on radio and in newspapers. Who can say whether television advertising caused the effect? Or what about statistical regression if toy manufacturers advertised those toys that were selling poorly during this period?

McKillip and Baldwin (1990) also used a nonequivalent dependent variable design and found that awareness of condom use increased more than awareness of alcohol abuse or of regular exercise after a media campaign about sexually transmitted diseases; and McNees, Gilliam, Schnelle, and Risley (1979) found that feedback about theft of potato chips from a snack bar reduced such theft but not theft of ice cream, milk, or sandwiches. This design is broadly useful and can often be causally interpretable when both dependent variables are plausibly exposed to the same set of environmental causes to the same degree.

The Removed-Treatment Design

This design adds a third posttest (O_3) to the one-group pretest–posttest design (O_1 and O_2) and then removes the treatment ($\not{X}$ symbolizes this removal) before a final measure is made (O_4):

$$O_1 \quad X \quad O_2 \qquad O_3 \quad \not{X} \quad O_4$$

The aim is to demonstrate that outcome rises and falls with the presence or absence of treatment, a result that could be otherwise explained only by a threat to validity that similarly rose and fell over the same time. The link from O_1 to O_2 is one experimental sequence, and the change from O_3 to O_4 is another that involves the opposite hypothesis to the O_1 to O_2 hypothesis. If the first sequence predicts, say, an increase from O_1 to O_2, the second sequence predicts a decrease (or a smaller increase). Of course, this pattern can occur only if the treatment effects

---

3. Rosenbaum (1995a, p. 137) references a similar idea when he notes "a systematic difference between treated and control groups in an outcome the treatment does not affect must be a hidden bias"; however, nonequivalent dependent variables are chosen to respond to particular threats to validity, providing more information about specific alternative causes than other outcomes that the treatment should not affect.

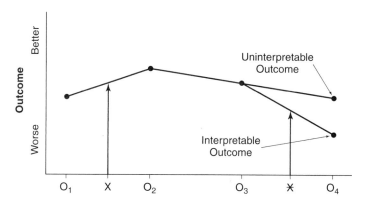

FIGURE 4.1 Generally interpretable outcome of the removed-treatment design

dissipate once treatment is removed. Even a partially persisting effect from O_2 to O_3 biases the analysis against the reversal of the treatment effect between O_3 and O_4. Thus the most interpretable outcome of the design is presented in Figure 4.1.

Statistical conclusion validity is a problem, because the pattern of results can be influenced by even a single outlier. So large sample sizes and reliable measures are a desideratum. Further, removing some treatments might be unethical or might arouse frustration that would be correlated with measures of aggression, satisfaction, or performance, operating similarly to resentful demoralization and compensatory rivalry. If so, it is unwise to use this design.

A naturally occurring version of this design occurs when respondents stop taking treatment, but only if their reasons for discontinuing are unrelated to treatment. That is rarely the case, so special care must be taken when respondents self-select out of treatment. To envision this, consider a study of the effects on attitudes of entering a new job role. For example, someone becomes a foreman (X); he or she develops promanagerial attitudes between O_1 and O_2 but dislikes the new contact with managers. By O_3 he or she has become less promanagerial (Lieberman, 1956). Such a person could then resign from the foremanship or be relieved of it, leading to less promanagerial attitudes from O_3 to O_4 when compared with O_1 to O_2. Given this pattern, the researcher must decide whether the O_3 to O_4 decrease reflects the job change or was already occurring by O_3. The latter would be more likely if the O_3 to O_4 difference were similar in size to the O_2 to O_3 difference (see the uninterpretable outcome in Figure 4.1). However, a steeper decrease in promanagerial attitudes between O_3 and O_4 when compared with O_2 to O_3 would suggest that entering the new role causes one to adopt promanagerial attitudes.

Lieberman (1956) actually used a simpler version of this design. He sampled men before they became foremen, after they became foremen, and then after they reverted to worker status—only three measurement waves. Hence, differences between O_1 and O_2 and O_2 and O_3 might be due to (1) a role change that influenced attitudes or (2) the demotion of foremen whose attitudes were becoming less managerial. Adding the fourth observation helps assess these possibilities.

Making observations at equally spaced intervals is important with this (and many other) designs because it permits assessment of spontaneous linear changes over time. Comparison of the differences between O_2 and O_3 and between O_3 and O_4 would be less meaningful if the O_3 to O_4 time interval were longer than the O_2 to O_3 interval because a constant rate of change would reveal larger O_3 to O_4 differences than O_2 to O_3 differences. If one has a *treatment-free* estimate of rate of change per time interval, the need for equal spacing is less; but an estimate of that rate is rarely possible with this design.

The Repeated-Treatment Design

It is sometimes possible to introduce, remove, and reintroduce treatment over time to study how treatment and outcome covary over time:

$$O_1 \quad X \quad O_2 \quad \cancel{X} \quad O_3 \quad X \quad O_4$$

Even more so than in the previous design, few threats to validity could explain a close relationship between treatment introductions and removals on the one hand and parallel changes in outcome on the other. Such threats would have to come and go on the same schedule as treatment introduction and removal. The latter is usually an unlikely event. However, if treatment effects are not transient, it is difficult for treatment removal to reverse the direction of effect; and if treatment creates a ceiling effect by O_3, that would prevent the reintroduction of the treatment from registering an effect.

The most interpretable outcome of this design is the case in which O_1 differs from O_2, O_2 differs from O_3 in the opposite direction, and the O_3 to O_4 difference resembles the O_1 to O_2 difference, not the O_2 to O_3 difference. Powers and Anglin (1993) adapted this design to demonstrate the effects of methadone maintenance on narcotic use. Narcotic use dropped dramatically while methadone was administered, rose when methadone was removed, and dropped again when methadone was readministered. This design is also frequently used by behavioral researchers in psychology (Barlow & Hersen, 1984). We suspect that this design has been used so much because it involves at least one replication of the treatment effect and because this replication meets a basic criterion for quality research: reproducibility.

A threat to internal validity is cyclical maturation. For example, if O_2 and O_4 were recorded on Tuesday morning and O_1 and O_3 on Friday afternoon, differences in productivity might be related to day-of-the-week differences in performance rather than to treatment. The researcher should also check whether unique historical events follow the pattern of treatment introduction and removal. In general, though, the design is strong for internal validity, especially when the investigator controls introduction and removal of treatment.

The design can be vulnerable on external and statistical conclusion validity
grounds. For example, many performance graphs in the Hawthorne studies (Roethlisberger & Dickson, 1939) are of individual female workers, sometimes as few as
six women, who displayed considerable variability in how they reacted to the treatments; so we cannot be sure how robust the results are to sampling error. Of course,
this design can use larger samples and statistical tests, which we encourage.

Construct validity of the cause is threatened when respondents notice the introduction, removal, or reintroduction of the treatment. Respondents may generate hypotheses about these treatment variations and respond to them. Resentful
demoralization can also be an issue when the treatment is removed between O_2
and O_3. The O_3 data point might then be affected, making it more difficult to interpret an increase between O_3 and O_4 when the treatment is reinstated.

So this design is better with transient effects, with unobtrusive treatments,
with a long delay between initial treatment and its reintroduction, and with no
confounding of temporal cycles with the treatment's introduction, removal, and
reintroduction. It is also more effective when reintroductions of the treatment are
frequent and randomly distributed across time, thus creating a randomized experiment in which time blocks are the unit of assignment (Edgington, 1987,
1992). Not all research projects can meet these conditions.

Implementing the Repeated-Treatment Design Using Retrospective Pretests

Powers and Anglin (1993) actually adapted this design by assessing retrospectively the effects of methadone maintenance on heroin addicts who had experienced multiple treatment episodes in the past. They asked addicts to recreate their
drug use and treatment history retrospectively. They found through these recol-
lected histories that methadone maintenance reduced drug use during treatment
periods but not between them. Unfortunately, retrospective judgments can be
quite biased (e.g., Silka, 1989). For example, people tend to overestimate "bad"
occurrences in the present compared with the past, and results from retrospective
self-reports can differ from prospective self-reports (Widon, Weiler, & Cottler,
1999; G. S. Howard et al., 1979; G. S. Howard, Millham, Slaten, & O'Donnell,
1981). Factors that influence the retrospective pretest include whether the material is easily distorted (e.g., cognition versus behaviors), length of time since the
events being recalled, demand characteristics (e.g., distorted responses of illegal
behaviors), specificity versus generality of information needed (specific events are
less accurately recalled), and the emotions elicited by the recall (e.g., remembering a trauma; Babcock, 1998). Sometimes retrospective pretests can be cross-
validated by other sources. For example, Powers and Anglin (1993) validated self-
reported treatment dates using stored administrative records. However, little is
known empirically about these matters in the context of experimental design, so
we repeat the opinion of Campbell and Stanley (1963): "Given the autistic factors

known to distort memory and interview reports, such data (i.e., retrospective pretest data) can never be crucial" (p. 66). Retrospective pretests should be a supplement to other design improvements, not used by themselves, and should be a method of last resort interpreted with great caution.

The Powers and Anglin (1993) study also had a problem of attrition over time. They could study only addicts who returned for treatment. Thus their sample sizes of addicts with one, two, three, or four treatment episodes were progressively smaller. If some patients returned to treatment because they had failed to stay clean, whereas others did not return because they had successfully withdrawn from heroin, then the general conclusion that methadone maintenance results in a success that is only temporary might not have held if the full sample had been followed. This is a general problem in any longitudinal study that follows the same people over time. Those who are not reinterviewed over time may differ systematically from those who are reinterviewed.

Many of the problems we have discussed in this section could be addressed better if an independent control group had been included. In the Powers and Anglin (1993) study, for example, the inclusion of addicts who were not on methadone maintenance might have clarified the frequency and timing of changes in retrospective pretest reports in untreated clients and might have clarified the effects of attrition over time. In the latter case, two controls could have been used: one that was required to return to the clinic for assessment in which the same sort of attrition might occur as in treated clients and one that was followed aggressively in the community, where such attrition might not occur. We turn now to discussion of such control groups, limiting discussion this time to quasi-experiments that have control groups but do not have pretests.

DESIGNS THAT USE A CONTROL GROUP BUT NO PRETEST

A classic method for supporting a counterfactual inference is to add a control group that receives no treatment, with the control group selected to be as similar as possible to the treatment group (D'Agostino & Kwan, 1995). Notationally, a dashed line (---------) between groups indicates that they were not randomly formed, and such groups are preceded by *NR* (nonrandom assignment). Table 4.2 summarizes quasi-experimental designs that have control groups but no pretest measures on the outcome variable.

Posttest-Only Design With Nonequivalent Groups

Here we add a control group to the one-group posttest-only design. This design might be used if a treatment begins before the researcher is consulted so that

TABLE 4.2 Quasi-Experimental Designs That Use Control Groups But No Pretest

---

Posttest-Only Design With Nonequivalent Groups

NR   X O_1

NR O_2

Posttest-Only Design Using an Independent Pretest Sample

NR O_1 ┆ X O_2

-----------------------┆------------

NR O_1 ┆ O_2

Posttest-Only Design Using Proxy Pretests

NR O_{A1} X O_{B2}

NR O_{A1} O_{B2}

---

pretest observations are not available on the scale used at posttest. Such a design can be diagrammed as:

$$NR \quad X \quad O_1$$
$$\text{------------------}$$
$$NR \qquad O_2$$

For example, Sharpe and Wetherbee (1980) compared mothers who received nutritional benefits from a Women, Infants, and Children (WIC) project in Mississippi with those who did not. Results indicated no significant posttest differences in infant birth weight or infant mortality between the two groups. However, groups may have differed on many variables related to these outcomes, such as prior nutrition status. This possibility of pretest group differences makes it very hard to separate treatment from selection effects.

A rationale sometimes offered for preferring this weak design is that pretest measurement may sensitize participants and so influence their posttest scores (Lana, 1969). But when different treatment groups are being compared, testing effects that are constant across groups do not threaten internal validity. Only differential testing effects do. They are rare, though they do occur (Aiken & West, 1990). They can be reduced by administering alternate forms of a test (one at pretest and the other at posttest), by using item response theory to calibrate different tests to the same scale (Hambleton, Swaminathan, & Rogers, 1991), by lengthening the time interval between pretest and posttest (Willson & Putnam, 1982), by using a Solomon Four Group Design to assess the presence and impact of such effects,[4] by using unobtrusive measures that are less reactive than self-report (Webb, Campbell,

---

4. In this design, participants are randomly assigned to one of two otherwise identical experiments, one with a pretest and one without, so the effect of the pretest can be measured empirically.

Schwartz, & Sechrest, 1966; Webb, Campbell, Schwartz, Sechrest, & Grove, 1981), by using techniques such as the bogus pipeline (Jones & Sigall, 1971), by using retrospective pretests, and by using explicit reference groups or behavioral criteria to anchor responding (Aiken & West, 1990). Thus, even if differential pretest sensitization is a problem, eliminating the pretests can entail much larger costs for detecting selection biases than dealing with them in the ways outlined here.

Improving the Posttest-Only Design Using an Independent Pretest Sample

Even when it is impossible to gather pretest data on the same sample both before and after treatment, one can sometimes gather pretest information from a randomly formed *independent* sample: a group that is drawn randomly from the same population as the posttest sample but that may have overlapping membership.[5] Such groups are useful when pretest measurements may be reactive, when it is too difficult or expensive to follow the same people over time, or when one wishes to study intact communities whose members change over time. The design is diagrammed here, with the vertical line indicating sample independence across time.

$$NR \quad O_1 \mid X \quad O_2$$
$$\text{-----------}\mid\text{----------}$$
$$NR \quad O_1 \mid \quad O_2$$

This design is frequently used in epidemiology, public health, marketing, and political polling and is preferable to a design without pretest data. However, if independent pretest and posttest samples are not randomly sampled from the same population, this design can introduce considerable selection bias into estimates of treatment effects. Nor is selection bias completely avoided by random sampling. First, random selection equates pretest and posttest only within the limits of sampling error, so comparability is more difficult to achieve with small, heterogeneous samples. Second, the populations being sampled may change in qualitative composition between measurement waves, particularly when waves are far apart in time, and those population changes can masquerade as treatment effects. Also, most internal validity threats that we describe in the next chapter as applying to control group designs with *dependent* pretest and posttest samples also apply when *independent* pretest and posttest samples are used. Finally, statistical conclusion validity can be lessened because independent samples at each measurement wave no longer serve as their own within-group statistical controls. Hence this design is recommended only when the need for independent groups is compelling or when problems with dependent groups are severe. If this design is necessary, the researcher should pay special attention to sample size, to how the sampling design is implemented, and to how comparability can be assessed using measures that are stable and reliable (Feldman & McKinlay, 1994).

5. In some literatures, these are called cross-sectional panels.

Improving the Posttest-Only Design Using Proxy Pretests

An alternative technique is to measure proxies for pretests—variables that are conceptually related to and correlated with the posttest within treatments. The design is diagrammed here, with A representing the proxy pretest and B the posttest:

$$NR \quad O_{A1} \quad X \quad O_{B2}$$
$$\overline{\hspace{3cm}}$$
$$NR \quad O_{A1} \qquad O_{B2}$$

Preferably, proxies should be conceptually related to outcome, not just readily accessible measures such as age, gender, social class, or race. For instance, when evaluating a calculus course for students who have never had calculus, a calculus pretest would yield little pretest variability; a proxy pretest of mathematical aptitude or achievement in algebra would be better. To the extent that proxies are correlated with the posttest, they index how much groups might have differed at pretest in ways that might be correlated with outcome (selection bias), and they index how much dropouts differ from those who stay in the study within and between groups (attrition bias). Even so, the indexing will usually be poorer than a pretest on the outcome variable itself.

Improving the Posttest-Only Design Using Matching or Stratifying

Lack of a pretest causes lack of knowledge about selection biases. Researchers often try to decrease the odds of such biases by forming treatment and control groups through matching or stratifying on likely correlates of the posttest.

Definitions. When **matching**, the researcher groups units with similar scores on the matching variable, so that treatment and control groups each contain units with the same characteristics on the matching variable.[6] For example, Levy, Matthews, Stephenson, Tenney, and Schucker (1985) studied the effects of a nutrition information program on product sales and market share in supermarkets owned by the same chain with a common set of management procedures. They used 10 treatment stores in Washington and 10 control stores in Maryland, creating 10 cross-state pairs, each matched on store size and socioeconomic characteristics because these variables predict sales and market share.

Twin studies provide a very special case of matching (e.g., Ashenfelter & Krueger, 1994). The presumption is that twins are more similar to each other than they are to other people, more so for identical twins, who share the same genetic

---

6. Some authors distinguish between blocking and matching, using blocking to indicate groups with similar scores and matching to identify groups with identical scores. In both cases, the number of units in a match-block is the same as the number of conditions in the experiment—for example, matched pairs with two conditions (such as treatment versus control) or matched triplets with three conditions (such as two different treatments and a control). We generally use the terms *block* and *match* interchangeably.

structure, than for fraternal twins, who share only some of the same genetic structure. In addition, twins are usually exposed to common environmental influences, for instance, being raised in the same family by the same parents with the same socioeconomic background. All these genetic and environmental similarities make using twins as matches in a quasi-experiment a very powerful approach.

A closely related technique is **stratifying,** which occurs when units are placed into homogeneous sets that contain more units than the experiment has conditions. An example is stratifying on gender; clearly, it is impossible to obtain a closer match than "male" among a large group of males, so a block will contain many more males than the number of experimental conditions. Sometimes, strata are formed from continuous variables, for example, by dividing achievement test scores at the median to form two large strata. With such a stratification, groups are less homogeneous than they would have been if participants had been matched because participants have more diverse achievement test scores in each stratum. If strata must be used, more strata are usually better than fewer; and five strata are usually sufficient to remove 90% of the variance that would have been accounted for with matching (Cochran, 1968). In the section that follows, we speak mostly of matching, but the same points usually apply to stratifying. Further, some of the methods we describe shortly, such as optimal matching, blur the conceptual distinction between matching and stratifying, though the practical implications should still be obvious.

Methods for Matching.   Diverse methods exist for matching (Cochran, 1983; Cochran & Rubin, 1973; Costanza, 1995; Dehejia & Wahba, 1999; Gu & Rosenbaum, 1993; Heckman, Ichimura, & Todd, 1997; Henry & McMillan, 1993; Marsh, 1998; Rosenbaum, 1995a; H. Smith, 1997). Exact matching requires units to have exactly the same score within a match. However, some units will not have an exact match if samples are small, if the distribution of participants between groups on the matching variable is uneven, or if variables are measured using very fine gradations. In caliper matching, the scores need not be identical but must be within a defined distance of each other (Cochran, 1965), though there are different ways of measuring that distance, such as nearest neighbor matching or Mahalanobis distance matching (Hill, Rubin, & Thomas, 2000; Rosenbaum, 1995a).

Sometimes more control units than treatment units exist, so if the researcher can select multiple controls (Henry & McMillan, 1993), it may be possible to improve the match and improve statistical power. For instance, index matching selects multiple control units above and below a treatment unit. Cluster group matching uses cluster analysis to embed the treatment group in a cluster of similar control units. Benchmark group matching selects control units that fall close to the treatment unit on a multivariate distance measure. Simulations suggest that cluster and benchmark methods may work better than index matching (Henry & McMillan, 1993). Finally, in optimal matching, each treatment unit may have multiple matched controls and vice versa (Bergstralh, Kosanke & Jocobsen, 1996; Rosenbaum, 1995a). A definitive review of the strengths and weaknesses of each matching method has yet to be done, with each compared with the other and with alternatives such as the analysis of covariance.[7]

Problems with Matching. Matching has a beleaguered history in quasi-experimentation because there is always the possibility of selection bias.[8] The minimum risk is *undermatching* because some nonredundant predictors of outcome were not included in the matching methodology. For example, although Levy et al. (1985) matched stores on two variables, other variables, such as the stores' product line and proximity to other stores, might have discriminated even more precisely between stores and might have been correlated with outcomes. If additional matching variables had been used, even greater equivalence might have been created between treatment and control stores. Further, because matching can never induce equivalence on variables not used in the matching, additional selection bias can never be ruled out with complete confidence.

However, skepticism about matching is due less to the concern for undermatching (which, after all, still gets one closer to the right answer) than for the possibility that matching may produce a result that is further away from the right answer than if matching had not been used at all. Campbell and Erlebacher (1970) showed how a common form of matching may have had the latter result. Their example was prompted by an evaluation of Head Start by Cicirelli and Associates (1969; Magidson, 2000) that seemed to show that Head Start children ended up doing worse than matched controls. Campbell and Erlebacher showed how this result could be caused by matching if the populations being matched do not overlap completely on the matching variable, so that matches for Head Start are taken from a different end of their distribution (say, the high end) than matched controls, who might be taken from the lower end of their distribution. If that variable is measured with error or is imperfectly correlated with outcome, statistical regression will occur that makes Head Start look harmful.

Marsh (1998) gives a similar example from the evaluation of programs for gifted and talented children in which the latter children come from a higher performing population than available controls. Matches could therefore be obtained from the overlap between the lower end of the gifted and talented population (the end with more negative random error) and the upper end of the control population (the end with more positive error). At posttest, the gifted and talented program children regress upward toward their population mean, and the controls regress down toward theirs. The resulting bias makes gifted and talented programs look effective even if they have no effect at all.

---

7. We discuss some relative advantages of matching and the analysis of covariance (ANCOVA) in the appendix to the next chapter and in the chapters on randomized experiments.

8. This discussion mostly applies to matching in quasi-experiments; in randomized experiments, matching is often a very useful adjunct to random assignment, as we discuss later in this book.

Principles to Guide Better Matching. A main lesson from these examples is that matching in quasi-experimentation works least effectively—and may be more harmful than helpful—when it is done on an unstable or unreliable variable and when the nonequivalent groups from which the matched sets are drawn are increasingly dissimilar when matched. Two methods help counteract these problems. The first is to select groups that are as similar as possible before matching, as much as the context and research question allow. If the distributions of the two groups on the matching variables overlap substantially, then many matches can be obtained without selecting extensively from opposite and extreme tails of the distributions. For example, nonequivalent groups might have more overlapping distributions if the control group is composed of applicants to the treatment group who would have been eligible but who applied too late than they would have if the control group is composed of those who are not eligible at all. When such selection is not possible, examination of the overlap of the two distributions will help alert the researcher to the possibility of regression among the matches.

The second method is to use matching variables that are stable and reliable. Some variables, such as gender and age, are measured with little error, and so they make good matching variables *if* they are correlated with outcome. The reliability of other matching variables can often be improved by aggregation—for example, by creating a composite of many pretest variables taken at the same time (e.g., the propensity score approach described in Chapter 5), by creating a composite of individuals (e.g., using school averages rather than individual student data), and by averaging two or more consecutive pretest performances rather than just one. This latter procedure also helps prevent the researcher from selecting groups *because* their pretest scores are extreme on one occasion (which also might result in statistical regression), given that random errors will tend to cancel out as more and more observations are averaged.

For example, we are much more optimistic about the kind of matching implemented in a recent study by Millsap, Goodson, Chase, and Gamse (1997) of the effects of a school development program (Comer, 1988) on student achievement in Detroit. They used a *stable matched bracketing* methodology in which 12 treatment schools were compared with 24 matched comparison schools. Matching was done (1) on variables that were measured reliably, in this case subdistrict location, school-level achievement test scores, and racial composition (achievement test scores *were* a true pretest in this case, but we ignore this for the sake of illustration); (2) by averaging over several years rather than just one year for the latter two variables; and (3) by using aggregate (e.g., school) rather than individual data. In addition, from a pool of four to six potential matches for each treatment school, two matching comparison schools were selected to bracket each treatment school: one that performed slightly above the treatment school on the prior achievement matching variable and another that fell just below it. Using two comparison schools for each treatment school increased study power at less cost than adding more treatment schools, because the expensive treatment did not have to be implemented in the comparison schools. The increase in power is particularly important when aggregates (e.g., schools) are being studied and when few aggregates are available.

Matching on more than one variable simultaneously becomes more difficult the more variables are used. However, reducing those variables to a multivariate composite makes matching more feasible. The previously described multivariate distance matching (Henry & McMillan, 1993) uses such a composite, as does matching on **propensity scores** (e.g., Rosenbaum 1995a; Dehejia & Wahba, 1999). A propensity score is obtained using logistic regression to predict group membership from pertinent predictors of group membership. Matching on the propensity score minimizes group differences across all the observed variables used in the propensity score equation and is robust over any **functional form** between propensity score and outcome. Propensity score matching can be supplemented by sensitivity analyses designed to probe whether the observed effect would be robust to biases of particular sizes. We discuss propensity scores and **hidden bias** analyses more extensively in an appendix to the next chapter.

The problems that matching must overcome in quasi-experiments are significant. Matching can occur only on observed measures, so hidden bias may remain. Removing unreliability will reduce the likelihood of regression artifacts, but such artifacts can occur when both the matching variables and the outcome are perfectly measured if they are still not perfectly correlated (Campbell & Kenny, 1999). Also, some threats to internal validity occur after pretest, as with history. There can be no direct match for this in the design planning. Still, we are modestly encouraged that the better matching procedures we have reviewed in this section will be more successful than the simplistic approaches to matching based on a single unreliable variable and on different populations that Campbell and Erlebacher (1970) rightly critiqued. Researchers who use matching should take advantage of these better procedures—the days of simple matching on single variables that are not reliably measured should be left completely behind.

Improving the Posttest-Only Design Using Internal Controls

Internal control groups are plausibly drawn from a population similar to that from which the treatment units are taken (Heinsman & Shadish, 1996; Shadish & Ragsdale, 1996). For example, Aiken, West, Schwalm, Carroll, and Hsiung (1998) used both a randomized design and a quasi-experiment to test the effects of a remedial writing program. Their nonequivalent internal control group was composed of eligible students who registered too late to be in the randomized experiment— a group that is plausibly similar to those eligible students who registered on time. In such cases, fewer selection biases are likely to be present than if the control group were external, such as students from another university or those whose ACT scores made them ineligible for the program. Internal controls do not guarantee similarity; for example, in some psychotherapy research the use of treatment acceptors (or completers) as a treatment group and treatment refusers (or dropouts) as a control group suggests obvious selection problems that might influence estimates of treatment effects. So there is no substitute for careful consideration of such potential selection biases when choosing good control groups.

Baker and Rodriguez (1979) used an internal control to study the effects of diverting criminal court defendants from the legal system to social and educational services. Legal aid attorneys objected to random assignment on legal grounds. However, twice as many clients were referred to diversion as could be accepted, so Baker and Rodriguez used a two-step assignment in which (1) time was divided into randomly distributed blocks of 11, 13, 15, 17, 19, or 21 hours in length and (2) the first 50% of clients expected during each block were assigned to treatment, with the remainder assigned to control. Program staff were unaware of the number of hours in the current block, so they could not easily predict when the 50% quota was met or whether the next client would be assigned to treatment. Nor could the courts funnel some clients preferentially to treatment, because they also did not know which block was in effect and because referrals came from multiple courts. Analysis of group differences suggested that treatment and control conditions were similar at pretest on the measured variables. This is a much stronger control than one from a nondiverted population. The random time feature probably increases the randomness of assignment if program staff were unaware when a new time block took effect and if research staff rather than program staff made assignments.

However, these conditions may often have been violated in a way that allowed program staff to selectively funnel certain cases into treatment. After all, the quota was always larger than one. So staff knew that when one referral was assigned to treatment, the next almost certainly would be, too; and assignment can easily be biased when program staff has knowledge of the next assignment (Chalmers, Celano, Sacks, & Smith, 1983; Dunford, 1990). The procedure also requires that the supply of referrals exceed program capacity. This requirement limits the situations in which it can be applied. Still, the procedure warrants use when better options are not feasible. It resembles two designs that we will later see are very strong: (1) a regression discontinuity design in which order of referral is the selection variable and (2) a study with random assignment of time blocks to conditions.

Improving the Posttest-Only Design Using Multiple Control Groups

It is often possible to use *multiple* nonequivalent control groups, as we pointed out in our discussion of matching. For example, Bell, Orr, Blomquist, and Cain (1995) compared a job training intervention group with four comparisons: those who failed to apply for the program, rejected applicants (screenouts), accepted applicants who failed to start treatment (no shows), and applicants who started treatment but dropped out before it ended (dropouts). Using multiple control groups can help in several ways. If the control groups differ from each other as much as they do from the treatment group, these differences obviously could not be caused by the treatment, and so they can index the magnitude of hidden biases that may be present (Rosenbaum, 1995a). If the direction of bias in each control group is known compared with the treatment group, it may be possible to bracket the treatment effect within a range of known biases. For example, Campbell (1969a) discussed both systematic variation controls and bracketing controls. In the former case, the researcher identifies a key threat to validity and then selects multiple controls that span the plausible range of that threat. If observed effects do not vary over that range, the plausibility of the threat is reduced. With bracketing, the researcher selects both a group expected to outperform the treatment group *if the treatment has no effect* and another group expected to underperform it. If the treatment group outperforms both groups, causal inference is strengthened.

Rosenbaum (in press) cites a similar example using multiple controls by Zabin, Hirsch, and Emerson (1989) on the effects on black teenage women of having an abortion. Zabin et al. compared pregnant women who obtained abortions with both pregnant women who had a child and women who sought abortions but were found after being tested not to be pregnant. They found that the treated women (with abortions) had a better educational outcome after 2 years than either of the two control groups, which showed educational outcomes that were about equal to each other. If the only control group had been the women who had children, the better educational outcomes found in women who had abortions could be challenged as being due to subsequent child care demands on the control group mothers rather than to the abortion itself. But that argument could not apply to the control group of women who turned out not to be pregnant and so did not have increased child care demands. These results make it more difficult to argue that abortion will *decrease* subsequent educational attainment.

Improving the Posttest-Only Design Using a Predicted Interaction

Sometimes substantive theory is good enough to generate *a highly differentiated causal hypothesis* that, if corroborated, would rule out many internal validity threats because they are not capable of generating such complex empirical implications. An example is Seaver's (1973) quasi-experiment on the effects of teacher performance expectancies on students' academic achievement. Seaver located children whose older siblings had previously obtained high (or low) grades and achievement scores in school. He divided these two (high- versus low-achieving) groups into those who had the same teacher their older sibling had had and those who had a different teacher. Seaver predicted that teacher expectancies should cause children with high-performing siblings to outperform children with low-performing siblings by a greater amount if they had the same teachers rather than different ones. The data corroborated this predicted statistical interaction. In this case, predicted interactions were useful because (1) substantive theory predicted a complex data pattern, (2) sibling control groups were available that, although nonequivalent, were plausibly similar on many family background factors, (3) outcome measures (academic achievement) were reliably measured, and

(4) large sample sizes allowed a powerful test of the interaction. These circumstances are rare in social research, but they illustrate the role that coherence of findings can play in strengthening an inference.

However, the researcher should be cautious even when a predicted interaction is confirmed—Reichardt (1985) showed that results from the Seaver study may be due to a regression artifact. When Seaver partitioned students into four groups, he also partitioned teachers. Suppose the older siblings with above-average performance had teachers whose abilities (not expectations) were above average. A younger sibling assigned to the same teacher would then receive above-average teaching; but a younger sibling assigned to a different teacher might receive closer to average teaching. A similar argument applies for older siblings who performed poorly and whose teachers may have been less able. Differences in teacher effectiveness might thus account for the crossover interaction Seaver obtained. But other internal validity threats still seem implausible, and this threat could be assessed empirically if measures of teacher ability were available.

Improving Designs Without Control Groups by Constructing Contrasts Other Than With Independent Control Groups

When it is not possible to gather prospective data on the kinds of independent control groups just discussed, it is sometimes possible to construct contrasts[9] that try to mimic the function of an independent control group. Three such contrasts are (1) a regression extrapolation that compares actual and projected posttest scores, (2) a normed comparison that compares treatment recipients to normed samples, and (3) secondary data that compares treatment recipients to samples drawn from previously gathered data, such as population-based surveys. All of these possibilities have great weaknesses, so our preference is that these constructed contrasts not be used by themselves. However, they are often inexpensive and convenient, and so a study can afford to combine them with other quasi-experimental design features to shed light on remaining alternative explanations at little added cost.

Regression Extrapolation Contrasts

This design compares the obtained posttest score of the treatment group with the score it was predicted to obtain based on other information. For example, Cook et al. (1975) studied the effects of viewing the television program *Sesame Street* in several parts of the country. A pretest was administered, followed 6 months later by a posttest. Age (in months) at pretest was then used to predict pretest academic achievement, resulting in an estimate of how much achievement gain is expected for

---

9. We call these contrasts because they would not generally be regarded as true control groups, even though the contrast of their results to those of the treatment group can sometimes help support a counterfactual inference.

each month a child aged. This monthly change estimate was then used to predict how much each child would have gained due to maturation in the 6 months separating pretest from posttest. The resulting prediction (which could not have been influenced by viewing *Sesame Street* because it was restricted to pretest measures) was then compared against the observed posttest data (which presumably was influenced by viewing *Sesame Street*). The regression equation generating the monthly gain estimate could also include measures of other threats to validity, such as parental socioeconomic status or other measures of selection bias.

However, by itself this approach has many severe problems. Without full knowledge of all threats to validity, predicted scores will rarely yield valid counterfactual inferences.[10] Moreover, the analysis depends on stable estimation using reliable measures and large samples. It also cannot address the possibility of history causing spurious effects after the pretest. Next, a testing artifact is possible because the obtained posttest is based on a second testing, whereas the first one obviously is not. And finally, this form of analysis is often used with aggregated school data to see if a school is doing better in a particular year than would be predicted for it on the basis of past academic performance and the nature of the student body and perhaps even the faculty. To do this well requires the use of multilevel data analytic approaches (Raudenbush & Willms, 1995; Willms, 1992) that respect the fact that individual responses are nested within schools. In our judgment, regression extrapolation contrasts are only worth doing when no other form of control group is possible or as an adjunct to a larger design. Indeed, Cook et al. (1975) used it as only one of many probes of the hypotheses about *Sesame Street*'s effectiveness, some of the others being much more conventional.

Normed Comparison Contrasts

In this case, obtained performance of the treatment group at pretest and posttest is compared with whatever published norms are available that might shed light on a counterfactual inference of interest. For example, Jacobson et al. (1984) compared couples treated for marital distress with norms for well-adjusted couples on the Marital Adjustment Scale to see if marital therapy made couples well-adjusted. Similarly, Nietzel, Russell, Hemmings, and Gretter (1987) reviewed studies that compared groups receiving therapy for depression with norms on the Beck Depression Inventory (Beck, Ward, Mendelsohn, Mock, & Erbaugh, 1961) to see if treated individuals eventually achieved levels of well-being similar to those reported by nondepressed adults. In each of these cases, the posttest score of the treated group was compared with the norm, with effects judged clinically significant if the treated group met or exceeded the normative standard.

This form of comparison is also routinely used in educational studies to assess whether a group of students, classrooms, or schools rises over time in its per-

---

10. The issues raised here are the same as those raised in **selection bias modeling** and structural equation **causal modeling** covered in the appendix to Chapter 5, so we defer more detailed discussion to that chapter.

centile ranking on some published test. The possible rankings are taken from published norms and are meant to reflect the students' performance and its change relative to how students in the original norming sample did. Studies using this method are severely limited. The normative contrast is a very weak counterfactual, providing little indication of how the actual treated participants would have performed without treatment. In fact, to the extent that the normative group is selected for being superior to the treated group, it becomes impossible for this comparison to reflect the treatment effect even if treatment improves outcomes greatly compared with what would have occurred without treatment. A treatment that is highly effective compared with a standard control group would often be judged ineffective against such a norm. The normative comparison group is also threatened by selection, because the normed sample usually differs from the treated sample; by history, because the norms were usually gathered well before data from the treated sample were; by testing, if the treated sample was pretested but the normative sample was not; by regression, if the treated sample was chosen because of high need (or high merit) but the normative sample was not; by instrumentation, if the conditions of measurement were much different for treated and normative groups; and by maturation, if the treated group was rapidly changing compared with the normative group. These threats can sometimes be ameliorated by using local norms gathered on the same population as the treated group, by ensuring that the conditions and timing of testing are similar over groups, and by selecting normative samples thought to have similar maturational experiences.

Secondary Source Contrasts

Even without published norms, researchers can sometimes construct opportunistic contrasts from secondary sources. For instance, medical researchers sometimes use clinical series, records of cases treated prior to a new treatment, for this purpose; medical data registers of all patients with a particular condition are similarly used; and historical controls from within the same institution are sometimes available (D'Agostino & Kwan, 1995). Studies of the effects of substance abuse prevention programs have supplemented their basic one-group designs with data from national or state surveys (Furlong, Casas, Corral, & Gordon, 1997; Shaw, Rosati, Salzman, Coles, & McGeary, 1997). Labor economists use national data sets this way, using current population surveys or panel studies on income dynamics to create contrasts against which to evaluate job training programs. These contrasts are all useful as preliminary indications of the possibility of treatment effects—for example, in Phase II trials in medicine to establish if a new treatment has promise.

However, any such use of archival or historical data faces daunting practical obstacles, including those just described for normative samples. The data may have been collected for different reasons from those that motivate the present study, despite superficial similarities in published descriptions, which may reduce comparability. Data may be of insufficient quality; for example, reliability checks used in treatment data may not have been used in the archival data, and missing data may be prevalent. The data may not include covariates that are needed to adjust for group differences and to diagnose group comparability. Such contrasts can add significant bias to effect estimates (Sacks, Chalmers, & Smith, 1982, 1983) because of changes in the populations who have a problem (e.g., the populations with AIDS have changed over time) or who are eligible for or have access to treatment (e.g., changes through which AIDS treatments are reimbursable). Again, then, the use of these secondary source contrasts best serves causal inference goals when coupled with other design features to create a more complex quasi-experiment.

The Case-Control Design

In the designs considered so far, participants are divided into groups that do or do not receive a treatment, and their subsequent outcomes are examined. This search for the effects of causes is characteristic of experiments. However, sometimes it is not feasible or ethical to experiment. For instance, in the 1960s the drug diethylstilbestrol (DES) was given to pregnant women who were at risk of miscarriage because of bleeding. DES became suspected of causing vaginal cancer in their daughters. It would be unethical to knowingly give this drug to some women and not to others to see if it caused cancer. In addition, vaginal cancer is so rare and takes so long to develop that enormous sample sizes and many years would be needed to reliably detect an experimental outcome. In such cases, an option is to use the **case-control design** (also called **case-referent**, case-comparative, case-history, or retrospective design) that was invented and is widely used in epidemiology. In this design, one group consists of cases that have the outcome of interest, and the other group consists of controls that do not have it.[11] The outcome in this design is typically dichotomous, such as pass or fail, diseased or healthy, alive or dead, married or divorced, smoke-free or smoking, relapsed or drug-free, depressed or not depressed, or improved or not improved. Cases and controls are then compared using retrospective data to see if cases experienced the hypothesized cause more often than controls. Herbst, Ulfelder, and Poskanzer (1971) identified 8 cases with vaginal cancer and matched them to 32 controls without vaginal cancer who had been born within 5 days of the case at the same hospital. Seven of eight cases had received DES, but none of the controls had.

The case-control design is excellent for generating hypotheses about causal connections. Causal relationships first identified by case-control studies include smoking and cancer, birth control pills and thromboembolism, and DES and vaginal cancer (Vessey, 1979). Case-control studies are more feasible than experiments in cases in which an outcome is rare or takes years to develop; they are often

11. We include this design in this chapter rather than the next one because case-control studies do not typically use a pretest, though it is possible to do so. The term "control" can be a bit misleading in case-control designs. In experiments, it implies a group that was not exposed to treatment. In case-control studies, however, some members of the control group may have received treatment even though they did not development the condition of interest.

cheaper and logistically easier to conduct; they may decrease risk to participants who could be needlessly exposed to a harmful experimental treatment; and they allow easy examination of multiple causes of a condition (Baker & Curbow, 1991).

Certain methodological problems are typical of case-control studies. The definition and selection of cases requires a decision about what counts as the presence or absence of the outcome of interest. But the relevant community of scholars may disagree about that decision; and even if they do agree, methods for assessing the outcome may be unreliable or of low validity. Moreover, definitions and measures may change over time, and so be different for cases diagnosed recently compared with cases diagnosed many years ago. Even when cases are diagnosed contemporaneously, they are often identified because their outcome brings them to the attention of a treatment source, as when women with vaginal cancer present for diagnosis and treatment. Controls rarely present this way, as they did not have the outcome. Hence the selection mechanism inevitably differs for the two groups. Attrition occurs when the outcome causes some cases to be unavailable (e.g., death from cancer occurs before the study begins). Those missing cases may have different characteristics than the available cases, a difference that can cause bias if the distribution of controls is not similarly truncated.

Selection of control cases is difficult. A common method is to choose controls to represent a general population. Randomly sampled controls are the exemplar. But when random sampling is not feasible, the control is often chosen by matching controls to cases on characteristics related to outcome. Neighborhood controls (exposure to a similar living environment) and hospital controls (exposure to the same facility) are common kinds of matched controls (Lund, 1989). Herbst et al.'s (1971) method of selecting controls from those born in the same hospital at the same time as the cases presumably increased the similarity of cases and controls on geographic influences, demographics, and birth cohort effects. However, matched controls still differ from cases in unobserved ways that can be confounded with the presumed cause and can be the actual cause of the outcome. For example, one study of children with diabetes used "friendly controls" in which parents of cases provided names of two age- and sex-matched friends of the children as controls (Siemiatycki, Colle, Campbell, Dewar, & Belmonte, 1989). Results suggested that children with diabetes were more likely to have school problems, few friends, trouble sleeping, hospitalizations and accidents, recent bereavements, and parental divorce. But are these causes or confounds? It turned out that parents tended to nominate sociable people as their children's friends, so the controls were disproportionately positive on social variables (Siemiatycki, 1989). The use of multiple controls can help avoid such problems (Kleinbaum, Kupper, & Morgenstern, 1982; Rosenbaum, 1995a)—a group from the same source of care as the cases, another from the same neighborhood, and a third sampled randomly from the general population (Baker & Curbow, 1991; Lund, 1989). Differences over controls in estimates of the causal relationship help to index the amount of hidden bias that may be present.

Further, which control population is most relevant depends greatly on the desired inference. For example, the use of a case's neighbors as controls is common. But if the question was whether traveler's diarrhea observed in U.S. citizens in a Mexican hospital is caused by drinking tequila, using neighbors would be inappropriate compared with using other non-Mexican travelers in the same hospital's catchment area (Miettinen, 1985). A general population control might be appropriate if little is known about specific causes, but a more narrowly defined control might be useful if the causal question is highly specific (Garber & Hollon, 1991). Also, cases that share the same problem are not always homogenous in the cause of that problem. For example, if cases are patients with a staphylococcus infection in a hospital, some may have contracted the infection outside the hospital and others within it (iatrogenic infection), requiring different controls.

Assessment of treatment exposure in case-control designs is retrospectively reconstructed from fallible sources such as memory or records. Hence classification as either having had exposure to treatment or not having had exposure is rarely fully accurate. Cases may have more incentive than controls to remember exposure to risk factors; for example, they may perceive that their diagnostic accuracy depends on an accurate history. Further, exposure to treatment is almost certainly confounded with other covariates. In the DES example, mothers were given DES because of increased risk of miscarriage due to bleeding, so the latter risk is confounded with exposure to DES. In this case that risk is implausible as a cause of vaginal cancer, given other correlational research supporting the link between DES and vaginal cancer, given randomized animal trials showing the effect, and given the lack of a theoretical expectation to link miscarriage risk and vaginal cancer (Potvin & Campbell, 1996). Still, exposure to treatment is usually confounded in case control studies, making the causal connection between treatment and outcome more tenuous.

These examples all illustrate that, because a case-control study probes causal inferences, the logic of ruling out threats to validity applies to it (Potvin & Campbell, 1996; Campbell & Russo, 1999). In fact, a literature about threats to validity with the case-control design has grown independently of the tradition presented in this book. Sackett (1979) lists these threats (Table 4.3)—although not all the items listed are necessarily sources of bias (e.g., the exclusion of outliers now has more extensive justification than it did 20 years ago). A large literature has developed to improve causal inferences from case-control studies, especially regarding analyses to adjust for potential confounds (Ahlbom & Norell, 1990; Greenland & Robins, 1986; Kleinbaum et al., 1982; Rothman, 1986; Schlesselman, 1982). Still, we believe that the case-control design deserves more widespread use in areas other than public health, although more for its ability to generate causal hypotheses than to test them well.

TABLE 4.3 Threats to Validity in Case-Control Studies

1. In *reading up* on the field:
   a. *The biases of rhetoric.* Any of several techniques used to convince the reader without appealing to reason.
   b. *The all's well literature bias.* Scientific or professional societies may publish reports or editorials that omit or play down controversies or disparate results.
   c. *One-sided reference bias.* Authors may restrict their references to only those works that support their position: a literature review with a single starting point risks confinement to a single side of the issue.
   d. *Positive results bias.* Authors are more likely to submit, and editors accept, positive than null results.
   e. *Hot stuff bias.* When a topic is hot, neither investigators nor editors may be able to resist the temptation to publish additional results, no matter how preliminary or shaky.
2. In *specifying and selecting* the study sample:
   a. *Popularity bias.* The admission of patients to some practices, institutions, or procedures (surgery, autopsy) is influenced by the interest stirred up by the presenting conditions and its possible causes.
   b. *Centripetal bias.* The reputations of certain clinicians and institutions cause individuals with specific disorders or exposures to gravitate toward them.
   c. *Referral filter bias.* As a group of ill are referred from primary to secondary to tertiary care, the concentration of rare causes, multiple diagnoses, and "hopeless cases" may increase.
   d. *Diagnostic access bias.* Individuals differ in their geographic, temporal, and economic access to the diagnostic procedures that label them as having a given disease.
   e. *Diagnostic suspicion bias.* A knowledge of the subject's prior exposure to a putative cause (ethnicity, taking a certain drug, having a second disorder, being exposed in an epidemic) may influence both the intensity and the outcome of the diagnostic process.
   f. *Unmasking (detection signal) bias.* An innocent exposure may become suspect if, rather than causing a disease, it causes a sign or symptom that precipitates a search for the disease.
   g. *Mimicry bias.* An innocent exposure may become suspect if, rather than causing a disease, it causes a (benign) disorder that resembles the disease.
   h. *Previous opinion bias.* The tactics and results of a previous diagnostic process on a patient, if known, may affect the tactics and results of a subsequent diagnostic process on the same patient.
   i. *Wrong sample size bias.* Samples that are too small can prove nothing; samples that are too large can prove anything.
   j. *Admission rate (Berkson) bias.* If hospitalization rates differ for different exposure/disease groups, the relation between exposure and disease will become distorted in hospital-based studies.
   k. *Prevalence-incidence (Neyman) bias.* A late look at those exposed (or affected) early will miss fatal and other short episodes, plus mild or "silent" cases and cases in which evidence of exposure disappears with disease onset.
   l. *Diagnostic vogue bias.* The same illness may receive different diagnostic labels at different points in space or time.
   m. *Diagnostic purity bias.* When "pure" diagnostic groups exclude co-morbidity, they may become non-representative.

TABLE 4.3 Continued

n. *Procedure selection bias.* Certain clinical procedures may be preferentially offered to those who are poor risks.

o. *Missing clinical data bias.* Missing clinical data may be missing because they are normal, negative, never measured, or measured but never recorded.

p. *Non-contemporaneous control bias.* Secular changes in definitions, exposures, diagnosis, diseases, and treatments may render non-contemporaneous controls non-comparable.

q. *Starting time bias.* The failure to identify a common starting time for exposure or illness may lead to systematic misclassifications.

r. *Unacceptable disease bias.* When disorders are socially unacceptable (V.D., suicide, insanity), they tend to be under-reported.

s. *Migrator bias.* Migrants may differ systematically from those who stay home.

t. *Membership bias.* Membership in a group (the employed, joggers, etc.) may imply a degree of health that differs systematically from that of the general population.

u. *Non-respondent bias.* Non-respondents (or "late comers") from a specified sample may exhibit exposures or outcomes that differ from those of respondents (or "early comers").

v. *Volunteer bias.* Volunteers or "early comers" from a specified sample may exhibit exposures or outcomes (they tend to be healthier) that differ from those of non-volunteers or "late comers."

3. In *executing* the experimental manoeuvre (or exposure):

a. *Contamination bias.* In an experiment when members of the control group inadvertently receive the experimental manoeuvre, the difference in outcomes between experimental and control patients may be systematically reduced.

b. *Withdrawal bias.* Patients who are withdrawn from an experiment may differ systematically from those who remain.

c. *Compliance bias.* In experiments requiring patient adherence to therapy, issues of efficacy become confounded with those of compliance.

d. *Therapeutic personality bias.* When treatment is not "blind," the therapist's convictions about efficacy may systematically influence both outcomes (positive personality) and their measurement (desire for positive results).

e. *Bogus control bias.* When patients who are allocated to an experimental manoeuvre die or sicken before or during its administration and are omitted or re-allocated to the control group, the experimental manoeuvre will appear spuriously superior.

4. In *measuring* exposures and outcomes:

a. *Insensitive measure bias.* When outcome measures are incapable of detecting clinically significant changes or differences, Type II errors occur.

b. *Underlying cause bias (rumination bias).* Cases may ruminate about possible causes for their illnesses and thus exhibit different recall or prior exposures than controls.

c. *End-digit preference bias.* In converting analog to digital data, observers may record some terminal digits with an unusual frequency.

d. *Apprehension bias.* Certain measures (pulse, blood pressure) may alter systematically from their usual levels if the subject is apprehensive.

e. *Unacceptability bias.* Measurements that hurt, embarrass, or invade privacy may be systematically refused or evaded.

f. *Obsequiousness bias.* Subjects may systematically alter questionnaire responses in the direction they perceive desired by the investigator.

TABLE 4.3 Continued

g. *Expectation bias.* Observers may systematically err in measuring and recording observation so that they concur with prior expectations.

h. *Substitution game.* The substitution of a risk factor that has not been established as causal for its associated outcome.

i. *Family information bias.* The flow of family information about exposure and illness is stimulated by, and directed to, a new case in its midst.

j. *Exposure suspicion bias.* A knowledge of the subject's disease status may influence both the intensity and outcome of a search for exposure to the putative cause.

k. *Recall bias.* Questions about specific exposures may be asked several times of cases but only once of controls. (See also the *underlying cause bias.*)

l. *Attention bias.* Study subjects may systematically alter their behavior when they know they are being observed.

m. *Instrument bias.* Defects in the calibration or maintenance of measurement instruments may lead to systematic deviation from true values.

5. In *analyzing* the data:

a. *Post-hoc significance bias.* When decision levels or "tails" for x and B are selected *after* the data have been examined, conclusions may be biased.

b. *Data dredging bias (looking for the pony).* When data are reviewed for all possible associations without prior hypothesis, the results are suitable for hypothesis-forming activities only.

c. *Scale degradation bias.* The degradation and collapsing of measurement scales tends to obscure differences between groups under comparison.

d. *Tidying-up bias.* The exclusion of outliers or other untidy results cannot be justified on statistical grounds and may lead to bias.

e. *Repeated peeks bias.* Repeated peeks at accumulating data in a randomized trial are not dependent and may lead to inappropriate termination.

6. In *interpreting* the analysis:

a. *Mistaken identity bias.* In compliance trials, strategies directed toward improving the patient's compliance may, instead or in addition, cause the treating clinician to prescribe more vigorously; the effect upon achievement of the treatment goal may be misinterpreted.

b. *Cognitive dissonance bias.* The belief in a given mechanism may increase rather than decrease in the face of contradictory evidence.

c. *Magnitude bias.* In interpreting a finding, the selection of a scale of measurement may markedly affect the interpretation.

d. *Significance bias.* The confusion of statistical significance, on the one hand, with biology or clinical or health care significance, on the other hand, can lead to fruitless studies and useless conclusions.

e. *Correlation bias.* Equating correlation with causation leads to errors of both kinds.

f. *Under-exhaustion bias.* The failure to exhaust the hypothesis space may lead to authoritarian rather than authoritative interpretation.

Source: Reprinted from "Bias in analytic research," by D. L. Sackett, 1979, *Journal of Chronic Diseases, 32,* pp. 51–63. Copyright 1979 by Elsevier Science. Reprinted with permission.

CONCLUSION

This chapter discusses and criticizes a wide variety of quasi-experimental designs that are often used but that frequently provide a weak basis for causal inference compared with the designs that follow in this book. These designs are weak primarily because they lack either a pretest or a control group. Nonetheless, these designs have a place in the methodologist's repertoire when many alternative causes are implausible on practical or theoretical grounds, when uncertainty reduction about cause is a low priority, and when the need is to generate causal hypotheses for further study with stronger designs. Fortunately, these designs can be strengthened by adding more design elements that are selected to address concerns about particularly salient threats to internal validity, particularly by adding both pretests and control groups, a design to which we now turn.

Quasi-Experimental Designs That Use Both Control Groups and Pretests

Con·trol (kən-trōl´): [Middle English *controllen*, from Anglo-Norman *controller*, from Medieval Latin *contrrotulre*, to check by duplicate register, from *contrrotulus*, duplicate register: Latin *contr-*, *contra-* + Latin *rotulus*, roll, diminutive of *rota*, wheel; see *ret-* in Indo-European Roots.] v. tr. con·trolled, con·trol·ling, con·trols. 1. a. To verify or regulate (a scientific experiment) by conducting a parallel experiment or by comparing with another standard. b. To verify (an account, for example) by using a duplicate register for comparison. n. 1. a. A standard of comparison for checking or verifying the results of an experiment. b. An individual or group used as a standard of comparison in a control experiment.

Pre·test (prē´tĕst´): n. 1. a. A preliminary test given to determine whether students are sufficiently prepared for a more advanced course of studies. b. A test taken for practice. 2. The advance testing of something, such as a questionnaire, a product, or an idea. v. tr. and intr. pre·test·ed, pre·test·ing, pre·tests (pr-tst.). To subject to or conduct a pretest.

THE HOMEMAKER–Home Health Aide Demonstration Program provided selected welfare recipients with up to 6 weeks of training, followed by subsidized employment as homemakers and home health aides. To determine if this intervention improved subsequent earnings, Bell et al. (1995) compared results from those who received training with three different nonrandomized control groups: (1) those who applied to the program but left before being screened for eligibility, (2) those who applied but were screened out by staff as ineligible, and (3) those who applied and were accepted but did not participate in the training.[1] Comparisons of results between treatment and all three control groups suggested that training improved subsequent earnings, although the size of the effect depended on which control group was used. Information about earnings before treatment was available for all these groups, and Bell et al. (1995) showed that those pretest differences were unlikely to account for posttest differences that later emerged.

DESIGNS THAT USE BOTH CONTROL GROUPS AND PRETESTS

This chapter focuses on quasi-experimental designs that, like that of Bell et al. (1995), have both control groups and pretests. The chapter explains how the use of carefully selected comparison groups facilitates causal inference from quasi-experiments, but it also argues that such control groups are of minimal advantage unless they are also accompanied by pretest measures taken on the same outcome variable as the posttest. Such pretests serve many purposes. They tell us about how the groups being compared initially differ and so alert us to the higher probability that some internal validity threats rather than others may be operating. They also tell us something about the magnitude of initial group differences on the variable that is usually most highly correlated with the outcome. The strong assumption is that the smaller the difference on the pretest, the less is the likelihood of strong initial selection biases on that pretest operating, though, unlike with random assignment, there can be no assumption that unmeasured variables at pretest are unrelated to outcome. And finally, having pretest measures helps enormously with the statistical analysis, especially if the reliability of these measures is known. No single variable will usually do as well as the pretest for these purposes. All these reasons explain why we like pretests and control groups in the widely implementable quasi-experimental designs that we cover in this chapter. Table 5.1 summarizes the quasi-experimental designs we consider.

The Untreated Control Group Design With Dependent Pretest and Posttest Samples

Frequently called the nonequivalent comparison group design, this may be the most common of all quasi-experiments. The initial variant we consider uses a treatment group and an untreated comparison group, with both pretest and

---

1. This study also included a randomized control, but that is not relevant for present purposes.

TABLE 5.1 Quasi-Experimental Designs That Use Comparison Groups and Pretests

---

Untreated Control Group Design with Dependent Pretest and Posttest Samples

NR O_1 X O_2

NR O_1 O_2

Untreated Control Group Design with Dependent Pretest and Posttest Samples Using a Double Pretest

NR O_1 O_2 X O_3

NR O_1 O_2 O_3

Untreated Control Group Design with Dependent Pretest and Posttest Samples Using Switching Replications

NR O_1 X O_2 O_3

NR O_1 O_2 X O_3

Untreated Control Group Design with Dependent Pretest and Posttest Samples Using Reversed-Treatment Control Group

NR O_1 X_+ O_2

NR O_1 X_- O_2

Cohort Control Group Design

NR O_1

....

NR   X O_2

Cohort Control Group Design with Pretest from Each Cohort

NR O_1 O_2

....

NR O_3 X O_4

---

posttest data gathered on the same units.[2] The latter is what makes the *dependent* samples feature. It is diagrammed:

$$NR \quad O_1 \text{ X } O_2$$

$$NR \quad O_1 \quad O_2$$

2. A variation is the regression point displacement design. It uses a posttest, a predictor of posttest scores that is taken prior to treatment (the predictor may be a pretest but often is not), and one treatment unit but many control units; each unit contributes a group mean but not data on individuals within groups (Campbell & Russo, 1999; Trochim & Campbell, 1996). The design can sometimes be useful when a single pretest (or other predictor) and posttest are available from so few treatment units that no other design is feasible. This might occur with administrative records in which data are not reported in a disaggregated way and many control units are available and in clinical contexts in which a treatment is given to a single client but records on many control clients are available.

The joint use of a pretest and a comparison group makes it easier to examine certain threats to validity. Because the groups are nonequivalent by definition, selection bias is presumed to be present. The pretest allows exploration of the possible size and direction of that bias.[3] For example, Carter, Winkler, and Biddle (1987) evaluated the effects of the National Institutes of Health (NIH) Research Career Development Award (RCDA), a program designed to improve the research careers of promising scientists. They found that those who received RCDAs did better than those not receiving them, but those who received them had also done better at pretest by a similar amount. So the final difference may have been due more to initial selection bias than to the effects of RCDA. The use of a pretest also allows examination of the nature of attrition, allowing researchers to describe group differences between who does and does not remain in a study. However, the extent to which the pretest can render selection implausible depends on the size of any selection bias and the role of any unmeasured variables that cause selection and are correlated with the outcome. The absence of pretest differences in a quasi-experiment is never proof that selection bias is absent.

When pretest differences do exist, the possibility increases that selection will combine with other threats additively or interactively. For example, selection-maturation may arise if respondents in one group are growing more experienced, tired, or bored than respondents in another group. To illustrate, suppose a new practice is introduced in a setting in which the average pretest level of performance exceeds the average pretest level in the control setting. If the treatment improves outcome, the posttest difference between groups might be even larger than the pretest difference. But this pattern might also occur if treatment group participants were, say, brighter on average and used their higher aptitude to learn at a faster rate than the controls—the rich get richer, so to speak.

A selection-instrumentation threat can occur when nonequivalent groups begin at different points on the pretest. On many scales, the intervals are unequal, and change is easier to detect at some points than at others (e.g., in its middle rather than at its extremes). On normed achievement test scores, for instance, getting a single item correct can have greater implications for percentile rankings at the extremes of a distribution than at the mean. Thus one item translates into different amounts of percentile change depending on the scale position of the respondent. Selection-instrumentation problems are probably more acute (1) the greater the initial nonequivalence between groups, (2) the greater the pretest-posttest change, and (3) the closer any group means are to one end of the scale, so that ceiling or floor effects occur. Sometimes, clues to the presence of such problems are apparent from inspecting pretest and posttest frequency distributions within each group to see if they are skewed or when group means and variances

---

3. This is typically done by seeing if groups differ significantly at pretest, but it might be better done using equivalency testing methods (Reichardt & Gollob, 1997; Rogers, Howard, & Vessey, 1993). The latter can be more sensitive to detecting pretest differences, although failure to find differences does *not* prove that groups are equal at pretest because groups may still differ on unobserved variables.

are correlated. Sometimes raw data can be rescaled to reduce such problems, whereas at other times a careful choice must be made to use groups that score close to each other at the middle of a scale.

A third example is selection-regression. In the 1969 Head Start quasi-experiment described in the previous chapter (Cicerelli & Associates, 1969), the treatment group of children who attended Head Start was potentially from a different population than the control group children, who did not attend. Recognizing this possibility, the Head Start researchers selected as matched controls only those controls who had the same sex, race, and kindergarten attendance status as the Head Start children. But this led to the problem of differential regression described in the last chapter.

A fourth problem is selection-history (or local history), the possibility that an event (or events) occurred between pretest and posttest that affected one group more than another. For example, a review of federal programs to improve pregnancy outcome (Shadish & Reis, 1984) found that many studies used the pretest-posttest comparison group design, and results suggested that such programs improved pregnancy outcome. But mothers who were eligible for these programs also were eligible for other programs that can improve pregnancy outcome, including food stamps and various health care programs. So it was impossible to know with confidence whether improvements in pregnancy outcome were caused by treatment or by these other programs.

How the Plausibility of Threats Depends Partly on the Observed Pattern of Outcomes

This list of relevant internal validity threats is daunting. However, the plausibility of a threat is always contextually dependent on the joint characteristics of the design, on extrastudy knowledge about the threats, and on the pattern of observed study results. Therefore, *possible* threats to validity are not always *plausible* ones. For example, maturation processes in children that cause *increased* academic achievement are not plausible explanations for *decreased* achievement. To make this point more generally, we now outline five outcome patterns that are observed with the pretest-posttest comparison group design and show how they render threats to validity more or less plausible. We focus mostly on selection-maturation but occasionally comment on other threats as well.

Outcome 1: Both Groups Grow Apart in the Same Direction. A common pattern of selection-maturation occurs when initially nonequivalent groups grow apart at different average rates in the same direction (Figure 5.1). This pattern has been called a fan-spread model of maturation because the groups grow apart over time like ribs in a fan, from the center out to the edges. Standardizing scores makes the fan spread disappear because the fan spread is a function of measured variances growing systematically over time, and standardization involves dividing scores by their variation and so putting scores at each time point on the same

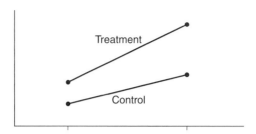

FIGURE 5.1 First outcome of the no-treatment control group design with pretest and posttest

scale instead of on different scales. This pattern is consistent with treatment effects, but can alternative interpretations be identified and ruled out?

Ralston, Anthony, and Gustafson (1985) examined the effects of flexible working hours (flextime) on productivity in two state government agencies. In the agency without flextime, productivity was initially lower and increased slightly over time; in the agency with flextime, it was initially higher but increased at a faster rate. This pattern is common in quasi-experiments, particularly when respondents self-select into condition. But even when administrators assign respondents, treatments are often made available to the especially meritorious, those most keen to improve, or to the more able or better networked, and such persons are also likely to improve at a faster rate for reasons that have nothing to do with treatment.

Several analytic clues can suggest whether nonequivalent groups are maturing at different rates. If group mean differences are a result of this selection-maturation threat, then differential growth *between* groups should also be occurring *within* groups. This could be detected by a within-group analysis in which higher performing members of the group with the higher pretest mean should be growing faster than lower performing members of that same group. This selection-maturation threat is also often associated with posttest within-group variances that are greater than the corresponding pretest variances. It may also help to plot *pretest* scores against the hypothesized maturational variable (e.g., age or years of experience) for the experimental and control groups separately. If the regression lines differ, different growth rates are likely. Such group differences in slope cannot be due to treatment because only the pretest scores have been analyzed.

Nothing makes initial group difference increase linearly; growth can be linear in one condition but quadratic in another. However, in our experience differential maturation of the fan-spread type is commonplace. In education, for example, children who show higher achievement often grow steadily ahead of their lower scoring contemporaries on the original metrics. We suspect that other longitudinal data sets will also show the fan-spread type of differential maturation. Nonetheless, some theoretical formulations predict a different selection-maturation pattern, even in some areas in education. For instance, Piaget's theory predicts sharp discontinuities in growth differences as some children suddenly acquire a concept and

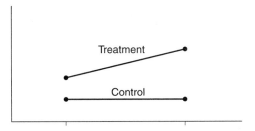

FIGURE 5.2 Second outcome of the no-treatment control group design with pretest and posttest

others do not. So each study using the basic design must present and justify its own assumptions about maturational differences. Sometimes pretest data will play an important role in this. Sometimes data from other longitudinal samples will serve a similar function, as with our assertion that a fan-spread model often fits longitudinal data on academic achievement. But at other times, theoretical speculation is all that can be presented.

Outcome 2: No Change in the Control Group. Narayanan and Nath (1982) used this design to examine how flextime influenced an existing unit of employees compared with another unit in the same company. Results showed improved supervisor-subordinate relations in the flextime group but no changes in the controls, as Figure 5.2 simulates.

When the controls do not change, the critic must explain why spontaneous growth occurred only in the treatment group. It is often easier to think about why both groups mature at different rates in the same direction or why neither group should be changing over time than to think about why one group improves whereas the other does not. Sometimes, within-group analyses can shed light on such between-group threats. For example, if the treatment group was maturing more quickly because the participants were older than those in the control group, then the data could be split by age. If treatment group participants continued to improve no matter what their age, this makes a selection-maturation hypothesis less plausible if it postulates that there should be growth in one group but not the other. Yet when all is said and done, not a lot of reliance can be placed on this particular pattern of differential change. The reason is that it is not unknown for one group to improve and another not to change. Moreover, the pattern of differential change we discussed as more prevalent is only more so in general. Yet each study is highly contextual, and generalities may not apply.

Outcome 3: Initial Pretest Differences Favoring the Treatment Group That Diminish Over Time. Figure 5.3 describes the scenario by which the pretest superiority of a treatment group is diminished or eliminated at posttest. This outcome occurred in a sample of Black third, fourth, and fifth graders in a study

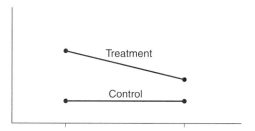

FIGURE 5.3 Third outcome of the no-treatment control group design with pretest and posttest

of the effects of school integration on academic self-concept (Weber, Cook, & Campbell, 1971). At pretest, Black children attending all-Black schools had higher academic self-concept than did Black children attending integrated schools. After formal school integration occurred, the initial difference was no longer found.

Some of the internal validity threats described for Figures 5.1 and 5.2 are also relevant to Figure 5.3. However, selection-maturation is less plausible, for it is rare that those who start off further ahead fall back later on or that those who start further behind subsequently catch up. It can happen, of course. For example, if in an educational context one group were slightly older than another but less intelligent, the older group might be further ahead at the earlier point due to their age advantage but lose this advantage as the younger but smarter group comes to perform better. But such phenomena are rare, and in the Weber et al. (1971) example, the two groups were equivalent in age. Thus the argument is that no presently known maturation process can account for the pattern of results in Figure 5.3, although some such process might be found in the future.

Outcome 4: Initial Pretest Differences Favoring the Control Group That Diminish Over Time. In this case, as in Figure 5.3, the experimental-control difference is greater at pretest than at posttest, but now the experimental group initially *under*performs the controls (Figure 5.4). This is the outcome desired when schools introduce compensatory inputs to increase the performance of the disadvantaged or when a firm makes changes to try to improve a unit's poor performance. Keller and Holland (1981) found this pattern when they assessed the impact of a job change on employee performance, innovativeness, satisfaction, and integration in three research and development organizations. Employees who were promoted or assigned to a different job were the treatment group, and all others were controls. Outcomes were measured twice, 1 year apart. Although this work had no explicit compensatory focus, the data fit the pattern under discussion, and those with the job change showed improved outcomes, whereas the outcomes for others stayed the same.

The outcome is subject to typical scaling (i.e., selection-instrumentation) and local history (i.e., selection-history) threats. But two special elements stand out. First, if the company changed the jobs of those employees whose performance was

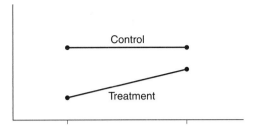

FIGURE 5.4 Fourth outcome of the no-treatment control group design with pretest and posttest

particularly poor at pretest, the outcome for those employees should regress upward at posttest, an outcome that could produce the results in Figure 5.4. If the treatment-control differences in Keller and Holland (1981) were temporally stable, something we could not tell with this design (but could if two pretests were used), then regression would not be a threat. In nonequivalent control group designs, therefore, it is imperative to explore the reasons for initial group differences, including why some groups assign themselves or are assigned to one treatment rather than to another.

The second special element of this design is that the outcome in Figure 5.4 rules out selection-maturation of the fan-spread type—or shows that the treatment overcame such an effect if there were one. However, other selection-maturation patterns could be invoked. In Keller and Holland (1981), for example, the job changers may have been junior staff members in the organization, accounting for their lower pretest scores, but they may also have been particularly open to learning from new experiences, making their performance rise disproportionately quickly. Data on age and time in the organization would have to be analyzed for this possibility. In general, this outcome is often interpretable causally. But it has to be explored seriously in any single study in case its specifics set up complex selection-maturation patterns like those just elaborated.

Outcome 5: Outcomes That Cross Over in the Direction of Relationships. In the hypothetical outcome of Figure 5.5, the trend lines cross over and the means are reliably different in one direction at pretest and in the opposite direction at posttest. This outcome is particularly amenable to causal interpretation. First, the plausibility of selection-instrumentation is reduced, for no simple data transformation can remove the interaction. For example, a ceiling effect cannot explain how the lower-scoring group came to draw ahead of a group that initially scored higher than it did. A convincing scaling artifact would have to postulate that the posttest mean of the treatment group is inflated because the interval properties of the test make change easier at points on the scale that are further away from its mean. However, this explains the exacerbation of a true effect and not the creation of a totally artifactual one.

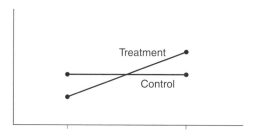

FIGURE 5.5 Fifth outcome of the no-treatment control group design with pretest and posttest

Second, selection-maturation threats are less likely with Figure 5.5, for crossover interaction maturation patterns are not widely expected, although they do occur. An example of the pattern in Figure 5.5 is Cook et al.'s (1975) reanalysis of Educational Testing Service (ETS) data on the effectiveness of *Sesame Street*. They found that children who were encouraged to view the show knew reliably less at pretest than children who were not encouraged to watch but that they knew reliably more than the control group at posttest. But were the encouraged children younger and brighter, thus scoring lower than controls at the pretest but changing more over time because of their greater ability? Fortunately, data indicated that the encouraged and nonencouraged groups did not differ in age or on several pretest measures of ability, reducing the plausibility of this threat.

Third, the outcome in Figure 5.5 renders a regression threat unlikely. Greene and Podsakoff (1978) found the depicted crossover when they examined how removing a pay incentive plan affected employee satisfaction in a paper mill. The employees were divided into high, middle, and low performers, and satisfaction was measured before and after removal of the pay incentive. Following removal, the high performers' satisfaction decreased reliably, that of the low performers increased, and that of the midlevel performers did not change. These slope differences might be due to regression if all three groups converged on the same grand mean (similar to Figure 5.4). But statistical regression cannot explain why the low performers reliably surpassed the high performers at posttest, though regression may have inflated treatment estimates.

Unfortunately, any attempt to set up a design to achieve the outcome shown in Figure 5.5 involves considerable risk. One reason is that the power to detect a statistically reliable interaction is low (Aiken & West, 1991). So such studies must be designed carefully. This is especially true when a fan-spread process such as that shown in Figure 5.2 is expected, for then a no-difference finding would leave it unclear whether the treatment had no effect or whether two countervailing forces (the treatment and fan-spread maturation) had canceled each other. Even if there were a difference in slopes, it would probably take the form of Figure 5.4, not Figure 5.5, and Figure 5.4 is less interpretable. So researchers should not rely on designing research to get the outcome in Figure 5.5. Instead, steps should be taken to add stronger design controls to the basic pretest-posttest design with control group.

Ways to Improve the Untreated Control Group Design With Dependent Pretest and Posttest Samples

As with the designs in the previous chapter, this basic design can be improved substantially by adding thoughtfully chosen design features to address threats to validity that are plausible in the context of the experiment. Examples include the following.

Using a Double Pretest. Here, the same pretest is administered at two different time points, preferably with the same time delay as between the second pretest and the posttest. The design is diagrammed as:

$$NR \qquad O_1 \qquad O_2 \quad X \quad O_3$$

$$NR \qquad O_1 \qquad O_2 \qquad O_3$$

The double pretest allows the researcher to understand possible biases in the main treatment analysis—if "treatment effects" emerge in the analysis of O_1 to O_2, similar biases may exist in the analysis from O_2 to O_3. Wortman, Reichardt, and St. Pierre (1978) used this design to study how the Alum Rock educational voucher experiment affected reading test scores. In this program, parents selected a local school for their child and received a voucher equal to the cost of education at that school. The aim was to foster competition between schools in the system. Initial data analysis by others had claimed that vouchers decreased academic performance, but Wortman and colleagues doubted the conclusion that had been drawn. So they followed a group of students through the first to the third grades in both voucher and nonvoucher schools and reanalyzed test scores using a double pretest. Furthermore, they divided the voucher schools into those with and without traditional voucher programs. The additional pretest allowed them to contrast pretreatment growth rates in reading (between O_1 and O_2) with posttest change in rates (between O_2 and O_3), and, because of this, the decrease in reading previously attributed to voucher schools was then attributed only to the nontraditional voucher group. The traditional voucher and nonvoucher groups showed no differential effect that could not be explained by the continuation of the same maturation rates that had previously characterized the traditional and voucher control schools.

The double pretest permits assessment of a selection-maturation threat on the assumption that the rates between O_1 and O_2 will continue between O_2 and O_3. That assumption is testable only for the untreated group. Moreover, the within-group growth rates will be fallibly estimated, given measurement error; and instrumentation shifts could make measured growth between O_1 and O_2 unlike that between O_2 and O_3. So the double pretest design with nonequivalent groups is not perfect. Yet the second pretest can help considerably in assessing the plausibility of selection-maturation by describing the pre-treatment growth differences. The double pretest also helps reveal regression effects if the O_2 observation in either group is atypically low or high compared with O_1. It further helps estimate more precisely the correlation between observations at different times, something of great value in the statistical analysis. Without the extra time point, the correlation between O_2 and O_3 in the treated group gives an unclear estimate of what the correlation would have been in the absence of a treatment.

Why are multiple pretests not used more often? Ignorance is surely one reason, but another reason is that it is sometimes infeasible. Often one is lucky to be able to delay treatment long enough to obtain a single pretest, let alone two, and let alone being able to space the pretests with the same time interval between pretest and posttest. Sometimes, archives will make possible a second or even more pretests, thus moving toward an even more powerful time series design. In addition, persons responsible for authorizing research expenditures are sometimes loath to see money spent for design elements other than posttest measures. Convincing them about the value of pretests and conventional control groups is hard enough. Convincing them of the value of double pretests can be even harder! Nonetheless, whenever the archival system, time frame, resources, and politics permit, the same pretest should be administered twice prior to treatment.

Using Switching Replications. With switching replications, the researcher administers treatment at a later date to the group that initially served as a no-treatment control. The resulting design is diagrammed as:

$$NR \qquad O_1 \qquad X \qquad O_2 \qquad\qquad O_3$$

$$NR \qquad O_1 \qquad\qquad O_2 \qquad X \qquad O_3$$

Besadur, Graen, and Scandura (1986) used a version of this design to study how training affected engineers' attitudes toward divergent thinking in solving problems. Measurement was taken prior to training, following the training of one group of engineers, and then following the training of a second nonequivalent group. The latter group served as controls in the first phase of the study, whereas the roles were switched in the second phase. However, the second phase is not an exact replication. The context surrounding the second treatment is different from the first, both historically and because the treatment has been removed from the first group. Even if the treatment was not removed, it is assumed to have no current impact. (However, the design is still useful even if the initial treatment continues to have an impact, especially if the control group catches up to the treatment group once the control group receives treatment.) Given the contextual differences between the first and second treatment, the second introduction of the treatment is a modified replication, probing both internal validity and an external validity issue of whether this new context changes the treatment effect.

The design can be extended to more groups than two. When it is, it is sometimes possible to assign groups at random to the particular time at which they start treatment, because by definition there must be many consecutively staggered times available if the design is to be implemented with many groups. This random component can help strengthen inferences, the more so when many groups at many time points are available. But even without the random assignment of treatments to time intervals, the analytic possibilities are productively expanded when more groups and time points are in the design (e.g., Koehler & Levin, 1998).

The major limitations of this design follow from the fact that later instances of groups serving as controls entail either (1) keeping the same treatment in place but presuming it to have no long-term discontinuous effects in the same direction as the treatment later applied to the initial controls or (2) removing the treatment from the original treatment group. This potentially sets up processes of compensatory rivalry and the like that must be thoroughly described, measured, and used in the analysis. Otherwise, the switching replications design is strong. Only a pattern of historical changes that mimics the time sequence of the treatment introductions can serve as an alternative interpretation.

Using a Reversed-Treatment Control Group. We diagram this version of the design as:

$$NR \qquad O_1 \qquad X_+ \qquad O_2$$

$$NR \qquad O_1 \qquad X_- \qquad O_2$$

where X_+ represents a treatment expected to produce an effect in one direction and X_- represents a conceptually opposite treatment expected to *reverse* the effect. Hackman, Pearce, and Wolfe (1978) used the design to investigate how changes in the motivational properties of jobs affect worker attitudes and behaviors. As a result of a technological innovation, clerical jobs in a bank were changed to make the work on some units more complex and challenging (X_+) but to make work on other units less so (X_-). These changes were made without the company personnel being told of their possible motivational consequences, and measures of job characteristics, employee attitudes, and work behaviors were taken before and after the jobs were redesigned. If treatment X_+ improved the scores of the treatment group, and if treatment X_- decreased the scores of the comparison group, a statistical interaction should result, suggesting a treatment effect.

The reversed-treatment design can have a special construct validity advantage. The causal construct must be rigorously specified and manipulated to create a sensitive test in which one version of the cause (job enrichment) affects one group one way, whereas its conceptual opposite (job impoverishment) affects another group the opposite way. To understand this better, consider what would have happened had Hackman et al. (1978) used an enriched-job group only and no-treatment controls. A steeper pretest-posttest slope in the enriched condition could then be attributed to either the job changes or to respondents feeling specially treated or guessing the hypothesis. The plausibility of such alternatives is lessened in this design if the expected pretest-posttest decrease in job satisfaction is found in the reversed-treatment group because awareness of being in research is typically thought to elicit socially desirable responses. To explain both an increase in the enriched group and a decrease in the reversed group, each set of respondents would have to guess the hypothesis and want to corroborate it in their own different way.

Interpretation of this design depends on producing two effects with opposite signs. It therefore assumes that little historical or motivational change would otherwise be taking place. When change is differential across treatments but in the same direction, results are less interpretable, because their relationship to a no-treatment control group is unknown. Adding such a control is helpful and should be done when it is feasible. Also in many contexts, ethical and practical considerations prevent using a reversed treatment. Most treatments have ameliorative and prosocial goals, but a conceptually opposite treatment might be harmful. However, that is not clearly the case with Hackman et al. (1978). Who is to say whether it is more beneficial to have one's job made more or less complex than it used to be?

Direct Measurement of Threats to Validity. These measurements allow the researcher to diagnose the possible presence of threats to validity. In Narayanan and Nath (1982), flextime was initiated in one unit of a company while another served as a no-treatment control. However, a history threat could be posed if supervisory practices changed in one group but not the other during the study. To explore this threat, Narayanan and Nath measured such changes and found none. Of course, this is only one example of history, and many others could be discovered, so researchers have to be vigilant lest finding that one study-specific threat is implausible lulls them into believing that all threats are implausible. Each individual threat has to be conceptualized, validly measured, and validly analyzed, making direct measurement of threats difficult. Still, measuring threats can facilitate later statistical analysis by allowing alternative interpretations to be built into whatever analyses are used to deal with initial group nonequivalence.

Matching Through Cohort Controls

Many institutions experience regular turnover as one group "graduates" to another level and their place is taken by another group. Schools are an obvious example, as most children are promoted from one grade to the next each year. Other examples include businesses in which one group of trainees follows another, families in which one sibling follows another, and prisons in which one group of inmates follows another. The term **cohort** designates the successive groups that go through processes such as these.[4] Cohorts are particularly useful as control groups

---

4. The term *cohort* is used in some other areas (e.g., developmental and longitudinal studies) to refer to any group that is repeatedly measured over time, a very different use from the present one.

if (1) one cohort experiences a given treatment and earlier or later cohorts do not; (2) cohorts differ in only minor ways from their contiguous cohorts; (3) organizations insist that a treatment be given to everybody, thus precluding simultaneous controls and making possible only historical controls; and (4) an organization's archival records can be used for constructing and then comparing cohorts.

The crucial assumption with cohorts is that selection differences are smaller between cohorts than would be the case between noncohort comparison groups. However, this assumption must be probed in each study through, for example, analyses of background characteristics presumed to correlate with outcomes. Even then, presumed comparability will never be as high with cohorts as with random assignment. Further, a review of behavioral genetics research found that, in the area of intellectual performance, environmental differences in the microworlds that siblings live in or create for themselves make two children from the same family as different from one another as are children paired randomly from the population (Plomin & Daniels, 1987). If this conclusion is true and generalizable to nonintellectual domains, it would seriously undermine the case for assigning special status to siblings as cohort controls. Yet many economists include sibling control designs among their preferred armamentarium for studying the effects of external variables on labor force participation or educational attainment (Aronson, 1998; Ashenfelter & Krueger, 1994; Currie & Duncan, 1995, 1999; Duncan, Yeung, Brooks-Gunn, & Smith, 1998; Geronimus & Korenman, 1992).

An example of the use of sibling controls is provided by Minton (1975). She examined how the first season of *Sesame Street* affected Metropolitan Readiness Test (MRT) scores of a heterogeneous sample of kindergarten children. She located a kindergarten in which the test was administered at the end of the child's first year. For a control group, she used MRT scores of the children's older siblings, who had attended the same kindergarten before *Sesame Street* began. So she had the scores from a time at which those siblings were at the same age and maturational stage as their siblings were during the run of *Sesame Street*. The design is diagrammed here; the dotted line (.......) between nonequivalent groups indicates a cohort control. We introduce a cohort design without pretest first and then add a pretest in the next section. The numerical subscripts refer to time of measurement, with the effect assessed by contrasting O_1 to O_2. The design clearly shows that the older sibling group is being used as the same-age, same-maturational-status, reduced-selection control group.

$$NR \qquad O_1$$
$$\text{...}$$
$$NR \qquad\qquad X \qquad O_2$$

Despite similarities between cohorts in maturation status and other family-based variables, to contrast just these two observations provides a weak test of the causal hypothesis. First, a selection problem remains because older siblings are more likely to be first-borns and first-borns tend to outperform later siblings on cognitive achievement tests (Zajonc & Markus, 1975). One way to reduce this threat is to analyze the data separately by birth order of the older child, because the birth-order effect should dampen as the birth order of the older sibling increases (Zajonc & Markus, 1975). The design is also weak with respect to history, for older and younger siblings could have experienced differential events other than watching *Sesame Street* that affected knowledge levels. One way to explore this threat is to break cohorts down[5] into those whose kindergarten experience was separated by 1, 2, 3, or more years from their siblings to see if the greater learning of the younger group held over the different sets of historical events that these cohorts presumably experienced. But even so, this procedure would still not control for those historical events that took place during the same year that *Sesame Street* was introduced. So a better solution would be to repeat the experiment in different schools in different years. If the effect occurred each time, any historical event or events that masqueraded as treatment effects would have to temporally mimic the introduction of the treatment from school to school across different years. As it turned out, not even this last possibility was feasible with *Sesame Street,* given its great initial popularity in private homes. Hence no school group with minimal exposure would have been possible.

Direct measurement can sometimes help assess selection and history. For instance, Devine, O'Connor, Cook, and Curtin (1990) conducted a quasi-experiment to examine how a psychoeducational care workshop influenced nurses' care of cholecystectomy (gallbladder) surgery patients and their recovery from surgery. Reports were collected from all relevant patients in a single hospital for 7 months before treatment and on another group at the same hospital for 6 months after treatment, thus creating pretreatment and posttreatment cohorts. An analysis of many background characteristics and hospital records revealed no differences between the two cohorts, minimizing the selection threat for the variables examined (but not for unmeasured attributes). Still, it would have been better if circumstances had allowed collecting both pretest and posttest data for a calendar year each instead of for 7 and 6 months, respectively, because the data collection procedure actually implemented is confounded with seasons. Regarding history, the research staff were in the target hospital most days and detected no major irrelevant changes that might have influenced recovery from surgery. This provides no guarantee, of course, and design modifications are better than measurement for ruling out this internal validity threat. So data were also collected from a nearby control hospital that was owned by the same corporation and

---

5. Such partitioning needs to be done with great caution, especially if it creates more extreme and less extreme groups. Our previous work gave an example of partitioning from the Minton study in which the treatment group was partitioned into four groups by level of viewing of *Sesame Street.* The sibling cohorts were then matched to the same partition. However, Mark (1986, p. 60) identified a plausible regression artifact that may have resulted from this partitioning: "Younger siblings who self-select into heavy 'Sesame Street' viewership are likely to be highly interested in learning, while those who self-select into light viewership are not. Given the less than perfect relationship between sibling's academic skills, we would expect that the older siblings would display less extreme behavior. The result of this regression effect would be a statistical interaction of the sort presented by Cook and Campbell (1979, p. 129) as an 'interpretable outcome.'"

had some of the same physicians. That control also supported the conclusion that the treatment effect was not due to history. What we see with this last point is important, with the cohort design being supplemented by a design feature such as a no-treatment control group. That kind of design improvement is what we now turn to, adding even more design features to improve causal inference.

Improving Cohort Controls by Adding Pretests

In a study comparing the effectiveness of regular teachers and outside contractors hired to stimulate children's achievement, Saretsky (1972) noted that the teachers made special efforts and performed better than would have been expected given their previous years' performances. He attributed this compensatory rivalry to teacher fear of losing their jobs if contractors outperformed them. Assume for pedagogic purposes that he compared the average gain in classes taught by teachers during the study period with the average gain from the same classes taught by the same teachers in previous years. The resulting design would be of the following form, with O_1 and O_2 representing beginning and end of year scores for the earlier cohort, who could not have been influenced by teacher fears, and O_3 and O_4 representing scores for the later cohort that might have been so influenced. The null hypothesis is that the change in one cohort equals that in the other. This design can be extended back over time to include multiple "control" cohorts rather than just one. Indeed, Saretsky reported data for 2 preexperimental years. In principle, if treatment is ongoing, the design could also be extended forward for several years to get multiple estimates of effects.

$$NR \qquad O_1 \qquad O_2$$
....
$$NR \qquad\qquad\qquad\qquad O_3 \quad X \quad O_4$$

As depicted, the design is similar to the basic nonequivalent control group design with pretest and posttest. The major differences are that measurement occurs at an earlier time period in the control group and that cohorts are assumed to be less nonequivalent than most other nonmatched groups would be. This last point can be explored by comparing cohort pretest means, one of the major advantages of including pretests in cohort design. The pretest also increases statistical power by allowing use of within-subject error terms. It enables better assessment of maturation and regression, and it enters into better (but still imperfect) statistical adjustment for group nonequivalence.

History is a salient internal validity threat in this design—it can involve any event correlated with the outcome that appears only during the O_3–O_4 period, even if there is a series of cohort control periods. Only if a nonequivalent control group is added to the design and measured at exactly the same time points as the treatment cohorts can we hope to address history. Sometimes the design can be strengthened by adding nonequivalent dependent variables if these are appropriate for the topic under investigation.

A variant of this design is what Campbell and Stanley (1963) called the *recurrent institutional cycle* design. With access to school records, or having at least 2 years to do a study with original data collection, the design is:

$$NR \quad X \quad O_1$$

....

$$NR \qquad\qquad\qquad\qquad O_2 \quad X \quad O_3$$

....

$$NR \qquad\qquad\qquad\qquad\qquad\qquad\qquad\qquad\qquad O_4$$

It involves the three cohorts entering, say, the second grade in 3 consecutive years. The first receives the treatment and a posttest, the second the treatment with both pretest and posttest, and the third no treatment and only one assessment. Note that O_1 and O_2 might not be simultaneously observed because one might be at the end of a school year and the other at the beginning of the next. This cycle is repeated again with O_3 and O_4. A treatment main effect is suggested by a certain pattern of results—that is, if O_1 and O_3 are, say, higher than O_2 and O_4; if O_2 does not differ from O_4; and if O_1 does not differ from O_3. A partial control for history is provided if, in addition to O_3 being greater than O_2, O_1 surpasses O_2, and O_3 surpasses O_4. Then there is presumptive evidence that the treatment could have been effective at two different times, though it is also possible for two separate historical forces to have operated or for one historical force to have reoccurred. But still, any single history alternative would have to repeat to explain both $O_1 > O_2$ and $O_3 > O_4$. Selection is also reduced in this version of a cohort design when the same persons are involved in the O_2–O_3 comparison.

Another threat, testing, is possible because some comparisons involve contrasting a first testing with a second testing (O_2 to O_3). Hence, Campbell and Stanley (1963) recommended splitting the group that is both pretested and posttested into random halves, one of which receives a pretest but the other of which does not. A reliable difference between these two groups at posttest might be due to testing; the lack of such differences would suggest that testing effects are not a problem. Finally, because causal interpretation depends on a complex pattern of outcomes in which three contrasts involve O_2, a change in elevation of O_2 would have crucial implications. Hence the design should be used only with reliable measures and large samples.

Improving Cohort Designs With a Nonequivalent Dependent Variable

Minton (1975) used a nonequivalent dependent variable to improve her study of how the first season of *Sesame Street* affected kindergarten children's learning. She showed, for those who watched *Sesame Street*, that their knowledge of letters that were taught on *Sesame Street* improved significantly more than did their knowledge of letters that were not taught. This outcome helped address maturation threats to validity, because children typically grow in their knowledge of letters of the alphabet over time as a result of many influences, including their own cognitive development. If only maturation explained the results, then we would expect no difference between knowledge of letters that were taught versus those that were not.

DESIGNS THAT COMBINE MANY DESIGN ELEMENTS

Throughout this chapter we have emphasized the value of adding design elements to aid causal inference. In this section, we describe three examples of designs that use many elements, examples that serve to clarify and extend the underlying rationale.

Untreated Matched Controls With Multiple Pretests and Posttests, Nonequivalent Dependent Variables, and Removed and Repeated Treatments

In an exemplar of good quasi-experimental design, Reynolds and West (1987) assessed the effects of Arizona's "Ask for the Sale" campaign to sell lottery tickets. Participating stores selling lottery tickets agreed to post a sign reading, "Did we ask you if you want a Lottery ticket? If not, you get one free," and they also agreed to give a free ticket to those customers who were not asked if they wanted one but who then requested one. Because participation was voluntary, the resulting nonequivalent control group design was supplemented in four ways. First, the authors matched treatment stores to control stores from the same chain (and when possible, from the same zip code area), as well as on the pretest market share of ticket sales. Second, they added multiple pretest and posttest assessments by examining mean weekly ticket sales for 4 weeks before and 4 weeks after the treatment started. Pretest sales trends were decreasing nearly identically in both the treatment and control groups, so that maturation differences could not explain increasing ticket sales. Similarly, regression to the mean was unlikely because the treatment group sales were *continuously* decreasing over four consecutive pretests and because control group ticket sales continued to decrease after treatment began. Third, Aiken and West studied treatment effects on three nonequivalent dependent variables in the treatment group, discovering that the intervention increased ticket sales but not sales of gas, cigarettes, or grocery items. Fourth, they located some stores in which the treatment was removed and then repeated or was initiated later than in other stores and found that the outcome tracked the introduction, removal, and reinstatement of treatment over time whereas sales in the matched controls remained unchanged. Nearly all these analyses suggested that the "Ask for the Sale" intervention increased ticket sales after the program began, making it difficult to think of an alternative explanation for the effect.

Combining Switching Replications With a Nonequivalent Control Group Design

Sometimes the researcher can introduce treatment to part of the original control group, with other controls remaining untreated over this later time period. Sometimes the researcher can even reintroduce treatment a second time to some of the original treatment group to evaluate the benefits of additional treatment. Gunn, Iverson, and Katz (1985) did this in a study of a health education program introduced into 1,071 classrooms nationwide. The design is diagrammed as follows, with R indicating a potential use of random assignment that is a useful but not necessary adjunct to the design:

Year 1					Year 2		
NR	O_1	X	O_2	R	O_3	X	O_4
				R	O_3		O_4
NR	O_1		O_2	R	O_3	X	O_4
				R	O_3		O_4

Classrooms were first divided into nonequivalent treatment and control groups. Students in each group were tested on knowledge of health before and after the first year of the program. Then the initial control group was divided randomly in half. One half received the health education program to replicate the treatment effect, and the other remained without instruction. In addition, a random sample of the original treatment group received a second year of instruction to explore the incremental benefit of additional health education. Here we see switching replications yoked to a continuation of the original controls and to a treatment booster. This yoking strengthens a switching replications design, especially if the second phase of the study uses random assignment or if those receiving the booster session are identified by falling to one side of a cutoff on a measure of need for the booster session—a regression discontinuity design (see Chapter 7).

An Untreated Control Group With a Double Pretest and Both Independent and Dependent Samples

To evaluate community-level interventions designed to reduce cardiovascular risk factors, both Blackburn et al. (1984) and Farquhar et al. (1990) combined a double pretest with samples in which the outcome was measured on both independent and dependent samples. We diagram the logic of the design here, using perpendicular lines between O's to show independent samples and glossing over some complexities in the actual designs used in these two studies.

R	O_1	$\mid$	O_2	$\mid$	O_3	$\mid$	O_4	$\mid$	O_5
R	O_1	$\mid$	O_2	$\mid X$	O_3	$\mid$	O_4	$\mid$	O_5
R	O_1		O_2		O_3		O_4		O_5
R	O_1		O_2	X	O_3		O_4		O_5

The first two rows of this diagram portray a randomized experiment with communities being assigned to intervention or control and with a cross-sectional panel survey being administered to independent samples of community households at each annual time point (however, relatively few communities were used in each study, and so there can be no presumption here that much initial equivalence was achieved). The two bottom rows of the diagram depict a longitudinal survey of respondents who were followed over time. The major study outcomes were annual physiological measures of heart problems, including blood pressure and cholesterol level. In the cross-sectional panel survey, independent random samples were drawn, both out of concern that obtrusive annual physiological measurement would sensitize repeatedly measured respondents to the treatment and out of desire to generalize to the community at large as it spontaneously changed over time. Because there were only three matched communities in Blackburn's study and two in Farquhar's, the double pretest was used to estimate preintervention linear trends. However, in the Blackburn study, variability between years within cities was greater than expected, and statistical adjustments for this were not very helpful. So Blackburn modified the design in midstream so that some pretest respondents were followed up at several posttests, thus creating the longitudinal sample to complement the independent samples that continued to be drawn. The Farquhar study was designed from scratch to include both independent and dependent samples.

The use of so many different design elements provided many ways to examine the threats to validity (Chaffee, Roser, & Flora, 1989). For example, Chaffee et al. examined history by comparing differences between successive waves of independent samples in the control cities, and they examined attrition by comparing differences between the dependent and independent treatment group samples with differences between the corresponding control group samples. The combined effects of testing and maturation are suggested by comparing the differences between changes over time in the dependent samples (in which testing and maturation are more likely to occur) with changes in the independent samples (although some maturation of the entire population might also occur in these). None of these ways of examining threats is perfect, each providing suggestive rather than definitive evidence.

The Farquhar study is interesting for another reason that is relevant when the unit of assignment is a large aggregate such as a community or a business. For reasons of cost and logistics, it is rarely possible to have many such aggregates. Indeed, the publication of the Farquhar study reported only two treatment and two control communities. Cardiovascular disease decreased in the two treatment communities and in one of the control communities by amounts that hardly differed. But the risk appears to have increased over time in the second control community, despite a national trend downward over the period studied. Omitting this one community from some analyses would have reduced the treatment-control differences to nearly zero. With so few units, there is no pretense of achieving comparability between treatment and control groups, however conscientiously communities were paired before assignment. To deal with this problem requires adding more communities (which will often be prohibitively expensive) or combining studies with similar treatments. In this last case, the treatments will not be identical, and other contextual and evaluation factors will surely also differ between the studies. There is no compelling reason why there should be as many control as experimental units, so adding more control communities is sometimes inexpensive and can increase power (Kish, 1987).

THE ELEMENTS OF DESIGN

We have shown how even the weakest quasi-experimental designs can be strengthened by adding thoughtfully chosen design elements that reduce the number and plausibility of internal validity threats. Here we summarize those design elements (Table 5.2). After all, quasi-experiments are nothing more than combinations of such elements selected to suit particular circumstances of research (Corrin & Cook, 1998). For convenience, we place them into four groups having to do with (1) assignment, (2) measurement, (3) comparison groups, and (4) treatments.

Assignment

In most quasi-experiments, assignment is not controlled by the researcher. Rather, participants self-select into conditions, or someone else makes the assignment decision, as when a physician decides who will receive surgery or a teacher or school board decides which student or school should receive new resources. There is considerable evidence that *nonrandom assignment* often (but not always) yields different results than random assignment does (Chalmers et al., 1983; Colditz, Miller, & Mosteller, 1988; Lipsey & Wilson, 1993; Mosteller, Gilbert, & McPeek, 1980; Wortman, 1992), more so when participants self-select into conditions than when others make the selection decision (Heinsman & Shadish, 1996; Shadish, Matt, Navarro, & Phillips, 2000; Shadish & Ragsdale, 1996)—so self-selection should be avoided if

TABLE 5.2 Design Elements Used in Constructing Experiments and Quasi-Experiments

Assignment

Random Assignment
Cutoff-Based Assignment
Other Nonrandom Assignment
Matching and Stratifying
Masking

Measurement

Posttest Observations
    Single Posttests
    Nonequivalent Dependent Variables
    Multiple Substantive Posttests
Pretest Observations
    Single Pretest
    Retrospective Pretest
    Proxy Pretest
    Repeated Pretests Over Time
    Pretests on Independent Samples
Moderator Variable with Predicted Interaction
Measuring Threats to Validity

Comparison Groups

Single Nonequivalent Groups
Multiple Nonequivalent Groups
Cohorts
Internal Versus External Controls
Constructed Contrasts
    Regression Extrapolation Contrasts
    Normed Contrasts
    Secondary Data Contrasts

Treatment

Switching Replications
Reversed Treatments
Removed Treatments
Repeated Treatments

possible. Certain nonrandom assignment methods such as alternating assignment can sometimes approximate random assignment decently well (McAweeney & Klockars, 1998; Staines, McKendrick, Perlis, Sacks, & DeLeon, 1999).

Assignment can often be controlled in other ways than by random methods. *Matching* and *stratifying* can both increase group similarity. However, matching requires significantly more vigilance in quasi-experiments than in randomized experiments, for when done with unreliable, single measures at one point in time it can create more problems than it solves. When feasible, *masking* (blinding) of investigators, participants, or other research and service staff to assignment can be useful. It prevents two biases: (1) investigator and participant reactivity to knowledge of the condition to which the participant has been assigned and (2) efforts by those involved in assignment to influence results from the condition to which a participant is assigned. In general, then, not all nonrandom assignments are alike, and nonrandom assignments can be improved by preventing self-selection and by using other experimental controls such as matching and masking in cases in which they are feasible.

Measurement

Researchers can improve causal inference by controlling the nature and scheduling of measurements in a study. The major reason for assessing *posttests* after a treatment is to eliminate ambiguity about the temporal precedence of cause and effect. This threat is most likely to occur when a measure of outcome is taken simultaneously with treatment, as occurs in many correlational studies in which the same questionnaire is used to assess both treatment exposure levels and outcome. It is obviously better to separate temporally the measurement of these two crucial attributes of causal analysis. The special posttest called a *nonequivalent dependent variable* requires posttest measurement of two plausibly related constructs (e.g., two measures of health), one of which (the target outcome variable) is expected to change because of the treatment, whereas the other (the nonequivalent dependent variable) is not predicted to change because of the treatment, though it is expected to respond to some or all of the contextually important internal validity threats in the same way as the target outcome (e.g., both would respond in the same degree to a maturational process that improves health across all health measures). If the target outcome variable changes in response to treatment but the nonequivalent dependent variable does not, the inference that the change is due to the treatment is strengthened. If both change, the inference is weakened because the change could have been due to the threats. The use of *multiple substantive posttests* allows the researcher to examine a pattern of evidence about effects. When this pattern is predicted based on prior knowledge about the pattern typically left by a particular cause, more confident causal inference is possible.

Adding a *pretest* to a design helps examine selection biases and attrition as sources of observed effects. Adding *repeated pretests* of the same construct on consecutive occasions prior to treatment helps reveal maturational trends, detect regression artifacts, and study testing and instrumentation effects. Sometimes when it is not possible to collect pretest information on the outcome variable, *retrospective* pretests ask respondents to recall their pretest status; or *proxy* pretests can be gathered on a variable that is correlated with the outcome. These options can help clarify selection and attrition biases, though more weakly than can pretests on the outcome variable itself. Or one can sometimes gather pretest information on an *independent pretest sample*—participants different from those in the posttest sample but presumed to be similar to them, such as a random sample from the same population.

A *moderator variable* influences the size or direction of an observed effect. It can aid causal inference when the researcher successfully predicts an interaction between the moderator and treatment in producing the observed effect. This confirmation usually allows few plausible threats to internal validity. Finally, *measuring threats to validity* that can be anticipated at the start of the study helps the researcher to detect the occurrence of the threat and whether its direction mimics the observed outcomes. Measuring the presumed selection process is one particularly crucial example.

Comparison Groups

Comparison groups provide data about the counterfactual inference, that is, about what would have happened in the absence of treatment. In quasi-experiments, the counterfactual inference often depends on a *nonequivalent comparison group* deliberately chosen to have maximum pretest similarity to the treatment group on as many observed characteristics as possible or on some particular feature that the researcher believes will be a particularly salient threat to validity. Using thoughtfully chosen *multiple nonequivalent comparison groups* rather than just one comparison can expand the researcher's ability to explore more threats to the causal inference and to triangulate toward a narrower bracket within which the effect is inferred to lie. A particularly useful comparison is to *cohort controls*, to groups that move through an institution (e.g., a school) in cycles (e.g., a new third-grade class each year). Cohorts are thought to be more comparable to each other (e.g., of the same age, same general socioeconomic status, etc.) than are most other nonequivalent comparison groups.

Nonrandom comparisons to an *internal* rather than an *external control group* can sometimes yield more accurate results (Aiken et al., 1998; Bell et al., 1995; Heinsman & Shadish, 1996; Shadish & Ragsdale, 1996). Internal controls are drawn from the same pool of participants (e.g., from students in the same school or class or from all program applicants). External controls are drawn from patently different pools (e.g., patients in different treatment settings) and are presumed to have less in common. Drawing the line between internal and external controls is sometimes difficult, however, and it is clear that all these nonequivalent comparison groups can yield significant biases (Stewart et al., 1993).

Sometimes counterfactual inferences are supported from less desirable sources, including (1) a *regression extrapolation* in which actual and projected posttest scores are compared, (2) a *normed* comparison in which treatment group scores are compared with normed samples from test manuals and the like, and (3) a *secondary data* comparison in which treatment respondents are compared with samples drawn from other studies. The usefulness of such comparisons depends on the extent to which similarity to the treatment group can be shown, on whether useful matching is possible, and on whether multiple comparisons can be constructed. In the case of the contrasts listed in this paragraph, it would be rare to discover that they adequately describe the missing counterfactual inference.

Treatment

The researcher's ability to control the application and scheduling of treatment is a powerful tool for facilitating a causal inference. The *switching replication* method replicates the treatment effect at a later date in a group that originally served as a control. Better still is the use of multiple comparison groups that each receive treatment at a different time. The *reversed treatment* method applies a treatment expected to reverse the outcome when compared with the expected outcome in the treatment condition. The *removed treatment* method first presents and then removes treatment to demonstrate that the pattern of outcomes follows the pattern of treatment application; and the *repeated treatments* method reintroduces the treatment after its removal, doing so as often as feasible (sometimes called the ABAB design, with A signifying treatment and B signifying treatment removal).

Design Elements and Ideal Quasi-Experimentation

Is there an ideal or best quasi-experimental design, one that assembles these elements optimally? The answer is "Usually not," because the best design for a given study depends on the particular hypotheses being probed, on the contextual relevance of various threats to inference, on knowledge from prior studies about the viability of those threats, and on what design elements are feasible to include. However, most quasi-experiments have used very few of the potentially available quasi-experimental design elements; and our impression is that most quasi-experiments would have benefited by more attention to both the threats to inference and the design elements that might help reduce the plausibility of those threats.

Our advice is in the spirit of R. A. Fisher, who advised researchers to "Make your theories elaborate" (cited in Rosenbaum, 1984, p. 41) in order to improve causal inference from nonrandomized experiments. It is also in the spirit of Holland (1989), who noted two competing principles in drawing causal inferences from quasi-experiments: (1) causal inference in nonrandomized studies requires more *data* than in randomized studies and (2) causal inference in nonrandomized studies requires more *assumptions* in data analyses than in randomized studies.

Holland encouraged researchers to put more emphasis on the former principle (gathering more data) than the latter (making more assumptions), for gathering more data is often the only way to test the assumptions necessary to make better analyses. Adding more design elements is a way to gather more elaborate and diverse data in the service of improving causal inference.

CONCLUSION

Our review in the previous two chapters has noted that the most frequently used quasi-experimental designs typically support causal conclusions that are somewhat ambiguous. In light of this, users must be prepared to tolerate the ambiguity, assume that alternative causal explanations are negligible, or use stronger designs. This chapter emphasizes building stronger designs through adding design features that reduce the plausibility of validity threats in the context under study. In the next chapter, we continue the same theme. By themselves, interrupted time series provide a particularly strong structure for supporting causal inferences. But when the design features just summarized (e.g., comparison groups, nonequivalent dependent variables, switching replications) are added to the interrupted time series, the result is a quasi-experiment whose inferential yield sometimes rivals that of the randomized experiment.

APPENDIX 5.1: IMPORTANT DEVELOPMENTS IN ANALYZING DATA FROM DESIGNS WITH NONEQUIVALENT GROUPS

Statisticians and economists have recently devoted substantial attention to the analysis of data from designs with nonequivalent groups. Much of it is highly statistical and beyond the scope of our focus on design. However, a chapter on quasi-experimentation would be remiss if it did not introduce these developments that we hope will serve not as alternatives to quality quasi-experimental designs but as adjuncts in dealing with whatever biases the best possible design cannot deal with. In a sense, the motto is "statistical adjustment only after the best possible design controls have been used." Winship and Morgan (1999) provide a superb review of this material.

Propensity Scores and Hidden Bias

Throughout the 20th century, statisticians have preferred randomized experiments, paying less attention to quasi-experiments (Shadish & Cook, 1999). This preference is partly due to the inherent intractability of selection bias, for it is difficult to develop statistical models when the underlying processes are by their very nature unknown. Recently, however, some statisticians have studied these problems with useful results (e.g., Holland, 1986; Rosenbaum, 1984, 1995a; Rubin, 1974, 1991). Much of that work is summarized by Rosenbaum (1995a); and useful examples now exist in epidemiology (C. Drake & Fisher, 1995), medicine (Connors et al., 1996; Smith, 1997; Stone et al., 1995), the evaluation of job training programs (Dehejia & Wahba, 1999), and high school education (Rosenbaum, 1986), to name a few.

A useful development is the propensity score: the predicted probability of being in the treatment (versus control) group from a logistic regression equation.[6] Careful measurement of likely predictors of selection into groups will improve the accuracy of propensity scores. The goal is to include all variables that play a role in the selection process (including interactions and other nonlinear terms; Rosenbaum & Rubin, 1984; Rubin & Thomas, 1996) and that are presumptively related to outcome, even if only weakly so (Rubin, 1997): "Unless a variable can be excluded because there is a consensus that it is unrelated to outcome or is not a proper covariate, it is advisable to include it in the propensity score model even if it is not statistically significant" (Rubin & Thomas, 1996, p. 253). Sample size allowing, some authors suggest also using as predictors *any* pretest variables that differentiate between nonequivalent groups (Canner, 1984, 1991; Cochran, 1965; Rosenbaum, 1995a; Rubin & Thomas, 1996) at a higher than usual Type I error rate (e.g., $p < .10$ or $p < .25$). Predictors should not be caused by the treatment, which usually entails using measures collected before treatment begins. Data tentatively suggest that correctly modeling the form of the regression (i.e., correct inclusion of interaction or nonlinear terms) is less important than including all the relevant predictors of group membership (Dehejia & Wahba, 1999; C. Drake, 1993). In cases of multiple treatments, propensity scores may be computed separately for each pairwise comparison (Rubin, 1997).

The logistic regression reduces each participant's set of covariates to a single propensity score, thus making it feasible to match or stratify on what are essentially multiple variables simultaneously. Standard matching can be used in which one treatment and one control unit are paired. But Rosenbaum (1995a) shows that such pair-matching usually will not minimize the distance between groups within strata on the propensity score. Instead, he recommends *optimal matching*, in which each subset consists of (1) a single treated participant and one or more controls or (2) a single control participant and one or more treated participants. Optimal matching uses an algorithm for minimizing aggregate sample differences between treatment and control conditions on the propensity score. It allows for eliminating prior matches to create new ones if that procedure yields the lowest total

---

6. Stone et al. (1995) illustrate an alternative method for creating propensity scores using classification tree algorithms rather than logistic regression.

difference over conditions (Rosenbaum, 1995a). Bergstralh, Kosanke, and Jocobsen (1996) provide a SAS macro for optimal matching, and Isserman and Rephann (1995) present a social science example of its application. Many other variations on matching algorithms are possible (e.g., Dehejia & Wahba, 1999; Gu & Rosenbaum, 1993; Heckman, Ichimura, & Todd, 1997; Marsh, 1998). For example, one can match on propensity scores while simultaneously matching on other variables, such as gender or age (Rosenbaum, in press). There is as yet no thorough review of the advantages and disadvantages of all these matching options.

If stratifying, "Cochran (1968) shows that five subclasses are often sufficient to remove over 90% of the bias due to the subclassifying variable or covariate" (Rosenbaum & Rubin, 1984, p. 516). So five strata are typically constructed that contain all the experimental and control cases that fall within the same quintile on the propensity score. That stratification is not affected by violations of linearity, and it balances treatment and control groups in the sense that within any stratum that is homogeneous in the propensity score, differences between treated and control participants on the predictors will be due to chance if the propensity score stratification worked well. The treatment group mean is then estimated as an unweighted average of the five treatment group strata means, and the control group mean is estimated similarly. Alternatively, Robins, Greenland, and Hu (1999) report a method for weighting proportional to the propensity of receiving the treatment actually received that may have advantages, particularly for time-varying treatments. The researcher should test how well stratification on propensity scores succeeded in adjusting for differences in observed covariates by submitting each covariate (separately) and the propensity score itself to a 2 (treatments) $\times$ 5 (strata) analysis of variance. A significant interaction suggests that the propensity score did not adjust well for observed covariates, a situation that is more likely to occur the more seriously discrepant the two groups are on pretest covariates. Sometimes this problem can be ameliorated by adding nonlinear terms to the propensity score equation.

Finally, the propensity score can be used as a covariate in ANCOVA. When the usual ANCOVA assumptions are met and the model is precisely correct (e.g., it models curvilinearity correctly), covariance adjustment is more efficient than matching or stratifying. However, if the model is not substantially correct, covariance adjustments may fail to reduce overt bias or may even increase it (Rosenbaum, in press). Some authors doubt how well covariance models can model the correct functional form (e.g., H. White, 1981; Winship & Morgan, 1999). Dehejia and Wahba (1999) found that matching performed better than covariance compared with a randomized experiment benchmark despite the addition of some nonlinear terms to the covariance model. Fortunately, matching or stratifying on propensity scores can be used in combination with a subsequent covariance analysis, the result being more efficient and robust than when either is used alone (Rosenbaum, 1998, in press). This ANCOVA may include predictors of group membership that were used to compute the propensity score (Rubin & Thomas, 2000; Stone et al., 1995). Although the latter may seem unusual, a predictor may account for both variability in group membership and variability in outcome. To the extent that those sources of variability are orthogonal (mostly an empirical question in any given case), including the predictor in the final outcome equation can increase the efficiency and decrease the bias of the final estimates.

Four caveats temper our excitement about the potential of propensity scores. First, they work best with larger samples (Rubin, 1997), but many quasi-experiments have small samples. Second, researchers should inspect the overlap between conditions on propensity scores. When overlap is extremely limited, it does not allow identification of many strata or matches with members from the treatments under contrast, which can severely limit sample size, generalizability, and accuracy of any causal conclusions. Third, methods for computing propensity scores when predictors are missing are just now being explored (e.g., D'Agostino & Rubin, 2000); this issue is crucial in practice, as missing data are common. Fourth, the method assumes that no further unknown confounding variable exists that predicts the propensity to be in condition and that is correlated with outcome. This is a strong assumption. Random assignment balances treatments on both observed and unobserved covariates on **expectation;** but propensity score adjustments balance treatments only on observed covariates, leaving hidden bias due to unobserved covariates. It helps reduce hidden bias if propensity scores are constructed from as many predictors of group membership and outcome as is contextually feasible. However, it is rarely possible to know all such variables; and cost or logistical constraints often prevent researchers from measuring those that are suspected to be operating. So hidden bias may remain in quasi-experimental estimates of treatment effects even when the best propensity score analysis is used.

A second relevant development in statistics derives directly from the likelihood of this hidden bias. It is the development of sensitivity analyses to assess whether hidden biases of various sizes would change the results of the study. Such analyses explore how much hidden bias would need to be present to change study outcomes, commonly from a significant observed difference between groups to a finding of no difference or vice versa. Rosenbaum (1991a, 1991b) provides a simple example of the computations (see also Gastwirth, 1992; Gastwirth, Krieger, & Rosenbaum, 1994; S. Greenhouse, 1982; Marcus, 1997b; Psaty et al., 1999; Rosenbaum, 1986, 1987, 1988, 1989, 1991a, 1991b, 1993, 1995a, 1995b, 1999b; Rosenbaum & Krieger, 1990). Similar research has emerged recently in the econometrics literature covered in the next section (Manski, 1990; Manski & Nagin, 1998).

The sensitivity analysis outlined by Rosenbaum (1991a, 1991b, 1995a) works as follows. In a randomized experiment using simple random assignment, the odds of being assigned to treatment or control conditions are even, so the probability of being assigned to treatment is .50. In this case, the significance level (i.e., the Type I error rate) yielded by the statistical test for the difference between the two groups is accurate. In nonrandomized experiments, however, these probabilities may depart from .50; for example, males may be more likely than females to be admitted to a job training intervention. As these probabilities depart from 50/50, the significance level yielded by a statistical test of the difference between groups can become less accurate, assuming that the omitted variable causing the bias is related to outcome. Unfortunately, without knowing the hidden biases that cause this change in assignment probabilities, we cannot know if the significance levels are too low or too high. A sensitivity analysis identifies how far the lowest and highest possible significance levels will depart from what would have been yielded by a randomized experiment. It does this separately for different assumptions about the degree to which the probabilities of being assigned to conditions depart from .50. This analysis can provide important diagnostic information about the degree of assignment bias on a variable related to outcome that would change the significance of the result.

Rosenbaum (1991a) provides an example in which the observed significance level in a quasi-experiment is $p = .0057$, suggesting that treatment is effective. Sensitivity analysis on the raw study data showed that possible significance ranges from a minimum of .0004 to a maximum of .0367 when the probability of being assigned to conditions ranges from .4 to .6. Both this minimum and maximum would support the conclusion that treatment is effective. However, that narrow assignment probability range (40/60) reflects relatively little departure from the randomized experiment due to hidden bias. If the probability of being assigned to conditions ranges from .25 to .75, then the minimum significance level is <.0001 but the maximum is .2420, the latter suggesting no significant effect. The probabilities suggest that if unmeasured variables exist that affect assignment to conditions in this study so that some people are more likely than others to be assigned to treatment by a factor of 3:1 (i.e., .75 to .25), then hidden bias may be creating a false treatment effect where none actually exists (or it may be masking even larger treatment effects).

The pattern of minimum and maximum significance levels and the disparities in assignment probabilities required to produce them will vary over studies. Some studies will seem invulnerable to all but the most extreme assumptions about hidden bias, and others will seem vulnerable to nearly any assumptions. However, sensitivity analyses do not actually indicate whether bias is present, only whether a study is vulnerable to biases of different degrees. Rosenbaum (1991a) describes one study that seemed invulnerable to hidden biases that caused assignment probabilities ranging from .09 to .91; but later research showed that an even larger bias probably existed in that study. The actual detection of hidden bias in a study is not easily accomplished; but sometimes the design elements we have outlined in this chapter and the previous one, such as use of nonequivalent dependent variables or of control groups that have known performance on some unobserved covariate, are useful. For example, Dehejia and Wahba (1999) suggest that when propensity score adjustments on multiple nonequivalent comparison groups yield highly variable results, the possible presence of hidden bias is suggested.

When sensitivity analysis is combined with matching on propensity scores, these new statistical developments provide an important new analytic tool in the arsenal of quasi-experimentation. We hope they are used more widely to help us gain more practical experience about their feasibility and accuracy.

Selection Bias Modeling

Given that propensity score analysis cannot adjust for hidden bias and that sensitivity analyses cannot indicate whether such biases are present, it would be desirable to have a method that remedies these weaknesses. For the past 25 years, a number of economists, notably Heckman (e.g., Barnow, Cain, & Goldberger, 1980; Cronbach, Rogosa, Floden, & Price, 1977; Director, 1979; W. Greene, 1985, 1999; Heckman, 1979; Heckman & Hotz, 1989a, 1989b; Heckman, Hotz, & Dabos, 1987; Heckman & Robb, 1985, 1986a[7]; Stromsdorfer & Farkas, 1980), have developed procedures they hoped would adjust for selection biases between nonequivalent groups to obtain an unbiased estimate of treatment effects. These methods are statistically complex and are not always easily implemented by those without advanced statistical training. They comprise a family of models that make different assumptions about selection. Accessible overviews are provided by Achen (1986), Foster and McLanahan (1996), Moffitt (1991), Newhouse and McClellan (1998), Rindskopf (1986), Winship and Mare (1992), and especially Winship and Morgan (1999).

A simple selection bias model might use two equations, a selection equation and an outcome equation. As with propensity score models, the selection equation predicts actual group membership from a set of presumed determinants of selection into conditions, yielding a predicted group membership score. This score may be substituted for the treatment dummy variable in the outcome equation or added to that equation in addition to the dummy variable. If the selection equation predicts group membership nearly perfectly, and if other assumptions, such as normality of observations, are met, then in principle the coefficient associated with the predicted dummy treatment variable in the effect estimation equation can yield an unbiased estimate of the treatment effect. Unlike propensity score methods, selection bias models can allow for correlation of errors in the selection equation and the outcome equation. This correlation is gained at a cost of assuming the nature of the bivariate relationship between the errors, usually as bivariate normal.

These models are closely related to regression discontinuity designs that achieve an unbiased estimate of treatment effects through full knowledge of the selection model by which participants were assigned to conditions, entering that model (i.e., the cutoff variable) directly into the effects estimation model. Regression discontinuity does not require a selection equation because the design forces perfect prediction of selection based on the cutoff score, so the residual of prediction into conditions is zero. In selection bias models, by analogy, if the residual of the selection equation departs much from zero (which is to say that predicted group membership does not match actual group membership well), then the selection bias model may fail to yield unbiased estimates of treatment effects. This primarily hap-

---

7. Wainer (1986, pp. 57–62, 108–113) reprints a spirited discussion by John Tukey, John Hartigan, and James Heckman of both the 1985 and 1986 versions of the Heckman and Robb papers.

pens if a variable that would improve prediction of group membership and that is related to outcome is omitted from the selection equation. This omission causes a correlation between the error terms and predictors in the selection and effect estimation equations, which will cause biased estimation of effects. As with regression discontinuity, the functional form of the selection equation must be correctly specified; for instance, if nonlinear or interaction terms that affect group membership are omitted, the effect estimation equation may yield biased estimates.

Selection bias models have been widely studied, praised, and criticized.[8] On the positive side, they address the very important question of taking hidden bias into account rather than just adjusting for observed covariates. And some empirical data can be interpreted positively (Heckman & Hotz, 1989a; Heckman, Hotz, & Dabos, 1987; Heckman & Todd, 1996; Reynolds & Temple, 1995), encouraging further work to develop these models (Moffitt, 1989). Less optimistically, sensitivity to violations of assumptions seems high, and many statisticians are skeptical about these models (e.g., Holland, 1989; Little, 1985; Wainer, 1986). Further, some studies suggest that these models do not well-approximate results from randomized experiments. For example, LaLonde and Maynard (1987) compared results from a randomized experiment with results from a selection bias analysis of the same data using a quasi-experimental control and found that the two answers did not match well. The presumption is that the randomized experiment is correct. Related studies have not yielded promising results (Fraker & Maynard, 1986, 1987; Friedlander & Robins, 1995; LaLonde, 1986; Murnane, Newstead, & Olsen, 1985; Stolzenberg & Relles, 1990; Virdin, 1993).[9] Thus even some economists have been led to prefer randomized experiments to nonrandomized experiments that use selection bias models (Ashenfelter & Card, 1985; Barnow, 1987; Burtless, 1995; Hollister & Hill, 1995). Advocates respond that some of these studies used data that did not meet certain tests for proper application of the models. For example, Heckman and Hotz (1989a, 1989b; Heckman, Hotz, & Dabos, 1987) suggest that a valid selection bias model should find no pretest difference between participants and controls and no posttest difference between randomized and nonrandomized controls (of course, if one has randomized controls, the selection bias estimate is of less interest). But even when those tests are passed, concern about the accuracy of resulting estimates can remain (Friedlander & Robins, 1995).

Work to develop better selection bias models continues (Heckman & Roselius, 1994, 1995; Heckman & Todd, 1996). Bell et al. (1995) note that several events in the 1970s encouraged use of external control groups, like those drawn from national survey archives in selection bias models, and discouraged use of internal controls. Today, there is renewed interest in internal control groups, on the assumption that they may be more similar to the treatment group a priori than are external

8. For a novel view of this debate from sociology of science, see Breslau (1997).

9. Dehejia and Wahba (1999) reanalyzed the Lalonde (1986) data using propensity score analysis and obtained point estimates that were much closer to those from the benchmark randomized experiment.

controls. This point has been widely suggested in the quasi-experimental literature for decades (e.g., Campbell & Stanley, 1963) but not appreciated in selection bias modeling until recently (e.g., Heckman & Roselius, 1994; Heckman et al., 1997). Friedlander and Robins (1995), for example, found that selection bias models of welfare experiments more accurately approximated estimates from randomized experiments when the nonrandomized controls were selected from within the same state as the program recipients rather than from other states. Bell et al. (1995) investigate various internal control groups formed from program applicants who withdrew, were screened out,[10] or did not show for treatment, with encouraging results.

Also, these models would probably work better if they used predictors that were selected to reflect theory and research about variables that affect selection into treatment, a procedure that requires studying the nature of selection bias as a phenomenon in its own right (e.g., Anderman et al., 1995). For example, Reynolds and Temple (1995) obtained effect size estimates from selection bias models that closely resembled those from randomized experiments on the effects of participation in a preschool program. The rules for eligibility to participate in the program were fairly clear, and the authors were able to predict participation fairly accurately. However, when less is known about participation, even authors who have made extensive efforts to select comparable controls and measure pertinent selection predictors have found results that made them question if the selection bias model worked (Grossman & Tierney, 1993).

Heckman (Heckman, Lalonde, & Smith, 1999; Heckman & Roselius, 1994, 1995; Heckman & Todd, 1996) has incorporated these lessons into various revised models that test the effects of employment and training programs under the Job Training Partnership Act (JTPA). The context is the National JTPA Experiment, commissioned in 1986 by the U.S. Department of Labor. It included program participants, a randomized control group, and a nonrandomized comparison group of people who were eligible for JTPA but did apply. Heckman tested several semiparametric selection bias estimators that do not require such strong assumptions, and they performed better than previous parametric models had.[11] However, making fewer assumptions usually results in weaker inferences, and the hard question of which assumptions are appropriate still remains to be solved in each study. In any case, the best performing models in Heckman and Todd used matching on a modified version of the propensity scores described in the previous

---

10. Bell et al. (1995) refer to this group as a regression discontinuity control group. Close examination of the procedures used to create this control make that unlikely, for two reasons. First, assignment does not seem to have been made *solely* on the basis of a quantitative cutoff. Second, staff who were making program selection decisions may have created the participant's score on the selection variable as a *result* of their judgments about who should get treatment rather than by first measuring the variable and then determining eligibility. Thus both the score and the cutoff may have been the effect of assignment rather than its cause.

11. All of these tests were conducted with knowledge of the outcome of the randomized experiment, so they leave doubt as to how well they would have performed under conditions in which the researcher does not know the correct answer—which is, after all, the likely context of application.

section. Heckman and Todd (1996) note that these matching methods "perform best when (1) comparison group members come from the same local labor markets as participants, (2) they answer the same survey questionnaires, and (3) when data on key determinants of program participation is (sic) available" (p. 60). Perhaps such results indicate the beginnings of a convergence among the statistical, econometric, and quasi-experimental design literatures in understanding of how to get better effect estimates from quasi-experiments.

Another indicator of convergence comes from Manski and his colleagues (e.g., Manski, 1990; Manski & Nagin, 1998; Manski, Sandefur, McLanahan, & Powers, 1992), who have explored nonparametric methods for placing bounds on treatment effects under conditions of selection bias, similar to the sensitivity analysis tradition. These methods do not make the strict assumptions of the parametric methods of Heckman. They result in a series of treatment estimate bounds that vary depending on the assumptions made. But the estimates that require the fewest assumptions also sacrifice power, so the bounds may be unacceptably wide; and point estimates of treatment effects can be attained only by making stronger assumptions about the process generating treatment assignment and outcome, that is, if one or more plausible selection models can be identified. Rosenbaum (1995b) suggests that Manski's bounds are analogous to the limit of a sensitivity analysis in which the key index of potential bias in the sensitivity analysis (Γ) approaches ∞; and he agrees that the bounds are conservative but that they contain some information. Copas and Li (1997) discuss the relationship between selection models and sensitivity analyses, arguing that selection models are so sensitive to assumptions that they should be used as sensitivity analyses by varying those assumptions deliberately rather than being used to estimate single treatment parameters—a point of view with which Heckman and others have expressed sympathy (e.g., Heckman & Hotz, 1986; Winship & Mare, 1992). All agree: sensitivity analyses are crucial in nonrandomized experiments.

Latent Variable Structural Equation Modeling

The work of Karl Joreskog and his colleagues on structural equation modeling (e.g., Joreskog & Sorbom, 1988, 1993) and the similar but more user-friendly work by Peter Bentler (e.g., Bentler, 1993, 1995) have led to widespread use of so-called "causal modeling" techniques. When these techniques were applied to data from quasi-experiments, the hope was to make causal inferences more accurate by adjusting for predictors of outcome that might be correlated with receipt of treatment and by adjusting for unreliability of measurement in predictors. If these two goals could be accomplished, an unbiased estimate of treatment effect could be obtained. In fact, adjustment for measurement error is feasible using latent variable models (see Chapter 12). Doing so requires using multiple observed measures of a construct that are, in essence, factor analyzed to yield latent variables shorn of random measurement error (multiple measurement can take place on a subsample to save costs; Allison & Hauser, 1991). Those latent variables can be used to model treatment outcome and may improve estimation of treatment effects. For instance, several reanalyses of the original Head Start data (Cicirelli & Associates, 1969) have been done with latent variables, all resulting in estimates of effects that are thought to be better than those the original analysis yielded (Bentler & Woodward, 1978; Magidson, 1977, 1978, 2000; Reynolds & Temple, 1995; Rindskopf, 1981).

However, the other goal of these models, to adjust outcome for variables correlated with treatment assignment and outcome, is problematic because it is rare in the social sciences to have sufficient knowledge of all the treatment-correlated predictors of outcome. The almost inevitable failure to include some such predictors leaves hidden bias and inaccurate effect estimates. Moreover, it is not enough that the model include all the predictors; it must correctly specify their relationship to each other and to outcome, including nonlinear and interaction terms, correct modeling of mediated versus direct relationships, and correct sequencing of lagged relationships. Reichardt and Gollob (1986) provide a readable introduction to the issues; Bollen (1989) has a detailed one; and Bentler and Chou (1988) give practical tips for the more productive use of these models. Ultimately, all agree that these causal models are only as good as the design underlying the data that go into them—even the developers of LISREL, who make clear that their program estimates causal parameters presumed to be true as opposed to testing whether the relationships themselves are causal (Joreskog & Sorbom, 1990).

The literature on structural equation modeling has developed largely independently of the literatures on selection bias modeling and propensity scores. In part, this is an accident of the different disciplines in which these developments first occurred; and in part it is because the methods attempt different adjustments, with structural equation models adjusting for predictors of outcome but with selection bias models and propensity scores adjusting for predictors of treatment selection. Yet Winship and Morgan (1999) make clear that there is a close relationship among all these methods (see also Pearl, 2000; Spirtes, Glymour, & Scheines, 2000). It is unclear whether such efforts at integrating these topics will be successful without making the same kinds of assumptions that have so far stymied prior analyses. But it is also clear that the attention being paid to causal inference is increasing across a wide array of disciplines, which at a minimum bodes well for further integration of this disparate literature.

6

Quasi-Experiments: Interrupted Time-Series Designs

Time (tīm): [Middle English from Old English *tima*; see *da* in Indo-European Roots.] n. 1. Abbr. t., T. a. A nonspatial continuum in which events occur in apparently irreversible succession from the past through the present to the future. b. An interval separating two points on this continuum; a duration: *a long time since the last war; passed the time reading.*

Time (tīm): adj. 1. Of, relating to, or measuring time.

Se·ries (sîr´ēz): [Latin series, from *serere*, to join; see *ser-*[2] in Indo-European Roots.] n., pl. series. Abbr. ser. 1. A number of objects or events arranged or coming one after the other in succession.

I N JULY 1982, the Arizona state legislature mandated severe penalties for driving while intoxicated. A comparison of monthly results from January 1976 to June 1982 (the control condition) with monthly totals between July 1982 and May 1984 (the treatment condition) found a decrease in traffic fatalities after the new law was passed. A similar finding occurred in San Diego, California, after January 1982, when that city implemented a state law penalizing intoxicated drivers. In El Paso, Texas, which had no relevant change in its driving laws during this period, monthly fatality trends showed no comparable changes near the months of either January or July 1982. The changes in trends over time in San Diego and Arizona, compared with the absence of similar trends in El Paso, suggest that the new laws reduce fatalities (West, Hepworth, McCall, & Reich, 1989). This interrupted time-series design is one of the most effective and powerful of all quasi-experimental designs, especially when supplemented by some of the design elements discussed in previous chapters (see Table 5.2), as we illustrate in this chapter.

WHAT IS A TIME SERIES?

Time series refers to a large series of observations made on the same variable consecutively over time. The observations can be on the same units, as in cases in which medical or psychiatric symptoms in one individual are repeatedly observed. Or the observations can be on different but similar units, as in cases of traffic fatalities displayed for a particular state over many years, during which time the baseline population is constantly changing.

In this chapter we describe a special kind of time series that can be used to assess treatment impact, the *interrupted* time series. The key here is knowing the specific point in the series at which a treatment occurred, for example, the date on which a mandatory seat belt law took effect. If the treatment had an impact, the causal hypothesis is that the observations after treatment will have a different slope or level from those before treatment. That is, the series should show an "interruption" to the prior situation at the time at which treatment was delivered. Such designs have been widely used to assess the impact of interventions in areas as diverse as attorney advertising (Johnson, Yazdi, & Gelb, 1993), community interventions to improve child-rearing practices (Biglan, Metzler, & Ary, 1994), epidemiology (Catalano & Serxner, 1987; Tesoriero, Sorin, Burrows, & LaChance-McCullough, 1995), consumer product safety (Orwin, 1984), gun control (Carrington & Moyer, 1994; O'Carroll et al., 1991), history of marriage (Denton, 1994), human rights (W. Stanley, 1987), political participation (Seamon & Feiock, 1995), real estate values (Brunette, 1995; Murdoch, Singh, & Thayer, 1993), environmental **risk analysis** (Teague, Bernardo, & Mapp, 1995), spouse abuse (Tilden & Shepherd, 1987), surgery (Everitt, Sourmerai, Avorn, Klapholz, & Wessels, 1990), substance abuse (Velicer, 1994), tax policy (Bloom & Ladd, 1982), workplace safety (Feinauer & Havlovic, 1993), and the effects of television (Hennigan et al., 1982). The interrupted time series is a particularly strong quasi-experimental alternative to randomized designs when the latter are not feasible and when a time series can be found. Here, we begin with the simplest interrupted time-series design, then introduce variants on that design, and finally discuss practical problems in implementing time-series studies.

Describing Types of Effects

A posttreatment time series can differ from a pretreatment series in several ways. First, there may be a sharp discontinuity at the point of the intervention, the time at which we expect the overall series to be "interrupted." Consider a short series with 20 observations, 11 before the intervention and 9 after it. If the values for the pretreatment series were 2, 3, 4, 5, 6, 7, 8, 9, 10, 11, and 12 and the values for the posttreatment series were 10, 11, 12, 13, 14, 15, 16, 17, and 18, then we would conclude that the values decreased following the intervention, for the 12th observation is a 10 and not the expected 13. The change from a value of 12 to 10 is called a change in *level* or *intercept,* because (1) the level of the series drops and (2) the pre- and posttreatment slopes would have different intercepts.

Second, there may be a change in the slope of the series at the point of interruption. Imagine that the pretreatment values are 2, 3, 4, 5, 6, 7, 8, 9, 10, 11, and 12 and the posttreatment values are 14, 16, 18, 20, 22, 24, 26, and 28. So before treatment the series shifted one score unit per time interval, but after it there were two score units of change per time interval. This is variously called a change in *drift, trend,* or *slope.*

Though changes in level and slope are the most common forms of change, they are not the only ones possible. For instance, posttreatment changes can occur in the variances around each mean if a treatment makes people more homogeneous or heterogeneous in the outcome measure compared with the preintervention time period. Or a cyclical pattern can be affected; for example, the introduction of air conditioning probably caused a new relationship between time of year and time spent indoors. Though one typically looks for changes in intercept and slope in interrupted time-series research, investigators should remain open to other kinds of effects.

Effects can be characterized along another dimension. A *continuous* effect does not decay over time. Hence, a shift in level of X units that is obtained immediately after an intervention is still noted in the later part of the total series. A *discontinuous* effect does not persist over time. Commonly, the initial effect drifts back over time toward the preintervention level or slope as the effect wears off. This is especially likely to occur if the intervention is introduced and then removed, but it can also occur if a treatment with transitory effects is left in place. Sometimes a discontinuous effect can take the opposite form, with an effect becoming larger over time, creating a sleeper effect (Cook et al., 1979). But in our experience this is rare.

Effects can also be *immediate* or *delayed* in their initial manifestation following the treatment. Immediate effects are usually simpler to interpret, for their onset can be matched exactly to the time of intervention. Delayed effects are more difficult to interpret unless there is a theoretical justification for how long a delay should elapse before an effect is expected (e.g., biology leads us to expect about a nine month delay between the introduction of a new birth control method and the first effects on birth rate). With delayed effects, the longer the time period between the treatment and the first visible signs of a possible impact, the larger the number of plausible alternative interpretations.

It clarifies an interrupted time-series effect to describe it on all three dimensions simultaneously, that is, the form of the effect (the level, slope, variance, and cyclicity), its permanence (continuous or discontinuous), and its immediacy (immediate or delayed). We provide examples of all these different kinds of effects in this chapter.

Brief Comments on Analysis

We focus almost entirely on design rather than analysis issues, although we occasionally mention some problems of statistical conclusion validity that particular examples highlight.[1] However, it is useful to know a few basic points about time-series statistics. Ordinary statistics cannot be used, for example, for comparing preintervention observations with postintervention observations using a *t*-test. Ordinary statistics assume observations are independent of each other. But time-series data are typically autocorrelated. That is, the value of one observation is usually related to the value of previous observations that may be one, two, three, or more lags away. Estimating this **autocorrelation** usually requires a large number of observations, typically 100, to facilitate correct model identification (Box, Jenkins, & Reinsel, 1994; Velicer & Harrop, 1983). However, the exact number of observations needed cannot be fully specified in advance. Statistically, one needs only enough to identify the model, and this identification depends on the amount of error in the data, any periodicity effects, the timing of the intervention within the series, and the number of lags to be modeled. Although having 100 observations is typically cited in the literature as desirable, some examples we use in this chapter have fewer observations.[2] Sometimes the reason is that the model can be identified adequately with fewer observations. Mostly, however, we present shorter time series to illustrate how even an abbreviated time series rules out many more threats to validity than is possible in cases in which there are only a few pretest or posttest time points. The interpretation of time series is not purely a statistical matter; it also depends on design features and the immediacy and magnitude of the effect.

1. Statistical methods for time-series analysis are classified into the time domain or the frequency domain (Shumway, 1988). Time domain approaches model time-series observations by predicting current values from past ones. The best known of these is the autoregressive integrated moving average (ARIMA) approach by Box and Jenkins (1970). Many econometric analyses are close to this tradition, sometimes labeled as structural regression models (Kim & Trivedi, 1994; Ostrom, 1990). Frequency domain approaches model time-series observations as a combination of periodic sine and cosine waves, often called spectral, harmonic, or Fourier analysis, an approach used most in the physical sciences and engineering. Shumway (1988) claims that both frequency and time approaches yield similar conclusions if the time series is long. We know of no strong consensus that one approach is preferable in general. Analysts are rapidly developing multivariate time series, methods for dealing with missing data, nonlinear time series, pooled time series that combine multiple time series on different units, and estimation of time series that are robust to outliers (Box, Jenkins, & Reinsel, 1994; Caines, 1988; Hannan & Deistler, 1988; Kendall & Ord, 1990; Sayrs, 1989; Tong, 1990; W. Wei, 1990). The *Journal of Time Series Analysis* offers cutting edge developments, and the *Journal of the American Statistical Association* includes pertinent articles on a regular basis. Many time series analysis books are available at both basic (Cromwell, Labys, & Terraza, 1994; Cromwell, Hannan, Labys, & Terraza, 1994; McDowall, McCleary, Meidinger, & Hay, 1980; Ostrom, 1990; Sayrs, 1989) and advanced levels (e.g., Box, Jenkins, & Reinsel, 1994; Fuller, 1995; Hamilton, 1994; Harvey, 1990; Judge, Hill, Griffiths, & Lee, 1985; Kendall & Ord, 1990; Reinsel, 1993; W. Wei, 1990). Some of them are accompanied by computer software programs (e.g., Brockwell & Davis, 1991; Shumway, 1988), and standard statistical packages have extensive time-series analysis capabilities (Harrop & Velicer, 1990a, 1990b; Newbold, Agiakloglou, & Miller, 1994; Kim & Trivedi, 1994).

2. Unless otherwise noted explicitly, none of the figures in this chapter aggregate raw data across time points; that is, all the time points available in the raw data are included in each figure.

SIMPLE INTERRUPTED TIME SERIES

A basic time-series design requires one treatment group with many observations before and after a treatment. A design with 10 observations might be diagrammed as:

$$O_1 \quad O_2 \quad O_3 \quad O_4 \quad O_5 \ X \ O_6 \quad O_7 \quad O_8 \quad O_9 \quad O_{10}$$

A Change in Intercept

Our first example of a simple interrupted time series (McSweeny, 1978) has 180 observations and is nearly ideal for ruling out many threats to internal validity (Figure 6.1). In March 1974, Cincinnati Bell began charging 20 cents per call to local directory assistance. Figure 6.1 clearly shows an immediate and large drop in local directory assistance calls when this charge began. A little thought suggests very few plausible rival hypotheses. Regression to the mean is implausible because the very long preintervention time series shows that a high number of calls to directory assistance were occurring for many years, not just immediately prior to the intervention (see Maltz, Gordon, McDowall, & McCleary, 1980, for a time series with prominent regression artifacts). Selection is implausible if the population making calls to local directory assistance in Cincinnati had no atypical changes over adjacent months before and after the intervention, so that pre- and postintervention samples should be largely the same on any variables affecting outcome. Similarly, attrition is implausible because it seems unlikely that such a large number of customers would disconnect their phones in response to the charge, and this could be easily checked with phone company records. Further, no known, naturally occurring maturation process could cause such a dramatic drop in local directory

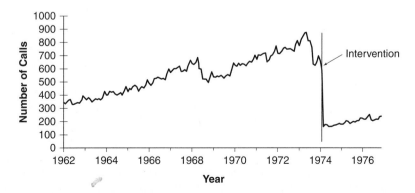

FIGURE 6.1 The effects of charging for directory assistance in Cincinnatii

assistance use. Testing effects are unlikely; here, the test is essentially the bill, and a testing effect would require that the phone company changed its billing to, say, highlight the number of directory assistance calls made prior to instituting the charge, so that customers changed their behavior based on that feedback rather than the charge. Whether they did so could be easily checked. History is plausible only if one could find another event that occurred simultaneously with the 20-cent charge and could have produced such a large effect, which seems unlikely. When effects are as immediate and dramatic as in this example, most threats to internal validity are usually implausible. Other examples of interrupted time series with immediate and dramatic effects include the effects of vaccinations on diseases such as tetanus (Veney, 1993) and of screening for phenylketonuria (PKU) on retardation (MacCready, 1974).

A Change in Slope

Figure 6.2 shows an example of an interrupted time series with 96 observations in which the outcome is a change of slope rather than of intercept. In 1983, Canada reformed its Criminal Code pertaining to sexual assault. The old law had two categories: rape and indecent assault. The new law used three categories of increasing severity and other provisions to increase the number of victims who report the crimes to the police, and it was implemented with much national publicity. To assess the impact of this change, Roberts and Gebotys (1992) used monthly data from the Canadian Uniform Crime Reporting System on sexual assault reports from 1981 through 1988. The resultant time series shows a seasonality effect, with more sexual assaults reported in summer and fewer in winter. Taking that into account, the slope was close to zero before the law was passed. After the law was passed the slope of the time series increased, suggesting that the law did have the desired effects on reporting sexual assaults.

Given the pattern of results, most threats to validity seem implausible. For example, maturation is unlikely because the slope changed dramatically at the point of the intervention, a result that does not mimic a known maturation process. For history to be plausible, another event must exist and have an abrupt effect on reporting of sexual assaults. With the exception of the publicity that surrounded the implementation of the law (which is arguably part of the intervention), no such event could be identified. However, the authors did present data suggesting that the publicity may have influenced people's attitudes toward sexual assault, which may have contributed to the increase in reports. This raises a question of the construct validity of the treatment. Should the treatment be construed as reform legislation or reform legislation with great publicity? The authors argue for the latter interpretation.

The intervention changed reporting categories, so Roberts and Gebotys (1992) identified four possible instrumentation threats. First, the new law allowed wives to charge their husbands with sexual assault, and it included assaults against

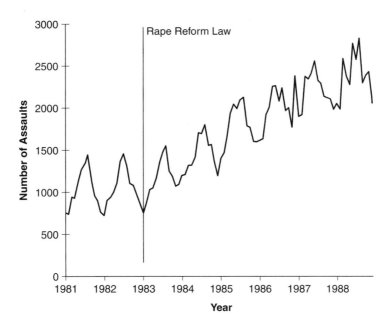

FIGURE 6.2 The effects of sexual assault law reform in Canada

From "Reforming rape laws: Effects of legislative change in Canada," by J. V. Roberts and R. J. Gebotys, 1992, *Law and Human Behavior, 16,* 555–573. Copyright 1992 by Kluwer Academic/Plenum Publishers.

both males and females. Countering this threat, the authors showed that the number of cases in which the suspect was either a woman or the husband increased only 5 percent after the law, insufficient to account for the far greater increase shown in Figure 6.2. Second, it could be possible that crimes that had been earlier reported as "other sexual assault" (and that therefore were not included in the preintervention section of Figure 6.2) were now being added to the sexual assault category and so were showing up only in the posttreatment series, which now for the first time included sexual exploitation, invitations to sexual touching, and bestiality. But analyses showed no change in reports of these highly specific crime categories over time, making it less likely that they caused the observed increase in slope. Third, perhaps these reports of other sexual assaults were rarely reported before reform but were reported more often afterward because of the publicity generated by the new law. The authors could find no data to directly rule out this threat, but they reported that indirect data suggested that it was unlikely. Fourth, some data suggested a temporal increase in the number of sexual assaults against children and juveniles. Was the increase shown in Figure 6.2 restricted to juvenile offenses? Unfortunately, the national statistics could not be disaggregated by age to test this possibility. But disaggregated crime statistics in cities such as Montreal showed too small an increase in the number of assaults against juveniles to account for the large increase in reporting sexual assaults shown in Figure 6.2.

Weak and Delayed Effects

Although interpretation of Figure 6.2 is not as clear as interpretation of Figure 6.1, few simple interrupted time-series designs are even as clear as Figure 6.2. Figure 6.3 presents a more common example. It includes 63 observations, and the effect seems both delayed in onset and weak in strength. This study (Hankin et al., 1993) examined the effects of an alcohol warning label law on the frequency with which pregnant women drank alcohol. Starting November 18, 1989, a federal law required a warning label on all alcohol containers. The label specifically warned that drinking alcohol during pregnancy can cause birth defects. The authors looked at how much alcohol was consumed by 12,026 pregnant African American women during the 2 weeks prior to their first prenatal visit to a Detroit clinic, both before and after the law took effect. The time series spanned September 1986 through September 1991 at monthly intervals. Visual inspection of the time series does not yield a clear-cut interpretation about whether the warning labels affected drinking.

The authors' statistical analysis, however, suggested a delayed rather than an immediate impact, beginning about 7 months after the law took effect. The reason to expect a delay is that the law affected newly produced containers, not those already on store shelves. Hence some time elapsed before bottles with warning labels could even appear on shelves in numbers sufficient to be noticed by consumers. Supporting this hypothesis, the authors asked women if they were aware of the labels, and they saw no increase in awareness until March 1990, 4 months after the implementation of the law. Hence a delayed effect would be expected, though not necessarily a 7-month delay. Furthermore, drinking among pregnant women appeared to have been decreasing before the intervention, and so maturation is a possible threat to validity given that the effect is a gradual change in slope, not in intercept. However, time series permits us to contrast the size of the pretreatment slope with the size thereafter. This contrast suggested that the (delayed) impact of the law was to speed up slightly the already occurring decrease in drinking among pregnant women.

We also see a seasonal trend in Figure 6.3. The rate of alcohol drinking goes up around the end of the year holidays and in the summer. However, seasonality is not a threat to validity in this case. Drinking actually increased very briefly immediately after the law took effect, coincidental with the approach of the Christmas season. Because the change in the law was supposed to decrease drinking, seasonality worked in the opposite direction to the hypothesis, and so cannot explain the obtained decrease. Indeed, Figure 6.3 shows that drinking during winter holidays and summer was visibly lower after the law's impact than before. However, if the law had been implemented in February, after the holidays, or in September, after summer ended, such seasonality effects could have been misinterpreted as a treatment effect. Good analytic practice requires modeling and removing seasonality effects from a time series before assessing treatment impact.

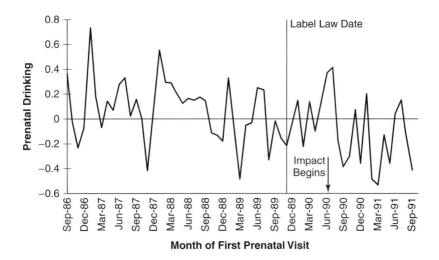

FIGURE 6.3 The effects of an alcohol warning label on prenatal drinking

From "A time series analysis of the impact of the alcohol warning label on antenatal drinking," by J. R. Hankin et al., 1993, *Alcoholism: Clinical and Experimental Research, 17,* pp. 284–289. Copyright 1993 by Lippincott, Williams & Wilkins.

The Usual Threats to Validity

With most simple interrupted time-series designs, the major threat to internal validity is history—the possibility that forces other than the treatment under investigation influenced the dependent variable at the same time at which the intervention was introduced. For example, in the Hankin et al. (1993) data, if the City of Detroit simultaneously passed laws restricting the sale of alcohol, this could have reduced drinking among pregnant women in a way that mimics the warning label effect. Several controls for history are possible, perhaps the best being to add a no-treatment time series from a control group, as we discuss shortly. But this is not always necessary. For instance, Hankin et al.'s measure of drinking was aggregated into monthly intervals, and the historical events that can explain an apparent treatment effect are fewer with monthly intervals than with yearly ones. Also, if a list is made of plausible effect-causing events that could influence respondents during a quasi-experiment, it should be possible using qualitative or quantitative means to ascertain whether most or all of them operated between the last pretest and the first posttest. If they did not, history is less plausible as a threat.

Another threat is instrumentation. For example, a change in administrative procedures sometimes leads to a change in how records are kept. Persons who want to make their performance look good can simply change bookkeeping procedures to redefine performance or satisfaction. Or persons with a mandate to change an organization may interpret this to include making changes in how records are kept or how criteria of success and failure are defined. This seems to have happened, for instance, when Orlando Wilson took charge of the Chicago police. By redefining how crimes should be classified, he appeared to have caused an increase in crime. But the increase was spurious, reflecting record-keeping changes, not criminal behavior. Similarly, the Hankin et al. (1993) time series relied on women's self-reports of drinking. Self-reports are subject to demand characteristics, and publicity surrounding the law might have increased such demand characteristics. That is, women's self-reports of drinking might have decreased when the law took effect—even if their actual drinking did not change—as the women became aware that it was socially undesirable to drink while pregnant.

Selection can be another threat if the composition of the experimental group changes abruptly at the time of the intervention. This might occur if the treatment causes (or even requires) attrition from the measurement framework. If so, the interruption in the time series might have been due to different persons being in the pretreatment versus the posttreatment series. One can sometimes check this by restricting a data analysis to the subset of units that were measured at all time periods, but this is not always possible (e.g., when the third-grade achievement scores from a single school over 20 years are involved; the third-grade children are mostly different each year). Alternatively, the characteristics of units can sometimes be analyzed to see whether a sharp discontinuity occurs in the profile of units at the same time the treatment is introduced.

The typical statistical conclusion validity threats apply as much to time series as to any other design, such as low power, violated test assumptions, and unreliability of measurement. But the Detroit study of labels against drinking highlights a particular problem. The time-series analyst must specify at what point the intervention began and must have some theory or data that maps its diffusion through the units exposed to treatment. But in the Detroit example, the intervention diffused slowly, with the exact diffusion rate and pattern being unknown. Hence the researcher has discretion over specifying at what time the intervention begins and so can inadvertently capitalize on chance by picking a start time to match the time of apparent maximum effect. Because a number of changes may occur by chance alone in a long time series, a poorly specified intervention point can seriously weaken the causal logic of the design. (If diffusion rates are known, a diffusion curve could be used to model the intervention rather than an abrupt start. We discuss this option later in this chapter.)

Those who use time series must also guard against all the generic issues of construct validity, such as inadequate explication of constructs or confounding of constructs. However, time series raises some special construct validity issues. Many time series use archived data such as driving records or school grades. In these cases, many reactivity-related threats are less relevant because it is often harder for respondents to affect the outcome measures. Indeed, respondents often do not know they are part of a study. Reactivity is more likely in clinical time series, especially when the time interval between observations is short and respondents can remember their past responses. So each time-series experiment has to be carefully examined on its own merits to determine whether the observed results might be due to evaluation apprehension, demand characteristics, or some similar threat to construct validity.

Also regarding construct validity, time-series work often uses only one outcome measure. The reason is partly that concerns about expense or old-fashioned definitional operationalist thinking led the persons who set up archives to measure, say, academic achievement, burglary, or unemployment in just one way. Compounding the problem, the researcher is often forced to use the outcome measures available, even if they are not fully relevant to the treatment being tested. This makes the available measures less sensitive for detecting outcome than they are when researchers collect their own dependent variable data, can tailor their measures to the treatment theory, and can add more items to increase reliability and validity. Of course, in time-series work in which several measures of an effect are available and each is reasonably reliable, changes in the time series can be separately examined for each measure. Furthermore, treatments are often events that respondents see as naturally occurring, such as changes in laws; and the outcomes are often (but not always) less obtrusively collected because respondents are used to government and corporations collecting data on them, at least more often than is the case with other kinds of research. So reactivity threats to construct validity of both treatment and outcome may be less.

Regarding external validity, it is sometimes possible to investigate it more actively by using available data on the background characteristics of units to stratify them into, say, males and females, or into different age groups, to see if the effect holds over such variability. There is no need to restrict such exploration to person variables. For example, setting variables can also be used to explore the range of an effect; and time variables can be used to see if an effect holds at different times of day (arrests during the day versus at night). This disaggregation has to be accomplished with caution, for statistical power can be reduced by creating subgroups. Moreover, in archival research one has a restricted flexibility in creating subgroups—necessary variables and cutoff points must be in the record. Thus, if the last age category is "over 65," and one is interested in studying the so-called old old (over 75), one cannot do so.

ADDING OTHER DESIGN FEATURES TO THE BASIC INTERRUPTED TIME SERIES

In previous chapters, we showed how to build stronger causal inferences by adding carefully chosen design features to basic quasi-experimental designs. The same principle applies to the interrupted time series, as well, as the following examples illustrate.

Adding a Nonequivalent No-Treatment Control Group Time Series

Consider the addition of a control group time series to the simple interrupted time-series design. The resulting design is diagrammed below:

$$O_1 \quad O_2 \quad O_3 \quad O_4 \quad O_5 \ X \ O_6 \quad O_7 \quad O_8 \quad O_9 \quad O_{10}$$

$$O_1 \quad O_2 \quad O_3 \quad O_4 \quad O_5 \quad O_6 \quad O_7 \quad O_8 \quad O_9 \quad O_{10}$$

An example of this design is given in Figure 6.4. In June 1992, the Spanish city of Barcelona passed legislation requiring riders of small motorcycles to wear helmets. Helmet use for large motorcycles had already been mandatory for several years. Ballart and Riba (1995) used a time series with 153 observations to examine the impact of that legislation. The outcome was the number of motorcycle accident victims with serious injuries or death. Both outcomes should decrease once the law took effect, but only for accident victims on small motorcycles. Victims riding large motorcycles, for whom the law had already been in effect for years, should show no such decrease, and so served as the control group. Figure 6.4 shows that the law had this hypothesized effect, and statistical analysis supported that interpretation.

Because the experimental and control groups rode their motorcycles and had accidents over the same time period, it is unlikely that a treatment-correlated historical event caused the decrease in serious injuries in the small-motorcycle group. Such an event should have decreased control group accidents, as well. The ability to test for the threat of history is the major strength of the control group time-series design. However, local history can be problematic if one group experiences a set of unique events that the other does not. Even then, local history can only threaten internal validity if the confounding event occurs *at the time of the intervention and would have an effect in the same direction as the intervention.* Such an event is unlikely with groups as comparable as those Ballart and Riba used. But with less comparable groups the probability of local history increases.

The untreated control series also allows tests of the other threats to internal validity that operate on the single time series. In the Ballart and Riba case, for example, the measurement instrument was the same between the treatment and control groups and before and after the law went into effect. Each group seemed to be changing at similar rates before the intervention (i.e., maturation). The intervention did not occur right after a particularly extreme observation, so statistical regression seems implausible. However, because the control group time series was formed nonrandomly, selection bias is a potential problem, though not often plausible. In the Ballart and Riba case, for example, perhaps the motorcycle riders most concerned with safety tended to ride large cycles until the law was passed because the law

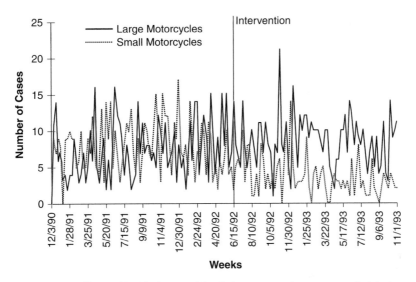

FIGURE 6.4 The effects of legislation requiring helmets on serious motorcycle injuries

From "Impact of legislation requiring moped and motorbike riders to wear helmets," by X. Ballart and C. Riba, 1995, *Evaluation and Program Planning, 18,* pp. 311–320. Copyright 1995 by Elsevier Science Ltd.

forced them to wear helmets. Then, when the law for smaller cycles changed, they felt free to go to such cycles. But it is possible that these safety-conscious individuals could have chosen to wear a helmet prior to the law about small cycles. We could add a corollary—perhaps that they would have been reluctant to wear helmets earlier because of peer pressure from other small cycle riders. How plausible this convoluted selection threat is for the Barcelona circumstance we cannot say.

Another interrupted time series (using 111 observations) with a control (Figure 6.5) shows the effects of a 1985 change in Iowa liquor laws on wine sales (Mulford, Ledolter, & Fitzgerald, 1992). On July 1, 1985, Iowa ended its public monopoly on liquor sales. Prior to then, only about 200 state-owned stores could sell liquor. After then, private sector liquor stores were licensed, and about 1,200 such private stores were rapidly established. Some people feared that increased availability of alcohol would lead to increased alcohol consumption with negative effects. Indeed, an early time-series analysis examined alcohol sales for 2.5 years after the law took effect (until December 1987) and found that wine consumption increased by 93% (Wagenaar & Holder, 1991). Mulford et al. (1992) investigated this matter further by adding a control series and extending the data to 1990. Figure 6.5 presents their data from 1981 through early 1990, nearly 5 years after the law took effect. As a control, they used national wine sales data for the same years. The Iowa wine sales time series shows an increase in wine sales when the law took effect. In fact, consistent with Wagenaar and Holder (1991), the increase persisted until early 1988, 6 months after Wagenaar and Holder stopped their data collection. After that time, Iowa wine sales returned to their preintervention levels. Mulford et al. (1992) were able to show that the sales

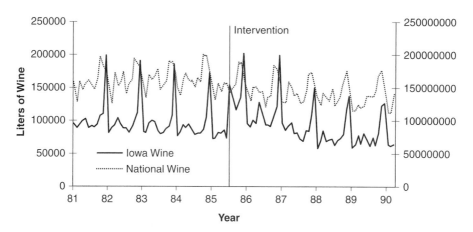

FIGURE 6.5 The effects of legislation in Iowa allowing private sector liquor stores on wine sales, using national data as a control

From "Alcohol Availability and Consumption: Iowa Sales Data Revisited," by H. A. Mulford, J. Ledolter, and J. L. Fitzgerald, 1992, *Journal of Studies on Alcohol, 53*, pp. 487–494. Copyright 1992 by Alcohol Research Documentation, Inc., Rutgers Center of Alcohol Studies, Piscataway NJ 08855.

increase was temporary and due partly to the 1,200 new liquor stores stocking their shelves rather than to increased consumption by retail consumers. Once these new stores fully stocked their shelves, sales returned to normal. A lesson from this example is that a long-duration time series may be needed to detect the temporal persistence of an effect. The addition of the national control in the Mulford et al. (1992) data helped to rule out history as an alternative explanation and made it easier to assess the temporal persistence of treatment effects.

Adding Nonequivalent Dependent Variables

The plausibility of many threats to internal validity in time series can be examined and the construct validity of the effect enhanced by collecting time-series data for a dependent variable that a treatment should affect and for a nonequivalent dependent variable that the treatment should not affect but that would respond in the same way as the primary dependent variable to a pertinent validity threat. The two dependent variables must be conceptually related. The design is diagrammed as:

$$O_{A1} \quad O_{A2} \quad O_{A3} \quad O_{A4} \quad O_{A5} \ X \ O_{A6} \quad O_{A7} \quad O_{A8} \quad O_{A9} \quad O_{A10}$$

$$O_{B1} \quad O_{B2} \quad O_{B3} \quad O_{B4} \quad O_{B5} \ X \ O_{B6} \quad O_{B7} \quad O_{B8} \quad O_{B9} \quad O_{B10}$$

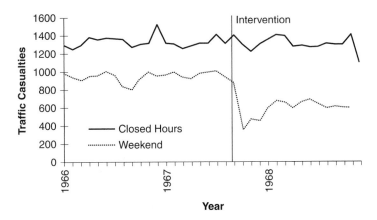

FIGURE 6.6 The effects of the British Breathalyzer crackdown on traffic casualties during weekend nights when pubs are open, compared with times when pubs were closed

From "Determining the social effects of a legal reform: The British 'breathalyser' crackdown of 1967," by H. L. Ross, D. T. Campbell, and G. V. Glass, 1970, *American Behavioral Scientist, 13,* pp. 493–509. Copyright 1970 by Sage Publications.

In this diagram, the A observation series represents the dependent variable of interest, and the B observation series represents the nonequivalent dependent variable.

McSweeny (1978) used a nonequivalent dependent variable in the Cincinnati directory assistance example, though it is not graphed in Figure 6.1. The new directory assistance charge was for local directory assistance, not long-distance directory assistance. If the effect were the result of the charge, only local calls should change; if the effect were the result of some other history event affecting all kinds of directory assistance calls, then long-distance directory assistance calls should change as well and at the same time that the local directory assistance time series changed. McSweeny plotted both time series and found that only local directory assistance calls changed; long-distance calls were unchanged.

Another example of this design comes from a study of the effectiveness of the British Breathalyzer crackdown (Ross, Campbell, & Glass, 1970; Figure 6.6). This time series has only 35 observations, but its effects are dramatic. The Breathalyzer was used to curb drunken driving and hence reduce serious traffic accidents. Under British drinking laws at that time, pubs could be open only during a limited time of day. If a large proportion of traffic casualties are due to drinking that takes place in pubs rather than at home, the Breathalyzer should decrease serious traffic accidents during the daytime hours or during weekend nights, when drinking was heaviest at pubs, and accidents should be less affected during commuting hours, when pubs were closed. Indeed, Figure 6.6 shows a marked drop in the accident rate on weekends (the outcome of interest) at the time of the intervention but little or no drop when pubs were closed (the nonequivalent dependent variable). Statistical analysis corroborated this decrease.

The distinction between accidents that occurred when pubs were either open or closed is important because most history threats to a decrease in serious accidents should affect *all* serious accidents *irrespective of the time of day*. This would be true for weather changes, the introduction of safer cars, a police crackdown on speeding, contemporaneous newspaper reports of high accident rates or particularly gory accidents, and so forth. So it is harder to find fault with either the internal or statistical conclusion validity of these data.

However, questions can be raised about external validity. For example, would the same results be obtained in the United States? Another concerns whether the effects are stronger with some kinds of drivers than with others. Another relates to possible unanticipated side effects of the Breathalyzer. How did it affect accident insurance rates, sales of liquor, public confidence in the role of technological innovations for solving social problems, the sale of technical gadgetry to the police, or the way the courts handled drunken driving cases? Such issues are examined by Ross (1973). Figure 6.6 reveals that some of the initial decrease in serious accidents on weekends is lost over time. The accident rate drops at first but then drifts part of the way back up toward the level in the control time series. Thus the effect is really only a *temporary and partial* reduction in serious accidents.

Ross also noted that the Breathalyzer was introduced with much nationwide publicity. Did the publicity make the public more aware of the desirability of not driving after drinking? Or did it make the police more vigilant in controlling the speed of traffic, especially during and immediately after pub hours? Did it reduce the overall number of hours driven? Did it cut down on drinking? Did it make drunken drivers drive more carefully? Ross very ingeniously ruled out some of these explanations. He took the regular surveys of miles driven done by the British Road Research Laboratory and showed that the introduction of the Breathalyzer was still associated with a decrease in accidents when the estimate of accidents per mile driven was used. This makes it less plausible to say that the Breathalyzer's effect is due to a reduction in the number of miles driven. Ross examined the sale of beer and spirits before and after the introduction of the Breathalyzer and found no evidence of a discontinuity in sales when the Breathalyzer was introduced, ruling out the interpretation that the Breathalyzer had reduced all drinking. He was able to show, for 10 months after the Breathalyzer was introduced, that more persons reported walking home after drinking than had been the case in the 10 months preceding the use of the Breathalyzer. Finally, he showed that fewer post-Breathalyzer traffic fatalities had high alcohol levels in their blood than had the corpses of pre-Breathalyzer fatalities. These analyses suggest that the explanation was a reduction in the number of heavy drinkers who drove, rather than a significant reduction in either aggregate drinking or driving. Ross's use of data to rule out alternative explanations of the causal construct highlights the importance of doing this, the difficulty and expense sometimes encountered in doing so, and the number of irrelevancies associated with the introduction of new practices into society.

Finally, Ross was faced with the problem of explaining why the effects of the Breathalyzer were not more permanent. His analysis suggested that the British

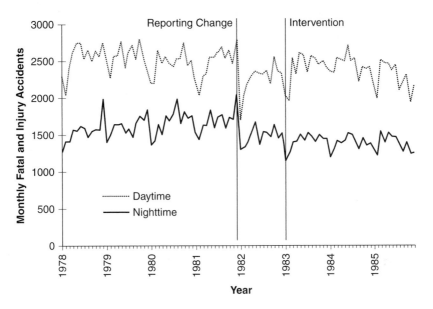

FIGURE 6.7 The effects of drunk driving legislation preceded by a change in accident reporting practices

From "The impact of drunk driving legislation in Louisiana," by M. W. Neustrom and W. M. Norton, 1993, *Journal of Safety Research*, *24*, pp. 107–121. Copyright 1993 by Elsevier Science.

courts increasingly failed to punish drinkers detected by the Breathalyzer so that it lost its deterrent power. Thus Ross's final inference took a highly useful form: A Breathalyzer will help reduce serious traffic accidents when it is used to restrict drunken driving, but it will have this effect only if the courts enforce the law about drinking and driving.

Neustrom and Norton (1993) provide a related time series with 96 observations (Figure 6.7) on the effects of drunk-driving legislation introduced in Louisiana in 1983. Neustrom and Norton (1993) hypothesized that the effects of this legislation would be stronger at night than in the day because past research had shown that alcohol-related accidents are more serious and frequent at night. Problematically, however, a temporary shortage of police resources had occurred earlier and had ended at the same time the drunk-driving law took effect. This event might have resulted in more police officers writing up more of the very accident reports that the new law was meant to decrease, thus setting up two countervailing forces that might cancel each other out. As Figure 6.7 shows, the control series helped clarify the effects of this confound. In the daytime accident time series, accident reports rose after the new law passed, but the nighttime series dropped very slightly. Taking into account the increase in accident reports caused by the end of the personnel shortage, Neustrom and Norton (1993) estimated that the new law caused a reduction of 312 accidents in the nighttime series and a reduction of 124 accidents in the daytime series. So the effects of a reporting change can sometimes be estimated if its onset is known and if the design has a nonequivalent dependent variable—in this case, day versus night, where the effect is expected to be stronger at night.

Removing the Treatment at a Known Time

The influence of treatment can sometimes be demonstrated by showing not only that the effect occurs with the treatment but also that it stops when treatment is removed. The removed-treatment design is diagrammed here, with X indicating the treatment and $\cancel{X}$ its removal.

$$O_1 \quad O_2 \quad O_3 \quad O_4 \; X \; O_5 \quad O_6 \quad O_7 \quad O_8 \quad O_9 \; \cancel{X} \; O_{10} \quad O_{11} \quad O_{12} \quad O_{13}$$

The design is akin to having two consecutive simple interrupted time series. The first, from O_1 to O_9 here, assesses the effects of adding treatment; and the second, from O_5 to O_{13}, tests the effects of removing an existing treatment. The most interpretable pattern of effects occurs if the intercept or slope changes in one direction between O_4 and O_5 and then changes in the opposite direction between O_9 and O_{10}.

Figure 6.8 shows an example with 36 observations by Reding and Raphelson (1995). In October 1989, a psychiatrist was added to a mobile crisis intervention team to provide immediate, on-the-spot psychiatric treatment in hopes of preventing subsequent state hospital admissions. This effect occurred. Six months later, several factors led to the termination of the psychiatrist's services, which led to a rebound in state hospital admissions. Although not pictured in Figure 6.8, the authors strengthened their causal inference even further by comparing these results with data on admissions to a local private psychiatric hospital at the same time, which showed no changes in admissions. Here three design features facilitated causal inference: the interrupted time series, the treatment removal, and the control private hospitals.

The treatment removal adds many strengths to a time-series design. One is that the threat of history is reduced because the only relevant historical threats are either those that operate in different directions at different times or those that involve two different historical forces operating in different directions at different times that happen to coincide with the treatment introduction and removal. Selection and attrition are less of a threat unless different kinds of people enter or leave at different time points. Instrumentation is less likely, though problems can be created by a ceiling effect or floor effect, that is, by participants reaching either the lowest or highest possible score on the scale so that further changes in that di-

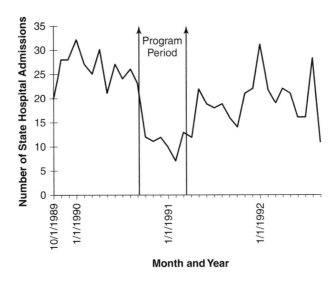

FIGURE 6.8 The effects of psychiatric crisis intervention on hospitalization

From "Around-the-clock mobile psychiatric crisis intervention: Another effective alternative to psychiatric hospitalization," by G. R. Reding and M. Raphelson, 1995, *Community Mental Health Journal, 31*, pp. 179–187. Copyright 1995 by Kluwer Academic Publishers.

rection are not possible, if the ceiling or floor is reached at the same point at which the treatment was removed. Other instrumentation effects may be implausible, insofar as the same instrumentation effect would have to account for both an increase and a decrease at different times.

The private hospital control series helped rule out history, the possibility that another event affected hospital admissions in general; and it helped rule out maturational trends such as cyclical patterns of admission to hospitals as the seasons change. The former threat is easily assessed using qualitative interviews with knowledgeable informants such as hospital directors. The latter threat is more plausible, as it is well known that some patients arrange to have themselves discharged from hospitals in cold climates during winter months, only to return during the summer to the cooler northerly climes.

Given this design and the effects in opposite directions at X and $\bar{X}$, it is sometimes plausible to argue that the disappearance of the original effect is not due to removing the treatment but is due instead to resentful demoralization at having the treatment removed. In the Reding and Raphelson (1995) case, the higher level of hospital admission after the psychiatrist was removed from the team might have been due to demoralization among remaining team members that such a successful intervention was discontinued. If so, then removed-treatment designs are probably more interpretable the less conspicuous treatment is to participants. However, such demoralization would not threaten the effect of introducing the treatment. When the removed-treatment design produces results in different directions, one usually needs two *different* alternative interpretations to invalidate a causal inference. Finally, the withdrawal design works well only if it is ethical to remove treatment and when the effects of treatment are temporary and end when treatment is removed. These conditions eliminate the design from consideration in the many cases in which treatment effects are presumed to last long.

Adding Multiple Replications

This is an extension of the previous design in which it is possible to introduce a treatment, remove it, reintroduce it, remove it again, and so on, according to a planned schedule. This design is diagrammed as:

$$O_1 \quad O_2 X O_3 \quad O_4 \bar{X} O_5 \quad O_6 X O_7 \quad O_8 \bar{X} O_9 \quad O_{10} X O_{11} \quad O_{12} \bar{X} O_{13} \quad O_{14}$$

A treatment effect is suggested if the dependent variable responds similarly each time the treatment is introduced and removed, with the direction of responses being different for the introductions compared with the removals. The design has often been used to assess the effects of psychological (Marascuilo & Busk, 1988; Wampold & Worsham, 1986) or medical (Weiss et al., 1980) treatments with individual patients. For example, McLeod, Taylor, Cohen, and Cullen (1986) compared the effects of a drug treatment with those of a placebo for a patient with inflammation of her continent ileostomy reservoir. Drug and placebo were assigned randomly (and with double-blind, although blinding is frequently difficult with this design) to 10 treatment periods of 14 days each (although data were gathered daily, they are only available aggregated to the 10 treatment periods). The patient reported outcomes on well-being, nausea, abdominal pain, abdominal gas, stool volume, watery stool, and foul odor. Figure 6.9 shows results for well-being and pain, both suggesting that treatment was effective because well-being increased and nausea decreased with treatment, though the effects were far stronger for pain than for well-being.

An issue with this design is the scheduling of treatment and removal. Although scheduling is usually done systematically or in response to the state of patient symptoms (Barlow & Hersen, 1984), many advantages ensue from random scheduling of treatment, though perhaps in a way that preserves an alternation of X and $\bar{X}$ (Edgington, 1987, 1992). Random scheduling rules out the threat of cyclical maturation, the possibility that the series would have exhibited a regular cycle of ups and downs even in the absence of a treatment. Other modifications increase the range of this design's application. For example, it can be used to compare two different treatments of theoretical interest, with X_1 being substituted for X and X_2

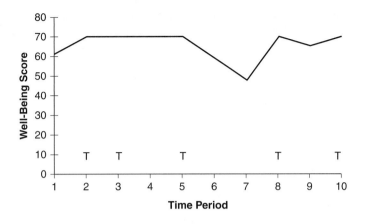

T = Treatment Time Period

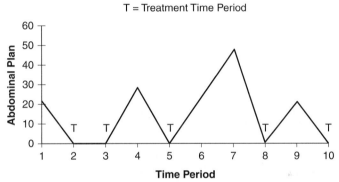

FIGURE 6.9 The effects of treatment for inflammation of continent ileostomy. In the graphs, the letter *T* indicates the time period during which treatment occurred

From "Single patient randomized clinical trial: Its use in determining optimal treatment for patient with inflammation of a Kock continent ileostomy reservoir," by R. S. McLeod et al., 1986, *Lancet, 1*, pp. 726–728. Copyright 1986 by The Lancet Publishing Group.

for $\overline{X}$. It is also possible to use a joint treatment factor $(X_1 + X_2)$, as O'Leary, Becker, Evans, and Saudargas (1969) did in examining how the disruptive behavior of seven children in a classroom responded to first giving rules, then adding educational structure plus rules, then using rules, structure, and praise for good behavior or ignoring bad behavior, and then adding a token economy to all this. Then, to demonstrate control over the total phenomena, all treatments were removed and reinstated. In another design variation, the treatment can be implemented at different (usually increasing) strengths to examine a dose-response relationship; for example, Hartmann and Hall (1976) examined the effects of increasingly high penalties for an increase in the number of cigarettes smoked each day.

The major limitations of this design are practical. First, as with the removed-treatment design, it can be implemented only when the effect of the treatment is expected to dissipate rapidly. Also, the design normally requires a degree of experimental control that can rarely be achieved outside of laboratory settings, certain **single-case design** treatment contexts, or enclosed institutional settings such as schools and prisons. When the design is feasible, however, Barlow and Hersen (1984) provide a thorough discussion of various design options.

Adding Switching Replications

Imagine two (or more) nonequivalent groups, each receiving treatment at different times and in an alternating sequence such that (1) when one group receives the treatment, the other serves as a control, and (2) when the control group later receives the treatment, the original treatment group then serves as a continued-treatment control. The design can be diagrammed as:

$$O_1 \quad O_2 \quad O_3 \; X \; O_4 \quad O_5 \quad O_6 \quad O_7 \quad O_8 \quad O_9 \quad O_{10} \quad O_{11}$$

$$O_1 \quad O_2 \quad O_3 \quad O_4 \quad O_5 \quad O_6 \quad O_7 \quad O_8 \; X \; O_9 \quad O_{10} \quad O_{11}$$

The design controls most threats to internal validity, and it enhances external and construct validity. External validity is enhanced because an effect can be demonstrated with two populations at two different moments in history, sometimes in two settings. There may be different irrelevancies associated with the application of each treatment and, if measures are unobtrusive, there need be no fear of the treatment's interacting with testing.

An example is presented in Figure 6.10, which plots annual crime rates (logged and standardized) in 34 cities in which television was introduced in 1951 and in 34 other cities in which television was introduced in 1955 (Hennigan et al., 1982; Mc-Cleary, 2000), the gap being due to an FAA freeze on television licenses between 1951 and 1955. In both series, the introduction of television led to an increase in property crimes in the subsequent year. This replication of the effect at two time points 5 years apart makes history implausible. For example, the Korean War began in 1951, and the exodus of men to the army may have left more unguarded homes that were then robbed; but this could not explain why the effect occurred only in the earlier cities, for the war should also have caused the same effect in the later cities. Similarly, a recession that began around 1955 may have caused an increase in crime, but again this should have affected both series. Regression artifacts could possibly explain the increase in earlier cities, but that hardly seems likely for the later cities. More generally, it is hard for any single threat to explain both in-

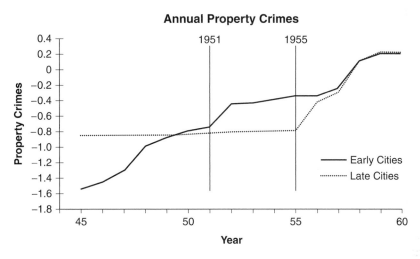

FIGURE 6.10 The effects of the introduction of television on property crime rates in cities in which television was introduced in 1951 versus 1955

From "The evolution of the time series experiment," by R. D. McCleary, 2000, *Research design: Donald Campbell's legacy, Vol. 2,* edited by L. Bickman, Thousand Oaks, CA: Sage. Copyright 2000 by Sage Publications.

creases. Threats such as selection-history or selection-instrumentation are possible alternative explanations—for example, if a critic can find two different historical events, one that occurred in most of the earlier cities (but not the later ones) and one that occurred in most of the later cities (but not the earlier ones), both of which could increase crime. But this possibility, too, seems implausible.

Another example is given in Figure 6.11, from a study of newborns who were screened for phenylketonuria (PKU) to prevent later mental retardation (Mac-Cready, 1974). This time series has 17 observations, the first 4 of which are aggregations of separate 3-year periods. PKU screening was introduced as a standard practice at birth into different U.S. states and Canadian provinces in different years—1962, 1963, 1964, and 1965—facilitating the replication feature of the design. The dependent variable was the number of annual admissions to state or provincial institutions with a diagnosis of retardation due to PKU. Figure 6.11 shows that such admissions dropped to zero and remained at zero the year after screening was implemented in each of the four time series. These results corroborated the hypothesis using archival measures, widely dispersed populations, different historical moments for introducing the treatment, different irrelevancies associated with how the treatment was introduced, and repeated measures to ascertain if an initial effect can be generalized over time.

But even the replicated time-series design can have problems of internal validity. Both the results in Figure 6.11 and anecdotal evidence suggest that some PKU screening occurred before it was officially introduced into some of the states or provinces. Medical professionals learned of the benefits of screening through

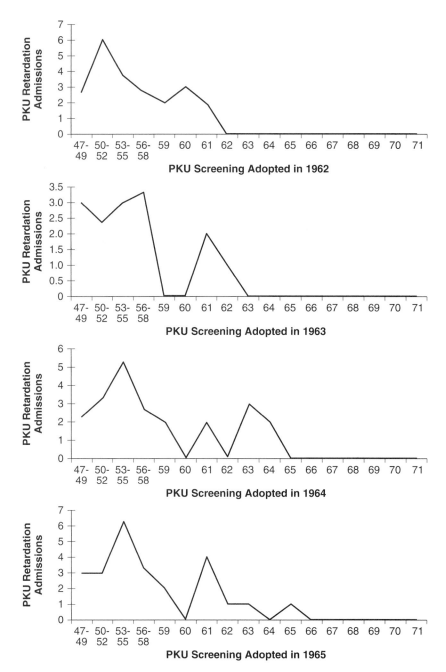

FIGURE 6.11 The effects of screening for phenylketonuria (PKU) on admissions for retardation due to PKU, with the implementation of screening staggered over 4 years in different locales

From "Admissions of phenylketonuric patients to residential institutions before and after screening programs of the newborn infant," by R. A. MacCready, 1974, *Journal of Pediatrics, 85,* pp. 383–385. Copyright 1974 by The National Medical Society.

journal articles, contact with newly trained physicians, and word of mouth at conferences and in discussions with colleagues. So a general trend toward reduced PKU admissions is observed even before the year in which screening was officially implemented—although admissions almost never dropped to zero before implementation. Perhaps such retardation was decreasing as mothers received better prenatal care, better nutrition, and better medical services at and right after birth. To investigate this possibility, MacCready (1974) gathered information on retardation from all causes from the 1950s through 1972 and reported finding no systematic upward or downward trend that could explain even part of the change in PKU admissions observed in Figure 6.11. Using nonequivalent dependent variables in this way renders this alternative explanation less plausible.

The switching-replications design can also help detect effects that have an unpredictable delay period. Assuming an equal delay of effect in each group, we would expect a discontinuity at an earlier date in one series than in the other. We would also expect the period between the discontinuities to be equal to the known period that elapsed between the implementations of the treatment with different groups. However, this will not always be plausible; for example, the effects of a treatment may be speeded up as new technologies for administering treatment are developed that make the treatment more effective. Therefore, it is more realistic to look for relative differences in the times at which an apparent treatment effect appears in each group. The switching-replication design is useful for probing delayed causal effects in cases in which there is no strong theory of the length of expected delay. However, it is most interpretable in the case in which the time difference between the groups receiving the treatment exactly matches the time period between effects appearing in each group—as is the case in Figure 6.11.

The replicated time-series design is practical wherever a time-series design with a no-treatment control group is feasible. Successful treatments will usually be of benefit to the groups or organizations that served as no-treatment controls. Representatives of these groups can be approached to see if they will agree to receive that treatment. For example, suppose Hankin et al. (1993; Figure 6.3) had been able to study the introduction of alcohol warning labels on bottled liquor introduced in different countries during different years. The causal inference would have been much clearer given their delayed, small effect.

SOME FREQUENT PROBLEMS WITH INTERRUPTED TIME-SERIES DESIGNS

As the previous examples begin to illustrate, a number of problems frequently arise in conducting interrupted time-series research:

- Many treatments are implemented slowly and diffuse through a population, so that the treatment is better modeled as a gradually diffusing process rather than as occurring all at once.

- Many effects occur with unpredictable time delays that may differ among populations and over time.
- Many data series are much shorter than the 100 observations recommended for statistical analysis.
- Many archivists are difficult to locate or are reluctant to release data.
- Archived data might involve time intervals between each data point that are longer than one needs; some data may be missing or look suspicious; and there may be undocumented definitional shifts.

We discuss all these in more detail below.

Gradual Rather Than Abrupt Interventions

Some interventions begin at a known point in time and quickly diffuse through the relevant population. The Cincinnati directory assistance intervention is an example; the financial charge took effect on a defined day and applied to all directory assistance calls. But other innovations diffuse quite gradually, so that the time span in which other events can occur that might affect the outcome increases, making history a more plausible threat to internal validity.

An example of a gradually implemented treatment is provided by Holder and Wagenaar (1994). They studied the effects on traffic crashes of mandated training for those who serve alcohol that was designed to reduce the intoxication levels and high-risk driving of alcohol drinkers. The State of Oregon introduced the training in December 1986, but not everyone could be trained at once. According to the Oregon Liquor Control Commission, about 20% of all servers were trained by the end of 1987, 40% by the end of 1988, and over 50% by the end of 1989. If the effect appears quickly for those individuals who receive treatment, then the immediate change in intercept should be small, but a gradual increase in slope should be apparent.

Knowledge of the form of the diffusion process is crucial to the analysis in such cases. For example, Holder and Wagenaar (1994) used the proportion of servers trained as their intervention variable rather than a dichotomous (1,0) dummy variable (sometimes called a **step function,** which assumes that all trainers received training on the day the law took effect). Treating a slower diffusion process as if it were a single step function can create serious problems. First, it can capitalize on chance and create false effects if the researchers assign the step function to a point in the time series at which the deviation in the outcome appears visually greatest. Second, one can overlook real but small early effects by assuming that the onset of the intervention (1986 for the Oregon law) occurred at the maximal point for potential impact (which was actually not reached until about 1988, and by then only 50% were trained in what is presumably a job with high turnover). Third, even when researchers carefully model treatment diffusion, they may look for patterns of effects that mirror that diffusion. However, to expect such patterns is often naïve, because causal thresholds can make the manifestation of an effect dependent on reaching a certain level of the treatment. Holder and Wagenaar (1994) speculated that training only one server in a bar that employs many servers may not be very effective (for example, if the other servers exert peer pressure to continue serving as usual), so a majority of servers must be trained to have the effect. Without knowledge of the exact rate and form of diffusion, often the best one can do is to look for delayed effects sometime after the onset of the treatment. The difficulty is ruling out the historical effects that could operate between treatment onset and a change in the time series—for example, changes in enforcement of drunk-driving laws.

In this connection, it is worth considering why the Breathalyzer data (Figure 6.6) were so clear-cut. If a new law is not well publicized or is poorly enforced, we might expect only a gradual buildup in public reaction to it and would not expect the visually dramatic decrease in traffic accidents displayed in the Breathalyzer example. Fortunately, we know from background data that the British Breathalyzer was widely publicized, as was the date at which the police would begin to use it. This probably speeded up the usual process of informing the public about the use of the Breathalyzer and also contributed to policemen using it at frequent intervals right after its implementation date. Under these conditions the actual diffusion process better approximates a step function.

Delayed Causation

Not all effects are instantaneous. Delayed causation can occur even when a treatment is abruptly implemented, as with the delayed effects of smoking on lung cancer. The cancer does not develop until decades after regular smoking has begun. Even more delay may occur if the treatment implementation is diffuse. For example, Figure 6.3 shows a delayed impact due to the time it took for newly manufactured liquor bottles with warning labels to make their way to retail shelves and into consumer homes. There is little problem with delayed causation when strong background theory permits us to predict a specific lag, such as the 9-month lag between human conception and birth that helps predict the point at which alcohol warning labels could first affect births. Many times, however, no such theory exists, so the interpretation of a delayed effect is obscured by historical events between treatment onset and the possible delayed effect. In such cases, a switching-replications design permits the researcher to examine whether the replications show similar delay intervals between the treatment onset and the manifestation of an effect, reducing the threat of history. However, this procedure assumes that the treatment does not interact either with the different kinds of units that receive the treatment at different times or with the different historical moments at which each group experiences the treatment. For example, chronic inebriates may respond to a drunk-driving program more slowly than social drinkers; or media publicity given to an accident related to driving while intoxicated (DWI) in one city may heighten the effects of a new DWI law compared with some other city in which the law was implemented without such publicity. Should there be such interactions, the delay between treatment onset and effect manifestation may differ over groups.

When delayed effects occur along with slow diffusion of treatments (as in Figure 6.3), causal inference is particularly difficult. This is true because no knowledge exists as to where to place the onset of the expected or desired effect, and effects might be expected at any point after treatment is implemented. The longer the time after implementation, the more plausible it is to interpret a possible delayed treatment effect in terms of historical factors. In these cases, the addition of control groups, nonequivalent dependent variables, removed treatments, or switching replications are all invaluable aids to inference.

Short Time Series

Textbooks dealing with the statistical analysis of time-series data suggest different rules of thumb for the number of time points required for a competent analysis. Most suggest making about 100 observations in order to model trends, seasonality, and the structure of the correlated error in the series before testing for an intervention impact. In Figure 6.4, for example, it is extremely difficult to tell from visual inspection whether trend or seasonality patterns exist. Visual inspection is sometimes more profitable if the data are graphed after aggregating them over time intervals. For example, when the data in Figure 6.4 are aggregated at the quarterly rather than the weekly level, seasonality patterns are not observed, though there does appear to be the hypothesized steadily decreasing trend in the small-motorcycle series. However, aggregation shortens the time series, which reduces the ability to model other aspects of the data. So large numbers of data points are preferable, all other things being equal.

Situations frequently arise, however, in which many more observations are available than just a single pretest and posttest, but the number is not close to 100 observations. Such short time series can still be useful for causal inference even if statistical analysis by standard methods is inadvisable. There are four principal reasons for this usefulness. First, the addition of the extra pretests will help address some threats to internal validity compared with designs with just one or two pretests. Second, the extra posttest observations help specify the delay and the degree of persistence of the causal impact. Third, the use of control groups or control time series is often feasible and can greatly strengthen inferences in the short series. Fourth, some analyses of short series are possible, for example, making assumptions about the error structure rather than describing it directly. Economists do this regularly (Greene, 1999; Hsiao, 1986; Hsiao, Lahiri, Lee, & Pesaran, 1999).

The Usefulness of Multiple Pretests and Posttests

Some advantages of a short interrupted time series are apparent in Figure 6.12, which shows how attendance in a job training program during 1964 affected sub-

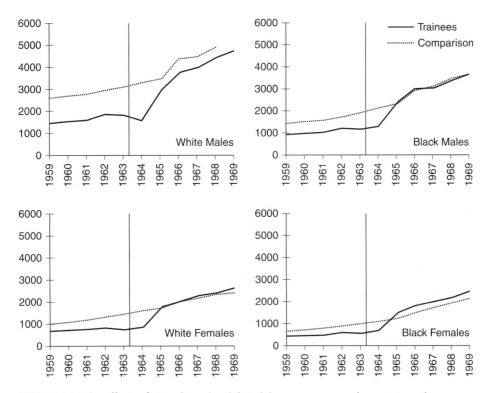

FIGURE 6.12 The effects of attendance in a job training program on subsequent earnings

From "Estimating the effects of training programs on earnings," by O. Ashenfelter, 1978, *Review of Economics and Statistics, 60*, pp. 47–57. Copyright 1978 by The MIT Press.

sequent earnings for groups of males and females who are Black or White (Ashenfelter, 1978). The treatment group comprised all those who began classroom training under the Manpower Development and Training Act in the first 3 months of 1964, a group that Ashenfelter noted were most likely to be successful. The control sample was constructed from the 0.1% Continuous Work History Sample of the Department of Labor, a random sample of earnings records on American workers. The outcome was earnings at eleven time points for each of the four groups.

Being in the work force, the controls had higher initial incomes (income data were taken from Social Security records). Figure 6.12 suggests a prompt causal impact in all four groups. Imagine now that only the 1963 and 1965 data had been available, the first full years before and after the program. An increase in earnings would still be suggested, but such a causal inference would be threatened by a number of alternative explanations. One is selection-maturation, the possibility that the training group was increasing its earnings faster than the control group but beginning at a lower starting point than the control group, even before 1963.

With the short pretest series, one can directly examine the plausibility of group differences in maturation.

Consider next the threat of regression. The persons eligible for job training programs in 1964 were those who were out of work in 1963. This fact could have depressed estimates of 1963 earnings for trainees relative to prior years if they had previously been employed and earning at the same level as the control group prior to 1963. If they were, and if their unemployment was just temporary, then the training group may have increased their posttreatment earnings in any case. Having 1963 as the sole pretest point does not allow us to estimate the plausibility of such regression, but having a few years of prior data does. In this case, regression may have added to the effect of training because a small decrease in earnings did occur in the treatment group between 1962 and 1963. But regression cannot account for all of the treatment effect because the average pretest earnings of the treatment group were much lower than those of the control group for many years, not just in 1963.

Without the later posttest years in Figure 6.12, one would not have been able to ascertain whether the effect of training was of any significant duration or quickly dissipated. Without the pretest series one might wonder, from consideration of only the years 1962 through 1965, whether the apparent change in earnings from 1962 to 1965 merely reflects a 4-year economic cycle within a general upward trend. The years from 1959 to 1962 help rule out this possibility, for they show no cyclical patterns. So the addition of multiple pretests and posttests greatly aids interpretation of quasi-experiments even when a full time series cannot be done (H. Bloom, 1984b, reanalyzed these data).

Strengthening Short Series with Design Features

The interpretability of short time series is enhanced by adding any of the design features discussed in this or previous chapters (e.g., Table 5.2), such as control groups, nonequivalent dependent variables, switching replications, treatment removals, and multiple replications (e.g., Barlow & Hersen, 1984; R. Franklin, Allison, & Gorman, 1997; Kratochwill & Levin, 1992; Sidman, 1960). For example, McKillip (1992) assessed the effects of a 1989 media campaign to reduce alcohol use during a student festival on a university campus. His primary dependent variable was a short time series (10 observations) on awareness of alcohol abuse in the targeted population. To strengthen inference in this short series, McKillip added two nonequivalent dependent variables (he calls them control constructs, to highlight their similarity to control groups) that were conceptually related to health and so would have shown changes if effects were due to general improvements in attitudes toward health. But these two variables (good nutrition, stress reduction) were not specifically targeted by the campaign, and so they should not have changed if the effect was due to the treatment. As Figure 6.13 shows, awareness of alcohol abuse clearly increased during the campaign, but

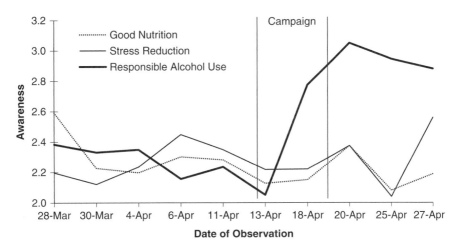

FIGURE 6.13 The effects of a media program to increase awareness of alcohol abuse

From "Research without control groups: A control construct design," by J. McKillip, 1992, *Methodological issues in applied psychology,* edited by F. B. Bryant, J. Edwards, R. S. Tindale, E. J. Posavac, L. Heath, & E. Henderson, New York: Plenum. Copyright 1992 by Plenum Press.

awareness of other health-related issues did not (see Fischer, 1994, for several similar applications that yielded more ambiguous results).

McClannahan, McGee, MacDuff, and Krantz (1990) added a switching-replications feature to their short time series (21 observations) that assessed the effects of providing regular feedback to married couples who supervised group homes for autistic children about the daily personal hygiene and appearance of the children in their home. The feedback was introduced after Session 6 in Home 1, Session 11 in Home 2, and Session 16 in Home 3. After each introduction, the personal appearance of the children in that home increased above baseline, and that improvement was maintained over time (Figure 6.14). However, both these examples illustrate a disadvantage of short time series, the difficulty in knowing how long the effect will last. Figure 6.13 shows this most clearly, with the beginnings of an apparent decrease in alcohol abuse awareness already apparent after the 2-week intervention.

Analysis of Short Time Series

When dealing with short time series, many researchers fail to do any data analysis. Some believe that visual analysis is adequate and that effects are not worth finding if they are so small that they require statistics to tease them out. But research suggests that visual inspection is fallible in the face of small or delayed effects (e.g., Furlong & Wampold, 1981; Ottenbacher, 1986; Wampold & Furlong,

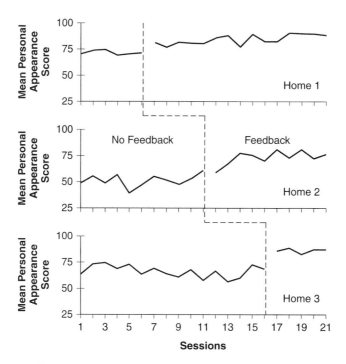

FIGURE 6.14 The effects of a parental intervention on the physical appearance of autistic children in three different homes

From "Assessing and improving child care: A personal appearance index for children with autism," by L. E. McClannahan et al., 1990, *Journal of Applied Behavior Analysis, 23*, 469–482. Copyright 1990 by The Society for the Experimental Analysis of Bahavior.

1981), and the belief that small effects are not important (e.g., Barlow & Hersen, 1984, p. 282) needs reconsideration given past demonstrations of important small effects (e.g., Rosenthal, 1994). Others have reviewed various analytic options but with mixed opinions about their worth (e.g., Franklin, Allison, & Gorman, 1997; B. Gorman & Allison, 1997; Matyas & Greenwood, 1997). Potentially accurate nonparametric options include randomization (exact) tests (Edgington, 1992; Gorman & Allison, 1997; Koehler & Levin, 1998) and bootstrapping methods (Efron & Tibshirani, 1993), although both often have low power for shorter time series. K. Jones (1991) and Crosbie (1993) suggest parametric alternatives, but critics point to significant problems with them (Reichardt, 1991). If the same people are measured over time, various kinds of repeated-measures ANOVAs can sometimes be used, as can growth curve models or event history analysis (e.g., Carbonari, Wirtz, Muenz, & Stout, 1994). Economists work with short time series by making assumptions about the error structure of the data to correct standard error estimates (Greene, 1999; Hsiao, 1986, 1999). If a short time series can be gathered on many individual units, then pooling time series can sometimes be useful (Sayrs, 1989; West & Hepworth, 1991). Perhaps the best advice is to apply several statistical methods to short time series (see Allison & Gorman, 1997, for a summary of the options). If results of diverse analyses converge and are consistent with visual inspection, confidence in the findings may be warranted.

However, facilitating visual analysis of time-series data is important. Good visual presentation uses the power of graphics to engage the reader. The study of graphical techniques has become a specialty in itself (e.g., Tufte, 1983, 1990), and an increasingly diverse array of graphical techniques is being made more accessible by computer. Both data analysis and visual analysis are important to time series, as is knowing the limitations of each.

Limitations of Much Archival Data

Much time-series data come from archives kept by public and private institutions. However, guides to archives are often difficult to obtain. Gaining access to data from the private business sector or from local institutions (e.g., schools and city governments) can be difficult. Frequently, a researcher may be assured that some particular data were available and may travel to the archive, only to find that the data are not on hand. Recent years have seen some improvements in this situation. For example, Kiecolt and Nathan (1990) have described some of the many sophisticated archive services that have been established across the United States. Similarly, a database of over 560 time series is available for sale ("Time Series Database," 1992) that may be useful for some general time-series purposes. Various computerized networks such as the Internet are making time-series data sets more convenient to locate and retrieve.[3]

Just as important is the possibility of construct validity problems in archival data. Because most data that are collected and stored are used for social and economic monitoring, variables that have an "outcome" rather than a "process" flavor are stressed, and direct archival measures of psychological and small-group processes are rare. Consequently, current archives may not be useful for testing causal explanations or psychological constructs.

All archived data need close scrutiny. Operational definitions have to be critically examined, and the construct label applied to a particular measure may not necessarily be a good fit. Inquiries have to be made about shifts in definition over the time a record is kept. When possible, the nature of the shift should be documented, and it helps if overlapping data are examined for any periods during which data were collected using both the old and new definitions. Shifts in definition may be suggested as soon as the data are plotted, but it is more convenient

---

3. A comprehensive list of economic and social time series is at *http://www.economagic.com/*, and some United States government time series are at *http://www.fedstats.gov/* and *http://www.census.gov/*.

to document such shifts when they first occur. In many cases, the data for some times will be missing and, if the problem is not too serious, will have to be imputed. If the plotted data show suspicious regularities, as when values remain constant for a section of the series or the increase per time unit is constant, it may be that the data were not properly collected or that someone has interpolated values for the missing observations without documenting that fact. Conversely, the data may vary widely and resist any rescaling to reduce the variability, perhaps as a result of sloppy data collection procedures rather than inherently unstable phenomena.

The major difficulty with archival data is their inflexibility. The time-series analyst prefers data that can be disaggregated into more frequent time intervals, local regions, individual demographics, and fine topical breakdowns (Campbell, 1976). But archives rarely allow this flexibility. Often, the researcher would like weekly, monthly, or quarterly data because they provide longer series than annual data, are more sensitive in detecting immediate causal impacts, and are better fitted for ruling out historically based alternative interpretations. But if the data are collected and stored in annual form, disaggregation into finer time units is not possible. The researcher often wants to disaggregate data by various social variables, including demographic characteristics such as race, class, or gender. Such disaggregation permits examination of how an effect varies over groups to explore external validity or over groups that did or did not receive a treatment, creating a control series. For instance, in studying the effects of the Breathalyzer, it would be useful to break the data down into drinkers versus nondrinkers or into different religious groups that do or do not proscribe drinking. Often, it would aid the researcher if more dependent variables were available, for then he or she might be able to find a nonequivalent dependent variable. In all these cases, however, the researcher usually has to be content with what the archive contains.

We should not be overly pessimistic about the rigidity of archives or the quality of their data. As the examples in this chapter show, interrupted time-series designs that permit confident causal inferences can often be implemented. Moreover, with sufficient ingenuity and perseverance, the researcher may uncover data one would not expect to find in an archive. For example, Cook, Calder, and Wharton (1979) obtained 25-year series covering a wide range of variables that can be classified under the general heading of consumption, leisure, political behavior, workforce participation, local economic structure, public health, and crime. Though some of the data came from federal archives, the majority came from obscure state records that seem to be rarely consulted for research purposes. States differ in the quality of the records they maintain. To cover a substantive area adequately, the researcher may have to collect some variables in one state and others in another. However, a surprising amount of time-series data is available. If recent and future data are of better technical quality than was sometimes the case in the past, we can hope to see increased use of time-series analyses based on all these data sources.

A COMMENT ON CONCOMITANT TIME SERIES

The interrupted time-series designs we have discussed in this chapter differ substantially from another use of time series that is sometimes advocated for causal inference—the concomitant time series. The interrupted time series requires a treatment that is deliberately manipulated and implemented. Sometimes a potential causative agent is not implemented in this way but rather varies in intensity without experimental control over a period of time during which the outcome is also observed to vary. In a concomitant time series, the investigator correlates the time series from the presumed causal variable with a time series on the presumed outcome, both series being measured on the same units over the same time. The researcher then looks at how rises and falls in the causal series are related to rises and falls at later times in the effect series. This gets at the temporal precedence issue so central to conceptions of cause. McCleary and Welsh (1992) cite a previously published example of the correlation of citations to the Rorschach and the Minnesota Multiphasic Personality Inventory (MMPI) personality tests, the hypothesis being that as more clinicians started to use the MMPI, it displaced the Rorschach as the test of choice. The correlations reported by the original authors supported that interpretation, though the original analysis had significant statistical problems such as the failure to take autocorrelation into account or to allow for a time lag by computing lagged correlations.

Crucially, however, the putative cause in a concomitant time series is not manipulated experimentally but rather fluctuates in an uncontrolled manner. It may seem strange, therefore, that such uncontrolled correlations are cited as evidence for causation, given the many well-known reasons why correlation does not prove causation. Some advocates cite the notion of "Granger causality" to justify the approach, relying on the logic of Granger (1969). Specifically, this logic maintains that if the causal relationship is known to be unidirectional at a particular lag period and if the two variables meet an analytic condition for "white noise," then the (appropriately time-lagged) correlation yields an unbiased estimate of the causal relationship. Unfortunately, although the white noise condition can be tested, it is unlikely that the other conditions will be met in practice. The simple unidirectional causation condition is very unlikely in most real world applications (McCleary & Welsh, 1992); Shonkoff and Phillips (2000) note that the problem is commonly called simultaneity bias. Cromwell, Hannan, Labys, and Terraza (1994) conclude, "When we speak of 'Granger causality,' we are really testing if a particular variable precedes another and not causality in the sense of cause and effect" (p. 33; see also Holland, 1986; Menard, 1991; Reichardt, 1991).[4]

---

4. Similar problems exist with other proposed models of inferring causation from uncontrolled observations of the relationships between two variables (e.g., Wampold, 1992).

CONCLUSION

Interrupted time series constitute an important class of designs for gaining causal knowledge when circumstances permit collecting the required data across many time points. They gain their advantage from the pretreatment series that allows many potential threats to be examined, from exact knowledge of the time at which the treatment was made available that partially helps to deal with history, and from the posttreatment data that allow the form of the causal relationship to be described in terms of the speed of onset and the degree of persistence of the effect. We are great fans of interrupted time-series designs and would like to see more of them, whether with data from archives or collected first-hand by researchers themselves. We are fans even when the number of observations is fewer than required for traditional statistical analyses. The principle we endorse is that the more information one has about the temporal aspects of pre- and postintervention performance, the better the resulting study can decrease uncertainty about whether an association is causal.

The same advantage follows from increased knowledge about the intervention under study, including the time of its onset and the form of its diffusion through the population under study. The specificity that comes from knowing precisely at what point an intervention is supposed to influence an outcome is of the greatest utility, especially when the intervention occurs at a specific point along an interval scale with many levels. In the time-series case, time is that scale, and interruptions in the form of the response at the time of the intervention provide diagnostic clues about causation.

In the chapter that follows, many of these principles are seen again in similar form. The design in question, called the regression discontinuity design, also requires knowledge of the onset of the intervention at a point on a continuum (although the continuum is not time but the ordered points on a measured variable used to assign units to conditions), with the effect demonstrated by an abrupt change in the outcome variable at that point. The regression discontinuity design also shares some characteristics in common with the randomized experiment we describe later in this book, so it helps to bridge from the interrupted time series to the randomized experiment.

7

Regression Discontinuity Designs

Dis·con·ti·nu·i·ty (dĭs-kŏn′tə-nōō′ĭ-tē): n., pl. dis·con·ti·nu·i·ties.   1. Lack of
continuity, logical sequence, or cohesion.   2. A break or gap.   3. Geol-
ogy. A surface at which seismic wave velocities change.   4. Mathematics. a. A point at which a function is defined but is not continuous. b. A
point at which a function is undefined.

W HEN PRISON inmates are first released, they often lack a job and other financial resources to help them become productive members of society. Do
some of them return to crime after leaving prison in order to get those resources? Will providing them with funds on their release reduce future offending?
Berk and Rauma (1983; Rauma & Berk, 1987) tried to answer the last question
when the State of California passed legislation giving unemployment compensation
to newly released prisoners, *but only if they had worked more than 652 hours over
the previous 12 months while in prison.* Those who had worked fewer hours were
ineligible. Berk and Rauma found that those receiving unemployment compensation
had a recidivism rate 13% lower than controls. For reasons we demonstrate shortly,
this estimate is statistically unbiased under certain assumptions.

Readers of the previous chapters on quasi-experiments must find it odd that
unbiased causal inference can result from a study with such obvious and massive
selection "problems." After all, released inmates were assigned to treatment or
control based on being different, not the same—one group worked more and the
other less than the 652-hour cutoff. This chapter shows why this design—the regression discontinuity design (RD)—capitalizes on selection but still provides unbiased causal estimates.

Work on the RD design began in 1958 (Campbell, 1984), with the first published example being Thistlewaite and Campbell (1960). Other authors independently reinvented the RD design in medicine and public health (Finkelstein,
Levin, & Robbins, 1996a, 1996b), in economics (Goldberger, 1972a, 1972b), in
education (Tallmadge & Horst, 1976; Tallmadge & Wood, 1978) and in statistics
(Rubin, 1977, 1978). Goldberger (1972a, 1982b), Lord and Novick (1968,
pp. 140–144), and Rubin (1977) provided formal statistical proofs that the design

(or cognates) yields unbiased estimates of treatment effects if its assumptions are met. Accessible summaries of the design are available (Huitema, 1980[1]; Judd & Kenny, 1981a; Marsh, 1998; Mohr, 1988, 1995), especially by Trochim and his colleagues (e.g., Cappelleri, 1991; Trochim, 1984, 1990; Trochim & Cappelleri, 1992).

The RD design was used more than 200 times in evaluations of local programs funded under Title I of the 1965 Elementary and Secondary Education Act (Trochim, 1980). Otherwise, only a score of studies claim to have used the design.[2] This low rate of use presumably results from practical problems that we will explore in this chapter that limit its implementation. Even so, the design can be more widely used than it has been, sometimes replacing better known quasi-experiments that are inferentially weaker, sometimes being added to existing quasi-experiments to improve causal inference, and sometimes being combined with randomized experiments to increase the power and ethics of both. We hope this chapter will elevate the importance of RD and contribute to its more frequent use by clarifying its benefits and the circumstances facilitating its implementation.

THE BASICS OF REGRESSION DISCONTINUITY

Table 7.1 summarizes the basic design and its variations that we feature in this chapter, including linking it to randomized experiments and quasi-experiments. We begin here with a description of the basic RD design.

The Basic Structure

The RD design requires the experimenter to control assignment of participants to two or more treatment conditions with a posttest. The experimenter assigns units to conditions on the basis of a *cutoff score on an assignment variable,* not by coin toss or lottery as in a randomized experiment. The **assignment variable** can be any measure taken prior to treatment, in which the units scoring on one side of the cutoff are assigned to one condition and those on the other side to another. The basic design can be represented as:

---

1. Huitema calls it the biased assignment experiment.

2. See Abadzi, 1984, 1985; Berk & DeLeeuw, 1999; Berk & Rauma, 1983; Braden & Bryant, 1990; Cahan, Linchevski, Ygra, & Danziger, 1996; Cahan & Davis, 1987; Cappelleri & Trochim, 1994; Carter, Winkler, & Biddle, 1987; Cullen et al., 1999; Deluse, 1999; DiRaddo, 1996; Finkelstein et al., 1996b; Havassey, 1988; Klein, 1992; Lipsey, Cordray, & Berger, 1981; Mark & Mellor, 1991; Rauma & Berk, 1987; Robinson, Bradley, & Stanley, 1990; Robinson & Stanley, 1989; A. Ross & Lacey, 1983; Seaver & Quarton, 1976; Stadthaus, 1972; G. Thomas, 1997; Visser & deLeeuw, 1984. It is clear that some of these studies do not meet the full requirements for the design or suffered from severe practical problems in its implementation; but they are included in this list anyway so that they can be examined in more detail by interested scholars.

TABLE 7.1 Summary of Regression Discontinuity Designs

1. *The Basic Design:* Assign participants to treatment or control based on whether they fall above or below a cutoff score.
   - The assignment variable may be any variable measured before treatment, including a pretest on the outcome variable.
   - The assignment variable does not have to be correlated with outcome.
   - The design is most powerful when the cutoff is placed at the mean of the assignment variable.
   - More than one assignment variable can be used.

2. *Variations on the Basic Design*
   - Compare two treatments rather than treatment to control.
   - Compare three conditions with assignment by two cutoffs.
   - Use two cutoffs to form a cutoff interval, with those between the cutoffs getting one condition and those outside the cutoff interval getting the other condition.

3. *Combinations of Regression Discontinuity with Randomization*
   - Use two cutoffs, assigning randomly within the cutoff interval, to treatment above (or below) the interval and to control below (or above) the interval.
   - Use one cutoff, randomly assign on one side of the cutoff, and assign all participants to one condition on the other side.
   - Use multiple cutoff intervals with randomization in some intervals and RD in others.
   - Use multiple cutoff intervals with increasing proportions of participants assigned to treatment over intervals.

4. *Combinations of Regression Discontinuity with Quasi-Experimental Design Features*
   - Use a cutoff interval with RD outside the interval and self-selection within the interval.
   - Use the basic RD design, but at the end of the study give treatment to all the control participants.
   - Add a double pretest to help diagnose functional form in the absence of treatment.
   - Add a cohort control that models the functional form in a cohort that did not receive treatment.

$$
\begin{array}{cccc}
O_A & C & X & O_2 \\
O_A & C & & O_2
\end{array}
$$

where O_A is a preassignment measure of the assignment variable and C indicates that units are assigned to conditions on the basis of a cutoff score. That is, if j is a cutoff score on O_A, then any score greater than or equal to j entails being in one group, and anything less than j entails being in the other. The assignment variable must have at least ordinal measurement characteristics, that is, be monotonically increasing; true nominal variables such as ethnicity are specifically excluded.

Figures 7.1 and 7.2 present two illustrations of a hypothetical RD study. The assignment variable could be a pretest score on a hypothetical outcome, say, a student achievement test or a measure of illness severity. Participants scoring above

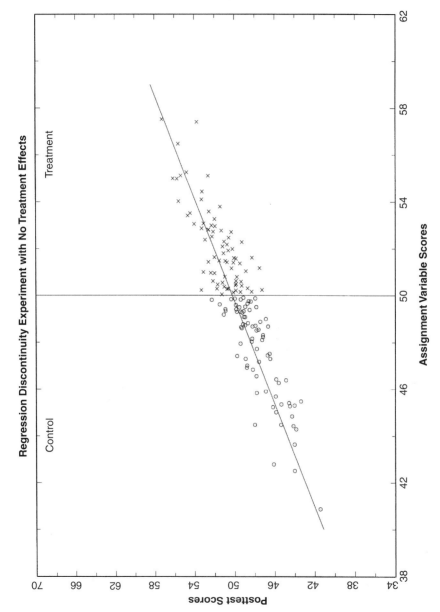

FIGURE 7.1 Regression discontinuity experiment with no treatment effects.

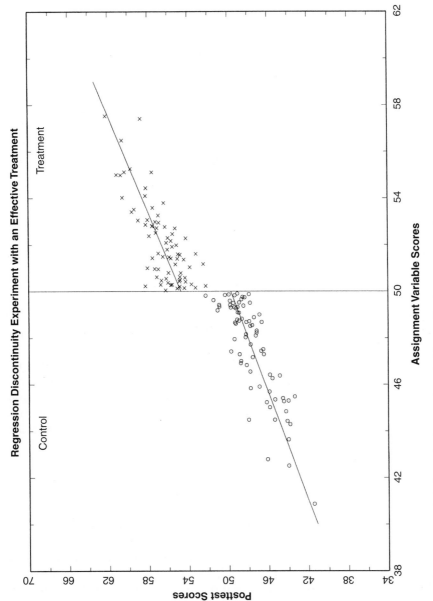

FIGURE 7.2 Regression discontinuity experiment with an effective treatment.

the cutoff, here set at 50,[3] are assigned to a treatment group and the others to a control group. Both figures graph a scatterplot of assignment variable scores against posttest scores. A vertical line at the cutoff score separates treatment from control participants. Otherwise, the figures look like any scatterplot graphing, in this case, a linear, positive relationship between two variables. Figure 7.1 illustrates the results we would expect if a treatment has no effect, and Figure 7.2 shows how the scatterplot would change if a treatment has an effect. The effect size we depict is about 5 units, an amount that has been added to the posttest scores of all treatment participants. The regression line in Figure 7.2 reflects this, showing a vertical displacement (or discontinuity) of about 5 points at the cutoff.

In actual studies, the assignment variable often assesses merit or need. The cutoff score then indicates either those who have done well who have received an award or those with a special need who are eligible for a compensatory service. By virtue of this, RD is useful in cases in which critics object that random assignment will deprive meritorious individuals of earned rewards or less fortunate individuals of needed treatments (Beecher, 1966; Marquis, 1983; Miké, 1989, 1990; Schaffner, 1986; Veatch & Sollitto, 1973), though the cost is that the RD design needs more participants to equal the power of a randomized experiment (Trochim & Cappelleri, 1992; Williams, 1990). As an example of a merit scale being used to define treatment eligibility, admission to a program for gifted and talented youth might be granted to students whose achievement test scores are greater than, say, the 98th percentile. As an example of a need-based eligibility criterion, extra tutoring might be given to students whose initial reading scores fall below the 25th percentile. In both cases, a treatment effect will cause an upward or downward displacement in the regression line relating assignment to outcome—either a change in mean in which outcome scores on one side of the cutoff are increased by the amount of the mean effect or a change in slope in which the regression line is steeper on one side of the cutoff than on the other. This displacement of the mean or slope should occur at exactly the point on the assignment variable at which the cutoff score defines the treatment contrast. It is this point-specific displacement (or discontinuity) of the regression line that gives the design the name **regression discontinuity.**

Examples of Regression Discontinuity Designs

Let us now consider some real examples of the design. In compensatory education, all children in a known pool would typically be pretested on, say, a reading test. Those scoring below the cutoff score would then be given a reading program, and those above it would not. Later, all children would receive a reading test (it need not be the same as the pretest), and the analysis would test for a regression

---

3. The choice of cutoff score will depend on the scale of the assignment variable; the use of 50 in these hypothetical data is arbitrary, reflecting the arbitrary scaling we used in constructing the example.

discontinuity. Trochim (1984) extensively analyzes data from such compensatory education examples in which the assignment variable was pretest reading scores. For example, his analysis of a second-grade compensatory reading program in Providence, Rhode Island, suggested that the program significantly improved children's reading abilities. The major alternative interpretation in this case is chance; Trochim (1984) points out that many other compensatory education programs he tested yielded zero or negative effects.

Mark and Mellor (1991) tested whether events with high personal relevance increase or decrease hindsight bias (a tendency to say an outcome was foreseeable after it is known—"I could have told you that"). The RD design was used because, among union workers in the large manufacturing plants studied, those with 20 years of seniority were not laid off, whereas those with fewer years were. The independent variable was losing employment, the assignment variable was years of seniority with a cutoff of 20 years, and the outcome was a rating of foreseeability. Results (Figure 7.3) showed that those laid off thought their layoffs were *less* foreseeable ("I didn't think I'd be laid off"). Note that Figure 7.3 plots group average responses formed by grouping together respondents within a range of years of seniority. Mark and Mellor did this primarily because their outcome was a 3-point rating scale, which would not have visually displayed the discontinuity as well as the group averages. But their data were analyzed at the individual level.

Another example is a study of how Medicaid affected doctor visits when the program was introduced in 1964 (Figure 7.4; Lohr, 1972; Wilder, 1972). Household income was the assignment variable, the legally specified income eligibility

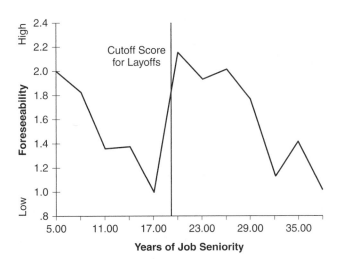

FIGURE 7.3 The effects of being laid off on hindsight bias

From "Effect of self-relevance of an event on hindsight bias: The foreseeability of a layoff," by M. M. Mark and S. Mellor, 1991, *Journal of Applied Psychology, 76,* pp. 569–577. Copyright 1991 by the American Psychological Association.

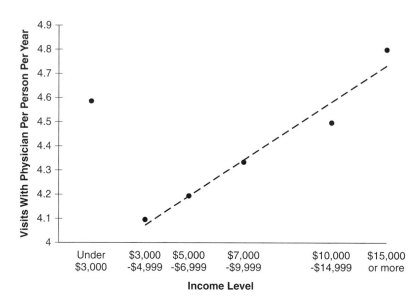

FIGURE 7.4 Quantified multiple control group posttest-only analysis of the effects of Medicaid. (After Lohr, 1972; Wilder, 1972).

level was the cutoff, the frequency of medical visits per year was the outcome, and, like the last example, group averages rather than individual scores were plotted. The regression line relating income to medical visits showed an overall positive relationship, perhaps because people with higher incomes can afford more medical care or because they tend to be older and therefore less healthy. For present purposes, the important result is that the number of physician visits visibly increases at the cutoff defining Medicaid eligibility, an effect that is as visually dramatic as the Cincinnati directory assistance time-series example (see Figure 6.1). Though the small sample size and the fact that only one treatment unit is observed are of concern in this study, any plausible alternative interpretation would have to involve non-Medicaid factors that increase physician visits *at exactly the same income eligibility criterion as Medicaid*. This is possible in the United States, where many social programs that might affect doctor visits also link program eligibility to family income around the Medicaid cutoff. To explore this explanation, Lohr (1972) examined data from the year before Medicaid was instituted, finding no discontinuity at the eligibility point that year. Given that result, no other program would increase doctor visits unless it used the same eligibility cutoff *and* was introduced in the same year as Medicaid, a possibility that can be checked.

A final example is Berk and DeLeeuw's (1999) evaluation of California's prison inmate classification system (Figure 7.5). Based on a classification score (the assignment variable) that is a composite of such variables as length of prison sentence, age, and prior incarcerations, inmates are sent to either high-security or low-security placements (the treatment), with the dichotomous outcome being

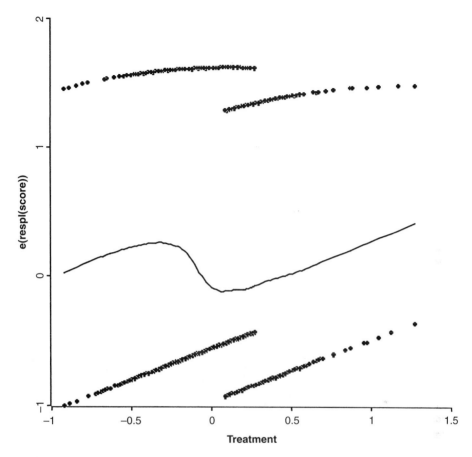

FIGURE 7.5. Added-variables plot of the effects of high- or low-security placement of prison inmates on subsequent misconduct. The horizontal axis label is the expectation of treatment receipt conditional on assignment score; and the vertical axis label is the expectation of outcome conditional on assignment score.

Prepared by Richard A. Berk for this book from "An evaluation of California's inmate classification system using a generalized regression discontinuity design," by R. A. Berk and J. DeLeeuw, 1999, *Journal of the American Statistical Association, 94, pp. 1045*–1052. Copyright 1999 by the American Statistical Association.

whether or not the inmate was reported for misconduct during the next 18 months. Statistical results suggested that high-security placements reduced the odds of inmate misconduct by about half. Figure 7.5 differs from previous plots in four ways: (1) the outcome is dichotomous, so the data points are separated into a group at the top of the plot and another at the bottom, reflecting the presence or absence of misconduct; (2) the plot does not graph raw data points but is an added-variables plot (Cook & Weisberg, 1994) in which both the response and the treatment indicator have been residualized for the assignment variable; (3) a treatment variable rather than the assignment variable is plotted on the horizontal axis; and (4) the plot includes a **lowess smoother** (Cook & Weisberg, 1994), the middle line in the plot, which is constructed to summarize the data points in a way that makes the relationship between treatment and outcome clearer. The discontinuity in the lowess smoother around the treatment variable score of zero shows the treatment effect. Clearly, Figures 7.3 to 7.5 show that plots of RD designs need not conform to any single model.

Structural Requirements of the Design

The Assignment Variable and the Cutoff

In an RD design, assignment to treatment must be based *only* on the cutoff score. In this, assignment in RD is as strict and unforgiving as assignment in the randomized experiment. One cannot override either assignment mechanism by removing a participant from a condition to which the cutoff (or coin toss) has assigned him or her. Considering that the assignment variable and cutoff score play a crucial role, how should they be selected?

The assignment variable cannot be caused by treatment. This requirement is met by an assignment variable that is measured prior to the start of treatment or by a variable that can never change, such as the year of one's birth (Judd & Kenny, 1981a). The assignment variable can be a pretest on the dependent variable—in the compensatory education example, both the pretest and posttest were reading tests. However, the assignment variable need not be a pretest. For example, in the crime-control study in which the binary (yes or no) outcome was recidivism, the assignment variable was the number of hours worked in prison. The assignment variable can even be totally unrelated to outcome and have no particular substantive meaning. For example, Cain (1975) suggested using order of application to a program as the basis for assignment, letting the first 20 applicants into a treatment, for example, with the remainder being controls; and Deluse (1999) did this in an RD study assigning couples to court-ordered divorce education based on the date they filed for divorce.[4] In this latter instance, RD would function like a ran-

---

4. This study, and the use of order of entry as an assignment variable in general, closely resembles an interrupted time-series design in which an intervention is implemented at some particular time. However, the two designs are typically (but not always) different in these cases. Typically, participants in an RD are independent of each other; but ITS participants are typically the same over time (or at least some subset is the same over time) so that points over time are autocorrelated in a way that does not occur in RD. But participants in an ITS could in principle be completely independent, just as in RD. Similarly, in a graph of an interrupted time-series design (e.g., Figure 6.1), the data points that occur prior to the intervention are typically *pretests*, that is, they physically occur before treatment begins. In a regression discontinuity design that uses order of entry (or cognates) as an assignment variable, the data points graphed before the cutoff (e.g., in Figure 7.2) are *posttests* that are physically taken after the treatment begins. However, it is hypothetically possible to imagine an RD design in which this latter distinction has no practical import, if the treatment (and control) condition is so brief that posttest is given very quickly after assignment to condition so that all control posttests occur before any participant has been treated. If so, a design meeting all these conditions and having completely independent data points might be considered both an RD and an ITS.

domized experiment in which the assignment process (a coin toss) is unrelated to the outcome on average. However, RD works whether the assignment variable is or is not related to the outcome.

The best assignment variable is a continuous variable, such as blood pressure in medical studies, annual income in job training studies, or achievement test scores in educational research. Such variables maximize the chance of correctly modeling the regression line for each group, which is crucial to the success of RD. Conversely, a dichotomous assignment variable, such as gender or status as a smoker or nonsmoker, cannot be used for assignment. With dichotomous variables, only one assignment score is possible below the cutoff (nonsmoker) and only one above (smoker), so no regression line for either group can be estimated; and the high correlation of the assignment variable with the treatment dummy variable would cause linear dependency among predictors.

Selection of Cutoff Point

Choice of cutoff score depends on many considerations. It may be chosen on substantive grounds, such as professional opinion about who needs a medical treatment or which children need compensatory education. Statistical power and the estimation of interactions are both facilitated if the cutoff is the mean of the distribution of assignment variable scores. However, locating the cutoff at the mean is not possible if participants trickle into the study slowly over time so that the mean cannot be computed until all units are available or if cost or merit or need limit treatment to those with especially high or low scores on the assignment variable. In the latter case, placement of the cutoff at an extreme value can harm the ability to model a regression line even with a continuous assignment variable. If a scholarship is restricted to those scoring above the 99.9th percentile on a test, there may be too few points above that cutoff to model the regression, and statistical power will also be severely reduced. Placement is crucial when the assignment variable is a polychotomy such as a 7-point Likert scale. Having only 1 or 2 points (e.g., 6 and 7) on one side of a cutoff hinders estimation of the regression line on that side. The most extreme example is shown in Figure 7.4, where only one unit is observed for the treatment condition so no regression line can be modeled at all to the left of the cutoff.[5]

It is possible to use many assignment variables simultaneously rather than just one. For example, if a 7-point Likert scale is used but the cutoff is too low, one can average several replicates of the variable to create a finely graded scale. For example, one might average the ratings of four physicians who each use a 7-point Likert scale to rate surgical candidates on their need for surgery, yielding

---

5. If one can model the regression line for the comparison group accurately, one can examine whether the treatment group *mean* lies significantly far from the projection of the comparison group line (by subtracting the treatment group's mean rather than the cutoff from the pretest scores).

an assignment variable with many more intervals. Or if several assignment variables are in different metrics, one could form a total score from them after first standardizing them and possibly weighting them differentially (Judd & Kenny, 1981a; Trochim, 1984, 1990). Participants are then assigned to conditions using a cutoff on the total score. Such averages and totals can help remedy the problems that arise if the available assignment variables have poor distributional properties that thwart an accurate regression model. Using such complex assignment strategies can increase the power of the design by reducing the correlation between the assignment variable and receipt of treatment (Cappelleri & Trochim, 1995; Judd & Kenny, 1981a). Or instead of combining separate indices of merit or need, one could set a cutoff on each and accept into treatment any participant who fell to the appropriate side of the cutoff on a specific number of indices—say, exceeding the cutoff on at least 6 of 12 indices or exceeding the cutoff on *all* assignment variables simultaneously. When these complex strategies are used, special analysis rules apply (see Judd & Kenny, 1981a; Trochim, 1984, 1990).

Assignment to treatment must be *controlled,* which rules out most retrospective uses of the design. An example is an initially uncontrolled nonequivalent comparison group quasi-experimental design in which the researcher then discarded all treatment participants falling to the intended control group side of a cutoff on some available variable and all control participants falling to the intended treatment side (Judd & Kenny, 1981a). Here, the initial assignment mechanism was not even known, much less controlled, which introduces selection biases that RD cannot remedy. Such post hoc elimination of misassigned cases can also induce curvilinearity in the true regression function, which can sometimes masquerade as a treatment effect (Goldberger, 1972a).

Additional Requirements

It is important to know the overall functional form that relates the assignment and outcome variables (i.e., whether it is linear, curvilinear, cyclical, etc.). A polynomial model may be appropriate for describing that form[6] (Trochim, 1984), or some other transformation may be used either for the assignment or posttest variable (e.g., a log transformation). Such functions can adequately describe most relationships. But if the functional form is misspecified in the analysis, treatment effects will be estimated with bias.

All participants must belong to one population prior to being assigned to conditions, though the RD literature is unclear about how to define a population. A definition such as that used in Rubin's causal model (Holland, 1986; Rubin, 1974, 1977, 1978, 1986) for randomized experiments might apply to RD as well. Rubin's model says that, prior to random assignment, it must have been possible for all units in an experiment to receive treatment. In RD, then, it must have been pos-

---

6. For example, an equation that includes, $X, X^2, X^3, . . , X^n$.

sible for all units in the study to receive treatment had the cutoff been set differently. For example, suppose a treatment was implemented in School A for students scoring above a cutoff and that the control group contained students in School B who scored below that cutoff. Because the treatment was not implemented in School B, it would not have been possible for School B students to receive the treatment even if their scores fell above the cutoff. Further, selection into School A and School B was determined by variables other than the cutoff that are unknown to the researcher. This introduces a selection bias that cannot be controlled in an RD design.

Ideally, as in a randomized experiment, those in treatment all should receive the same amount of treatment, and those in control no treatment at all. However, some treatment group participants may receive less treatment than others, or treatment diffusion may make some controls comparable with the treatment group. Dropping such treatment crossover participants compromises the integrity of assignment. So, in both RD and the randomized experiment, it is common to retain all participants in the conditions to which they were assigned (Lavori, 1992; Pocock, 1983).[7] Similarly, suppose the percentage of treatment implementation covaries systematically with scores on the assignment variable, so that those with progressively lower scores receive progressively less treatment. A treatment that is equally effective for all participants might then appear to have smaller effects for those with lower pretest scores, producing an artifactual interaction effect.

Variations on the Basic Design

Now that the basic principles underlying RD are clear, it is simple to extend those ideas to more complicated variations. Here are examples:

- One could compare two treatments with each other instead of comparing treatment with control, and both analysis and design are otherwise the same as before.
- One could compare three conditions, say, a standard treatment, an innovation, and a control, with participants assigned on the basis of multiple cutoffs (two cutoffs for three conditions, three cutoffs for four conditions, and so forth).
- Treatments can be administered at different doses to different groups so that those with higher need receive higher doses.[8]
- Even if two conditions are administered, two cutoff scores on the assignment variable can be used to divide participants into three groups. The middle group

---

7. Recently developed analyses to address this problem in randomized experiments (Angrist, Imbens, & Rubin, 1996a; Rubin, 1992a) may apply to RD as well.

8. In these second and third variations, the standard analysis we describe later for the basic design must now include multiple dummy variables, Z, to represent each treatment, subject to the usual dummy variable coding constraints. However, only one cutoff can be subtracted from the assignment variable term in the model (Trochim, 1984, pp. 134–135).

receives one condition, say, the treatment; and the two extreme groups receive the other condition. If treatment is effective and the control has no effect, the relationship between the assignment variable and the dichotomous variable recording treatment condition would be curvilinear. This increases the power of the design by reducing colinearity between these two predictors of the outcome variable in a linear model.

Several authors (e.g., Judd & Kenny, 1981a; Trochim, 1984) provide detailed advice about the implementation and analyses of these and other variations on the basic RD design.

Once one thinks about cutoff-based assignment strategies, possible applications proliferate (Atwood & Taylor, 1991). Here are four examples. First, Rubin (1977) suggested that at the end of a randomized experiment those who score below a certain cutoff on outcome could get booster sessions or those who score below a cutoff on a measure of treatment compliance could get extra attention. A second example is the "Clinical Laboratory Improvement Amendments" passed by the U.S. Congress in 1988 to mandate medical laboratory inspections. Labs falling below a quantified evaluation score had to receive special remedial attention from the Centers for Disease Control (CDC). An evaluation of that program would have lent itself to the use of RD. A third example occurred during a consultation to a study using a 2 mg dose of nicotine gum to prevent relapse among those who quit smoking. The drug manufacturer had a 4 mg dose that it believed was too strong for most smokers. A solution would be to assign the 4 mg dose to those smokers above a certain cutoff on a measure of addiction to smoking (e.g., Fagerstrom, 1978) and 2 mg to those below it. As the fourth example, Head Start programs rank children on their need for preschool services, and this plays a role in the decision as to who eventually gets services. If it played the only role, then an RD design would be possible.

RD may have greater applicability than its infrequent past use might indicate. In this regard, the randomized experiment itself was developed and introduced in the 1920s but did not find widespread acceptance among practitioners in social and health sciences until the 1950s (Pocock, 1983). Perhaps the same 30-year lag between invention and wide use is true of RD and it will be used more frequently over the next 30 years.

THEORY OF THE REGRESSION DISCONTINUITY DESIGN

Many readers will think it implausible that the regression discontinuity design would yield useful, much less unbiased, estimates of treatment effects. In this section, we explain why the design is successful. The first explanation shows that randomized experiments also use regression discontinuities to estimate effects, and the second links regression discontinuity to the conditions under which selection biases can be successfully modeled in any quasi-experiment.

Regression Discontinuities as Treatment Effects in the Randomized Experiment

Suppose that participants are pretested, randomly assigned to treatment or control, and then posttested, using the same tests as in Figures 7.1 and 7.2. If the treatment is ineffective, that randomized experiment would produce a scatterplot of pretest against posttest scores like Figure 7.6, with a regression line that is positive, as in Figures 7.1 and 7.2. But Figure 7.6 differs from Figure 7.1 in two ways. First, it has no cutoff line because assignment was random across all pretest scores rather than occurring at a cutoff score. Second, in Figure 7.1 all treatment participants fall to the right of the cutoff score and all control participants to the left. But in Figure 7.6 the treatment and control participants are randomly intermixed because random assignment ensures that there is no systematic relationship between treatment group membership and any pretest scores.

Figure 7.7 shows a scatterplot that would result if the treatment in the randomized experiment had the same 5-point effect previously used for the RD design. We can graph two regression lines now, one for each condition. Both lines show a positive slope between pretest and posttest scores, but the treatment group regression line is now 5 points higher than the control group line. Note how similar this figure is to the RD design in Figure 7.2. Indeed, if we add a vertical line in Figure 7.7 at a pretest score of 50, the displacement of the regression lines at that cutoff would be an unbiased estimate of the effect.[9] And if in Figure 7.7 we deleted all treatment participants to the left of the cutoff line and all control participants to the right, the resulting graph would be visually identical to Figure 7.2.

Such deletions illustrate another important difference between RD and the randomized experiment. In Figures 7.6 and 7.7, the pretest means of the treatment and control groups are nearly identical at about 50 because groups have been equated probabilistically through random assignment. By contrast, cutoff-based assignment creates groups with maximally different pretest means—indeed, with nonoverlapping pretest distributions! How can RD yield an unbiased estimate of treatment effects if the groups have such different pretest means from the start? Given such compelling differences in pretest group equivalence between RD and the randomized experiment, we must explain why this objection, although plausible, is wrong, and why this design can be stronger for causal inference than any design except the randomized experiment.

---

9. In fact, a weighted average of this discontinuity across the entire range of values in the pretest is a traditional estimator of treatment effect in a randomized experiment (Rubin, 1977).

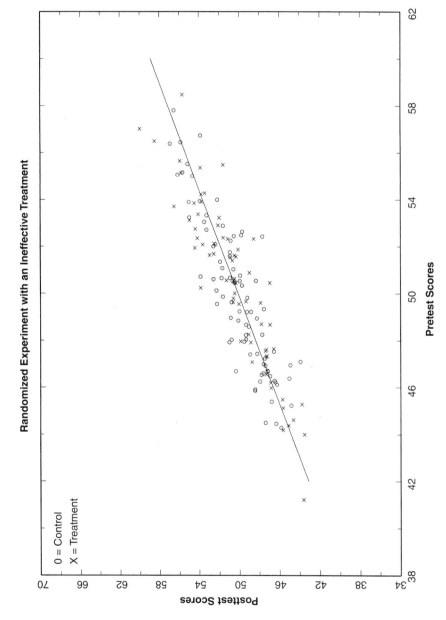

FIGURE 7.6 Randomized experiment with an ineffective treatment.

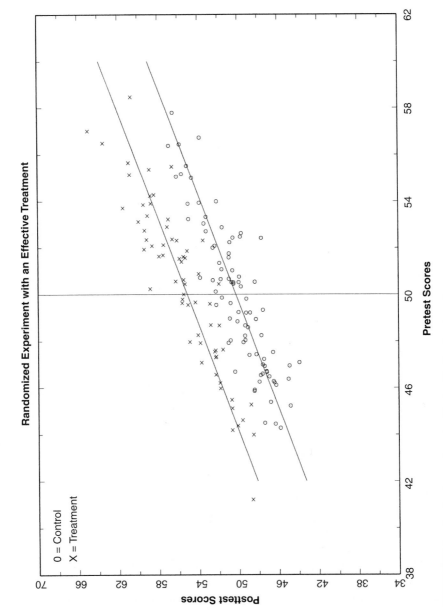

FIGURE 7.7 Randomized experiment with an effective treatment.

In randomized experiments, the treatment effect is inferred by comparing the treatment group posttest mean with the control group posttest mean. The strong assumption required here is that the groups being contrasted are probabilistically equivalent, which random assignment helps make the case at pretest (though not necessarily at posttest). In regression discontinuity, however, the comparison is not between means but between regression lines—comparing the treatment group regression line with a control group regression line that is estimated from scores on the other side of the cutoff from the treatment cases. Absent a treatment effect, we assume that the functional forms are equivalent on both sides of the cutoff—the regression lines have the same intercepts, slopes, and other attributes—rather than assume that pretest means are equivalent.

Regression Discontinuity as a Complete Model of the Selection Process

In most other quasi-experiments in which assignment to treatment is uncontrolled, the selection process is sometimes totally unknown, often partially known, but almost never fully known. For example, how can the researcher know the roles that motivation, ability, socioeconomic status, and other variables have played in determining who enters treatment? And even when they know some selection variables, they rarely measure them perfectly. However, if the selection process could be *completely known* and *perfectly measured,* then one could adjust for differences in selection to obtain an unbiased estimate of treatment effect. In theory, these conditions are met in both RD and the randomized experiment, and so both designs can be viewed as special (successful) cases of selection bias modeling (see Appendix 5.1). In a randomized experiment, the assignment mechanism is completely known and is equivalent to a coin toss. It is also fully known for RD, as it consists of whether the score on the assignment variable is above or below the cutoff. In neither case does an unknown variable determine to which condition participants were assigned. In both cases, the assignment mechanism can be perfectly measured and implemented—that is, the researcher records correctly whether the coin came up heads or tails or whether a person's score is above or below the cutoff. Of course, recording errors occur, and social processes can override assignment in both RD and randomized experiments (Conner, 1977; Dennis, 1988); but theoretically, the assignment process is completely known and perfectly measured. That is the key that allows simple statistics such as analysis of covariance (ANCOVA) to yield unbiased effect estimates in RD (Overall & Woodward, 1977). In other quasi-experiments, selection into conditions is neither fully known nor perfectly measured (Lord, 1967; Overall & Woodward, 1977). At best, the assignment variable is a partially **observed variable** (or set of variables) measured with error.

Consider this in more detail. Imagine assigning participants to conditions based on a cutoff IQ test score of, say, 130. That score is just a number. People often use the score to make inferences about a construct, and they often disagree about how well it measures that construct. Some claim that IQ measures intelligence, but others say it measures exposure to educational opportunities. For each of these inferences, the IQ score will have error—the IQ score of 130 that you received at any given testing is not a perfect measure of either your intelligence or your opportunities. But in the RD design IQ scores are not used to measure intelligence or opportunity. They only measure how participants got into conditions, and they contain no error for this purpose when assignment to conditions is based only on that score.

In all other quasi-experiments, assignment occurs on a construct that can only be measured *with error*. To illustrate, Figure 7.8 presents three scatterplots with pretest scores plotted on the horizontal axis, posttest scores on the same variable plotted on the vertical axis, and pretest scores perfectly correlated with posttest scores (the argument generalizes to an assignment variable other than pretest and to imperfectly correlated variables). In each plot, the data points on the right are the treatment group ($N = 200$) and those on the left are the control group ($N = 200$). In all three plots, treatment has no effect, but random measurement error varies in instructive ways. In Figure 7.8a, neither pretest nor posttest has such error. So the intersection of pretest and posttest scores for each participant falls on a straight, diagonal line, because the perfectly measured posttest scores are the same as pretest scores. This line is the base from which we infer the effects of measurement error.

In Figure 7.8b, error is added to the *pretest*, as is typical in most quasi-experiments. Each point that was formerly on the diagonal line in Figure 7.8a is now displaced horizontally and randomly to the left or right of that line. Neither of the slopes in Figure 7.8b is as steep as in 7.8a, due to regression to the mean attributable to measurement error. For example, a treatment group pretest score of 63 regressed down to 60.99 on the posttest, whereas a pretest score of 57 regressed up to 58.09. Put differently, measurement error in the pretest caused the regression lines for the observed scores to change slope, even though the regression lines for the true scores (in Figure 7.8a) remain the same. If we fit a regression line to the two groups separately, as in Figure 7.8b, we observe an artifactual treatment effect, a gap between regression lines even though we know no such effect exists. This false effect is what occurs in nonequivalent comparison group designs when our measure of assignment to conditions is measured with measurement error.

No such bias exists if we add error to the *posttest* (Figure 7.8c). Each point that was formerly on the diagonal line in Figure 7.8a is now displaced vertically and randomly above or below that line. If regression lines are plotted separately for each group, the lines overlap and, as in Figure 7.8a, there is no discontinuity, correctly showing no treatment effect.[10] Figure 7.8c is exactly the situation of the regression discontinuity design with no treatment effect (notice the similarity between Figures 7.8c and 7.1). In RD, the posttest undoubtedly has error, but the

---

10. Random measurement error in the posttest can cause random regression discontinuities in any given study, but the *expectation* of the discontinuities is zero, so the estimate is still considered unbiased.

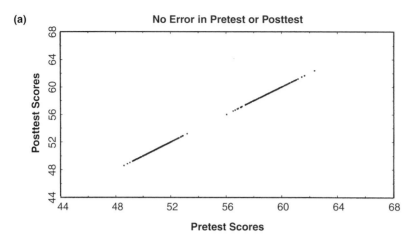

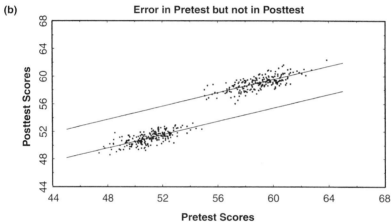

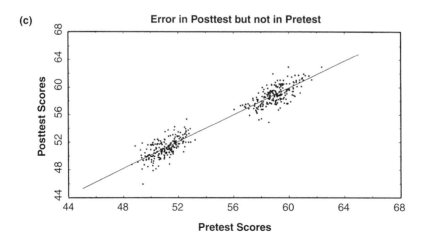

FIGURE 7.8 The effects of errors in pretests and posttests.

pretest (in this case, the assignment variable) has no error *when used as a measure of the selection mechanism into treatment.*

Regression lines are unaffected by posttest errors but biased by pretest ones because ordinary least squares (OLS) regression minimizes errors in the variable being predicted (placed by convention on the vertical axis). In RD, the posttest variable (i.e., the outcome) is being predicted, so OLS regression minimizes the squared differences between the observed and predicted *posttest* scores. Graphically, it minimizes errors in the vertical direction; so the regression line in Figure 7.8c will fall exactly where the true scores were in Figure 7.8a. None of this is true for errors in the pretest because errors are added horizontally (i.e., to the pretest) but regression still minimizes squared errors vertically. Simple visual inspection of Figure 7.8b shows that the resulting regression line will now shift in the direction indicated, causing biased treatment effects to result.

ADHERENCE TO THE CUTOFF

Critical practical problems in the implementation of the regression discontinuity design concern adherence to the cutoff when assigning participants to conditions. Adherence problems stem from many sources.

Overrides of the Cutoff

In RD, treatment assignment must follow the cutoff, but this often violates the expectations of treatment professionals that their judgment should decide whether a participant gets treatment. If this judgment is not quantified and made part of the assignment variable, the use of such judgmental strategies violates the assumptions of the design. For example, Robinson, Bradley, and Stanley (1990) assigned participants to conditions based not only on a cutoff but also on a qualitative committee judgment. Similarly, school district administrators often want discretionary power to override treatment assignment (Trochim, 1984) in order to exercise favoritism or to override "close calls" when professional judgment and test scores clash as to who needs treatment. When judgment indicates need but test scores do not, it is not easy to get administrators to act on the scores alone. Including cases that are admitted to a program regardless of their cutoff score is likely to produce bias. If feasible, such cases should be identified and removed from the research sample prior to assignment, preferably without examining eligibility scores and without knowing what their assignment would have been.

If cases like this cannot be eliminated in advance, one could retain them in the analysis if they are classified by their eligibility scores rather than by the treatment actually received. This yields an unbiased effect estimate, but an estimate of the effects of assignment to treatment rather than of treatment itself. One can also do the analysis both including and then excluding such cases to see how estimates change. Trochim (1984) found that excluding participants provides reasonably accurate estimates of effects, but presumably the extent of treatment misassignment makes a difference. However, if misassignment is the product of deliberately falsifying the assignment score, there is no methodological cure, though one might be able to estimate the likely direction of bias.

Cutoff-based assignments may be difficult to implement if participants trickle in too slowly or too quickly, creating pressure to adjust the cutoff score so as to keep the program filled (Havassey, 1988). If sample sizes are sufficiently large, one can adjust the cutoff occasionally but then analyze each group admitted using a different cutoff as a separate RD design. Or, if more eligible participants arrive than can be treated, one can randomly assign a proportion of the overflow to no treatment, embedding a randomized design into the basic regression discontinuity design.

If a cutoff score is public, potential participants can manipulate their own score to get into treatment. In the Berk and Rauma (1983) RD study of the impact of unemployment benefits on recidivism among ex-prisoners, those prisoners close to the cutoff might try to work more hours so they can get into treatment, whereas others do not try if they know they already made it or that they have little chance of doing so. This would affect the distribution of prisoners' scores on the assignment variable, in the worst case leaving a gap just below the cutoff that could result in bimodal data. Another example is the Irish School Leavers Examination, in which graders showed a marked reluctance to assign scores just below the cutoff point (Madaus & Greaney, 1985). Non-normally distributed data such as these can cause nonlinear regression surfaces that complicate analysis.

Crossovers and Attrition

Treatment crossovers occur when those assigned to treatment do not take it or those assigned to control end up in treatment. For example, Robinson and Stanley (1989) included in their control condition some participants who were assigned to treatment but did not attend. In a later chapter, we outline how such crossovers may be partially taken into account in randomized experiments; some of the same principles might apply to RD.

A related problem is attrition from the study after assignment has occurred. Seaver and Quarton (1976) studied the effects of making the dean's list due to obtaining a GPA of 3.5 or greater in the prior semester. But they excluded any student "who was not enrolled for the fall, winter, and spring terms consecutively, who changed campuses, or who enrolled for fewer than nine credits in any term" (p. 460). Such exclusions are warranted if they simply define the study population (the 9-credit-hour requirement), and some attrition is inevitable in most field research. But excluding participants based on measurements that could have been caused by assignment to treatment is a problem. For example, if making the dean's list allows a student to get into a better college and if that is the reason for his or her transfer, then attrition is probably treatment correlated, and so biased estimates may again result. Again, partial solutions that we outline later for randomized experiments may apply to RD, as well.

Fuzzy Regression Discontinuity

Trochim (1984) calls cases in which assignment to treatment does not adhere fully to the cutoff (e.g., Cahan & Davis, 1987) a fuzzy regression discontinuity design. Strictly speaking, an RD with a fuzzy cutoff is not an RD at all. But just as a slightly degraded randomized experiment may still produce better effect estimates than many quasi-experiments (Shadish & Ragsdale, 1996), a fuzzy cutoff RD design may produce better estimates than many other quasi-experiments if the fuzziness is not too great.

If the range of misassignment is confined around the cutoff score to a narrow range, say, between assignment variable scores of 49.5 and 50.5 in Figure 7.2, then participants within that range can be eliminated, with the remainder of the participants treated as a strict RD design (Mohr, 1988, 1995). This solution works well only if the range being deleted is narrow, for otherwise it will be difficult to accurately model the regression line near the cutoff. If no more than 5% of the participants are misassigned, one can exclude misclassified participants and probably obtain reasonable treatment estimates (Judd & Kenny, 1981a; Trochim, 1984). For other cases in which the percent of misassigned participants is higher or over a wide range of the assignment variable, Berk and deLeeuw (1999) outline useful sensitivity analyses to explore effects of violations of the assignment process on outcome. Finally, use of selection bias models or propensity score analyses outlined in Chapter 5 might also improve estimates in such cases, though we know of no research on this possibility.

THREATS TO VALIDITY

The statistical rationale for RD is responsible for wider recognition of the design's special status among cause-probing studies when random assignment is not possible. But the strength of the design becomes clearer by comparing it with the quasi-experiment to which it is conceptually most similar, the interrupted time series (ITS).

Regression Discontinuity and the Interrupted Time Series

In both ITS and RD, an effect is predicted to occur at a specific point on a continuum. In ITS, time is the continuum, and in RD the continuum is the assignment variable. In ITS, the intervention occurs at a known time point, and in RD it occurs at a known cutoff score. If the treatment is effective in ITS, it will alter the mean or slope of the time series at the point at which treatment occurs; and in RD, an effective treatment will alter the slope or intercept the regression line at the known cutoff point. Even the graphs of ITS and RD look similar!

Not surprisingly, then, threats to validity for RD are not too different from those for ITS. With the simple interrupted time series, the most relevant threats are point specific, occurring at the same time as the intervention. Simple forms of maturation or selection are rarely relevant; but history (extraneous events occurring contemporaneously with treatment) and instrumentation changes at the intervention time are sometimes plausible. We will find that the same is true for RD. Similarly, ITS requires that we accurately model autocorrelation, trend, cycles, and drift to estimate the effects; that is, we have to know the naturally occurring shape of the time series in order to detect changes to that shape. The statistical analysis of RD is similarly complex.

Statistical Conclusion Validity and Misspecification of Functional Form

When treatment effects in ITS are large and coincide with the introduction of treatment, the effects are often plausible without statistical analysis. Similarly with RD, when the discontinuity is large at the cutoff, as with the Medicaid example in Figure 7.4, little statistical analysis may be needed. However, such dramatic effects are as rare in RD as they are in ITS, so correct modeling of the shape of the regression is needed to tease out RD effects. In the simplest case, that in which the underlying regression line is linear, an analysis of covariance (ANCOVA) such as the following is used:

$$Y_i = \hat{\beta}_0 + \hat{\beta}_1 Z_i + \hat{\beta}_2 (X_i - X_c) + e_i \qquad (7.1)$$

where Y is the outcome,[11] $\hat{\beta}_0$ is the intercept, Z is a dichotomous (0,1) variable that records which treatment condition the participant received (0 = control, 1 = treatment), X is the assignment variable, the regression coefficient predicting outcome from the assignment variable is $\hat{\beta}_2$, the effect of treatment is measured by the regression coefficient $\hat{\beta}_1$, and e is a random error term. The subscript i indexes the N units in the study, from $i = 1$ to N. Subtracting the cutoff value from the assignment variable ($X_i - X_c$, which is the same as centering the assignment variable if the cutoff is the mean) causes the equation to estimate the effect of treatment at the cutoff score, the point at which groups are most similar. One could estimate the effect anywhere on the range of the assignment variable by varying which value is subtracted or estimate it at the intercept by subtracting zero.

---

11. Judd and Kenny (1981a) outline analysis possibilities and problems if more than one outcome variable is used; and Berk and Rauma (1983) demonstrate analysis for a dichotomous outcome.

This simple analysis yields an unbiased estimate of the size of the treatment effect. The proofs of this are sufficiently statistical that we do not present them here (see Appendix 7.1). Understanding those proofs clarifies both how the RD design resembles randomized experiments and how it resembles the selection bias models in Appendix 5.1. However, treatment effect estimates in RD are unbiased only if the simple model in (7.1) is correct. Two problems are especially likely to make the model wrong: nonlinearity and interactions.

Nonlinearity

The model in (7.1) specifies that the relationship between the selection variable and the outcome is linear. Suppose it is really *nonlinear,* a function of, say, X^2 or X^3 rather than just X? If the model does not incorporate this nonlinear term, then it is misspecified and the estimates of the regression discontinuity may be biased, as Figure 7.9 illustrates. In this figure, the data were constructed so that posttest is a cubic function of the assignment variable (a function of X^3), and the treatment actually has no effect. If the data are incorrectly fit to (7.1) instead of to a model with a cubic term, a significant but incorrect discontinuity between the two regression lines would appear at the cutoff. In this case, it would mistakenly suggest a significant negative effect of treatment. To reach the correct answer, the equation must also include X^3. Cook and Campbell (1979) presented an example in their reanalysis of Seaver and Quarton's (1973) dean's list RD experiment. The latter found an effect for being on the dean's list, but the effect was nonsignificant once a curvilinear model was substituted for a linear one.

Nonlinearity can also occur if the underlying variables are not normally distributed. Trochim, Cappelleri, and Reichardt (1991) illustrate this in their figures 1 and 2, using data distributed uniformly (i.e., roughly equal numbers of units at each pretest point) rather than normally. The resulting curvilinearity resembled Figure 7.9, and a pseudoeffect resulted from fitting the data with a linear model. Inspecting distributions of the posttest and assignment variables is useful to detect this; transforming data will sometimes help solve these distribution problems (Trochim, 1984). Nonlinearity can also result from chance outliers or from floor and ceiling effects. Fortunately, in all these cases, a cubic function would still fit the data, indicate no effect, and be consistent with the impression of no discontinuity provided by visual inspection.

Interactions

Nonlinearity can also arise from *the failure to model statistical interactions between the assignment and treatment variables.* Equation (7.1) specifies only a treatment main effect term but no interaction terms. What if units assigned to treatment with scores near the cutoff benefit less than those with more extreme scores? In this case, a product term for the interaction must be added to the equation to get an

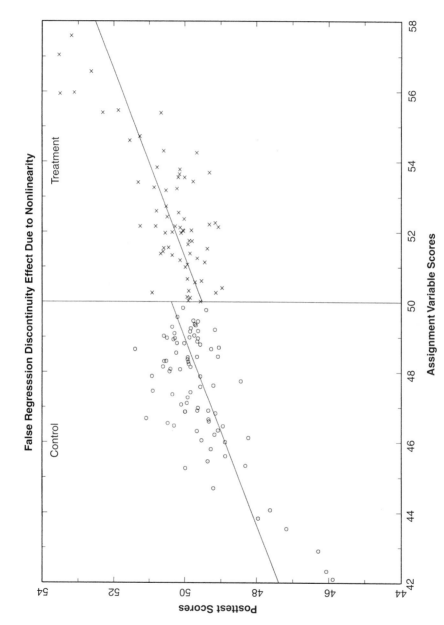

FIGURE 7.9 False regression discontinuity effect due to nonlinearity

unbiased effect.[12] If the data were generated by an underlying interaction effect but no main effect and if the interaction term is omitted, the coefficient for the main effect is biased, as indicated by the false discontinuity at the cutoff in Figure 7.10. In that figure, the coefficient associated with Zi should be zero, but instead it is significant at $\hat{\beta}_1 = 1.42$; other coefficients in the equation will also be biased.

Figure 7.11 shows a correctly modeled case with a main effect for treatment and an interaction between treatment and pretest scores; in addition to the regression discontinuity at the cutoff, the slope of the line is steeper to the right than to the left of the cutoff. In this example, all treatment participants benefit more than controls, but those who scored higher on the assignment variable do better than those who scored lower, so the size of the discontinuity varies depending on where it is measured on the assignment variable. The analysis will correctly yield different estimates of the effect depending on which score is subtracted from the assignment variable.

Figure 7.12 shows a shift in slope with no discontinuity at the cutoff produced by an interaction but no other effect of treatment. Some interpret this situation as no effect because of the lack of a discontinuity at the cutoff, but others interpret it as indicating a possible effect among those far from the cutoff. The latter interpretation has two problems. One is that the logic of the RD design is partly tied to finding discontinuities at the cutoff because participants are most similar there. The other is that it is difficult to distinguish Figure 7.12 from a nonlinear relationship generated by a quadratic function with no treatment effect. Sometimes it helps to sort out these possibilities to combine RD with other design features that we cover shortly.

Advice About Modeling Functional Form

If interactions or nonlinearities are suspected, the analysis should overfit the model by starting with more polynomial and interaction terms than is probably needed, dropping nonsignificant terms from higher to lower order. When in doubt, keep terms rather than drop them; such overfitting yields unbiased coefficients, although it reduces power (Cappelleri & Trochim, 1992). The researcher should also study whether substantive conclusions are stable over varied assumptions about functional form. Standard regression diagnostics and remedies (e.g., J. Cohen & Cohen, 1983; Cook & Weisberg, 1994; Neter, Wasserman, & Kutner,

---

12. The term would be $Z_i(X_i - X_c)$ for the case in which the cutoff score is subtracted from the assignment variable X. So to model both nonlinearities and interactions, the equation may use functions of the assignment variable that increase in polynomial degree ($X, X^2, X^3, \ldots, X^n$), along with interaction terms for each of these polynomials ($ZX, ZX^2, ZX^3, \ldots, ZX^n$):

$$Y_i = b_o + \hat{\beta}_1 Z_i + \hat{\beta}_2(X_i - X_c) + \hat{\beta}_3 Z_i(X_i - X_c) + \hat{\beta}_4(X_i - X_c)^2 + \hat{\beta}_5 Z_i(X_i - X_c)^2 \\ + \ldots + \hat{\beta}_{n-1}(X_i - X_c)^S + \hat{\beta}_n Z_i(X_i - X_c)^S + e_i \qquad (7.2)$$

where the terms are as defined previously, where S is the degree of the highest polynomial fitted to the model, where $\hat{\beta}_n$ is the regression coefficient for the last polynomial or interaction term in the model.

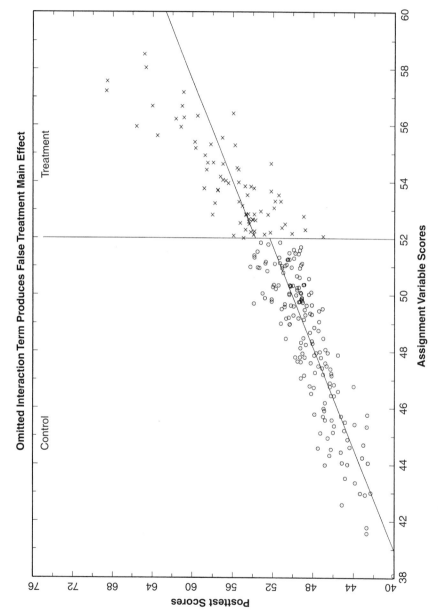

FIGURE 7.10 Omitted interaction term produces false treatment main effect.

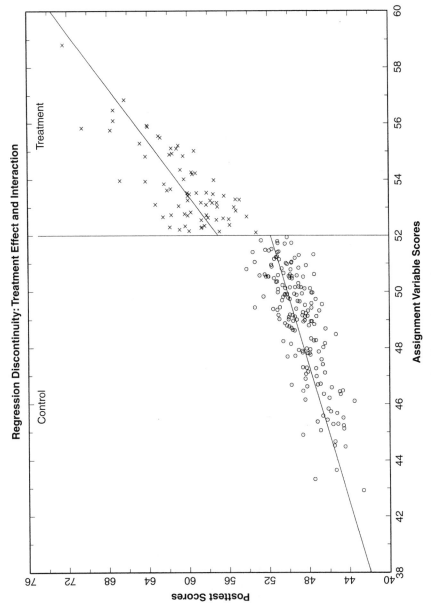

FIGURE 7.11 Regression discontinuity: Treatment effect and interaction.

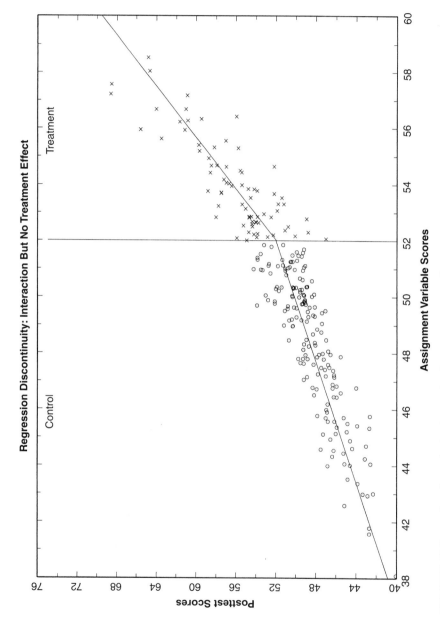

FIGURE 7.12 Regression discontinuity: Interaction but no treatment effect.

1983; West et al., 2000) can also help diagnose these problems. Often, additional data can be gathered to provide a baseline functional form that is not affected by treatment, for example, pretreatment data on both the assignment and outcome variables or data on both the assignment and outcome variables on related but untreated samples of participants. If this is not possible but the sample size is large, one can split the sample, using the first half to develop a model and the second to cross-validate it. Finally, one can combine RD designs with randomized experiments to address this problem, as we discuss shortly. But first, we examine the performance of RD on internal validity threats.

Internal Validity

A threat to internal validity in RD would have to cause a sudden discontinuity in the regression line that exactly coincides with the cutoff. This is almost always implausible. Indeed, except for the scatterplots in this chapter, most readers will probably *never* see a scatterplot that demonstrates a naturally occurring discontinuity. It almost always takes a treatment effect, given only to persons to one side of a cutoff, to produce that discontinuity.

Selection would not cause that discontinuity. In part the reason is that we can model selection successfully given that it is fully known and perfectly measured. But even if the latter statistics are not transparent to the reader, a more common sense rationale should be: If participants with assignment scores at 50.05 in Figure 7.1 perform remarkably better on the outcome variable than participants at 49.95, surely the .05 difference between them on the assignment variable is unlikely to account for that improvement. *History* is plausible if events that could affect outcome occur only to people to one side of the cutoff, as happened in the Medicaid example in Figure 7.4; but that is often both unlikely and easy to assess. *Testing* is unlikely to influence the size of the discontinuity because both groups receive the same tests; and *instrumentation* changes that occur exactly at the cutoff are again unlikely and easy to assess. *Maturation* would imply that the outcome variable is, say, naturally improving for those high on the assignment variable faster than for those low on it; this would cause a curvilinearity that would need accurate modeling. *Mortality* is always a threat in RD, just as it is in randomized experiments, when correlated with treatment assignment (Shapiro, 1984).

Many readers think that *statistical regression* is plausible because groups were formed from the extremes of the assignment variable distribution. But regression is already captured totally in the regression line between assignment variable and posttest. The correlation coefficient, r, between the two tests measures the amount of regression that will occur. In fact, both the term *regression* and the symbol r were coined to indicate that they measure regression to the mean. Yes, a person scoring high on the assignment variable will not score as high on the outcome variable; and a person scoring low on the assignment variable will not score as low on the outcome. But this just causes the regression line to become more horizontal; it does not cause a discontinuity at the cutoff.

Other threats are possible. For example, a *selection-instrumentation* effect could occur when ceiling or floor effects are present in the measures. Cappelleri and Trochim (1992) describe a floor effect in their study of the effects of the drug Xanax on anxiety; the drug was so effective that many treated participants reported "no symptoms" on the outcome measure, flattening out the regression at that floor. This causes a biased estimate of the interaction effect in RD designs if improperly modeled. In general, however, RD does well regarding internal validity threats.

COMBINING REGRESSION DISCONTINUITY AND RANDOMIZED EXPERIMENTS

If feasible, combining the randomized experiment with RD is much better than using RD alone. For example, instead of using a single cutoff score, one could define a cutoff interval lying between two scores. Above the upper score, all participants are assigned to one condition; below the lower score all participants are assigned to the other. In between, participants are assigned randomly to conditions. The result is a randomized experiment embedded in a regression discontinuity design. In Figure 7.13, for example, participants with assignment scores less than 48 are assigned to the control condition, those with scores above 52 to treatment, and those between 48 and 52 are assigned randomly to conditions. All participants are analyzed in equation (7.1), but one must choose which cutoff score to subtract from assignment variable scores. Trochim (1991) suggests using the cutoff that assigns all participants in the treatment group to the same side of the cutoff. His rationale is that an interaction between assignment and treatment would affect all treated participants, including those in the interval; so subtracting that cutoff helps estimate that interaction more accurately. In Figure 7.13, this means subtracting 48, because all participants who received treatment are to the same side of 48. If there is no interaction, however, using the median of the interval as the estimation point will increase the power of the test (Trochim & Cappelleri, 1992). If the researcher's initial hypothesis about this interaction is wrong, the alternative analysis can then be done, as long as it is clearly described as exploratory.

The randomized experiment can be combined with RD in many different ways (Boruch, 1975; Cappelleri, 1991; Trochim, 1984, 1990; Trochim & Cappelleri, 1992). First, all patients to one side of a cutoff could be deemed needy and given the treatment and the rest could be randomly assigned to conditions. Second, an RD design could be added to an existing randomized experiment that is already using a quantified eligibility cutoff (e.g., Cappelleri & Trochim, 1994). Those who do not pass that cutoff could be kept as a regression discontinuity con-

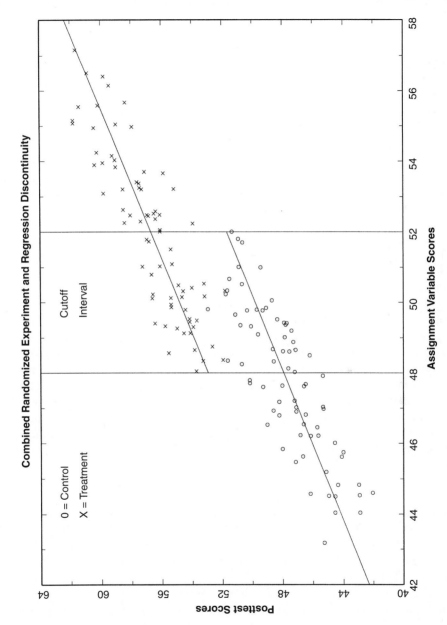

FIGURE 7.13 Combined randomized experiment and regression discontinuity.

trol rather than just being discarded. This would increase measurement costs but also increase power without having to administer treatment to more participants. Third, one could use several cutoff intervals spread across the assignment variable, for example, one interval in the middle, one at the upper end, and one at the lower end. The advantages are increased generalizability of the effect across the range of the assignment variable, rather than just at the cutoff, and the use of randomization at the points on the regression line where the influence of floor and ceiling effects in estimating the regression line is most problematic. Fourth, one could assign participants to multiple intervals randomly but with varying probabilities of receiving treatment across the different intervals. For instance, three cutoff intervals with a 25:75, 50:50, and 75:25 probability of being assigned to treatment might be sandwiched in between the 0:100 and 100:0 probabilities that define the regression discontinuity part of the design. This variation reduces concern that close calls might be inappropriately assigned, because the greater the participant's measured need or merit on the assignment variable, the greater the chances the participant will get treatment. Fifth, the probability of random assignment within the interval could be changed over sites or within sites, and the size of the intervals can vary at different sites or within sites over time. Sixth, the randomization interval can be placed at a point at which curvilinearity is suspected, in order to minimize problems modeling functional form. Seventh, participants in a cutoff interval could be randomly assigned, but all others could be assigned to just one condition. In the case of a hazardous drug, for example, all other participants could be given the placebo to minimize their risk; in the case of a likely efficacious treatment, all others could be given the treatment to maximize their benefit. For all these models, readers should consult Cappelleri (1991); Cappelleri, Darlington, and Trochim (1994); Trochim (1984, 1990); and Trochim and Cappelleri (1992) for crucial details about design, power, and analysis.

One advantage of the combined design is that randomization increases the power of the test of treatment effects. The increase is proportional to the increasing size of the randomization interval relative to the total range of the assignment variable (Cappelleri, 1991; Trochim & Cappelleri, 1992).

A second advantage is that it allows estimation of the regression lines for both treatment and control participants over the same range of assignment scores within the randomization interval. This helps ameliorate the problem in the basic RD design of having to project lines to the cutoff score, a projection that requires accurate modeling of the functional form of the regression. The overlap of regression lines within the randomized portion of the design helps assess the accuracy of this projection.

A third advantage is the amelioration of practical problems that arise when it is not clear where the cutoff should be set. In medical studies it is often clear that all participants below a certain point do not need a treatment and that those above a higher point do need it; but the need of those in between is unclear. Random assignment may be most ethical for those middle participants. Conversely, in many randomized experiments, those in most need are excluded because they must be treated, those whose needs are minimal are often excluded from the start, and the experiment is conducted on only those participants whose needs fall into a narrow interval. Using the combined design to include both those least and most needy participants who would otherwise be excluded will increase the power of the total experiment (Luft, 1990).

One explanation of RD appeals to a notion that is related to the combined designs just discussed, that is, a tie-breaking randomized experiment. Consider only those participants in Figure 7.1 who fall very close to the cutoff score of 50—say, those between 49.5 and 50.5. These are the participants for whom most controversy might exist about assigning them to one condition in an RD design. For instance, administrators may believe that a certain child deserves treatment, but her score of 49.5 might make her ineligible. For these participants, one might conduct a randomized experiment. If we then plotted the treatment and control groups means for just the participants in that interval, we would see the same distance between means that the regression discontinuity design would yield. So RD can be viewed as projecting the regression lines to the results of this hypothetical tie-breaking randomized experiment, with the cutoff interval going to zero.

COMBINING REGRESSION DISCONTINUITY AND QUASI-EXPERIMENTS

In all the combined designs just described, one could use a quasi-experiment instead of a randomized experiment. In medical settings, those whose scores fall within the cutoff interval would get treatment at the discretion of a physician or treatment team, with those above and below the interval being assigned in an RD design. In compensatory education, administrators could have the discretion to assign or not assign children to treatment within the interval. In psychotherapy, clients could choose or not choose to self-select into therapy.

This combination of quasi-experimentation and regression discontinuity is particularly useful when a decision has already been made to do a nonequivalent comparison group quasi-experiment. Often, adding RD to that quasi-experiment will make great practical sense to those very same administrators, physicians, and psychotherapists who want the discretion a quasi-experiment gives them or their clients. After all, even their preferred quasi-experiment is likely to use some exclusion criteria. Why throw those participants away? Both the power of and the estimates from that quasi-experiment will be improved by adding an RD component whose only costs are quantifying the exclusion criteria and measuring assignment and outcome variables for those who otherwise would have been excluded anyway.

Similarly, one can combine any other quasi-experimental design feature with RD. One could run a traditional RD design, then at the end of the RD study give the control participants the treatment. Or one can run an otherwise identical regression discontinuity on a nonequivalent control group that is predicted *not* to display an effect because it did not receive the treatment (e.g., Cullen et al., 1999). Or, if a major internal validity problem is dissociating the intervention under analysis from other interventions that might have used the same cutoff, one can replicate the analysis using data from a period before the intervention to show that there is no discontinuity prior to the intervention and a discontinuity after it—as previously described for the study of the effects of Medicaid eligibility on the number of doctor visits.

REGRESSION DISCONTINUITY—EXPERIMENT OR QUASI-EXPERIMENT?

Both in this book and in our previous work (Campbell & Stanley, 1966; Cook & Campbell, 1979; Cook & Shadish, 1994), we categorized the regression discontinuity design as a quasi-experiment. This is partly due to our understanding of a quasi-experiment—a design that has structural features of an experiment but that lacks random assignment. Clearly the RD design is a quasi-experiment by this understanding. Moreover, other good reasons make us reluctant to give RD a status equal to the randomized experiment. First, it is newer and its design and analytic shortfalls are not yet as clear as with the randomized experiment (Ahn, 1983; Cappelleri, Trochim, Stanley, & Reichardt, 1991; Reichardt, Trochim, & Cappelleri, 1995; Robbins & Zhang, 1988, 1989, 1990; J. Shapiro, 1984; T. Stanley, 1991; T. Stanley & Robinson, 1990; Trochim, Cappelleri, & Reichardt, 1991; Visser & deLeeuw, 1984; Williams, 1990). Second, accurate modeling of the functional form of the relationship between the assignment variable and the outcome is crucial in RD, requiring a more demanding statistical analysis than is the case for the more straightforward analyses that are often sufficient with randomized experiments. Third, the RD design has less power than the randomized experiment (Cappelleri et al., 1994), due principally to colinearity between the assignment and treatment variables, especially as the cutoff is placed at the third decile or lower (Cappelleri, 1991). But even with cutoffs at the mean, for small effect sizes the RD design requires 2.73 times as many participants as in a balanced randomized experiment to reach .80 power; with medium effect sizes, the ratio is 2.54; and with large effects, it is 2.34 (Cappelleri et al., 1994). Table 7.2 summarizes various strategies for increasing power in the RD design. Of course, standard advice, such as to increase the reliability of measurement and the size of the effect, apply to RD, too.

However, other authors say the RD design is more than just a quasi-experiment. Mosteller (1990), for example, claimed that "by this author's definition—which is that in an experiment the investigator controls the application of treatments—the regression-discontinuity design actually is an experiment" (p. 225). Similarly, if one defines an experiment as any design that is known to yield an unbiased estimate of

TABLE 7.2 Methods for Increasing Power in Regression Discontinuity

1. Place the cutoff at the mean on the assignment variable.
2. Use a continuous assignment variable or one with more ordinal categories rather than fewer.
3. Choose an assignment variable that is as little correlated with treatment as possible (which can sometimes be done by creating a composite from multiple assignment variables).
4. Be careful not to overfit nonlinear and interaction terms to the analysis model; if unnecessary, they use up degrees of freedom.
5. Assign those who fall into a middle cutoff interval to one condition and those who fall on either side of the interval to the other condition; this reduces colinearity between assignment variable and treatment variable.
6. Combine RD with a randomized experiment, with the study being more powerful the wider the range of the cutoff interval in which participants are randomly assigned.

treatment effects, then the RD design would be an experiment by that definition, too. We will elaborate some of these similarities further as we turn to the topic of the next chapter in this book, the randomized experiment.

APPENDIX 7.1: THE LOGIC OF STATISTICAL PROOFS ABOUT REGRESSION DISCONTINUITY

Several authors give proofs that RD provides unbiased estimates of treatment effects (Cappelleri, 1991; Goldberger, 1972a, 1972b; Rubin, 1977). The details of such proofs are beyond the scope of this chapter, but it is worth explaining their general logic to highlight the difference between RD and other quasi-experiments. Some of the arguments pertain to the points about measurement error made graphically for the special cases in Figure 7.8, so that is a good starting point. We start with the simplifying assumption that only treatment and the assignment variable can affect outcome (we generalize the argument shortly). The statistical proofs then hinge on showing that "the population partial regression coefficient obtained by regressing measurement error, u, on the perfectly measured treatment variable, Z, controlling for or holding constant the fallibly measured covariate, X" is equal to zero: $B_{u,Z|X} = 0$ (Cappelleri, Trochim, Stanley, & Reichardt, 1991, p. 406; see also Cappelleri, 1991, p. 178). Conceptually, this means that at any given score on the assignment variable (X), assignment is completely and perfectly known, so the partial correlation is zero between errors of measurement in the assignment variable (u) and the dummy variable representing treatment assignment (Z)—once we know X, we know Z perfectly, and information about u tells us nothing more about Z (here we follow Cappelleri, 1991, and use u rather than e to refer to error). When this latter condition holds, as it does in regression discontinuity, the regression coefficient for Z is an unbiased estimate of the treatment effect. Note that this condition also holds for the randomized experiment, because at any given level of a pretest (X), assignment to treatment (Z) is randomly determined, and so Z is only randomly related to any other variable, including both of the components of X: the true score (T) and errors of measurement (u).

By contrast, in correlational data and in nonequivalent control group designs, errors of measurement in covariates are often correlated with assignment to treatment for at least some levels of X. This is illustrated in Figure 7.8. Suppose the true selection mechanism is some unknown and unobserved true score, T, rather than the observed score, X; for example, any participant with T at pretest of 56 or higher is selected into the treatment group. If the pretest X has no error (it is a perfect measure of T), looking only at pretest scores, we would correctly identify to which condition each participant was assigned, as is seen in Figures 7.8a and 7.8c. But in a nonequivalent control group design, we cannot observe T; we can only observe the fallibly measured covariate X as a proxy for the true selection mechanism T. Some participants who belong in the treatment group because their true scores are greater than 56 in 7.8a are now incorrectly predicted to be in the control group because their observed pretest scores are less than 56 in 7.8b. This misassignment occurred because some negative errors were added to some of the true scores just above 56 that caused the observed scores to fall below 56. It is clear that these errors are now one of the causes of Z, so $B_{u,Z|X}$ no longer equals zero. In plain English, if assignment to treatment really was caused by the true score (T) being greater than 56, we are making a mistake when we say that only those participants with observed scores (X) greater than 56 were in treatment, and that mistake was clearly caused by, and therefore correlated with, random measurement error. The coefficient $B_{u,Z|X}$ simply indicates how large a mistake we made.

Now we generalize the argument. The previous paragraphs treated u as if it consisted only of random measurement error. In fact, the same proof generalizes to the case in which u is a disturbance term that includes not only measurement error but also any **omitted variables** that affect outcome. This more general argument is intuitively as follows (Mohr, 1988, 1995, provides more detail). Some omitted variables will be related to outcome but will be uncorrelated with the predictors in the regression equation. Such variables will not cause problems for estimating the treatment effect because they have no mechanism through which to influence the relevant regression coefficients; this much is the same as a randomized experiment. Other omitted variables will be correlated with both outcome and with some variables in the regression equation. If a child's achievement test score is the assignment variable, for example, the mother's education may well be correlated with it and influence study outcome. But to understand why this is not a problem in RD, we must distinguish between that part of the omitted variable that is correlated with the assignment variable and that which is uncorrelated. Definitionally, the uncorrelated part cannot influence the regression coefficient of the assignment variable. The influence of the correlated part on outcome is already captured by the regression coefficient for the assignment variable by virtue of the nature of correlation. This means that this regression coefficient now reflects the *confounded* influence of the assignment variable and the omitted variable; hence it is not an unbiased estimate of the effects of the assignment variable on outcome. But this is not a problem because the regression coefficient of the assignment variable is not the coefficient of interest; rather, the regression coefficient of the treatment dummy variable is the one of interest. So how is the regression coefficient for treatment affected by the omitted variable in RD? Not at all. That part of the omitted variable that is correlated with X is already partialed out of the coefficient for Z; it is represented in the coefficient for X. That part of the omitted variable that is uncorrelated with X must also be uncorrelated with Z because Z is perfectly known once X is known.[13] Notice also that this uncorrelated part of the omitted variable is in the error term of the regression equation, so the error term is uncorrelated with the treatment dummy variable—just as is the case in the randomized experiment.

It is crucial to note that the key to the preceding logic was that Z was perfectly predicted by X; this is not the case when selection is not determined totally by the assignment variable, as in other nonequivalent control group designs. In such cases, parts of the omitted variables in the error term that are uncorrelated with X may then still be correlated (confounded) with Z. Because OLS regression *always* chooses beta coefficients to minimize this correlation, those weights will be wrong to the degree that such a correlation is present in the data, for then the data do not fit the assumptions of the OLS regression model. The resulting beta weight for treatment effect may be biased as a result.

---

13. Notice that this does not mean that Z is perfectly correlated with X; in fact, it is better that Z not be perfectly correlated with X as long as any remaining factors depend solely on chance. At the extreme, when X and Z have zero correlation, assignment based on X is effectively random. As an example, X might be a coin toss or a roll of dice.

8

Randomized Experiments: Rationale, Designs, and Conditions Conducive to Doing Them

Ran·dom (răn′dəm): [From at random, by chance, at great speed, from Middle English *randon*, speed, violence, from Old French from *randir*, to *run*, of Germanic origin.] adj.   1. Having no specific pattern, purpose, or objective: *random movements; a random choice*. See Synonyms at chance.   2. Statistics. Of or relating to the same or equal chances or probability of occurrence for each member of a group.

DOES EARLY preschool intervention with disadvantaged children improve their later life? The Perry Preschool Program experiment, begun in 1962, studied this question with 128 low-income African-American children who were randomly assigned to receive either a structured preschool program or no treatment. Ninety-five percent of participants were followed to age 27, and it was found that treatment group participants did significantly better than controls in employment, high school graduation, arrest records, home ownership, welfare receipt, and earnings (Schweinhart, Barnes, & Weikart, 1993), although early IQ and academic aptitude gains were not maintained into early adulthood. Along with other experimental evidence on the effects of preschool interventions (e.g., Olds et al., 1997; Olds et al., 1998), these results helped marshal continued political support and funding for programs such as Head Start in the United States. In this chapter, we present the basic logic and design of randomized experiments such as this one, and we analyze the conditions under which it is less difficult to implement them outside the laboratory.

In the natural sciences, scientists introduce an intervention under circumstances in which no other variables are confounded with its introduction. They then look to see how things change—for instance, whether an increase in heat affects the pressure of a gas. To study this, a scientist might place the gas in a fixed enclosure, measure the pressure, heat the gas, and then measure the pressure again to see if it has changed. The gas is placed in the enclosure to isolate it from anything else that would affect the pressure inside. But even in this simple example, the intervention is still a molar treatment package that is difficult to explicate fully. The enclosure is made of a certain material, the heat comes from a certain kind of burner, the humidity is at a certain level, and so forth. Full control and full isolation of the "intended" treatment are difficult, even in the natural sciences.

In much social research, more formidable control problems make successful experimentation even more difficult. For example, it is impossible to isolate a person from her family in order to "remove" the influences of family. Even in agricultural tests of a new seed, the plot on which those seeds are planted cannot be isolated from its drainage or soil. So many scientists rely on an approach to experimental control that is different from physical isolation—random assignment. The randomized experiment has its primary systematic roots in the agricultural work of statistician R. A. Fisher (1925, 1926, 1935; see Cowles, 1989, for a history of Fisher's work). Randomization was sometimes used earlier (e.g., Dehue, 2000; Gosnell, 1927; Hacking, 1988; Hrobjartsson, Gotzche, & Gluud, 1998; McCall, 1923; Peirce & Jastrow, 1884; Richet, 1884; Stigler, 1986). But Fisher explicated the statistical rationale and analyses that tie causal inference to the physical randomization of units to conditions in an experiment (Fisher, 1999).

THE THEORY OF RANDOM ASSIGNMENT

Random assignment reduces the plausibility of alternative explanations for observed effects. In this, it is like other design features such as pretests, cohorts, or nonequivalent dependent variables. But random assignment is distinguished from those features by one very special characteristic shared only with the regression discontinuity design: it can yield unbiased estimates of the average treatment effect (Rosenbaum, 1995a).[1] Moreover, it does this with greater efficiency than the

---

1. Three observations about the phrase "unbiased estimates of average treatment effects" are worth noting. First, some statisticians would prefer to describe the advantage of randomization as yielding a consistent estimator (one that converges on its population parameter as sample size increases), especially because we never have the infinite number of samples suggested by the theory of expectations discussed shortly in this chapter. We use the term *unbiased* in this book primarily because it will be more intuitively understood by nonstatistical readers and because it fits better with the qualitative logic of bias control that undergirds our validity typology. Second, in a random sampling model, sample means are always unbiased estimates of population means, so differences between sample means are always unbiased estimates of differences between population means. The latter estimates can be obtained without using random assignment. But such estimates are not the same as unbiased estimates of treatment effects. It is the latter that random assignment facilitates; hence its ability to facilitate the causal inference that we refer to with the shorthand phrase "unbiased estimates of treatment effects." Third, the phrase correctly refers to the average effect over units in the study, as distinguished from the effects on each unit in the study, which is not tested in a randomized experiment.

regression discontinuity design in a greater diversity of applications. Because unbiased and efficient causal inference is a goal of experimental research, it is crucial that researchers understand what random assignment is and how it works.

What Is Random Assignment?

Random assignment is achieved by any procedure that assigns units to conditions based only on chance, in which each unit has a nonzero probability of being assigned to a condition. A well-known random assignment procedure is a coin toss. On any given toss, a fair coin has a known (50%) chance of coming up heads. In an experiment with two conditions, if heads comes up for any unit, then that unit goes into the treatment condition; but if tails comes up, then it becomes a control unit. Another random assignment procedure is the roll of a fair die that has the numbers 1 through 6 on its sides. Any number from 1 to 6 has a known (1/6) chance of coming up, but exactly which number comes up on a roll is entirely up to chance. Later we recommend more formal randomization procedures, such as the use of tables of random numbers. But coin tosses and dice rolls are well-known and intuitively plausible introductions to randomization.

Random *assignment* is not random *sampling*. We draw random samples of units from a population by chance in public opinion polls when we ask random samples of people about their opinions. Random sampling ensures that answers from the sample approximate what we would have gotten had we asked everyone in the population. Random assignment, by contrast, facilitates causal inference by making samples randomly similar to *each other,* whereas random sampling makes a sample similar to *a population.* The two procedures share the idea of "randomness," but the purposes of this randomness are quite different.

Why Randomization Works

The literature contains several complementary statistical and conceptual explanations for why and how random assignment facilitates causal inference:

- It ensures that alternative causes are not confounded with a unit's treatment condition.
- It reduces the plausibility of threats to validity by distributing them randomly over conditions.
- It equates groups on the expected value of all variables at pretest, measured or not.
- It allows the researcher to know and model the selection process correctly.
- It allows computation of a valid estimate of error variance that is also orthogonal to treatment.

These seemingly different explanations are actually closely related. None of them by itself completely captures what random assignment does, but each sheds light on part of the explanation.

Random Assignment and Threats to Internal Validity

If treatment groups could be equated before treatment, and if they were different after treatment, then pretest selection differences could not be a cause of observed posttest differences. Given equal groups at pretest, the control group posttest serves as a source of counterfactual inference for the treatment group posttest, within limits we elaborate later. Note that the logic of causal inference is at work here. The temporal structure of the experiment ensures that cause precedes effect. Whether cause covaries with effect is easily checked in the data within known probabilities. The remaining task is to show that most alternative explanations of the cause-effect relationship are implausible. The randomized experiment does so by distributing these threats randomly over conditions. So treatment units will tend to have the same average characteristics as those not receiving treatment. The only systematic difference between conditions is treatment.

For example, consider a study of the effects of psychotherapy on stress. Stress has many alternative causes, such as illness, marital conflict, job loss, arguments with colleagues, and the death of a parent. Even positive events, such as getting a new job or getting married, cause stress. The experimenter must ensure that none of these alternative causes is confounded with receiving psychotherapy, because then one could not tell whether it was psychotherapy or one of the confounds that caused any differences at posttest. Random assignment ensures that every client who receives psychotherapy is equally likely as every client in the control group to have experienced, say, a new job or a recent divorce. Random assignment does not prevent these alternative causes (e.g., divorce) from occurring; nor does it isolate the units from the occurrence of such events. People in a randomized experiment still get divorces and new jobs. Random assignment simply ensures that such events are no more likely to happen to treatment clients than to control clients. As a result, if psychotherapy clients report less stress than control clients at posttest, the cause of that difference is unlikely to be that one group had more new jobs or divorces, because such stressors are equally likely in both groups. The only systematic difference left to explain the result is the treatment.

The only internal validity threat that randomization prevents from occurring is selection bias, which it rules out by definition, because selection bias implies that a systematically biased method was used for selecting units into groups but chance can have no such systematic bias. As for the other internal validity threats, randomization does not prevent units from maturing or regressing; nor does it prevent events other than treatment from occurring after the study begins (i.e., history). Pretests can still cause a testing effect, and changes in instrumentation can still occur. Random assignment simply reduces the likelihood that these threats are confounded with treatment.

Equating Groups on Expectation

In statistics, the preceeding explanation is often summarized by saying that random assignment equates groups on expectation at pretest. What does this mean? First, it does not mean that random assignment equates units on *observed* pretest scores. Howard, Krause, and Orlinsky (1986) remind us that when a deck of 52 playing cards is well shuffled, some players will still be dealt a better set of cards than others. This is called the luck of the draw by card players (and sampling error by statisticians). In card games, we do not expect every player to receive equally good cards for each hand, but we do expect the cards to be equal in the long run over many hands. All this is true of the randomized experiment. In any given experiment, observed pretest means will differ due to luck of the draw when some conditions are dealt a better set of participants than others. But we can expect that participants will be equal over conditions in the long run over many randomized experiments.

Technically, then, random assignment equates groups on the *expectation* of group means at pretest—that is, on the mean of the distribution of all possible sample means resulting from all possible random assignments of units to conditions. Imagine that a researcher randomly assigned units to treatment and control conditions in one study and then computed a sample mean on some variable for both conditions. These two means will almost certainly be different due to sampling error—the luck of the draw. But suppose the researcher repeated this process a second time, recorded the result, and continued to do this a very large number of times. At the end, the researcher would have a distribution of means for the treatment group over the samplings achieved and also one for the control group. Some of the treatment group means would be larger than others; the same would be true for the control group. But the average of all the means for the treatment group would be the same as the average of all the means for the control group. Thus the expectation to which the definition of random assignment is linked involves the mean of all possible means, not the particular means achieved in a single study.

When random differences do exist in observed pretest means, those differences will influence the results of the study. For example, if clients assigned to psychotherapy start off more depressed than those assigned to the control group despite random assignment, and if psychotherapy reduces depression, posttest depression scores might still be equal in both treatment and control groups because of the pretest group differences. Posttest differences between treatment and control groups then might suggest no treatment effect when treatment did, in fact, have an effect that was masked by sampling error in random assignment. More generally, the results of any individual randomized experiment will differ somewhat from the population effects by virtue of these chance pretest differences. Thus summaries of results from multiple randomized experiments on the same topic (as in psychotherapy meta-analysis) can yield more accurate estimates of treatment effects than any individual study. Even so, we still say that the estimate from an individual study is unbiased. Unbiased simply means that any differences between the observed effects and the population effect are the result of chance; it does not mean that the results of the individual study are identical to the "true" population effect.

The preceding explanation uses pretest means to illustrate how randomization works. However, this is merely a teaching device, and the use of actual measured pretests is irrelevant to the logic. Randomization equates groups on expectations of *every variable before treatment, whether observed or not.* In practice, of course, pretests are very useful because they allow better diagnosis of and adjustment for attrition, they facilitate the use of statistical techniques that increase statistical power, and they can be used to examine whether treatment is equally effective at different levels of the pretest.

Additional Statistical Explanations of How Random Assignment Works

Randomization ensures that confounding variables are unlikely to be *correlated* with the treatment condition a unit receives. That is, whether a coin toss comes up heads or tails is unrelated to whether you are divorced, nervous, old, male, or anything else. Consequently, we can predict that the pretest correlation between treatment assignment and potential confounding variables should not be significantly different from zero.

This zero correlation is very useful statistically. To understand this requires a digression into how to estimate treatment effects in linear models. Let us distinguish between the *study* and the *analysis* of the study. In a *study* of the effects of psychotherapy, stress is the dependent variable (Y_i), psychotherapy is the independent variable (Z_i), and potential confounds are contained in an error term (e_i). In the *analysis* of that study, the effects of treatment are estimated from the linear model:

$$Y_i = \mu + \hat{\beta}Z_i + e_i \qquad (8.1)$$

where μ is a constant, $\hat{\beta}$ is a regression coefficient, and the subscript i ranges from 1 to n, where n is the number of units in the study. Thus Y_i is the score of the ith unit on a measure of stress, Z_i is scored as 1 if the unit is in psychotherapy and 0 if not, and e_i consists of all potential confounding variables. In the analysis, if $\hat{\beta}$ is significantly different from zero, then psychotherapy had a significant effect on stress, and $\hat{\beta}$ measures the magnitude and direction of that effect.

For all this to work properly, however, the model that is specified in the analysis must match the reality of the study. Failure to achieve this match is called **specification error**—an incorrect specification of the model presumed to give rise to the data. Specifically, the statistical techniques used to estimate models such as equation (8.1) choose values of $\hat{\beta}$ so that correlations between the resulting errors and the predictor variables are zero (Reichardt & Gollob, 1986). The statistics do this whether or not that correlation really was zero in the study. Fortunately, random assignment assures that the correlation in the study will be zero for reasons outlined in the previous section; so the study matches the analysis. However, in nonrandomized studies, many confounds are probably correlated with receipt of treatment, but the computer program still chooses $\hat{\beta}$ so that the error is minimally correlated with the predictors in the data analysis, yielding a mismatch between the study and the analysis. The result is an incorrect estimate of treatment effects.[2]

A related way of thinking about the benefit of randomization is that it provides a valid estimate of error variance (e.g., Keppel, 1991; R. Kirk, 1982). Two possible causes of total variation in outcome (i.e., of how much people differ from each other in stress levels) exist—variation caused by treatment conditions (e.g., whether the person received psychotherapy) and variation caused by other factors (e.g., all the other causes of stress). Random assignment allows us to separate out these two sources of variability. Error variation is estimated as the amount of variation among units within each condition. For example, for those clients who were assigned to psychotherapy, variation in whether or not they received psychotherapy cannot contribute to their different stress levels because there was no such variation—they all got psychotherapy. So any variance in outcome among people randomly assigned to psychotherapy must be caused only by confounds. The average of each of these computed error terms from within each condition serves as our best estimate of error. This error term is the baseline against which we see if differences *between* treatment conditions exceed the differences that normally occur among units as a function of all the other causes of the outcome.

Summary

Random assignment facilitates causal inference in many ways—by equating groups before treatment begins, by making alternative explanations implausible, by creating error terms that are uncorrelated with treatment variables, and by allowing valid estimates of error terms. These are interrelated explanations. For example, groups that are equated before treatment begins allow fewer alternative explanations if differences later emerge, and uncorrelated errors are necessary to estimate the size of the error term. But randomization is not the only way to accomplish these things. Alternative explanations can sometimes be made implausible through logical means, as is typically the aim with quasi-experimentation; and uncorrelated errors can be created with other forms of controlled assignment to conditions, as with the regression discontinuity design. But randomization is the only design feature that accomplishes all of these goals at once, and it does so more reliably and with better known properties than any alternatives.

2. One way to think about the selection bias models in Chapter 5 is that they try to make the error terms orthogonal to the predictors in a statistically acceptable way, but this is hard, so they often fail; and one way to think about the regression discontinuity design is that it is able to make this correlation zero for reasons outlined in the Appendix to Chapter 7.

Random Assignment and Units of Randomization

We have frequently used the word "unit" to describe whatever or whoever is assigned to experimental conditions. A unit is simply "an opportunity to apply or withhold the treatment" (Rosenbaum, 1995a, p. 17).

Kinds of Units

In much field experimentation, the units being assigned to conditions are people—clients in psychotherapy, patients in cancer trials, or students in educational studies. But units can be other kinds of entities (Boruch & Foley, 2000). R. A. Fisher (1925) assigned plots of land randomly to different levels of fertilizer or different strains of seed. In psychological and medical research, animals are often randomly assigned to conditions. Researchers in the New Jersey Negative Income Tax experiment (Rees, 1974) randomly assigned families to conditions. Gosnell (1927) randomly assigned neighborhoods to conditions. Edgington (1987) discussed single-participant designs in which treatment times were randomly assigned. Schools have been randomly assigned (Cook et al., 1998; Cook, Hunt & Murphy, 2000). Nor is randomization useful just in the social sciences. Wilson (1952) describes a study in which the steel plates used in gauges were randomized prior to testing different explosives, so that variations in the strength of the plates would not be systematically associated with any one explosive. The possibilities are endless.

Higher Order Units

Units such as families, work sites, classrooms, psychotherapy groups, hospital wards, neighborhoods, or communities are aggregates of individual units such as family members, employees, students, clients, patients, neighbors, or residents. Studies of the effects of treatments on such higher order units are common, and a literature has developed specific to experiments on higher order units (e.g., Donner & Klar, 2000; Gail, Mark, Carroll, Green, & Pee, 1996; Moerbeek, van Breukelen, & Berger, 2000; Murray, 1998; Sorensen, Emmons, Hunt, & Johnston, 1998). For example, the National Home Health Agency Prospective Payment Demonstration experiment assigned 142 home health agencies to different Medicare payment options to see how use of care was affected (Goldberg, 1997); the San Diego Nursing Home Incentive Reimbursement Experiment assigned 36 nursing homes to different Medicare reimbursement options (Jones & Meiners, 1986); the Tennessee Class Size Experiment randomly assigned 347 classes to large or small numbers of students (Finn & Achilles, 1990); and Kelly et al. (1997) randomly assigned eight cities to two conditions to study an HIV prevention intervention. The higher order unit need not be a naturally occurring entity such as a work site or a neighborhood. The researcher can create the higher order unit solely for the research, as in the case of a stop-smoking program that is administered in small groups so that participants can benefit from mutual support. Nor is it necessary that the individual units know or interact with each other. For instance, when physicians' practices are randomized to conditions, the physician's practice is a higher order unit even though the majority of the physician's patients will never meet. Finally, sometimes a treatment cannot be restricted to particular individuals by its very nature. For example, when a radio-based driving safety campaign is broadcast over a listening area, the entire area receives treatment, even if only some individual drivers are formally included in the research (Reicken et al., 1974).

There are often good practical and scientific reasons to use aggregate units. In a factory experiment, it may not be practical to isolate each worker and give him or her a unique treatment, for resentful demoralization or diffusion of treatment might result. Similarly, in the first evaluation of "Plaza Sesamo," Diaz-Guerro and Holtzmann (1974) randomly assigned some individual children in Mexican day care centers to watch "Plaza Sesamo" in small groups. They were in a special room with two adult monitors who focused attention on the show. At the same time, other children watched cartoons in larger groups in the regular room with no special monitors. Because treating classmates in these different ways may have led to a focused inequity, it would have been desirable if the experimenters' resources had permitted them to assign entire classes to treatments.

The research question also determines at which level of aggregation units should be randomized. If effects on individuals are at issue, the individual should be the unit, if possible. But if school or neighborhood phenomena are involved or if the intervention is necessarily performed on an aggregate, then the unit of randomization should not be at a lower level of aggregation.[3] Thus, if one is investigating whether frequent police car patrols deter crime in a neighborhood, different amounts of patrolling should be assigned to neighborhoods and not, say, to blocks within neighborhoods.

In aggregate units, the individual units within aggregates may no longer be independent of each other because they are exposed to common influences besides treatment. For example, students within classrooms talk to each other, have the same teacher, and may all receive treatment at the same time of day. These dependencies lead to what used to be called the **unit of analysis** problem (Koepke & Flay, 1989) but what is more recently discussed as multilevel models or hierarchical linear models. Because this book focuses on design rather than analysis, we do not treat the analytic issues in detail (Feldman, McKinlay, & Niknian, 1996; Gail et al., 1996; Green et al., 1995; Murray, 1998; Murray et al., 1994; Murray, Moskowitz, & Dent, 1996). But from a design perspective, using higher order units raises several issues.

3. The nesting of participants in higher order units can still pose problems even when individuals are assigned to treatment. For example, if individual cancer patients who each have multiple tumors are randomly assigned to treatment but treatment is administered separately to each tumor and tumor response is observed separately for each tumor, those responses are not independent (Sargent, Sloan, & Cha, 1999).

Studies that use higher order units frequently have fewer such units available to randomize. Consider the limiting case in which students in one classroom are given the treatment and those in a second classroom serve as controls. Treatment conditions are then totally confounded with classrooms, making it impossible to tell if performance differences at posttest are due to differences in treatment or in classroom characteristics, such as the charisma of the teacher, the mix of students, or the physical conditions of the class. When more than one, but still few, higher order units are assigned to conditions, randomization may result in very different means, variances, and sample sizes across conditions. Such cases are surprisingly common in the literature (e.g., Simpson, Klar, & Donner, 1995); but they incur substantial problems for internal and statistical conclusion validity (Varnell, Murray, & Baker, in press). Such problems occur most often with studies of schools and communities, because it is expensive to add new sites. Random assignment of higher order units from within blocks or strata can reduce such problems. For example, McKay, Sinisterra, McKay, Gomez, and Lloreda (1978) studied the effects of five levels of a program of nutrition, health care, and education on the cognitive ability of chronically undernourished children in Cali, Colombia. They divided Cali into 20 relatively homogeneous neighborhood sectors. Then they rank-ordered sectors on a standardized combination of pretreatment screening scores and randomly assigned those sectors to the five conditions from blocks of five. The Kansas City Preventive Patrol experiment followed a similar procedure in its study of whether the visible presence of police patrols deterred crime (Kelling, Pate, Dieckman, & Brown, 1976). The researchers placed 15 patrol districts into blocks of three that were homogenous on demographic characteristics; they then randomly assigned districts from these blocks into the three experimental conditions.

Planning proper sample size and analysis of designs with higher order units is more complex than usual because individual units are not independent within aggregate units (Bock, 1989; Bryk & Raudenbush, 1992; Bryk, Raudenbush, & Congdon, 1996; H. Goldstein, 1987; Raudenbush, 1997; Snijders & Bosker, 1999). Given the same number of individual units, power is almost always lower in designs with higher order units than in those with individual units; and special power analyses must be used.[4] Moreover, power is improved more by increasing the number of aggregate units (e.g., adding more classrooms) than by increasing the number of individuals within units (e.g., adding more students within classrooms). Indeed, at a certain point the latter can rapidly become wasteful of resources without improving power at all, depending on the size of the dependencies within cluster (as measured by the intraclass correlation).

4. See Donner (1992); Donner and Klar (1994); Feldman et al. (1996); Gail, Byar, Pechacek, and Corle (1992); Gail et al. (1996); Hannan and Murray (1996); Koepsell et al. (1991); Murray (1998); Murray and Hannan (1990); Murray, Hannan, and Baker (1996); Raudenbush (1997); and Raudenbush and Liu (2000). Both Orr (1999) and Raudenbush and Liu (2000) address tradeoffs between power and the cost of adding more participants within and between treatment sites.

Often resources will prevent the researcher from including the number of higher order units that the power analyses suggest is required to conduct a sensitive statistical analysis. In such situations, it helps to treat the study as if it were a quasi-experiment, adding features such as switching replications or double pretests to facilitate causal inferences. Shadish, Cook, and Houts (1986) discuss this strategy and provide illustrations. For example, in the Cali study, McKay et al. (1978) staggered the introduction of treatment across the five treatment groups, so that some received treatment for the full length of the study but others received treatment progressively later. All had a common final posttest time. Their demonstration that effects started concurrent with implementation of treatment in each group helped to bolster the study's interpretability despite its use of only four higher order units per condition. Finally, measurement of the characteristics of higher order units helps diagnose the extent to which those characteristics are confounded with treatment.

Researchers sometimes create an unnecessary unit of analysis problem when, in order to save the extra costs and logistical complexity of treating participants individually, they administer to a group a treatment that could have been administered to individuals. By doing this, the researcher may thus create dependencies among participants within groups. For example, suppose a treatment for insomnia is administered to 50 participants in 10 groups of 5 people each; and suppose further that the treatment could have been administered individually in the sense that it does not involve transindividual theoretical components such as mutual interpersonal support. Nonetheless, group members are now exposed to many common influences. For example, some of them might become romantically involved, with possible consequences for their sleep patterns! These group influences may vary from group to group and so affect outcome differentially. So researchers should administer the treatment to individual units if the research question makes this possible; if not, then group membership should be taken into account in the analysis.

The Limited Reach of Random Assignment

Though random assignment is usually better than other design features for inferring that an observed difference between treatment and control groups is due to some cause, its applicability is often limited. Random assignment is useful only if a researcher has already decided that a local molar causal inference is of most interest. Such inferences are a common goal in social research, but they are not the only goal. Yet random assignment is conceptually irrelevant to all other research goals. Further, random assignment is just one part of experimental design, and experimental design is only part of an overall research design. Experimental design involves the scheduling of observations, the choice of treatments and comparisons, the selection of observations and measures, the determination of who should be the respondents, and the manner of assigning units to treatments. Random assignment deals with only the last of these issues, so to assign at random does not guarantee a useful experimental or research design.

Thus, if a randomized experiment is conducted with units that do not correspond to the population of theoretical or policy interest, the usefulness of the research is weakened even if the quality of the causal inference is high. Rossi and Lyall (1976) criticized the New Jersey Negative Income Tax Experiment because the respondents were working poor, but most guaranteed incomes in a national scheme would go to the jobless poor. Similarly, Cook et al. (1975) criticized Ball and Bogatz (1970) for manipulating levels of social encouragement to view "Sesame Street," thus confounding viewing with encouragement. Larson (1976) criticized the Kansas City Patrol Experiment because the amount of police patrolling that was achieved in the high-patrolling condition was not even as high as the average in New York City and because the contrast between high- and low-patrol areas in Kansas City was reduced due to police squad cars crossing atypically often over the low-patrol areas with their lights flashing and sirens screaming. These are all useful criticisms of details from social experiments, though none is a criticism of random assignment itself. Such criticisms have implications for the desirability of random assignment only to the extent that implementing such assignment caused the problems to emerge. This is rarely the case.

SOME DESIGNS USED WITH RANDOM ASSIGNMENT

This section reviews many variants of randomized experimental designs (see Table 8.1; for other variations, see Fleiss, 1986; Keppel, 1991; Kirk, 1982; Winer, Brown, & Michels, 1991). The designs we present are the most commonly used in field research, providing the basic building blocks from which more complex designs can be constructed. This section uses the same design notation as in earlier chapters, except that the letter R indicates that the group on that line was formed by random assignment. We place R at the start of each line, although random assignment could occur either before or after a pretest, and the placement of R would vary accordingly.

The Basic Design

The basic randomized experiment requires at least two conditions, random assignment of units to conditions, and posttest assessment of units. Structurally, it can be represented as:

$$R \quad X \quad O$$
$$R \quad \quad \quad O$$

TABLE 8.1 Schematic Diagrams of Randomized Designs

The Basic Randomized Design Comparing Treatment to Control

R	X	O
R		O

The Basic Randomized Design Comparing Two Treatments

R	X_A	O
R	X_B	O

The Basic Randomized Design Comparing Two Treatments and a Control

R	X_A	O
R	X_B	O
R		O

The Pretest-Posttest Control Group Design

R	O	X	O
R	O		O

The Alternative-Treatments Design with Pretest

R	O	X_A	O
R	O	X_B	O

Multiple Treatments and Controls with Pretest

R	O	X_A	O
R	O	X_B	O
R	O	O	

Factorial Design

R	X_{A1B1}	O
R	X_{A1B2}	O
R	X_{A2B1}	O
R	X_{A2B2}	O

Longitudinal Design

R	$O \ldots O$	X	O	$O \ldots O$
R	$O \ldots O$		O	$O \ldots O$

A Crossover Design

R	O	X_A	O	X_B	O
R	O	X_B	O	X_A	O

Note: For simplicity, we place the R (to indicate random assignment) at the front of the schematic diagram; however, assignment sometimes occurs before and sometimes after the pretest, so that the placement of R could be varied accordingly.

A good example of the use of this design with a single treatment and a control group is the test of the Salk polio vaccine in 1954. More than 400,000 children were randomly assigned to receive either the vaccine or a placebo (Meier, 1972).

A key issue is the nature of the control condition. Selection of a particular kind of control group depends on what one wants to control. For example, a no-treatment control condition tests the effects of a molar treatment package, including all its active and passive, important and trivial components. However, when interest is in the effects of a part of that package, the control should include everything but that part. In drug studies, for example, the researcher often wants to separate out the effects of the pharmaceutically active ingredients in the drugs from the effects of the rest of the package—things such as swallowing a pill or having contact with medical personnel. A placebo control does this, with medical personnel providing patients with, say, an inert pill in a manner that includes all the extraneous conditions except the active ingredients (Beecher, 1955).

Many types of control groups exist, for example, no-treatment controls, dose-response controls, wait-list controls, expectancy controls, or attention-only controls (Borkovec & Nau, 1972; Garber & Hollon, 1991; International Conference on Harmonization, 1999; Jacobson & Baucom, 1977; Kazdin & Wilcoxon, 1976; O'Leary & Borkovec, 1978; Orne, 1962; Seligman, 1969; Shapiro & Shapiro, 1997). The variations are limited only by the researcher's imagination. But in all cases the question is always, "Control for what?" For instance, Rossi and Lyall (1976, 1978) criticized the New Jersey Negative Income Tax in part on this basis—that the control group differed not only in failure to receive the treatment of interest but also in receiving far fewer and less intrusive administrative experiences than the treatment group.

Two Variants on the Basic Design

One variation compares two treatments by substituting X_A and X_B for the X and blank space in the previous diagram:

$$
\begin{array}{ccc}
R & X_A & O \\
R & X_B & O
\end{array}
$$

If X_A is an innovative treatment, for example, X_B is often a "gold-standard" treatment of known efficacy. The causal question is then, "What is the effect of the innovation compared with what would have happened if units had received the standard treatment?" This design works well if the standard treatment has a known track record against no-treatment controls. But if not, and if those receiving X_A are not different from those receiving X_B at posttest, the researcher cannot know if both treatments were equally effective or equally ineffective. In that case, a control group helps:

$$
\begin{array}{ccc}
R & X_A & O \\
R & X_B & O \\
R & & O
\end{array}
$$

This design was used in Boston to study the effects of an experimental housing project designed to improve the kinds of neighborhoods in which poor families lived (Katz, Kling, & Liebman, 1997; Orr, 1999). Poverty families in Treatment A received housing vouchers good for use only in low-poverty areas so that if they moved, they would move to better neighborhoods; those in Treatment B received vouchers for use anywhere, including in high-poverty areas; and those in the control group did not receive any vouchers at all.

Risks to This Design Due to Lack of Pretest

Omitting a pretest is a virtue whenever pretesting is expected to have an unwanted sensitization effect; and it is a necessity when a pretest cannot be gathered (as in some studies of cognitive development in infants), is seriously impractical (as with expensive and time-consuming interviews of patients by physicians), or is known to be a constant (as in studies of mortality in which all patients are alive at the start). Otherwise, the absence of a pretest is usually risky if there is any likelihood of attrition from the study; in fact, some observers cite the need for a pretest as one of the most important lessons to emerge from the last 20 years of social experiments (Haveman, 1987). Attrition occurs often in field experiments, leaving the researcher with the need to examine whether (1) those who dropped out of the study were different from those who remained and, especially, (2) if those who dropped out of one condition were different from those who dropped out of the other condition(s). Pretreatment information, preferably on the same dependent variable used at posttest, helps enormously in answering such questions.

Of course, attrition is not inevitable in field experiments. In medical trials of surgical procedures that have immediate outcomes, the treatments happen too quickly to allow much attrition; and patient follow-up care is often thorough enough and medical records good enough that posttests and follow-up observations on patients are available. An example is Taylor et al.'s (1978) study of short-term mortality rates among 50 heart attack patients randomly assigned to receive either manual or mechanical chest compression during cardiopulmonary resuscitation. The intervention was started and finished within the space of an hour; the heart attack patients could not very well get up and leave the hospital; and the dependent variable was quickly and easily gathered. A second situation conducive to minimal attrition is one in which the outcome is a matter of mandatory public record. For instance, in both the LIFE (Living Insurance for Ex-Offenders) experiment and the TARP (Transitional Aid for Released Prisoners) experiment (Rossi, Berk, & Lenihan, 1980), the main dependent variable was arrests, about which records were available for all participants from public sources. In general, however, attrition from conditions will occur in most field experiments, and pretests are vital to the methods we outline in Chapter 10 for dealing with attrition.

The Pretest-Posttest Control Group Design

Consequently, adding pretests to the basic randomized design is highly recommended:

$$R \quad O \quad X \quad O$$
$$R \quad O \quad \quad O$$

Or, if random assignment occurred after pretest,

$$O \quad R \quad X \quad O$$
$$O \quad R \quad \quad O$$

This is probably the most commonly used randomized field experiment. Its special advantage is its increased ability to cope with attrition as a threat to internal validity, in ways we outline in Chapter 10. A secondary advantage, however, is that it allows certain statistical analyses that increase power to reject the null hypothesis (Maxwell & Delaney, 1990). S. E. Maxwell (1994) says that allocating 75% of assessment to posttest and 25% to pretest is often a good choice to maximize power with this design. Maxwell, Cole, Arvey, and Salas (1991) discuss tradeoffs between ANCOVA using a pretest as a covariate and repeated-measures ANOVA with a longer posttest as a method for increasing power.

Although the researcher should try to make the pretest be identical to the outcome measures at posttest, this need not be the case. In research on child development, for example, tests for 8-year-old children must often be substantially different in content than those for 3-year-old children. If the pretest and posttest assess the same unidimensional construct, logistic test theory can sometimes be used to calibrate tests if they contain some common content (Lord, 1980), as McKay et al. (1978) did in the Cali study of changes in cognitive ability in 300 children between the ages of 30 and 84 months.

Alternative-Treatments Design with Pretest

The addition of pretests is also recommended when different substantive treatments are compared:

$$R \quad O \quad X_A \quad O$$
$$R \quad O \quad X_B \quad O$$

If posttests reveal no differences between groups, the researcher can examine pretest and posttest scores to learn whether both groups improved or if neither did.[5] This design is particularly useful when ethical concerns mitigate against comparing treatment

---

5. Here and elsewhere, we do not mean to imply that change scores would be desirable as measures of that improvement. ANCOVA will usually be much more powerful, and concerns about linearity and homogeneity of regression are at least as important for change scores as for ANCOVA.

with a control condition, for example, in medical research in which all patients must be treated. It is also useful when some treatment is the acknowledged gold standard against which all other treatments must measure up. Comparisons with this standard treatment have particularly practical implications for later decision-making.

Multiple Treatments and Controls with Pretest

The randomized experiment with pretests can involve a control group and multiple treatment groups:

$$
\begin{array}{cccc}
R & O & X_A & O \\
R & O & X_B & O \\
R & O & & O
\end{array}
$$

H. S. Bloom's (1990) study of reemployment services for displaced workers used this design. More than 2,000 eligible unemployed workers were assigned randomly to job-search assistance, job-search assistance plus occupational training, or no treatment. Note that the first treatment included only one part of the treatment in the second condition, giving some insight into which parts contributed most to outcome. This is sometimes called a **dismantling study,** though the dismantling was only partial because the study lacked an occupational-training-only condition. Clearly, resources and often logistics prevent the researcher from examining too many parts, for each part requires a large number of participants in order to test it well. And not all parts will be worth examining, particularly if some of the individual parts are unlikely to be implemented in policy or practice.

This design can be extended to include more than two alternative treatments or more than one control condition. An example is the National Institute of Mental Health Treatment of Depression Collaborative Research Program (NIMH-TDCRP; Elkin, Parloff, Hadley, & Autry, 1985; Elkin et al., 1989; Imber et al., 1990). In this study, 250 depressed patients were randomly assigned to receive cognitive behavior therapy, interpersonal psychotherapy, antidepressant chemotherapy (imipramine) plus clinical management, or a placebo pill plus clinical management.

This design is also used to vary the independent variable in a series of increasing levels (sometimes called *parametric* or *dose-response* studies). For example, the Housing Allowance Demand Experiment randomly assigned families to receive housing subsidies equal to 0%, 20%, 30%, 40%, 50%, or 60% of their rent (Friedman & Weinberg, 1983). The Health Insurance Experiment randomly assigned families to insurance plans that required them to pay 0%, 25%, 50%, or 95% of the first $1,000 of covered services (Newhouse, 1993). The more levels of treatment are administered, the finer the assessment can be of the functional form of dosage effects. A wide range of treatment levels also allows the study to detect effects that might otherwise be missed if only two levels of a treatment that are not powerful enough to have an effect are varied. The Cali, Colombia, study (McKay et al., 1978), for example, administered a combined educational, nutritional, and medical treatment in four increasing dosage levels—990 hours, 2,070 hours, 3,130 hours, and 4,170 hours. At the smallest dosage—which itself took nearly a full year to implement and which might well be the maximum dosage many authors might consider—the effects were nearly undetectable, but McKay et al. (1978) still found effects because they included this wide array of higher dosages.

Factorial Designs

These designs use two or more independent variables (called *factors*), each with at least two levels (Figure 8.1). For example, one might want to compare 1 hour of tutoring (Factor A, Level 1) with 4 hours of tutoring (Factor A, Level 2) per week and also compare tutoring done by a peer (Factor B, Level 1) with that done by an adult (Factor B, Level 2). If the treatments are factorially combined, four groups or cells are created: 1 hour of tutoring from a peer (Cell A1B1), 1 hour from an adult (A1B2), 4 hours from a peer (A2B1), or 4 hours from an adult (A2B2). This is often described as a 2×2 ("two by two") factorial design written in the notation used in this book as:

$$
\begin{array}{lll}
R & X_{A1B1} & O \\
R & X_{A1B2} & O \\
R & X_{A2B1} & O \\
R & X_{A2B2} & O
\end{array}
$$

This logic extends to designs with more than two factors. If we add a third factor in which the tutor is or is not trained in effective tutoring methods (Factor C, Levels 1 and 2), we have a $2 \times 2 \times 2$ design with 8 possible cells. The levels of the factors can include control conditions, for example, by adding a no-tutoring condition to Factor A. This increases the number of levels of A so that we have a $3 \times 2 \times 2$ design with 12 cells. This notation generalizes to more factors and more levels in similar fashion.

Factorial designs have three major advantages:

- They often require fewer units.
- They allow testing combinations of treatments more easily.
- They allow testing interactions.

First, they often allow smaller sample sizes than would otherwise be needed.[6] An experiment to test for differences between peer versus adult tutoring might require

6. Two exceptions to this rule are (1) detecting interactions of special substantive interest may require larger sample sizes because power to detect interactions is usually lower than power to detect main effects; and (2) if the outcome is a low base rate event (e.g., death from pneumonia during the course of a brief clinical trial) and if the treatments in both factors reduce death, their combined effect may reduce the number of outcome events to the point that more participants are needed in the factorial design than if just one treatment were tested.

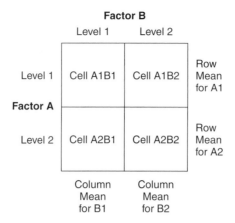

FIGURE 8.1 Factorial Design Terms and Notation

50 participants per condition, as might a second experiment to test for differences between 1 versus 4 hours of tutoring—a total of 200 participants. In a factorial design, fewer than 200 participants may be needed (the exact number would have to be determined by a power analysis) because each participant does double duty, being exposed to both treatments simultaneously.

Second, factorial designs allow the investigator to test whether a combination of treatments is more effective than one treatment. Suppose that an investigator runs both an experiment in which participants are assigned to either aspirin or placebo to see if aspirin reduces migraine headaches and a second experiment to test biofeedback versus placebo for the same outcome. These two experiments provide no information about the effects of aspirin and biofeedback applied jointly. The factorial design provides information about the effects of aspirin only, biofeedback only, aspirin plus biofeedback, or no treatment.

Third, factorial experiments test interactions among factors (Abelson, 1996; D. Meyer, 1991; Petty, Fabrigar, Wegener, & Priester, 1996; Rosnow & Rosenthal, 1989, 1996). Treatments produce *main effects;* for example, the main effect of aspirin relative to a placebo pill is to reduce headaches. Main effects are *average* effects that may be misleading if, for example, some kinds of headaches respond well to aspirin but others do not. Interactions occur when treatment effects are not constant but rather vary over levels of other factors, for example, if aspirin reduces tension headaches a lot but migraine headaches very little. Here the treatment (aspirin) interacts with a moderator variable (type of headache), the word *moderator* describing a second factor that interacts with (moderates the effect of) a treatment. The same general logic extends to designs with three or more factors, though higher order interactions are more difficult to interpret.

Interactions are often more difficult to detect than are main effects (Aiken & West, 1991; Chaplin, 1991, 1997; Cronbach & Snow, 1977; Fleiss, 1986), so large sample sizes with appropriate power analyses are essential whenever inter-actions are an important focus.[7] Indeed, some authors have argued that predicted interactions are sufficiently important in advancing scientific theory to warrant testing them at a larger than usual Type I error rate (Meehl, 1978; Platt, 1964; Smith & Sechrest, 1991; Snow, 1991). If testing a predicted interaction is at issue, deliberate oversampling of observations that are extreme on the interacting vari-ables provides a more powerful (and still unbiased) test of the interaction, al-though it gives a poorer estimate of the total variance accounted for by the pre-dictors. The test for the interaction could be done using an unweighted sample, and the test for total variance could be done using a sample that is weighted to re-flect the population of interest (McClelland & Judd, 1993). This is a special case of optimal design theory (e.g., A. Atkinson, 1985) that can help select treatment levels and combinations that maximize the power of the design to detect parame-ters that may be of particular policy or theoretical interest.

When using a factorial design, the researcher need not actually assign units to all possible combinations of factors, though empty cells can reduce power. It might waste resources to test treatment combinations that are of no theoretical in-terest or unlikely to be implemented in policy. The New Jersey Negative Income Tax (NJNIT) experiment, for example, studied proposals for dealing with poverty and welfare reform (Kershaw & Fair, 1976)—specifically, the joint effects of two independent variables: the guarantee level and the tax rate. Guarantee level was an amount of money paid to poor families or individuals if they had no other in-come; it was defined as 50%, 75%, 100%, or 125% of the poverty level. The tax rate was the rate at which that guaranteed income was reduced as a family's other income rises: 30%, 50%, or 70%. So the design was a 4 × 3 factorial experiment that could assign participants to 12 different cells. However, the investigators as-signed the 725 participants only to the eight cells that were not too costly and that were considered politically feasible for eventual policy implementation. The empty cells can complicate data analysis, but the flexibility of this option often outweighs the complications. This design is an example of a fractional factorial design that allows estimates of some higher order interaction terms even when the full factorial design is not implemented (Anderson & McLean, 1984; Box, Hunter, & Hunter, 1978; West, Aiken, & Todd, 1993).

Nested and Crossed Designs

In a **crossed** design, each level of each factor is exposed to (crossed with) all lev-els of all other factors. For example, in an educational experiment, if some stu-dents in each classroom are exposed to treatment and some to control, then the

---

7. Interactions are ordinal (when you graph the cell means, the resulting lines do not cross) or disordinal (they do cross) (Maxwell & Delaney, 1990). Tests of ordinal interactions frequently have lower power than main effects, but tests of disordinal interactions are often more powerful than the test of either main effect. Rosnow and Rosenthal (1989) explain which lines should and should not cross when interactions are present.

treatment factor is crossed with classroom. In a **nested design,** some levels of one factor are not exposed to all levels of the other factors. For example, when some classrooms receive the treatment but not the control condition, classrooms are nested within treatment conditions. Crossed designs yield unconfounded statistical tests of all main effects and interactions, but nested designs may not. The distinction between nested and crossed designs is particularly relevant in the presence of higher order units (e.g., schools, hospitals, work sites). Often the researcher will nest treatments within these units to minimize the chances of diffusion and communication of treatment within higher order units. The dilemma is that the crossed design yields separate statistical estimates of the effects of higher order units, treatment conditions, and their interaction; but crossing increases problems such as diffusion of treatment. Each researcher will have to review the specifics of this tradeoff as it applies to the experiment at hand before deciding whether nesting or crossing is to be preferred.

A Disadvantage of Factorial Designs

Factorial designs are common in laboratory research and in highly controlled settings, such as those of some medical research. They are more difficult to implement in many field settings. They require close control over the combination of treatments given to each unit, but such control is difficult as more factors or more levels are included—especially if each cell has different eligibility criteria, as in pharmaceutical studies in which rules for who can receive which drug combinations can be complex. In addition, much field research is conducted to assess the policy implications of a proposed innovation. Yet the ability of policymakers to legislate or regulate interactions is low, given traditions of local control and professional discretion in the delivery of services and given difficulties in ensuring that social interventions are implemented as intended (Pressman & Wildavsky, 1984; Rossi & Wright, 1984). Policymakers are often more interested in generalized inferences about which treatments work than in the highly specific and localized inferences about the effects of particular combinations of particular levels of particular factors in a particular setting that factorial designs sometimes provide.

Longitudinal Designs

Longitudinal designs add multiple observations taken before, during, or after treatment, the number and timing of which are determined by the hypotheses under study:

$$R \quad O \ldots O \quad X \quad O \quad O \ldots O$$
$$R \quad O \ldots O \quad \quad O \quad O \ldots O$$

These designs closely resemble the time-series studies in Chapter 6, but they have far fewer pre- and posttest observations. Longitudinal designs allow examination of how effects change over time, allow use of growth curve models of individual differences in response to treatment, and are frequently more powerful than designs with fewer observations over time, especially if five or more waves of measurement are used (Maxwell, 1998). So especially when sample sizes are small, adding pretests and posttests can improve power.

Longitudinal randomized experiments with multiple pretests are rare. Bloom (1990), for example, randomly assigned displaced workers to three treatment or control conditions designed to help them get jobs. He reported quarterly earnings at four pretests and four posttests. The pretests showed that participants experienced an acute drop in earnings during the one or two quarters immediately preceding assignment to conditions, perhaps reflecting a short-term job loss by workers who move rapidly into and out of the labor market. So regression effects might cause some improvement in all groups even if treatments did not work. Indeed, control participants did improve, though not as much as treatment participants.

The use of multiple posttests is more common. For example, the Cambridge-Somerville Youth Study began in 1939 when 650 adolescent boys were randomly assigned from blocked pairs either to a counseling program or to no treatment (W. McCord & McCord, 1959; Powers & Witmer, 1951), with a follow-up taken 37 years later in 1976 (J. McCord, 1978). A current study in a health maintenance organization aims to follow patients for their entire lives (Hillis et al., 1998). Here the multiple posttests explore whether treatment gains are maintained or changed over time. This is especially important if the primary outcome can be measured only many years later—for example, children's eventual educational and occupational achievement after participating in Head Start, mortality rates from AIDS among gay men after exposure to a program teaching safe sex, or lifetime earned income among Job Corps trainees. Sometimes longitudinal studies follow different outcomes simultaneously over time to explore the validity of a hypothesized causal chain of effects—for example, that a treatment to help children of lower socioeconomic status to rise out of poverty will first improve their aspirations, which will affect expectations, which will affect achievements in grammar school, which will help them successfully complete high school and college, which will finally lead to a better paying or higher status job as an adult. Here the timing of the observations follows the hypothesized schedule of events to be observed in order to explore if and at what point the chain breaks down.

Practical problems plague longitudinal designs. First, attrition rises with longer follow-up periods as, for example, participants move to unknown locations or simply tire of the research. Still, we are impressed with what tireless follow-up procedures can achieve with most populations (Ribisl et al., 1996). Second, some long-term outcomes, such as lifetime earned income, are nearly impossible to assess given current technology and limited access to such relevant data sources as the Internal Revenue Service or the Social Security Administration (Boruch & Cecil, 1979). Third, it is not always ethical to withhold treatments from participants for long periods of time, and the use of longitudinal observations on no-treatment or wait-list control-group participants is rare because such participants often simply obtain treatment elsewhere. An example of all these problems is provided by Snyder and Wills (1989; Snyder, Wills, & Grady-Fletcher, 1991), who randomly assigned 79 distressed couples to receive behavioral marital therapy ($N = 29$), insight-oriented marital therapy ($N = 30$), or a wait-list control group ($N = 20$). At 6-month and 4-year follow-ups they assessed outcomes only on the two treatment group conditions because control participants had already begun dropping out of the study despite the agreed-upon 3-month waiting period between pretest and posttest. Despite participant death, medical problems, and relocation out of state, Snyder and Wills (1989) were able to gather 4-year follow-up data on 55 of the 59 treatment couples—a remarkably high retention rate, although still a loss of participants such as one nearly always experiences in longitudinal research. Finally, a 4-year follow-up is far longer than most psychotherapy outcome studies use, but it is still far short of such long-term outcomes as distress levels over the life of the marriage or lifetime divorce rates. Even exemplary longitudinal studies such as this experience such problems.

Crossover Designs

Imagine an experiment in which some participants are randomly assigned to receive either Treatment A or B, after which they receive a posttest. In a crossover design, after that posttest the participants cross over to receive the treatment they did not previously get, and they take another posttest after that second treatment is over. In our design notation this crossover design is written:

$$
\begin{array}{ccccccc}
R & O & X_A & O & X_B & O \\
R & O & X_B & O & X_A & O
\end{array}
$$

Sometimes the interval between treatments is extended so that the effects of the first treatment can dissipate before the second treatment begins.

This design is often used in medical research, as in cases in which several drugs are given to participants in a within-participants design and the crossover is used to counterbalance and assess order effects.[8] It is also used to gather even more causal information from a study that would otherwise stop after the first posttests were administered. In either use, the crossover design is most practical when the treatments promise short-term relief (otherwise carryover effects will occur), when the treatments work quickly (otherwise the experiment will take too long), and when participants are willing and able to continue through both treatments even if the first treatment fixes the problem. If analysis finds an interaction between treatments and

---

8. The crossover design is a variation of a more general class called Latin squares (Cochran & Cox, 1957; Fisher & Yates, 1953; Fleiss, 1986; R. Kirk, 1982; Pocock, 1983; Rosenthal & Rosnow, 1991; Winer et al., 1991). Latin squares are widely used to counterbalance treatments in within-participants factors and to estimate effects in very large factorial designs in which all possible combinations of conditions cannot be administered.

TABLE 8.2 Ten Situations Conducive to Randomized Experiments

---

1. When demand outstrips supply
2. When an innovation cannot be delivered to all units at once
3. When experimental units can be temporally isolated
4. When experimental units are spatially separated or interunit communication is low
5. When change is mandated and solutions are acknowledged to be unknown
6. When a tie can be broken or ambiguity about need can be resolved
7. When some persons express no preference among alternatives
8. When you can create your own organization
9. When you have control over experimental units
10. When lotteries are expected

---

order, then the effect of the second round of treatments cannot be interpreted without taking order effects into account, although the first round of treatment is still just as interpretable as would have been the case without the crossover.

CONDITIONS MOST CONDUCIVE TO RANDOM ASSIGNMENT

This section (and Table 8.2) explicates the situations that increase the probability of successfully doing a randomized field experiment.

When Demand Outstrips Supply

When demand for service outstrips supply, randomization can be a credible rationale for distributing service fairly. For example, Dunford (1990) describes an experiment on the effects of a summer youth employment program. Initially, program personnel objected to randomly assigning some youths to jobs and others not. However, they also recognized that far fewer jobs were available than there were applicants, and they eventually agreed that random allocation of those jobs was fair. They later reported that the obviously unbiased nature of randomization helped them to show a vocal group of critics that entry into the program discriminated neither for nor against minority youth. Similarly, the Omnibus Budget Reconciliation Act of 1981 allowed states to experiment with novel approaches to welfare reform. Many states wanted to do so, but few states could afford to implement programs that could be given to all welfare recipients; random assignment was again accepted as a fair mechanism for distributing services in one experiment

(Gueron, 1985). Finally, the Milwaukee Parental Choice Program tested the use of school vouchers by random selection of participants when there were more applicants to a particular school and grade than could be accommodated (Rouse, 1998).

When demand exceeds supply, applicants originally assigned to the comparison condition sometimes reapply for the treatment. Experimenters need to be clear about whether they will have this right, and if they do, whether reapplicants will have priority over new applicants. Sometimes the right to reapply cannot be denied on ethical or regulatory grounds, as in the case of a distressed psychotherapy client assigned to a wait-list who becomes severely symptomatic or that of welfare recipients who have a regulatory right to reapply to a job-training program. It is crucial to negotiate support from everyone in the experiment about dealing with reapplicants, for dissenters can thwart those arrangements (Conrad, 1994). For example, the Rockefeller Foundation's Minority Female Single Parent (MFSP) program could not afford to provide services to all eligible candidates right away, so randomization was proposed as an ethically appropriate way to distribute services among the many eligible women (Boruch, 1997). However, some local program managers disagreed and spread their resources more thinly over a large number of women rather than limit the number of women served. Ultimately, if a large proportion of rejected applicants is likely to reapply and be accepted into treatment, the feasibility of a randomized experiment is questionable. If the proportion of successful reapplicants is likely to be small, methods that we discuss in Chapter 10 for dealing with treatment implementation problems may be useful.

When an Innovation Cannot Be Delivered to All Units at Once

Often it is physically or financially impossible to introduce an innovation simultaneously to all units. Such situations arise in education as curricula are slowly changed, as new teaching devices filter down through the schools in a system, or as computers are introduced or new training schemes are implemented. In these situations, the experiment can deliberately introduce the innovation in stages, with some units receiving it before others on a random basis. This provides an experimental and control comparison until the point at which the controls get their turn for treatment. It is even better if it can be done using the switching-replications design feature described for previous quasi-experimental designs, but with replications now randomly assigned.

When Experimental Units Can Be Temporally Isolated: The Equivalent-Time-Samples Design

Although we typically think of randomly assigning people, schools, communities, or cities to conditions, we can also randomly assign times to conditions (Hahn,

1984). Campbell and Stanley (1963) called this an "Equivalent Time Samples Design" to highlight that randomization equates the time periods in which the treatment was present to those in which it was absent. Edgington (1987) provides several examples of single-participant designs in which treatments were presented and removed randomly over time—a comparison of three drugs for narcolepsy, of a medication with a placebo for an intestinal disorder, and of the effects of artificial food colorings with placebo on the behavior of hyperactive children. The effect must be of short duration so that it can decrease in magnitude when treatment is withdrawn; and the effect must continue to respond to repeated exposure to treatment so that it can increase when treatment is readministered.

But the principle applies to more than just single-participant designs. It can be used when there are naturally occurring rotations of groups and each group is isolated from the others in time. Thus, when 24 groups of persons came for sequential 2-week stays at a pastoral counseling center, Mase (1971) randomly assigned those groups to one of two kinds of sensitivity training, twelve groups receiving each kind. In this example, the creation of simultaneous treatment and control conditions might have led to diffusion of treatment or other reactive threats to validity, but the equivalent-time-samples design avoided such problems. Note, however, that participants are now nested within time samples in the same way they could be nested within some aggregate such as a school or a neighborhood; the analysis should take this into account.

When Experimental Units Are Spatially Separated or Interunit Communication Is Low

When units are geographically separated and have minimal contact with one another, or when they can be made this way, those units can be randomly assigned. This often occurs in organizations that have many branches, for example, supermarkets, units in the armed forces, university alumni, schools within school districts, wards within hospitals, residential units of religious orders, branches of health clubs in large cities, and dealerships that sell automobiles, appliances, and the like. However, spatial isolation does not guarantee minimal contact, so care should be taken to check that this is indeed the case.

For example, an experiment in Peru studied the effects of providing gynecological and family planning services to clients of 42 geographically separated community clinics (Population Council, 1986). Clinics were assigned randomly to receive one, two, or four physician visits per month. The geographical separation of clinics meant that women tended to visit the same clinic over time, so little diffusion of treatment was likely. If some diffusion was possible (e.g., if women regularly visited two clinics very close to each other), the researchers could have blocked clinics by geographic area and assigned areas rather than individual clinics. Similarly, Perng (1985) randomly assigned people to six different methods that the Internal Revenue Service was considering for collecting delinquent income tax returns. Most people were separated geographically. But even if they had been in close physical proximity to each other, by law the very fact that their tax return was part of a study was confidential, and people are generally reluctant to discuss their income tax returns; so it was unlikely that communication between people in different conditions would occur.

These experiments had an additional strength; both took advantage of the natural appearance of the interventions to randomize treatments unobtrusively. After all, patients expect that physicians will visit clinics and are not likely to notice minor variations in the number of times those visits occur. Those receiving delinquent tax letters from the IRS are rarely familiar enough with specific IRS procedures to know that any variation on normal routine was occurring. Unobtrusiveness is a worthy goal to strive for, except when treatment is deliberately designed to stand out from what respondents expect.

When Change Is Mandated and Solutions Are Acknowledged to Be Unknown

Sometimes, all concerned parties agree that an undesirable situation needs changing, but it is not clear which changes we should make despite passionate advocacy of certain alternatives by interested parties. If administrative, political, and economic conditions allow, trying out several alternative changes in a formal experiment is more likely to win acceptance. An example is the Minneapolis Spouse Abuse Experiment (Berk, Smyth, & Sherman, 1988). Spouse abuse is a serious felony that can lead to the murder of the spouse, and so police officers who are called to such a crime must take some action. But concerned parties disagreed about whether that action should be to do on-the-spot counseling between the two spouses, to require the offender to leave the premises for 8 hours, or to arrest the offender. An administrator who had an attitude favoring experimentation in finding a solution allowed the implementation of a randomized experiment to test which of these three options worked best. Similarly, a randomized experiment to treat severely mentally ill patients with either standard care or a radically different form of community care could be done in part because all parties acknowledged that they were unsure which treatment worked best for these patients (Test & Burke, 1985).

Though such planned variation studies promise important results, each variation may not define its goals *exclusively* in terms of the same target problem. In the Minneapolis Spouse Abuse Experiment, this potential disagreement was not a problem because most parties agreed that the end point of interest was a decrease in postintervention repeat violence. However, disagreement may be more likely if participants are assigned to projects with different management, staff, and funders than to projects in which all variations are implemented by the same people. Nor will the directors of the various projects always agree which measures should be used to measure those things they are trying in common to change.

When a Tie Can Be Broken or Ambiguity About Need Can Be Resolved

Assignment of people to conditions on the basis of need or merit is often a more compelling rule to program managers, staff, and recipients than is randomization. Such considerations are one justification for the regression discontinuity design. However, the need or merit of some people is often ambiguous. In those cases, the ambiguity can sometimes be resolved by randomly assigning people of ambiguous need to conditions, perhaps in combination with the regression discontinuity design. Similarly, Lipsey, Cordray, and Berger (1981) used random assignment to resolve ambiguity in their evaluation of a juvenile delinquency diversion program. In a quasi-experimental design, police officers used their best judgment as to whether an arrested juvenile needed to be counseled and released, referred to probation, or diverted to a more intensive social service project that provided counseling, remedial education, recreation, and substance abuse services. However, when the officer was unsure which assignment was most needed and also judged that either counseling and release or diversion would be appropriate, the officer randomized juveniles to one of these two conditions.

In such tie-breaking experiments, generalization is restricted to persons scoring in the area of ambiguous need, the group about which we know least as far as effective treatment. However, if an organization specializes in treating the best, the worst, or the full range of participants, its officials may well object that evaluating their performance with "ambiguous" participants is insensitive to what they really do. Fortunately, it may be possible to link a tie-breaking experiment with some form of interpretable quasi-experiment, as Lipsey et al. (1981) did, to satisfy these objections.

When Some Persons Express No Preference Among Alternatives

Even if ethics or public relations require that people be allowed to choose which option they will receive, persons who express no preference from among the options can be assigned by chance. For example, Valins and Baum (1973) wanted to study some effects of physical environment on university freshmen who entered one of two kinds of living quarters that differed in the number of persons a resident was likely to meet each day. The authors restricted the study to the 30% of freshmen who expressed no preference for either kind of living quarters. College authorities assigned this 30% to living units on a haphazard basis; but it would presumably have been easy to do the assignment randomly. Of course, limiting the experiment to persons who have no preference does make generalization beyond such persons more problematic. If the full range of decisive and no-preference respondents is of interest, the randomized experiment with the no-preference respondents could be conducted along with the best possible quasi-experiment with the decisive respondents. Then the results of the studies can be compared, with the weakness of one study being the strength of the other. Where the results coincide, a global overall inference is easier.

When You Can Create Your Own Organization

Random assignment is an accepted part of the organizational culture of laboratory experimentation, but most field experiments are conducted in organizational cultures in which randomization is mostly foreign. Yet sometimes researchers can create their own organizations in which they can make the practice of randomization a more usual norm. For example, university psychology departments often set up a psychological services center to facilitate the training of graduate students in clinical psychology and to allow department faculty members to exert more experimental control than would typically be possible in most clinics (Beutler & Crago, 1991). In such centers, researchers can better control not just randomization but also such features as treatment standardization, measurement, and case selection. Freestanding research institutes and centers focused on particular problems frequently allow similar levels of broad control. The California Smokers' Helpline, for example, provides free smoking cessation help to smokers in that state who call the helpline (Zhu, 1999). Randomizing callers to treatment and control was not feasible. All callers received a treatment mailing with instructions to call back when they were ready to start treatment. Those who did not call back were then randomized into two groups: no further action or proactive callback from the treatment staff to begin treatment. In principle, this procedure could be used to randomly subdivide the nonresponders in any quasi-experimental treatment group into treatment and control—for example, those who request psychotherapy but fail to show for appointments, those who are given prescriptions but fail to fill them, those who are accepted to a job training program but fail to attend, and so forth. Finally, researchers can sometimes set up organizations just to control randomization, as is often done in multisite medical trials in which a central clearinghouse controlled by the researcher is created to do randomization. The National Institute of Mental Health (NIMH) Collaborative Depression Project (Collins & Elkin, 1985) used this clearinghouse method to control randomization.

When You Have Control over Experimental Units

Being able to establish one's own organization or randomization clearinghouse is rare. Most field researchers are guests in someone else's organization, and they derive many of their possibilities for control from their powerful hosts. An example comes from an evaluation of solutions to the "peak load" problem by utility companies (Aigner & Hausman, 1980). Electricity usage varies by time of day, and the utility company must have enough capacity to meet peak demand even if that capacity is largely unused at other times. Building that capacity is expensive. So utility companies wanted to know whether charging more for electricity during peak demand periods would reduce demand and so reduce the need to build more capacity. Experimenters were able to randomly assign households to higher peak demand rates versus standard rates because their hosts completely controlled electricity supply to the affected households and were interested in getting an answer to this question with experimental methods.

Randomization is also more likely whenever major funders insist on it. For example, both the National Institute on Drug Abuse and the National Institute on Alcohol and Alcohol Abuse have offered funding for innovative service provision contingent upon evaluation of those services by rigorous experimental designs, both paid for by the grant (Coyle, Boruch & Turner, 1991). The NIMH Collaborative Depression project used the same approach (Boruch & Wothke, 1985). However, especially when funder and fundee have a long-term relationship, the use of the purse strings for control can lead to tension. Lam, Hartwell, and Jekel (1994), for example, noted the "contentious codependence" (p. 56) that developed between Yale University and the city of New Haven, in which Yale is located, due to the fact that Yale researchers frequently offer social services to the city that it might not otherwise be able to afford but with a research string attached. There is a thin line between contentious codependence and oblique coercion, and it is even self-defeating to conduct a randomized experiment in a way that directly or indirectly demeans hosts or respondents. After all, the motivation for hosts and participants to volunteer tomorrow may well be related to how we treat them in experiments today.

When Lotteries Are Expected

Lotteries are sometimes used as a socially accepted means of distributing resources. Examples include a lottery used to assign female students to dormitories at Stanford (Siegel & Siegel, 1957), a lottery to choose among applicants to a newly developed "magnet" school (Zigulich, 1977), and the 1970 draft lottery in the United States (Notz, Staw, & Cook, 1971). In the latter case, Hearst, Newman, and Hulley (1986) asked whether being randomly assigned an eligible draft number elevated mortality and found that it did do so. Angrist et al. (1996a) confirmed this finding, with the average causal effect on mortality of being randomly assigned an eligible draft number equal to less than one tenth of one percent. In these cases, the motivation for randomization was not to do research but rather to capitalize on the perception that randomization is an unbiased way of distributing a resource. These social uses of randomization create a natural randomized experiment that the investigator can exploit. Unfortunately, formal social lotteries do not occur frequently, so they cannot be relied upon as a means of creating probabilistically equivalent groups very often.

WHEN RANDOM ASSIGNMENT IS NOT FEASIBLE OR DESIRABLE

Even when interest exists in whether a treatment is effective, some circumstances mitigate against using a randomized experiment to answer the question. First, randomized experiments may not be desirable when quick answers are needed. Typically, several years pass between the conception of a major field experiment and the availability of results—particularly if the treatment requires time (as with long-term psychotherapy) and if medium- to long-term outcomes are of interest (as with lifetime earnings). In the New Jersey Negative Income Tax Experiment, for example, "the four years of the operating phase were sandwiched between 44 months of planning and design and 16 months of data analysis" (Haveman, 1987, p. 180)—8 years total. So, if information is needed rapidly, alternatives to randomized experiments may be better. For example, the Program Evaluation and Methodology Division (PEMD) of the U.S. General Accounting Office (GAO) frequently fielded questions from legislators who wanted answers quickly about pending decisions. Some of those questions involved the effects of programs or policies. A delay of a few years might delay the decision too long—indeed, the question may no longer be of policy interest, and the legislator who asked the question may no longer be serving. Consequently, PEMD rarely used randomized experiments, relying instead on combinations of quasi-experiments, surveys, and reviews of existing literature about the effects of related policies (Chan & Tumin, 1997; Datta, 1997; Droitcour, 1997). Such procedures may be weaker for inferring cause than a new randomized experiment, because even when the literature contains randomized experiments, they are rarely on the exact question of legislative interest. But GAO's methods are almost always more timely than those of a new randomized experiment and often of reasonable accuracy.

Second, randomized experiments provide a precise answer about whether a treatment worked (Cronbach et al., 1980). But the need for great precision may be low in many cases. For example, when much high-quality prior information exists about the treatment, a review of existing literature may be a better use of resources than would be a new randomized trial. When a causal question is of secondary interest to a noncausal question, such as whether services are being provided as intended, program monitoring procedures may be better. When an effect is so large and dramatic that no one doubts it resulted from the treatment, as with the dramatic effects of screening for PKU on PKU-based retardation among children, investing in an additional randomized experiment may be superfluous.

Third, randomized experiments can rarely be designed to answer certain kinds of questions. It is not possible to assign persons at random to variables that cannot be manipulated, such as age or race, or to manipulate events that occurred in the past, such as the effects of the death of President John F. Kennedy or of the Great Depression in the 1930s. It is unethical to assign persons at random to many manipulable events that cause significant harm, such as to cigarette smoking or to having a spinal cord injury.

Fourth, before conducting an experiment, a good deal of preliminary conceptual or empirical work must be done. The Federal Judicial Center (1981) recommends that, before an experiment is conducted, it should be demonstrated that the present conditions need improvement, that the proposed improvement is of unclear value, that only an experiment could provide the necessary data to clarify the question, that the results of the experiment would be used to change the practice or policy, and that the rights of individuals would be protected in the experiment. Similarly, the National Cancer Institute's five-phase model of testing a potential cancer control method suggests that, before a randomized experiment is conducted, the existing scientific literature should be identified and synthesized to see if an empirically supportable and testable hypothesis can be generated; pilot tests should be done to investigate the feasibility or acceptability of an intervention; studies assessing participation and adherence in the population should be conducted; data collection forms should be developed and validated; and quasi-experimentally controlled studies should be used to provide preliminary evidence about treatment effects (Greenwald & Cullen, 1984). Premature experimentation can be a great waste of resources—indeed, it can undermine potentially promising interventions for which there has not yet been time to develop recruitment procedures, identify and fix implementation problems, and serve the clientele long enough to make a difference.

DISCUSSION

The randomized experiment is often the preferred method for obtaining a precise and statistically unbiased estimate of the effects of an intervention. It involves fewer assumptions than other methods, the validity of those assumptions is usually easier to check against the data and the procedures used, and it requires less prior knowledge about such matters as selection processes and unit characteristics than do quasi-experiments, causal modeling, and selection bias models. Given all these strengths, it is easy to forget the many practical problems that can arise in implementing randomized experiments.

One practical problem concerns the feasibility and desirability of experimenting in particular cases. Some experimental manipulations are not ethical, as in the case of a physician deciding that a certain class of patients must be given a certain treatment and so cannot be randomized, or of an experimental treatment producing positive or negative effects that are so large that it would be unethical to continue to study them. Other times, it is not acceptable to wait the years that a well-designed and implemented experiment can take. Still other times, legal problems arise, not only because ethical violations can become legal problems but also because the law is often involved in certain experimental situations, for instance, when it mandates experimental evaluations of a program; when participants are directly under legal scrutiny, as with prisoners; or when legal systems are themselves the target of study.

A second practical problem is that a sufficiently large number of people (units) may not exist who are both eligible and willing to receive the treatment if assigned to it at random. Many is the experiment that has failed on this count. Frequently, especially with researchers who have never run a large field experiment before, the number of eligible people is vastly overestimated, as is the ease with which they can be located. When they are located, they often refuse to participate. In the worst case, the result is the death of the experiment for lack of participants.

A third practical problem is that the randomization procedure is not always properly designed and implemented. Sometimes this problem occurs because the researcher does not understand what random assignment is and so substitutes a seemingly haphazard assignment procedure. Or the researcher may introduce ad hoc adjustments to a random assignment procedure that seems to be yielding groups that are unequal before treatment, all the while thinking that these procedures are random when they are not. Other times the researcher correctly designs random assignment procedures but fails to create or supervise the procedures for implementing random assignment, so the assignment is implemented improperly. Whenever randomization is incorrectly or incompletely implemented, its benefits may be thwarted.

A fourth practical problem is that the treatment assigned is not always the treatment received. Participants may fail to fully receive the treatment to which they are assigned or may not receive it at all, as in the case of patients assigned to drug therapy who fail to take the drug or take only part of it. They may cross over to another condition (in a design that does not call for a crossover), as in the case of participants in a control condition who reapply for treatment and are accepted. Diffusion of treatment may occur through such means as treatment-related communication between participants in different conditions. Here, too, the participant is now receiving some part of both conditions. In all these cases, the intended treatment contrast is thwarted. If so, although the inference that *assignment to condition caused outcome* is still clear, the construct validity of the treatment is not clear. Hence it can be useful to prevent these failures of treatment implementation or measure their occurrence in many experiments in which pure treatment contrasts are desired.

A fifth problem is attrition. The randomized experiment does not just aim to make groups equivalent before treatment begins; it also aims to make groups equivalent at posttest in all respects except for differences in treatment conditions. Differential attrition from conditions after initial random assignment can vitiate this latter aim. Such attrition occurs often in field experiments. So preventing attrition, coping with attrition, measuring attrition, and analyzing data with attrition all become crucial adjunct topics to the study of the randomized experiment.

This chapter, being mostly about the design and logic of randomized experiments, has skirted all these problems in the interests of presenting the simplest case and its variants. But the researcher needs to know about these problems because they bear on the decision whether to use the randomized experiment at all, and if the decision is to do so, then they bear on how well the experiment is implemented and subsequently interpreted. So we turn to these problems in more detail in the next two chapters.

9

Practical Problems 1: Ethics, Participant Recruitment, and Random Assignment

Prac·ti·cal (prăk´tĭ-kəl): [Middle English *practicale*, from Medieval Latin *practicalis*, from Late Latin *practicus*, from Greek *praktikos*, from *prassein*, to make, do.] adj.   1. Of, relating to, governed by, or acquired through practice or action, rather than theory, speculation, or ideals: *gained practical experience of sailing as a deck hand.*   2. Manifested in or involving practice: *practical applications of calculus.*   3. Actually engaged in a specified occupation or a certain kind of work; practicing.   4. Capable of being used or put into effect; useful: *practical knowledge of Japanese.*

Eth·ic (ĕth´ĭk): [Middle English *ethik*, from Old French *ethique* (from Late Latin *ethica*) (from Greek *ethika, ethics*) and from Latin *ethice* (from Greek *ethike*) both from Greek *ethikos, ethical,* from *ethos, character.*] n.   1. a. A set of principles of right conduct. 1b. A theory or a system of moral values: *"An ethic of service is at war with a craving for gain"* (Gregg Easterbrook).   2. ethics. (*used with a sing. verb*) The study of the general nature of morals and of the specific moral choices to be made by a person; moral philosophy.   3. ethics. (*used with a sing. or pl. verb*) The rules or standards governing the conduct of a person or the members of a profession: medical ethics.

Re·cruit (rĭ-kroot´): [French *recruter,* from obsolete *recrute,* recruit, variant of *recrue,* from feminine past participle of *recroître, to grow again* from Old French *recroistre:* re-, re- + croistre, *to grow* (from Latin *crescere*).] v. *tr.*   1. To engage (persons) for military service.   2. To strengthen or raise (an armed force) by enlistment.   3. To supply with new members or employees.   4. To enroll or seek to enroll: colleges recruiting minority students.   5. To replenish.   6. To renew or restore the health, vitality, or intensity of. **re·cruiter** *n.* **re·cruitment** *n.*

VEN VERY good experiments encounter practical problems. For instance, the Perry Preschool Program experiment violated randomization protocols in minor ways, and even their heroic effort to follow participants until age 27 was only 95% successful. Such problems are sometimes so severe that they thwart the experiment completely. In the Madison and Racine Quality Employment experiment, the pool of applicants was too small, and the treatment program could not develop many good jobs for those who did apply. Consequently, the intervention could never show the expected impact on getting good jobs, so the experiment was ended prematurely (Greenberg & Shroder, 1997).

Experienced researchers know that designing a good experiment is only half (or less!) of the battle. Successfully implementing that experiment requires coping with many practical problems. In this chapter and the next, we outline these problems and describe strategies to address them. This chapter focuses on problems that occur early in experiments: ethical and legal issues, getting enough participants to be in the study, and correctly implementing random assignment. In the next chapter, we address problems that occur later: treatment implementation issues and coping with post-assignment attrition. Except for issues that are specific to random assignment itself, most of these practical problems apply to nonrandomized experiments just as much as to randomized ones, and some of them (e.g., tracking participants, using appropriate informed consent, guarding confidentiality) apply to nonexperimental research, such as surveys, as well.

ETHICAL AND LEGAL ISSUES WITH EXPERIMENTS[1]

Ethics should be considered from the very start of the process of designing an experiment. Here we address a few key ethical and legal questions that philosophers, lawyers, and scientists have raised about both experimentation and randomization:

- the ethics of experimentation on human beings;
- the ethics of withholding a potentially effective treatment from control or comparison participants;
- the ethics of random assignment compared with alternatives such as assignment based on need;
- the conditions under which experiments might be discontinued for ethical reasons; and
- some legal problems that bear on experiments.

---

1. This section focuses on problems specific to experimentation. However, the conduct of science involves many other ethical problems. For example, concerns about fraud in some clinical trials (e.g., Ranstam et al., 2000) have led to useful protocols for ensuring the integrity of data (Knatterud et al., 1998); similarly, the management of data to insure its integrity presents a host of practical problems with ethical features (McFadden, 1998).

The Ethics of Experimentation

In the name of scientific experimentation, great wrongs have been done. Abusive medical experiments during World War II, especially in Nazi concentration camps, are well-known (Greenberg & Folger, 1988). In the United States, researchers in the Tuskegee syphilis study withheld effective treatment from African-American males suffering from syphilis so that scientists could observe the long-term course of the disease (J. Jones, 1981). Less extreme examples are prevalent (Beecher, 1966; Veatch & Sollitto, 1973). Indeed, it seems inevitable that a methodology that depends on manipulation would encounter objections to such manipulations—especially when the manipulation can cause harm, as with medical treatments or decisions about punishment of criminals. To counter these problems, experimenters use three sources of help:

- Ethical Codes
- Informed Consent
- Institutional Review Boards

Ethical Codes and Principles

To reduce abuse and foster ethics, governments have adopted various codes of ethics for scientific research, for example, the Nuremberg Code adopted by the United Nations General Assembly (Nuremberg Code, 1949; although Miké, 1990, points out that reasonable ethical codes were present in Nazi Germany and did not prevent abuse); and ethicists have proposed other similar ethical standards (Emanuel, Wendler, & Grady, 2000; World Medical Association, 2000). The U.S. Public Health Service's Belmont Report (National Commission for the Protection of Human Subjects of Biomedical and Behavioral Research, 1979)[2] proposed three ethical principles for scientific research with human participants:

1. *Respect for Persons:* that individuals are autonomous agents with the right to decide whether to enter a study (hence the need for informed consent) and, if their autonomy is diminished by a disability, have the right to be protected from harm;
2. *Beneficence:* that researchers must maximize benefits and minimize harms to participants (hence the need to reveal potential harms and benefits);
3. *Justice:* that the benefits and harms of treatment be distributed fairly (hence the need to recruit participants fairly), and that persons not be deprived of efficacious treatments to which they would otherwise be entitled (hence the need to inform of alternative treatments).

The latter requirement was motivated partly by the observation that abuses in experiments often fell disproportionately on disadvantaged or vulnerable persons

2. See http://grants.nih.gov/grants/oprr/humansubjects/guidance/belmont.htm.

such as Black males in the pre–civil rights era in the Tuskegee study or concentration camp prisoners during World War II.

Informed Consent and Experiments

To operationalize these principles, participants are often asked to give their written *informed consent* to being in the experiment (Protection of Human Subjects, 1983[3]). The U.S. Public Health Service requires that human participants in research studies that it funds should read and sign a consent statement that includes:

1. A statement that the study involves research, an explanation of the purposes of the research, the expected duration of the participant's participation, a description of the procedures to be followed, and identification of any procedures that are experimental.
2. A description of any reasonably foreseeable risks or discomforts to the participant.
3. A description of any benefits to the participant or to others that may reasonably be expected from the research.
4. A disclosure of appropriate alternative procedures or courses of treatment, if any, that might be advantageous to the participant.
5. A statement describing the extent, if any, to which confidentiality of records identifying the participant will be maintained.
6. For research involving more than minimal risk, an explanation as to whether any compensation and any medical treatments are available if injury occurs and, if so, what they consist of or where further information may be obtained.
7. An explanation of whom to contact for answers to pertinent questions about the research and research participants' rights and whom to contact in the event of a research-related injury to the participant.
8. A statement that participation is voluntary, that refusal to participate will involve no penalty or loss of benefits to which the participant is otherwise entitled, and that the participant may discontinue participation at any time without penalty or loss of benefits to which the participant is otherwise entitled.

Boruch (1997, pp. 44–49) provides sample informed consent forms from past experiments. New experimenters should consult those with experience to help generate a contextually appropriate informed-consent protocol.

The Public Health Service (PHS) does not require informed consent for surveys or confidential educational tests. For prisoners, pregnant women, or those with diminished mental capacity, more stringent requirements apply (Federal Judicial Center, 1981; Mastroianni, Faden, & Federman, 1994; Stanley & Sieber, 1992). Research with children requires either active or passive consent from parents (Esbensen et al., 1996). Some other federal agencies in the U.S. government

---

3. See http://ohrp.osophs.dhhs.gov/humansubjects/guidance/45cfr46.htm.

have adopted these rules, including the Departments of Education, Agriculture, Justice, and Health and Human Services (Boruch, 1997), as have many professional associations whose members study human participants. For example, the American Psychological Association's (1992) ethical principles require many of these procedures of psychologists who study human participants (J. Greenberg & Folger, 1988; Sales & Folkman, 2000; Sieber, 1992). Many individual researchers and research firms use these procedures voluntarily (e.g., Gueron, 1999; Orr, 1999), both for ethical reasons and because obtaining informed consent can help protect the experimenter against liability for harms that experiments might cause.

Institutional Review Boards

The Code of Federal Regulations (Protection of Human Subjects, 1983) also established a limited requirement for Institutional Review Boards (IRBs) at institutions receiving PHS funding for research with human participants, including many universities, government agencies, and private research firms. The IRB monitors research with human participants by reviewing the experimental and informed consent procedures for ethical problems. It may also review the scientific quality of research, such as whether the experiment has adequate statistical power, because to conduct a seriously underpowered experiment would waste both resources and the time of the participants.

These particular procedures are not always uniformly applicable to all human research. They were developed mostly in medical research, and other substantive areas sometimes have different needs. For example, the Guiding Principles of the American Evaluation Association (American Evaluation Association, 1995) do not include the Belmont Report's (National Commission for the Protection of Human Subjects of Biomedical and Behavioral Research, 1979) principle of beneficence because evaluations by their very nature sometimes do harm to the interests of some people—for example, identifying poorly performing programs is often part of the evaluator's contract, even though the program might be terminated and program personnel lose their jobs (Shadish, Newman, Scheirer, & Wye, 1995). Similarly, some researchers object that telling research participants about other services to which they are entitled without being in the research might destroy our ability to form control groups (Rossi, 1995); and the American Psychological Association allows deception under limited conditions. But in matters of informed consent, our belief is that exceptions to customary practice require careful thought and consultation with experts and colleagues about the justification.

Withholding a Potentially Effective Treatment

Arguments for and Against Withholding Treatment

In experiments, treatments are deliberately withheld from or reduced for some participants, or a different (and potentially less effective) treatment is given to some participants than to others. This practice can be ethically questionable if beneficial treatments are withheld from persons who might need or deserve them. Fetterman (1982), for example, questioned the ethics of assigning disadvantaged high school dropouts to a no-treatment control when they had expressed interest in a remedial "second-chance" treatment because this second chance might be their last chance. Similarly, a debate in AIDS research concerns whether treatments that are promising in preliminary research should be released to patients before results from more extensive tests are done (Marshall, 1989). For both ethical and practical reasons, there is some obligation to err on the side of benefiting the patient when doubt exists about the most ethical action. Consequently, the health care establishment has experimented with procedures such as the establishment of "group C" cancer therapies that could be given to patients prior to typical rigorous FDA testing; the Fast Track Accelerated Approval process for moving drugs into use more quickly; and the "parallel track" structure for distributing AIDS drugs that are safe and promising in preliminary tests (Marshall, 1989; Expanded Availability, 1990). AIDS research has benefited enormously from interaction with the AIDS patient community and their advocates. Many of their concerns have now been better addressed, both within and outside the accepted principles of experimental design (Ellenberg, Finkelstein, & Schoenfeld, 1992).

However, good ethical arguments exist *for* withholding treatments in experimental comparisons. If such treatments are released too early, toxic side effects may not be found until after they have harmed people; long-term effects are more difficult to study; drug companies may sell treatments that have little effect; and physicians who prescribe such drugs may become liable for toxic effects (and should follow special informed consent procedures). The tradeoffs are obvious, but the solutions are not.

Withholding treatment is sometimes ethical when scarce resources make it impossible to provide treatment to everyone. In the former case, the investigator can use a crossover design (Fleiss, 1986; Pocock, 1983) to provide the treatment, or a refinement of it, at a later date to control participants if the treatment is successful and resources allow. However, this solution works best when the problem being treated is not progressive and does no permanent damage. For example, a patient with cancer may experience a more rapid progression while being treated with a less effective comparison treatment, and the later crossover to treatment may not compensate for that loss (Marquis, 1983). Similarly, a disadvantaged high school dropout with few options who is denied entry into a second-chance educational program may experience lifelong educational, social, and economic damage if no other chance comes along (Fetterman, 1982). But if the problem will not get worse without treatment, this option helps ensure that everyone will finally receive a treatment that turns out to be useful. It also benefits the experimenter, who can confirm preliminary findings on the former comparison group participants.

Withholding treatment can also be ethical when alternative treatments, each of approximately equal desirability, are compared. The strategy of "planned variations" in the evaluation of educational programs is an example (e.g., Rivlin & Timpane, 1975). However, the strategy is difficult to implement, as researchers often found more variation within a planned treatment over sites than they found between different treatment variants. Further, different variations are often targeted at different parts of the same problem (e.g., cognitive performance versus academic self-concept) and so should include measures of those particular problems, as well as measures of the general problem to which all the variants are aimed (e.g., educational achievement). Another example is a study of computer-assisted instruction (CAI; Atkinson, 1968). Entire classrooms were randomly assigned to receive CAI in either mathematics or English, and each group was tested on both subjects, so that mathematics was the experimental and English the control topic for some students, whereas the reverse was true for other children. This design works when several equally pressing problems are to be treated and when the particular form of one treatment (CAI in English) would not be expected to affect very much the tests pertaining to the other form of the treatment (CAI in mathematics). Such conditions do not hold in many areas, such as AIDS research.

Options When Withholding Treatment Is Problematic

Most other cases of withholding treatment are problematic, especially for severe, deteriorating, or permanently damaging problems. Then, useful options include:

- Using dose-response designs
- Offering all participants an intervention prior to randomization
- Using a "treatment-on-demand" control

First, in dose-response studies participants receive one dose from a range of doses from lower to higher. For example, in a spousal assault intervention experiment, those arrested could be assigned either to normal arrest and release condition in which they were held only a few hours or to an extended arrest condition in which they were held as long as the law allowed (Boruch, 1997). Once the dose of the intervention is reduced to a certain point, the lower end is like a placebo control (although placebos can themselves show a dose-response relationship; Clark & Leaverton, 1994).

Second, one can offer all participants an intervention that occurs *prior* to randomization so that everyone gets something. Some sites used this option as part of the Rockefeller Foundation's Minority Female Single Parent (MFSP) program (Boruch, Dennis, & Carter-Greer, 1988) that provided employment training, day care, and other support services to economically disadvantaged minority women who were single parents. Women were randomly assigned either to receive the intervention or to a control group that could not receive some of the employment and training services. Before random assignment, one site held meetings to help all women to develop a plan to solve some of their problems in case they were assigned to the control condition. Of course, this change may reduce the chance of finding a treatment effect.

A third solution is the treatment-on-demand (TOD) control condition, particularly if fewer participants are assigned to that control than to treatment. Snyder and Wills (1989), in a study of marital therapy, created such a control condition to which fewer couples were assigned than to the treatment conditions. Couples in this control condition could request therapeutic consultations up to 1 hour biweekly for crises that jeopardized the couple's ability to tolerate the 3-month waiting period. Couples who requested more than three consultations were dropped from the study. This procedure has fewer ethical problems than one with a control group receiving no treatment. Attrition is not severe if few couples actually reached the attrition threshold or if such couples are kept in the control anyway and then analyzed using methods discussed in the next chapter.

Imposing Undesirable Treatments

Finally, some experiments involve imposing a potentially undesirable treatment. Such treatments may contain a noxious element, such as a nausea-producing agent in certain aversion-training procedures. They may cause harmful side effects, such as the loss of hair and fatigue in chemotherapy. They may be costly or time-consuming. For example, one study randomly assigned 21 schools to two treatment conditions and one control condition (Moberg, Piper, Wu, & Serlin, 1993). The intensive-treatment condition required a large investment of time and resources by the schools, so some schools refused to be in that condition. This problem was caught early and remedied by allowing schools to self-select their preferred treatment condition with the understanding that they would then be assigned at random either to that treatment or to a control but not to the treatment they objected to. Solutions discussed in the previous sections might apply here to these kinds of experiments, as well.

The Ethics of Random Assignment

Many experiments involve the distribution of scarce and desired resources, such as income supplements, educational grants, or new medicines. Decisions about who will receive these resources must be made ethically. Randomized experiments make the decision by lottery, no matter what the applicants' needs or merits, no matter whether they applied first or last, and no matter who they know or what their connections or power may be (cronyism). We have seen no arguments for treatment allocation by cronyism, for this seems to violate our basic sense of fairness. We could imagine an argument for allocation by order of application, for example, to reward those who made the effort to apply first. But the argument would be weak because effort is confounded with the resources one has to apply—for example, those who apply first may have better access to transportation or more leisure time. So need, merit, and randomization are usually the main options.

The case for assignment by need is strongest when a treatment is known to be the most effective in meeting that need. For example, antibiotics are widely acknowledged to be the most effective treatment for pneumonia, so it is difficult to imagine a case in which it would be ethical to withhold them from such a patient. A similar case can be made for assignment by need to a proven compensatory education program intended to help students from impoverished inner-city schools. Examples of assignment by merit are similarly easy to find, as with the awarding of a National Merit Scholarship for high performance on the National Merit Exam. Bolstering these arguments is the fact that the regression discontinuity design (Chapter 7) can yield unbiased estimates of effects when assignment is made by need or merit (although it is less powerful than the randomized experiment and has its own implementation problems).

Arguments Against Randomization

Given the arguments for assignment by need or merit, some philosophers assert that randomization is ethical only if the conditions being compared may be therapeutically equivalent and if no better treatment exists (Marquis, 1983). They argue that even if the difference between two treatments is based on poor designs and is small, say, only one chance in one thousand of doing better with one treatment, the ethical principle of autonomy contained in the Belmont Report (National Commission for the Protection of Human Subjects of Biomedical and Behavioral Research, 1979) requires that participants be told of these results in the informed-consent process so that they can judge the relevance and weight of such evidence for themselves—especially in areas such as medicine, in which participants usually have some discretion in choosing treatment. These scholars ask the reader to imagine being a cancer patient whose life is at stake before assuming that one is not entitled to all information, no matter how preliminary. Failure to recognize such simple realities can have drastic consequences for the feasibility of the research, as in the example provided by Berg and Vickrey (1994) in which "funding was withdrawn for another trial of epilepsy surgery after an insufficient number of patients were willing to have the decision of whether to have part of their brains surgically removed decided at random" (p. 758).

Other arguments against randomization appeal to practical realities that impede it. Those who sign informed consents may frequently not understand either the forms or their legal rights (T. Mann, 1994). Attitudes toward randomization are not always favorable, even when resources are scarce (Hillis & Wortman, 1976), especially if harm may occur from some treatment conditions (Innes, 1979). Women in the Rockefeller MFSP program thought randomization was less fair than assignment by need or by test scores (but more fair than assignment by "first come, first served" or by "who you know"). About 25% of patients eligible for the NIMH Collaborative Depression Project refused to sign the informed consent because it included a consent to randomization (Collins & Elkin, 1985). Some participants wrongly believe that by signing the form, they have signed away their rights to sue for negligence (T. Mann, 1994). Service providers can react equally negatively, sometimes blaming randomization for problems actually caused by other factors, such as poor referral practices (Lam et al., 1994). Respondents may not believe that a truly random procedure was used, particularly if they receive a less desirable treatment (Boruch, Dennis, & Carter-Greer, 1988; Lam et al., 1994; Wortman & Rabinowitz, 1979), though the latter can sometimes be ameliorated by doing random assignments in a forum open to public participation and scrutiny, as with the U.S. military draft of the 1970s.

Arguments for Randomization

Advocates of randomization respond that we frequently do not know which treatment works best, particularly for innovative treatments with little empirical track record (Miké, 1989). Especially when the sample size is small, as it is likely to be in small trials, or at the time interim results first appear, sampling error is quite likely and quite large, so early results can be misleading. Often the data available about such innovations are based on poorly controlled or executed research that has been advanced to the stage of a proposed clinical trial precisely in order to get larger samples, better designs, and more trustworthy outcome data. In order to advance as far as a clinical trial, the innovation has to show promise, but that promise often proves to be illusory, or worse yet, the innovation causes harm. For example, in observational studies beta-carotene reduced cancer risks, but in clinical trials it increased risk (Liebman, 1996). Indeed, a review of randomized trials showed that medical innovations produce better results than standard treatment only about half the time (Gilbert, McPeek, & Mosteller, 1977b). As Chalmers (1968) put it: "One has only to review the graveyard of discarded therapies to discover how many patients might have benefited from being randomly assigned to a control group" (p. 910). Given the complexities of the statistical issues surrounding the uncertainty of evidence, the researcher presumably has some obligation to point to better and worse evidence.

Other Partial Remedies

Clearly this controversy has no quick fixes. Following are additional solutions that are sometimes used (see Table 9.1). Random assignment can include a "safety valve" mechanism, holding a certain number of program slots for the most needy applicants who are not entered into the experiment, though this may decrease power if the most needy are also most likely to benefit. This strategy was used in the Rockefeller MFSP program, in which staff could fill 10% of program slots with women they judged to be most needy (Boruch et al., 1988).[4] One can divide participants into strata from least to most needy and assign proportionately more of the most

---

4. If the judgment can be quantified, this becomes a regression discontinuity design.

TABLE 9.1 Partial Remedies to Ethical Problems with Random Assignment

1. Use a regression discontinuity design to assign based on need or merit instead of randomly.
2. Use a safety valve mechanism for treating the most needy participants.
3. Divide participants into strata by need, assigning proportionately more of the most needy to treatment.
4. Assign proportionately more participants to the treatment in highest demand.
5. Use a dose-response design.
6. Use an adaptive design to increase the proportion of assignment over time to the most successful condition.
7. Use the informed-consent procedure to ensure that participants are willing to be assigned to all conditions.
8. Use public lotteries for assignment to increase perceived fairness.

needy persons to treatment (Coyle et al., 1991); or similarly, one can assign participants to conditions that vary only in the intensity of treatment (say, dose), so that no participant goes without treatment entirely. When the experiment can use multiple sites but has only limited resources, the treatment can be implemented at some of the sites. A final option is to use adaptive designs that use Bayesian logic in which the proportion assigned to a condition increases over the life of an experiment as the number of successes produced by that condition increases (Flournoy & Rosenberger, 1995; Kadane, 1996; Tamura, Faries, Andersen, & Heiligenstein, 1994).

Discontinuing Experiments for Ethical Reasons

Ethics sometimes demands that ongoing experiments be halted if negative side effects unexpectedly occur or if one treatment condition is producing dramatically better results than another (Marquis, 1983). This happened in the Physicians' Aspirin Study, which examined whether aspirin reduced heart attacks in physicians more effectively than a placebo (Steering Committee of the Physicians' Health Study Research Group, 1988). Of 22,071 patients, 104 had heart attacks while on aspirin and 189 had heart attacks while on the placebo—an effect that objectively seemed small statistically ($r = .034$)[5] but that was large enough to end the study early on grounds that it was unethical to withhold such an effective treatment from controls. Similar decisions to end randomized trials on ethical grounds have occurred in other areas of medicine (Marx, 1989; R. Rosenthal, 1994), though we know of no examples in the social sciences.

Hence it is common to do preliminary analyses of early returns at fixed intervals to determine whether to stop the experiment (Choi & Pepple, 1989; Choi, Smith, & Becker, 1985; S. Emerson, 1996; Spiegelhalter, Freedman, & Blackburn,

5. This correlation is somewhat higher ($r = .16$) if computed differently (Haddock, Rindskopf, & Shadish, 1998); in either case, however, the effect size is undeniably small.

1986; Tan & Xiong, 1996). The issue is not entirely statistical, for it also involves determining who decides to stop the study and whether treatment providers get to see the preliminary results if the experiment is not stopped. These decisions are often made by a data and safety monitoring board (Dixon & Lagakos, 2000). In addition, important outcomes may be revealed only after long periods of time, so terminating a trial after only short-term outcomes have been observed may miss crucial findings (Armitage, 1999). Presenting interim results without ensuring that these problems are clearly understood may mislead participants into selecting a treatment that later proves ineffective or harmful.

Legal Problems in Experiments

Ethical problems can be grounds for legal action. This occurred in the New Jersey Negative Income Tax Experiment. Confidentiality was promised to participants. But a Mercer County grand jury, suspecting that some respondents were fraudulently receiving both experimental payments and welfare, subpoenaed the experimenters' records in order to identify respondents. This action placed the experimenters in a difficult dilemma: to protect possible lawbreakers who had been promised that their responses would be kept confidential, the experimenters would have had to defy the grand jury. Eventually a legal settlement was made by the experimenters out of court.

The law provides certain legal guarantees of confidentiality, such as prohibitions against revealing Internal Revenue Service (IRS) income records of individuals in most circumstances or the confidentiality of the physician-patient relationship. However, the confidentiality of research data is not routinely guaranteed in the law. No matter what an informed consent says, researchers may have to respond to a court subpoena, a warrant for their data, or a summons to appear in court with their data to answer questions. Research participants can also be summoned to court to answer the same questions that they were asked in an interview—although these are rare occurrences in practice (Cecil & Boruch, 1988). Some laws have been enacted to safeguard the confidentiality of data in specific cases. Boruch (1997) lists relevant statutes and the kinds of guarantees given—for example, immunity from legislative inquiry, provisions for secondary analysis of data, and so forth. In research in which legal complications are possible, such as with drug abusers or parole violators, the researcher should identify statutes that are pertinent to such research. However, many of these statutes have never been tested in court, so the extent to which they can be relied on is unclear. Hence researchers should consider using research procedures that can ensure confidentiality, such as using randomized response methods or determining not to gather any data about potential identifiers, and, just as important, they should ensure that such procedures are followed.

The legality of randomization has sometimes been challenged; for example, in criminal justice research some have argued that randomization is arbitrary and so violates both our sense of fairness and the due process and equal protection rights of the accused (Baker & Rodriguez, 1979; Erez, 1986; but see Lind, 1985). This complaint is also heard in entitlement programs such as social security or welfare. Resolutions are legislative, judicial, and procedural (Boruch, 1982, 1997). Sometimes, specific laws authorize randomization, as in the evaluation of the Job Opportunities and Basic Skills Training Program, for which a federal law mandated that "a demonstration project conducted under this subparagraph shall use experimental and control groups that are composed of a random sample of participants in the program" (Family Support Act, 1988). At other times that randomization has been contested in courts, the courts have ruled that it is legal, establishing some case law precedent for later uses of similar randomization (Breger, 1983). Sometimes procedures can be approved to authorize randomization after a law is passed. Gueron (1999) describes a case in which a welfare reform was mandated by law. Although participants could ordinarily not opt out of these legally imposed program requirements, it was possible to arrange afterward for some recipients to be excused from them in the interests of the evaluation. Informed-consent procedures provide some defense, especially if an IRB reviewed and approved the work. Still, many managers and service providers fear being sued if they participate in the experiment. In one experiment on police methods for dealing with domestic violence, the city government initially demanded that the experimenters provide liability insurance coverage for lawsuits incurred as a result of their participating in experiments (Dunford, 1990). Fortunately, this case was successfully resolved without the purchase of insurance.

A report by the Federal Judicial Center Advisory Committee on Experimentation in the Law (Federal Judicial Center, 1981) noted that the law has long viewed experimentation as a legitimate means of exploring public policy issues but with many stipulations. The principle of equality of treatment requires that individuals who are similar in relevant ways be treated similarly. Randomization can violate this principle if needy people are randomly divided into conditions rather than being treated the same way. Regarding benefits and harms, they noted that large harm to individuals is typically not justified in the law by appeals to some larger benefit to those who might receive the treatment in the future. The committee also expressed concern about any experiments that might undermine public faith in the justice system. The committee discussed how these principles might apply to harm caused by disparate treatments, the use of mandatory treatment, confidentiality issues, and deception in experiments. The committee recommended that before an experiment be conducted, it should be demonstrated that:

- the present conditions need improvement,
- the proposed improvement is of unclear value,
- only an experiment could provide the necessary data to clarify the question,
- the results of the experiment would be used to change the practice or policy, and
- the rights of individuals would be protected in the experiment.

RECRUITING PARTICIPANTS TO BE IN THE EXPERIMENT

An experiment cannot begin without locating participants who are willing and eligible to participate. Failure to do so can kill an experiment entirely, as with the Madison and Racine Quality Employment experiment cited at the start of this chapter, or can reduce its power dramatically. Moreover, the characteristics of those who do eventually participate will affect both construct and external validity in obvious ways. For example, the Systolic Hypertension in the Elderly Program experiment (Cosgrove et al., 1999) sent out over 3.4 million letters of invitation, contacted 447,921 screenees, found 11,919 eligible people, and randomized 4,736 to conditions—that is, those who were assigned were just a small subset of those eligible, who were themselves only a small subset of volunteers from a large population that also included nonvolunteers who might have been eligible if screened. In one alcohol treatment outcome study, 76% of a pool of alcoholics were screened out, another 15% refused random assignment to conditions, and the remaining 9% differed greatly from the original pool on many variables (Howard, Cox, & Saunders, 1988). And Pearlman, Zweben, and Li (1989) showed that participants who were solicited for alcohol treatment research by media advertisements differed significantly from the usual alcohol clinic patients on many key characteristics.

Sometimes the problem is that the target population is not clearly defined but merely labeled as unemployed, inner-city residents, or educationally disadvantaged children. More often, the target population is defined but cannot be located (Bickman, 1985; Boruch, 1997; Boruch et al., 1988; Dennis, 1988; Dunford, 1990; Ellenberg, 1994; Orwin, Cordray, & Huebner, 1994). To ensure that they can be located, experimenters can use: (1) preexperimental surveys to locate and characterize potential participants, (2) pipeline studies to follow what happens to them over time, (3) pilot tests of the solicitation procedures to see who will learn about the experiment and who will attend if eligible, (4) trained outreach specialists skilled in communicating and generating interest about a program, (5) intake specialists who aggressively recruit potential participants, and (6) efforts to learn what features of the intervention cause people to decline to enroll, such as lack of child care or finding the training to be in a career that they do not ultimately want to pursue.

If the number of eligible participants is lower than anticipated despite these efforts, the researcher can (1) extend the time frame for the experiment if time and resources are available and if program staff are willing; (2) divert additional resources to intensified outreach efforts; (3) alter eligibility requirements so that more participants are eligible, though this may require testing interactions between eligibility requirements and treatment; (4) reduce the proportion assigned to treatment if power analyses suggest it would still be feasible to find an effect; or (5) terminate the experiment, which is sometimes better than spending funds on an experiment that cannot find the expected treatment effect, especially if the decision is made early in the life of the experiment.

From among those selected as the target sample of interest, the volunteers who agree to be in the experiment may have different characteristics than non-volunteers do. For example, Klesges et al. (1988) offered a workplace smoking cessation program to 66 eligible smokers in two work sites. The 44 who agreed to participate in the experiment differed from those who did not participate in being less successful in previous attempts to quit, in having smoked longer, and in perceiving themselves to be more vulnerable to smoking-related diseases. Such characteristics suggest that these 44 participants were more tenacious smokers who would presumably find it more difficult to quit than those who did not volunteer, possibly biasing the experiment toward finding smaller effects. Notice how this situation affects many kinds of validity—power is reduced given the smaller sample size, the program can only be described as effective with volunteers, and we do not know if the program would work with nonvolunteers.

Sometimes decisions about who is eligible for the experiment are affected by awareness of randomization procedures (Dunford, 1990). For example, in a randomized experiment testing three different methods of police response to domestic violence, individual police officers knew the condition to which the next case would be assigned. They also had responsibility to judge if a case met experimental eligibility criteria. As a result, if they did not believe the next case merited the condition to which it had been assigned, they sometimes defined the case as ineligible. If this problem occurred systematically for one condition more than the others (e.g., if officers were reluctant to assign comparatively minor disputes to the arrest condition and so defined those cases as ineligible when the arrest condition was next to be assigned), both internal and external validity would be affected simultaneously. Here, separating the eligibility and recruitment judgment from the assignment process would help.

Some researchers have proposed design and statistical methods for estimating the effects of these preassignment selection problems. Marcus's (1997a) method requires conducting parallel randomized and nonrandomized experiments, both experiments being identical except that participants willing to be randomized are in the randomized experiment but those wishing to choose their treatment are in the nonrandomized experiment. Ellenberg's (1994) method studies a random sample of participants at each stage of elimination (e.g., those with a diagnosis who are eliminated as inappropriate for treatment, those appropriate patients who cannot be screened, those who are screened but deemed ineligible for randomization, and those who are randomized but refuse to accept assignment) to provide data about the biases that are introduced at each step. Braver and Smith's (1996) design randomizes the entire pool of eligible participants to three conditions: (1) a lottery condition in which participants are randomized to both treatment and control, (2) an invitation to treatment in which participants are offered the chance to participate in treatment, and (3) an invitation to control in which participants are offered the chance to participate in the control. In all three conditions, some participants will refuse participation; but the design takes advantage of these refusals by using a number of randomized and nonrandomized comparisons that shed light on what the effects of treatment might have been in the full population. This design might be usefully combined with the instrumental variable statistical methods presented in the next chapter to estimate the effects of receipt of treatment rather than just invitation to treatment.

IMPROVING THE RANDOM ASSIGNMENT PROCESS

After participants are recruited to a randomized experiment, they have to be randomly assigned to conditions. Successfully implementing and monitoring random assignment in field settings requires great practical expertise and craft knowledge. Few experimenters have that knowledge, in part because statistical textbooks rarely include it and in part because many researchers have little prior experience doing experiments (Haveman, 1987). More than half those funded to conduct an experiment by the National Institute of Justice over 15 years had never conducted one before (Dennis, 1988).

Methods of Randomization

Units can be randomly assigned to conditions in many ways (Table 9.2). We present here some common techniques and their advantages and disadvantages (see also Kalish & Begg, 1985; Lachin, Matts, & Wei, 1988). The techniques sometimes can be used jointly if a particular design has characteristics that would warrant it.

Simple Random Assignment

The procedures for implementing the best known random assignment procedures—the toss of a coin or the roll of a die—are so well known as to need no explanation. Similar possibilities include shuffled cards, spinners, roulette wheels, and urns filled with numbered balls. These procedures have considerable public relations value when the decision that random assignment makes is sensitive and public (as with winning a lottery or being drafted into the military) given the personal consequences of winning or losing. When implemented properly, these easily understood and publicly transparent procedures result in perfectly good random assignments.

But they have two key practical drawbacks. One stems from the physical structure of some devices. A coin only has two sides and so is best adapted to assignment of units to two conditions; a die has six sides, making it useful for up to six conditions. Yet many experiments, for example a 3×3 factorial design, have more conditions than this. Coins and dice can be adapted to more conditions, but

TABLE 9.2 Varieties of Random Assignment

1. Simple Random Assignment
   - Any procedure for assigning units to conditions by chance with nonzero probability (without replacement).
   - Typically done with table of random numbers or computer-generated random numbers.
2. Restricted Random Assignment to Force Equal Sample Sizes
   - Particularly useful with small sample sizes to prevent severely unequal splits over conditions.
   - Equal sample sizes tend to maximize power for testing treatment main effects in many (but not all) designs.
   - Preferred method is to assign from matches or strata (see #7 below).
3. Restricted Random Assignment to Force Unequal Sample Sizes
   - Can be done to cope with practical limitations, such as restriction in the number of units that can receive treatment or ethical objections to depriving many participants of treatment.
   - Can increase power to test certain limited hypotheses (see optimal design theory).
4. Batch Randomization
   - Refers to cases in which small groups with more units than experimental conditions, but not the whole sample, are available to be randomized to conditions.
5. Trickle Process Randomization
   - Refers to cases in which units trickle in slowly and assignment must be made from batches that are smaller than the number of conditions.
   - The key problem is to ensure that desired proportions are assigned to conditions over time.
6. Adaptive Randomization Strategies
   - Methods for correcting imbalances in the desired proportions assigned to conditions by changing the proportions over time.
   - Can be unbiased if unit characteristics remain stable over time; if not, certain analytic adjustments may be required.
7. Random Assignment from Matches or Strata
   - Placing units into groups and then assigning separately for each group.
   - In matching, groups contain as many units as conditions; in stratifying, groups contain more units than conditions.
   - Always helps control proportion assigned to conditions.
   - If matching or stratifying variable is related to outcome, this can also increase the power of the design.
   - Useful to match or stratify on variables expected to interact with treatment.

it can be logistically complex to do so, and the possibilities for errors increase and public transparency may decrease. The second drawback is that these procedures can be biased by systematic behavior by experimenters, as when they (perhaps unknowingly) always place the coin heads up prior to tossing it. For example, the 1970 draft lottery used capsules containing birthdays that were chosen blindly out of a 2-foot-deep bowl—seemingly random. But the capsules were initially placed in a container in chronological order, and that container was probably not shuffled enough. When the capsules were poured from the container to the bowl with no further mixing, the early birth dates were on top of the bowl and were overrepresented among the first picks that sent some young people into the military (Fienberg, 1971). When these more publicly accepted procedures must be used, Fienberg (1971) suggests ways to increase the likelihood that the randomization process is reliable.

The main alternative is to use a table of random numbers. Many statistics texts contain them (e.g., Fleiss, 1986; Rosenthal & Rosnow, 1991). They are convenient and useful for experiments with any number of conditions, and they are often generated by computer algorithms that severely curtail the possibility of systematic biases. Over the years, they have been examined for many different kinds of latent nonrandomness, and biased columns or pages have been deleted and substituted. Though they are not perfect, such tables are the most accessible source of reliable random numbers.

Another alternative is to use a computer to generate one's own list of random numbers. Most common statistical packages can do this, including SPSS, SAS, and Excel (Appendix 9.1). These programs have great flexibility, but they can still have problems. For instance, one large city school system assigned eligible students at random to either a regular city school or to a new and innovative magnet school that spent four times more per pupil. A study of how the magnet school affected achievement and attitudes showed that attempts during one year to make the computerized random number generator more efficient actually made it more biased (Zigulich, 1977)! In the Spouse Assault Replication Program (SARP; Boruch, 1997), researchers discovered that a string of random numbers was being repetitively duplicated when the computer was rebooted after "going down" because the program started anew with the same algorithm generating the same numbers. Further, if the researcher does not fully understand the programming algorithms, a faulty randomization may result. Most researchers are well served if they continue to rely on tables of random numbers.[6]

The general principle in using any of these methods is to make all the allocation decisions as random as possible. Consider a psychotherapy experiment in which the experimenter wishes to assign 20 clients to either a treatment or control condition. First, the experimenter might pick a random start in a table, which may be done haphazardly by simply turning to a random page, closing one's eyes, and touching a spot on the page (Wilson, 1952), or more formally by using numbers picked haphazardly to identify the page, column, and row for the random start. Then the researcher simply moves down the column or across the row from

---

6. Creative researchers have invented many more randomization techniques. In the Spouse Assault Replication Program (Boruch, 1997; Garner, Fagen, & Maxwell, 1995), for example, the exact time of each complaining phone call to police was recorded to the second by a computer. All cases ending with an even-numbered second were assigned to the arrest condition for the alleged assault, and all those that ended in an odd-numbered second were assigned to the mediation condition.

that starting point, searching in this case for either the numbers 1 or 2 to indicate that the participant is assigned either to treatment or control (the pair can be 1 or 0, or any other plausible pair; or one could use odd numbers to assign participants to one condition and even numbers to the other). Suppose the numbers after the random start are 73856 20392 34948 12637. Moving left to right, the number 2 is encountered first, so the first participant is assigned to control. Continuing the search for 1 or 2, one encounters 2, 1, and 2 in that order. So the second and fourth participants are assigned to the control condition, but the third participant goes to the treatment group; and so on until all participants have been assigned. If the experiment has three conditions, then the search is for the numbers 1, 2, or 3 (or 1–3 for the first condition, 4–6 for the second, 7–9 for the third, ignoring 0); and the logic extends to any number of conditions. Such a procedure is called **simple random assignment** without replacement. It is "simple" because no prior stratification has occurred, and it is "without replacement" because any unit already assigned will be skipped if and when its number comes up a second time in the random number listing.

Restricted Random Assignment to Force Equal Sample Sizes

Simple random assignment often results in unequal sample sizes in each condition, especially when the sample of units is small. In the psychotherapy example, it is extremely unlikely that simple random assignment will split the 20 clients into two groups of 10 each. The reason is simple: in any random number list, it is extremely unlikely that one will encounter exactly 10 ones and 10 twos among the first 20 eligible numbers. More likely one will encounter 9 ones and 11 twos or 12 ones and 8 twos. With small samples, splits can be very uneven. One of us (Shadish) once accidentally demonstrated this to a class of graduate students by using the flip of a coin to publicly assign 10 students in the class to one of two conditions. The coin came up heads all 10 times, resulting in a treatment group with 10 participants and a control group with none! Unequal sample sizes can complicate the estimation of effects (Keppel, 1991), make the statistical analysis more sensitive to departures from homogeneity of variance (S. Maxwell & Delaney, 1990), and jeopardize power as the split exceeds a ratio of 2:1 or 3:1 (Pocock, 1983). Researchers should probably avoid simple random assignment with total sample sizes less than 200. Pocock (1983, Table 5.3) has shown with 200 units that a split as large 57–43% would be expected by chance only 5% of the time. The researcher must also consider whether interim results are desired. Unequal sample size splits are more likely early in a trial if strict procedures are not followed to ensure otherwise. If the researcher knows that interim results on less than the full sample will be computed or disseminated to the press, the funding agent, service providers, participants, or other scientists, then smaller group sizes are desirable to ensure equal sample sizes early on.

With smaller samples or when interim results are to be used, the researcher should consider methods that equalize sample sizes across conditions. One way to do so is to randomize from within groups of size equal to the number of conditions—from pairs in studies with two conditions, from triplets in experiments with three conditions, and so on. With two conditions, the researcher takes the first two units, randomly assigns one to the first condition, and then places the second unit into the second condition. Often this method is used when the design calls for matching or stratifying on some predictor of outcome, a topic we cover later in this chapter. Whether or not matching is done on a substantive variable, masking of random assignment may then be required to prevent those involved in the experiment from using knowledge of assignment from matches to anticipate the next assignment. Thus in medical trials a physician who knew that matches of two were being used might be able to predict the next assignment, systematically directing patients toward or away from being the next treatment to be assigned, for example, by claiming that the next person to be assigned does not meet the eligibility criteria. The researcher can also keep the size of the matches confidential or even vary the size of the matches, though this would complicate analyses. Berger and Exner (1999) present a method for detecting selection biases that might have occurred as a result of such anticipation. However, when the experiment uses several stratification variables, has multiple factors with several levels each, or is a double-blind or multisite experiment, then the chances of being able to predict the next assignment are much smaller.

When units become available for treatment slowly over time—that is, when they "trickle" into a study—an adaptive assignment design is another option to equalize sample size over time (Kadane, 1996). Here the proportion assigned to conditions is changed over time to assign more units to the condition that has the smallest number of units. Like matching or stratifying, this method can also be used to equalize groups on substantive variables that have been measured prior to assignment, and this method also makes it harder for those involved in the experiment to predict the next assignment, so that the need to mask assignment is smaller.

The least desirable solution usually occurs when the researcher has not anticipated this problem at the start—to force equal cell sizes by starting with simple random assignment, to stop assigning units into a condition when it receives its planned share, and to continue in this way with all the other treatments until the last units are placed into the last remaining condition. The problem here is that this procedure increases the possibility of confounding if the last units differ systematically from earlier units (e.g., due to seasonality effects). In a trial of a program to prevent smoking, for example, the last people to volunteer may be systematically less motivated to quit than the first people who eagerly sought the opportunity. In a trial of a new cancer chemotherapy, eligibility criteria may be strict for early clients; but if the desired sample size seems unattainable in the time available, the researcher may loosen eligibility criteria to hasten inclusion into the study, with the result that the last patients may be different from the first ones. If these last participants are disproportionately assigned to the last condition so as to force equal sample size, significant bias may result.

Restricted Random Assignment to Force Unequal Sample Sizes

Randomization does not require equal sample sizes. In fact, a common definition of random assignment, that participants must have an equal chance of being in all conditions, is wrong. All random assignment requires is assignment by chance, with each eligible unit having a nonzero chance of assignment to each condition. Procedurally, forcing unequal sample sizes is easy. For example, to assign two thirds of the participants to one condition and one third to the other with a table of random numbers, one could use the numbers 1 through 6 to assign to the first condition and 7 through 9 for the second, without using 0. The options here are obvious enough to need little elaboration.

Unequal sample sizes are useful for two reasons. One is statistical. Although common belief is that equal sample sizes increase power, this is not always true. In optimal design theory (e.g., McClelland, 1997), unequal assignment of observations to conditions can increase power to detect certain effects. For example, when comparing more than two conditions, power for some contrasts may be maximized with a weighted sum of detectable differences, in which the weights reflect unequal sample sizes. To know if unequal sample sizes increase power, researchers must identify the basic design (number of factors and levels per factor) and know which effects are of most interest (e.g., linear versus higher order polynomial; main effects versus interactions; nonordinal effects) in more detail than most social scientists are accustomed to (Atkinson & Donev, 1992; Mead, 1988; Orr, 1999). McClelland (1997) suggests some practical guidelines. First, use the same number of levels of an independent variable as it requires parameters to estimate the effect: two levels for a linear effect, three for quadratic, and so on. Second, consider an extra level to guard against underfitting the model: for example, add a third level to guard against a quadratic effect when a linear effect is hypothesized. Third, allocate observations disproportionately to extreme levels of the variable if nonlinear effects are likely. Fourth, in those rare cases in which random sampling of levels is used, power is maximized in analysis by using as few polynomial and interaction terms as necessary or by using one-degree-of-freedom focused tests for categorical variables.

The second reason to use unequal sample sizes is to respond to practical demands. For example, when only a small number of participants can be given a treatment but the pool of applicants is large, using more control participants can improve statistical power compared with equal sample size (Kish, 1987). Similarly, when contrasting two treatments with each other and with a control group, primary interest sometimes lies in the contrast between the two treatments, for instance, if both treatments have often been compared with control in the past studies. In this case, a smaller control group may be warranted. Another example is to compare a well-known treatment with a new treatment when precise estimates of the effects of the latter are needed so that more participants may be assigned to the latter. In another case, one can maximize the number of people receiving treatment for ethical reasons, as when Klesges, Haddock, Lando, and Talcott (1999) assigned 75% of new Air Force trainees to a program to help them maintain smoking cessation and only 25% to the control. In yet another instance, treatment may be more expensive than control, and the optimum distribution of a fixed budget over treatment and control is at issue (Orr, 1999; Zucker et al., 1995). Suppose the experimenter has a fixed $50,000 budget. It costs $1,000 to include a treatment participant who receives an expensive medical regimen and outcome tests, but only $250 to include a control participant who receives just the outcome tests. If the investigator opts for an equal sample size of 40 per cell, with an effect size of $d = .50$ and $\alpha = .05$, power is .60. But if the same resources are allocated to 30 treatment participants and 80 controls, power rises to .64. However, power drops dramatically as sample sizes become very discrepant. With 25 treatment participants and 100 controls, power is back to .60; and as cell sizes become even more discrepant, power drops rapidly. Power is more complex with designs to test multiple conditions or interactions, in which case consulting a statistical expert is good advice.

Batch Randomization

Batch randomization occurs when only small groups of units are available for assignment to conditions at any one time (Reicken et al., 1974), as with a new cancer trial in which the flow of eligible patients is slow and out of the experimenter's control. The experimenter cannot wait months or years to obtain a complete list of all patients before assigning them to conditions, because some of them would die and the rest would undoubtedly find another physician. So assignment decisions might be made for each batch of patients periodically. The experimenter must then decide ahead of time what proportion of participants are to be assigned to each condition and arrange a randomization procedure that anticipates these proportions and applies them consistently to each batch. The previously described procedures can all be adapted to these conditions, but keeping track of batches is essential for later analyses of differences over batches.

Trickle Process Randomization

Trickle process randomization occurs when units trickle in slowly and must be assigned immediately for practical or ethical reasons (e.g., Goldman, 1977)—for example, psychotherapy clients whose symptoms require immediate help. Here, fixed proportions of units are randomly assigned to conditions based on the expected proportion of treatment group openings for new clients. Thus, in an inpatient medical study, the experimenter might know that about 10 eligible patients arrive each week and that about four beds are available each week. Then a fixed proportion of about 40% of patients are randomly assigned to treatment each week. Braught and Reichardt (1993) review trickle process assignment and describe a computer protocol for implementing it.

Adaptive Randomization Methods

These methods adapt the assignment proportion over time to correct imbalances in sample size (or covariate levels) when the initial randomization is not producing the desired ratio of participants in each condition. This happened in the National Job Training Partnership Act (JTPA) study, in which staff found it difficult to recruit enough eligible youth to fill program slots. Halfway through the study they decreased the proportion of eligibles assigned to the control group from a 1:2 control:treatment ratio to a 1:6 ratio at some sites (Orr, 1999). The rationale and procedure were outlined in Efron (1971), adapted to batch or trickle process assignment in L. Freedman and White (1976) and Pocock and Simon (1975), and adapted to random assignment from strata (under the rubric of urn randomization or play-the-winner randomization) in Lachin (1988), Wei (1978), and Zelen (1974). Palmer and Rosenberger (1999; Rosenberger, 1999) review the strengths and weaknesses of all these methods.

In the simplest case, when an imbalance is noted, the probability of assignment of subsequent participants is adjusted until the originally envisioned proportions are achieved. Then the original assignment proportions are used again. For example, in a trial with a desired 50:50 proportion over two groups but in which an imbalance has developed, Pocock (1983) suggests shifting to a new ratio of 2:3 if the trial is small (or 3:2, depending on the direction of the imbalance to be remedied) or to 3:5 for larger trials of 100 units or more. The NIMH Collaborative Depression project used adaptive randomization to remedy a developing imbalance over conditions in the assignment of both males and minorities (Collins & Elkin, 1985). In a more complex case (often called urn randomization), the adjustment occurs after each assignment—after each participant is assigned to one group, the probability of assignment to that group is decreased and is increased to the other group(s). The result is a long-run balance of sample size.

However, some kinds of adaptive assignment can cause problems. If the first 50 participants were assigned using simple random assignment and resulted in a 15:35 split, and if the remaining 50 participants were assigned with a different proportion to remedy this split, then bias could result if the last 50 participants were systematically different from the first 50. For instance, they might have been subject to different eligibility standards or to different seasonality effects. During the 3-year San Diego Job Search and Work Experience Demonstration experiment, the San Diego job market tightened, so later applicants differed from earlier applicants in some job-related characteristics (Greenberg & Shroder, 1997). In such cases, pooling applicants assigned before the change in proportion with those assigned after it can create biases because the different kinds of applicants in the pools before and after the change are assigned to groups in different proportions. If the investigator recognizes from the start of the project that imbalances may arise, urn randomization would be far less subject to this problem. Otherwise, one could randomly discard cases separately from treatment and control conditions for each batch, so that each batch contributes equal proportions of experimentals and controls; but this is only viable with sample sizes large enough to avoid too much loss of power. Finally, batches can be analyzed as strata in the statistical analysis.

Haphazard Assignment

Some investigators substitute haphazard assignment, that is, a procedure that is not formally random but has no obvious bias, for random assignment. For example, alternating assignment was used in an evaluation of a pretrial arbitration procedure in Connecticut courts (Lind, 1985). In the Illinois On-Line Cross-Match Demonstration experiment, applicants with odd last-digit identification numbers were experimentals, whereas those with even last-digit identification numbers were controls (Greenberg & Shroder, 1997). In the Teen Outreach program experiment, some sites assigned by choosing every other name on an alphabetized list (Allen, Philliber, Herrling, & Kuperminc, 1997). Some haphazard procedures approximate random assignment reasonably well (Mosteller, Gilbert, & McPeek, 1980; McAweeney & Klockars, 1998), and if random assignment is not feasible, they may be a good choice. Even when haphazard assignment procedures may have a bias, they can be a source of stronger quasi-experiments than letting participants choose their own conditions (Staines et al., 1999).

However, whenever haphazard assignment is feasible, some form of random assignment is usually feasible, too. It makes little sense to substitute the former for the latter, because the latter's characteristics are so widely studied and understood, whereas the former's characteristics are not. Haphazard procedures can *appear* to be random when they actually have selection biases. For example, if two clients come to a psychotherapy clinic for therapy each day, one in the morning and one in the afternoon, alternating assignment will be biased toward using "morning persons" in the treatment group and "afternoon persons" in the control group. Such persons may differ systematically from each other in ways we rarely fully understand, in circadian rhythms or sleep patterns, for example. Similarly, some haphazard methods such as alternating assignment allow one to anticipate which treatment will be given next; a person knows that because the date is even-numbered, the patient will be assigned to control rather than treatment. If so, that person might encourage a particularly needy patient to delay coming until a day on which he or she can be assigned to treatment, thereby biasing the treatment group toward more needy patients. Because the possibility of such selection biases can never be fully ruled out in haphazard assignment, formal random assignment is usually preferred when it is feasible.

Sometimes investigators begin their studies with random assignment but later override randomization with a nonrandom procedure to compensate for an observed difference between groups. For example, the original Perry Preschool Project evaluation randomly assigned 128 children from 64 matched pairs to two conditions (Schweinhart et al., 1993). Subsequently, some of these pairs were exchanged so that groups would be better balanced for sex and socioeconomic status (Spitz, 1993; Zigler & Weikart, 1993). This is tempting because it appears to do exactly what randomization intends—to make groups more equivalent before treatment begins. It is particularly tempting when the imbalance is on a variable known to predict outcome. However, it is not recommended. Differences between groups on observed means are to be expected because random assignment equates on expectations, not on observed means; and overriding randomization can even create biases on unobserved variables. If variables such as age are known to be important prognostic indicators, then the investigator should have done random assignment from matches or strata formed by age. It is rarely a good idea to override random assignment, for there are almost always better options, such as those we cover now.

What to Do If Pretest Means Differ

It is not a "failure of randomization" if some observed means are significantly different across conditions at pretest after random assignment.[7] Indeed, from sampling theory we expect that the fewer the number of participants assigned to conditions, the larger are the differences in pretest means that may be found. Conversely, large sample sizes greatly reduce the likelihood of substantial differences among observed pretest means and so enhance the interpretability of any single randomized trial. Similarly, using units that are very homogeneous also decreases the likelihood of such differences emerging. But as long as randomization was implemented properly, any pretest differences that occur will always be due to chance, even with small sample sizes, heterogeneous populations, and obtained pretest means that are greatly discrepant.

However, the fact that balance is expected in the long run over multiple experiments is little comfort in an experiment that is imbalanced here and now. One has to interpret the results of one's own experiment, imbalances and all. Hence researchers sometimes test whether pretest differences between conditions are statistically significant (or fall into a certain acceptable range; Hauk & Anderson, 1986; Makuch & Simon, 1978; Westlake, 1988). When these tests suggest that the observed pretest means differ by more than seems desirable, the researcher may then wonder whether to proceed with the experiment or to redo the randomization procedure until pretest means are observed that are more nearly equal. Unfortunately, redoing random assignment compromises posttest hypothesis tests whose underlying sampling distributions are based on the assumption of a single randomization. To rerandomize makes standard hypothesis testing a bit more conservative, failing to detect real effects too often. But some methodologists do allow rerandomization (e.g., Cox, 1958; Pocock, 1983) if the criteria under which

---

7. Huitema (1980) and Mohr (1995) call this unhappy randomization; Maxwell and Delaney (1990) call it fluke random assignment.

it will occur are specified in advance and if it is done prior to the start of the experiment. After all, even if rerandomization results in conservative tests, such conservative biases are often viewed as acceptable in science.

However, in most cases, there are better options. One can legitimately use the analysis of covariance (Huitema, 1980) to adjust results for random pretest differences, though this procedure is usually inferior to choosing covariates that are correlated with outcome (Begg, 1990; Maxwell, 1993; Permutt, 1990). Using large sample sizes also helps prevent pretest discrepancies of large magnitude from occurring, though the increased power they provide also increases the likelihood of finding significant differences on pretreatment measures. Even better, unhappy randomizations can be prevented from occurring at all through the use of random assignment from matches or strata, to which we now turn.

Matching and Stratifying

Units can be matched or stratified before being randomly assigned to conditions. For example, in an experiment on the effects of psychotherapy on stress, participants will differ from each other on initial stress levels and a host of other variables, such as marital status, that may be related to stress. Simple random assignment may yield observed mean differences between treatment and control groups on any of these variables. Such differences can be minimized by first matching participants on a relevant variable and then randomly assigning from these matches. For example, to match on age in a two-group experiment, the two oldest participants form a pair; and one member of the pair is randomly assigned to treatment and the other to control. Then the next oldest pair is treated similarly, and so on through the youngest pair. Diament and Colletti (1978), for example, used a behavioral counseling group and a wait-list control group to study the effects of a treatment of parental control problems with learning disabled children. Prior to the study, they placed 22 mothers into 11 pairs based on age and then randomly assigned from those pairs. Better still, the experimenter can match on pretest scores when they are available. Bergner (1974), for example, randomly assigned 20 couples to either marital therapy or a control group by using pairs formed by matching on pretest scores of behavior ratings of couple communication patterns, and similar behavior ratings at posttest were the outcome variable.

Stratifying is similar except that strata contain more units than conditions, unlike matches that contain the same number of units as conditions. For example, we might stratify psychotherapy clients on gender, randomly assigning females to treatment and control separately from males; or, in a multisite experiment, sites could be strata with random assignment to treatment and control within each site, as was done in the NIMH Treatment of Depression Collaborative Research Program (Elkin, Parloff, Hadley, & Autry, 1985; Imber et al., 1990). When either matching or stratifying can be used, matching is preferred if it is convenient, but stratifying into five strata is often sufficient to remove over 90% of the bias due to the stratification variable (Cochran, 1968). Although we primarily discuss matching here, our comments also apply to stratifying unless otherwise indicated.

Both matching and stratifying greatly increase the likelihood that conditions will have similar pretest means and variances on the matching/stratifying variable and on any variables correlated with it. When properly analyzed, the variance due to the matching variable can then be removed from overall error variance (Keppel, 1991; Kirk, 1982). This produces a more powerful statistical test.[8] In general, we recommend random assignment from matches or strata whenever it is feasible and a good matching variable can be found. We especially recommend it when sample sizes are so small that simple random assignment may not result in equal means, variances, and sample sizes. This is important when subanalyses are planned (e.g., stratifying on gender to aid a test for a treatment by gender interaction). Without matching, there may be too few participants in individual cells to do the planned subanalyses.

We note three caveats. First, matching on variables completely unrelated to outcome produces little benefit and can decrease statistical power by using up degrees of freedom. Second, more care must be taken with matching in quasi-experiments, in which the issues we outlined in Chapters 4 and 5 come to bear (Campbell & Erlebacher, 1970; Costanza, 1995). Third, the benefits of matching and stratifying mostly apply to their use *prior to* randomization (Fleiss, 1986). For example, prestratification on gender with subsequent random assignment is far more likely to yield equal sample sizes than will post-randomization stratification on gender during data analysis.

A good matching variable in randomized experiments is often the pretest score on the main outcome of interest. So in the psychotherapy-for-stress example, matching participants on pretest stress levels prior to random assignment is preferred. If that is not possible, then the researcher can match on variables that are highly correlated with the outcome variable. For example, the researcher may not want to give a pretest on the exact same stress test to be used at posttest for fear of sensitizing clients to the outcome. But a simple one-item question about overall stress levels that is embedded in the initial application form that clients complete might be surreptitious enough to avoid sensitization effects but still be correlated with outcome. Or if it is known that overall stress levels are lower in married than in single clients, then stratifying on marital status may be worthwhile.

Adaptive randomization strategies can also be used to help equate groups on observed scores, in addition to their benefits for equating on sample size that we described earlier (e.g., Wei, 1978). The Project MATCH Research Group (1993)

---

8. There are two main exceptions. First is the case in which the number of units is very small (e.g., less than 10 per condition), as when schools or communities are matched and then assigned to conditions (Diehr, Martin, Koepsell, & Cheadle, 1995; Gail et al., 1992; Gail et al., 1996; Martin, Diehr, Perrin, & Koepsell, 1993). Second, if the between-match variance is not much larger than zero (e.g., if males do not differ appreciably from females on the outcome variable), then a randomized design without matching is more powerful because its error term will have more degrees of freedom.

used this method to ensure that the conditions in their alcohol treatment study were balanced for current drinking severity, prior treatment for drinking, prior psychiatric treatment, sociopathy, marital and employment status, gender, and education.

Finally, the Propensity Matched Pairs Design (PMPD) uses propensity score matching in randomized experiments (Hill, Rubin, & Thomas, 2000).[9] It can be used if a small proportion of a population is selected randomly to receive treatment, but there are insufficient resources to follow all remaining controls in the population. If sufficient pretreatment information is available to compute propensity scores on all treatment and nontreatment participants in the population, then a control can be selected from the population for each treatment participant by matching on propensity scores. This requires enumeration of the entire population of eligibles before the study starts. Presumably, methods for selecting multiple controls from the population for each treatment participant (e.g., Henry & McMillan, 1993; Rosenbaum, 1995a) could be adapted to this design.

Matching and Analysis of Covariance

The analysis of covariance (ANCOVA) can be used as an alternative or as a complement to matching or stratifying (Huitema, 1980; Maxwell & Delaney, 1990). ANCOVA is especially useful to adjust for variables that were not used for matching because their correlation with outcome was not anticipated or because it was too logistically complex to match on all variables that were known to predict outcome.[10] For example, in the NIMH Treatment of Depression Collaborative Research Program experiment (Elkin et al., 1985; Elkin et al., 1989; Imber et al., 1990), marital status was included as a covariate in the analysis because it proved to be correlated with outcome, though this was not anticipated. Similarly, Bloom (1990) used age, education, ethnicity, socioeconomic status (SES), earnings, employment, and unemployment benefits received as covariates in his study of the effects of reemployment services on the earnings and employment of over 2,000 displaced workers randomly assigned to conditions. The researcher could also covary propensity scores to adjust for random selection differences between conditions.

---

9. The true propensity for randomization into two conditions is a probability of .50 for each condition with simple random assignment. However, randomization equates conditions only on expectations, not on observed scores, so randomization does not equate observed propensity scores either. Predicting group membership in a randomized experiment will yield propensity scores that vary randomly from the true propensity scores of .50. Those propensity scores can then be used to adjust the randomized experiment for random assignment sampling fluctuations.

10. Researchers frequently make the mistake of choosing covariates that are significantly different between groups, but it is usually better to covary variables that are highly correlated with the outcome whether or not they distinguish between groups at pretest (Begg, 1990; Maxwell, 1993; Permutt, 1990). Beach and Meier (1989) present a method that takes into account the correlation of the covariate with both assignment and outcome.

The temptation is to add many covariates, but each uses up a degree of freedom. So adding covariates that do not predict outcome or that are highly correlated with each other will waste a degree of freedom while providing little new information.[11] Covariates also cost money to administer and score. Allison (1995) provides an algorithm for judging when the cost of adding a covariate exceeds the savings realized from needing fewer participants; Allison, Allison, Faith, Paultre, and Pi-Sunyer (1997) cover power-cost optimization with covariates, multiple measures, optimal allocation of participants to conditions, and optimal selection of participants to enter the experiment.

ANCOVA may be preferable to matching or stratifying on the covariate for control of extraneous variance due to the covariate if the relationship between covariate and outcome is linear or if the researcher is confident that the form of any nonlinearity can be adequately modeled. Matching and stratifying are not affected by such nonlinearities and so may be preferable if the relationship between the covariate and outcome is not known to be nonlinear or if the form of the nonlinearity is not confidently known (Maxwell & Delaney, 1990; Maxwell, Delaney, & Dill, 1984). Many statisticians are not confident that such nonlinearities can be well-modeled (Dehejia & Wahba, 1999). Matching may also be preferable if the matching variable has many small unordered categories, such as "type of alcoholic." Or matching and ANCOVA can be used together by randomly assigning from matches and then analyzing with ANCOVA; this allows all the benefits of matching for similar sample sizes and observed means at pretest.

The Human Side of Random Assignment

To judge from anecdotal evidence and research, problems in executing random assignment are prevalent (Berk, Smyth, & Sherman, 1988; Boruch & Wothke, 1985; Conrad, 1994; Dunford, 1990; Gilbert, McPeek, & Mosteller, 1977a; Greenberg & Shroder, 1997; Marcus, in press; Rezmovic, Cook, & Dobson, 1981; Sackett, 2000; Schulz, 1995; W. Silverman, 1977; Test & Burke, 1985).[12] Conner's (1977) analysis of 12 projects found that planned randomization was less likely when (1) randomization was done by researchers working for the project being evaluated rather than by outside researchers; (2) random assignment was controlled by operating personnel from the agency under study rather than by researchers; (3) loopholes exempted some individuals from random assignment; and (4) randomization was done by several persons rather than one individual. Similarly, Dennis (1988) found

---

11. The interpretation of ANCOVA results is complicated if the covariate is caused by treatment, a result that should generally be avoided by, for example, using a covariate measured prior to treatment beginning. If not, adjusting for the covariate may remove some of the treatment effect (Maxwell & Delaney, 1990, pp. 382–384).

12. The *Canadian Medical Association Journal* recently started a new series on why randomization fails (Sackett & Hoey, 2000).

that covert manipulation of randomization occurred often in 30 randomized experiments in criminal justice, especially when it was not controlled by the researcher or when the person doing the assignment knew to which conditions specific individuals were being assigned. These are the sorts of problems that field researchers often face. We know too little about their prevalence and about their likely influence on estimates of program effects, though available evidence suggests they can cause significant biases in experiments (Berger & Exner, 1999; Chalmers et al., 1983; Schulz, Chalmers, Hayes, & Altman, 1995).

Fortunately, we have learned much about how to increase the likelihood of successfully implementing random assignment (Boruch, 1997; Gueron, 1999; Orr, 1999). Boruch and Wothke (1985) suggest seven lessons that provide a convenient framework (Table 9.3). First, the researcher should plan how to explain the nature and purpose of randomization to those who will be affected, how to respond to arguments about why randomization could or should not be done, and how to provide incentives for doing randomization (Kruse et al., 2000). After all, it is naive to expect that research assistants, service delivery agents, program managers, or research participants will understand random assignment fully. The explanations need to be simple, scripted, learned in advance, and written and delivered at a level appropriate to the recipient. The researcher should anticipate the objections that are commonly raised to randomization and be prepared to discuss all sides of them, for such questions invariably arise and must be discussed hon-

TABLE 9.3 Seven Lessons About Implementing Random Assignment

1. Plan in advance how to explain the nature and purpose of randomization to those who will be affected, how to respond to various arguments about why randomization could or should not be done, and how to provide incentives for doing randomization.
2. Pilot test the randomization procedure to discover problems that can be remedied with further planning.
3. Develop clear procedures for implementing, controlling, and monitoring the randomization process throughout the entire experiment.
4. Have meetings at which to negotiate the randomization procedures with those who will be affected by them.
5. Develop fallback options that can be used to bolster estimates of program effects in the event that randomization fails.
6. Take advantage of naturally occurring opportunities that facilitate the conduct of randomization.
7. Carefully examine the match between the proposed design and those factors that will make randomization more likely to be successful in the particular context of the experiment.

Note: This table is a synthesis of a chapter on this topic by R. F. Boruch and W. Wothke, 1985.

estly and ethically. Gueron (1999) gives an example from an employment training experiment that required staff to randomly assign applicants to a control group:

> We met with these staff and told them what random assignment involved, why the results were uniquely reliable and believed, and how positive findings might convince the federal government to provide more money and opportunities for the disadvantaged youth they served, if not in San Jose, then elsewhere. They listened; they knew first-hand the climate of funding cuts; they asked for evidence that such studies had ever led to an increase in public funding; they sought details on how random assignment would work and what they could say to people in the control group. They agonized about the pain of turning away needy young people, and talked about whether this would be justified if other youth, as a result, gained new opportunities. Then they asked us to leave the room, talked more, and voted. Shortly thereafter, we were ushered back in and told that random assignment had won. This was one of the most humbling experiences I have confronted in 25 years of similar research projects, and it left me with a sense of awesome responsibility to deliver the study and get the findings out. (p. 11)

The worst mistake a researcher can make is not to take these staff and administrative concerns seriously. The ethical problems and the risk of failed randomization are too great. The experiment should often be abandoned if these concerns cannot be overcome.

Second, the researcher should pilot test the randomization procedure to discover problems that can be remedied. Gueron (1999) recommends that randomization schemes take no more than 1 minute per person to implement. Each person doing randomization should be instructed several times on how to randomize by an expert in randomization. In fact, there is probably no better way to find context-specific problems. For example, staff who have been cajoled into silence rather than persuaded of the value of random assignment may reveal their remaining objections through the actions they take as assignment is implemented. When piloting is not feasible, many implementation problems can be detected by using a brief "run-in" period during the start of the study in which procedures are tested but resulting data are not used in the analysis. If neither of these options is feasible, the researcher should pay particular attention to the initial randomization process to find and remedy problems before most experimental participants have been assigned.

Third, the researcher should develop clear procedures for implementing, controlling, and monitoring the randomization process throughout the entire experiment. It is usually better (1) to prepare the randomization procedures as early as possible, (2) to use tables of random numbers, except when public relations value requires mechanical methods, (3) to separate the randomization process from the process of determining eligibility so as to prevent covert manipulation of randomization by manipulation of eligibility judgments, (4) to have a single person who is part of the research team in charge of random assignment, (5) to keep the master list of assignments in a secure place (and keep a backup of it elsewhere), (6) to make that list accessible only to those doing assignment and to the principal investigator,

(7) to monitor the procedure closely and frequently for correct implementation throughout the experiment, (8) to check whether a new applicant has already been admitted into the study (because people often drop out and then reapply), (9) to keep a log of the assignment process and especially of violations of it, (10) to keep as many people as possible blind to assignment, (11) to have regular meetings with those doing randomization to review randomization decisions made since the last meeting and to identify and resolve problems with the procedure, and (12) where appropriate, to provide incentives to randomize correctly, such as monetary payments.[13]

Fourth, the researcher should have meetings at which to negotiate the randomization procedures with those who will be affected by them. Doing this when the randomization procedure is first designed allows the researcher to benefit from staff members' more intimate knowledge of what is likely to go wrong, to enlist their active cooperation in implementing randomization, and to minimize both the costs and the objections to randomization by those stakeholders. This includes those who will do randomization and also others in the organization who might be affected by randomization, such as service providers. Sherman and Berk (1985) note that implementing randomization is like implementing any other organizational change—such change always requires special attention. In the Minneapolis Spouse Abuse Experiment, Sherman and Berk spent considerable time in numerous meetings negotiating random assignment with the funding agency, the mayor of the city, representatives of the police who had to implement randomization, and various interest groups who cared about the problem. Through this negotiation procedure a feasible randomization procedure emerged. Some authors have even formalized these agreements in contracts (Bickman, 1985; Fairweather & Tornatsky, 1977).

Fifth, the researcher should develop fallback options that can be used to bolster estimates of program effects in the event that randomization fails. The addition of design elements such as staggered implementation of treatment over sites can provide alternative sources of causal evidence in the event that randomization fails in a serious way. Sixth, the researcher should take advantage of opportunities that facilitate the conduct of randomization. We covered a wide range of these opportunities in more detail at the end of the previous chapter. Seventh, the researcher should carefully examine the match between the proposed design and those factors that will make randomization more likely to be successful in the particular context of the experiment. For example, sometimes aggregate units such as classrooms or schools could be randomized more feasibly than individual units such as students, and the researcher should be prepared to adopt either design feature if possible. Conversely, the researcher should be skeptical of designs that rely on the promise that a site can generate a large number of experimental participants if that site has

---

13. Marcus (2001) discusses sensitivity analyses that can be helpful if it is suspected that randomization has been subverted.

not previously participated in experiments and can provide little evidence that large numbers of qualified participants exist and can be attracted.

All these matters are most difficult to ensure in multisite experiments in which participants within sites are assigned to conditions, particularly when a more complex design is used (Hausman & Wise, 1985). In such evaluations, the choice may be between allowing someone at the local level to randomize within each site or using a central office to randomize via telephone. The latter allows the researcher to retain control over the integrity of assignment but is more difficult to implement efficiently and quickly (Pocock, 1983). In multisite evaluations, different sites will also have different experience with randomization. Boruch et al. (1988) describe one site in a large multisite study that became distressed when all their referrals were assigned randomly to the control condition (stratifying by site prior to randomization can prevent this problem). Multisite evaluations require more complex randomization procedures that, in turn, require more resources to implement correctly, so researchers with few resources should minimize any complexity.

CONCLUSION

This chapter concerns what researchers can do to design an ethical experiment, to ensure that enough participants will be eligible to enter the experiment, and to plan a feasible and successful random assignment procedure. The next chapter takes up from this point and concerns problems that arise when those randomly assigned to treatment do not fully receive it or refuse to participate further in the measurement of their outcomes.

APPENDIX 9.1: RANDOM ASSIGNMENT BY COMPUTER

SPSS and SAS

The random number generators in programs such as SPSS and SAS are well-tested to produce reliable random assignments. Here is an SPSS syntax that will assign equal numbers of units randomly to conditions.[14] To run the program, begin by making the changes noted in the capitalized comments.

---

14. Both programs were suggested by Virgil Sheets of Indiana State University, used by permission.

input program.
*YOU SHOULD LOOP TO THE TOTAL N.
loop #I=1 to 200.
*DIVIDE THE N BETWEEN GROUPS.
if (#I<101) group=1.
if (#I>100) group=2.
compute x=normal(1).
end case.
end loop.
end file.
end input program.
sort cases by x.
print table/ $casenum group.
execute.

The number of cells in the design can be varied by adding more "if (#I>x) group=y" lines, and unequal cell sample sizes can be obtained by appropriate changes to the same statements. For example, to divide 200 units into three cells of 50, 50, and 100 each, use:

if (#I<101) group=1.
if (#I>100 and (#I<151)) group=2.
if (#I>150) group=3.

The following SAS syntax will also accomplish the task:

```
OPTIONS LS=80;
DATA WORK;
**Set number after 'to' as # in intended sample;
**change q to reflect # of groups in study;
**set intervals as equal division of sample by q;
DO I=1 TO 300;
IF I<61 THEN Q=1;
IF (I>60 AND I<121) THEN Q=2;
IF (I>120 AND I<181) THEN Q=3;
IF (I>180 AND I<241) THEN Q=4;
IF (I>240 AND I<301) THEN Q=5;
X=RANUNI(0);
OUTPUT;
END;
PROC SORT; BY X;
PROC PRINT; VAR Q;
```

World Wide Web

The World Wide Web contains numerous sites that can perform random assignment tasks. At the time of printing of this book, these sites included:
http://members.aol.com/johnp71/javastat.html#Specialized
http://www.assumption.edu/html/academic/users/avadum/applets/applets.html
http://lib.stat.cmu.edu/

Excel

Open a new workbook. Enter the number 1 in Cell A1 and 2 in A2; then drag the AutoFill handle (highlight Cells A1 and A2, and the handle appears as a dot at the lower right corner of A2) to Cell AN, where N is the number of units to be randomized. In B1, enter "=rand( )" (without the quotation marks); highlight B1 and drag the AutoFill handle to Cell BN. In Cell D1, enter the number 1, and drag the AutoFill handle to Cell Dx, where x is the number of units to be assigned to the first condition. In Cell D(x+1), enter the number 2, and drag the AutoFill handle to Cell D(x+y), where y is the number of units to be assigned to the second condition. If the study has a third condition, then in Cell D(x+y+1), enter the number 3, and drag the AutoFill handle to Cell D(x+y+z), where z is the number of units to be assigned to the third condition. Continue this process until all N cells in Column D are filled. Pick any cell in Column B and click the Sort Ascending button; this randomizes the original N units. Column A is the unit identification number, and Column D is the condition to which they are assigned. Highlight Columns B and C and delete them. Then either print the list (which is now ordered by condition number) or highlight Columns A and B and sort them in ascending order on Column A for a list ordered by unit identification number. Those who choose to use this procedure should note that errors in statistical procedures in Excel have been documented (McCullough & Wilson, 1999), at least for Excel 97; whether these errors have been fixed in subsequent versions is unknown. The nature of the errors is probably such that they would not compromise random assignment, but as other options do exist, those options should be used where feasible.

10

Practical Problems 2: Treatment Implementation and Attrition

Im·ple·ment: (ĭm′plə-mənt) v. *tr.* [Middle English *supplementary payment,* from Old French *emplement, act of filling,* from Late Latin *implementum,* from Latin *implere.*]   1. To put into practical effect; carry out: implement the new procedures.   2. To supply with implements. **imple·men·tation** n. **imple·menter** n.

At·tri·tion (ə-trĭsh′ən): n. [Middle English *attricioun, regret, breaking,* from Old French *attrition, abrasion,* from Late Latin *attritio,* attrition- *act of rubbing against,* from Latin *attritus,* past participle of *atterere, to rub against:* ad-, *against.*]   1. A rubbing away or wearing down by friction. 2. A gradual diminution in number or strength because of constant stress.   3. A gradual, natural reduction in membership or personnel, as through retirement, resignation, or death.

I N AN ideal world, those who are assigned to an intervention would receive it properly and would be measured on all outcomes, and those assigned to the comparison condition would also receive the proper treatment (or receive no treatment, according to the design) and be measured. But field experiments are rarely ideal. The intervention may not be implemented properly, fully, or even at all. Sometimes, those assigned to the intervention group refuse the treatment either before or after the experiment starts; and sometimes, the controls insist on receiving the intervention. Other people drop out of the study entirely so that no outcomes are ever observed on them, whether or not they received the intervention. All these problems fall under two headings, treatment implementation and attrition. These two problems threaten the very reason for doing an experiment:

to get a good estimate of a treatment effect. In this chapter, we describe both design and statistical approaches to both these problems.

PROBLEMS RELATED TO TREATMENT IMPLEMENTATION

In a randomized experiment that studied a program to increase medication adherence for newly diagnosed patients with high blood pressure, each patient in the treatment group was given a form on which to record his or her medication intake as an aid to improve adherence (Saunders, Irwig, Gear, & Ramushu, 1991). After 6 months, only 28% could even produce the form, and only 40% knew how to fill it out correctly. Another study found that only 30–40% of patients took their medications within 2 hours of the time of day they were supposed to be taken, even with weekly reminders (Rudd, Ahmed, Zachary, Barton, & Bonduelle, 1990). In the Minneapolis Spouse Abuse Experiment (Berk et al., 1988), 18% of participants received a treatment other than the one to which they were assigned. Bloom (1990) found that about 3% of the unemployed workers who were assigned to the no-treatment condition crossed over into one of the treatment conditions. In a psychotherapy outcome study, the same therapists administered both treatments, and one therapist used extensive techniques from the behavioral condition when he was doing therapy with clients in the eclectic condition (Kazdin, 1992).

These examples point to three related problems—failure to get the full intervention, crossing over to get a different treatment, and treatment diffusion—that are common in field experimentation. Indeed, few experiments achieve full implementation of the intervention, in which every participant in each condition is offered the intervention, fully receives the intervention, and fully complies with the intervention to which they were assigned and no other intervention. Knowledge of treatment implementation helps characterize the intervention and its context, facilitates the detection of problems in the intervention, and helps distinguish between the effects of assignment and the effects of the intervention. This section discusses practical methods for assessing and inducing implementation and then presents statistical analyses that account for levels of implementation.

Inducing and Measuring Implementation

Experiments benefit from making sure treatment is implemented as intended (induction), and from having very specific information about the extent to which the intervention is actually delivered and then received and implemented by the recipient. Such information helps to ensure that the intervention was actually manipulated, to detect and remedy problems with the intervention before they progress too far, to describe the nature of the intervention, to explore not just whether the intervention works but how it works, and to examine covariation between intervention and outcome. All these issues bear directly on the cause-effect relationship that is the central justification for doing a randomized experiment in the first place.

The Components of Implementation

Treatment implementation is not just one thing but rather is a multifaceted process that includes **treatment delivery, treatment receipt,** and **treatment adherence** (Lichstein, Riedel, & Grieve, 1994). To use a simple medical example, *delivery* refers to whether a physician writes a prescription for a patient, *receipt* refers to whether the patient gets the prescription and has it filled, and *adherence* refers to whether the patient takes the prescribed medication and does so according to the instructions. For some cases, these three processes blend together. For example, delivery, receipt, and adherence often blend together completely for a surgical intervention in which the delivery and receipt of, say, an incision are two sides of the same action. In other cases, these three processes could be broken down further, especially in the kind of complex social interventions that occur in, say, whole school reform, job training, or programs such as Head Start.

Adherence is what most researchers probably mean when they talk about treatment implementation. But adherence clearly depends on delivery and receipt in most of the interventions studied in social experiments. Consequently, the researcher should consider doing things to increase the chances that delivery, receipt, and adherence will occur and to measure how much delivery, receipt, and adherence actually happened in the experiment. Here are some examples.

Inducing and Measuring Treatment Delivery. The odds that an intervention will be delivered can be increased by using treatment manuals, by training service providers, by giving verbal reminders to those providers to include all treatment procedures, by providing on-the-spot instructions to them during treatment, or by administering treatment by videotape or audiotape. In addition, treatments may be delivered with less integrity when they are more complex, burdensome, of long duration, inconvenient, or expensive or when they require the recipient to alter his or her lifestyle; so reducing all these problems when possible can increase service delivery. Delivery can be measured in staff meetings by supervisors of service providers or by reviewing or even formally scoring tapes of the sessions at which service is provided. Assessing differential delivery (e.g., that the treatment *excludes* key components of a comparison treatment) is important when many treatments are being compared to each other. For example, the NIMH Treatment of Depression Collaborative Research Program used ratings of psychotherapy sessions to show that therapists in three different therapy conditions performed those behaviors appropriate to the condition to which they were assigned more often than they performed the behaviors appropriate to the other conditions (Hill, O'Grady, & Elkin, 1992).

Inducing and Measuring Treatment Receipt.   Ways to improve treatment receipt include giving written handouts to recipients that summarize key treatment points, using established communication strategies such as repetition of the message or making the treatment deliverer appear expert or attractive, questioning the recipient about key treatment features to induce cognitive processing of treatment, and having recipients keep logs of their treatment-related activities. In many cases failure of treatment receipt is due to failure of communication between the deliverer and the recipient if the provider is a poor communicator or if the recipient is poorly motivated or inattentive. Receipt can be measured using manipulation checks, written tests of change in recipients' knowledge related to treatment, talk-aloud assessments of the recipients' experience during treatment, monitoring physiological changes that the treatment should induce when it is received, or asking the recipients if they are confident applying treatment skills.

Inducing and Measuring Treatment Adherence.   Adherence is reduced when treatment participants lack the time to carry out the treatment, forget to do it, are unsure of the correct treatment procedures, are disappointed by initial results from trying treatment, lack access to an appropriate setting in which to carry out the treatment, or simply lose motivation to change (Lichstein, 1988). Each of these suggests strategies for improving adherence; for example, by assigning the recipient written homework to do and return, by using family members to encourage adherence, by making available physical aids such as tape recordings or motivational cards to guide practice of the skills taught in the intervention, or by giving reinforcements such as raffle tickets for demonstrated adherence. Adherence can be measured by interviewing the recipient and other informants about the recipient's treatment-relevant activities outside of treatment or by using biological assays when adherence to the treatment would result in a detectable biological change, such as the presence of a medication in the blood or the absence of nicotine residuals in saliva for a stop-smoking treatment. Adherence has been particularly heavily studied in medicine; entire monographs (Cramer & Spilker, 1991; Haynes, Taylor, & Sackett, 1979; Okene, 1990; Sackett & Haynes, 1976; Schmidt & Leppik, 1988; Shumaker & Rejeski, 2000) are devoted to the topic, and even a journal (the *Journal of Compliance in Health Care*) dedicated to adherence existed for 4 years (1986–1989).

Overlooked Targets for Implementation Assessments

Three kinds of implementation assessments are often overlooked in experiments. First, researchers often forget to assess the *extra-study* treatments that participants are getting while they are in an experiment. In AIDS research, for example, patients who are not assigned to the treatment they prefer often seek their preferred treatment elsewhere, all the while remaining in the treatment arm to which they were assigned (Marshall, 1989). Some AIDS patients are enrolled in more than one experiment simultaneously (Ellenberg et al., 1992). Similarly, in studies of the effects of social programs to improve pregnancy outcome, participants often sought and used other programs to improve the health of their babies (Shadish & Reis, 1984).

Second, researchers often forget to assess the treatments received by those who are assigned to a no-treatment control condition, for it is naive to think that they experience nothing between a pretest and posttest. The clearest examples occur in medical trials in which some patients must be taken off placebo medication and treated actively for ethical reasons. Often, however, those assigned to control groups actively seek treatment elsewhere. For example, Margraf et al. (1991) questioned patients and physicians in a randomized, double-blind experiment that compared two medications for treatment of panic disorder with a placebo and found that the great majority of both patients and physicians could guess accurately whether they received active medication or the placebo (see also Greenberg, Bornstein, Greenberg, & Fisher, 1992). Given the extreme distress that panic disorder patients often experience, some patients assigned the placebo probably sought and received treatment elsewhere.

Third, researchers often forget to assess the unplanned things that service providers do in treatment. For example, those who administer treatment may depart from the protocol by adding new components based on their experience of what works, making a treatment more powerful (Scott & Sechrest, 1989; Sechrest, West, Phillips, Redner, & Yeaton, 1979; Yeaton & Sechrest, 1981). By definition, planning to measure such unplanned deviations is difficult. So the experimenter may need some capacity for discovery. Qualitative methods such as participant observation or open-ended interviews with providers and recipients can provide that capacity.

Assessing Program Models

To this point, we have been speaking of implementation issues as if they are limited to the intended treatment. We have done so in order to emphasize the role that these matters play in improving the construct validity of the treatment and in allowing the use of the statistical analyses described in the next section that tease out the difference between the effects of assignment to treatment and receiving the treatment. But in an important sense, implementation issues are larger than what we have covered to this point. They may include inputs that the treatment requires, including client flow, treatment resources, provider time, and managerial support. They may include contextual issues such as local politics and social setting peculiarities that constrain how treatment is done. And they may include funding or insurance reimbursement rules for paying for treatment. Information about all of these matters is important for two reasons. One is to anticipate potential breakdowns in the intervention so that they can be monitored and prevented before they undermine the study; the other is to provide descriptions of the context of implementation that can be crucial to those who are considering using it in another context.

Two methods help accomplish these goals. One is to construct a **process model** of the treatment that portrays the intervention and its context, typically a figure complete with boxes for inputs, processes, and outputs, with causal arrows connecting them to portray the time flow of events that are supposed to occur. A number of authors have provided detailed instructions for how such models can be constructed, along with practical examples (Becker, 1992; Rossi, Freeman, & Lipsey, 1999; Sechrest et al., 1979; Weiss, 1998). The second method is good description of all these matters in study reports, the more detailed the better. In both cases, the use of these methods should occur from the start of the study, be maintained throughout its implementation, and be included in reports. In some cases, such as multisite experiments, for example, it may help to have an ongoing newsletter in which useful information about these issues is presented and in which individuals can exchange experiences regarding difficulties they have met in implementing their treatment or procedures they have adopted for alleviating these problems.

Treatment Implementation in Efficacy and Effectiveness Studies

Although much can be learned from *assessing* treatment implementation, *inducing* full treatment implementation is not always necessary or desirable. In particular, the internal validity of the inference that *assignment to condition caused outcome* does not require the treatment to be fully implemented. Researchers in public health recognize this fact in their distinction between tests of treatment efficacy versus effectiveness:

> Efficacy denotes the degree to which diagnostic and therapeutic procedures used in practice can be supported by scientific evidence of their usefulness under optimum conditions. Whether or not these procedures are applied adequately in practice, and whether they produce the intended results when so applied, are matters of effectiveness. (Starfield, 1977, p. 71)

In **efficacy** trials, treatments often are standardized, and full implementation is the goal, so the treatment is given every possible chance to show its effects. This procedure is particularly desirable when a treatment is first being studied because it would make little sense to pursue a treatment that does not perform satisfactorily under optimal circumstances. But in **effectiveness** trials, because researchers recognize that treatments are often administered in the real world with less than full standardization and implementation, inclusion criteria may be loosened and recipient compliance may be left to be variable, all because researchers want to know how a treatment will perform in such less-than-ideal circumstances. Indeed, haphazard standardization and implementation are so characteristic of many social interventions that stringent standardization would not well represent treatment in practice. A randomized trial in which treatment standardization and implementation are left to vary according to the contingencies of practice still yields an internally valid estimate of the effectiveness of that treatment-as-standardized-

and-implemented. However, the construct validity of the treatment characterization clearly depends on the nature of treatment implementation—indeed, the words *efficacy* and *effectiveness* are simply construct labels we choose to use to distinguish different kinds of conditions to which we assign people in experiments.

Analyses Taking Implementation into Account

When treatment implementation data are available, experimenters may analyze them in three ways:

- An intent-to-treat analysis.
- An analysis by amount of treatment actually received.
- By one of a variety of newly-developed analyses that try to combine some of the benefits of the first two options.

Intent-to-Treat Analysis

In an **intent-to-treat analysis,** participants are analyzed as if they received the treatment to which they were assigned (Begg, 2000; Lachin, 2000; Lavori, 1992; Lee, Ellenberg, Hirtz, & Nelson, 1991; Rubin, 1992a). This analysis preserves the benefits of random assignment for causal inference but yields an unbiased estimate only about the effects of being assigned to treatment, not of actually receiving treatment. The inference yielded by the intent-to-treat analysis is often of great policy interest because if a treatment is implemented widely as a matter of policy (say, by being mandated by law or funded by an insurance company), imperfect treatment implementation will occur. So the intent-to-treat analysis gives an idea of the likely effects of the treatment-as-implemented in policy. But the inference is not of universal interest. Moreover, the intent-to-treat analysis can yield biased results in the presence of nonrandom missing outcome data, requiring additional assumptions and analyses to yield valid effects (Frangakis & Rubin, 1999). Consequently, although researchers should conduct and report an intent-to-treat analysis, they should supplement it with other analyses.

Analysis by Amount of Treatment Received

If treatment implementation has been measured, the researcher can compare outcomes for those who received treatment with outcomes for those who did not. However, this comparison is quasi-experimental (compared with the intent-to-treat analysis) because participants were not assigned to receipt of treatment at random. For example, all things being equal, if outcome improves as the amount of treatment implemented increases within the treatment group (and within the comparison group, if relevant), the improvement constitutes only weak circumstantial evidence that the treatment caused the outcome. It is weak because people may have self-selected into receiving greater levels of treatment based on, say, being more motivated than those who chose to receive lower levels of treatment. Treatment effects are then confounded with those unknown selection biases, just as they are in any quasi-experiment. Hence analyses by amount of treatment ought to be done in addition to, rather than instead of, a standard intent-to-treat analysis.

Instrumental Variable Analyses

The state of the art of these kinds of analyses is rapidly improving (West & Sagarin, 2000). In one of the most influential of these works, Angrist, Imbens, and Rubin (1996a) use random assignment as an **instrumental variable** (Foster & McLanahan, 1996) to obtain an unbiased estimate of the average causal effect for those who receive treatment.[1] They consider a randomized experiment with a binary outcome and a binary measure of whether participants in both conditions complied with treatment or not. They make five *strong* assumptions, three of which are straightforward and often plausible: (1) that one person's outcomes do not vary depending on the treatment someone else is assigned (e.g., if two friends were assigned to different conditions, one to get a flu vaccine and the other not, the probability of one friend getting the flu might decrease because the other was vaccinated); (2) that, by virtue of random assignment, the causal effects of assignment both on receipt and on outcome can be estimated using standard intent-to-treat analyses; and (3) that assignment to treatment has a nonzero effect on receipt of treatment. The remaining two assumptions can be problematic, but Angrist et al. (1996a) describe sensitivity analyses to explore the magnitude of bias that results from violations: (4) that random assignment (the instrumental variable) affects outcome only through its effects on receipt of treatment, and (5) that there are no "oppositional" participants who would always refuse treatment if assigned to it but take treatment if not assigned to it. Although both assumptions can be plausible, both have exceptions we discuss shortly.

Angrist et al. (1996a) illustrate the method and the assumptions with the Vietnam draft lottery, in which birth dates were assigned random numbers from 1 to 365, and those below a certain number were then subject to the draft (in effect, being randomly assigned to draft eligibility). However, not all those subject to the draft actually served in the military. Suppose the question of interest is whether serving in the military (not draft eligibility) increases mortality. The standard intent-to-treat analysis uses randomization to examine whether draft eligibility increases mortality, which

---

1. See comments on this method and example by Heckman (1996); Moffitt (1996); Robins and Greenland (1996); Rosenbaum (1996a); and Angrist, Imbens, and Rubin (1996b). Heitjan (1999) compares the method with others. Special cases of the method were presented more intuitively by Bloom (1984a) and Zelen (1979), though certain ethical issues can arise (Snowdon, Elbourne, & Garcia, 1999; Zelen, 1990) with some implementations of Zelen's randomized consent design in which participants are randomized to conditions before they have given informed consent (see also Braunholtz, 1999; Elbourne, Garcia, & Snowdon, 1999).

yields an unbiased estimate of effects but is not quite the question of interest. We can address the question of interest by comparing the mortality of those who served in the military with that of those who did not, but the comparison is then quasi-experimental, biased by the many unknown factors other than the draft that caused people to serve in the military (e.g., volunteering to maintain a family tradition, being cajoled by peers who enlisted). The Angrist et al. (1996a) method provides an unbiased instrumental variable estimate of the question of interest if the aforementioned assumptions are met. Clearly the first three assumptions are no less plausible than they are in any randomized experiment. As to the fourth, however, a potential draftee's knowledge that he was now eligible for the draft might cause him to stay in school to gain a deferment, which might improve mortality rates through education and income. The fifth assumption is that no one is so oppositional that if drafted he would refuse to serve but if not drafted he would volunteer. This is generally plausible, but one can imagine exceptions, such as the person whose family history would have encouraged him to volunteer for the military in the absence of being drafted but who objected to the government draft and so refused to serve in protest. If we know the prevalence of such violations of assumptions, sensitivity analyses can show the magnitude of expected biases. Using these analyses, Angrist et al. (1996a) showed that violations of the fourth assumption might significantly bias results in this example.

Variations on this method are rapidly appearing for use in studies with variable treatment intensity, such as drug dosage or hours of exam preparation; with multivalued instrumental variables; with providing bounds on estimates rather than point estimates; and with quasi-experiments and other observational studies (Angrist & Imbens, 1995; Balke & Pearl, 1997; Barnard, Du, Hill, & Rubin, 1998; Efron & Feldman, 1991; Fischer-Lapp & Goetghebeur, 1999; Goetghebeur & Molenberghs, 1996; Goetghebeur & Shapiro, 1996; Imbens & Rubin, 1997a, 1997b; Little & Yau, 1998; Ludwig, Duncan, & Hirschfield, 1998; Oakes et al., 1993; Robins, 1998; Rosenbaum, 1995a; Sommer & Zeger, 1991). The plausibility of assumptions may decrease in some of these applications. Developments on this topic are so rapid that readers are well-advised to search the literature before relying solely on the preceding references.

An issue is that the answer these methods yield may depend on the measure of implementation that is used. Heitjan (1999) shows that even a simple classification of a participant as a complier or noncomplier is fraught with subjectivity. Similarly, an implementation measure with low reliability might attenuate results, and a measure with low validity would presumably call the construct validity of the treatment into question. Further, these models currently use only one measure of implementation, but if one can develop several measures of delivery, receipt, and adherence, no single measure may best capture implementation (though it seems that adherence is the intended target in the Angrist et al. method). If several measures exist, the implementation analysis could be run repeatedly, once for each available implementation measure, and results inspected for more or less consistent results. A version of the method that could use several implementation measures simultaneously would be desirable.

POST-ASSIGNMENT ATTRITION

In this section, we start by defining the problem of post-assignment attrition and the difficulties it causes. Then we discuss how to, first, prevent attrition and, second, statistically analyze data when attrition has occurred.

Defining the Attrition Problem

Post-assignment attrition refers to any loss of response from participants that occurs after participants are randomly assigned to conditions. Such losses can range from an inadvertent failure to answer a single questionnaire item to the loss of all data on predictors and outcomes that occurs when a participant refuses any further participation. Post-assignment attrition should usually include cases in which, after assigning a participant to conditions, an experimenter deliberately drops that participant from the data. Such deliberate drops are a problem if they could have been caused by assignment. For example, researchers often drop participants for failing to meet an eligibility criterion. In some cases this is plausible, as when a study eligibility criterion was that all participants be female and a male was accidentally included. Treatment could not have caused gender, so dropping this person will cause no bias. In many other cases, however, this judgment is subject to considerable unreliability, as when a researcher decides to drop a participant as not really being bulimic or anorexic. The latter judgments are made with sufficient error to allow inadvertent biases based on experimenter or participant expectations. Even with such seemingly reliable rules as dropping those who move from the area, treatment assignments (e.g., to a less desirable control condition) can push a participant over the edge to decide to move, thereby making the move treatment-correlated. Given such ambiguities, it is rarely a good idea to deliberately drop participants after assignment to conditions.

All attrition lowers statistical power, and treatment-correlated attrition of participants from conditions threatens internal validity in a randomized experiment. Many of the benefits of random assignment occur because it creates equivalence of groups on expectations at pretest, an equivalence that is presumed to carry over to posttest. But when attrition is present, that equivalence may not carry over, particularly because attrition can rarely be assumed to be random with respect to outcome. In such cases, the nonrandom correlates of attrition may be confounded in unknown ways with treatment, compromising inference about whether treatment caused posttest outcomes.

Moderate to high attrition from treatment outcome studies has been reported in such widely diverse areas as smoking cessation (Klesges et al., 1988), alcohol treatment (Stout, Brown, Longabaugh, & Noel, 1996), substance abuse treatments (Hansen, Tobler, & Graham, 1990), psychotherapy (Epperson, Bushway, & Warman, 1983; Kazdin, Mazurick, & Bass, 1993; Weisz, Weiss, & Langmeyer, 1987), and early childhood education (Lazar & Darlington, 1982). In a meta-analysis of

85 longitudinal cohorts in adolescent substance abuse research, Hansen, Tobler, and Graham (1990) found that the average attrition rate was 18.6% at 3 months posttreatment and 32.5% at 3 years. Other reviews have found attrition rates greater than 40–50% in studies of substance abuse, homelessness, and child behavior problems (Ribisl et al., 1996).

Both lore and evidence suggest that attrition is often systematically biased rather than random (Bloom, 1990; Klesges et al., 1988; MacKenzie, Funderburk, Allen, & Stefan, 1987; Mennicke, Lent, & Burgoyne, 1988; Stout et al., 1996). For example, lore says that individuals who drop out of job training programs that guarantee an income during training are likely to be the more able, because they are more likely than others to find work that pays well; that individuals who drop out of parole programs will be those with the lowest chance of "rehabilitation"; or that individuals who drop out of an experimental group designed to evaluate the effectiveness of day care for the elderly will be the oldest and most infirm and those who are less gregarious. Data support such lore. Kazdin, Mazurick, and Bass (1993) found substantial differences between those who drop out of child psychotherapy and those who stay for treatment. MacKenzie, Funderburk, Allen, and Stefan (1987) found that alcoholics lost to follow-up differ from those who could be found and interviewed. Adolescents who drop out of a substance abuse study have different drug use patterns than those who stay (Brook, Cohen, & Gordon, 1983; Tebes, Snow, & Arthur, 1992). Examinees who leave questions unanswered on tests differ on a variety of personal characteristics from those who answer all questions (Grandy, 1987). Given such data, the burden of proof should be on the researcher to show that attrition is *not* treatment-correlated when it occurs and that the failure to find such a relationship is not due to low power.

By virtue of treatment-correlated attrition, many randomized experiments in practice become more similar to quasi-experiments. However, this does not mean that randomized experiments with attrition are no better than quasi-experiments. After all, these same attrition biases may exist in quasi-experiments, adding attrition biases to the selection biases already present in such designs. Meta-analytic evidence suggests that effect sizes from randomized experiments with attrition fall between those from randomized experiments with no attrition and quasi-experiments (Shadish & Ragsdale, 1996). It is likely, therefore, that initial randomization can often reduce the overall magnitude of posttest bias when compared with quasi-experimental approaches, even when attrition occurs.

Preventing Attrition

The most desirable solution to attrition is to prevent it from occurring. Preventing all attrition is rarely possible, but minimizing attrition is still important if the effects of attrition are cumulative. Not all attrition is preventable—for example, that due to natural disasters, death, and riots (Clarridge, Sheehy, & Hauser, 1977). And the costs of minimizing attrition could be used for other purposes, such as increasing sample size, so balancing such expenditures is a consideration (Groves, 1989). However, much attrition can and should be prevented.

Attrition Caused by Treatment or by the Research Procedures

Treatment dropout is not unique to experiments. Psychotherapists refer to "premature termination" of therapy as a substantive problem, and in medicine, noncompliance with medication is common. Not surprisingly, then, some attrition from an experiment is due to features of treatment. Some women declined to be trained in elevator repair in the Rockefeller MFSP program because they perceived it to be a traditionally male job (Boruch et al., 1988). Many depressed outpatients refused randomization to a drug treatment condition that they found unattractive (Collins & Elkin, 1985). Counseling clients are less likely to drop out when their therapists are seen as expert, attractive, and trustworthy (Mennicke et al., 1988). Some of these features can be manipulated to decrease attrition, as with pretherapy training about the nature of treatment and the expectations a client should have, and by tailoring treatments to more closely match client expectations (such as offering brief therapy because many clients expect that). However, there are limits to how much manipulation can be done while still maintaining the original research question. One could not offer brief therapy if the question concerns an extended treatment. Sometimes the offending features of a treatment are inherent to it, as with the deliberate administration of nausea drugs in aversion therapy for sex offenders.

Other times attrition is caused by the research process. The demands of research exceed those normally expected by treatment recipients. An example is the tradeoff between the researcher's desire to measure many relevant constructs as accurately as possible and the respondent's desire to minimize the time spent answering questionnaires. Interpersonal conflict between research staff and participants can cause attrition, as can requests made of participants that exceed their resources, such as requiring mothers to leave their children at home without day care, research staff's failure to keep promises to participants such as providing feedback about how they performed on tests, participant fear of lack of confidentiality, and scheduling difficulties that the participant may have little incentive to resolve. Researchers can identify such problems in pilot studies before the main experiment begins, but even these fail to locate all such sources of attrition. After the fact, the researcher can identify these problems by **debriefing** participants about their study experience and by asking dropouts why they failed to return. These can be done by a staff member not involved in other aspects of the study, for those staff members might minimize reports of negative experiences that might reflect poorly on their work.

Retention and Tracking Strategies

Attrition is especially likely in studies of research populations that are mobile or afraid to make their locations known or that lack phones or employment, such as the homeless, drug abusers, or abused spouses. Special efforts to retain and track these populations have been developed, and these efforts are equally applicable to any other populations. A thorough review with a rich trove of advice on retention and tracking strategies is provided by Ribisl et al. (1996; see also Boruch, 1997). They summarize their recommendations in eight parts (see Table 10.1 for detail): (1) gather complete location information at baseline from the participants, friends, or relatives and any available records or agencies that might know their whereabouts, including release of information forms giving permission to contact them; (2) establish formal and informal relationships with public and private agencies, such as driver's license bureaus, that might help find participants; (3) create a project identity with such means as a logo and identification badge; (4) emphasize the importance of tracking to project staff dedicated to that task and ensure that those staff are well-supported and compensated; (5) use the simplest and cheapest tracking methods first, saving more extensive methods for hard-to-find participants; (6) make research involvement convenient and rewarding for participants by such means as providing day care or lotteries for participation and by using alternative means of data collection, such as phone interviews if in-person interviews are not feasible; (7) expend the greatest amount of tracking effort at the initial follow-up periods, when most attrition occurs; and (8) customize tracking efforts to the individual participant's situation and to the study's circumstance. Such specifically tailored advice has been published on tracking and retention for prevention research (Biglan et al., 1991), childhood behavioral problems (Capaldi & Patterson, 1987), the homeless (Cohen et al., 1993), youth at high risk for AIDS (Gwadz & Rotheram-Borus, 1992), and smoking prevention research (Pirie et al., 1989).

Consider a longitudinal study that interviewed 141 abused women six times over 2 years (Sullivan, Rumptz, Campbell, Eby, & Davidson, 1996). Interviewers were trained in how to establish trust with these women, including explaining why the research was important and stressing the confidentiality of the women's identity, location, and response. Interviewers obtained names, addresses, and phone numbers of all contact persons who would know where the woman was living if she moved, including family, friends, neighbors, employers, coworkers, clergy, individuals in local organizations, and government agents, such as their social workers or the local social security office. Release of information forms giving permission to contact these people were obtained. The woman received a business card with information about how to contact the project (including a toll-free number) with the date of the next interview, the amount she would be paid for that interview, and a request to call the project if she moved. Finally, the project paid each woman an increasing amount of money for each interview as an incentive for her to make contact if she moved. Halfway between any two interviews, the project staff called the woman to remind her of the upcoming interview, and then a week before the interview would try to locate her and set up the interview. If phone calls, letters, and home visits did not locate the woman, then they called, visited, and sent letters to the alternative contacts and made trips into the woman's community to find people who might know her location.

TABLE 10.1 Comprehensive Listing of Retention and Tracking Techniques

Information collected from participant

Demographics of participant	• First and last name, middle initial (or name) and all aliases, nicknames • Intentions to change name • Social Security number • Medicaid/Medicare number • Date of birth and place (city, town, state, hospital) • Home address(es), mailing address(es), and phone number(s) • Current and previous occupation, work address(es), and phone number(s) • Veteran status—if applicable, claim number and dates of service • Student status, name and address of school, school district • Driver's license number • Participant's moving plans in the next year
Demographics of relatives (parents, spouse, significant other, stepparents, siblings, children)[a]	Obtain the following information on at least two people: • Full names (maiden or birth names for women if married and changed name) • Addresses and phone numbers • Date of birth
Demographics of collaterals[a]	• Name, address, phone number of significant others/friends • Name, address, phone number of representative payee, state welfare worker, and religious contacts, if applicable • Name, phone number of landlord, if applicable
Demographics of professionals[a]	Identifying information for: • Community mental health caseworker or primary therapist • Department of Social Services caseworker • Parole/probation officer—note times and dates of incarceration • Medical doctor and/or clinics/hospitals utilized • Names of shelter workers or shelters the participant frequents

a. You must have a signed "Release of information" form for each of these individuals.

TABLE 10.1 Continued

Relatives, correspondents, and professionals (optional)	• Contact these people to check the accuracy of information • If the participant is institutionalized, verify contacts before his or her release and discuss with them any conflicting or inaccurate information
Retention and tracking procedures	
Participant	• Request that participant call project office if any tracking information changes or give him or her prepaid change of address cards • Call or write 2–3 weeks after initial contact (or midway between end of treatment and first follow-up), as the "trail is fresh," and contact again at least 2 weeks before follow-up data point • After locating the person, go over all current tracking information and add any new information (keep copies of all old information) • Schedule interview appointment for difficult-to-locate participants on the same day of contact or within 1 week, at a time most convenient for the participant • Give participant an interview card with the logo featuring: the name, address, and phone number of the study; a description of the incentive for completing an interview (if offered); time and place of next interview; and a reminder to call the office if any location information changes • Offer to help defray the costs that participants incur for getting to the interview (cab or bus fare, baby-sitting costs, etc.) • Send participants cards on their birthdays and any other appropriate occasions
Relatives/correspondents	• If you cannot locate the actual participant, call or write to relatives or correspondents • If the relative does not know the person's whereabouts, ask him or her if you can call again in a week or so, because people tend to resume contact eventually. Also send the collateral an interview card to forward to the participant if they see him or her • Contact other participants who were in treatment, jail, and so forth, at the same time as the participant (see McCoy & Nurco, 1991; Nurco, Robins, & O'Donnel, 1977, for a method to do this and still maintain confidentiality)

TABLE 10.1 Continued

Public records	• Telephone—check phone directory, call directory assistance, use criss-cross directory for participant and collaterals
	• Mail—contact post-office for change of address information for participants and collaterals, use U.S. Postal Service forwarding and record updates, certified mail, registered mail, stamped return envelope
	• Government records—check police and prison records, check parole and probation information—check names and addresses of visitors to jails or prisons. Contact marriage license bureaus; city, county, and state tax rolls; drivers' license bureaus; the Social Security Administration; the state welfare office; the FBI; population statistics. Contact State Departments of Public Health or Vital Statistics to inquire if the participant is deceased
	• Contact agencies: Alumni offices, local utility companies, high school records, professional organizations, treatment centers, credit agencies, psychiatric institutions, Veterans Administration hospital
Neighborhood environment	• Contact next-door neighbors when the participant has moved
	• Go to participant's home and workplace
	• Talk to landlord and neighbors and walk around the neighborhood and ask anyone "hanging out"
	• Go to corner restaurants, convenience stores
Preventing refusals	
	• Have same interviewer track participant over time to build rapport, or switch interviewers to see if participant likes the new one better
	• Provide immediate reinforcement for attending appointments
	• Provide snacks and beverages during interviews or treat participant if conducting interview at a restaurant or coffee shop
	• If participant has a history of missing interviews, send appointment reminder card or remind by telephone; mention incentives
	• Be nonjudgmental and open

TABLE 10.1 Continued

Potential dropouts	• Stress that all information will be held strictly confidential • Discuss incentives, if any, for participation • Remind the participant of the importance of the study and his or her participation • Have study director personally call or visit participant • Ask if you can call the participant back after a few days so he or she can think about the decision to drop out of the study • Do not coerce participant
Relatives, correspondents, and professionals	• From the beginning, have the participant inform contacts that researchers may contact them • Describe, mail, or show in-person the "Release of information" form that the participant has signed mentioning that person's name

Note: Not all of the information featured in this table typically needs to be collected, nor do all of the tracking procedures need to be attempted for all populations. The purpose of this list is to be as comprehensive as possible. The information in this table is from "Minimizing participant attrition in panel studies through the use of effective retention and tracking strategies: Review and recommendations," by K. M. Ribisl, M. A. Walton, C. T. Mowbray, D. A. Luke, W. S. Davidson, and B. J. Bootsmiller, 1996, *Evaluation and Program Planning, 19,* pp. 1–25. Copyright 1996 by Elsevier. Adapted with permission.

With this intensive protocol, the researchers located about 95% of the women over 2 years. Phoning or going to the house of the woman more than once and phoning alternative contact persons accounted for 70–85% of successful contacts. The remaining strategies were necessary to get the overall success rate to 95%. If the project had relied solely on techniques that did not require them to leave the office, they would have lost 40% of their sample in the first 10 weeks after treatment—doubly crucial because this 40% of difficult-to-locate women had different characteristics than other women, and so would otherwise increase attrition bias greatly.

Preventing Treatment Attrition Versus Measurement Attrition

Measurement attrition (the topic of this section of the chapter) refers to a failure to complete outcome measurement, whether or not treatment is completed. **Treatment attrition** (part of the previous section on treatment implementation) refers to those research participants who do not continue in treatment, whether or not they continue taking the measurement protocol. In studies using archival sources to measure outcomes such as arrest records, hospital mortality, or student grades, it is possible to obtain outcomes on everyone assigned to treatment, even those who did not complete treatment—such studies contain treatment attrition but no measurement attrition. Conversely, in brief studies that use captive participants (literally or figuratively), such as prisoners or elementary school students, it is possible to administer the treatment completely to every participant. But equipment failures, illness, objections to burdensome measurement, or careless responding may all lead to failure to obtain outcome measures—such studies contain measurement attrition but no treatment attrition.

The distinction is practically important for several reasons. First, measurement attrition prevents the inclusion of the participant in the analysis (except via missing data imputation methods), but treatment attrition does not preclude inclusion as long as the participant completed the measures. Second, many dropouts can be convinced to complete the measurement protocol even when they refuse to complete treatment. Third, if measurement attrition can be eliminated, the researcher can do a classic intent-to-treat analysis and, if a good implementation measure is available, can sometimes use the Angrist et al. (1996a) implementation analysis. So a good rule to follow is this: Prevent measurement attrition even when you cannot prevent treatment attrition.

Minimizing Time and Obstacles Between Randomization and Treatment

Attrition is lower when the time and obstacles between random assignment and treatment implementation are minimized. Bloom (1990), for example, reported results from three randomized experiments of programs in three different Texas cities to help employ displaced workers. In one site with participation rates of 87%, the intake process was quick, with little time and few obstacles between random assignment and receipt of treatment; in another site with more obstacles and time between those two steps, participation rates were only 60%. This leads naturally to the suggestion that assignment to treatment be delayed until the last possible moment.

For example, in a study to which one of us (Shadish) consulted, the aim was to examine the effects of different medications in preventing weight gain among participants who had just quit smoking. The study recruited smokers and asked all of them to quit over a 4-week period, during which they received identical quit-smoking interventions. The medication was administered in the 4th week, with both smoking cessation and medication continuing for several months. Originally, assignment was to occur at the start of Week 1, prior to smoking cessation. But a little thought shows that this may be too soon. The treatments to which participants were randomized were the different medications, not the program to help them quit smoking. The latter merely provided a pool of newly quit smokers on which to test the medications. In the final design, then, random assignment occurred at the start of Week 4 instead. Doing so minimized the attrition of participants who decided they did not want to be in the study and of participants who could not quit smoking and thus could not be used in testing the main hypothesis. A very similar strategy uses a "running-in" procedure in which all participants are given one of the treatments, usually a standard treatment or one perceived as less desirable, for a period of time prior to randomization (Coyle, Boruch, & Turner, 1991). Many of those who would drop out of the study would have done so before the end of this run-in period. Those who remain are then randomized either to continue in the condition they began or to the innovative or more desirable treatment.

These methods to minimize attrition also increase selectivity of participants into the experiment, which may reduce generalizability. In the smoking cessation example, the causal inference about the effects of medication in reducing postcessation weight gain is more likely to generalize to smokers who were able to quit for more than 4 weeks and who were willing to be randomly assigned to different medications or a placebo. This excludes a substantial portion of the smoking population. However, given that the same experiment without a run-in period would still contain attrition, external validity would still be restricted by participant attrition. If the characteristics of preassignment dropouts and perhaps their reasons for dropping out are measured, valuable information about generalizability can be obtained, for example, about the kind of person who judges the treatment unacceptable. Methods outlined in Chapter 9 for getting better estimates of both treatment effects and generalizability can also be applied to this problem (Braver & Smith, 1996; Ellenberg, 1994; Marcus, 1997a).

Minimizing Treatment-Correlated Attrition

Differential attrition is more important than total attrition as a threat to internal validity. Differential attrition may be present even when equal percentages of treatment and comparison participants drop out, if they drop out for different reasons or have characteristics that relate to outcome. For example, in the New Jersey Negative Income Tax Experiment (Reicken et al., 1974), control group losses may have resulted from low economic motivation to cooperate, whereas the experimental losses may have resulted from unwillingness to accept charity. If so, equivalent attrition rates (7.9 versus 8.6) may mask differential selection factors that could produce group differences on outcome.[2]

Differential attrition occurs for many reasons. Differential vigilance by the research team during follow-up can keep more experimentals remaining in the study than controls. Similarly, no matter how late in the sequence randomization is deferred, some attrition may occur when treatments differ in desirability. For example, in the smoking and weight gain study described earlier, the medications were

---

2. Sometimes the dropout rate over conditions is an outcome of interest in its own right. In such a case, attrition rates are zero and can be analyzed with no attrition threat to internal validity.

administered to some participants through a chewing gum and to others using a skin patch. A disproportionate number of participants perceived the patch as more convenient and less unsightly and so refused their assignment to the chewing gum and dropped out of the study entirely. In studies using aggregate units such as schools, differential attrition can occur but can be harder to detect. For example, families may decide to remain in experimental school districts so that their children can receive an attractive treatment, but control families may leave more often; yet this might not be detected just by counting the number of schools in conditions (Reicken et al., 1974). When randomly assigning organized social units such as schools, it is particularly important to assign from among volunteers who agree to receive any treatment. This is because one is often dealing with so few units that the loss of any of them after randomization has serious consequences for the integrity of the design. Although this procedure does not guarantee that all units will accept the assignment—using this procedure, Cook, Hunt, and Murphy (2000) had one of 24 schools pull out after it learned it was a control—it reduces the problem considerably. But one must be willing to pay the price in terms of external validity.

One way to reduce treatment-correlated dropout is to use an informed-consent procedure in which the participant agrees to accept assignment to any experimental condition. However, this solution also reduces generalizability to similarly compliant ex-smokers; and it will not prevent the problem entirely because many participants will give consent in hopes of receiving the more desirable treatment, only to balk when they are assigned to the less desirable treatment. Here an option is a two-stage informed-consent procedure similar to that described by Reicken et al. (1974) in their commentary on the New Jersey Negative Income Tax Experiment. The first informed consent requests the participant's cooperation with measurement. Assignment to conditions is made from those who consent. The second informed consent requests agreement to the experimental treatments from those participants assigned to a treatment (but not necessarily from those assigned to the control condition unless an ethical constraint required it). Those who refused this consent are continued in the measurement protocol to which they already consented, reducing measurement attrition. However, those participants who agree to accept assignment to any condition are aware of all the treatment conditions by virtue of informed consent. So those who then receive less desirable treatments may envy recipients of the more desirable ones. This may lead to problems of compensatory rivalry or resentful demoralization. Sometimes this problem can be reduced by providing treatment-irrelevant incentives, such as more money or the chance to participate in a lottery for prizes, to those assigned to the less desirable condition.

Preventing Measurement Attrition

Reviews of the literature have suggested strategies for reducing measurement attrition depending on the kind of outcome measure used (Day, Dunt, & Day, 1995;

Lockhart, 1984; Yu & Cooper, 1983). They report that higher response rates occur with the use of personal or telephone (versus mail) surveys, the use of incentives to answer (either monetary or not, the more the better), providing prior notice of the questionnaire's arrival, using the foot-in-the-door method that gets the respondent to agree to a smaller task first and a larger one later, personalizing letters and other forms of contact, and using follow-up letters. Appealing to social values or flattering the respondents were not effective.

Some experiments take advantage of an established measurement framework that has been developed and maintained independently of the experiment, for example, court records or records of withholding tax. Even if a respondent drops out of the experiment, he or she can still be included in the measurement system. However, even with this approach some research participants will be missing from the record-keeping system, and the researcher is limited to using archival measures of unknown reliability and validity for answering the questions of interest.

A Flawed Approach—Replacing Dropouts

When participants drop out of an experiment, some researchers replace them with new participants who may even be randomly selected from the same pool of applicants as those originally assigned to conditions and who may also be randomly assigned to conditions (e.g., Snyder & Wills, 1989). Although this approach does keep the sample size at a specified level, which may be important for purposes of power, such replacement would only solve attrition as an internal validity threat if (1) both attrition and replacement are random, which is unlikely to be the case with attrition unless shown otherwise (and showing otherwise requires analyses that usually occur long after it would be feasible to add replacements), or (2) both former and replacement participants have the same latent characteristics, especially as pertains to outcome, which again is unlikely because we cannot know the latent characteristics of dropouts and so cannot match replacements to them. This problem is similar to the discussion in Chapter 4 of why matching does not substitute for random assignment (it only matches on observed but not latent characteristics), but in this case the selection bias is out of treatment rather than into it.

Analyses of Attrition

Ultimately, the goal of all analyses of attrition is to understand how much it threatens the validity of a conclusion about treatment effectiveness. There is no single best way to gain this understanding. So the researcher should usually do several analyses to shed light on the problem from different perspectives (see Table 10.2 for a summary). Unfortunately, reviews of the literature suggest that few studies undertake such analyses (Goodman & Blum, 1996).

TABLE 10.2 A Summary of Possible Attrition Analyses

Simple Descriptive Analyses

- Overall attrition rate
- Differential attrition rates for treatment and controls
- Whether those who completed the study differed from those who did not on important characteristics
- Whether those who completed the treatment group differed from those who did not on important characteristics and the same for the control group
- Whether those remaining in the treatment group differed from those remaining in the control on important characteristics

Identifying Different Patterns of Attrition

- Whether different groups have different patterns of attrition
- Whether different measures have different attrition patterns
- Whether certain subsets of respondents or sites have complete data that could be used to salvage some randomized comparisons

Accounting for Attrition When Estimating Effects

- Impute values for missing data
- Bracket the possible effects of attrition on effect estimates
- Compute effect estimates that are adjusted for attrition without using imputed data

Simple Descriptive Analyses

First, experimenters should provide simple descriptive data about attrition. A basic template for such analyses (Lazar & Darlington, 1982) reports (1) overall attrition rate, (2) differential attrition rates for treatment and controls, (3) whether those who completed the study differed from those who did not, (4) whether those who completed treatment differed from those who did not and the same for the control group, and (5) whether those remaining in treatment differed from those remaining in the control. For analyses (3) through (5), particularly important variables to analyze include reasons for dropping out, pretest scores on the measures that will subsequently be used as indicators of a treatment effect, and other pretest variables correlated with outcome. Pretests on the outcome measure provide the best available single estimates of the direction of bias for that outcome. After all, if the direction of the bias runs opposite to the empirical results of the study, attrition is much less of a threat to those results. For example, if those who scored best on the pretest dropped out differentially more often from treatment than from control, but posttest results suggest the treatment did better than the control despite this bias, it is less plausible to think that differential attrition is the cause of the observed effect. Moreover, the pretest difference of experimental and control units who remain frequently gives a helpful estimate of the magnitude of the pseudo-effect that would be expected at the posttest (Heinsman & Shadish, 1996;

Shadish & Ragsdale, 1996). This, in combination with the difficulty of maintaining randomly formed groups over time in complex field settings, is one reason why we recommend the use of pretests, even though they are not needed if randomization is successfully initiated and maintained without attrition.

Identifying Different Patterns of Attrition

A study may show several different patterns of attrition. Sometimes we define those patterns conceptually, as when we distinguish between those who could not be located, those who were located but would not complete the outcome variable, and those who died. Alternatively, we can search for patterns of missing data empirically. For example, BMDP's AM program explores data sets to try to discover missing data patterns[3]; and several stand-alone personal computer programs have extensive missing-data-analysis capabilities, including SOLAS (Statistical Solutions, 1998) and ESTIMATE (Marcantonio, 1998). Then the experimenter can explore whether different patterns of attrition have different predictors. MacKenzie, Funderburk, Allen, and Stefan (1987) found different predictors of attrition in alcohol treatment studies depending on how attrition was defined. Mennicke et al. (1988) found that early dropouts from counseling showed worse adjustment than later dropouts. Willett and Singer (1991) used survival analysis to differentially predict attrition that occurred at different times. Such definitional differences hold between studies, as well. Kazdin (1996) suggested that discrepancies among child psychotherapy researchers in their estimates of the rates and correlates of attrition was due partly to their use of different definitions of dropout.

Within the same study, different measures may have different attrition patterns. For instance, in the New Jersey Negative Income Tax Experiment (Reicken et al., 1974), Internal Revenue Service (IRS) records of labor force participation had a different attrition pattern than did personal interviews about labor force participation. Attrition from the IRS records occurred because some persons do not file tax returns and because employers may not file earnings data with the IRS in some cases. Some of this missing data might be found using periodic interviews. Attrition from the interviews was more strongly related to the financial value of the experimental treatment—more people refused to be interviewed in the less lucrative conditions. The latter point favors the IRS measures to the extent that any underrepresentation of persons in IRS records would probably affect experimentals and controls alike, which was not the case with interviews.

Sometimes treatment-correlated attrition is restricted to certain subgroups of respondents or sites. If examination of pretest data and attrition rates suggests that there are sites or subgroups where pretest comparability can reasonably be assumed, these deserve special attention in the data analysis. But although the search for randomly comparable subgroups or sites is worthwhile, it must be done

---

3. BMDP was purchased by SPSS in 1996 and is available through that company.

cautiously, because sample sizes will be reduced (making tests of comparability less powerful) and the possibility of capitalizing on chance will be increased if multiple tests are done without some correction for overall error rate. Nonetheless, careful disaggregation will sometimes help salvage some true experimental comparisons that have been compromised by attrition.

Accounting for Attrition When Estimating Effects

Here the goal is to estimate what the study would have shown had there been no attrition. Two general approaches are common: one that imputes values for the missing data points so that they can be included in the analyses and another that tries to estimate effects without imputing missing data.

Imputing Values for Missing Data.   Programs such as SOLAS (Statistical Solutions, 1998) and ESTIMATE (Marcantonio, 1998) are specifically designed to do most of the imputations we cover here, and many other programs have some capacity to impute data, too (e.g., EQS; Bentler & Wu, 1995). Imputation methods vary from simple to complex, with the simpler methods yielding the least satisfactory imputations. For example, the simplest but least satisfactory approach is to substitute the sample mean on a variable for the missing data point. The implicit assumption underlying mean substitution is that data are missing at random,[4] which is usually implausible.

At the other extreme are methods that use maximum likelihood algorithms to estimate missing data, the best of which is multiple imputation (Jennrich & Schlucter, 1986; Rubin, 1987; Little & Rubin, 1987; Little & Schenker, 1995). The latter uses multiple regression to predict missing data points from a set of measured predictors, does this several times, and then adds random error to each imputed data point. The average of these multiple imputations is then used. However, these methods make strong distributional assumptions, and they generally assume that the mechanisms generating missing data are either known or ignorable, that is, unrelated to the actual value of the missing data, which is unlikely to be true in many settings. For example, people who drop out of a drug abuse study often do so because they return to drug use, which *is* the outcome variable often missing and needing imputation.

---

4. Little and Rubin (1987) distinguish between data missing completely at random (MCAR) versus data missing at random (MAR). Data are MCAR if data are missing for reasons that are completely unrelated to any information in the available data—randomly discarded data, for example. Data are MAR if they are missing for reasons related to the value of another observed variable that has no missing data, but specifically not because of the value on the missing variable itself. Because missing data on the outcome variable is often of interest, this latter requirement implies that data cannot be MAR if, say, drug addicts dropped out of a drug treatment study because they started using drugs again when drug use is the outcome of interest. If missing data are MCAR or MAR, they are ignorable for likelihood-based inferences; and any other kind of missing data are nonignorable. Ignorability implies that unbiased estimates of treatment effectiveness can be obtained with proper analyses (Little & Rubin, 1987). Ignorability is probably rare in most data sets.

In between are a host of other imputation options that are occasionally good choices for particular situations, such as the last value forward method for longitudinal data sets, hot deck imputation, and single imputation (Little & Schenker, 1995; Little & Yau, 1996; Speer, 1994; Speer & Swindle, 1982; Statistical Solutions, 1998). Most of these methods work well only when good predictors of missing data are available. If not, two strategies may help. One strategy is to gather additional data on a random sample of dropouts. In principle, this would give good data on which to impute the values of all missing participants (Graham & Donaldson, 1993) and would yield much other valuable information pertaining to attrition. A key problem with this approach is whether small samples of missing participants would yield sufficiently small confidence intervals. If not, resources may be required to examine virtually all dropouts, which is prohibitive. However, preliminary work suggests that the samples might not have to be too large (Graham & Donaldson, 1993; Hansen & Hurwitz, 1996).

The other strategy is to try to bracket the effect within a range of plausible values. When using model-based predictions such as hot decking or multiple imputation, one can vary the imputation model to see how different assumptions about predictors change the imputed values and the treatment effect estimate (Little & Yau, 1996). When outcomes are dichotomous (success-failure, pass-fail, married-divorced, diseased–disease-free) or can reasonably be dichotomized for purposes of exploring the effects of missing data, an option is to explore the distribution of all possible outcomes that could have been observed under different assumptions about attrition (Delucchi, 1994; Shadish, Hu, Glaser, Kownacki, & Wong, 1998; Yeaton, Wortman, & Langberg, 1983). Shih and Quan (1997) present a similar method for bracketing the effects of attrition when outcome data are continuous; but their method depends on having covariates capable of equating treatment and control completers, something that cannot always be assumed.

Estimating Effects in Data Sets with Attrition.   Though no clear winner has emerged here, a number of approaches are being investigated to estimate effects in data sets with attrition, and researchers should consider trying several of them. Allison (1987) and Muthen, Kaplan, and Hollis (1987) use multigroup structural equation models to estimate effects in the presence of missing data. The idea is to identify a small number of groups with different missing data patterns (perhaps using the methods discussed previously) and then analyze the same model for all groups in a multigroup analysis to see whether parameter estimates are stable for all groups despite the missing data. However, if sample size per group is small, results may not be stable; and if the number of groups is too large, the technique may be too computationally intensive. If the data are missing at random, the approach yields accurate inferences about parameters. Even when this condition is not met, as will generally be the case, the technique yields useful information about whether groups with different missing data patterns yield the same parameter estimates. Several structural equation modeling programs have examples of how to implement this approach (e.g., Arbuckle, 1997; Bentler, 1995).

In longitudinal designs with large numbers of repeated measures, several analytic techniques can be tried without imputing missing data. Kraemer and Thiemann (1989; see also S. Maxwell, 1998) propose estimating the slope (rather than a change score or an endpoint score) as the outcome in a design having many repeated measures, though the power of this method may be poor (Delucchi & Bostrom, 1999). The slope can be estimated from as few as two time points, so some missing data can be tolerated and the slope can still be estimated accurately. Similarly, growth curve analysis techniques do not require observations at all time points on all research participants or even that the observations be taken at fixed time points (e.g., Bryk & Raudenbush, 1992; Rogosa, 1988). However, in both these techniques nonrandom missing data points can bias results.

Economists have proposed methods to estimate treatment effects in the face of attrition that model the dropout process itself (Leaf, DiGiuseppe, Mass, & Alington, 1993; Welch, Frank, & Costello, 1983). Doing this well requires the researcher to think about and measure why people drop out of conditions. However, these models make strong assumptions about normal distributions and about finding variables that affect attrition but not outcome. When these assumptions are not met, these models may produce substantially worse estimates than no correction at all (Hartman, 1991; Stolzenberg & Relles, 1990). Some economists have proposed semi-parametric methods making fewer assumptions (e.g., Scharfstein, Rotnitzky, & Robins, 1999), though questions still arise about bias in these methods (Little & Rubin, 1999). Little (1995) presents a method for repeated measures designs that combines these econometric models with missing data imputation.

As with imputation, it is often good practice to conduct a variety of analyses under different assumptions about the nature of attrition, finishing up with a range of estimates of effect (e.g., Scharfstein et al., 1999). In some situations, all of the estimates will be in essential agreement and final inference will be easy. But in others, the estimates will bracket a range of contradictory outcomes and will thus serve as a warning that attrition artifacts may be masquerading as treatment effects.

Economists have also suggested some relatively simple diagnostic tests to examine whether attrition may be a problem in a study. Verbeek and Nijman (1992) suggest comparing fixed and random effects estimates of model parameters and comparing results on respondents with complete data to those for the sample as a whole (including dropouts). In both comparisons, the resulting estimates should not differ significantly if attrition is not biasing results. They also suggest certain variations to the correction factor used in the econometric models that should also be nonsignificant if attrition is not a problem. Foster and Bickman (1996) illustrate the use of these methods using data from a large quasi-experiment. If these tests indicate that attrition is a problem, the researcher may still be left with a puzzle as to what the correct effect size estimate really is.

It should be clear from this discussion that a wide array of options now exists for constructively analyzing experiments with missing data. When both total and differential attrition are low (e.g., less than 10%) *and* the effect size is high, these analyses will rarely change the qualitative conclusion about whether treatment works compared with analyses that do not take attrition into account. Under most other circumstances, however, it is possible for the qualitative conclusion to change completely (e.g., Shadish et al., 1998), in which case careful attention to the results of multiple attrition analyses is required to understand the implications of attrition.

DISCUSSION

The material that we have covered to this point in the book is in some sense just an extension of the tradition of field experimentation begun by Campbell (1957) and reflected in Campbell and Stanley (1963) and Cook and Campbell (1979). As with those prior works, the primary focus has been on how to use experimental design to improve internal validity, though we have often tried to show how these design choices can also affect all the other validity types at the same time. In the next three chapters of the book, however, we move considerably beyond this traditional focus by providing a conceptual analysis and practical methods for improving construct and external validity. We do so in a way that remains consistent with the history of Campbell's ideas and preferences, especially in focusing on how randomized and quasi-experimental designs can still be used to support such generalizations.

11

Generalized Causal Inference: A Grounded Theory

Gen·er·al·ize (jĕn´ər-ə-līz´): v. **gen·er·al·ized, gen·er·al·iz·ing, gen·er·al·iz·es.** v.
tr.   1. a. To reduce to a general form, class, or law. b. To render indefi-
nite or unspecific.   2. a. To infer from many particulars. b. To draw inferences or a general conclusion from.   3. a. To make generally or universally applicable. b. To popularize.

Ground·ed (ground´ĕd): v. tr.   1. To place on or cause to touch the ground.
2. To provide a basis for (a theory, for example); justify.   3. To supply
with basic information; instruct in fundamentals.

T HE STRENGTH of the randomized experiment is its capacity to facilitate the
causal inference that a change in A caused a change in the probability that B
would occur. However, one of the oldest criticisms of the randomized experiment is that it is so locally defined that this clear causal inference comes at the cost
of one's ability to generalize the causal connection found. Fisher (1935) himself
criticized the randomized experiment on this point, and it is evident in the Campbell and Stanley (1963) claim that internal and external validity can be negatively
related. Campbell's (1986) relabeling of internal validity as local molar causal validity highlights the same point—the embeddedness of experimental results in a
particular local context seems to provide little basis for generalizing results beyond that context.

As we saw in Chapters 1 and 3, generalizing a causal inference involves generalizing about four entities—treatments, outcomes, units (usually persons), and
settings. We also saw that we can make two different kinds of generalizations
about each of these four entities: (1) generalizations about the constructs associated with the particular persons, settings, treatments, and outcomes used in the
study (construct validity) and (2) generalizations about the extent to which the
causal relationship holds over variation in persons, settings, treatment, and measurement variables (external validity). This chapter presents a grounded theory of

generalized causal inference that shows how scientists address both these issues. The two chapters that follow present methods for implementing that theory in single studies and multiple studies, respectively.

However, to write about generalized causal inference is very difficult, more difficult than writing about internal validity. The latter is built upon centuries of thinking about causation and on nearly a century of experimental practice. Although there is a comparable history of concern with generalization to human populations, mostly through random sampling in statistics, and with generalization to entities, mostly through construct validity in psychometrics, we lack a systematic history of concern with generalized causal inference. Of course, all sciences are concerned with such inferences. But most of this knowledge about generalization is the product of multiple attempts at replication, of reflection on why successful or failed generalization might have occurred, and of empirical tests of which reasons are true. This procedure is very useful in fields in which experiments can be conducted quickly, one after the other, and in which traditions of replication are well-established. But this is not the case in most of the social sciences. Social scientists therefore need theory about how to plan research in order to increase the yield for construct and external validity. Such theory is not available, but there are practices in various disciplines that are used to improve the quality of claims about general causal inference. We describe a sample of these practices in this chapter and then describe a set of principles to justify generalized causal inferences that are consistent with these practices. The resulting theory is not as simple, as internally consistent, and as consonant with history as has been achieved for internal validity. Nonetheless, we hope this analysis begins a process of thinking even more systematically about such claims and sets an agenda for future methodological work on generalized causal inference.

Before we describe this grounded theory, we must first consider the solution that is most commonly proposed for problems of generalization—formal sampling methods such as random sampling. Though this method is indeed a powerful solution, it is rarely practical for the problem of generalized causal inference.

THE RECEIVED VIEW OF GENERALIZED CAUSAL INFERENCE: FORMAL SAMPLING

Formal probability sampling procedures are a common solution to generalization problems in a wide range of practical (nonexperimental) applications, especially in survey research and in quality control in industry. The crucial element in sampling theory involves selecting units by chance with known probability from a clearly designated population of units, where the population is simply the larger set of units from which the study units were sampled (Frankel, 1983). Such sampling yields a match between the sample and population distributions on all (measured and unmeasured) attributes within known limits of sampling error. For example, the mean and variance of the sample will be the same on expectation as in the population.

The universe is generally designated in one of two ways. The first method is to obtain a full enumeration of the members of the population, such as a list of all hospitals in a city. It helps if this enumeration also includes details on unit characteristics that might be related to the outcome of interest, such as whether the hospital is public or private. When such conditions are met, formal sampling strategies can facilitate generalization from sample to population. The best known case is *simple random sampling*, in which each unit in the population has an equal chance of being selected into the sample and is chosen using a chance process, such as a table of random numbers. If one were interested in estimating the failure rate of all 20,000 students on the initial enrollment roster of a school system of a large city (the population) but one could afford to study only 1,000 of those students in detail (the sample), one might select that 1,000 at random. Failure rates calculated on this sample will be unbiased estimates of the rates in the entire population of students within known probabilities. Sometimes research calls for more complicated sampling schemes (Cochran, 1977). For example, suppose failure rates are thought to be different in public than in private schools, and one wants separate estimates for each of these two groups. Under *stratified random sampling*, one would first divide the schools into those two strata and then randomly sample students separately from each stratum using the procedures outlined for simple random sampling.

When full enumerations are not possible, the researcher can still sometimes be certain that all members of the population are identified by knowing the boundaries within which the population lies. Suppose that one wanted to estimate how many residents of a given city have had a cholecystectomy (a gall bladder operation) but that there exists no list of city residents who have had such an operation. We could use a census map to number and identify city blocks, randomly select blocks, randomly select households on each block, and then randomly select people within each household. Such a *cluster sample* procedure would yield an unbiased estimate of cholecystectomy prevalence in the city among domiciled citizens, although the estimate usually will have wider confidence intervals than is the case with simple random sampling. Although sampling all citizens to find the subset that has had a gall-bladder operation is less efficient than having a list of all such patients at the start, such a cluster sample is still guaranteed to represent the population quite well. Many other formal sampling techniques are available for more specialized needs (e.g., Cochran, 1977; Hansen, Hurwitz, & Madow, 1993; Rossi et al., 1983; S. Thompson, 1992).

Without doubt, formal sampling procedures would facilitate generalized causal inference if they could be applied to experiments. Indeed, some statisticians write as though they were confident that generalization depends on random sampling (Draper, 1995). For instance, Lavori, Louis, Bailar, and Polansky (1986) suggest that experimenters should follow a two-step process: first randomly sample a subset of patients from the total population of patients, and then randomly as-sign the sampled patients to experimental or control conditions. They write:

> So far we have dealt with methods for ensuring that the analysis of a parallel-treatment study correctly assesses the relative effects of treatment on patients enrolled in that study. The investigator must also consider whether the results can properly be extended to patients outside the study; we refer to this issue as generalizability. . . . Un-less there is random sampling from a well-defined population (not to be confused with random allocation of treatment), the question of generalizability may not be com-pletely resolvable. Nevertheless a brief discussion of selection criteria and a concise de-scription of the clinically relevant facts about the patients chosen for study can go a long way toward meeting this objective. (pp. 62–63)

We will elaborate this last disclaimer later, for it suggests that researchers need not throw in the towel if random selection is not possible. Note also that Lavori et al. (1986) mention only one study feature across which causal connections are to be generalized—persons. We need also to ask about the relevance of the formal sampling ideal for generalizations about treatments, outcomes, and settings.

Kish (1987) also advocates the statistician's traditional two-step ideal: the random selection of units for enhancing generalization and the random assign-ment of those units to different treatments for promoting causal inference. But Kish frankly acknowledges that the random sampling part of this ideal is rarely feasible; and he explicitly chooses not to deal with how manipulations and meas-ures might be selected so as to represent cause-and-effect constructs, even though such constructs are as indispensable to generalized causal inference as statements about populations of units. Kish's book suggests that the statistical theory he prefers cannot constitute a comprehensive practical framework for generalized causal inference, though it may sometimes promote generalizing to populations of persons and settings. The theoretical and practical reasons for being so pessimistic about the two-step ideal need clear explication. To elaborate these concerns, we start with sampling causes and effects because they most dramatically illustrate both the practical and theoretical difficulties involved.

Formal Sampling of Causes and Effects

Sampling theory requires a clearly designated population from which one can sample. A prototype is sampling individuals from a national or state population in order to conduct a survey. In experiments, however, one needs to sample not just people but also settings, treatments, and observations. Sampling treatments and observations is more difficult than sampling people or settings. A key prob-lem is the difficulty in locating comprehensive lists of the population of treatments or outcomes from which to sample. Regarding treatments, for example, full enu-meration is occasionally possible, as when a computer generates every two-digit addition or subtraction possibility to create the universe of all two-digit arithmetic problems. But this is an atypical case, of interest primarily in basic laboratory rather than in field research. The latter researchers rarely generate long lists of treatments from which they then select one for study. More typically, they select treatments by crafting one or a few manipulations to meet some treatment specification of theoretical or practical interest rather than by selecting from a list.

Still, field researchers sometimes produce lists of possible manipulations (Steiner & Gingrich, 2000) or outcomes (e.g., B. Bloom, 1956; Ciarlo, Brown, Edwards, Kiresuk, & Newman, 1986). But random selection rarely occurs from such lists, for good practical reasons. Given a choice, most researchers would prefer to add new *theory*-based treatments or outcomes or even to improve other features of the design entirely by, say, increasing the number of units in each cell. Indeed, in experiments it is mostly impractical to implement even two random variants of the same causal construct. How can a second treatment variant be justified when one is already available? And anyway, sampling theory requires many more such variants if confident generalization is to result. This large sample requirement makes it unrealistic to expect to see many random variants of the same treatment within a single experiment.

To increase the number of measures of an effect *is* often feasible, especially when paper and pencil tests are used. Yet researchers prefer to select those measures to reflect either theory or pertinent stakeholder interests, and we know of no instances of random measurement selection. Further, including too many measures and items can increase participant response burden to a point that encourages poor responding or even attrition and can trade off sampling breadth with measurement reliability and validity. Field research usually involves outcome measures that are shorter than they are when the same construct is measured in personality or aptitude testing. Field experimenters are usually under pressure to measure simultaneously many different outcome (and moderator and mediator) constructs while restricting the total time spent testing. So measuring just a few constructs with a high degree of validity is often (but not always) a lower priority than assessing many constructs with a few items for any one of them.

Further complicating the random sampling of outcomes, social and psychological constructs often have many components. The construct of depression, for example, seems to consist of negative attitudes, performance difficulty, and physiological symptoms (Tanaka & Huba, 1984). Each component requires many items to be assessed well, and it is better if those measures are not limited to self-reports. So even if a population of pertinent items existed from which to sample at random to assess any one component, doing this is only practical when an experiment involves few constructs with few components. This is a situation field experimenters rarely face, and so item selection tends to drift toward rational selection based on human judgments about the degree to which particular components are prototypical of a construct and then about the degree to which specific items are prototypical of those components. Early in his career Cronbach called for random item selection (Cronbach, Rajaratnam, & Gleser, 1967), but he later argued that how items are selected is less important than ensuring (Cronbach, Gleser, Nanda, & Rajaratnam, 1972) and justifying (Cronbach, 1989) that a construct description has captured all the construct components of theoretical relevance.

Formal Sampling of Persons and Settings

In theory, it is easier to use formal sampling techniques to generalize to specific populations of persons and settings. Sometimes, lists of the relevant populations exist. This is most obviously the case for lists of persons but sometimes is also true for settings. For example, the *National Directory of Mental Health* (Neal-Schuman Publishers, 1980) contained a list of all community mental health centers in the United States as of that date. Moreover, new community mental health centers were rarely being built at that time, and centers that were under construction could probably have been identified through the federal offices that helped provide construction funds. Hence a list could be constructed that contained all the mental health centers in the United States. Even when such lists do not exist, the population can sometimes be circumscribed because one knows the boundaries within which they must be located. This makes it possible to use the cluster sampling techniques described earlier. For example, because these centers must be located in the 50 states, a list might exist of the state directors of mental health services, who could be contacted to help create the list of mental health centers.

However, practical constraints still limit the experimenter's ability to sample settings or people formally. Not all the persons or settings selected for a cause-probing study will consider participating; and after they read the informed consent, still more will decline. As the study progresses, those assigned to less desirable conditions may drop out; and because most cause-probing field research is also of long duration, some will die, move, or become bored by the demands of treatment or measurement. When added to initial refusal rates, these dropouts will reduce the correspondence between the intended and achieved populations. They do not render random selection meaningless or even inferior to its alternatives. But they do attenuate its advantages.

Even for the most practical use of random sampling—sampling people—examples of individuals being randomly selected to participate in a randomized experiment are rare. When they do occur, the population is often only trivially larger than the sample that would have been studied anyway (e.g., Mallams, Godley, Hall, & Meyers, 1982; Wagoner, 1992). But some examples do exist that were sampled from very large populations. For example, Perng (1985) describes an experimental test of six different methods for collecting delinquent taxes based on randomly sampling from all delinquent accounts at a centralized Internal Revenue Service collection center before randomly assigning these accounts to one of six tax-collection methods. Puma et al. (1990) randomly assigned individuals either to or not to participate in the Food Stamp Employment and Training program after generating a nationally representative sample through a multistage procedure in which they first randomly sampled food stamp agencies and then chose a random sample of participants within each agency. The Health Insurance Experiment (Newhouse, 1993) randomly sampled the nonelderly population at six sites using screening interviews and then randomly assigned them to experimental conditions. Wallace, Cutler, and Haines (1988) randomly sampled patients with drinking problems from hundreds of thousands of patients in 47 physician practices, and they then randomly assigned those patients to treatment or control.

When possible, selecting units at random prior to assigning at random is the best way to explore generalizability to populations of units (see also Page, 1958; Vinokur, Price, & Caplan, 1991; Wolchik et al., 1993). However, such studies usually encounter real problems getting randomly sampled units to comply with random assignment. In the Wallace et al. (1988) example, only 61% of patients who were randomly selected would agree to go to treatment. Replacing those who refuse random assignment, even with other randomly sampled units, does not solve the representativeness problem because those who refuse participation are usually systematically different from those who comply. Researchers cope with this problem in various ways if they still want to pursue the goal of both randomly sampling and randomly assigning. For example, those who refuse random assignment are sometimes retained in a quasi-experimental version of the same study, thereby providing some information about causation pertinent to the entire population and about how refusers differ from compliers (Marcus, 1997a). When units are nested within aggregates, as with Wallace et al. (1988), willingness on the part of the aggregate (physician practices) to participate in the randomized experiment can sometimes be increased by decreasing the number of people who are randomly assigned and increasing the number of aggregates sampled. This has the added benefit that, in such nested designs, using large numbers of aggregates improves power faster than using large numbers of people within a smaller number of aggregates (D. Murray, 1998).

Sampling different settings at random is somewhat more problematic than sampling individuals, given the financial costs of mounting an intervention at more than a few sites. Many interventions are expensive and are studied precisely because their efficacy is not yet established, let alone their effectiveness. It rarely makes sense to fund a study with many randomly selected sites in order to test something whose efficacy under controlled conditions with well-implemented treatments at just one site is not clear. Hence, few studies of ameliorative treatments have involved randomly chosen samples of persons and settings that were then randomly assigned to different treatments. Even in these few cases, random selection was usually from within some entity that was known to be smaller than the population of real interest—for instance, from within a small number of physician practices or within the hospitals in a particular city rather than across all practices or all the hospitals in the nation.

Summary

To summarize, formal sampling methods are of limited utility for generalized causal inference because: (1) the model is rarely relevant to making generalizations about treatments and effects; and, as for persons and settings, the formal model assumes (2) that sampling occurs from a meaningful population, though ethical, political, and logistical constraints often limit random selection to less meaningful populations; (3) that random selection and its goals do not conflict with random assignment and its goals, though probing the generality of a *causal* connection clearly supposes some reason to believe such a connection will be supported in the study at issue or has been supported in prior research; and (4) that budget realities rarely limit the selection of units to a small and geographically circumscribed population at a narrowly prescribed set of places and times. Moreover, (5) the formal model is relevant only to generalizing to populations specified in the original sampling plan and not to extrapolating to populations other than those so specified. Finally, (6) random sampling makes no clear contribution to construct validity, that is, to how we label the persons, settings, treatments, and outcomes that are in any given experiment, except in the trivial case in which the correct construct that characterizes the population is already known. Taken together, these factors indicate that the two-step model of random sampling followed by random assignment cannot be advocated as *the* model for generalized causal inference, despite the claims on its behalf by some statisticians (Kish, 1987; Lavori et al., 1986). Though we unambiguously advocate it when it is feasible, we obviously cannot rely on it as an all-purpose theory of generalized causal inference. So researchers must use other theories and tools to explore generalized causal inferences of this type. We turn to such theories and methods now.

A GROUNDED THEORY OF GENERALIZED CAUSAL INFERENCE

Scientists routinely make generalizations without using formal sampling theory, often without any formally articulated guiding theory at all. In this section, we attempt to make explicit the concepts and methods that are used in such work. By grounding our ideas in scientific practice, we hope to present a theory of generalized causal inference that is more practical than random sampling for daily scientific work. However, this theory is not new with this book. Rather, its roots can be found in a variety of works on generalization (Brunswik, 1956; Campbell, 1986; Cronbach, 1982; Cronbach & Meehl, 1955); and its initial conceptualization was formalized a decade ago (Cook, 1990, 1991) as a construct validity theory of causal generalization, that is, with its principles grounded in ideas that were already present in the construct validity literature. In the intervening years, however, we have come to realize that these principles are also present and used in a wider array of scientific efforts to generalize. So we call this a grounded theory not to imply that it was developed inductively by examining all those endeavors but rather to capture the idea that these principles are broadly consistent with practices that scientists have used to generalize across many areas over many decades.

Exemplars of How Scientists Make Generalizations

We begin by presenting brief exemplars of the generalizations that scientists make and the methods they use to make them (Matt et al., 2000, give more details). These examples help to bolster the credibility of the claim that generalizations without formal sampling are made all the time, and at the same time they point to some of the methods that scientists use in doing so. We *italicize* terms in this section that point to those key notions and practices that these scientists seem to use in making generalizations and that foreshadow the five principles of generalized causal inference we present at the end. We first give examples from basic research and then move to more applied examples, in the process illustrating both construct and external validity generalizations.

Category Membership

Perhaps the most common form of human generalization is placing instances into categories, such as saying that robins and eagles are both birds, that books and journal articles are both publications, or that photo albums, pets, and children all belong to the category of things to take out of a house that is on fire. Psychological theories of classification and category membership (Lakoff, 1985; Rosch, 1978; E. Smith & Medin, 1981) propose that decisions about category membership usually rely on some form of *assessing the similarities* between the characteristics of an instance (say, a penguin) and the *prototypical characteristics* of a category (say, birds). Birds are animals with feathers and wings. These prototypical features are crucial to *discriminate* birds from other animals that may seem similar but for which different labels are more accurate; insects and bats have wings but not feathers, for example, so they fall outside the *boundaries* of the category of birds. Other features are *irrelevant* to the category even though they may be correct descriptions; for example, birds range in size from tiny finches to large ostriches, but size does not *distinguish* them from bats and insects.

Measurement Theory

Researchers regularly use a small number of items to represent more general constructs that they think those items measure, and their selection of those items is rarely random. For example, researchers who may have gathered information only from self-reports on 21 items on the Beck Depression Inventory (Beck et al., 1961) commonly say that they have measured the general construct of depression. Measurement theorists have well-developed ideas and methods for making this generalization to constructs (Cook, 1990). Conceptually, for example, Cronbach and Meehl (1955) argued that such generalizations required an *explanatory theory* that covers (1) the *prototypical features of the construct* and its component parts, (2) how these parts relate to each other and to various instances that might represent them, (3) how the construct relates to other constructs and to instances that are *similar* and *dissimilar* to it, (4) which components of the related constructs are *essential* to these relationships and which are *irrelevant,* (5) how the construct might *respond differently* to different manipulations, and (6) what other processes or constructs are required to *mediate or moderate such relationships.* Following this line of thought, Campbell and Fiske (1959) proposed a method for assessing construct validity that they called the multitrait-multimethod matrix. The matrix included different measures of *similar* traits to assess *convergent validity* and measures of *different* traits to show *discriminant validity,* all assessed using *heterogeneous* methods to rule out the possibility that correlations are due to *irrelevant method variance.*

General Propositions in Cognitive Science

Cognitive science offers many examples of causal propositions of wide generalizability. For example, the "Magic Number Seven" finding, that people remember best in chunks of about 7 categories, is the product of a program of research that found *similar results* over *heterogeneous instances*—that respondents could only remember about seven numbers or words when these were randomly ordered and presented in a sequence, that to remember more than seven they created about seven more superordinate categories in which to place the words, and so forth. These findings were similar over many laboratories with otherwise *irrelevant characteristics* such as location, quality of the university, and exact methods used. A second example is risk aversion, that individuals tend to avoid potential losses. The basic finding comes from laboratory demonstrations that again varied in *irrelevant characteristics:* a wide variety of subjects in many countries who are confronted with many different choice dilemmas that are *similar in certain prototypical ways:* although the material gains from one choice are absolutely equivalent to the gains from the other, in one case the potential gains are more salient and in the other, the potential losses are.

Animal Models of Human Psychopathology

In the neurochemistry of major psychiatric disorders, animal researchers have developed theories about how generalization from animal models to human application is warranted (Willner, 1991). First, the drug must show *similar* chemical markers in both animals and humans. For instance, in an animal model for anxiety, known anti-anxiety agents produce a particular chemical marker in both animals and humans. If a new anti-anxiety drug fails to produce that marker in the animal, generalization to humans is called into question. Second, there must be *phenomenological similarities* between the model and the condition and no major dissimilarities. For example, many animal models of depression use decreased locomotor activity as the indicator that the animal is depressed, because this behavior seems similar to psychomotor retardation and loss of motivation in depressed humans. Third, we must be able to *explain the mechanism* by which a drug affects both animals and humans, even if it produces different symptoms in different animal species. For example, when stimulants are given, rats rear on their hind legs more often, but primates tend to scratch themselves more. Yet the same physiological mechanisms cause these two apparently disparate behaviors.[1]

Toxic Chemicals

The U.S. Environmental Protection Agency (EPA) sets limits for human exposure to toxic chemicals by relying on data from animal research. The EPA takes animal data about the highest dose of a chemical that still produces no toxic effect in an animal species and *extrapolates* to humans, using a formula that adjusts for (1) the weight of a human adult, child, or infant, (2) interspecies differences in surface areas, (3) a large safety margin to account for interindividual differences in human responsiveness to chemicals, (4) an adjustment for how long outcomes on the animals were observed, and (5) a safety margin for effects on infant development.

Secondhand Smoke and Lung Cancer

Researchers have debated whether the causal connection between secondhand smoke and lung cancer in adult nonsmokers observed in epidemiological studies would generalize to settings such as workplaces and restaurants in which public policy might ban smoking. Gross (1993) grants the overall connection in these studies, though he says it is comparatively weak. But he *distinguished among* three kinds of studies. In the first kind, nonsmoking spouses married to smokers contracted cancer more often than when both partners did not smoke. The second kind also suggested that secondhand smoke caused cancer, but it consisted of studies conducted outside the United States, where living conditions at home, ventilation systems, and smoking patterns differ considerably from those in the United States. The third kind was a subset of studies conducted in the United States on workplace exposure, and they report no statistically significant association. Gross

---

1. One well-known animal researcher made a well-taken point about the role that pragmatism plays in the selection of animal models. When asked why vision researchers use cats instead of macaques to study vision, he answered that cats are cheap to buy and maintain and that their eyes are something like human eyes, even though the vision system of macaques would be even more proximally similar to humans than are cats. Practicality drives the choice of species that researchers generate to extrapolate to humans, especially considering publishing and funding pressures. To use the words of Herb Simon (1976), scientists are satisficing in their choice of models more than optimizing.

argued that these studies were *most similar* to the public policy debate at issue and so did not support policies against smoking in U.S. public settings. Rockette (1993) responded that generalization should be based on a broader set of evidence than just the epidemiological literature, including knowledge of biological *mechanisms*, supporting evidence from animal models, and existence of a *dose-response relationship* across these three kinds of settings that might be obscured in these epidemiological studies in which dose was not measured.

Safe and Effective Drugs

The U.S. Food and Drug Administration (FDA) warrants that new drugs are safe and effective in humans, making generalizations about the dosage of the drug, its long- and short-term outcomes whether intended or not, and the populations and settings in which it can be used. To do this, FDA relies on interrelated investigations that proceed in stages. The first stage is preclinical research to evaluate a drug's toxic and pharmacological effects using in vitro and in vivo laboratory animal testing, including clarifying some key biological *mechanisms* such as absorption rates and metabolic processes. The second stage involves seeing if the pharmacological activity and safety observed in animals is *similar* to that observed when the drug is applied to a few humans. Then, a series of clinical trials, gradually increasing in sample size and methodological rigor, are done in humans to examine biological *mechanisms* in humans, *dose-response relationships*, and effects in both the *short- and long-term*. At first, the particular patient diagnosis is mostly assumed to be *irrelevant*, but subsequent trials examine whether particular diseases or conditions *make a difference to outcome*.

Generalizing from Cancer Studies to Individual Patient Decision Making

Medical research has yielded extensive knowledge about the treatments that are more or less effective in the treatment of cancer. Individual patients who have cancer are certainly interested in average effects over many patients; but they are even more interested in knowing if the treatment will work for them, with their particular disease characteristics. Consider the case of a man who is diagnosed with prostate cancer and has the recommended surgery. It helps him to know that, in general, over 80% of men who have that surgery will survive at least 15 years without developing metastases. However, he can get more specific information by looking at the outcomes of men whose characteristics are most *similar* to his. Suppose his Gleason score (a measure of cancer aggressiveness) is very high at 9 (out of 10) and his preoperative PSA (a measure of prostate cell products in the blood that is correlated with cancer) was low at less than 4.0. With that more specific information, he can find out that this kind of man is cured over as long as 15 years if his PSA remains low postoperatively but dies in an average of 5 to 8 years if his PSA rises within 2 years of surgery (Pound et al., 1999).

Psychotherapy Effects

Smith and Glass (1977) statistically summarized the results of about 300 psychotherapy outcome experiments. Results suggested that psychotherapy clients had better outcomes than did clients in control groups, and few studies produced negative effects. For the most part, differences in kinds of patients, therapist characteristics, treatment variations, settings, and times proved *irrelevant*. That is, the effects of therapy were quite generalizable over all these variations. However, other scientists subsequently criticized this meta-analysis for failing to make the right *discriminations* and so failing to find relevant *moderators of effects*. One such discrimination is between research therapy and clinic therapy. Most parties agree that the former is effective and is what is studied in most meta-analyses, but in research therapy there are procedural differences, such as using graduate students as therapists and treatment standardization manuals, that are unrepresentative of clinical practice. Clinic therapy uses experienced therapists and does not constrain what the therapist can do in therapy, and its effectiveness has been questioned in at least some meta-analysis of child psychotherapy (Weisz et al., 1992).

Five Principles of Generalized Causal Inferences

A review of the italicized ideas in these exemplars suggests that some occur and recur many times (e.g., similarity) and others point to a single underlying process (e.g., discriminate, distinguish, boundaries). We believe that they illustrate five simple principles that scientists use in making generalizations:

1. *Principle 1: Surface Similarity.* Scientists generalize by judging the apparent similarities between the things that they studied and the targets of generalization—for example, locomotor retardation in animals looks like psychomotor retardation in depressed humans, studies of the effects of secondhand smoke in the workplace seems more similar to the public settings at issue in policy debates than do studies of smoking in private residences, and animals with wings seem more similar to our prototypical understanding of birds than do animals without wings.
2. *Principle 2: Ruling Out Irrelevancies.* Scientists generalize by identifying those attributes of persons, settings, treatments, and outcome measures that are irrelevant because they do not change a generalization—for example, that size is irrelevant to membership in the category of bird, that length of follow-up is irrelevant to the effect of psychotherapy, or that the location of a cognitive science research lab is irrelevant to the finding that people tend to use groups of seven to remember things.
3. *Principle 3: Making Discriminations.* Scientists generalize by making discriminations that limit generalization—for example, that child psychotherapy works in the lab but might not work in the clinic, that a claim to have a new measure of a trait involves discriminating that trait from other ones, or that any animal

with both feathers and wings falls within the boundaries of the category of birds, but all other animals fall outside that category.

4. *Principle 4: Interpolation and Extrapolation.* Scientists generalize by interpolating to unsampled values within the range of the sampled persons, settings, treatments, and outcomes and, much more difficult, by extrapolating beyond the sampled range—for example, that the effects of cytotoxic chemotherapies for cancer increase as the dose increases until the point at which they would cause the patient to die or that effects of toxic chemicals on small mammals will generalize to much larger and more biologically complex humans.

5. *Principle 5: Causal Explanation.* Scientists generalize by developing and testing explanatory theories about the target of generalization—for example, that the construct called "effects of stimulants" includes both scratching in primates and rearing in rats because the biological mechanisms underlying both these behaviors are the same.

None of the five principles is, by itself, necessary or sufficient for generalized causal inference. However, our knowledge of generalized causal inference is not complete unless we can provide the knowledge required by all five principles. Further, although the principles are not independent, they are worth presenting separately because each calls our attention to a different practical strategy for clarifying generalized causal inference. We will elaborate the ideas behind these principles in more detail in this chapter and the methods that can be used to implement them in the next two chapters.

The Use of Purposive Sampling Strategies

Another lesson is apparent in the preceding exemplars. None of them used formal sampling techniques to make generalized causal inferences; rather, they mostly use **purposive sampling** strategies. In the case of secondhand smoke, for example, the epidemiological studies did not randomly sample the sites at which smoking was occurring but rather *used a heterogeneous array* of sites at which secondhand smoke occurred, such as homes or workplaces. Animal researchers who modeled psychiatric disorders did not randomly select outcomes but rather selected decreased locomotor activity as *typical* of the kinds of outcomes of interest in humans with major depressive episodes. Meta-analysts examine the effects of psychotherapy over *heterogeneous* characteristics of persons, settings, treatment variations, and outcomes.

This observation about the prevalence of purposive sampling strategies in how scientists talk about generalization was reported previously by Kruskal and Mosteller (1979a, 1979b, 1979c). They analyzed how the phrase *representative sampling* is used in both scientific and non-scientific literatures and found it used nine different ways: (1) in general acclaim of data, (2) for absence of selective forces, (3) as a miniature of the population, (4) as a typical or ideal case, (5) as coverage of the population, (6) as a vague term to be made precise later with a longer description, (7) as a more specific and formal sampling method, (8) as a method that permits good estimation, and (9) as a method that is good enough for a particular purpose. They set aside (1), (2), and (8) as typically being either unwarranted or unjustified without formal sampling, (6) as being superfluous to the longer description, and (9) as being rarely applicable (e.g., finding one negative side effect in a pertinent sample of treated cases is often sufficient to reject the claim that no negative side effects occur); and (7) refers to formal sampling methods that are not at issue here. The remainder of these uses, (3), (4), and (5), describe samples that are representative in a purposive sense. Moreover, they map well onto the two purposive sampling methods that Cook and Campbell (1979) had simultaneously suggested and that we mentioned in Chapter 1—deliberately heterogeneous sampling, (3) and (5), and modal instance sampling, (4).

Cook and Campbell's method of modal instance sampling aimed to explicate the kind of units, treatments, outcomes, and settings to which one most wants to generalize and then to select at least one instance that is similar to the class mode. Kruskal and Mosteller's typical or ideal case sampling is similar to this, though it is a bit broader in allowing *typical* to be defined not just by the mode but by the mean, median, or ideal case, as well. We are entirely sympathetic to using the mean or median to represent typical cases. As a practical matter, however, the mode has three advantages over the mean and median: (1) sampling to approximate the mode is more widely applicable (e.g., to categorical variables) than is sampling to approximate the mean or median; (2) the mode will equal the mean and the median in normally distributed continuous data; and (3) when such data are not normally distributed, the mode may often be more informative about central tendencies (e.g., in bimodal distributions) and is less susceptible to the presence of outliers. So we will usually prefer the mode in most cases. As to ideal instance sampling,[2] we think this refers more to a substantive consideration about whether one is interested in ideal instances, a consideration that is orthogonal to which measure of central tendency is used to represent that ideal (e.g., by sampling the modal ideal instance).

Cook and Campbell's (1979) method of deliberate sampling for heterogeneity aimed to include a set of instances chosen deliberately to reflect diversity on presumptively important dimensions, even though the sample is not formally random. Kruskal and Mosteller's (1979a, 1979b, 1979c) usage (3)—miniature of the population—does this by knowing the key characteristics of the population and then ensuring (without the use of formal sampling) that some members with each level of each characteristic are in the sample. Their usage (5)—coverage of the

---

2. In the Weberian notion of an ideal type that predominates in sociology (Burger, in press), ideal types are always multi-attribute and need not describe the world as is. Rather, they are an ideal about the world constructed by overlooking the probabilistic nature of links between attributes in the real world. In an ideal type, related attributes are presented as inevitably related to each other and through this mechanism an ideal is constructed.

population—simply requires heterogeneity on some rather than all key characteristics and so requires less knowledge about all those characteristics. But in both cases, the key methodological implication is to deliberately sample for heterogeneity on as many key population characteristics as are known and practical.

To reflect Kruskal and Mosteller's points on these matters, henceforth in this book we will refer to Cook and Campbell's modal instance sampling as **purposive sampling of typical instances** (PSI-Typ). And in parallel, we will also refer to Cook and Campbell's deliberate sampling for heterogeneity as **purposive sampling of heterogeneous instances** (PSI-Het). Replacing *deliberate* with *purposive* in these labels is consistent with statistical usage of the term *purposive sampling* (Marriott, 1990) as a nonrandom sampling method intended to represent a population.

Like Kruskal and Mosteller (1979a, 1979b, 1979c), however, we remind the reader that these purposive sampling methods are not backed by a statistical logic that justifies formal generalizations, even though they are more practical than formal probability sampling. Still, they are by far the most widely used sampling methods for generalized causal inference problems, so we provide more details about them in the next two chapters, in which we describe practical methods that are used in single studies and multiple studies to address these problems.

Applying the Five Principles to Construct and External Validity

Generalized causal inference involves two tasks: (1) identifying construct labels for persons, settings, treatments, and outcomes (construct validity) and (2) exploring the extent to which a causal relationship generalizes over variations in persons, settings, treatments, and outcomes (external validity). In this section, we show how the five principles are used in science to clarify both these tasks. Table 11.1 summarizes the main points in this section.

Principle 1: Surface Similarity

Construct Validity and Surface Similarity.   From measurement theory, the somewhat outdated notion of face validity captures part of the meaning of surface similarity used here. Face validity referred to a simple judgment about the construct that an assessment "appears superficially to measure" (Anastasi, 1968, p. 104). As much as face validity has fallen out of favor in modern test theory (e.g., Messick, 1995), it is extremely widely used to cope with the scores of construct decisions that scientists have to make about how to label multiple outcomes (sometimes dozens), several treatments and occasionally several settings, subcategories of persons studied, and the large number of other constructs used in relating the experiment to the larger scientific literature. We should not be surprised that scientists make most of these decisions rather casually, probably relying as much on surface

TABLE 11.1 Five Principles of Generalized Causal Inference Applied to Construct and External Validity: A Summary of Concepts and Methods

---

Surface Similarity: Assessing the apparent similarities between study operations and the prototypical characteristics of the target of generalization.

Applications to Construct Validity

1. Face Validity: What constructs do the study operations appear to reflect?
2. Content Validity: What are the prototypical characteristics of the target persons, settings, treatments, and outcomes that study operations are thought to reflect? Do different language communities have different understandings of those prototypical characteristics? Which parts of those characteristics are represented in study operations?

Applications to External Validity

1. What are the prototypical characteristics of those variants of persons, settings, treatments, or outcomes to which generalization of the causal relationships is sought?
2. Campbell's Principle of Proximal Similarity: The judgment that causal relationships that have been demonstrated with one kind of person, setting, treatment, or outcome will generalize to persons, settings, treatments, or outcomes that appear to be similar on important prototypical characteristics.

Ruling Out Irrelevancies: Identifying those attributes of persons, settings, treatments, and outcome measures that are irrelevant because they do not change a generalization.

Applications to Construct Validity

1. Construct Irrelevancies: Features that are present in study operations but are irrelevant to the prototypical characteristics of the construct.
2. Convergent Validity: Two different assessments of the same study operations should correlate with each other despite any irrelevancies associated with each assessment.
3. Multiple Operationalism: The operations used to index a construct are relevant to the construct of interest, but across the set of operations, there is heterogeneity in conceptually irrelevant features.
4. Heterogeneity of Irrelevancies: Make irrelevancies heterogeneous so inferences about the construct are not confounded with the same irrelevancy or with different irrelevancies whose direction of bias is presumptively in the same direction.

Applications to External Validity

1. What variations in persons, treatments, settings, and outcomes are irrelevant to the size or direction of a cause and effect relationship?
2. Fisher's (1935) insight: Causal results that are demonstrably robust across many irrelevancies constitute failed attempts to disconfirm the hypothesis of a generalized causal relationship.

Making Discriminations: Identifying those features of persons, settings, treatments, or outcomes that limit generalization.

Applications to Construct Validity

1. Campbell and Fiske's (1959) argument: When a construct is proposed, the proponent invariably has in mind distinctions between the new dimension and other constructs already in use. One cannot define without implying distinctions, and the verification of these distinctions is an important part of the validation process.
2. Discriminant Validity: The construct validity of an assessment is questioned if it correlates too highly with other assessments purporting to measure different constructs.
3. We can interpret and label the operations used in a study more accurately if we can discriminate between different constructs that usually have overlapping content.

TABLE 11.1 Continued.

Applications to External Validity
1. The aim is to discriminate between the two versions of a causally implicated construct when one version would substantially change the magnitude or direction of the causal relationship.

Interpolation and Extrapolation: Generalizing by interpolating to unsampled values within the range of the sampled persons, settings, treatments, and outcomes and by extrapolating beyond the sampled range.
Applications to Construct Validity
1. When a label applies to both the lowest and highest observed value, it usually applies to levels in between.
2. Does the nature of the construct change in important ways at different points along a continuum?
3. Confounding Constructs with Levels of Constructs: An error of extrapolation that occurs when inferences about the constructs best representing study operations fail to describe the limited levels of the construct that were actually studied.
4. Ceiling and Floor Effects: Scale compressions at the low or high end hide distinctions of kind among persons, settings, treatments, or outcomes.
Applications to External Validity
1. Interpolation uses the results observed at various points on a continuum to infer the results that would have occurred between any two of those points.
2. Extrapolation uses the results observed at various points on a continuum to infer the results that would have occurred below the lowest observed point or above the highest observed point on that continuum.
3. These strategies work best when more levels are observed, when the functional form is well identified over those observations, and when the extrapolation is to levels close to those originally sampled.

Causal Explanation: Developing and testing explanatory theories about the target of generalization.
Applications to Construct Validity
1. Deep or Structural Similarity: Similarities in underlying structural relations in different operational instances that give rise to a common concept that characterizes all the instances. Deep similarities do not always give rise to the same surface similarities.
2. Construct network: A theory that relates a construct to similar and dissimilar constructs and that predicts how that construct might respond to various manipulations.
Applications to External Validity
1. The Transfer Argument: To specify (a) which parts of the treatment (b) affect which parts of the outcome (c) through which causal mediating processes in order to accurately describe the components that need to be transferred to other situations to reproduce the effect.

similarity as on any other principle. That is, they choose plausible-sounding labels that appear to be reasonable, as when they describe the research as taking place in a large urban university or the participants as being undergraduate introductory psychology students. Presumably, the more peripheral the construct to the key issues in the study, the more likely surface similarity is used, with the scientist accepting the label on faith because it is impossible in any one study to exercise skepticism about the vast majority of them. Nonetheless, as anyone knows who has reviewed manuscripts for publication, many of both the implicit and explicit labeling decisions in such manuscripts are questionable and become grounds for negative reviews.

The best applications of this principle move beyond face validity to a more thoughtful matching of the surface characteristics of an operation to those that are prototypical of a construct. This is what test theorists mean when they say that content relevance and representativeness are important to the construct validity of a test, especially "that all important parts of the construct domain are covered" (Messick, 1995, p. 745). The same criteria of content relevance and representativeness should apply to characterizations of the persons, settings, and treatments in an experiment, as well. Suppose a researcher wants to do an experiment using participants to be described as "unemployed." Most people take the concept of unemployment to refer to adults of working age who do not hold jobs currently and who have no alternative career that temporarily removes them from the job market (e.g., homemaker or graduate student). However, in official policy circles, unemployment has ancillary meanings—a person is not considered to be unemployed unless he or she is actively looking for work and has been without paid work for less than 6 months. Otherwise, he or she is put into the category of a "discouraged" (rather than "unemployed") worker. But active search and being out of work for less than 6 months are peripheral to lay understandings of unemployment, and they serve to shade the official understanding toward favoring those who are out of work but eminently employable and eliminating those who are more hard-core unemployable. Which version of "unemployed" is the study going to use? Similarly, the study might look at participant income as an outcome. How is income to be measured, and will that measure be relevant and representative? For example, is last year's reported income on IRS Form 1040 well-described with the label "income"? To answer this, one must know how much underreporting of income occurs among tax filers and how much income is earned by those who do not file any return at all. We see in these examples the iterative interplay between construct explication and assessment, making decisions about each to increase their match.

External Validity and Surface Similarity. The exemplars of generalization that we cited at the start of this chapter included a number of illustrations of how scientists use surface similarity for external validity questions. These included researchers who generalize from decreased locomotor activity in animals to psychomotor retardation and loss of motivation in humans, researchers who claim that epidemiological studies of secondhand smoking in public places are more similar to the public settings in which secondhand smoke would be banned in proposed policies than are studies done in private homes, and a prostate cancer patient who looks at the outcome of that subset of all patients in a cancer treatment study who had a similar Gleason score and postoperative PSA level to determine his predicted time to metastasis under that treatment. All these cases involve a prediction that findings that hold for one kind of person, setting, treatment, or outcome will generalize to persons, settings, treatments, or outcomes that appear to be similar on important prototypical characteristics.

Campbell (1966b, 1986) called this the principle of proximal similarity, saying that we generalize an experimental effect "with most confidence where treatment, setting, population, desired outcome, and year are closest in some overall way to the original program treatment" (1986, pp. 75–76). Consider the preceding example of whether last year's reported income on IRS Form 1040 is well-described with the label "income." In the case of external validity, we might ask how well results on this particular income measure generalize to another outcome measure, say, employment tenure. Surface similarity instructs us to examine how similar reported income on IRS Form 1040 is to the prototypical characteristics of employment tenure. The answer is probably not very similar, for income does not reflect such things as weeks or years spent on the job that are prototypical of employment tenure. In light of this, surface similarity gives us little grounds for generalizing to job tenure based on a study of income. Of course, income is not unrelated to tenure; and it probably plays an important role in the individual's decision to stay with a job, along with such other factors as fringe benefits or working conditions. Some generalization to this new outcome construct might not be surprising, but proximal similarity offers little insight into how much generalization is likely to occur.

We can see from this example that matching operations by surface similarity to prototypical elements of the construct is a judgmental process that is weaker but more feasible than formal sampling. It emphasizes rational matching on those components that theoretical analysis suggests are central to the construct description, always remembering that what is central can vary depending on the purpose of the research. The similarity so achieved is superficial because the operations and constructs match on certain manifest characteristics and not necessarily on any more latent components that may be central in bringing about the effect. And that similarity judgement is hampered by the fact that not everyone will agree about which components are prototypical. By itself, then, surface similarity rarely makes a persuasive case for external validity, despite its wide use.

Sometimes, however, surface similarity is entirely sufficient, even for generalizations to instances that have never been studied before. For example, sometimes the need for action is sufficiently great that scientists and practitioners are willing to act as if the research will generalize to their as yet unstudied application despite considerable ambiguity. For instance, in the 1990s scientists discovered a treatment for cancer called metronomic dosing that appeared to work very well in animals by using low doses of long-term chemotherapy supplemented by angiogenesis inhibitors. This treatment had never been studied in humans, but several physicians were willing to try it in their patients because it worked in animals, because the drugs were not experimental and were commonly approved for clinical practice, because the doses of chemotherapy were so low that it seemed almost certain that side effects would be fewer and smaller than in the standard high-dose chemotherapy regime, and because the patients asking for the treatment had extremely advanced cancers that had failed to respond to other available treatments. Surface similarity is probably also used by policymakers when deciding whether to legislate a new program to as yet unstudied people or settings, by practitioners who experiment informally with new ways of providing services, by scientists who write narrative reviews of the literature, and perhaps most important, by scientists as they generate new studies based on their predictions about what will work in applications they have not yet studied.

Principle 2: Ruling Out Irrelevancies

Construct Validity and Ruling Out Irrelevancies. Scientists demonstrate generalization when they show that a source of variability is irrelevant to a generalization, for example, that physical size is largely irrelevant to membership in the category of birds. Measurement theorists call this *construct irrelevancies*, things that are present in the instance but are presumed to be irrelevant to the prototypical characteristics of the construct itself. In Campbell and Fiske's (1959) multitrait-multimethod matrix, for instance, the method by which a trait is assessed is assumed to be irrelevant to valid measurement of the trait construct, so that two measures of the same trait construct should correlate highly even if assessed by different methods. For instance, the Beck Depression Inventory (Beck et al., 1961) is a self-report measure, but the fact that it is self-report is presumed to be irrelevant to the construct of depression. The presumption is that the same level of depression will be observed whether self-report, spousal report, or any other method is used. This idea is called **convergent validity** in measurement, that two different measures of the same thing should correlate with each other no matter what the many unique irrelevancies associated with each of them.

More generally, when we select particular people, treatments, outcomes, and settings to be in our experiment, we nearly always introduce some surplus attributes that are not part of the construct description. The omnipresence of such conceptual irrelevancies has spurred the call for multiple rather than single operationalism (Webb et al., 1966). **Multiple operationalism** requires that all the operations used to index a construct are relevant to the construct of interest but that, across the set of operations, there will be heterogeneity in conceptually irrelevant features. Imagine a study of the effects of "moving to the suburbs" on earnings for poor families. The request to be part of that study can come from a city official, a local community leader, the representative of a research firm, or any other person—all attributes that are irrelevant to "moving to the suburbs." Likewise, earnings might be measured by self-report or by tax records, each of which is imperfect in different ways. Such irrelevancies are also germane to populations of persons and settings, as when we draw a sample of individuals who turn out to be all volunteers; or when we select settings that look like the type of setting to which generalization is sought but turn out to be all settings with younger managers more open to research (and other innovations?) than older managers. The age of managers is presumed to be an irrelevancy, as is the volunteer status of individuals. But each is confounded with the target construct in the sampling particulars achieved. The task is to somehow unconfound the irrelevancies from the descriptively necessary attributes of the constructs under examination. Campbell coined the term **heterogeneity of irrelevancies** to capture the problem (how to deal with irrelevancies that often have to be part of the sampling particulars but not the target constructs) and to capture the solution (make those irrelevancies heterogeneous so inferences about the construct are not confounded with the same irrelevancy or with different irrelevancies whose direction of bias is presumptively in the same direction). For example, some individuals are invited to join the study by researchers and others by city officials or local political figures; earnings can be assessed in several ways; one can find persons to be in the study who are not volunteers; and one can examine different kinds of suburbs into which people move who leave the inner city.

Brunswik (1956) is also associated with the notion of heterogeneity of irrelevancies applied to the construct validity of presumed causes. Brunswick worked mostly in human perception and assumed perception to be context-dependent. But he realized that this context, although sometimes necessary to perception, is also sometimes irrelevant to the construct under particular study. To illustrate this, he used the homely example of studying facial characteristics. Imagine studying whether persons who squint are judged to be more sly than people who do not squint. Because squints exist only on faces, Brunswik maintained that they cannot and should not be abstracted from faces. He would not favor studies in which respondents rate squints on otherwise fully masked faces. Given this position, decisions have to be made about which facial attributes to build into the research. Should there be details about eyes (their color or size), noses (their size or shape), facial contours (round or oval), chin forms (square, pointed, rounded), or other features? The size of pores, the length of eyelashes, and the number of wrinkles could also be incorporated into the facial stimulus materials. But in any one study we typically cannot make heterogeneous all these facial attributes. Hence fallible judgments based on theory or personal experience have to be made to decide on which attributes are more prototypical and so deserve to be deliberately varied. Brunswik recommends sampling combinations of facial attributes that meet two criteria: they co-occur with some regularity in the world, and they are maximally different from each other.

External Validity and Ruling Out Irrelevancies. When this principle is applied to external validity problems, the issue is to identify variations in persons, treatments, settings, and outcomes that are irrelevant to the size or direction of a cause and effect relationship, for then the causal relationship can be said to generalize over those features. For example, in selecting unemployed persons to participate in a job training experiment, we might assume that it is irrelevant to the construct of unemployment whether those persons are introverted or extraverted or how many brothers and sisters their parents had. Of course, what researchers consider conceptually peripheral or irrelevant is sometimes shown to be in error when subsequent research reveals that the variable in question conditions a causal relationship. This is why it is desirable to study the unemployed of different ages and with many different educational backgrounds—thereby making these irrelevancies heterogeneous. Any causal conclusions that are then drawn are less likely to be limited to a subclass such as those unemployed persons who went to college or lived in a small town.

Fisher (1935) himself explicitly noted the advantage of including irrelevancies when probing cause-effect relationships:

> Any given conclusion . . . has a wider inductive base when inferred from an experiment in which the quantities of other ingredients have been varied, than it would have from any amount of experimentation, in which these had been kept strictly constant. . . . Standardization weakens rather than strengthens our ground for inferring a like result, when, as is invariably the case in practice, these conditions are somewhat varied. (p. 99)

His insight is presumably based on the supposition that causal results that are demonstrably robust across many irrelevancies constitute failed attempts to disconfirm the hypothesis of a *generalized* causal relationship. The presumption is that causal connections are worth provisionally treating as general if researchers have deliberately incorporated into their research many sources of irrelevant heterogeneity, especially those that theory or critics suggest are most likely to make a causal connection disappear.

This latter point highlights a logical conundrum. If the source of irrelevant heterogeneity makes the causal connection disappear (or weaken considerably or change directions), then it obviously is not irrelevant. For both construct validity and external validity, initial judgments are always about *presumed* irrelevancies. Data help decide what is and is not actually irrelevant. But investigators have to start by presuming that a relatively limited number of features are relevant and by leaving a much larger number of features provisionally judged to be irrelevant. The latter may be later found to be relevant, requiring a change in the meaning we attach to variables. We may assume that method of assessment is irrelevant to the construct of anxiety, but we slowly come to learn that this is not the case if the causal relationship depends on how anxiety is measured: by self-report, observer ratings, or physiological methods. The same is true for our assumptions about irrelevancies in assessing persons, settings, and treatments. The researcher's *aspiration* may be to show that a cause-effect finding is robust to irrelevancies. The eventual *achievement* may be otherwise and indicate a set of contingencies modifying the strength of a cause-effect relationship.

Principle 3: Making Discriminations

Construct Validity and Making Discriminations. In the exemplars given earlier in this chapter, scientists also clarified generalizations from operations to constructs by discriminating one construct from another—for example, that having feathers and wings is what distinguishes birds from other creatures. In measurement theory, this is partially captured by the idea of **discriminant validity** (Campbell & Fiske, 1959; Miller, Pedersen, & Pollock, 2000). This involves an analysis capable of discriminating a target construct from its alternatives or cognates: "When a construct is proposed, the proponent invariably has in mind distinctions between the new dimension and other constructs already in use. One cannot define without implying distinctions, and the verification of these distinctions is an important part of the validation process" (Campbell & Fiske, 1959, p. 84). If so, then the construct validity of a measure "can be invalidated because of too high correlations with other tests purporting to measure different things" (p. 84).

The major point is that we can interpret and label the operations used in a study more accurately if we can discriminate between different constructs that usually have overlapping content.[3] Thus, in research on inner city neighborhoods, one theory postulates that "collective efficacy" (high social control and high social consensus) should reduce crime because neighborhoods with such efficacy can mobilize against internal dangers (Sampson, Raudenbush, & Earls, 1997). But these particular neighborhood attributes are usually highly correlated with other characteristics of a "quality neighborhood," such as its resource levels, parent participation in neighborhood organizations, and adult or teenage satisfaction with the neighborhood (Cook, Shagle, & Degirmencioglu, 1997). All these other attributes could influence crime; they are conceptually related to what makes a good neighborhood; and they are all empirically related to each other in non-trivial ways. As a result, it is crucial to show that collective efficacy has an effect when the other conceptually related and empirically correlated neighborhood attributes are controlled for, as Sampson et al. (1997) did.

Similar construct validity issues arise for the persons, settings, and outcomes measured in a study. Regarding persons, differential diagnosis in medicine or mental health is a classic example of a discriminant validity challenge. I may claim to have studied persons with a diagnosis of schizophrenia, but you might challenge this by noting that the nursing home chart diagnoses I recorded are notoriously invalid indicators of diagnosis and that many of these patients would be given a diagnosis of Alzheimer's disease if better diagnostic assessments were done. Regarding settings, my claim to have studied mental health long-term care settings

---

3. Strictly speaking, these alternative constructs do not need to have overlapping content. However, it is the overlapping content that usually leads us to mistake one construct for another; we rarely make construct validity mistakes about highly dissimilar constructs.

might be challenged by the observation that I included only nursing homes, leaving out small, proprietary board-and-care homes in which substantial numbers of mental health clients live. Regarding outcomes, a critic might note that all my measures of patient psychiatric symptomatology were self-reports and that research suggests that such measures may assess the more general construct of demoralization rather than specific symptomatology (Dohrenwend, Shrout, Egri, & Mendelsohn, 1980).

External Validity and Making Discriminations. In some of the exemplars given earlier in this chapter, the scientists made discriminations that show the points at which a causal relationship is substantially reduced, goes to zero, or even changes direction—for example, that secondhand smoke research gave different results depending on whether the setting was a U.S. home, a U.S. workplace, or a setting outside the United States. We can easily think of other examples of persons, outcomes, times, and treatments. For example, we might find that quitting smoking causes much greater weight gain in females than in males. We might find that caffeine causes more arousal in the morning than in the evening for those scoring high on a test of impulsivity (Revelle, Humphreys, Simon, & Gilliland, 1980). Or we might find that the positive effects of psychotherapy are more pronounced for behavioral psychotherapies than for other forms of therapy. In all these cases, the challenge is to discriminate between the two versions of the causally-implicated construct, with the hypothesis being that one version would substantially change the magnitude or direction of the causal relationship.

These examples also suggest that discriminant validity challenges to both construct and external validity can take one of two forms. In one, an entirely different construct is proposed to replace the conceptualization I prefer. In the other, some *part* of the construct I prefer is involved in the effect, but other parts are not. In the latter case, probes of the challenge are aided by multiple operations of the construct that tap the different parts of the construct at issue, such as differentiating symptomatology from demoralization by including measures of both, and by assessing symptomatology using expert psychiatric ratings rather than just patient self-reports. It is particularly important not to let the same source of bias run through all operational instances. When all the outcome measures come from self-report data, this precludes studying the correlation between them and non–self-report measures. Constant bias is a major problem in construct validation, precluding the analysis required for empirically ruling out alternative interpretations.

In the vast majority of cases in which discriminant validity is challenged, as in the previous examples, the challenge is made from variables at the same level of reduction—that is, the level at which the constructs involved are both psychological constructs, both social constructs, or both biochemical constructs. This is done because constructs at one level are usually compatible with constructs at another level. The light switch example used in Chapter 1 to explain the difference between descriptive and explanatory causation provides a good example. The cause could be conceptualized at a mechanical level that the electrician might use (stringing wires into circuits, connecting light fixtures and switches), but it could simultaneously be explained at an atomic level that a physicist might use (the channeling of electrons, the excitation of photons). Here, the mechanical and atomic explanations are compatible—both may be true. But it is occasionally possible for a discriminant validity challenge to cross levels of reduction. The example of ulcers used several times in this book illustrates this possibility. For decades the cause of ulcers was thought to be stress, a psychological variable. The *H. pylori* bacterium that eventually proved to be the cause, however, was biological rather than psychological. This discriminant validity challenge did cross levels.

Principle 4: Interpolation-Extrapolation

External Validity and Interpolation-Extrapolation. This principle is used almost exclusively for external validity inferences, so we start with those inferences and then discuss the smaller role of this principle in construct validity. Several of the exemplars discussed earlier in this chapter illustrate these external validity inferences, including extrapolations from animals to humans that occur when EPA sets limits on exposure to toxic chemicals and identification of dose-response relationships in smoking research that predict the dosage level below which secondhand smoke may not cause cancer. Studying drug dosage effects is prototypical. Imagine examining the differential effects of 100 mg, 250 mg, and 500 mg of a pain reliever. Interpolation uses the pattern of obtained results to infer what might have been observed if 375 mg had been studied. Extrapolation infers what might have been observed below the sampled range at, say, 50 mg, or above the range at, say, 650 mg. Both interpolation and extrapolation work best when more levels are sampled, when the functional form is well-identified over the sampled range, and when the extrapolation is to levels close to those originally sampled.

Although these examples focus on inferences about different levels of treatment, the same argument applies to generalizations about different levels of outcomes, times, and setting and person characteristics. In many medical studies, for example, the primary dependent variable is a conveniently available dichotomous indicator of whether the patient lived or died. Yet between life and death lie a range of better or worse health states to which we often implicitly interpolate, viewing a treatment that produced 80% survival rates as indicating better overall patient health than one that produced 20% survival. Conversely, survival rates are often inferred from data gathered at follow-ups of no more than 5 years, with survival rates beyond that point being extrapolated. Similarly, in achievement testing for schoolchildren, we often extrapolate that achievement gains level off at an upper bound (e.g., a logistic test score model) rather than continue upward indefinitely, even though we often have very few observations at the upper bound on which to make the extrapolation. Regarding generalizations about times, very few psychotherapy studies include follow-ups of more than 1 year; thus it can be debated whether observed gains at 6 months or 1 year can be extrapolated to longer time spans (Jacobson, Schmaling & Holtzworth-Munroe, 1987; Nicholson & Berman, 1983; Snyder, Wills, & Grady-Fletcher, 1991). Finally, debates about dose-response curves in psychotherapy research reflect efforts to interpolate with more accuracy to the point in a small range of therapy sessions at which the benefits of therapy might level off (Kopta, Howard, Lowry, & Beutler, 1994).

Extrapolation and interpolation also apply to generalizations about person and setting characteristics that can be quantitatively ordered. In school-based research, schools can often be rank-ordered on a poverty index such as the percent of free lunches provided. But it is rare that investigators can afford to represent all possible percents, and so they must interpolate results to those that fall in between, or outside of, the range on the schools actually sampled. Regarding person characteristics, investigators often use exclusion criteria that eliminate from study any person who falls outside some range on the criterion. The NIMH Collaborative Depression experiment (Elkin et al., 1985; Elkin et al., 1989; Imber et al., 1990), for example, selected depressed patients falling in a narrow range of observed clinical depression, leaving ambiguity about whether results of that work could be extrapolated to more or less severely depressed patients.

Confidence in extrapolation depends on the gap between the end of the sampled distribution and the level of desired application. Short extrapolations seem easier to justify, presumably because qualitative transmutations are less likely—transmutations such as when water boils and turns to steam at one temperature and freezes at another, or when a metal cracks at one temperature or melts at another, or when sibling relations go from shouting to blows as personal stress escalates. Shorter extrapolations also entail a lower likelihood of exogenous variables affecting the causal relationship—as when only a very high body temperature brings in the doctor or only a bank's extreme financial woes bring in special federal auditors. Unless the relevant theory is good enough to specify such inflection points, there will inevitably be uncertainty about extrapolation, especially when an impressionistically large gap exists between the sampled treatment values and those to which generalization is sought.

Construct Validity and Interpolation-Extrapolation. Although the primary use of this principle is with external validity, some applications to construct validity exist. A mundane example is that we give different names to the chemical H_2O depending on its temperature: *ice* when it is below 0° Celsius, *steam* when it is above 100° Celsius, and *water* when it is in between those two temperatures. Most construct inferences involve interpolation because only a finite number of discrete levels of a variable are usually studied, but the construct label typically covers a wider range of possible levels. For example, suppose an experimenter studied five overweight people with body mass indices (BMI) of 25 to 29.9. Because BMI is a continuous variable, it is obvious that these five people cannot represent all possible values on the BMI scale. Yet we usually have no problem with the plausibility of the interpolation that someone who would have had a BMI of, say, 28.3 would still be called overweight even though a person with exactly that BMI was not in the sample. More generally, whenever we can construct a label that accurately represents both the lowest and highest value in the sample on some continuous variable, by interpolation that label usually covers all values in between, observed or not.

This is also often true of extrapolation, but extrapolation again entails greater risk for construct validity, just as it does for external validity. Indeed, one threat to construct validity discussed in Chapter 3 is confounding constructs with levels of constructs, a threat that occurs when inferences about the constructs best representing study operations fail to describe the limited levels of the construct that were actually studied. When this mistake is made, the researcher has extrapolated the construct too far beyond the range that was studied. For example, experts on weight and health say that a person with a BMI of 30 or above is obese rather than overweight, the distinction being important given its implications for comorbidity with other diseases. Ceiling and floor effects can also give rise to extrapolation problems in construct validity. Some group intelligence tests, for example, give compressed estimates at the high and low ends of the range of possible scores they can yield, so that people who have above average scores are lumped together with people who would have scores at a much higher level if an individually administered test were used. Calling all these people above average might then hide further useful distinctions among them, particularly at the high end.

Principle 5: Causal Explanation

Construct Validity and Causal Explanation. Sometimes a key underlying feature of a construct is known. Then it is possible to identify operational instances with the same feature that at first might even appear to be quite different from each other. As a simple example, consider a truck, a bus, a sedan, and a lawn mower, each of which belongs to the class of objects propelled by an internal combustion engine. This engine is at first out of sight and, if it were examined, would look quite different in size and complexity depending on the kind of vehicle. Yet in each case the same underlying process is involved in furthering propulsion. Here the similarity is not on the surface. It is beneath it, though there is still an abstract notion (of an internal combustion engine in this case), and there are still instances that can be related to this notion. Yet the instances one sees representing this category are quite different at first sensory inspection.

In contrast to surface similarity, then, causal explanation refers to what cognitive psychologists call *deep* or *structural* similarity (Vosniadou & Ortony, 1989). This term refers to similarities in the underlying structural relations in different operational instances that give rise to a common concept that characterizes all the instances. For example, once physicians learned that most ulcer cases were caused by a particular bacterium that responded to antibiotic treatment, even though some ulcers were caused by stress, they began to use construct labels that differentiated pathogenic from psychosomatic ulcers because their origins and their treatment are different. In this case, the surface similarity (pain and bleeding) is caused by an underlying deep similarity (the *H. Pylori* bacterium) that is common across many patients. However, deep similarities do not always give rise to the same surface similarities. Among the exemplars cited earlier in this chapter, a good example is the fact that when stimulants are given, rats rear on their hind legs more often, but primates tend to scratch themselves more; yet the same physiological mechanisms in reaction to stimulants cause these two apparently disparate behaviors. In Chapter 3, another good example was that laypersons attend to whether trees shed their leaves (deciduous or coniferous), but botanists attend to how they reproduce (angiosperms or gymnosperms). The latter is a deep similarity given its key role in species survival, but it is imperfectly correlated with the surface similarity of whether leaves are shed.

This use of causal explanation to advance construct validity has clear precedent in the traditional construct validity literature (e.g., Cronbach & Meehl, 1955; Messick, 1989). In that literature, test theorists emphasize that a construct, and any proposed measure(s) of that construct, should be embedded in a theory that relates it to other observations and constructs. The theory should include both similar and dissimilar constructs and also predictions about how constructs relate to each other and how they might respond to various manipulations. This same emphasis is reflected in modern test theory (e.g., Messick, 1995) in the call for measures of constructs to reflect "theoretical rationales for the observed consistencies in test responses, including process models of task performance (Embretson, 1983), along with empirical evidence that the theoretical processes are actually engaged by respondents in the assessment tasks" (Messick, 1995, p. 745), and also that "the theory of the construct domain should guide not only the selection or construction of relevant assessment tasks but also the rational development of construct-based scoring criteria and rubrics" (Messick, 1995, p. 746).

External Validity and Causal Explanation. Causal explanation is widely invoked as a means for transferring knowledge across variations in persons, settings, treatments, and outcomes. The key is to specify (1) which parts of the treatment (2) affect which parts of the outcome (3) through which causal mediating processes in order to accurately describe the components that need to be transferred to other situations if we are to reproduce the effect. For instance, knowledge of how electricity is generated allows us to provide such power to satellites in space where electricity may never have been available or studied before; and knowledge of the pharmacologically active ingredients of aspirin might allow inventive persons to create the drug's equivalent out of local plants that have never before been used to cure headaches. The presumption is that knowledge of the complete causal system (as with electricity) or of the total set of causally efficacious components (as with aspirin) makes it easier to reproduce a given causal connection in a wide variety of forms and settings, including previously unexamined ones (Bhaskar, 1975). This is why causal explanation is often considered a primary goal of science.

This sort of explanatory rationale has long undergirded basic theory development (Westmeyer, in press). For instance, in his review of major developments in social psychology over 50 years, Edward Jones (1985) said:

> Without some kind of bridging theory of interpersonal process, would-be experimenters were thwarted by what might be called the generalization question. How could an experimenter claim that his findings on thirty male college sophomores were in any important sense generalizable to a broader population of human beings or even to college males? Sociology essentially confronted the generalization question by abjuring the laboratory experiment and constructing or testing theories through survey methods in which sample representativeness was an important consideration. Psychologists, on the other hand, developed and refined experimental techniques that would test the plausibility of general process theories in restricted concrete contexts. In the late 1920s and 1930s this effort increased particularly in studies of animal behavior in which psychologists like Hull and Tolman attempted to theorize about general learning processes from data produced by rats in mazes. Thus there developed a broad context in U.S. psychology nurturing the importance of theory as a bridge between concrete experimental findings. As the experimental tradition developed in social psychology, researchers became more preoccupied with the conceptual generality of their findings than with the representativeness of their samples. Theories were useful to the extent that they predicted superficially different but conceptually similar relations in a variety of contexts. (p. 67)

Social psychology has many examples, such as Latané's work on bystander apathy (Brown, 1986; Latané & Darley, 1970) and Rosenthal's (1973a, 1973b) work on experimenter expectancy effects.

The explanation for an effect often includes features of the treatment that might not have been considered the "intended" treatment by the investigators. An example described in Chapter 1 concerned the effectiveness of endostatin in shrinking cancers by reducing their blood supply (Rowe, 1999). Although the effect occurred in the original investigator's lab, transferring the effect to other labs proved difficult until researchers discovered which aspects of the drug's manufacture, handling, and administration were crucial to its effectiveness. Some of those aspects are not usually considered part of the explanatory scientific theory as such theory is usually conceived and written. But they are essential for explaining how to produce the effect.

Unfortunately, such complete knowledge is rare in the social sciences. Explanatory questions such as, "Why does patient education promote recovery from surgery?" presuppose valid answers to the descriptive causal issue of whether such education does, in fact, promote recovery. Such descriptive causal connections are often far from certain. And each proposed explanation supposes that other explanatory models—with or without the same constructs—cannot be fit to the data equally well or better. We can rarely be confident that this is true (Glymour, Scheines, Spirtes, & Kelly, 1987). So we do not yet know why patient education is effective, despite about 150 studies on the topic (Devine, 1992). Nor do we know why Whites flee schools as more and more Blacks enter them. Although complete explanatory causal knowledge is useful for knowledge transfer, the key question is whether such knowledge can be gained often enough to be useful, given that *complete* causal knowledge is a rarity. We suspect that the answer is positive in much basic experimental research; but the answer is still pending in much social science, in which the incorporation of explanatory methods into experimental designs is still in its infancy. However, we want to see more attempts made to do just this, and we believe that some advantages follow from even the marginal gains in explanation that single studies typically achieve. We hope the concepts and methods that we outline in the next two chapters may encourage such work.

Should Experimenters Apply These Principles to All Studies?

Researchers typically initiate experiments to answer a circumscribed question prompted either by requests for proposals from government or private funding agencies, by the theoretical interests of the policy shaping or research communities, or by intriguing results from a prior study. In all these cases, large parts of the original research question are heavily constrained from the start. These constraints imply resource allocations to some possible design features over others, and these allocations cannot easily be changed without changing the question being studied. This is most salient when granting agencies convey budget expectations to potential applicants based on their experience of what it will take to answer a particular question. It would be unreasonable to expect applicants for such grants to endanger their chances of funding by changing either the question or the budget. Because few initial research questions deal specifically with generalizability, it is not surprising that few investigators who operate under such constraints opt to funnel resources into generalizability. Such constraints are also salient to researchers such as faculty members who are free to shape their own research questions, though their funding constraint is a lack of resources rather than inflexibility in moving resources.

Also, the principles themselves differ in how practical they are for application to single studies. The most practical are probably surface similarity and causal explanation. In its least expensive forms, the latter requires little more than conceptualizing possible mediators between cause and effect, measuring those mediators, and then using them in data analyses of mediation. Finding surface similarities is also feasible, requiring only an analysis of apparent similarities between the treatments, measures, persons, and settings used in a study and the targets of construct or external validity inferences. However, there are limits to its feasibility because the costs of some prototypical features (e.g., the measurement of long-term employment success in job training studies) may exceed reasonable bounds. The remaining three principles (making discriminations, ruling out irrelevancies, and interpolation-extrapolation) all call for the diversification of study features (e.g., more diverse kinds of participants, multisite studies, heterogeneous measurement methods, or several treatments that differ in dosage from existing treatments). These inevitably incur substantial practical costs, and the funds for them will only infrequently be available. Even so, such diversification is highly practical for *programs of research* on the same topic and even for large multisite studies.

Another feature that affects the applicability of the principles to the design of single experiments is the tradeoff between design features that facilitate generalizability and those that facilitate the local causal inferences that are the usual justification for experiments and that provide knowledge about the causal relationship whose generalization is at issue. Decisions that facilitate generalization will frequently come at the cost of decisions that facilitate other goals. For example, making irrelevancies heterogeneous may increase construct validity at the cost of decreasing statistical power. Both making discriminations and interpolation-extrapolation will often suggest adding additional features to a study so as to clarify external validity, but adding those features may take resources away from features that improve statistical conclusion or internal validity. Although such tradeoffs may well be warranted in some studies, it is difficult to forward rules for making them that would apply routinely. To paraphrase what we said in Chapter 3, existing knowledge lends strength to different kinds of inferences in experiments, so that any given experiment may need to repair knowledge weaknesses of different kinds. Sometimes, when that need is for knowledge about external or construct validity, the five principles will be of use.

But the principles do not apply just to planning studies. When applied to one or more completed studies, the five principles clarify which questions about generalization were or were not answered clearly. When just one study report is available, the options for using these principles to generate answers about construct and external validity may be quite limited. Sometimes reanalysis of the data set from that study will help resolve a question, as when critics ask whether the observed effects generalize separately to both males and females, given that the original authors did not report such a breakdown even though the data were available to do so. Sampling limitations will place significant restrictions on the extent to which a review of a single study will ever be able to answer all the interesting questions about generalization. However, when summary statistics from multiple studies are available, researchers can apply the five principles using the research synthesis techniques outlined in Chapter 13 that take advantage of the likely broader array of sampling options in multiple studies compared with a single one.

Prospective and Retrospective Uses of These Principles

The preceding discussion mixed prospective and retrospective uses of these five principles, but this distinction does have some implications. The prospective use of these principles and methods in individual experiments is more often (but not exclusively) in the service of construct validity, that is, to design experiments that support better inferences to intended constructs and to analyze and report results that more accurately characterize achieved constructs because of slippage between the intended constructs and what actually occurred in the study. Of course, scientists may also try to anticipate during the design of the study any external validity issues that might arise in the future by, for instance, gathering data about potential moderators of treatment effects to have on hand in case reviewers ask if the effect holds, say, for both males and females. But in general, external validity concerns are rarely a high priority in the prospective design of individual studies because designing more generalizable studies takes resources away from other priorities, because the number of questions about external validity is orders of magnitude larger than the number of questions that initially motivate the study, because the ability of scientists to anticipate such questions is understandably limited, and because most such questions arise only after the study has been reported.

The retrospective use of these principles and methods with single studies is almost always to criticize a study either for mischaracterizing the constructs that it achieved or for a lack of external validity regarding some variations of units, treatments, observations, settings, or times that were not reported in it. Because a study is designed only once but is retrospectively read and criticized much more often, these retrospective applications are almost by far the most common. But the distinction is not totally orthogonal, for it is sometimes possible to reanalyze the original data to respond to a criticism of study generalizability. For example, even if the study was not intentionally designed to examine generalizability of results over males and females, if data on gender were retained in the archived data set, then an analysis by gender can still be done in response to criticism. Indeed, if the practice of archiving data sets becomes more widespread in the 21st century and beyond, we hope that such reanalyses will be more common.

DISCUSSION

In this chapter, we have reviewed the most widely accepted approach to generalization, random sampling, and found that it is an inadequate solution to either of the two problems of generalization from experiments. We then pointed out the obvious: that scientists routinely make such generalizations in their daily work without using random sampling. They do so using five principles of generalized causal inference: surface similarity, ruling out irrelevancies, making discriminations, interpolation-extrapolation, and causal explanation. We then showed how these five principles help both construct validity generalizations and external validity generalizations. In the next two chapters, we present methods for implementing these ideas in single studies and multiple studies, respectively.

Generalized Causal Inference: Methods for Single Studies

Meth·od (mĕth′əd): [Middle English *medical procedure*, from Latin *metho-dus*, *method*, from Greek *methodos*, *pursuit*, *method*: meta-, *beyond*, *after*; see meta- + hodos, *way, journey*.] n.   1. A means or manner of procedure, especially a regular and systematic way of accomplishing something: *a simple method for making a pie crust; mediation as a method of solving disputes.*   2. Orderly arrangement of parts or steps to accomplish an end: *random efforts that lack method.*   3. The proce-dures and techniques characteristic of a particular discipline or field of knowledge: *This field course gives an overview of archaeological method.*

Sin·gle (sĭng′gəl): [Middle English *sengle*, from Old French from Latin *singu-lus*] adj.   1. Not accompanied by another or others; solitary.   2.a. Consisting of one part, aspect, or section: *a single thickness; a sin-gle serving.*   2.b. Having the same application for all; uniform: *a single moral code for all.*   2.c. Consisting of one in number: *She had but a single thought, which was to escape.*

THIS CHAPTER describes a variety of methods for exploring generalized causal inference in single studies, methods that do not rely on random sampling. They include purposive sampling, selected statistical techniques such as re-sponse surface modeling, and an array of qualitative and quantitative methods for studying causal explanations.

PURPOSIVE SAMPLING AND GENERALIZED CAUSAL INFERENCE

Here we describe in more detail the two purposive sampling options that we in-troduced in the last chapter—purposive sampling of typical instances (PSI-Typ), and purposive sampling of heterogeneous instances (PSI-Het). We also show how these methods are used with the first four principles of generalized causal inference (the fifth principle, causal explanation, is treated in more detail in the second half of this chapter).

Purposive Sampling of Typical Instances

Purposive sampling of typical instances requires clearly defining the characteristics of the typical persons, settings, times, treatments, or outcomes to which one wants to generalize and then trying to select a sample that matches this target. If this can be done, the researcher increases the likelihood that the causal inference may generalize to typical instances—not a trivial accomplishment if typical instances are defined by things such as modes that are more frequently occurring than other instances.

Defining typical instances and selecting samples to represent those instances are easiest when the target of generalization is a clearly delineated single instance or set of instances (e.g., a school, or all the public schools in a city) that available data describe on various characteristics (e.g., the size or ethnic composition of the school). Then, typicality is usefully defined with reference to a statistical measure of central tendency such as the mean, median, or mode on those characteristics, and in the simplest case the researcher can select a single public school that is close to the central tendency on those characteristics. If there are multiple modes, one can define more than one typical instance and obtain at least one instance of each mode. Thus, in many urban school districts in which ethnic diversity is not normally distributed over schools, one might find three modes corresponding to all-Black, all-White, and more racially desegregated schools. Then a minimal choice would be of one school from each of these classes.

Defining typical instances is more difficult when no suitable data exist to describe the target of generalization. This situation often occurs when the target of generalization is changing rapidly over time, as in the case of U.S. Census data; these data are collected only once every decade, but population changes in some areas of the United States occur so quickly that census data rapidly become dated. It also occurs with newly emergent targets of generalization, as with the very rapid evolution of angiogenesis inhibitor treatments for cancer in the late 1990s, when virtually no descriptive data about these treatments in humans were available but they nonetheless sparked an enormous amount of basic and applied research (Folkman, 1996). Even in such cases, however, the researcher can sample the opinions of experts and interested parties to obtain their impressions of what a typical instance is like. A composite impression could then be derived for all the single impressions, and this composite forms the framework for deciding which samples to include.

Defining typicality becomes substantially a qualitative judgment when the target of generalization is a construct (e.g., disadvantaged children), for then the issue is deciding exactly what characteristics constitute the construct (e.g., that disadvantaged children are those who fall below the federal poverty line, who live in poverty neighborhoods, and who are performing below average on achievement tests).

Once typical instances are defined, the researcher still faces the task of sampling one or more of them. Such sampling is probably most easy in consultant work or project evaluation, in which the available sample is highly constrained by the very nature of the project. For instance, an industrial manager who hires a consultant knows that he or she wants to generalize to the present work force in its current setting carrying out its present tasks, the effectiveness of which is measured by means of locally established indicators of productivity, profitability, absenteeism, lateness, and the like. Consultants or evaluators know that they have to select respondents and settings to reflect these circumscribed targets. In other cases, however, researchers have more discretion. They can sample one typical instance; multiple instances, each of which is typical; or multiple instances that match the target on average, even if each particular sampled instance is not itself typical. Given resource constraints, treatments and settings are often represented by only one typical instance, but persons and outcomes allow more flexibility. We provide examples of each of these kinds of sampling in subsequent sections.

Purposive Sampling of Heterogeneous Instances

The starting point for purposive sampling of heterogeneous instances is the same as the starting point for purposive sampling of typical instances—defining the characteristics of the persons, settings, treatments, or outcomes to which one wants to generalize. However, whereas PSI-Typ aims to create a sample that *is* typical on those characteristics, PSI-Het aims to create a sample that is heterogeneous and that need not include a typical instance at all. For example, if one's goal was to measure marital satisfaction in an experiment on the effects of marital therapy, PSI-Typ might lead the researcher to select the Marital Adjustment Scale (MAS; Locke & Wallace, 1959), which is the most widely used measure of this construct. PSI-Het, on the other hand, would lead the researcher to select an array of marital satisfaction measures that are heterogeneous in construct representation and methods used and that need not include the MAS at all. Similarly, if one's goal was to study elderly residents of nursing homes, PSI-Typ would lead the researcher to include residents whose ages were all about, say, the mean age of nursing home residents in the population of interest, or at least whose average age was about the mean of all residents. But PSI-Het would lead the researcher to select patients whose ages vary widely, from the youngest to the oldest such patients. Not only would PSI-Het *not* require including a patient whose age was actually at the mean, it would not even require the average age of the sample to match that mean.

Achieving heterogeneity is what is important to PSI-Het. This heterogeneity has two advantages. First, causal relationships are usually easier to find when samples are homogenous, not heterogeneous, because heterogeneous samples often increase the error variance in an analysis, especially the more that source of heterogeneity is correlated with outcome. So a causal relationship that holds despite heterogeneity will often have greater strength and so is presumed to have greater generalizability by virtue of that strength. That is a very fragile presumption but still one that is incrementally greater than would be the case with an effect in a homogenous sample. The quote from Fisher (1935) in Chapter 11 on the disadvantages of standardization makes this point. Second, PSI-Het gives the researcher far greater ability than does PSI-Typ to identify irrelevancies, to make discriminations, to explain which parts of the outcome are most affected by which parts of the treatment through which mediators, and, in the case of a continuous variable, to interpolate and extrapolate. In the next section, we show how this is so.

Sometimes it is advantageous to obtain heterogeneous samples that differ as widely as possible from each other. Thus if it were possible, one might choose to implement a treatment both in a "magnet school," that is, a school established to exemplify teaching conditions at their presumed best, and also in one of the city's worst problem schools. If each instance produced comparable effects, then one might begin to suspect that the effect would hold in many other kinds of schools. However, there is a real danger in having only extreme instances at each end of some implicit, impressionistic continuum. This problem can be best highlighted by asking, "What would you conclude about generalizability if an effect were obtained at one school but not the other?" One would be hard pressed to conclude anything about treatment effects in the majority of schools between the extremes. So it helps if PSI-Het includes at least one instance of the mode of the population under investigation, as well as instances at each extreme. In other words, at least one instance should be representative of the typical school of a particular city and at least one instance representative of the best and worst schools.

PSI-Het is also useful for avoiding the limitations that result from failing to consider secondary targets of inference—for instance, questions about the social class of those testing children as opposed to the social class of schoolchildren. Unless one has good reasons for matching the social class of testers and children, the model based on PSI-Het indicates how desirable it is to sample from a heterogeneous group of testers with different class backgrounds, given that social class might plausibly affect certain kinds of child outcomes and in many cases can be made heterogeneous at little or no extra cost.

However, PSI-Het can reduce power. If an overall treatment main effect is found, this problem is moot; but otherwise, the problem manifests itself in two ways. One is greater width of confidence intervals around the effect size and hence an increased likelihood of a Type II error for the main hypothesis of treatment effect. The other is that the effect size may not vary significantly over levels of the variable that was made heterogeneous. The researcher might then conclude that the effect generalizes over levels of that variable when, in fact, the test had too little power to detect differential treatment effects over this source.

Purposive Sampling and the First Four Principles

We noted previously that PSI-Het aims to create heterogeneous samples and that PSI-Typ aims to create samples that are typical. But heterogeneous on what? Typical on what? These two purposive sampling methods provide researchers with insufficient guidance about the particular selection of variables on which typicality or heterogeneity is desired. Fortunately, the first four of the principles outlined in the previous chapter (surface similarity, ruling out irrelevancies, making discriminations, interpolation, and extrapolation) provide additional guidance about the variables to make typical or heterogeneous. In this section, we provide both methodological guidance and examples of how purposive sampling is combined with these principles to facilitate generalized causal inference. The fifth principle, causal explanation, relies much less on sampling than it does on other qualitative and quantitative methods for probing explanations, which we cover in the second half of this chapter.

Surface Similarity

This principle highlights surface similarities between the target of generalization and the instance(s) representing it. For example, Triplett (1898) was interested in factors that might improve real-world bicycle racing and especially in whether bicycle riders went faster in competition than alone. To study this, he ensured that the salient features of field competition (the presence of competition and the activity of bicycling) were recreated in the laboratory. His laboratory bicycles had wheels and pedals just like typical bicycles (though they were stationary and outfitted with mileage indicators), and his apparatus allowed for competitors to bicycle either side by side or alone (to see if competition made a difference) while a marker signaling the end of the race drew nearer. This example illustrates a purposive sample of a single typical instance guided by surface similarity between the lab treatment and the field competition. Triplett thereby improved the construct validity of the laboratory treatment, with the obvious hope that the laboratory results would also hold in field settings by virtue of the surface similarity between the laboratory bicycle and those used in field competitions.[1]

Triplett only used one version of treatment, but sometimes several levels of a treatment are of interest, and the task is to deliberately sample those levels. The New Jersey Negative Income Tax experiment (Rees, 1974) studied income support treatments that were most likely to be adopted as policy, and several such levels of support were under consideration in the relevant policy discussions. So the researchers identified the lowest and highest income guarantees and benefit reduction rates that were within that likely policy range (PSI-Het of extreme instances) and then studied several purposively sampled options within that range.

---

1. Often empirical studies show a high degree of correspondence between the results of lab and field studies (e.g., C. Anderson, Lindsay, & Bushman, 1999; Shadish et al., 1997; Shadish et al., 2000).

Purposive sampling gave more control over the spacing of the intervals between levels than random sampling of levels would have allowed, a desirable feature for modeling the form of the relationship between level of support and outcome. This example used PSI-Het to improve the construct validity of multiple treatments. And it simultaneously improved the ability of the researcher to make external validity inferences, not only because it allowed the researchers to study how treatment effects varied over levels of the treatments but also because the researchers could later interpolate and extrapolate to unstudied levels of the treatment—unlike the Triplett study, which provided no data for investigating such external validity questions.

Obtaining a typical sample does not require that *each* sampled instance be typical. Sometimes the researcher can ensure that the *average* of the sampled instances is typical. For example, researchers evaluating the Washington State Self-Employment and Enterprise Development Demonstration purposively sampled sites to minimize a weighted index of the average differences between sampled sites and the average characteristics of all sites in the state (Orr, 1999; Orr, Johnston, Montgomery, & Hojnacki, 1989).[2] Also, though settings were not purposively sampled for their heterogeneity, the researchers could also use whatever heterogeneity did exist over sites to explore how variability in site characteristics might change the effects of the program.

Surface similarity can be undermined if researchers rely on operations that are easily available. For instance, Pearlman et al. (1989) questioned the increased use of media advertisements to solicit participants in alcohol treatment research, showing that they differed from usual clinic clients on many surface characteristics. Similar arguments apply to settings—participation in many studies is often voluntary, and the settings that volunteer often have staff who are unusually willing to try innovations or who are led by a particularly dynamic administrator. Although such features may be crucial to the results of a study, they may be irrelevant to the intended setting construct. Intensive effort is required to convince other settings without those features to participate. In the early stages of research, when efficacy is most at issue, experimenters may justifiably argue that they are trying to see if the intervention will work under optimal conditions. But if so, they need to qualify their reported conclusions accordingly.

Such qualifications are too rarely acknowledged, and setting limitations can quickly become paradigmatic over research programs involving many investigators. Weisz, Weiss, and Donenberg (1992), for example, argued that after considering scores of child and adolescent psychotherapy outcome studies, they could find only a handful that examined the effects of treatments that were currently being used in clinic settings. When they looked at those studies, their claim was that psychotherapy had no effects. The Weisz et al. (1992) study illustrates the *retrospective* use of

---

2. This is sometimes called **balanced sampling** in statistics (Marriott, 1990).

surface similarity to judge the kinds of construct and external validity inferences that might be warranted—they coined the term *"research therapy"* to refer to the treatment construct actually shown to be effective in these studies, and they pointed out that inferences about the effects of "clinic therapy" were less warranted because such therapies were mostly unstudied in that literature.

Harold Brown (1989) did a similar retrospective criticism of Gholson and Houts (1989), who had used college students to study how scientists test hypotheses. Brown (1989) claimed that this choice of participants was so far removed from real scientists as to be irrelevant to how scientists think. Houts and Gholson (1989) rightly responded that surface similarity is not the only issue in generalization, and our use of four other principles bolsters their point. But still, Brown's (1989) criticism of the lack of surface similarity in Gholson and Houts (1989) remains valid. College students do not appear to be much like practicing scientists (see also Shadish et al., 1994).

Ruling Out Irrelevancies

This principle calls on the researcher to identify those attributes of persons, settings, treatments, and outcome measures that are presumed to be irrelevant because they would not change a generalization and then to make those irrelevancies heterogeneous (PSI-Het) in order to test that presumption. The multitrait-multimethod matrix that Campbell and Fiske (1959) first outlined is an exemplar of this strategy for construct validity. In one example from their article, the irrelevancy was whether the researcher measured attitudes by interview or by a trait checklist; and in another example, the irrelevancy was whether the researcher measured popularity by self-rating, sociometric assessments by others, or observations by raters. As these examples illustrate, Campbell and Fiske especially emphasized ruling out methodological irrelevancies, for constructs in measurement theory are usually tied to substantive characteristics of the thing being measured, and methods are rarely an intended part of the construct. Methodological irrelevancies, however, are just a special case of things that are not considered relevant to the theory of the construct.

This argument extends from measurement to all other aspects of a cause-probing study. For example, many demonstration projects are evaluated using volunteer participants when volunteerism is hoped to be conceptually irrelevant to the persons served by the program. Regarding treatments, the intervention we call Head Start is often evaluated in different centers, and the identities of particular personnel are presumed to be conceptually irrelevant. Regarding settings, the income maintenance experiments of the 1970s and 1980s were implemented in a limited number of cities (e.g., Seattle, Denver), the identities of which were also thought to be conceptually irrelevant to the effect. In these cases, the task is to identify the levels of the irrelevancy (e.g., volunteers versus nonvolunteers) and then to deliberately select at least one instance to represent each level. This allows testing the presumption of irrelevancy.

Many researchers do not have the resources to sample heterogeneously, and so they rely on a more narrowly defined sample of people, settings, measures, manipulations, and times. But even then, cases are rarely identical but rather are likely to differ from each other in a host of ways that are irrelevant to the major research question. Measuring those irrelevancies sometimes adds little cost to the research. In research in which a broader sampling frame is possible, one can probe how robust a causal relationship is across, say, regions of the country, ages of the hospitals, average tenure of physicians, types of patient diagnoses, or any other patient attributes.

Special problems occur when the sample of instances is small—as it often is for settings in particular. How many states, hospitals, schools, and the like can a research budget accommodate? Given small samples, how should cases be selected, as heterogeneity can be deliberately achieved on only a small number of presumptively irrelevant attributes? In some cases, purposive sampling of heterogeneous instances is impossible, especially when the guiding research question specifies substantively relevant moderator variables that have to be included in the sampling design and without which the study's major purpose would be undermined. Including such moderators consumes resources that might otherwise be used to facilitate heterogeneity. Imagine being able to sample 20 hospitals—10 in each of two treatment groups. After stratifying on any potential moderator of relevant theoretical or practical interest (say, public versus private hospitals and large versus small ones), the only remaining room for heterogeneity may be that which has been spontaneously generated. Sampling theorists may throw up their hands at this point and contend that small samples and the plethora of potential causal determinants make sampling theory irrelevant in cases such as these. We understand and share their exasperation. But such limitations regularly confront researchers testing causal propositions with modest budgets. We cannot give up on the need for generalized causal inferences solely because methodologies based on large samples and random selection are not applicable. However, we also have to be clear that, in the small sample context, there is no perfect algorithm for selecting which variables to make heterogeneous. The best course may be a falsificationist one—select variables that the experimenter believes are irrelevant but that critics might claim would change the sign or direction of a causal relationship.

When a potential irrelevancy is not varied or even measured but may be subject to criticism by other researchers, it should be noted as a study assumption and described with whatever measures or relevant qualitative observations are available. It is in this spirit that Lavori et al. (1986) said that researchers should analyze why individuals and organizations have agreed to participate in a study. Were all the units volunteers? Were they selected because they seemed to be exemplary cases of good practice? Or were the units experiencing special problems and so needed special help? Lavori et al. (1986) seem to assign a special status to this set of (presumably) irrelevant ways in which samples differ from their intended target populations, highlighting them as part of the necessary sample description that must substitute when random selection is not feasible. Such descriptions are vital, whatever the variation randomly or deliberately achieved, so that they can be subject to critical scrutiny by those who believe the feature is not irrelevant.

Making Discriminations

This principle calls on the researcher to make discriminations about kinds of persons, measures, treatments, or outcomes in which a generalization does or does not hold. One example is to introduce a treatment variation that clarifies the construct validity of the cause. For instance, many studies show that a brief psychosocial intervention successfully reduces hospital stay for surgical patients. But if physicians or nurses know who is receiving an intervention, it is then crucial to discriminate effects of the education from effects of the professionals' expectations for recovery. To do this requires manipulating whether professionals know of the patient's experimental condition. However, practical reasons dictate that there is a very low ceiling for adding manipulations to studies.

Discriminations can also be made with stratification variables, often to clarify external validity generalizations. For example, researchers evaluating how the Job Training Partnership Act (JTPA) affected subsequent earnings suspected that effects would be stronger among women who had been on welfare longer (Orr, 1999). So they stratified their sample into women who had been on Aid to Families with Dependent Children (AFDC) (1) never, (2) less than 2 years, or (3) more than 2 years. JTPA was clearly effective only for the last of the groups. Although JTPA effects on the first two groups depended on how the analyses were done, they were never as large as for the last group. Length of time on welfare seems to be an important moderator of the generalizability of JTPA effects. However, as with adding new manipulations, there is a limit to the number of strata that can be added to a study.

Similarly, in large multisite experiments, researchers often find that sites differ from each other in outcome, and these site differences can be the source of searches for variables that moderate effects by site. Ioannidis et al. (1999), for example, found that the response of AIDS patients to a preventive treatment for pneumonia varied significantly across the 30 clinical sites in the randomized trial. In a series of exploratory analyses, they found that these differences were predicted by site differences in the administration of treatment, the types of diagnoses offered, and the risk levels of patients. Although this study did not set out to create as much heterogeneity as possible through its sampling design, the authors nonetheless took advantage of the heterogeneity that did occur to explore generalizability of treatment effects.

But there is also a limit to the amount of stratification that is feasible in a study and to the number of settings or treatments that can be added. So the easiest way to study discriminations is to add differentiating measures. Consider length of hospital stay as a measure of recovery from surgery. Although a shorter stay might indicate that patient education helped speed recovery, hospital administrators are under pressure from insurance companies and the government to reduce length of stay. For a given diagnosis, hospitals are now reimbursed for only a prespecified number of hospital days; there is no open-ended commitment. However, if patients left the hospital sooner because of this financial-administrative component of length of stay, they might well be in poorer physical health and so run a greater chance of being rehospitalized or delayed in their return to normal activities at home or work. To distinguish between a genuinely speedier recovery and a premature discharge due to reimbursement policies, valid measures are required of such variables as patients' physical condition on leaving the hospital, their rehospitalization rates, and the time it takes them to resume normal activities. Differentiating between target and cognate outcomes should be widespread in individual studies given the relative ease with which additional outcome measures can be collected.

It is similarly easy and valuable to add differentiating measures concerning persons, settings, and treatments. For example, if prior research shows that depressed patients who see primary care physicians have different levels of well-being and functioning than patients who visit mental health specialists (Stewart et al., 1993), varying provider type might be advised. Similarly, initial tests of bee-sting immunotherapy were done on beekeepers, with results suggesting that a preparation made of ground-up whole bees did as well as a bee venom preparation. Later, however, it was proved that beekeepers had a special sensitivity to both preparations because of their daily exposure to bees. Subsequent trials on other persons showed that only the bee venom worked well (Lichtenstein, 1993).

Interpolation and Extrapolation

Both extrapolation and interpolation are facilitated by having many different levels of the variable at issue. With outcomes, this is most saliently illustrated by the problem of interpolating effects in between the extremes of a dichotomous outcome—what happens to quality of life in between life and death in medical research or to marital satisfaction in between getting divorced or deciding to stay together in marital therapy research or to GPA in between passing and failing in education? Fortunately, the ease with which measures can often be added to studies offers great opportunity to measure at a fine-grained level.

Having many different levels of times and persons can also usually be done by extending the range sampled and by measuring their characteristics at even finer intervals. Regarding times, for example, longitudinal studies with multiple assessments of outcome over time allow greater interpolation about what happens in between assessments, for the more times that are included, the easier it is to model the form of the relationship between time and outcome. Often overlooked are assessments of outcome during treatment itself, which facilitate dose-response assessments when dose is a function of time (e.g., number of sessions of therapy). Some growth curve analyses allow time of assessment to differ for each participant, interpolating and even extrapolating that participant's outcomes at times not observed based on the data that are available for that participant augmented by data from the entire sample (e.g., Bryk & Raudenbush, 1992; Hedeker & Gibbons, 1994).[3] Similarly, persons can often be scaled on continuous variables that may predict response to treatment—aptitude scores for educational interventions, poverty levels for job training, cancer cell differentiation for cancer treatments, or readiness to change for smoking cessation programs.

Diversifying treatments and settings is far more difficult. Field experiments with many deliberately manipulated levels of the independent variable are rare. The reason for this highlights some of the most pressing practical problems involved in social experimentation. Typically, only two levels of a treatment are sampled—the treatment itself and some control group. The contrast between them is the diversity available for study. Thus researchers might specify patient education as the cause but then manipulate only an average of 3 hours of it. Because the control groups will also experience some patient education in the course of normal hospital treatment, the achieved contrast in patient education will be less than 3 hours—say, 2. But written research conclusions will rarely refer to the cause as either "3 hours of patient education" or as the more exact "2-hour-differential in patient education." The unqualified causal construct "patient education" will tend to be invoked.

The ideal solution describes the form of the function relating the full range of the independent variable to the full range of the dependent variable. To do this entails a dose-response study. The best version of this study entails independent samples of units randomly assigned to many levels of a unidimensional independent variable that can be expressed quantitatively (at least ordinally). These requirements are rarely practical except for experimental studies in the laboratory. Multicomponent interventions and few comparison levels are the reality elsewhere. The practitioners' dilemma, then, is to decide how many levels to choose and what range to represent.

When studying a very novel intervention about which little is known, it is wise to include, at a minimum, one level of treatment that is as high or as powerful as practical and another as equivalent to a no-treatment control group as possible. But then conclusions can be drawn about the effect of A only as it varies between these two levels, not about A more generally. With more resources, a treatment group in between these two levels could be added. If an effect were then observed at both treatment levels, one might conclude that the effect would also have been observed at (unsampled) levels in between the two treatment levels. This suggests an empirically bounded generalization based on interpolating between the two treatment levels (and also assuming that the cause and effect are not curvilinearly

---

3. Care is needed to avoid endogeneity of time points in growth curve models, because time points are predictors and so must be exogenous. For example, if outcome measures occur at a time that is not predetermined (e.g., suppose a psychotherapist decides to end therapy based on the client's progress or lack thereof and outcome is then measured at termination), then that particular assessment is endogenous (e.g., potentially determined by another variable in the system such as client status on the outcome), and estimates may be biased. This is not to say that such data cannot be gathered for use in, say, hazard rate analysis but only to say that it may cause problems for growth curve analyses.

related within the range studied). If, on the other hand, the data analysis revealed that an effect is found at the higher but not the lower level of the independent variable, this suggests that the treatment has a causal threshold higher than that lower level.

Complicating the choice is the fact that applied researchers are often interested in the level of treatment implementation that would be anticipated as modal if an intervention were to be routinely adopted (Glasgow, Vogt, & Boles, 1999). This requires selecting (and justifying) a treatment level corresponding to what regular practice is likely to be. But this choice alone would not inform us about the treatment when implemented at its best. Establishing this is often a concern of both substantive theorists and program developers, especially in the early stages of a theory or program. Hence the presumed modal implementation is best incorporated into experimental designs as intermediate between the high-intensity and no-treatment levels. Although such strategies move the analysis toward the desirable circumstance of describing the functional relationship between the independent and dependent variables, outside of the laboratory treatments are often so multidimensional that they cannot be neatly scaled ordinally.

The preceding refers to planned manipulation of heterogeneous levels of treatment; but unplanned variation nearly always occurs, as well, given that treatments are rarely implemented with full fidelity and that some people refuse to complete all treatment. In Chapters 4 and 5 we noted the dangers of interpreting outcomes related to this unplanned variability, especially the selection bias confound that occurs when people self-select into levels of treatment dose. However, if this variability has been measured, it can be useful for exploring two generalizability questions. One is whether an effect remains relatively constant despite the unplanned variability, or at least above a certain threshold level of treatment; and the other is to suggest possible causal thresholds below which no effect may be likely.

The preceding problems apply with equal force to generalizations about settings—indeed, in one sense the problems may be worse. Except in large, well-funded trials, many studies implement treatment in just one setting, making extrapolations or interpolations about setting variability all but impossible. Some researchers avoid using more than one setting to simplify close monitoring of the research and to avoid the reduction in statistical power that can occur in some group randomized or setting-stratified designs. However, the decision to use a single setting is often made only for convenience so that investigators need not travel far, can obtain human participants' permission more easily, and can avoid the interpretive difficulties that arise when treatment effects vary by setting. Although we have used such rationales to the same end ourselves, they become harder to justify intellectually when certain setting characteristics may dramatically affect outcome. The previously mentioned review of psychotherapy outcome in clinically relevant settings (Weisz et al., 1992) is an excellent example. Given that controlled psychotherapy clinical trials have rarely been run in the conditions in which most psychotherapy takes place and that there is controversy about whether studies run in clinic settings find no effects (Shadish et al., 2000), avoiding this setting variability for the sake of convenience is very hard to defend.

Statistical Methods for Generalizing from Purposive Samples

The preceding section emphasizes the ways in which study design affects generalizability. Partly, this reflects our focus in this book on the design of experiments more than on their analysis; and partly, it reflects the reality that few statistical methods are available for studying the generalizability of experimental results when random sampling is not used. However, some methods are available that, especially when used in concert with better purposive sampling, can be informative. We describe those methods here. Such models were not necessarily developed for the purpose of generalized causal inference from experiments to constructs or to instances not studied, so they do not cover the full range of the conceptual theory we outline. Their applicability will also depend on appropriate data being available, which will often not be the case.

Sample Reweighting

In principle, experimental results on purposive samples can be made to approximate the results that would have occurred in the population through reweighting the sample characteristics. Survey researchers routinely use reweighting to correct random samples for participant loss that may be systematic and for improving the match between nonrandom samples and populations (Cochran, 1977; Rossi et al., 1983). Such reweighting also occurs in field experiments in economics, combining results from randomized experiments with knowledge of pertinent population characteristics to predict population effects (Orr, 1999). Constructing the necessary weights requires knowledge of the pertinent characteristics of the population to which generalization is sought. When that knowledge is available, the sample data are reweighted to reflect the composition of that population regarding those characteristics. The results will usually be less precise relative to the results that would have been obtained had a random sample been used (Orr, 1999), but they will usually be less biased as estimates of what would have happened in the population than would the unweighted results of the study (Hedges, 1997b).

Two problems impede widespread use of such reweighting techniques. First, the use of this method requires some estimate of population characteristics in order to do the appropriate weighting. When those estimates are not available, the researcher must obtain them through further research studies (e.g., sample surveys of the pertinent population). Hedges (1997b) suggests doing so only if there is reason to think that the money would not be better invested in improving the internal and statistical conclusion validity of the primary experiment. Often the latter are higher priorities given low funding levels for many experiments.

Second, these methods focus mostly on weights for characteristics of people. Although an extension to settings seems plausible, extensions to treatments and outcomes are less so. After all, if a population is defined as it usually is in statistics as "any finite or infinite collection of individuals" (Marriott, 1990, p. 158), lists of treatments or outcomes are rare and are generally not thought to be complete. In many areas, for example, available outcomes are typically self-report measures; but physiological or observer measures are often completely absent from the list despite well-accepted theoretical desirability for generalizing over such sources of method variance. Still, this second objection carries less force to the extent that the researcher is willing to restrict inference to how well this particular treatment-outcome combination generalizes to populations of persons and settings instead. Often such a limitation is plausible.

Response Surface Modeling

Response surface modeling (RSM) refers to a general set of methods for empirical model building and the subsequent use of that model to predict outcomes as a function of predictors such as treatment duration and intensity or person and setting characteristics, as long as those predictors can be quantified. Box and Draper (1987) give the example from psychology that "an investigator might want to find out how a test *score* (output) achieved by certain subjects depended upon the *duration* (input 1) of the period during which they studied the relevant material, and the *delay* (input 2) between study and test" (p. 1). With these three variables, for example, a three-dimensional response surface can be constructed that graphically portrays the relationship among the variables. One use of that surface is to see what combination of duration and delay maximized test scores by finding the highest predicted test score on the surface—even if the researcher had not included that particular combination of duration and delay in the experiment. When more predictors are included, it is usually impossible to graph and visualize the resulting *n*-dimensional response surface. But the graphical visualization is simply a convenient tool reflecting the underlying regression equation giving rise to the surface, and it is really that equation that is used to make the prediction.

Under the RSM logic, generalized causal inference is a prediction about the likely effect that would be obtained with persons, settings, treatments, or outcomes specified by the analyst as the target of generalization. Consider the example of the lab-versus-clinic debate in psychotherapy (e.g., Weisz et al., 1992) in which the question was whether the results from research studies of the effects of psychotherapy would generalize to more clinically representative contexts. The target of interest would probably include clinic settings, experienced professional therapists, clients presenting through usual referral routes, and the like, so an RSM would project results from existing data—which may not actually have any studies representing this particular combination of characteristics—to a study that did have such characteristics. Similarly, RSM allows examination of whether outcome varies over levels of predictors that are presumed to be irrelevant, especially if critics suggest they might prove to be relevant—such as whether the presenting problem involved a child or an adult. It allows examination of whether outcome varies over levels of predictors that are thought to moderate outcome, such as whether or not the study randomly assigned psychotherapy clients to treatment or control.

And it allows examination of how outcome changes over predictors that vary on a continuum, such as dose of therapy or duration of posttherapy follow-up.

In all these senses, RSM is an ideal method for exploring generalized causal inference. So West et al. (1993) suggested using RSM to identify which particular combination of components of multiple component prevention programs maximized outcome, even though that particular combination might never have actually been studied. However, their examples were all hypothetical; we know of no applications of RSM to the problem of generalized causal inference from field experiments in the social sciences, except for some parts of economics. For example, the several income maintenance experiments varied multiple levels of some of the independent variables in order to create "parameters that can be applied to project the effects of national policy proposals affecting low-income people" (Greenberg & Shroder, 1997, p. 374).

In practice, the usefulness of RSM is often limited in single experiments by a lack of variability on irrelevancies and important discriminating variables and by the usual failure to deliberately vary or even measure the quantitative dimensions required for extrapolation and interpolation. These lacunae are understandable given the usual lack of the resources that it takes to implement more than one level of some variables, such as setting or treatment, and the usual conflict between the benefits of variability for generalization and the costs of variability for statistical power. Other researchers may be intimidated by the traditional statistical literature on RSM because it is not couched in familiar terms and because the examples come primarily from industrial production (Box & Draper, 1987). But these impediments are more apparent than real, for the required statistics are mostly simple regression equations. Provision of a few exemplars would probably encourage far more experimenters to do the requisite analyses.

Other Methods

The literature contains many other statistical methods that could be adapted to generalized causal inference—probably many more than we report here. SenGupta (1995), for example, used multidimensional scaling procedures to identify the prototypical features of those chronically mentally ill individuals who most benefited from supportive employment. The assumption is that these same treatments for other individuals in other locations may be more effective to the extent that they share these prototypical characteristics. Similarly, in the Washington State Self-Employment and Enterprise Development Demonstration, researchers nonrandomly selected sites to minimize a weighted index of the differences between sites and the entire state on a set of characteristics presumed to be important for representing the state (Orr, 1999; Orr et al., 1989). Further, some statistics described in previous chapters for generalizing from those who accept random assignment to conditions to those invited to the experiment (some of whom declined random assignment) could probably be extended to model generalization to even larger populations (Braver & Smith, 1996; Ellenberg, 1994).

Finally, Glasgow et al. (1999) proposed a mixed approach that combines available statistical and experimental information with judgmental ratings to make (partially data-based) assumptions about matters such as efficacy, likely coverage, and degree of anticipated implementation, all of which are then combined to estimate likely effects in the more generalized populations.

At the most general level, Hedges (1997b) described a broad statistical model that incorporates some of the conceptual theory that we outline here. Essentially, the model defines a global (generalizable) causal effect as the average of a set of unbiased estimates from individual experiments conducted over admissible methods, contexts, operations, and participants. The difference between an individual experiment and this global causal effect may be due to estimation error (typically, sampling error and measurement error), local causal inference error (sources of internal invalidity in the individual experiments), and error of generalized causal inference (limited generalizability across contexts). Though Hedges' model does not lead immediately to practical statistical methods that can improve generalized causal inference, it does indicate that statisticians are working on this problem and that additional practical methods may be forthcoming in future years.

METHODS FOR STUDYING CAUSAL EXPLANATION

The fifth principle of generalized causal inference is causal explanation. In many respects, methods for studying causal explanation are more diverse and better developed than they are for any of the other four principles. Here we present three general approaches: (1) qualitative methods that primarily help to discover and explore possible explanations, (2) statistical methods such as structural equation modeling that combine experimental information with measures of mediating processes, and (3) programs of experiments that manipulate explanatory variables in experiments. The order of presentation is intentional, moving from methods that are more discovery oriented through those that measure but do not manipulate and ending with those that provide a stronger basis for asserting the causal role of mediational variables.

Qualitative Methods

Qualitative methods provide an important avenue for discovering and exploring causal explanations. They are now widely accepted and acknowledged—if not always used—as a unique part of the social science repertoire. Old classics in qualitative methods are still widely read (Dallmayr & McCarthy, 1977; Glaser & Strauss, 1967), and new volumes keep expanding the relevant literature about participant observation, interviewing, and content analysis of written records, as well as methods from investigative journalism and litigation, history, and even connoisseurship (Berg, 1989; Della-Piana, 1981; Denzin & Lincoln, 2000; Gephart, 1981; E. Smith, 1992; S. Taylor & Bogdan, 1984). Although these methods have a wide array of uses that are beyond the scope of this book, here we focus on how various methods can be used in experiments to improve our understanding of *how* interventions work (Griffin & Ragin, 1994; Leviton et al., 1999).

The first example (Estroff, 1981) is an **ethnography** that used **participant observation** of psychiatric clients who were part of a well-known model program in Madison, Wisconsin, that was being studied with a randomized experiment (Stein & Test, 1980; Test & Stein, 1980). Estroff lived among these clients, observing and participating with them in most aspects of their daily life (e.g., taking the same medications that they took in order to understand their effects). The ethnography presented a much richer picture than the quantitative results did. For instance, quantitative results suggested that medications did help clients remain in the community rather than having to return to the hospital. The ethnography showed the costs of this success—the drugs had side effects that included sexual dysfunction and physically unappealing mannerisms—and so many clients stopped taking their medications even though they knew that their psychiatric symptoms would return and they would likely be rehospitalized. This ethnography was done independently of the experiment, exploring issues that might not have occurred to those who designed the experiment.

A second example used open-ended *interviews* (Bos et al., 1999). The New Hope program aimed to increase the income, financial security, and employment of low-income workers in Milwaukee. Eligible people were randomly assigned either to the New Hope program or to a control group and assessed on a host of outcomes after 2 years, at which time they were also given an open-ended interview that was then used for several purposes (Morales, 2000). First, they created narrative descriptions that could be used to illustrate the most important study results and to clarify the context and dynamics of the families in the study. Second, they used the interviews to learn more about puzzling results from the study. For instance, quantitative results suggested that the program improved the behavior of boys more than of girls. The qualitative interviews suggested that this was because parents thought boys were more vulnerable to gang influences, so those parents used more program resources to help their boys than their girls. Third, the interviews discovered some moderator effects, for instance, that the program had little effect both on families experiencing large barriers to success and on those with no barriers who could succeed even without the program. It was families in the middle with only a few barriers who benefited the most.

A third example (J. Maxwell, Bashook, & Sandlow, 1986) combined a quasi-experiment with *unstructured observation and interviews* to assess the value of medical care evaluation committees (MCEs) in educating physicians about medical practice. This study used quasi-experimental thinking to clarify causal inferences in an ethnographic context. For instance, the authors noted that "the concept of 'controlled comparison' has a long and respected history in anthropology (Eggan, 1954), and our use of specific comparison incorporated into the research design is a logical extension of Eggan's use of historical and geographical controls in comparing societies" (Maxwell et al., 1986, p. 126). The authors used a non-equivalent control group design in which they compared physicians participating in the committee with those who did not participate. In subsequent qualitative exploration of why committees might work, they found that the most successful committees had lengthy, high-level discussions of a patient or problem. When the six MCE committees were subdivided on this variable into three that used high-level discussions and three that did not, the former yielded significant effects compared with the nonequivalent control group, but the latter did not.

The fourth example (M. Gorman, 1994) used *observation* of people's behavior in a series of laboratory experiments on reasoning. The experiments examined how participants' reasoning was affected by giving them explicit instructions either to confirm or disconfirm hypotheses that they had developed to explain card sequences provided to them by the experimenter. One experiment compared participants assigned to develop these hypotheses in groups with those assigned to develop them individually and found that group production was more likely to result in the correct hypothesis. Observation of the decision-making process showed that a strong leader could lead the group down the right or wrong path, to some degree overriding the evidence of the cards themselves. In another experiment, participants were told that the feedback they received about whether their hypothesis was right or wrong might be incorrect, introducing the possibility of random error into the task. This greatly disrupted problem solving. Observation suggested that groups responded differently to the possibility of error. Some used it to immunize their hypothesis against falsification, declaring cards that were inconsistent with their hypothesis to be errors. Others ignored errors entirely, searching instead for confirmations of their hypothesis that yielded no errors at all. Still other groups combined disconfirmation strategies with replication, playing sequences again and again to try to falsify in the face of error. The latter group had the best performance, a fact revealed only by the qualitative examination of the actual operations of groups.

Qualitative methods sometimes generate information that is inconsistent with quantitative data. Trend (1979) gives an example of an intervention that provided direct cash payments to needy families so they could obtain better housing. At one site the quantitative data suggested that the program accomplished this goal and that it had been implemented and monitored in an efficient, precise, and rational way. However, the qualitative data suggested that although the cash transfer improved the financial condition of needy families, it did not improve the quality of housing, was tarnished by racial biases, and alienated a potentially overworked staff. Some of this discrepancy could be reconciled. At one of the two branch offices of the site, financial contingencies pressured the staff to enroll more White families because such families tended to get smaller subsidies. This appeared racist to some staff members, who quit in protest. In the qualitative data, this reflected problems with the program, but in the quantitative data it looked as though the program efficiently saved money. Other discrepancies between the quantitative and qualitative results were less easily resolved. For instance, the quantitative data indicated that the site in question obtained high-quality housing for recipients, but the qualitative data did not show this. The researchers could not explain this, and so let it stand in the report as a discrepancy. Later reanalyses of the quantitative data found a mistake that had indeed led to overestimating the quality of the housing obtained, thus vindicating the qualitative results. Such conflicts can also emerge between two different sets of quantitative data, of course, or even two different analyses of the same data. But they may be more frequent when more divergent methods are used for gathering data.

Our currently preferred causal explanations also have to be examined historically and cross-nationally to see what limits to their generalization might become apparent (Eggan, 1954). It also helps to take causal findings and get multitheoretical perspectives on why they occur. The aim is to produce interpersonal deliberation on the basic descriptive causal finding from people who hold different theoretical perspectives in science and those who hold different perspectives on the phenomenon in the world of practical action. This is exploratory but worthwhile because an interpersonal process of theoretically and practically informed deliberation helps discipline any one model and helps set up the competing models to deliberately test against each other. At issue in all these cases—on-site intense observation, historical and national comparison, and soliciting critical perspectives—is the attempt to elucidate the more temporal, spatial, and micromediational processes that explain an effect. Such explorations of explanation help identify hypotheses about possible causal contingencies to be tested in the next round of studies.

Statistical Models of Causal Explanation

A second set of methods for exploring explanatory mechanisms involves measurement and statistical manipulation. Here the researcher measures the independent, dependent, mediating, and moderating variables, perhaps including measures of different components of each. Using the covariances (or correlations) among all these measures as input data, the researcher then models the presumed causal relationships among the variables (Bollen, 1989), trying to control for various confounds using statistical manipulation. This general set of methods goes under a variety of names, including causal modeling, structural equation modeling, and covariance structure analysis (Tanaka, Panter, Winborne, & Huba, 1990), names that incorporate a host of more specific applications such as path analysis, cross-lagged panel designs, and complete latent variable structural models. The literature in this area grew rapidly over the last 3 decades of the 20th century, including excellent introductory and advanced texts (Bollen, 1989; Loehlin, 1992; Pearl, 2000), computer programs (Arbuckle, 1997; Bentler, 1995; Bentler & Wu, 1995; Hox, 1995; Joreskog & Sorbom, 1988, 1993), textbooks on how to use these programs for common problems (Byrne, 1989, 1994; Hayduk, 1987), and even a journal—*Structural Equation Modeling.* In general, this kind of modeling benefits from large sample sizes (e.g., $N = 300$; Boomsma, 1987; MacCallum, Browne, & Sugawara, 1996; MacKinnon, Warsi, & Dwyer, 1995; but see Tanaka et al., 1990).[4]

Path Diagrams with Measured Variables

Common to all applications of these techniques is the path diagram—a graphical model that portrays the hypothesized causal and correlational relationships among all the measures. The path diagram is useful for two reasons. First, it forces the researcher to specify explicitly the details of the model that relates antecedents of the treatment to the treatment and moderator variables and from there to mediators and from there to the outcome(s). Second, a given path model implies that certain covariances (or correlations) among measures should be observed if the model is correctly specified. So the observed covariances from the data can be compared with the implied covariances to test the goodness of fit of the hypothesized model. Hence it is worth reviewing some simple conventions for constructing and depicting path models. In doing so, we use the notation conventions of the EQS computer program for describing structural equation models (Bentler, 1995).[5] The notation is intuitive, does not require knowledge of matrix algebra, and provides the reader with a simple and user-friendly introduction that might encourage more mediational modeling of experimental data.[6]

Consider the example in Figure 12.1a, in which observed (measured) variables are listed as V1, V2, and so forth. Figure 12.1a depicts the hypothesis that a measured variable V1 causes a measured variable V2, whether in an experiment, a quasi-experiment, or nonexperimental research. In an experiment, V1 might be the (1,0) dummy coding for whether someone was assigned randomly to the treatment or control group; and V2 might be the dependent variable.[7] In a quasi-experiment,

---

4. Mediational modeling in hierarchical or multilevel data raises additional problems not covered in this chapter (Krull & MacKinnon, 1999).

5. The passage of time renders any computer program obsolete, so our emphasis is on issues that are likely to remain valid for a longer time. One can conduct the analyses we describe using other structural equation programs such as AMOS or LISREL (Arbuckle, 1997; Joreskog & Sorbom, 1988, 1993; Hox, 1995) and even using other statistical techniques entirely, including two- and three-stage least squares regressions and various econometric models (Goldstein, 1986; Greene, 1999)—even ordinary regression programs in some cases (Baron & Kenny, 1986; MacKinnon et al., 1991).

6. We do not much discuss such crucial issues as distribution assumptions (West, Finch, & Curran, 1995), estimation methods, model identification, input of covariance versus correlation matrices, specification searches, various optional or required parameter constraints, missing data, testing nested models, or assessment of fit. Bentler (1987) provides a tutorial on these matters. Our aim is only to expose readers to the basics of explanatory modeling, given its role in generalizing causal connections.

7. Joreskog & Sorbom (1988, pp. 112–116) show how the structural equation analysis of this model can yield the standard F-ratios from an analysis of variance.

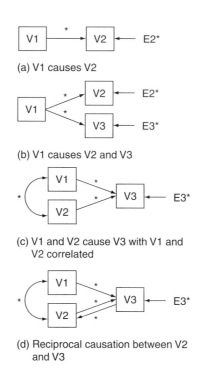

(a) V1 causes V2

(b) V1 causes V2 and V3

(c) V1 and V2 cause V3 with V1 and
    V2 correlated

(d) Reciprocal causation between V2
    and V3

FIGURE 12.1 Path diagrams

V1 is also likely to be a (1,0) dummy coding, say, for whether or not a child participated in Head Start; and V2 might be that child's academic achievement score. In nonexperimental research, V1 could be categorical but is often likely to be continuous, such as the number of cigarettes smoked; and V2 might be the severity of lung cancer the person contracted. Finally, Figure 12.1a could represent a longitudinal study in which the same measure is observed twice, say at pretest and posttest, with pretest scores causing posttest ones (e.g., Anderson, 1987; Bentler, 1987). By convention, a presumed causal path is indicated by a straight arrow with a single arrowhead on it, going from cause to effect. In Figure 12.1a, the arrow indicates that the direction of this causal influence is from V1 to V2. Asterisks (*) indicate parameters to be estimated; the asterisk on the causal arrow indicates that the researcher wishes to estimate the **path coefficient** for the arrow on which the asterisk lies.

A path coefficient measures the magnitude of the presumed causal influence of V1 on V2. Statistically, it is essentially a regression coefficient. **Endogenous** variables in the model receive causal inputs from other variables that are in the path diagram, whereas **exogenous** variables do not. In Figure 12.1a, V2 is endogenous and V1 is exogenous. V2 also has an arrow entering it from variable E2, an error term whose number matches that of the variable it causes. One must usually estimate the variance of such error terms, indicated by the asterisk next to the term. In path diagrams, all endogenous variables have error terms associated with them because there are almost always causes of an observed score on V2 other than the presumed cause V1. These other causes of endogenous variables include random measurement error, as well as omitted causes of V2 that were not measured in this study. By contrast, the exogenous variable V1 does not have an error associated with it, even though V1 will usually be measured with error and caused by **omitted variables.** Before we can describe why this is so, more background is necessary.

Our hypotheses will often be more complex than depicted in Figure 12.1a. Figure 12.1b depicts a model with two endogenous variables and one exogenous variable. In a randomized experiment, this could represent the case in which assignment to treatment causes changes in two distinct outcomes; in a correlational study, it might represent the case in which smoking causes both heart disease and cancer. Figure 12.1c depicts a model with two exogenous variables and one endogenous variable. This could represent a two-factor randomized experiment (without an interaction) in which V1 is the (1,0) dummy variable for the first factor, V2 is the dummy for the second factor, and V3 is the dependent variable. Exogenous variables can also be covariates. Hence, in a repeated measures randomized experiment, V1 could be the treatment dummy variable, V2 the pretest used as a covariate, and V3 the posttest. Similarly, in a quasi-experiment V1 could be participation (or no participation) in Head Start, V2 could be the covariate of family socioeconomic status (SES), and V3 could be achievement. In postulating such a model, the researcher may assume that membership in Head Start is correlated with SES, and if so, indicate this by a curved, two-headed arrow between the correlated variables. The asterisk (*) then indicates that the correlation is to be estimated. If no correlation is hypothesized, then the arrow is omitted, as it would be in the randomized experiment example, because pretest variables should not be correlated with random assignment. The addition of the correlation does not make V1 and V2 endogenous. Only variables with *causal* arrows entering them are endogenous.

Sometimes variables cause each other. In Head Start, for example, SES may influence subsequent achievement, and achievement may change subsequent SES. This is variously called mutual causation, bidirectional causation, reciprocal causation, or **nonrecursive causation.**[8] Figure 12.1d is the most common portrayal of mutual causal influence in a path diagram, with two straight causal arrows linking the two variables, one in each direction. However, this diagram (and the equations it suggests) may be seriously misleading because it implies no time lag between cause and effect, and this conflicts with the requirement that cause precede effect. A more satisfactory portrayal of mutual causal influence is the cross-lagged panel design at the end of this chapter (Figure 12.10).

---

8. The word **recursive** is used differently in other literatures (P. Winston & Horn, 1989).

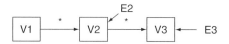

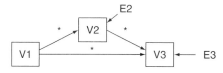

(a) A mediational model where V1 affects V3
    indirectly through V2

(b) V1 affects V3 both directly and indirectly

FIGURE 12.2 Path diagrams with mediator variables

Figure 12.2 depicts two mediational models. In Figure 12.2a, V1 directly causes V2, which then directly causes V3. In this model, V1 influences V3 only indirectly, through the mediator V2. For example, if smoking (V1) causes heart disease (V3), it might do so by increasing carbon monoxide in the blood (V2), which in turn causes damage to the heart by depriving it of oxygen. Paths that connect two variables with no other variable in between are called **direct paths; indirect paths** connect two variables through some other variable(s); **compound paths** consist of two or more direct paths connected together. The size of a direct effect is measured by the path coefficient for that effect. The size of an indirect effect is obtained by multiplying all the path coefficients along the indirect path. For instance, suppose that the path coefficient between V1 and V2 was .3, and that between V2 and V3 was .4; then the indirect effect of V1 on V3 is $.3 \times .4 = .12$. Figure 12.2b depicts a model that allows both a direct and an indirect path from V1 to V3. The total effect of one variable on another is equal to the sum of all of the direct and indirect paths between the two variables. In Figure 12.2b, if the direct path between V1 and V3 was .4 and the indirect paths were the same as before, adding this to the previously computed indirect effect of .12 yields a total effect of .52.[9]

In a three-variable system with cause, mediator, and outcome, three conditions must be met to claim *complete* mediation (Judd & Kenny, 1981b). First, the unmediated relationship between cause and effect must be statistically significant. Otherwise, there is no effect to mediate. Second, both of the mediational paths (from cause to mediator and from mediator to effect) should be statistically significant. Otherwise, the notion of a causal chain breaks down. Third, when the mediational paths are included in the model, the direct path from the cause to the effect (i.e., the path from V1 to V3 in Figure 12.2b) is no longer significant; otherwise, the mediation is not complete but only partial. However, these three conditions apply

---

9. The estimation of indirect and total effects can be more complicated than this oversimplification, especially as multiple mediation paths are used. More appropriate estimates are available in common structural equation programs (e.g., Bentler, 1995).

only to a three-variable system. Once a second mediational path is added independently of the first, things become more complicated. For instance, it is possible for the indirect effect through one mediator to have the opposite sign to the indirect effect through the other mediator. In that case, the two indirect effects could cancel each other, resulting in zero total relationship between cause and effect.

Consider how the path models in Figures 12.1 and 12.2 can be used to explain causal relationships. Figure 12.1b might depict the case in which the outcome construct is broken down into constituent parts; and in Figure 12.1c the same is done for the cause. The intervening variable in Figure 12.2 might represent a causal mediating process, and more mediators can be chained together to create longer paths and more complex relationships with many indirect paths through different mediators. In all cases, the model represents a pattern of relationships among presumed causes, effects, and mediators. Such a model is often called a *structural model* in the sense that it represents the underlying structure that is thought to give rise to the observed data.

Path Equations

Path diagrams also lend themselves to full matrix algebra representations (e.g., Bollen, 1989) that we do not cover here. However, the elementary rules for constructing individual path equations from path diagrams are quite simple:

1. One equation exists for every endogenous variable (every variable with a causal arrow entering it);
2. The left side of the equation is the endogenous variable;
3. The right side of the equation is the sum of:
    a. the path coefficient for the first variable that directly causes the endogenous variable, multiplied by the variable; plus
    b. continuing this process for every variable that directly causes this particular endogenous variable until the last one is added to the equation; plus
    c. an error term.

For example, the path diagram in Figure 12.1a has only one endogenous variable and requires only one equation: $V2 = {}^{*}V1 + E2$, where the asterisk ($*$) indicates the regression weight (path coefficient) to be estimated.[10] Notice that this equation has the same basic form as all regression equations, even though the notation is different. For example, Equation 8.1 was used to model the basic randomized experiment: $Y_i = \mu + \hat{\beta}Z_i + e_i$. Comparing that equation with the present one, $V2$ takes the place of Y_i; $V1$ takes the place of Z_i; $E2$ takes the place of e_i; and the asterisk takes the place of $\hat{\beta}$.[11]

---

10. The use of the asterisk simply follows conventions in the EQS program. However, this should not be read as implying that path coefficients will be equal to each other (they rarely are). A more formal presentation would assign subscripts to each path coefficient to indicate which variables are involved in the relationship.

11. For reasons that need not concern us here, the constant term is not included in the path diagram equation using Bentler's (1995) EQS approach.

Now consider more complicated path diagrams and the equations they imply. Figure 12.1b, for instance, has two endogenous variables and so requires two equations:

$$V2 = {}^*V1 + E2;$$
$$V3 = {}^*V1 + E3.$$

Figure 12.1c has only one endogenous variable and requires only one equation. But it has two exogenous variables, and so rule 3b increases the number of terms on the right side of the equation: $V3 = {}^*V1 + {}^*V2 + E3$; it results in an equation like the typical multiple regression equation in which a set of predictors is used to model a dependent variable. Figure 12.1c, then, is a specific case of the generic kind of path diagram for a single multiple regression equation with more than one predictor. The generalization to more predictors simply involves adding more exogenous variables as causes of the single endogenous variable.

Figure 12.2 presents path diagrams with mediators, which always require more than one equation to represent them because they always have more than one endogenous variable. In Figure 12.2a, both the outcome and the mediator variable are endogenous, so each requires an equation:

$$V2 = {}^*V1 + E2;$$
$$V3 = {}^*V2 + E3.$$

Figure 12.2b also has two endogenous variables and so requires two equations:

$$V2 = {}^*V1 + E2;$$
$$V3 = {}^*V1 + {}^*V2 + E3.$$

Notice in both these examples that V2, an endogenous variable, causes V3, another endogenous variable. More generally, endogenous variables can cause each other. Thus the term *endogenous variable* is not equivalent to *dependent variable* or *outcome*—an endogenous variable can serve roles other than being the outcome.

Once these equations are constructed, the next step would be to solve them to get estimates of the path coefficients represented by the asterisks (*). Programs such as EQS and LISREL do not solve these equations directly. Instead, for reasons that go beyond the scope of this chapter, they solve the implied covariance equations for the parameters. When taken together, the previous steps are often referred to as path analysis (Wright, 1921, 1934) or structural equation modeling. The aim is always the same—to predict and justify a set of causal relationships involving cause(s), effect(s), and substantively interesting mediators, moderators, and covariates and then to test the strength of the relationships postulated in the model. However, the model does not "confirm" causal relationships. Rather, it assumes causal links and then tests how strong they would be if the model were a correct representation of reality.

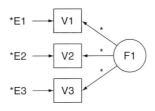

FIGURE 12.3 The latent variable F1 causes the measured variables V1, V2, and V3, with errors E1, E2, and E3

Latent Variables

All the path diagrams in Figures 12.1 and 12.2 included measured or observed variables. But researchers are rarely interested in scores on such measures. Their interest is often in the latent constructs the measures are presumed to represent. Latent variable modeling attempts to separate the variance due to the latent construct from the variance due to the unique and random error components of the measure. The most familiar form of latent variable modeling is factor analysis, which models obtained scores as a function of latent variables and measurement error. In a path diagram, latent variables (factors) are portrayed as F1, F2, and so on. Figure 12.3 gives an example in which one latent variable (F1) causes scores on three measured variables (V1, V2, V3), and in which scores on each measured variable are also caused by measurement error (E1, E2, E3). Path coefficients are represented by asterisks (*)—factor loadings in factor analytic terms. By convention, latent variables are enclosed in circles and observed variables in rectangles so the two can be easily distinguished visually.

Although a variety of factor structures can be modeled with these techniques (Hayduk, 1987), our present interest is in the use of latent variables in causal modeling. In Figure 12.4, a latent variable F1 causes a latent variable F2. Each latent variable causes three measured variables. Also, because there will be some error in predicting F2 from F1, an error term is added that also causes F2. Errors that cause latent variables are called *disturbances* to distinguish them from measurement errors. Hence the disturbance for F2 is D2. Disturbances are composed of omitted variables, because it is assumed that measurement errors are captured by E1 through E6 in the factor analytic part of the model. The EQS equations to represent the model in Figure 12.4 are:

$$F2 = {}^*F1 + D2;$$
$$V1 = {}^*F1 + E1;$$
$$V2 = {}^*F1 + E2;$$
$$V3 = {}^*F1 + E3;$$
$$V4 = {}^*F2 + E4;$$
$$V5 = {}^*F2 + E5;$$
$$V6 = {}^*F2 + E6.$$

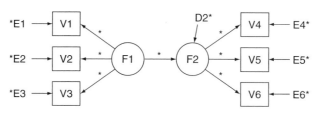

FIGURE 12.4 The latent variable F1 causes the latent variable F2, plus a disturbance D2

The first of these seven equations is generally referred to as the structural model because it portrays the underlying causal structure presumed to give rise to the data. The remaining six are the measurement model because they show how latent variables and random measurement error give rise to measured variables.

The causal models presented to this point involve either measured variables that cause other measured variables or latent variables that cause latent variables. When measured variables are causally related to latent variables, other labels are often used. Cohen, Cohen, Teresi, Marchi, and Velez (1990) use the term emergent variable to refer to unobserved variables caused by measured variables. Bollen (1989) refers to the measured variables as cause indicators if they cause a latent variable and as effect indicators if they are caused by the latent variable (Bollen, 1989; Edwards & Bagozzi, 2000). An example might be a child's socioeconomic status (SES) as measured by mother's education, father's education, and family income, where we clearly mean that the measured education and income cause the inference about SES. The opposite causal relationship, that the child's SES caused the parent's income, makes little sense. So the three measured variables are cause indicators, and SES is an emergent latent variable. Cohen et al. (1990) give more examples and show the negative consequences of modeling the causal direction incorrectly.

Each latent variable should be assessed with at least three (Bentler & Chou, 1988) or four (Cohen et al., 1990) measured variables. It is better if those variables are composites rather than single items because single items are usually quite unreliable and have large error variances. In reality, researchers often have several measures for some of the constructs in the model but not all of them. Fortunately, it is possible to model any mix of measured variables that cause latent variables and of latent variables that cause measured ones. The relevant graphs and equations are straightforward extensions of examples already presented.

A particularly relevant example of a measured variable causing a latent variable is a randomized experiment in which the cause (assignment to treatment) is recorded as a 1,0 dummy variable and in which the effect is a latent variable assessed by several measures. Figure 12.5 is a graphic depiction of that experiment. The advantage of this model over the standard analysis (e.g., regression or ANOVA) is reduced unreliability of measurement in the dependent variable, thus increasing statistical power. However, latent variables also make a model more

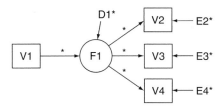

FIGURE 12.5 A randomized experiment with V1 representing assignment to treatment and F1 a latent dependent variable associated with three measured variables

complex in the number of parameters estimated, and their inclusion can complicate specification searches in a host of ways (Spirtes et al., 2000). Further, latent variable approaches are not necessary (Spirtes et al., 2000; Pearl, 2000) if instrumental variable approaches to estimating effects are used (Bollen, 1989; Foster & McLanahan, 1996) or if the emphasis is on bounding effects rather than estimating them (Manski & Nagin, 1998).

The Two Key Problems for Inferring Cause in Causal Models

Now that the basics of causal modeling have been covered, we can turn to its key problems—measurement error (errors in variables) and specification error (errors in equations). Understanding these errors clarifies causal inference in both experimental and nonexperimental data. Bollen (1989, especially Chapter 2) describes these problems in more statistical detail. Our goal is less ambitious: to expose the reader to the conceptual nature of the problem.

Measurement Error (Errors in Variables). The problem of measurement error is often called the problem of errors in variables, as observed variables almost always contain measurement error. Most researchers believe that such error always attenuates the relationship among variables. But this conclusion only applies to simple correlations or the multiple correlation between one variable and a composite of predictors. With regression and path coefficients, the effects of measurement error can be more complicated. First, the effects of measurement error in the predictor are different from those in the outcome—and much more devastating to causal inference. Errors in the predictor cause bias in regression estimates of the predictor's causal impact, whereas errors in the outcome do not cause this bias in unstandardized coefficients.[12] The basic reasons for this were outlined in Chapter 7,

---

12. Standardized coefficients are always reduced by unreliability in the outcome, whereas unreliability in the predictor can produce biases in any direction.

especially in the text describing Figure 7.8. Second, the effects of measurement error are complex when using more than one predictor. In multiple regression:

> If only one explanatory variable is subject to error, its regression coefficient is attenuated, but the extent of attenuation depends on the relation of the latent variable to the measured variable as well as its relation to the other explanatory variables. Furthermore the coefficients of the variables free of error are affected as well. Thus error even in a single variable can make itself felt through all of the coefficients. . . . The situation is further complicated if more than one variable is measured with error. Here any generalizations are difficult. In particular, measurement error does not always attenuate regression coefficients. Coefficients from equations that ignore error in variables can be higher, lower, or even the same as the true coefficients. (Bollen, 1989, pp. 166–167)

The coefficients can even change signs (e.g., from positive to negative) if error is ignored. The same conclusions extend to multiple equation path analysis models in which relationships among variables are even more complicated than in multiple regression. And all these problems get worse when reliabilities are unequal.

Hence, the goal of latent variable modeling is to separate errors of measurement (e.g., E1 through E6 in Figure 12.4) from omitted variables (e.g., D2 in Figure 12.4) and then estimate causal relationships only among latent variables from which errors of measurement have been removed. F1 represents only variance that V1, V2, and V3 share in common, as assessed by common covariance (or correlation). F1 cannot contain random measurement error because a variable that takes on only random values over participants (as random error must do by definition) cannot correlate with anything else, so it cannot contribute to shared covariance (within the limits of sampling error). Similarly, F1 cannot contain unique variance because unique variance by definition is not shared with other measures, and F1 contains only shared variance. Therefore F1 represents the reliable latent variable made up of what V1, V2, and V3 share in common.

Of course, the researcher still faces a construct validity question about what that latent variable is. For example, if the three measured variables are all measures of depression, the latent variable might be depression. But if all three measures are self-reports, the construct might well be self-report method or some combination of method and trait variance (e.g., self-reports of depression). In principle, we cannot know for sure what the correct label for the construct is. In both factor analysis and latent variable causal modeling, construct validity problems are always present.

Specification Error (Errors in Equations).   Unbiased path coefficients require a correctly specified path model, as well as perfectly reliable predictors. Models can be specified so many different ways that it is difficult to list all the requirements for accurate specification. Most generally, both the variables individually and the structural relationships among these variables must constitute the structure that gave rise to the data. We will see later that there are some ways of testing parts of the structure. But to overstate a little, to avoid specification error requires knowing in advance what the crucial constructs are and how they relate to each other. Causal modeling does not test this but only tests the strength of the relationships assuming that the model is true.

The best known cause of model misspecification is omission of relevant variables. A model is misspecified if it omits a variable that directly causes the effect *and* is related to a cause or a mediator in the model. A model is also misspecified if it incorrectly identifies whether a relationship is causal or correlational, what the functional form of that relationship is, what the direction of causality is, or whether a causal relationship is reciprocal or not. Finally, a model is misspecified if it incorrectly imposes (or fails to impose) possible parameter constraints, such as whether errors are correlated for the same variable measured consecutively over time. If such errors could be identified, they would change the path diagram, and therefore also the equations implied by the diagram. This is why the problem of specification error is sometimes called the problem of errors in equations. The problem concerns which variables belong in which equations, not whether there is error in those variables.

Except when modeling a simple randomized experiment without mediators, causal models typically yield path estimates of ambiguous internal validity. To explore the accuracy of these coefficients, Karlin (1987) suggests (1) examining the robustness of results when outliers in the data are present or removed, (2) replacing variables in the model with other variables alleged to assess the same construct, and (3) cross-validating the results with new samples. Mauro (1990) and Reichardt and Gollob (1986, 1987) suggest testing the effects that omitted variables might have on path coefficients, although they note that the results will frequently indicate that the bias might be large (James & Brett, 1984). None of these methods gives the same confidence as experimental control and will often decrease confidence in the coefficients from causal models by showing how sensitive results are to model assumptions.

A special model specification problem concerns equivalent models—models that propose different causal and correlational relationships among the same set of variables but yield *exactly* the same goodness of fit indices (e.g., chi-square tests of how well the model fits the data; Lee & Hershberger, 1990; MacCallum, Wegener, Uchino, & Fabrigar, 1993; Stelzl, 1986). For example, in Figure 12.1a, if the causal arrow ran from V2 to V1 instead of from V1 to V2 (deleting E2 and adding E1), the fit would still be identical to the fit in the model originally portrayed. Similarly, in Figure 12.2b the arrow between V2 and V3 could be reversed in direction, but the fit would be the same. However, the interpretation would be radically different in each case. Causal modeling by itself is incapable of telling us which model is correct. The addition of randomized or quasi-experimental design features can solve some of these problems (Pearl, 2000). In particular, such designs typically deliver treatment prior to measuring the outcome, and because cause does not operate backward in time, we know that the direction of causation must be from the treatment to the outcome. Similarly, if we measure mediators prior to the outcome, it would again make no sense to reverse the direction of the arrow between, say, V2 and V3 in

Figure 12.2b. So combining causal modeling with experimental and quasi-experimental design features can help rule out at least some equivalent models.

Fortunately, when the data analysis suggests that a model should be rejected, the chances are very good that it is not correctly specified (assuming the test of fit is not overly dependent on sample size; Bentler & Bonett, 1980). Given model rejection, most researchers engage in a specification search to find a different model that fits the data. Various technical aids to such searches have been developed (Bentler & Chou, 1990; Bollen, 1990; Glymour et al., 1987; Joreskog & Sorbom, 1990; MacCallum, 1986; Spirtes, Scheines, & Glymour, 1990a, 1990b), but they may capitalize on chance. So cross-validation on a new sample or on a random half of the original sample is desirable, although single sample criteria that try to approximate cross-validation are worth trying when sample sizes are small (Camstra & Boomsma, 1992). But even when specification searches are combined with cross-validation, there is no guarantee that the answer reached is the correct one.

Examples of Causal Modeling

Causal Modeling Within Randomized Experiments. The simplest randomized experiment tells us that an effect occurred. The addition of causal modeling helps explain the effect by modeling possible relationships among many molecular components of (1) the independent variable, (2) mediating variables, (3) moderating variables, and (4) the dependent variable. Therefore, the addition of causal modeling methods to randomized experiments is a welcome development, albeit one that is far too rarely used today. We distinguish this situation from using causal modeling techniques in quasi-experimental and nonexperimental research in which the underlying causal inference is itself often still in question and in which specification errors and measurement error will often add uncertainty about explanatory processes.

Wolchik and colleagues (1993) studied an intervention designed to help children at risk for poor mental health who lived in families in which the parents had divorced within the last 2 years. All mothers ($N = 70$) and one randomly selected child from each family were randomly assigned either to a wait-list control group or to an immediate intervention group. Although this sample is too small to give us much confidence in the exact results, that does not decrease the study's value for pedagogical purposes. The treatment group received 10 weekly sessions and 2 individual sessions designed to affect five mediators of positive mental health—the quality of the mother-child relationship, discipline, negative divorce events, contact with fathers, and support from nonparental adults. Wolchik et al. (1993) examined models for each mediator separately because the sample size made it statistically impractical to test a full model containing all five mediators. Figure 12.6 presents their model postulating that the quality of the mother-child relationship mediates effects. Note from the results that the intervention increased the quality of the mother-child relationship at posttest and that this in turn decreased the child's total behavior problems at posttest. The connection to generalization is that if we can

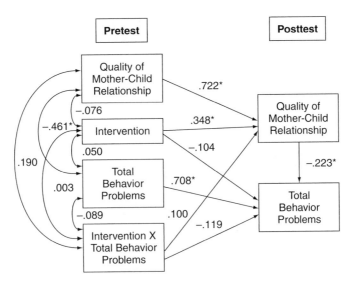

FIGURE 12.6 A mediational model from a randomized experiment

From "The Children of Divorce Parenting Intervention: Outcome evaluation of an empirically based program," by S. A. Wolchik, S. G. West, S. Westover, I. N. Sandler, A. Martin, J. Lustig, J.-Y. Tein, & J. Fisher, 1993, *American Journal of Community Psychology*, 21, p. 319. Copyright 1993 by Kluwer Academic/Plenum Publishers.

find other ways to increase the quality of the mother-child relationship, then these too should increase the odds that positive effects would be obtained.

Figure 12.6 has several instructive features. First, it includes pretest information, which in structural equation modeling functions much the same as analysis of covariance and so can improve the fit of the model. In this case, both pretests are highly related to their respective posttests. Second, assignment to the intervention is not significantly correlated with other variables at pretest, exactly what we expect to observe with random assignment. Third, the mediator was measured at posttest, so it is not really a mediator. It should have been measured between pretest and posttest at a time when it is believed from theory to exercise its mediating effect. Fourth, the model includes a term for the interaction of pretest status with the intervention, because previous analysis had shown that treatment group members with high pretest scores did better at posttest than control group members with high scores, whereas low scorers did about the same at posttest no matter which group they were in. This makes sense because treatment has little room to improve children with few behavior problems, but children with problems can be helped by an effective treatment.[13]

---

13. The programming of interaction terms as product variables in latent variable models can be complex (Kenny & Judd, 1984). Interactions can also be represented using multigroup models (Bentler, 1995).

Berk, Lenihan, and Rossi (1980) studied the Transitional Aid Research Project (TARP), which assumed that released prisoners return to crime because they have difficulty getting legal employment and are rarely eligible for welfare benefits. So released prisoners were randomly assigned to a control group or to several treatment groups that received varying levels of welfare payments over varying amounts of time. Analysis showed no overall causal relationship between the provision of payments and subsequent crime and showed that the treatments may have reduced rather than increased employment.

But the authors did not stop there. They constructed an explanatory model that is partially reproduced in Figure 12.7. Using (+) to indicate positive effects and (−) negative ones, we see that TARP payments were expected to decrease crime, to decrease a prisoner's incentive to gain legal employment, and so to decrease the time worked. In general, the hypothesized relationships are intuitive and need little explanation. However, the model postulates reciprocal causal relationships that introduce analytic complications. Also, the authors did not model assignment to conditions. They did not do so because not all the released prisoners who were assigned to receive payments actually did receive them. Because the authors reasoned that receipt of payment was the theoretically active variable, they included it in the model instead of the formal random assignment to eligibility for receipt of payments. This is a reasonable exploratory procedure, but it vitiates the integrity of causal inference because of the selection complications arising from the large numbers of prisoners receiving no payment at all. Today, instrumental variable approaches to modeling partial treatment implementation might be preferable (Angrist et al., 1996a).

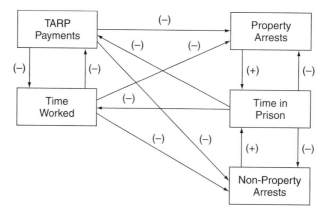

FIGURE 12.7 A model to explain TARP effects From "Crime and poverty: Some experimental evidence from ex-offenders," by R. A. Berk, K. J. Lenihan, and P. H. Rossi, 1980, *American Sociological Review, 45*, p.774. Copyright 1980 by the American Sociological Association. Adapted with permission.

The overall analysis suggested that the effects of random assignment to TARP were zero. The model helps explain why. Figure 12.7 contains mediating processes with different causal signs. The direct effects of TARP payments on arrests are negative; that is, TARP payments reduced subsequent arrests, as predicted. But the indirect effects of TARP payments on arrests are positive; that is, TARP payments indirectly increased arrests. We can see why this may have occurred. TARP payments decreased the amount of time a prisoner worked in legal employment, and the more an ex-prisoner worked on the job, the less time was spent in crime. Statistically, the path from TARP payments to time worked is negative, as is the path from time worked to both arrest variables. Because the effect of this indirect path is calculated by multiplying the component paths together, multiplying two negative path coefficients yields a positive number that cancels the negative direct effect of TARP on arrests and so leads to the overall conclusion of no effect. Thus the mediational model paints a more complex and perhaps informative picture than the analysis without mediators. Both are legitimate, though, because TARP did not make a difference in the aggregate, and policymakers need to know this. But knowing about the mediational process helps us better understand the exact circumstances under which we might and might not expect an effect in the future. Berk et al. (1980) conclude that future research should use incentives for the ex-felon to gain legitimate employment by increasing payments temporarily even when legitimate employment is obtained.[14]

Alwin and Tessler (1985) illustrate the use of latent variables in a $2 \times 2 \times 2$ randomized factorial design that sought to simulate an initial session between a counselor and client. The three dichotomous factors were therapist experience, value similarity between client and counselor, and formality of the counselor. Ninety-six females were randomly assigned to one of the resulting eight cells. The outcome constructs were client self-reports of satisfaction with the counselor-client relationship and with progress in solving the presenting problem. Each independent variable was assessed with three manipulation checks and each dependent construct with four observed measures, thus allowing analysis using latent variables. The resulting model is portrayed in Figure 12.8. To keep the figure tractable, it does not include the measurement models for the latent variables; the full portrayal is in Alwin and Tessler (1985, Figure 4.9).

Figure 12.8 has several interesting characteristics. First, it illustrates how an explanatory model benefits by breaking the dependent variable down into components (relationship satisfaction versus problem satisfaction). The coefficients show that the independent variables affected these two components differently. Relationship satisfaction is lower when the counselor is more formal but is hardly related to therapist experience, whereas problem satisfaction is highest with greater therapist experience and is hardly related to formality. Value similarity has

---

14. See Cronbach (1982) for useful critiques of both the experimental and nonexperimental features of the TARP study.

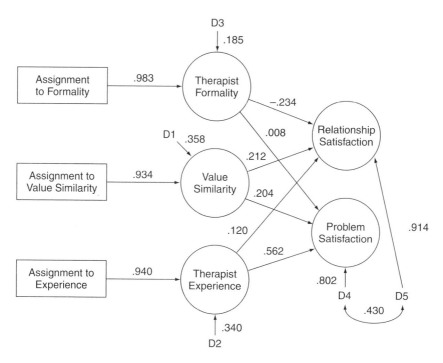

FIGURE 12.8 Randomized experiment with latent variables and multiple component outcome Adapted from "Causal models, unobserved variables, and experimental data," by D. F. Alwin and R. C. Tessler, 1985, *Causal models in panel and experimental designs,* edited by H. M. Blalock, New York: Aldine.

very modest but consistently positive influences on both kinds of satisfaction. This allows us to specify better the conditions under which each cause will be effective. Second, Figure 12.8 includes a measured (dummy) variable with values of 1 or 0 for each of the three independent variables. They are part of the structural equation rather than the measurement model. Each assignment variable is assessed by three manipulation checks. The large coefficients from treatment assignment to the manipulation checks indicate a high degree of convergent validity, whereas the lack of need to postulate paths from assignment variables to checks for a different manipulation indicates a high degree of discriminant validity. The construct validity of each manipulation is supported thereby.

Some Problems with Causal Models That Are Built into Randomized Experiments. Adding causal modeling to randomized experiments is not problem free. As in any causal model, when constructs are represented only by variables with measurement error, path coefficients may be biased. Figures 12.6 and 12.7 incur

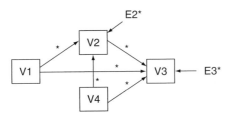

FIGURE 12.9 If V4 is omitted from the model, biased path estimates may result

this problem because all their mediators and outcomes presumably have measurement error. However, the independent variables in a randomized experiment may be assumed to be measured without error, as with the intervention main effect in Figure 12.6. But in Figure 12.7, the TARP payments variable may be measured with error. Figure 12.8 reduces many of these errors-in-variables problems by using latent variables. However, even when all variables are measured perfectly, omitted variables can still cause bias in mediational models used to explain the results of randomized experiments. Figure 12.9 illustrates this problem (Judd & Kenny, 1981b). Suppose that another variable (V4) causes both the mediator and outcome and is not included in the model. If the model is estimated as Figure 12.2a or 12.2b, or as Figures 12.6 or 12.7, then the path coefficients may be biased.[15]

Also, such models are more complex than the simple ANOVA or regression models often used to test explanations, and the individual parts of the model may be tested with somewhat less power than otherwise unless sample size is increased. If maximum likelihood techniques are used to estimate model parameters, then assumptions of multivariate normality must hold (West, Finch, & Curran, 1995, describe how to deal with nonnormality). Such models can be unstable or biased if some relationships among variables are nonlinear but are modeled as linear (Kenny & Judd, 1984). And estimates are most accurate and stable with large sample sizes (e.g., N = 300; Boomsma, 1987; but see Tanaka et al., 1990) or when cross-validation is possible (Camstra & Boomsma, 1992). Such sources of potential instabilities should always be explored by respecifying the model in competing ways, omitting some variables and changing relationships among others, to see if the value of the path(s) of interest changes.

---

15. Hence, although Figure 12.8 solved many important measurement problems by using latent variables, it introduced a model specification problem. Each of the three assignment variables was assumed to be measured perfectly and each caused a latent variable represented by the manipulation checks. As pointed out earlier with this model, the cause-effect relationships between treatment assignment and the manipulation checks are part of the structural rather than the measurement model. In effect, therefore, the latent manipulation checks caused by the assignment variables have the same statistical status as any mediator variables and therefore potentially bias path coefficients for the reasons outlined in the previous paragraph. Exactly which coefficients are biased depends on the model being tested.

A final problem in mediational modeling occurs if the mediator and the dependent variable are measured simultaneously (Baron & Kenny, 1986), as in Figure 12.6. We do not know then if the mediator caused the outcome, if the outcome caused the mediator, or if there is reciprocal causation between the two. Researchers should measure the mediator at the time the causal mediating process is presumed to be maximal in impact and certainly prior to assessing the dependent variable. Unfortunately, few theories are specific enough to predict such time periods. This is a problem because there is little value to using a mediator before it has varied much as a consequence of treatment or before it has had a chance to affect the major outcomes of interest. Thus it is best if the tests of a mediational model could be followed by another randomized experiment in which the mediator itself becomes the independent variable to see if it affects the outcome in question. We describe such research shortly.

Summary. Overall, then, the use of causal modeling within randomized experiments has many advantages (Baron & Kenny, 1986). It forces the researcher to be more specific about the theoretical model that is thought to bring about the effect. It allows the researcher to investigate the antecedents and consequences of any mediational process measured and to test whether the independent variable directly causes the dependent variable or indirectly causes it through one or more mediating variables, or whether both direct and indirect effects occur. And, if several measures of a construct are gathered, it is possible to analyze relationships among latent variables to get more accurate effect estimates.

Causal Modeling with Quasi-Experimental and Nonexperimental Data. Imagine the causal models in Figures 12.1 through 12.5 being generated from a quasi-experimental or nonexperimental study. The key problems for causal modeling are still the same—measurement error and specification error. Latent variable models can still be used to reduce measurement error. But specification error is much more problematic than with causal modeling within an experimental framework. Sometimes the researcher is willing to assume that treatment and control groups were practically equivalent at pretest even though they were not formally equivalent on expectations, thus justifying the use of causal modeling to explore potential explanations for an effect. But such an assumption is almost always tenuous in the absence of random assignment, even when tests suggest that the groups are quite similar on observed scores at pretest (Rogers, Howard, & Vessey, 1993). Sometimes causal modeling is the only available means to examine the potential causal role of variables that cannot be experimentally manipulated (e.g., gender) or that would be unethical to manipulate (e.g., assignment to carcinogens). Rather than give up causal language entirely for such topics, causal modeling is a viable alternative

---

16. Type I error rates were not corrected for the number of tests done, so this one significant result may have been due to chance. However, MacKinnon et al. (1991) also note that statistical tests of mediated effects have reduced power (Baron & Kenny, 1986).

(Shadish, 1992a). Depending on the particular circumstances, each of these might be a good reason to try causal modeling, even though none of the reasons gives the same confidence that a well-implemented randomized experiment gives.

An example from a quasi-experiment is provided by MacKinnon and colleagues (1991). They examined 42 schools participating in a study of the effects of a drug prevention program. Of these schools, 8 were randomly assigned to treatment or control groups, 14 were assigned to the control group because they would not reschedule their activities to accommodate the research, and 20 were assigned to the treatment group because they were willing to reschedule. Comparison of the treatment and control groups showed few significant differences on a host of pretest variables. However, students in the treatment group reported more resistance skills and stronger negative attitudes toward marijuana than did control group students, both of which probably bias results toward making the treatment look effective. Using the LISREL 7 structural equation models program (Joreskog & Sorbom, 1988), MacKinnon et al. (1991) reported 12 mediational analyses of these data, of which only one was clearly significant.[16] Students who participated in treatment seemed to care more about their friends' reactions to drug use, which in turn discouraged alcohol use. In this example, it might have been useful to examine the mediational models separately for those 8 schools randomly assigned versus those 34 not randomly assigned to see if they yielded the same results, though the small number of randomized schools might make this test relatively insensitive. Finally, MacKinnon et al. (1991) used school means as the unit of analysis, an appropriate choice given the limited technology available for doing multilevel mediational modeling at that time. However, that technology is rapidly improving, so that more appropriate analyses might now be possible (e.g., Krull & MacKinnon, 1999; MacKinnon et al., 1995).

An example from a nonexperimental study is provided by Tracey, Sherry, and Keitel (1986), who studied how psychological distress among college students was affected by (1) student sense of self-efficacy, (2) the discrepancy between what students wanted in their dorm and what they perceived their dorm to be like (perceived person-environment discrepancy), and (3) the discrepancy between what students wanted and the average of what the other students in the dorm perceived the dorm to be like (actual person-environment discrepancy). A mediational analysis found that both self-efficacy and perceived person-environment discrepancy had direct effects on distress but that the effects of actual person-environment fit were mediated through help seeking—the more the actual discrepancy, the more help seeking, which then reduced distress—presumably because the help seeker obtained treatment for distress. This model also used latent variables to cope with measurement error. However, specification error is clearly a problem, given likely selection biases in particular. Do students have greater self-efficacy because they have less psychological distress? Do those who perceive social relationships to be congruous also have less distress? These models represent what the world could be like, which may or may not be the same as what it is like. Too many untested assumptions are involved to ever confidently believe in the test.

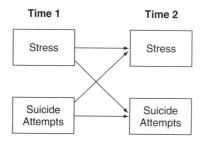

FIGURE 12.10 A cross-lagged panel correlation study

Another nonexperimental example is the **cross-lagged panel** correlation design, first suggested by Lazarsfeld (1947, 1948), and reinvented by Pelz and Andrews (1964) and Campbell (1963; Campbell & Stanley, 1963). Its simplest form consists of two variables, one presumed to be the cause and the other the effect, each measured at two times ideally separated by the length of time it takes for the cause to influence the effect. As Figure 12.10 shows, it is possible to compute six correlations among these four variables. The correlation between cause and effect measured at the same time is called a synchronous correlation. The correlation between the same variable at different times is called a stability correlation (or autocorrelation); and the correlation between the two different variables at different times is called a cross-lagged correlation. As originally conceived, the intuition was that if we have identified the true causal agent correctly, then the cross-lagged correlation between cause at Time 1 and effect at Time 2 should be larger than the correlation between the effect at Time 1 and the cause at Time 2. Today, the emphasis would be on estimating the path coefficients rather than the observed correlations (e.g., Bagozzi & Warshaw, 1992; Bentler & Speckart, 1981; Cramer, 1990). The design can be extended by adding more variables at each time and more times (panels).

However, this design is subject to the same general problems that all passive observation studies are—measurement and specification errors (Rogosa, 1980). Although the measurement problem can be ameliorated with latent variable modeling, the specification errors cannot be so easily addressed, particularly those associated with omitted variables that causally produced the data. Unless the reader is willing to become an advanced student of the design (e.g., Campbell & Kenny, 1999; Kenny, 1979; Kenny & Harackiewicz, 1979; Mayer, 1986), we cannot recommend the design any more highly than other causal modeling techniques within a nonexperimental framework. There are some special circumstances in which it might be more useful than the standard cross-sectional path analysis (Campbell & Kenny, 1999), but it will take a student familiar with both methods to recognize them.

Numerous other examples exist of the application of causal modeling techniques to quasi-experimental and nonexperimental data (e.g., Crano & Mendoza, 1987; Gallini & Bell, 1983; Kline, Canter, & Robin, 1987; Patterson, 1986). Critiques of these applications are numerous, often compelling (Freedman, 1987), with complexities acknowledged even by advocates of the techniques (Schoenberg, 1989; see also the entire issue of *Journal of Educational Statistics,* 1987, Volume 12, Number 2). It is difficult to appreciate how tenuous causal inferences really can be in such data. So it is worth ending with a simple and memorable observation. Measurement error and specification error combine with quasi-experimental or nonexperimental data to make nearly any empirical result possible no matter what the true causal relationships may be. Even the commonly made observation that a nonzero correlation indicates the possibility of causation—because correlation is a prerequisite to causation—is wrong with nonexperimental data:

> Many researchers suggest that a bivariate association between a cause and effect is a *necessary* condition to establish causality. The occurrence of suppressor relations casts doubt on this claim: no bivariate association can occur although a causal relation links two variables. The old saying that correlation does not prove causation should be complemented by the saying that *a lack of correlation does not disprove causation.* It is only when we isolate the cause and effect from all other influences that correlation is a necessary condition of causation. (Bollen, 1989, p. 52; italics in original)

Observed bivariate correlations can be too high, too low, spurious, or accurate (as indices of causation) depending on the pattern of relationships among the variables in the structure that actually generated the data (Alexander, Barrett, Alliger, & Carson, 1986); and controlling confounding variables does not ensure that bias is reduced in nonexperimental data (Greenland & Robins, 1986).

Instrumental Variable Approaches to Mediational Models

Some recent work has approached mediational modeling using instrumental variables (Robins, 2000; Robins & Greenland, 1992). The principle is similar to that outlined in Chapter 10 for using random assignment as an instrument to measure the effects of treatment-as-received in a study with incomplete treatment implementation (Angrist et al., 1996a), but the mediator takes the place of the treatment implementation. Holland (1988) used this approach to study mediational effects in an experiment in which students were randomly assigned to being encouraged or not encouraged to study. To meet the conditions for an instrumental variable, he made the plausible assumption that random assignment to encouragement did not directly affect test scores but rather only indirectly affected them through the mediator of amount of time studied. Similarly, Ludwig, Duncan, and Hirschfield (1998) used this method to analyze mediational effects in the Moving to Opportunity Experiment that randomly assigned participants to one of two interventions (or a control) to improve housing and so reduce juvenile crime, with the mediator being neighborhood poverty rates. Sobel (2000) notes that this approach may be more appropriate than structural equation modeling but also that it makes the restrictive assumption that the effect of the mediator on outcome is identical for all participants. The recency of the method and the rarity with which it has been used makes it difficult to know its flaws or whether its assumptions will generally prove plausible (e.g., no interactions between cause and mediator). Given the rapid development of instrumental variable models in general in statistics, however, we suspect that this approach will be used more often as its strengths and weaknesses become more widely understood.

Experiments That Manipulate Explanations

In the example earlier in this chapter of medical care evaluation (MCE) committees, Maxwell et al. (1986) identified lengthy, high-level discussions of patients and problems as likely explanations of why some MCEs were more successful than others. But there is a problem with their approach of splitting the six MCEs into those with and without such discussions. MCEs were not randomly assigned to different levels of discussion, and so selection biases are confounded with the nature of the discussion. Did MCEs with higher levels of discussion also have physicians who were more extraverted and so better at interacting with patients and at obtaining better diagnostic information? Is it physician extraversion rather than MCE discussions that explained the relationship obtained? Because we do not know the answers to such questions, a logical next step would be to do an experiment in which physicians are randomly assigned to MCEs with or without high-level discussions.

For instance, family therapy research suggests that behavior modification procedures are effective in reducing child behavior problems. Eyberg and Johnson (1974) conducted a study exploring the causal mechanisms. Behavioral theory and anecdotal evidence from therapists suggested that behavior therapy effects might be mediated by the number of contingent reinforcements, with the effect increasing as the number of reinforcements grows. Hence they assigned parents randomly to two conditions that received standard behavior modification techniques, but they varied whether parents were or were not required (1) to make a financial deposit that would be returned if participation in treatment was satisfactory, (2) to make sure tasks that the therapist assigned to the family between therapy sessions were complete before another session could be scheduled, and (3) to contact the therapist only rarely by phone unless the family had completed those assigned tasks. Although both groups improved, the group with more contingencies improved significantly more than the other group. The principle involved here is to vary the presumed explanatory mechanism systematically to show its operations, to distinguish it from other possible explanations, and to identify any variables on which the relationship between the cause and effect is stably dependent.

Similarly, Klesges, Vasey, and Glasgow (1986) noted that many antismoking programs had been implemented in work sites at which it was possible to reach large numbers of smokers quickly and easily. But the results were mixed. One possible explanation of this was that employee participation in the antismoking programs was highly variable, and such participation was a prerequisite to reducing smoking through this program. Hence they designed a quasi-experiment in which all participating employees at five worksites received a stop-smoking program, but at four of them employees also participated in various competitions and incentive programs aimed at increasing participation. As predicted, the competition conditions increased participation and also resulted in better quit rates at 6 months.

There is some general methodological theory to help guide this explanatory research (Mark, 1986). The first two suggestions are borrowed from medicine. *Blockage models* assume that a certain drug operates through a particular physiological process, as when a drug decreases psychological depression through producing an opiatelike chemical. To provide evidence for this mechanism, the researcher may inject patients with a chemical known to block the production of opiates, and if the action of the drug to reduce depression is then reduced or eliminated, this supports opiate production as a mediating mechanism. If this version of the model is not practical to test in field experimentation—as when ethical considerations preclude it—the researcher can still use a laboratory analogue study to complement knowledge gained from the field experiment. In *enhancement models,* the researcher hypothesizes a mechanism that may enhance effectiveness, then injects a drug known to produce that mechanism to see if the overall effect is increased. And finally, Mark (1986) suggests a *pattern matching model* in which the researcher hypothesizes more than one mediating process, each of which would produce a different pattern of outcomes. Suppose that researchers accepted that psychotherapy of Type X produced Outcome A, and suppose further that one could develop at least two different mechanisms to explain this result. Explanation 1 might predict Outcome A but also Outcome B and C, whereas Explanation 2 might predict Outcome D and E. If information on all five outcome measures is obtained and is approximately equally valid, then the data analysis can explore which pattern of results is obtained. Mark (1986) points out that, by the logic of predicted pattern matching outlined in our earlier chapters on quasi-experimentation, such pattern matching also helps the basic local molar causal inference.

However, all these examples are about how single experiments can manipulate potential mediators to determine their effects. Given the large number of potential mediators that it is usually reasonable to hypothesize in a full mediational model, any single study can make, at best, only a partial contribution to understanding the full mediational model that may apply. Consequently, experimental manipulations of mediators are more productive and more convincing when done as programs of research. The next chapter discusses this further.

CONCLUSION

It may be useful to remind ourselves of the overall argument of the last two chapters. The classic method in statistics for constructing generalizable knowledge is formal probability sampling. But such sampling is rarely feasible when generalizing about causal connections. These two chapters outlined an alternative theory: that useful knowledge about the generalized causal inference can be constructed using five principles that are grounded in how scientists make such generalizations in their daily work. This chapter discussed methods for implementing this theory in single studies. But single studies are inevitably limited in how they represent persons, settings, treatments, and outcomes. Fortunately, researchers are not always limited to generalizing from single studies. Sometimes many studies have been conducted on the same general causal questions. In these cases, it can be quite beneficial to apply the five principles to these multiple studies. In the next chapter we develop this theme, with a special focus on the use of meta-analysis.

13

Generalized Causal Inference: Methods for Multiple Studies

Mul·ti·ple (mŭl′tə-pəl): [French from Old French from Late Latin *multiplum, a multiple*: Latin *multi*-, multi- + Latin -plus, *-fold*]. adj. Having, relating to, or consisting of more than one individual, element, part, or other component; manifold.

Meta - or **met-**: [Greek from *meta,* beside, after; see *me-²* in Indo-European Roots.] pref. 1. a. Later in time: *metestrus.* b. At a later stage of development: *metanephros.* 2. Situated behind: *metacarpus.* 3. a. Change; transformation: *metachromatism.* b. Alternation: *metagenesis.* 4. a. Beyond; transcending; more comprehensive: *metalinguistics.* b. At a higher state of development: *metazoan.*

SMITH AND Glass (1977) reported the results of a massive quantitative summary of 375 studies of psychotherapy effectiveness (later expanded to 475 studies; M. Smith, Glass, & Miller, 1980). The studies were conducted over many years, over different geographic areas with diverse clients, using different kinds of therapies and outcome measures. Over all this variability, clients receiving psychotherapy had better outcomes than control clients who received no treatment. Therapy outcomes were similar whether the therapies were behavioral or nonbehavioral, whatever the level of therapist experience, and however long therapy lasted. With a few exceptions, the effects of therapy generalized over great heterogeneity in many moderators across these studies. This study was a meta-analysis, a powerful tool for generalized causal inference that has emerged over the past few decades, and one of several methods we discuss in this chapter for generalizing from multiple studies.

GENERALIZING FROM SINGLE VERSUS MULTIPLE STUDIES

The previous chapter discussed generalizations from single studies. Unfortunately, single studies rarely have the large and heterogeneous samples of persons, settings, times, treatments, and outcome measures that are useful for confident generalization; and single studies rarely use diverse methodologies. By contrast, multiple studies usually have greater diversity in most or all of these things. This variation in study features allows us to conduct better tests of generalized causal inference.

One way this can be done is with programs of research on the same topic by the *same* researcher (or in the same lab). Such programs allow a more directed investigation of variables that bear on generalized causal inference. A researcher can systematically vary important variables from study to study, slowly homing in on a more refined understanding of the targets of generalization, the variables that might bound or limit generalization, and the mediators that might explain it. Another way this can be done is with summaries of multiple studies on the same topic by *different* researchers, especially quantitative summaries from meta-analyses. These summaries allow both more precise estimates of effects than could be had from single studies and better exploration of how causal relationships might change over variation in study features. This kind of analysis helps clarify the nature of the relationship, its boundaries, its behavior within those boundaries, and its explanations. Further, the wider base on which this knowledge is based often results in more credibility than claims based on single studies. This is especially the case when an intervention nearly always does better than an alternative or remains robustly positive over many potential contingencies. Conversely, an intervention that sometimes does better and sometimes worse or that sometimes causes harm may be less valued, especially if the contingencies leading to negative outcomes are unknown or cannot be easily modified. In the material that follows, we present more details about these different ways in which generalized causal inferences are facilitated by using multiple studies.

MULTISTUDY PROGRAMS OF RESEARCH

Multistudy programs of research offer the researcher great control over exactly which aspects of generalized causal inference are examined from study to study, so that the researcher can pursue precisely the questions that most need answering at any given moment in time. However, these programs also require much more time and funding than any other method we cover. Sometimes that funding is provided by government agencies that direct programs of research using many investigators, sites, and methods; and sometimes it is available on a much smaller level to individual investigators who, using both external and intramural support, direct programs of research in their labs over time.

Phased Models of Increasingly Generalizable Studies

One approach to generalized causal inference is the so-called *phase* model that appears in several closely related guises. In the United States, several federal agencies fund or review health research, for example, the National Institutes of Health or the Food and Drug Administration. These agencies often fund research that proceeds in phases, from basic research discoveries to applications to human health in real world settings. The details of those phases differ from agency to agency and over time, but Greenwald and Cullen's (1984) description of five phases of cancer research is typical. Before the phases begin, basic research occurs on the effects of a treatment on particular kinds of cancer cells in test tubes and on artificially induced tumors in animals. Eventually, an idea for a treatment seems plausible based on this research. Phase I then reviews existing basic and applied research to see if a testable hypothesis about a new cancer agent can be developed. Phase II moves to method development to ensure that accurate and valid research procedures and technology are available to study the effects of that agent. Phase III is the conduct of controlled intervention trials to test the efficacy of the cancer agent, that is, whether it will work under ideal circumstances that may differ from the circumstances of eventual application. Phase IV consists of **effectiveness** studies with defined populations to see if the treatment works in particular populations of interest under conditions of real-world implementation. In Phase V field studies aimed at entire communities are done to see whether the treatment will affect public health at large.

Doing all this is time-consuming and expensive. For example, Folkman's (1996) program of research on angiogenesis inhibitors occurred over several decades in the late 20th century, beginning with basic laboratory research to understand how cancers develop blood supplies and how those supplies could be impacted. Promising results in animal models occurred in the mid-1990s, and it took more time for other scientists to learn how to replicate those results so they could be used elsewhere. The first human clinical trials on the pertinent agents (e.g., endostatin) began in 1999, testing a range of possible doses on small numbers of diverse cancer patients so as to gauge toxicity and maximum effective doses. Preliminary results from those trials came out in late 2000 showing a small but promising benefit, and more trials will be forthcoming, probably for decades. Those trials might explore whether the drugs work best alone or in combination with other treatments, whether they affect different cancer outcomes differentially (e.g., blood tests, time to metastases, survival time), whether they are equally effective with different kinds of cancers, and so forth. Fields such as medicine have a strong tradition of supporting such time-consuming and expensive research.

Other fields have insufficient funding or interest in doing so. We address the latter problem in the last chapter.

Nonetheless, this phased approach excels at exploring generalized causal inference. It relies on purposive sampling of persons, settings, times, outcomes, and treatments, and all five principles of causal explanation can be seen, for example: (1) surface similarity in the use of human cancer cell lines to create comparable tumors on animals; (2) ruling out irrelevancies in deliberately making patient characteristics diverse, such as the type of cancer, age, and gender of patient in early dosage-toxicity trials; (3) making discriminations about which kinds of cancers are most and least affected; (4) interpolation and extrapolation in varying drug doses in initial trials to see how both toxicity and clinical response might vary over that continuum; and (5) causal explanation in developing models of how a drug acts on human cancer cells so that the potency of that action can be increased.

Directed Programs of Experiments

In these programs, the aim is to systematically investigate over many experiments the explanatory variables (moderators, mediators, constructs) that may account for an effect, gradually refining generalizations. These programs may be conducted by one investigator in one lab over time or by multiple investigators in multiple labs at the same time. A series of experiments on diffusion of responsibility illustrates. The experiments were partly prompted by the 1964 murder of a woman named Kitty Genovese who was stabbed repeatedly for over half an hour while nearly 40 neighbors watched but did nothing to help. Why would no one help, or even call the police? In more than 30 experiments, Latané and his colleagues (Latané & Darley, 1970; Latané & Nida, 1981) demonstrated that one explanation was diffusion of responsibility: when many other people are present, people assume that surely someone else will act, and this assumption increases in strength the more people are present. All the experiments embodied prototypical features of the constructs of interest (surface similarity). For example, all had bystanders present who could offer help with a problem they witnessed; the situation always involved an event of some obvious and immediate harm, such as a medical problem or a robbery; and the key outcome always involved helping behavior appropriate to the problem. The experiments were done in diverse venues—a woman falling and spraining her ankle, smoke coming into a room from a fire, someone having an epileptic seizure, shoplifting, or a cash register being robbed (ruling out irrelevancies). The researchers also varied the number of bystanders present, finding that one bystander who is watching alone is very likely to help, but with more than three bystanders the probability of helping is very low and gradually levels off at a low level of helping with very large numbers of bystanders (interpolation-extrapolation). However, if one bystander is particularly qualified to help by virtue of his or her social role—if a medical student or emergency room nurse is known to be present during a medical emergency—then the number of bystanders becomes nearly irrelevant, and that expert is nearly always expected to respond in place of the other bystanders (making discriminations).

In this example, the experiments were relatively short, inexpensive, and simple to do. So they could be repeated many times, facilitating greater confidence that the mechanism being studied does indeed generalize over settings, persons, treatments, outcome, and times. Such programs are less feasible for the larger social experiments with which this book is primarily concerned because the latter are costly, time-consuming, and logistically complex. Still, examples of such programs do exist. Olds and his colleagues (Kitzman et al., 1997; Korfmacher, O'Brien, Hiatt, & Olds, 1999; Olds et al., 1997; Olds et al., 1998; Olds, Henderson, Kitzman, & Cole, 1995) have investigated the effects of home visits by nurses to pregnant women and parents of young children. In that program, they investigated the generalizability of effects over (1) low socioeconomic status urban African American women versus low socioeconomic status rural European-American women, (2) nurses versus paraprofessionals, (3) immediate outcome to 15-year follow-up, and (4) diverse outcomes such as child abuse and neglect, maternal life course, child malnutrition, childhood injuries, repeated childbearing, pregnancy outcome, and children's subsequent criminal and antisocial behavior. Here we see diversity in persons, settings, treatments, outcomes, and times, with primary emphasis on searching for moderators (both irrelevant and discriminating) to clarify the bounds of the effect, on treatment implementation to understand mediating mechanisms, and on interpolation and extrapolation over time.

Similarly, Lichtenstein, Glasgow, and Abrams (1986) reported five smoking cessation experiments that manipulated a mediator. Preliminary research and observations had led them to hypothesize that the effects of smoking cessation interventions were mediated by how much social support the participant received. So, in these five studies, the investigators compared a cognitive-behavior-therapy smoking cessation program with the same program with a social support component added to it. Although four of the five studies found correlational evidence that social support was related to outcome, the manipulations themselves showed no difference between conditions with and without support. The authors offered a number of possible explanations for this failure, for example, that the manipulations did not induce social support at a level that was adequate to affect outcome and that significant effects might have been revealed had breakdowns by gender or by need for social support been done.

NARRATIVE REVIEWS OF EXISTING RESEARCH

Given the time and expense of conducting programs of research that explore generalizability, a more common strategy is to review existing literature for clues about generalized causal inference. The advantages and disadvantages of such reviews are the opposite of programs of research: they take substantially less time and funds to do, but they limit the researcher to questions and variables that have already been studied in the literature. This section describes narrative reviews, and a subsequent section describes quantitative reviews.

Narrative Reviews of Experiments

These reviews describe the existing literature using narrative descriptions without attempting the quantitative syntheses of study results that are characteristic of the meta-analyses we cover shortly. For instance, Gurman and Kniskern (1978) reviewed more than 200 studies on the effects of marital and family psychotherapy, describing the characteristics of studies and the general direction of results using extensive tables and text. The studies they reviewed were conducted by different authors who used diverse methodologies and outcome assessments with different kinds of clients and in different settings, applying different versions of marital or family therapies of varying duration. Gurman and Kniskern (1978) concluded that these therapies were generally effective, as assessed by whether those who received family or marital therapies significantly outperformed those given the control conditions. For example, they found that marital-family therapies outperformed no-treatment control groups in 18 studies, performed no better than controls in 11 studies, and did worse in 2 studies. Similarly, behavioral marital therapies outperformed controls in 7 of 11 studies, and behavioral family therapies were superior to controls in all 5 relevant studies. This kind of counting of wins, ties, and losses is often referred to as the *box score* or *vote counting* approach to reviewing effectiveness studies (Hedges & Olkin, 1985, in press). The reviewer relies on statistical significance levels to draw conclusions about intervention effectiveness, counting one vote in favor of intervention effectiveness if a therapy significantly outperformed the comparison group, one vote against it if it significantly underperformed, and a tie vote if the two groups were not significantly different. Summarizing these votes suggests whether treatment works over studies.

Such a review also allows examination of potential moderators of the generalizability of intervention effects. For example, Gurman and Kniskern (1978) reported that short-term therapies tended to be as effective as long-term therapies and that clients did as well with a less experienced therapist as with a more experienced therapist—so the effect generalized over dose and therapist experience levels. Failure to generalize can also be of great interest. For instance, marital therapy worked better when both partners were involved in therapy compared with treating only one partner. And with chronic and acute hospital inpatients, only interventions based on systems theory were reported to work well—nothing else.

Narrative Reviews Combining Experimental and Nonexperimental Research

Narrative reviews may include not only field experiments but also evidence from surveys, animal studies, and basic laboratory bench work in order to match the evidence across these studies to a pattern that would be consistent with and explain an effect and clarify its generalizability. For example, Dwyer and Flesch-Janys (1995) summarized a pattern of evidence to support a causal link between the spraying of Agent Orange during the Vietnam War and the subsequent incidence of cancer among those exposed to spraying. Some studies showed that tissue and blood toxin levels among those in sprayed areas were 6 times greater than among those in unsprayed areas, whereas there was no such difference for other toxins. They also showed that sources of the toxin other than Agent Orange were not locally available in highly sprayed areas. Next, they used both animal experiments and human epidemiology studies to show that this toxin was associated with increased cancer—even in animals who were typically most resistant to acute toxic effects and in humans in both the United States and Germany who had unusually high exposure levels (in Germany because they manufactured Agent Orange). The findings held over a variety of kinds and sites of cancer. The authors also showed a consistency of evidence about the causal mechanisms through which Agent Orange might produce cancer in both humans and animals. By combining these multiple sources of evidence, Dwyer and Flesch-Janys (1995) made a convincing case for the plausibility of the link between Agent Orange and cancer in Vietnam, the explanation for that link, and its generalizability.

Such reviews are particularly useful when direct experimental manipulation of the treatment would be unethical with humans (e.g., Agent Orange) or impossible (e.g., gender, past events). In such cases, experimental manipulation with animals, basic laboratory research, and existing theoretical knowledge can be combined with quasi-experimental and observational data on naturally occurring variability in the treatment to clarify an effect and its generalizability. However, results of these reviews can be controversial, with critics pointing to methodological inadequacies in the research. The causal relationship between smoking and cancer is a case in point. For ethical reasons, much of the research on this topic is correlational and quasi-experimental. Though the link seems reasonably well accepted today, it was disputed by such eminent scientists as Sir Ronald Fisher and Hans Eysenck (Grossarth-Maticek & Eysenck, 1989; Pearl, 2000). Today, the connection between second-hand smoke and cancer is similarly controversial, with the controversies rising substantially from methodological uncertainties (Gross, 1993; Rockette, 1993).

Problems with Narrative Reviews

Narrative reviews have great strengths that cannot be matched by the quantitative methods we cover below—for hypothesis generation, for thick description of a literature, and for theory development with qualitative categories and relationships among variables. But for the assessment of generalized causal inference, narrative reviews have some disadvantages.[1]

First, as the number of studies increases, it becomes increasingly difficult for reviewers to keep straight all the relationships between effects and potential moderators that might be important. Here the situation is no different from that of primary studies in which we find it difficult to summarize all the data from all respondents using only narrative descriptions. Partly for this reason, we use numbers to represent observations. They help us to keep track of data, to organize it more efficiently, and to analyze relationships among data more readily. Something is inevitably lost in going from narrative description to numbers, of course, leading many researchers to use both methods in primary studies (Reichardt & Rallis, 1994). But still, the benefits of numbers can be considerable.

Second, narrative reviews traditionally rely on box score summaries of results generated from the significance tests of study outcomes. But this information is very limited. A significant effect means that the observed group differences are unlikely to occur by chance in a population in which there is no intervention effect. It tells us very little about the size of the difference between groups. A very small difference between groups might be statistically significant in a study with a very large sample size, even if the size of the difference has no practical importance at all. Or a very large difference might be nonsignificant in a study with a small sample size, even if it were important practically (Kazdin & Bass, 1989; Mosteller et al., 1980). So information about effect size has come to be highly valued by those who review literatures on the effects of interventions.

Third, narrative reviews are not very precise in their descriptions of study results. Suppose that a reviewer uses a box score approach, and it suggests that 5 of 10 studies produced nonsignificant results. This summary could result from one of two patterns. In one, the five statistically significant results could report Type I error rates of $p < .001$ and the five nonsignificant ones $p = .10$; small sample sizes are involved in all cases. In the second pattern, suppose the five statistically significant results are about $p = .04$, the five nonsignificant ones have rates between $p = .50$ and .99, and all tests are based on large sample sizes. A box score approach would yield the same answer for both patterns—5 "yes" and 5 "tie" votes. But a more precise cumulation of results might indicate a very large effect in the first pattern and a quite small one in the second.

Fourth, matters become even more complex when a narrative reviewer tries to examine relationships among outcomes and potential moderator variables. Now the reviewer must also deal with imprecision in the moderators, with monitoring an even larger number of relationships between variables, and with questions about whether differences vary in size over moderator levels and variables. In the face of such problems, narrative reviews of intervention literatures can be overwhelmed.

---

1. In work on a related topic that we do not pursue here, Wortman, Smyth, Langenbrunner, and Yeaton (1998) compare results of meta-analyses to those from scientific consensus panels.

It is no surprise, then, that narrative reviews of the literature have increasingly given way to reviews that combine quantitative and qualitative methods (C. Mann, 1994). These latter reviews use numbers to describe primary studies in the same ways and for the same reasons that primary studies use numbers to describe their participants. But the use of numbers does *not* entail a rejection of narration or qualitative analysis. Just as primary studies benefit from using both quantitative and qualitative methods (Reichardt & Rallis, 1994), so also literature reviews benefit from both approaches. Indeed, it is difficult to conceive of how numbers could be used without narrative support.

QUANTITATIVE REVIEWS OF EXISTING RESEARCH

The use of quantitative techniques to summarize the results of scientific studies has a long history. In the early 18th century, the English mathematician Roger Cotes computed weighted averages of measurements made by different astronomers. Sir Karl Pearson (1904) used quantitative methods to average results from six studies of the effects of a newly developed inoculation against typhoid (Shadish & Haddock, 1994; see Cooper & Hedges, 1994b; Dickerson, Higgins, & Meinert, 1990; and Hunter & Schmidt, 1990, for other historical examples). However, widespread adoption of such methods did not occur until Glass (1976) coined the term *meta-analysis* to describe quantitative techniques for cumulating effect sizes over studies. Though other scholars preceded Glass in applying quantitative methods to literature reviews, Glass was the first to detail a general method for cumulating effect sizes over studies from any literature.

The essential innovation was the use of the effect size as a common metric over studies. A common metric is needed because different studies rarely use identical outcome measures, even if they address similar questions and invoke similar outcome constructs. Thus one study of psychotherapy for depression might have used the Beck Depression Inventory, whereas another used the MMPI Depression scale. These measures have different metrics with different means and standard deviations, so averaging scores without converting them into a common metric would yield nonsensical results. Meta-analysis converts each study's outcomes to a common effect size metric, so that different outcomes have the same means and standard deviations and can be more readily averaged across studies.[2]

2. An alternative is combining probability levels. Intervention studies commonly test the significance of a contrast between, say, an intervention and a control group, accompanying this with a probability level estimating the Type I error rate—the chance of incorrectly rejecting a true null hypothesis. A variety of methods is available for cumulating probability levels (B. Becker, 1994; R. Fisher, 1932), and the result is a combined significance test of the null hypothesis that the effect is not present in any of the populations represented across the studies. The alternative hypothesis is that at least one sample among those reviewed was from a population with a nonzero effect. Most researchers prefer to have information about effect sizes rather than simply knowing that at least one study had a nonzero effect. However, these combined significance level methods may be useful when sufficient information to compute effect sizes is not available but significance levels are available. Wang and Bushman (1999) present a method for combining effect sizes and probability levels.

Meta-analysis was originally applied to the effects of psychotherapy (M. Smith & Glass, 1977) and the influence of class size on student achievement (Glass & Smith, 1979).[3] Today meta-analyses of intervention effectiveness can be found in areas as diverse as medicine (Stroup et al., 2000), labor economics (Hedges, 1997a) and entomology (Koricheva, Larsson, & Haukioja, 1998). However, the general principles of quantitative reviews are not limited to summaries of intervention outcome literatures. Meta-analysis has also been applied to questions without any intervention, such as whether boys and girls differ in science achievement (B. J. Becker, 1992), to the validity of tests used in personnel selection (F. Schmidt & Hunter, 1977), and to the correlates of interpersonal expectancy effects (Rosenthal & Rubin 1978); and it can be applied to purely descriptive questions such as the percent of former mental patients who commit violent crimes after discharge from a mental hospital. In these latter cases, use of the term *effect size* must be understood broadly as a quantitative index of magnitude.

The Basics of Meta-Analysis

Here we review the essential steps and terminology of meta-analysis in order to help the reader understand how meta-analysis is useful in generalized causal inference. The reader who wishes to actually do a meta-analysis will generally require more detailed guidance (Boissel, Blanchard, Panak, Peyrieux, & Sacks, 1989; Cook et al., 1992; Cooper, 1998; Cooper & Hedges, 1994a; Durlak & Lipsey, 1991; Fink, 1998; Hedges & Olkin, 1985, in press; Hunter & Schmidt, 1990; Lipsey & Wilson, 2000). Quantitative and qualitative reviews both go through stages that include but are not limited to problem formulation, data collection, data evaluation, analysis and interpretation, and public presentation of results (Cooper & Hedges, 1994b). As in any research, these stages are iterative and highly dependent on each other, not rigid steps taken and finished one at a time. In the next section we present some uniquely meta-analytic perspectives on these otherwise common research tasks.

Identifying the Problem and Doing the Literature Review

All reviews require thoughtfulness about the problem to be addressed. It can be very broad, such as assessing the overall effects of psychotherapy (Smith, Glass, & Miller, 1980), or very narrow, such as assessing whether the use of paradoxical

---

3. This chapter is primarily concerned with meta-analysis of multigroup experiments. However, a literature is developing about meta-analysis of uncontrolled experiments and single subject designs (e.g., D. Allison & Gorman, 1993; Becker, 1988; Faith, Allison, & Gorman, 1997; Gibbons, Hedeker, & Davis, 1993; Kollins, Newland, & Critchfield, 1999; Kromrey & Foster-Johnson, 1996; Li & Begg, 1994; Looney, Feltz, & Van Vleet, 1994; Smoot, 1989; Swanson, & Sachselee, 2000; Viswesvaran & Schmidt, 1992; White, Rusch, Kazdin, & Hartmann, 1989), case control designs (Stroup et al., 2000; Thompson, Rivara, & Thompson, 2000), and interrupted time series (Grilli, Freemantle, Minozzi, Domenighetti, & Finer, 2000).

interventions in psychotherapy improves outcome (Shoham-Salomon & Rosenthal, 1987). The problem can concern the main effect of an intervention compared either with control groups or with some other intervention, or it can concern moderators of effects, such as whether psychotherapy effects are maintained at both posttest and follow-up (Nicholson & Berman, 1983; Shadish & Sweeney, 1991). Or the problem might be to find possible mediators of observed effects (Cook et al., 1992). Little about the question formation process in meta-analysis is different from question formation in primary studies or narrative reviews. The aim is to develop a clear research question and, based on this, a tentative framework of criteria for including studies in the meta-analysis.

Meta-analysts then need to conduct a literature search to find relevant studies. Many studies can be located from computerized databases, by inspecting reference lists of previous reviews, by scanning tables of contents of recent journals, by identifying registers of past and ongoing trials, and by contacting the "invisible college" of colleagues with special interest in the research question (Dickerson, 1994; Dickerson et al., 1990; Reed & Baxter, 1994; White, 1994). But some studies will be hard to locate and are often called the *fugitive literature* (M. C. Rosenthal, 1994). These may be unpublished dissertations and master's theses, final reports of grants or contracts, convention papers, technical reports, and studies subject to the **file drawer problem**—papers rejected for publication that are then relegated to the file drawer (Rosenthal, 1979). The size of this fugitive literature is unclear, but in some areas it may be sizable and may entail somewhat smaller effects than appear in the published literature on the same topic (e.g., Shadish, Doherty, & Montgomery, 1989; Simes, 1987; M. Smith, 1980; B. Sommer, 1987). If so, it is important to locate such fugitive studies (assuming they otherwise meet the criteria for inclusion in the meta-analysis) lest their omission result in biased estimates of effects. M. C. Rosenthal (1994) outlines methods for locating the fugitive literature, though one can never be sure of having found it all.

The studies included in the review must meet substantive criteria. They must address the question of interest and be relevant to the treatments, units, settings, measures and times outlined in the guiding problem formulation. There may also be methodological criteria, some of which are controversial, for example, whether a minimum sample size or level of power is required for each included study (e.g., Kraemer, Gardner, Brooks, & Yesavage, 1998; Wortman, 1992), whether only published studies are included, and whether only randomized studies are included if the review is of a causal issue (Boissel et al., 1989). Such decisions depend greatly on the context of the meta-analysis. For example, randomized studies of neonatal care are rare for ethical reasons, and so meta-analyses are limited to quasi-experiments by necessity (e.g., Ozminkowski, Wortman, & Roloff, 1989). Other times, the number of randomized experiments is so large as to consume all available resources to code them (e.g., Shadish et al., 1993). When there is doubt about these choices, our bias is to include more rather than fewer studies and then to code the methodological criterion at issue in order to probe in later analyses whether it makes a difference to outcome.

How many studies addressing a common question are required for a meta-analysis? This is a power question. Power is not computed in the standard ways that are used with single studies. Rather, methods specific to meta-analytic power must take into account between-study variance, the power of some tests that are peculiar to meta-analysis (e.g., homogeneity tests), and the differential power of fixed versus random effects models. Hedges and Olkin (in press, Chapter 7) provide the requisite equations for such cases (see also Harwell, 1997; Overton, 1998).

Coding of Studies

Meta-analyses use a common coding scheme to quantify study characteristics and results (Lipsey & Wilson, 2000; Stock, 1994). Individual codes should, first and foremost, reflect the researcher's hypotheses. In a study of interventions for child and adolescent obesity, for example, the researcher may be interested in whether the intervention included behavioral, educational, exercise, or dietary features, in the age of the child, in whether parents were involved in the intervention, and in whether outcome is measured as body mass or body fat (e.g., Haddock, Shadish, Klesges, & Stein, 1994). Codes for each of these must be developed. Codes often include characteristics of the study report (e.g., date published, publication form), the participants (e.g., presenting problem, gender composition), the intervention (e.g., type of intervention and dosage; who provides the intervention and where), intervention process (e.g., use of manual to increase intervention fidelity, level of fidelity achieved), and the methodology (e.g., sample size, method of assignment to conditions, attrition, kinds of measures).

Such coding is more difficult than it might seem. One reason is ambiguities and omissions in primary study reports (Orwin & Cordray, 1985; Pigott, 1994). These can sometimes be remedied by contact with the original authors; but finding authors for older studies is a problem, and authors often have little record and faulty memory even about what they did recently. And some codes are contingent on other codes; for example, two coders might have computed the same effect size for a dependent variable, but if one classified that variable in one way (e.g., as reactive) and the other another way (as nonreactive), overall effect size reliability may be decreased for the reactive-nonreactive comparison (Wortman, 1992; Yeaton & Wortman, 1993). Further, some codings require detailed instructions and seasoned judgments, as when rating the reactivity of a measure or categorizing the theoretical orientation of a psychotherapy. Hence the initial scheme should have explicit coding rules, should be tested for interrater reliability, and should be revised until adequate reliability is attained. Periodic reliability checks and retraining are also wise to ensure that coding practices do not drift over time (Orwin, 1994).

Finally, coding protocols should be developed with an eye toward how the database will be entered for subsequent computer analysis (Woodworth, 1994) and whether initial coding will be done directly into computer files. The problems of data entry are more complex than for most primary studies because several layers of nesting usually occur in meta-analysis—for example, effect sizes within measures at different times within intervention comparisons within studies. This usually results in a complex file structure that must be taken into account when creating coding and data entry protocols. Lipsey and Wilson (2000) provide helpful guidance on these structures.

Computing Effect Sizes

It is rare for the same outcome measure to be used in all or even most studies of a given topic. A meta-analysis of the effects of presurgical psychoeducational interventions to improve postsurgical outcome might include studies that use several different measures of postsurgical pain, including number of pain pills requested, number of complaints to the nursing station, and self-reports of pain on a rating scale. Such studies might also measure a variety of constructs, not just pain but also postsurgery length of stay, consumer satisfaction, or anxiety. In all these cases, the measures are on a different metric, having different raw score means and standard deviations. Consequently, the various study outcomes must be converted to a common metric before outcomes can be meaningfully compared over studies. This is the function of effect size measures.

Many different effect size measures are possible (Fleiss, 1994; R. Rosenthal, 1994). Here we describe the two most appropriate for meta-analyses of experiments:[4]

- the standardized mean difference statistic (*d*)
- the odds ratio (*o*)

The **standardized mean difference statistic** is defined as:

$$d_i = \frac{\overline{X_i^t} - \overline{X_i^c}}{s_i}$$

where $\overline{X_i^t}$ is the mean of the treatment group in the *i*th study, $\overline{X_i^c}$ is the mean of a comparison group in the *i*th study, and s_i is the pooled standard deviation of the two groups. The latter is easily computed with knowledge of the sample sizes and standard deviations of the two groups being compared (Shadish & Haddock, 1994, p. 273). A correction for small sample bias (Hedges & Olkin, 1985, p. 81) should be routinely used in meta-analyses that include small sample studies. The comparison group may be either a control group or an alternative intervention.

---

4. The correlation coefficient is another common effect size measure. It is most obviously appropriate when the aim of the meta-analysis is to summarize studies that have examined the same correlational relationship among variables (e.g., Ones, Viswesvaran, & Schmidt, 1993; Rosenthal & Rubin, 1978). Most authors recommend using R. A. Fisher's (1925) variance stabilizing *z* transformation prior to combining correlations over studies (R. Rosenthal, 1994; but see Hunter & Schmidt, 1990, for a counterargument). In treatment outcome research, the correlation between the dichotomously scored treatment condition (e.g., treatment = 1, control = 0) and a continuous outcome measure (e.g., depression levels, number of days in the hospital) can be an effect size measure (but for dichotomous outcomes, the odds ratio is the estimate of choice), though it is generally rare to find that correlation between treatment and outcome reported in treatment outcome studies.

Suppose, for example, that a marital therapy for distressed couples produced a mean posttest score of 103.97 on a measure of marital satisfaction, compared with a mean at posttest of 97.13 for control group participants. If the pooled standard deviation was 22.06, then $d = .31$. This means that the intervention group did about one third of a standard deviation better than the control group at posttest (see Shadish et al., 1993, p. 994, for other ways to interpret d). When the necessary means, standard deviations, and sample sizes are not available, it is often possible to use other statistics reported in a study to compute d or an approximation to d (e.g., Smith, Glass & Miller, 1980, Appendix 7; Shadish, Robinson, & Lu, 1999). The properties of these approximations have not been much investigated. Many are quite good, but a few can provide poor approximations to the exact methods (Shadish et al., 1999).

The standardized mean difference statistic assumes that study outcome is measured continuously. But sometimes study outcomes are measured dichotomously. For example, each participant is scored as a success or failure in marital therapy, or each patient receiving a new cancer therapy is classified as having survived or not. Such studies can be diagrammed as a fourfold table with intervention-control as one factor and the two levels of the dichotomous outcome as the other (Table 13.1). In these cases, both the standardized mean difference statistic and the correlation coefficient can yield problematic effect size estimates (Fleiss, 1994; Haddock, Rindskopf, & Shadish, 1998). Hence the appropriate effect size index is usually the odds ratio, defined as:

$$o_i = \frac{AD}{BC}$$

where A, B, C, and D are cell frequencies depicted in Table 13.1. If a cell size is zero, then .5 should be added to all cell sizes for that sample. The odds ratio can also be computed from other information such as data about the proportion of successful participants in each group (Fleiss, 1994; Shadish et al., 1999). Suppose, for example, the intervention group received an experimental vaccine against a

TABLE 13.1 Notation for a Fourfold Table

| | | Outcome | |
		Absent	Present
Cause	Present	A	B
	Absent	C	D

disease and the control group did not. The outcome might be the number in each group who did or did not get the disease. Suppose that $A = 265$ inoculated participants who remained immune, and $B = 32$ who contracted the disease in that group; $C = 204$ untreated participants in the control group who remained immune, and $D = 75$ of them who became ill. The odds of being immune to the disease if you were inoculated were $A/B = 265/32 = 8.28$; so inoculated persons were about eight times more likely to be immune than to contract the disease. In the control group, the same odds were $C/D = 204/75 = 2.72$. The ratio between these two odds is $o_i = 3.04$; that is, the odds that inoculated participants were immune to the disease were roughly three times larger than the odds for participants not inoculated.

On rare occasions, all studies use the same outcome measure. For instance, studies of obesity interventions may all report outcome in pounds or kilograms (Haddock et al., 1994), studies of depression treatment may all assess outcome on the Beck Depression Inventory (L. Robinson, Berman, & Neimeyer, 1990), or studies of presurgical interventions may all report number of days hospitalized postsurgically (Mumford, Schlesinger, Glass, Patrick, & Cuerdon, 1984). In these cases, it may make sense to use the difference between raw means as the common outcome metric (Shadish & Haddock, 1994). After all, the data are already in a common metric, and the original variable in pounds, days, or dollars may be far more intuitively interpretable than another effect size measure.

Analyzing Meta-Analytic Data[5]

Conceptually, meta-analytic data in the form of effect sizes are analyzed just like any other social or behavioral data, using both descriptive and inferential statistics with univariate and multivariate techniques (Cooper & Hedges, 1994a; Hedges & Olkin, 1985, in press). Meta-analysis simply substitutes study-based data for individual-level data (though a few things about it are statistically unique, as we cover shortly). Indeed, in the early years of meta-analysis, researchers simply borrowed the statistics already in use in primary studies, for example, computing an average effect size over all relevant studies and its variance. Thus Smith et al. (1980) averaged 1,766 standardized mean difference statistics from 475 controlled studies of psychotherapy (most studies produced multiple effect sizes) and obtained an average $d = .85$ with a standard error of .03. Confidence intervals were also constructed in the usual way by multiplying the standard error times some critical

5. Computer programs specifically written for doing meta-analytic statistics are increasingly prevalent (Borenstein & Rothstein, 1999; Johnson, 1989, 1993; Mullin, 1993; Rosenberg, Adams, & Gurevitch, 1997; Shadish, Robinson, & Lu, 1999), although many meta-analysts adapt standard statistical packages or spreadsheet programs to the task (e.g., Hedges, 1994; Lipsey & Wilson, 2000; Shadish & Haddock, 1994; Wang & Bushman, 1999; Woodworth, 1994). Multivariate models like those required by Raudenbush, Becker, & Kalaian et al. (1988) require matrix algebra that can be implemented in standard statistical packages; but those packages have little capacity to implement hierarchical analyses, so stand-alone PC programs for that purpose may also be useful (Bryk, Raudenbush, & Congdon, 1996).

value (often 1.96, the z-score for a two-tailed test at $\alpha = .05$), with the product added to and subtracted from the mean to make the interval. In the present case, this 95% confidence interval ranges from .79 to .91; because it excluded zero, Smith et al. concluded that the mean effect size differed significantly from zero. Similarly, it is common to compute means for finer-grained categories of studies. For example, Smith et al. (1980) found that the average effect size for psychodynamic therapies was $d = .78$, for behavioral $d = .91$, for cognitive $d = 1.31$, for humanistic $d = .63$, for developmental $d = .42$, and for cognitive-behavioral $d = 1.24$. More generally in meta-analysis, hypotheses can also be tested about differences between kinds of interventions, participants, or methodologies; effect sizes can be correlated with continuous study or intervention characteristics; multivariate tests can be conducted to try to identify redundancies and to adjust for study-level irrelevancies that have been measured; and stratification can be used to assess how a potential modifier influences the size or direction of an effect.

However, several features about meta-analytic statistics are unusual:

- The desirability of weighting effect size estimates by a function of study sample size
- The use of tests for homogeneity of effect sizes
- The hierarchical nature of meta-analytic data
- The dependency of effect sizes within studies
- The presence of publication bias

First, individual studies are often weighted prior to averaging, which can yield substantially different answers than unweighted (ordinary least squares) analyses (Shadish, 1992a). The most common scheme weights effect sizes by sample size or a function of sample size on the assumption that studies with more participants should yield more accurate estimates of population parameters (Sanchez-Meca & Marin-Martinez, 1998). Such weighting reduces the variance of the average effect size, making inferential tests more powerful. Other possible schemes include weighting for reliability and validity of outcome measures (Hunter & Schmidt, 1994), and for study quality (Amato & Keith, 1991; Begg et al., 1996; Franklin, Grant, Corcoran, Miller, & Bultman, 1997; Jadad et al., 1996; Moher et al., 1995; Moher & Olkin, 1995; Wampler & Serovich, 1996; Wortman, 1994). In general, however, only sample size and psychometric weighting schemes are well justified both logically and statistically. Examination of variables such as study quality is probably better done during subsequent data analyses rather than by weighting (Shadish & Haddock, 1994).

A second feature of meta-analytic data analysis that may be unfamiliar is homogeneity testing. This tests whether a set of observed effect sizes vary only as much as would be expected due to sampling error—the part of the difference between the population effect size and the sample estimate of that effect size that is due to the fact that only a sample of observations from the population were observed. If so, then the observed effect sizes are said to be homogenous, and the remaining variance is taken to be random and so unpredictable. If homogeneity is rejected, then the distribution of effect sizes contains more variance than we would expect by chance given the sample sizes in the individual studies being pooled; and that additional variance may be predictable by other substantive or methodological variables. For example, Lipsey (1992) examined the effects of juvenile delinquency interventions in 397 studies and found a weighted average effect size of $d = .103$. However, the hypothesis that these effect sizes were homogenous was rejected, with the effect sizes having more than three times the variability than would be expected by chance. So Lipsey explored various regression models to see which variables accounted for this variance. Of course, to reject homogeneity in the univariate case is not a surprise, for homogeneity in that case implies that one and only one variable (receiving juvenile delinquency intervention of some kind) accounts for *all* the systematic variance in juvenile delinquency intervention outcomes. We would rarely expect that to be the case. Rather, in the social sciences, we routinely expect to use several explanatory variables before accounting for much variance in the phenomena we study, and this is a successful strategy in meta-analysis, as well (e.g., Shadish, 1992a).

Sometimes homogeneity is rejected even after all available covariates are taken into account (e.g., Lipsey, 1992). This leaves two possibilities. One is that more covariates can be coded that might result in homogeneity. The other is that the population from which the effect sizes were drawn is characterized by a *distribution* of effect sizes (a *random effects* model) rather than a *single* effect size (a *fixed effects* model). If this is the case, then simply adding more covariates will never achieve homogeneity, and random effects estimators and analyses can be computed to take this possibility into account (Hedges & Vevea, 1998; Louis & Zelterman, 1994; Raudenbush, 1994; Shadish & Haddock, 1994). Indeed, Bayesian analysts advocate random effects models as a matter of principle no matter what the homogeneity test results. They do this in order to reflect better the inherently uncertain nature of inferences in all data, including meta-analytic data (Raudenbush, 1994). Random effects models typically increase standard errors and confidence intervals, reflecting greater uncertainty about inferences to the population.

A third way in which meta-analytic data are unusual is that respondents are always nested within studies. We have already discussed nested data, as with students nested within classrooms in randomized experiments. Then the so-called unit of analysis problem arises, as it routinely does in meta-analysis. The best analyses to take this nesting into account also rely on multilevel models (e.g., Bryk & Raudenbush, 1992; Kalaian & Raudenbush, 1996). These models are random effects models, so that their use helps address the problems in the previous paragraph, too. Goldstein, Yang, Omar, Turner, and Thompson (2000) describe a multilevel model that can be used to combine study level data with individual level data for use when some studies report summary statistics, but individual level data are available for other studies.

The fourth different feature of meta-analytic studies is that, when a study has multiple effect sizes, they are stochastically dependent. This situation can arise when a study has multiple outcome measures, when it reports results on those outcomes at more than one time point, or when it compares several interventions with a common control condition on just one measure. Such dependencies violate the statistical assumption of independent effect sizes. So it is common to average effect sizes from different measures within a study prior to combining studies; doing so essentially assumes that the effect sizes are perfectly correlated. If correlations between measures are known, more efficient (less variable) average effect size estimates can be obtained using certain multivariate procedures (Gleser & Olkin, 1994; Hedges & Olkin, in press; Kalaian & Raudenbush, 1996; Raudenbush, Becker, & Kalaian, 1988). When the correlation between measures is high, very little gain in efficiency occurs. When the correlation approaches zero, the gain in efficiency can be as much as 10–15%. But when the correlation is that low, it is not clear that the various dependent variables *should* be combined or analyzed separately (e.g., Harris & Rosenthal, 1985).

The fifth unusual feature is the presence of **publication bias**. This problem results because many reviewers are prejudiced against recommending the publication of studies with nonsignificant findings (Greenwald, 1975). So such studies tend to go unpublished, making them more difficult to find and include in a meta-analysis when compared with studies with significant effects. Because significance and effect size are correlated, published studies tend to overestimate effect size compared with the population of studies. A common way of addressing this problem is to compute the number of nonsignificant studies that would be needed to make an average effect size become nonsignificant statistically (Orwin, 1983; Rosenthal, 1979; Iyengar & Greenhouse, 1988, and Schonemann, 1991, have criticized this method). More sophisticated techniques for dealing with publication bias are available (Begg, 1994; Duval & Tweedie, 2000; Greenhouse & Iyengar, 1994; Hedges, 1992; Hedges & Olkin, in press; Hedges & Vevea, 1996; Silliman, 1997).

Interpreting and Presenting Results

In general, interpretation and presentation of meta-analytic results poses few special problems, although a specialized literature does exist (Halvorsen, 1994; Light, Singer, & Willett, 1994; Wang & Bushman, 1998). Interpretation inevitably extends beyond the data to attributions about the meaning of data that will usually be fallible and imbued with the theoretical biases of the interpreter. But when interpreting meta-analytic results, particularly for purposes associated with causation, one particular issue should be kept in mind. With a few exceptions, meta-analytic data are correlational (Louis, Fineberg, & Mosteller, 1985; Shadish, 1992a). We never randomly assign studies to the person, setting, time, cause, and effect categories we analyze. Indeed, it is difficult to see how such assignment would even be possible. Similarly, we rarely use quasi-experimental design features in meta-analysis to rule out threats to validity, although Shadish and Sweeney (1991) cite a few such examples. In almost all cases, the meta-analyst records data observationally in a manner most akin to a survey, making causal inferences about the effects of category membership on effect size subject to the same kinds of validity threats as any correlational data. The categories of causal interest in a meta-analysis are usually confounded with many other categories that are as unknown and unmeasured in meta-analysis as they are in primary correlational or quasi-experimental studies (e.g., Knight, Fabes, & Higgins, 1996).

The only significant exception occurs when reviewing a set of randomized experiments of the same intervention. In that case, the meta-analytic causal inference about the effect of that intervention over all the studies is no weaker than the inference from the individual studies themselves. For instance, a meta-analysis of 71 randomized experiments of the effects of marital and family psychotherapies compared with randomized controls yielded a $d = .51$ at posttest (Shadish et al., 1993). We may conclude that these psychotherapies caused this effect size, at least as strongly as we could conclude it in the studies themselves. Indeed, it would be odd if it were otherwise, for then the aggregate would somehow have become weaker than the studies themselves. However, this warrant extends only to the single conclusion about the effect of the common intervention. Inferences about other categories, such as the comparative effectiveness of different therapy subtypes examined in different studies or methodological details such as whether dissertations gave different outcomes than publications are still correlational.

Meta-Analysis and the Five Principles of Generalized Causal Inference

From the start, meta-analysis had obvious implications for generalization. After all, taking an average over multiple studies is one means of characterizing the general (central) tendency of those studies. Some early criticisms of meta-analysis questioned the appropriateness of such generalizations (e.g., Eysenck, 1978; Presby, 1978) because effect sizes are the product of myriad judgments by both primary analysts and meta-analysts. These include judgments about whether to do a study at all, how to design it, whether to write it up, what to include in the write-up, whether to archive the results, and whether to include the study in the review given its topic and methodological quality. At best, averaging over all these judgments seems to lose information and at worst might hide important variability. The criticisms went even deeper, contending that the effect sizes under analysis are probably not drawn at random from the population of all possible effect sizes for a given research question. So meta-analysts emphasized finding all the studies ever conducted on an issue (but see Rubin, 1990, 1992b). But even if all these fugitive studies could be found, this would still constitute a census of all conducted studies and would not represent the more relevant population of all possible studies.

Moreover, reviews are of less use, even if every published and unpublished study is found, if all share the same constant bias. This may have happened, for example, in meta-analyses of how school desegregation affects the academic achievement of Black children. Though children stay in school for 10 years or more, the available studies cover only the first 2 years after desegregation (Cook, 1985), probably leading to underestimates of desegregation's total impact. The reality is that meta-analysts work with purposive but heterogeneous samples of studies, the population referents of which are rarely clear and not necessarily devoid of constant biases.

Yet these samples of studies are still extremely useful for generalized causal inference. In the remainder of this chapter, we show why this is the case by applying the five principles of generalized causal inference outlined earlier.

Surface Similarity

With this principle, the emphasis is on assessing the match between research operations and the prototypical features of the targets of generalization. Reviews of multiple studies facilitate this in two ways. First, multiple studies typically represent many more constructs than any one study can do, thus increasing the number of construct inferences that can be made. For logistical reasons, most single studies of patient education programs limit themselves to one kind of patient (e.g., those receiving gall bladder surgery) or at most a few kinds of patients. But over multiple studies, many different kinds of patients have been examined (e.g., abdominal, thoracic, orthopedic, gynecological, urological). Similarly, nearly all single studies are conducted in a single setting, say, a large for-profit hospital in a major city, but multiple study reviews can draw conclusions about settings that are large or small, for-profit or nonprofit, urban or suburban, and even hospital versus outpatient clinics (Devine, 1992).

Second, such reviews greatly increase the chances of finding studies with operations that reflect constructs that may be of particular policy or research interest. This is especially important when a construct is rare. For example, certain schools of psychotherapy advocate a comparatively rare technique called paradoxical interventions in which the therapist gives the client suggestions that seem contrary to common sense or unlikely to be curative. By reviewing hundreds of psychotherapy studies, Shoham-Salomon and Rosenthal (1987) were able to find 10 studies of this rare treatment construct. Similarly, though the prototypical features of clinically representative psychotherapy are themselves a matter of debate, they probably include the use of experienced therapists in clinic settings treating clients referred through normal routes. Though psychotherapy experiments with this particular combination of persons, treatments, and settings are rare, meta-analytic reviews of multiple studies have been able to locate a number of them and then summarize their results (e.g., Shadish et al., 1997; Shadish et al., 2000; Weisz et al., 1992).

In the end, though, sometimes no studies exist at all on a target of generalization. In that case, one of the main benefits of reviews is that they highlight important constructs that a literature has mostly ignored so that future research can be aimed at them. For example, even those who may disagree about the effects of psychotherapy in clinically representative conditions do agree that few if any existing studies are both well designed and have *all* the prototypical features that such therapies might have (Shadish et al., 1997; Shadish et al., 2000; Weisz et al., 1992). Partially in response to such observations, U.S. federal funding agencies such as the National Institute of Mental Health have initiated special funding programs to generate more clinically representative research.

It is not necessary that the researcher know the prototypical attributes of the construct independently of what has been done in the studies in the meta-analysis. After all, constructs can be inferred inductively from the operations in the multiple studies and from the meta-analyst's existing knowledge base. But independent knowledge about the targets of generalization can be the source of support for or challenges to the construct validity of meta-analytic conclusions. Sometimes data about the target of generalization exists, so that the sample operations can be compared with it. For instance, Shadish et al.'s (1997) review of clinically representative psychotherapy supported its claims about modal psychotherapy practice by reference to empirical data that had previously been collected to describe such practice. Other times, knowledge is available from common sense or clinical lore. For example, Meyer and Mark (1995) noted that nearly all of the 45 studies they reviewed of psychosocial interventions with adult cancer patients were conducted with White women in the United States, noting that this obviously is a small subset of all adult cancer patients.

Ultimately, what is considered prototypical reflects understandings that are shared within the relevant language community of those who authorize, fund, and conduct social research. Components that the community sees as prototypical will tend to be represented in more of the operational instances available, and those it sees as less central will be less frequently represented. For example, the construct of depression is understood by the relevant research community as including physiological, cognitive, and affective features (Tanaka & Huba, 1984). Because the Beck Depression Inventory (BDI; Beck et al., 1961) assesses those features, many studies use the BDI, and reviews of those studies allow for conclusions about depression that better reflect that consensus about the construct of depression.

Of course, future researchers may come to see contemporary understandings of the prototypical characteristics as flawed or biased. Such biases arise because understandings of prototypical features can change as more is learned, because research practices that were widely adopted for convenience later prove to be problematic, and because researchers can no more easily escape larger social forces than can other citizens, witnessed by claims about widely shared sexist, racist, ageist, or first-world biases of social scientists. Reviews are superior to individual studies in their *potential* to represent prototypical attributes better. But potential is not achievement, and researchers must continually search to identify hidden sources of constant bias in how constructs are represented by the sampling operations even when multiple studies are being reviewed.

Ruling Out Irrelevancies

By itself, the principle of surface similarity cannot uncover such biases. We need to distinguish those deviations from the shared understanding of a construct that would not change a causal conclusion from those that would. Those that would not change a causal conclusion are irrelevant, and we can average over them without loss of generality in our conclusion. The principle of ruling out irrelevancies calls on us to consider some of the deviations from the prototype that might *not* make a difference. It does this partly through emphasizing the ongoing dialogue among members of a research community about what are important moderators of a causal connection; and it also does so by emphasizing the importance of exploratory analyses to search for deviations that do indeed make a difference. Neither procedure is perfect, and some constant biases are only identified in criticism from outside the relevant research community, or from within it over long time periods. Still, the serious search for causal moderator variables helps identify which sources of heterogeneity are irrelevant and which are relevant because they identify specific limits to the generalization of a causal claim.

To continue the patient education example used previously (Devine, 1992), the generally shared understanding is that such education should work about the same (within sampling error) no matter what type of hospital is studied. If researchers realize this and select hospitals haphazardly because funders and reviewers place little special emphasis on the type of hospital, then the hospitals represented in a review will tend to come from all regions of the country and represent many different patterns of ownership, financial health, size, and so forth. The principle of ruling out irrelevancies instructs the meta-analyst to show that a given causal relationship holds over all these irrelevant features. Because these irrelevancies are likely to be more heterogeneous in the typical review than in the individual study, the potential exists for promoting more confident generalized causal inferences from meta-analysis than from single studies.

When the number and range of setting variables is impressionistically large, an average effect size can be computed across all the available types of hospitals to evaluate whether a causal connection is so robust that it persists despite this variability. Such an analysis increases the likelihood that a causal connection is not completely confounded with a particular type of hospital, thus indicating that the link can be found despite the great variability in the kinds of hospitals in the review. But rather than lump together a heterogeneous set of hospitals, it may be preferable to create an explicit typology of hospitals and to build these types into the data analysis, sample sizes permitting. Probes can then be conducted of whether a causal relationship persists over each type of hospital, region, patient, or way of conceptualizing the cause. Indeed, Devine (1992) did just this, demonstrating that patient education consistently improved recovery from surgery no matter what the types of patient, types of hospital, time periods, and ways of conceptualizing patient education and recovery from surgery. Such robust effectiveness in a sample of over 150 studies strengthens the conclusion that patient education probably has highly generalized causal impacts. However, we must be careful if the sample of units in each stratum/type is small, for then low power may mislead the meta-analyst into thinking a feature is irrelevant when, in fact, the meta-analysis had too few units to test it well.

The enhanced number and range of irrelevancies also helps careful reviews to promote inferences about target cause-and-effect constructs. The same-labeled cause is manipulated many more ways in a review, and the same-labeled effect is measured in many different ways that reflect researcher-specific understandings of an effect and of the irrelevancies associated with any one understanding. Also evident in the typical review are diverse modes of measurement, different time lags between the manipulation and the outcome measurement, different kinds of data collectors, and so on. Any causal finding achieved despite such heterogeneity of irrelevancies is all the more firmly anchored conceptually, the more so when the individual irrelevancies have been used as stratification variables and the causal connection fails to disappear when the irrelevancy is present.

Sometimes there is no variation in a construct presumed to be irrelevant, thus precluding analyses of whether it truly is irrelevant. For instance, Devine and Cook (1983, 1986) showed that nearly all the available studies of patient education had used researchers rather than regular staff nurses to provide the intervention. Yet staff nurses may not be as intensively trained in the intervention as researchers, and they have many more competing responsibilities to contend with in the hospital. Can they ever implement the intervention enough for it to be useful? At the time of the review, regular staff nurses had been used in only 4 of the 102 studies then available, and effect sizes were smaller in these studies than in those in which researchers provided the intervention. However, the interventions in these 4 studies were less comprehensive than in the more optimal patient education protocols, and a later study conducted with regular nurses and a presumptively powerful intervention achieved the same effect as found in the review (Devine et al., 1990). Even so, the fact that the type of person providing patient education was systematically correlated with intervention intensity across 102 studies suggests that the number of studies in a review is less important than their relevance to conceptual issues. Director (1979) has made the same point about job training, contending that it had been systematically provided to applicants with worse education and work histories, resulting in a constant source of bias that could not have been controlled no matter how many similar studies had been conducted.

Of course, some meta-analyses aim to decrease, not increase, heterogeneity of irrelevancies. Thomas Chalmers and his colleagues (1988) routinely conducted meta-analyses of the available randomized clinical trials of particular drugs or surgical procedures; Ian Chalmers and his colleagues (e.g., Chalmers, Enkin, & Keirse, 1989) did the same for randomized trials in pregnancy and childbirth.[6] Their meta-analyses

---

6. The latter study reflects a larger effort called the Cochrane Collaboration (www.cochrane.org), an organization that prepares, maintains, updates, and promotes systematic reviews of the effects of health care interventions. A similar organization, the Campbell Collaboration (http://campbell.gse.upenn.edu), was recently organized in the United States to do the same for social, behavioral, and education interventions.

deliberately try to find studies using similar independent variables, outcome measures, experimental designs, diagnoses, physician specialties, and criteria of methodological adequacy for entering the review. This research model is close to an exact replication ideal, with the intent being to achieve the clearest possible picture of the causal efficacy of the intervention under well-controlled and highly standardized conditions designed to maximize the detection of an effect if there is one.

Contrast this with the priority in meta-analyses on other topics in which the desire is to assess effectiveness under conditions of real-world implementation, in which a different attitude toward sources of heterogeneity is common. In patient education, the diagnoses studied meta-analytically are more variable (from transurethral resections of the prostate to limb amputations); the outcome measures legitimately vary from study to study (including length of hospital stay, the amount of pain medication taken, satisfaction with the hospital stay); and the interventions vary from study to study depending on local understandings of patient education and the time and resources available for the intervention. There is no pretense here of exact replication—of repeated "pure" tests. Indeed, heterogeneity is welcomed to the extent that it resembles the heterogeneity found in the social settings of desired application. Moreover, the greater the robustness of effects over heterogeneity in persons, settings, treatments, measures, and times examined, the greater the confidence that the cause-effect relationship will also be obtained in still unexamined contexts. Reviews of a sample of highly standardized studies cannot have this positive result.

Making Discriminations

Here the strategy is to demonstrate that an inference holds only for the construct as specified, not for some alternative or respecified construct. Sometimes these discriminations serve the same purpose they do in measurement theory, to discriminate between different versions of a construct in order to clarify theoretical and policy discourse. For example, Shadish and colleagues (1997) were inspired to study the construct of clinically representative psychotherapy in part by prior work by Weisz et al. (1992) on clinic therapy. Yet subsequent dialogue suggested that these two seemingly similar constructs were not really the same—clinic therapies were intended by Weisz et al. to have existed in the clinic prior to the start of the experiment (though this was not explicit in Weisz et al., 1992), but this was not part of Shadish et al.'s definition of clinically representative therapy at all. A review of the Shadish et al. (1997) database indeed suggested that their clinically representative studies included few that reflected Weisz et al.'s intended construct. One function of meta-analytic work, then, is to clarify discourse about such important constructs in a literature, so that one can better characterize the constructs that have and have not been studied in that literature.

As or more important, however, is the role of such discriminations in clarifying the range and boundaries of causal relationships. In psychotherapy research, for example, the target treatment construct might be the specific verbal content of the therapist's message or the homework the therapist assigns to get clients to monitor and change their behavior. But some researchers might claim that the treatment really is better characterized as a general placebo or that the causal relationship is due to paying money to an individual who is called a therapist and who has visible diplomas and certificates attesting to acumen in helping others. Consequently psychotherapy researchers try to see if the effects of psychotherapy can be reliably discriminated from a placebo effect (Critelli & Neumann, 1984). In medicine, the power of the placebo is so well known that **double-blind studies** are routinely recommended to rule out that interpretation. But placebos are not the only threat to generalizing psychotherapy effects. Sometimes the challenge comes with a respecification of the active treatment ingredients. Suppose they are not the verbal content or out-of-therapy assigned activity but rather the expectation of feeling good? One creative researcher explored this possibility by comparing psychotherapy with the effects of a vacation in the Florida Keys (McCardel, 1972).

The aim here is to make discriminations about the parts of the target persons, settings, measures, treatments, and times for which a cause and effect relationship will *not* hold—for example, that the effects of SAT coaching will be minimal for students who are not assigned homework exercises, that the effects of reduced class size will disappear if those new smaller classes must be placed in temporary classrooms such as trailers, that a new treatment for prostate cancer will reduce blood flow to tumors but not decrease the number of tumors, that the effects of reduced class size will diminish or disappear if new, smaller classes are taught by inexperienced teachers, or that the effects of psychotherapy will be strong for 6 months after therapy ends but will disappear after 5 years. Such challenges stem from the fact that each construct can be thought of as having many parts. The strategy is to break each construct down into those components that are and are not important for producing the effect. Devine and Cook (1986) found a subset of studies that permitted discrimination of the target outcome—recovery from surgery—from some of its cognates. For example, some studies measured the time it took patients after their discharge to get back to work or normal activities in the home, and these measures showed that patient education decreased the period required to resume normal activities. This reduced the plausibility of the argument that the recovery measures had tapped into hospitals' need to reduce costs rather than into a genuine recovery from surgery. The larger the sample size of studies, the greater is the likelihood of finding some variables that help unconfound interpretations of the outcome.

Sometimes, of course, variations that the research community presumes to be relevant are later shown to be irrelevant. The psychotherapy research community, for example, tended to assume that therapist experience was relevant to treatment outcome, with increases in experience improving the client's outcome. Yet meta-analyses that have explored this relationship have so far found experience to be irrelevant (J. Berman & Norton, 1985; M. Smith et al., 1980; Shadish et al., 1993). This leads to rethinking of the role of such sources of variation. For example, does therapist experience interact with other variables such as severity of the presenting problem, even though it does not engender a main effect (Shadish, 1992b)? Both shared understandings and empirical findings about relevance and irrelevance are always subject to revision over time.

Interpolation and Extrapolation

We generalize most confidently when we can specify the range of persons, settings, treatments, outcomes, and times over which the cause and effect relationship holds more or less strongly or not at all. This requires empirical exploration of the existing range of instances to discover how effect sizes vary with position along the range. In medical research, examples include a range of treatment doses between none and the maximum expected safe dose, a range of settings between a small 100-bed and a large 5,000-bed hospital, a range of cancer patients between the ages of 25 and 75, and a range of follow-up times between immediate posttreatment and 5 years later. In each of these cases it is possible to rank order the instances of the construct. Meta-analysis holds more promise than any individual study for these tasks. The extremes are likely to be further apart in a review, and the intermediate values more numerous; by contrast, the levels represented in any one study are more likely to fall within the extremes achieved across all the studies.

An example pertaining to treatment dose is provided by Howard, Kopta, Krause, and Orlinsky (1986), who studied the relationship between number of sessions of psychotherapy and patient benefit. Fifteen primary studies reported tables showing patient improvement as a function of varying lengths of treatment. For each study, Howard et al. used probit analysis to project percent of patients improved at 0, 1, 2, 4, 8, 13, 26, 52, and 104 sessions of once-a-week psychotherapy. Of course, no individual study actually reported percentage improved at each of these nine time points. Also, none of the studies actually reported percentage improvement at 0 sessions, and eight studies stopped following outcomes after more than 100 sessions. So improvement estimates had to be extrapolated for these cases.

An example pertaining to time concerns the length of follow-up in psychotherapy research. Some meta-analytic evidence suggests that the effect size from psychotherapy at posttest is not significantly different from that at follow-up (Nicholson & Berman, 1983). But that conclusion depends in part on an extrapolation from the longest follow-up to what would have been observed had an even longer follow-up been used. In marital and family psychotherapy, for example, length for follow-up averaged about 5 months, and the longest follow-up observed in any study was only 9 months (Shadish et al., 1993). Even though follow-ups of this length resulted in effect sizes similar to posttest, some evidence suggests that follow-ups of a year or longer might have seen more marked deterioration (Jacobson, Schmaling, & Holtzworth-Munroe, 1987; Snyder, Wills, & Grady-Fletcher, 1991). So the extrapolation to follow-ups of this length is risky.

Interpolation and extrapolation are often studied by correlating effect size with the variable of interest. For example, Becker (1992) found that the correlation between student abilities and their science achievement was positive at $r =$

.33 for males and $r = .32$ for females. In general, this leads us to posit an increasingly strong positive relationship along the continuum. But the correlations being aggregated here are linear, and we could better interpolate and extrapolate if we saw a graph of the relationship, along with nonlinear correlations, in order to detect deflections in the relationship. Becker could not do this because she was aggregating the correlations reported by primary authors, all of which were linear. But sometimes meta-analysts construct their own quantitative continuums that can be related to effect size using nonlinear techniques. Shadish et al. (2000), for example, studied how effect sizes in psychotherapy outcome studies varied as a function of the clinical representativeness of the conditions in which therapy was studied. Clinical representativeness was coded for each study on 10 items (e.g., were experienced professional therapists used, did clients come from standard referral sources), the sum of which yielded a total clinical representativeness score for each study ranging from 1 to 10. A scatterplot of the relationship between effect size and those scores suggested an overall linear trend, and adding nonlinear terms to a statistical model of these data did not improve prediction significantly.

The Shadish et al. (2000) study also illustrates a particularly useful if somewhat preliminary application of a statistical method for interpolations and extrapolations in meta-analysis, response surface modeling (Rubin, 1990). The previous chapter described how this method applied to single studies, but the range on each variable in single studies is often too small to apply the method well or to many predictors. For example, the vast majority of experiments in the Shadish et al. (2000) meta-analysis used only one level of clinical representativeness within any one study. In meta-analysis, however, that range is considerably increased; so Shadish et al. (2000) used 90 studies that ranged from very low to very high representativeness. In a random effects regression, they first predicted effect size from clinical representativeness and from a host of potential covariates and confounds such as study design, therapy dose, measurement characteristics, and publication status of the report. These adjustments are particularly important because more clinically representative studies tend to be systematically different from less clinically representative ones. For example, the former studies are less likely to use random assignment than the latter. Then the authors used the resulting regression coefficients to extrapolate to the results that would have been obtained by an ideal study of clinical representativeness in this literature—one that used the strongest design for estimating treatment effects and that obtained the maximum score on clinical representativeness. No single study existed that actually had these characteristics, but the response surface model used data that are available to project the results of that ideal study. The results suggested that psychotherapy was about as effective under clinically representative conditions as it is in more research-oriented conditions.

Causal Explanation

Explorations of causal explanation can occur in three ways in meta-analysis. First, meta-analysis makes it easier for the researcher to break down persons, settings, treatments, and outcomes into their component parts in order to identify their causally relevant components. For instance, Devine and Cook (1986) were able to break down patient education into three components: providing information, skills training, and social support, even though no single study included all these combinations. The effects of different combinations of these components were then assessed, and analyses showed that each component was minimally effective by itself but that combining components increased the size of effect in additive fashion. The major limitations to using meta-analysis for identifying causally relevant intervention components are practical rather than theoretical. They include (1) the paucity of detail about intervention components in many journals and books (dissertations often prove to be a godsend here!), (2) published intervention descriptions that are often based on what researchers intended to do as an intervention rather than what they actually accomplished, and (3) the need for large samples of studies if sensitive analysis of individual cause-and-effect components is to take place. Nonetheless, there are many published meta-analyses with reasonable probes to identify crucial components of the more global cause and effect constructs (Lipsey, 1992).

Second, meta-analysts can use multiple regression equations to identify redundancy among variables that moderate study outcome, helping to narrow the explanation and to better assess the magnitude of effect associated with different predictors. For example, Lipsey (1992) analyzed the results of hundreds of studies of the effects of juvenile delinquency treatments, and he coded over 100 potential predictors of those results. Regression analyses suggested that larger pretest differences between groups were associated with larger posttest differences, that treatments provided by researchers had larger effects, that treatment in public facilities such as custodial homes had lower effects, and that behavioral and multimodal treatments had larger effects. Some other predictors were nonsignificant in those regressions, including most of the personal characteristics of the juveniles and some of the most widely publicized kinds of treatments, such as the "Scared Straight" programs aimed at deterring juvenile crime by exposing juveniles to frightening admonishments from prisoners incarcerated in unpleasant environments.

Third, full explanation also requires analysis of the micromediating causal processes that take place after a cause has been varied and before an effect has occurred. An example concerns Rosenthal's expectancy effects. Rosenthal (1973a, 1973b) proposed a four-factor theory of the mediation of teacher expectancy effects. The four factors are (1) *climate,* that high expectations lead to a warmer socioemotional climate, (2) *feedback,* that high expectations lead to more differentiated feedback about accuracy of student responses, (3) *input,* that teachers will teach more, and more difficult, material to high-expectancy students, and (4) *output,* that teachers will give high-expectancy students more opportunity to respond. In 1985, M. Harris and Rosenthal (1985) located 135 studies that examined relationships between expectancies and these mediators or between the mediators and the outcome. All effect sizes were converted to the common metric of correlations and then aggregated over studies separately for each of the four factors. Results suggested that all four factors helped mediate the effect. Armed with such knowledge, we are better able to know exactly how to produce (or minimize) the effect across diverse situations, thus fostering generalized causal inference. Other examples of meta-analytic explorations of causal mediation processes are discussed by Shadish (1996).

However, these examinations of causal mediating processes can be very difficult in meta-analysis (Shadish, 1996). A central problem is that so few primary studies examine mediators at all; and when they do, it is rarely with the more sophisticated causal modeling or instrumental variable methods that were outlined in the previous chapter. The result is a paucity of well-done and well-analyzed mediational studies to aggregate (Becker, 1992). Some meta-analysts (e.g., Shadish & Heinsman, 1997; Shadish & Ragsdale, 1996) bypass this problem by having coders rate studies on potential mediators. But such indirect and post-hoc ratings may be less reliable and valid than would have been measures taken in the primary study itself; and some mediators simply cannot be rated that way. Finally, the statistical methods that are so useful for mediational modeling in primary studies in the previous chapter have not been adapted to meta-analysis. For example, their fit statistics often fail to take random effects into account, and they are often only able to fit fixed effects models. However, work on these topics is developing (Becker, 1992; Becker & Schram, 1994; McDonald, 1994; Muthen, 1994), and computer programs with the capacity to do random effects (multilevel) mediational models are appearing as this book goes to press.

These latter problems with mediational modeling notwithstanding, meta-analysts can do much to improve the usefulness of meta-analytic work for purposes of causal explanation by using the first two methods outlined in these sections, by using the simpler mediational methods like Harris and Rosenthal (1985) did, and most important, by beginning to think about mediational models in general in both their primary and meta-analytic work. The former, after all, is what will provide the data for the latter.

Discussion of Meta-Analysis

In the early years after meta-analysis was first introduced, numerous criticisms of it appeared (e.g., Eysenck, 1978; Presby, 1978). Although some of these amounted to little more than name calling (e.g., Eysenck's "mega-silliness"), others raised thoughtful questions about the meaningfulness of the enterprise. Indeed, meta-analysts themselves have been among the most thoughtful and persistent critics of their own efforts, both identifying key problems and trying to devise ways to solve them (e.g., Hedges & Vevea, 1996; Ray & Shadish, 1996). So our enthusiasm for the methodology must be tempered by realistic understandings of its limitations. In this spirit, the appendix to this chapter contains a list of threats to the validity of inferences that are generated from meta-analyses.

The flaws of meta-analysis notwithstanding, however, the problems with narrative literature reviews are often even more serious. So one must read criticisms of meta-analysis keeping in mind whether a particular problem is specific to meta-analysis or would be true of any literature review and whether the problem is severe enough to warrant a return to all the problems of narrative review techniques. For example, Kraemer et al. (1998) suggest excluding underpowered studies from a meta-analysis because this would reduce the bias due to the file-drawer problem and due to results reported only as nonsignificant. However, in some literatures it is difficult to locate any studies that are adequately powered by standard criteria (e.g., power of .80). Yet in those literatures, narrative reviews will still be done; and those narrative reviews will contain all the flaws that meta-analysis aims to remedy. Including quantitative methods for **research synthesis** in such reviews would still seem worthwhile, power problems or not. The alternatives (either banning all literature reviews that cannot meet this criterion or relying solely on narrative reviews) are not only unrealistic but also a cure that is worse than the problem.

Not surprisingly, new criticisms continue to appear. Though they sometimes gain significant attention, they do not always withstand careful scrutiny of their validity. For example, LeLorier, Gregoire, Benhaddad, Lapierre, and Derderian (1997) reported finding serious discrepancies between results from meta-analyses of smaller experiments and those from single large randomized trials. However, the alleged problems turn out not to be very convincing on many counts. For example, their use of a fixed rather than random effects model may have resulted in an inflated Type I error rate; nearly all their confidence intervals comparing meta-analyses with single trials in fact overlapped despite their claim that the results disagreed; their methods are poorly described in certain critical respects (e.g., did the meta-analyses include nonrandomized trials?); and some reason exists to think that the findings reported in this article that are interpreted as disagreement are, in fact, very close to the findings one would expect (given power theory) from studies that are estimating exactly the same population parameter (personal communication, Larry V. Hedges, November 7, 1997). Indeed, another study that remedied some of these difficulties (Cappelleri et al., 1996) concluded the opposite from LeLorier et al., that large trials and meta-analyses of smaller trials yielded about the same answer.

Ultimately, our advice to the reader is to be as critical of meta-analysis as you would be of any other scientific method, but no more so. Because meta-analysis is so new, new criticisms will continue to appear, followed by criticisms of the criticisms and by solutions to those that can be solved. This is what happens with any new method in science. But this should not blind us to the reality that the addition of quantitative methods to our repertoire of literature review techniques remains one of the most important social science developments in the second half of the 20th century.

APPENDIX 13.1: THREATS TO THE VALIDITY OF META-ANALYSES

Generalizations from meta-analyses can be wrong for a variety of reasons. Here we summarize threats to the validity of generalized causal inferences in meta-analysis. Matt and Cook (1994) presented the first version of this list. We have modified a few of their entries and added some new ones. First, we discuss threats that apply to meta-analyses that seek only to describe the degree of association between two variables. Second, we discuss threats to the inferences that the relationship between two variables is causal. Third, we address validity threats that apply when generalizing to particular target constructs. Fourth, we present threats to inferences about how effect size is influenced by variation in persons, settings, times, outcomes, and treatments. These lists are not definitive. All threats are empirical products, and any list of threats should change as theories of method are improved and as critical discourse about research synthesis accumulates. So we anticipate these lists will change, too.

Our main focus is threats that are particular to research syntheses. These threats usually have analogs in general principles of research design and statistics. Thus the review-related threat called publication bias can be construed as merely a particular instance of selection bias. However, publication bias is one very concrete way in which practicing research synthesists encounter selection bias, and we prefer to formulate individual threats in forms that are as close as possible to how research synthesists will encounter them in practice.

Threats to Inferences About the Existence of a Relationship Between Treatment and Outcome

These threats can lead the research synthesist to conclude falsely that there is no relationship between two variables when there really is one (Type II error) or that there is a relationship when there really is not (Type I error). These errors occur because of deficiencies in either the primary studies or the meta-analytic review process. Deficiencies in primary studies are carried forward cumulatively to the meta-analysis and are especially critical when the same direction of bias operates across multiple studies.

Unreliability in Primary Studies

Unreliability in implementing or measuring variables attenuates effect sizes from primary studies. Attenuation corrections can correct estimates during the meta-analysis (Hunter & Schmidt, 1990, 1994; R. Rosenthal, 1994; Wolf, 1990). Data needed to make these corrections (documentation of treatment implementation and reliability of outcome measures) are often not reported in the primary study; but they can sometimes be estimated, for example, using reliability estimates reported in test manuals.

Restriction of Range in Primary Studies

Restriction of range in the outcome variable can attenuate effect sizes in a primary study, and these attenuated effect sizes will carry forward to the meta-analysis. In that case, corrections exist to adjust for this meta-analytically if valid estimates of the population range or variance are available (Hunter & Schmidt, 1994; R. Rosenthal, 1994). Restriction of range in any other variable in primary studies may or may not attenuate effect sizes; for instance, it may reduce effect size if treatments being contrasted are minor variations of each other, but it may increase effect size if homogenous samples of persons are studied. Thus the effects of restriction of range must be examined separately for each study, in light of the effect size measure used and the variable that is restricted.

Missing Effect Sizes in Primary Studies

Missing effect sizes occur when researchers in primary studies (1) fail to report details about statistically nonsignificant findings or (2) mention using an outcome measure but never discuss results for it. The former increases average study effect size if nonsignificant findings are omitted, but the effect of the latter is mostly unknown. The meta-analyst can contact study authors to obtain unreported data (e.g., Premack & Hunter, 1988), can conduct sensitivity analyses of the effects of different assumptions about missing data (e.g., Shadish, 1992a; Shadish, Hu, Glaser, Kownacki, & Wong, 1998), or can impute missing data (Pigott, 1994; Statistical Solutions, 1998).

Unreliability of Codings in Meta-Analyses

The variables used in meta-analytic coding can be unreliable and can attenuate meta-analytic relationships, particularly given common practice of coding only one item to represent a construct. Strategies for reducing unreliability include pilot testing the coding protocol, thorough coder training, using coders with expertise in the substantive areas being coded, using multi-item codes, contacting primary authors to clarify codes, and separately analyzing codes by confidence ratings.

Capitalizing on Chance in Meta-Analyses

Meta-analyses conduct many tests to probe relationships between effect size and various predictors. To reduce capitalization on chance, the researcher can adjust error rates using Bonferroni corrections or use multivariate procedures such as regression. In meta-analyses with small numbers of studies, such techniques may be impractical; in those cases, exploring only a few a priori hypotheses is warranted.

Biased Effect Size Sampling

Bias occurs when a meta-analyst codes only some of the plausibly relevant effect sizes from a study if the omitted ones differ from the coded ones on average. For example, Matt (1989) tried to follow M. Smith et al.'s (1980) rules but extracted almost three times as many effect estimates with mean effect size of about .50, compared with .90 from Smith et al. Clarity of selection rules is crucial, as is training of coders in implementing the rules and exploration of coder differences in results.

Publication Bias

Published studies may be a biased sample of all studies ever done and may also overestimate effects (D. Atkinson, Furlong, & Wampold, 1982; Greenwald, 1975; Rosenthal, 1979; Shadish et al., 1989). Minimizing this bias requires (1) strenuous attempts to find unpublished studies, (2) testing separate effect size estimates for published and unpublished studies, and (3) assessing potential consequences of this bias using one of the several methods now available for doing so (Begg, 1994; Dickerson, 1994; Hedges, 1984; Hedges & Olkin, in press; Reed & Baxter, 1994; M. C. Rosenthal, 1994; White, 1994).

Bias in Computing Effect Sizes

Primary studies often fail to provide the data needed to compute an effect size, and approximations to these effect size estimates vary in accuracy. When such approximations are necessary, meta-analysts should empirically examine whether estimates differ by computation method. Further, some meta-analysts use an effect size estimate that may not be appropriate for the kind of data analyzed (Haddock et al., 1998).

Lack of Statistical Independence Among Effect Sizes

Effect size estimates may lack statistical independence because (1) several effect size estimates are calculated on the same respondents using different measures; (2) several effect sizes compare different interventions with a common comparison group; (3) effect sizes are calculated on different samples in one study; and (4) different studies are conducted by the same research team over time. The typical solution is to analyze only one effect size per study (e.g., usually the mean estimate, but sometimes a randomly selected or theoretically relevant estimate). Multivariate statistics that model dependencies among effect sizes are better (Gleser & Olkin, 1994; Hedges & Olkin, 1985, in press; Raudenbush, Becker, & Kalaian, 1988; Rosenthal & Rubin, 1986), but they require estimates of covariances among within-study effect sizes, and the gain in better estimates can be relatively small.

Failure to Weight Study Level Effect Sizes Proportional to Their Precision

Studies with larger sample sizes should receive more weight in order to increase the precision of the average over studies. Weighting by the inverse of effect size sampling error (a function of sample size) minimizes the variance of the weighted average effect size (Hedges & Olkin, 1985, in press). Weighting by sample size (Hunter & Schmidt, 1990) does not have this latter advantage but improves precision considerably compared with no weighting at all.

Inaccurate Homogeneity Tests

Homogeneity tests (Hedges & Olkin, 1985, in press) influence several decisions in meta-analysis, such as the choice between fixed and random effects models or the decision to continue searching for moderators of effect size. When primary studies have very small sample sizes, the tests may have lower power (Harwell, 1997; Overton, 1998). Hence meta-analysts may temper purely statistical rules with judgments that take such mitigating circumstances into account, for instance, continuing to search for moderators even if homogeneity is not rejected with small sample size studies.

Underjustified Use of Fixed Effects Models

Fixed effects models are often used, but not as often well justified in meta-analysis. The reason is that homogeneity of effect size is often rejected in meta-analysis, which should lead most meta-analysts to consider whether random effects models ought to be used. However, fixed effects models can sometimes be justified despite rejection of homogeneity, for example, if adding predictors to a regression equation accounts for remaining heterogeneity (e.g., Shadish et al., 1993; though even then, univariate results should be reported as random effects) or if the researcher has an interest in the robustness of observed studies to sampling error (Hedges & Vevea, 1998). Frequently the latter is plausible, though it would imply a joint use of both fixed and random effects models to the same meta-analytic data rather than just the use of fixed effects models alone (e.g., Shadish et al., 2000).

Lack of Statistical Power

All other things being equal, statistical power is higher in meta-analyses than in primary studies. But that power may still be low when meta-analytic data are finely disaggregated into subcategories, and especially when that category has few studies with small sample sizes. Power tests (Hedges & Olkin, in press) help clarify this.

Threats to Inferences About the Causal Relationship Between Treatment and Outcome

When the covariation between two variables in a meta-analysis is presumed to be causal, new threats apply.

Failure to Assign to Primary Treatments at Random

Many meta-analyses examine questions about treatment effects. Meta-analysts may have confidence in causal inferences about treatment contrasts to which participants were randomly assigned in the primary studies—certainly no less confidence than in the primary studies themselves—subject to the usual caveats such as low and nondifferential attrition that usually apply to those studies. However, if primary studies failed to assign units to those treatments at random, meta-analytic causal inferences suffer accordingly. A solution is to contrast estimates for comparisons to which participants were randomly assigned with those on the same question to which they were not randomly assigned, giving primacy to the former when results differ over designs (e.g., Shadish et al., 2000). Where too few randomized studies exist to do this, a careful explication of possible biases is necessary, and adjustments for pretreatment differences in effect sizes can sometimes be useful (e.g., Shadish et al., 2000; Shadish & Ragsdale, 1996; Wortman, 1994).

Primary Study Attrition

Attrition is routine and differential in some areas. In Lipsey's (1992) meta-analysis of juvenile delinquency interventions, the more amenable juveniles dropped out of treatment groups and the more delinquent juveniles out of control groups. In Stanton and Shadish's (1997) meta-analysis, family therapy retained more substance abusers, especially those more likely to fail, compared with other therapies, which made family therapy appear less effective when attrition was ignored. The effects of attrition on meta-analyses can easily be explored with sensitivity analyses when outcomes are dichotomous (Shadish et al., 1998); when they are continuous, disaggregating studies by levels of both total and differential attrition can help.

Moderator Variable Confounding

Even when participants were randomly assigned to treatment contrasts that are the primary focus of a meta-analysis (e.g., does family therapy work better than a control condition), neither participants nor studies are randomly assigned to potential moderators of that effect, such as publication status, measurement techniques, or study setting. Even though meta-analysts often make causal claims about such moderators, those causal attributions are frequently wrong because those moderators are almost always confounded with other variables. Some of these confounds can be ruled out by analyzing within-study comparisons of the treatment at issue (Shadish et al., 1993). Confounds that are ruled out this way include any variable that must be constant over the two treatments compared within one effect size— for example, certain study-level variables, such as publication status, and certain measurement characteristics, such as reactivity. But other confounds that covary with levels of the moderator variable will still be confounded. A multivariate adjustment for such mediators is useful but not definitive, given that the confounds are definitionally unknown selection biases of the kinds that plague correlational data of all kinds.

Threats to Inferences About the Constructs Represented in Meta-Analyses

The main point of this chapter has been to show how meta-analysis facilitates generalized causal inference. But as valuable as meta-analysis is for this task, such generalizations face constant threats to validity. Here we identify threats to the construct validity of meta-analytic inferences. The majority of them pertain to the primary source of construct inference in meta-analysis—the coding protocol.

Underrepresentation of Prototypical Attributes

Studies often do not contain representations of all of the prototypical elements of a target construct. For instance, the construct of school desegregation prototypically includes educating together children from mixed racial backgrounds for many years. A meta-analysis in which none of the studies has implemented desegregation for more than 3 years does not match this prototype well (Cook, 1984). In such cases, the description of the construct actually studied needs to reflect those study operations; and the meta-analysis prompts the research community about the missing features of the prototype that still need testing.

Mono-Operation Bias

This threat and the next draw attention to the typically poor measurement properties of the vast majority of meta-analytic coding. Typically, each construct of interest in a meta-analysis is measured with a single item. Single items are notoriously unreliable, and too few meta-analyses report appropriate interrater reliability statistics. Single items also underrepresent the construct of interest and measure irrelevant constructs. Some of these biases can be reduced by using standard scale development procedures, as was done in developing the 10-item clinical representativeness scale described earlier in this chapter (Shadish et al., 2000), though this is almost never done in meta-analysis.

Monomethod Bias

Similarly, the vast majority of construct measurement in meta-analysis relies on a single method—the use of one coder who exercises largely independent judgment in assessing the properties of a study. Other methods are sometimes possible. For example, L. Robinson et al. (1990) rated researcher allegiance to therapy type as a predictor of effect size; but they also used a second measure of allegiance in which they located any previous publication by that same researcher in which that same therapy type had been studied and shown to be effective. Similarly, meta-analysts occasionally mention contacting the original authors to provide data for effect size computation (e.g., Kirsch, 1996), a method that could plausibly be extended to having original authors do additional coding, as well.

Rater Drift

This threat is similar to Treatment Sensitive Factorial Structure in Table 3.1, and refers to changes in consecutive ratings by the same rater over time. Causes of the drift include such things as practice effects, fatigue effects, and changing cognitive schema as a result of exposure to study reports of data that do not easily fit the existing codes. Monitoring for such drift helps, as do explicit procedures for public changes to the coding manual as new ways of understanding a code emerge.

Reactivity Effects

Parallel to the several reactivity and expectancy effects in Table 3.1, this refers to certain extraneous forces in the meta-analytic coding protocol. For example, coders are rarely masked to the hypotheses of the study and so may be influenced by explicit or implicit messages about the expectations of the principal investigator conveyed through such channels as meetings to develop study hypotheses, participation in the development of the coding manual, and meetings to monitor study progress. Where feasible, masking raters to such influences is desirable. For example, some meta-analysts ensure that coding effect sizes is kept separate from coding substantive variables so that those doing the latter are not influenced by knowledge of study outcomes (Shadish et al., 2000).

Confounding Constructs with Levels of Constructs

Just as in primary studies, meta-analysts may use construct labels that fail to describe the limited levels of the construct that were actually studied. Regarding the treatment construct, for example, Weisz et al. (1992) made such a construct validity challenge when they said the proper label for the treatment in hundreds of previously meta-analyzed studies was research therapy rather than clinic therapy—pointing out that the provision of therapy was confounded with a host of theoretically extraneous clinic, therapist, treatment, and patient characteristics.

Confounding Constructs with Other Study Characteristics

In meta-analysis, constructs of one kind (e.g., treatment constructs) are often confounded with those of another kind (e.g., settings, times, outcomes, persons). For example, Shadish and Sweeney (1991) found that studies using behavioral psychotherapies disproportionately used behavioral outcome measures (e.g., counts of marital fights) and that the latter yielded higher effect sizes than did nonbehavioral measures (e.g., self-reports of marital satisfaction). Here the label "behavioral therapies" may be more accurately described as "behavioral therapies assessed on behavioral outcome measures." Because such confounds are themselves prototypical of meta-analytic data, construct labels are especially problematic in meta-analysis.

Misspecification of Causal Mediating Relationships

Few meta-analyses of mediating processes exist, and those few utilize different strategies. Such efforts are frequently subject to criticisms about doing causal modeling in correlational data, about having severe missing data problems, and about using inappropriate statistical methods (Shadish, 1996). These models are a good source of hypotheses about mediation, but their validity must be suspect until some of these problems are solved or demonstrated in any given study to have little effect on the results.

Threats to Inferences About External Validity in Meta-Analyses

Here we describe threats to meta-analytic inferences about whether a cause-effect relationship holds over variation in persons, settings, treatment variables, and measurement variables.

Sampling Biases Associated with the Persons, Settings, Treatments, Outcomes, and Times Entering a Meta-Analysis

The persons, settings, treatments, outcomes, or times that are reported in primary studies are rarely sampled randomly. This nonrandomness worsens in meta-analysis because the studies entering into a meta-analysis are also not randomly sampled from a larger population of studies. Some of those sampling biases will be irrelevant to the generalization at issue. However, some will make a difference, so that it seems almost certainly the case that meta-analytic generalizations are frequently overstated, remaining so until critics find a sampling bias and show that it makes a difference to outcome.

Restricted Heterogeneity in Classes of Populations, Treatments, Outcomes, Settings, and Times

Even if sampling from a class were random, inferences about the robustness of a relationship may be wrong if those classes are not themselves heterogeneous. For example, some have suggested that meta-analysts rely only on studies with exemplary and standardized treatments, outcomes, settings, populations, and times

(Chalmers et al., 1988; Slavin, 1986). Such a strategy is useful in areas in which research is fairly standardized and represents well a consensually agreed-upon construct. But if carried to extremes, it can limit the ability of the meta-analyst to test for robustness over heterogeneous designs, treatment implementations, outcome measures, recruitment strategies, participant characteristics, and the like.

Failure to Test for Heterogeneity in Effect Sizes

Rejection of a homogeneity test implies that systematic variance in effect sizes remains to be accounted for, and further analyses may change results by, for example, identifying a variable that moderates the effect. Because such moderation limits generalization, failure to do homogeneity tests can lead to premature conclusions that an effect is generalizable. Of course, testing for generalizability in meta-analysis should not rely solely on homogeneity tests. Rather, consistent direction of effect is qualitatively important, too. But the failure to do homogeneity testing almost certainly leads to overstated generalizations.

Lack of Statistical Power for Studying Disaggregated Groups

To explore generalizability, meta-analysts often disaggregate classes of treatments, outcomes, persons, times, or settings to examine whether an effect changes significantly over subgroups. But such subgroup analyses rely on fewer studies, lowering statistical power, thereby leading the meta-analyst to find no significant result and then to conclude incorrectly that an effect generalizes over subgroups to the class. Hedges and Olkin (in press) give examples in which power of a random effects test of means will not reach the common standard of .80 even when the category has 10 studies with 100 participants each (though fixed effects tests are more powerful, they are often less appropriate). So some caution about generalizations is probably warranted in many cases in which subgroups have smaller numbers of studies and participants.

Restricted Heterogeneity of Irrelevancies

A threat arises if a meta-analysis cannot demonstrate that an effect holds across presumed irrelevancies. For instance, if private schools are those in which school expenses come from private sources rather than from taxes, it is irrelevant whether the schools are Catholic, Jewish, Muslim, or Protestant or whether they are military or elite academic schools. To generalize to private schools requires being able to show that relationships are not limited to one or a few of these contexts. This applies to methodological irrelevancies as well. Indeed, the wider the range and the larger the number of irrelevancies across which a finding holds, the stronger the belief that it will generalize over similar but unexamined irrelevancies.

A Critical Assessment of Our Assumptions

THIS BOOK covers five central topics across its 13 chapters. The first topic (Chapter 1) deals with our general understanding of descriptive causation and experimentation. The second (Chapters 2 and 3) deals with the types of validity and the specific validity threats associated with this understanding. The third (Chapters 4 through 7) deals with quasi-experiments and illustrates how combining design features can facilitate better causal inference. The fourth (Chapters 8 through 10) concerns randomized experiments and stresses the factors that impede and promote their implementation. The fifth (Chapters 11 through 13) deals with causal generalization, both theoretically and as concerns the conduct of individual studies and programs of research. The purpose of this last chapter is to critically assess some of the assumptions that have gone into these five topics, especially the assumptions that critics have found objectionable or that we anticipate they will find objectionable. We organize the discussion around each of the five topics and then briefly justify why we did not deal more extensively with nonexperimental methods for assessing causation.

We do not delude ourselves that we can be the best explicators of our own assumptions. Our critics can do that task better. But we want to be as comprehensive and as explicit as we can. This is in part because we are convinced of the advantages of falsification as a major component of any **epistemology** for the social sciences, and forcing out one's assumptions and confronting them is one part of falsification. But it is also because we would like to stimulate critical debate about these assumptions so that we can learn from those who would challenge our thinking. If there were to be a future book that carried even further forward the tradition emanating from Campbell and Stanley via Cook and Campbell to this book, then that future book would probably be all the better for building upon all the justified criticisms coming from those who do not agree with us, either on particulars or on the whole approach we have taken to the analysis of descriptive causation and its generalization. We would like this chapter not only to model the attempt to be critical about the assumptions all scholars must inevitably make but also to encourage others to think about these assumptions and how they might be addressed in future empirical or theoretical work.

CAUSATION AND EXPERIMENTATION

Causal Arrows and Pretzels

Experiments test the influence of one or at most a small subset of descriptive causes. If statistical interactions are involved, they tend to be among very few treatments or between a single treatment and a limited set of moderator variables. Many researchers believe that the causal knowledge that results from this typical experimental structure fails to map the many causal forces that simultaneously affect any given outcome in complex and nonlinear ways (e.g., Cronbach et al., 1980; Magnusson, 2000). These critics assert that experiments prioritize on arrows connecting A to B when they should instead seek to describe an explanatory pretzel or set of intersecting pretzels, as it were. They also believe that most causal relationships vary across units, settings, and times, and so they doubt whether there are any constant bivariate causal relationships (e.g., Cronbach & Snow, 1977). Those that do appear to be dependable in the data may simply reflect statistically underpowered tests of moderators or mediators that failed to reveal the true underlying complex causal relationships. True variation in effect sizes might also be obscured because the relevant substantive theory is underspecified, or the outcome measures are partially invalid, or the treatment contrast is attenuated, or causally implicated variables are truncated in how they are sampled (McClelland & Judd, 1993).

As valid as these objections are, they do not invalidate the case for experiments. The purpose of experiments is not to completely explain some phenomenon; it is to identify whether a particular variable or small set of variables makes a marginal difference in some outcome over and above all the other forces affecting that outcome. Moreover, **ontological** doubts such as the preceding have not stopped believers in more complex causal theories from acting as though many causal relationships can be usefully characterized as dependable main effects or as very simple nonlinearities that are also dependable enough to be useful. In this connection, consider some examples from education in the United States, where objections to experimentation are probably the most prevalent and virulent. Few educational researchers seem to object to the following substantive conclusions of the form that A dependably causes B: small schools are better than large ones; time-on-task raises achievement; summer school raises test scores; school desegregation hardly affects achievement but does increase White flight; and assigning and grading homework raises achievement. The critics also do not seem to object to other conclusions involving very simple causal contingencies: reducing class size increases achievement, but only if the amount of change is "sizable" and to a level under 20; or Catholic schools are superior to public ones, but only in the inner city and not in the suburbs and then most noticeably in graduation rates rather than in achievement test scores.

The primary justification for such oversimplifications—and for the use of the experiments that test them—is that some moderators of effects are of minor relevance to policy and theory, even if they marginally improve explanation. The most important contingencies are usually those that modify the sign of a causal relationship rather than its magnitude. Sign changes imply that a treatment is beneficial in some circumstances but might be harmful in others. This is quite different from identifying circumstances that influence just how positive an effect might be. Policy-makers are often willing to advocate an overall change, even if they suspect it has different-sized positive effects for different groups, as long as the effects are rarely negative. But if some groups will be positively affected and others negatively, political actors are loath to prescribe different treatments for different groups because rivalries and jealousies often ensue. Theoreticians also probably pay more attention to causal relationships that differ in causal sign because this result implies that one can identify the boundary conditions that impel such a disparate data pattern.

Of course, we do not advocate ignoring all causal contingencies. For example, physicians routinely prescribe one of several possible interventions for a given diagnosis. The exact choice may depend on the diagnosis, test results, patient preferences, insurance resources, and the availability of treatments in the patient's area. However, the costs of such a contingent system are high. In part to limit the number of relevant contingencies, physicians specialize, and within their own specialty they undergo extensive training to enable them to make these contingent decisions. Even then, substantial judgment is still required to cover the many situations in which causal contingencies are ambiguous or in dispute. In many other policy domains it would also be costly to implement the financial, management, and cultural changes that a truly contingent system would require even if the requisite knowledge were available. Taking such a contingent approach to its logical extremes would entail in education, for example, that individual tutoring become the order of the day. Students and instructors would have to be carefully matched for overlap in teaching and learning skills and in the curriculum supports they would need.

Within limits, some moderators can be studied experimentally, either by measuring the moderator so it can be tested during analysis or by deliberately varying it in the next study in a program of research. In conducting such experiments, one moves away from the black-box experiments of yesteryear toward taking causal contingencies more seriously and toward routinely studying them by, for example, disaggregating the treatment to examine its causally effective components, disaggregating the effect to examine its causally impacted components, conducting analyses of demographic and psychological moderator variables, and exploring the causal pathways through which (parts of) the treatment affects (parts of) the outcome. To do all of this well in a single experiment is not possible, but to do some of it well is possible and desirable.

Epistemological Criticisms of Experiments

In highlighting statistical conclusion validity and in selecting examples, we have often linked causal description to quantitative methods and hypothesis testing. Many critics will (wrongly) see this as implying a discredited theory of positivism. As a philosophy of science first outlined in the early 19th century, positivism rejected metaphysical speculations, especially about unobservables, and equated knowledge with descriptions of experienced phenomena. A narrower school of logical positivism emerged in the early 20th century that also rejected realism while also emphasizing the use of data-theory connections in predicate logic form and a preference for predicting phenomena over explaining them. Both these related epistemologies were long ago discredited, especially as explanations of how science operates. So few critics seriously criticize experiments on this basis. However, many critics use the term *positivism* with less historical fidelity to attack quantitative social science methods in general (e.g., Lincoln & Guba, 1985). Building on the rejection of logical positivism, they reject the use of quantification and formal logic in observation, measurement, and hypothesis testing. Because these last features are part of experiments, to reject this loose conception of positivism entails rejecting experiments. However, the errors in such criticisms are numerous. For example, to reject a specific feature of positivism (like the idea that quantification and predicate logic are the only permissible links between data and theory) does not necessarily imply rejecting all related and more general propositions (such as the notion that some kinds of quantification and hypothesis testing may be useful for knowledge growth). We and others have outlined more such errors elsewhere (Phillips, 1990; Shadish, 1995a).

Other epistemological criticisms of experimentation cite the work of historians of science such as Kuhn (1962), of sociologists of science such as Latour and Woolgar (1979) and of philosophers of science such as Harré (1981). These critics tend to focus on three things. One is the incommensurability of theories, the notion that theories are never perfectly specified and so can always be reinterpreted. As a result, when disconfirming data seem to imply that a theory should be rejected, its postulates can instead be reworked in order to make the theory and observations consistent with each other. This is usually done by adding new contingencies to the theory that limit the conditions under which it is thought to hold. A second critique is of the assumption that experimental observations can be used as truth tests. We would like observations to be objective assessments that can adjudicate between different theoretical explanations of a phenomenon. But in practice, observations are not theory neutral; they are open to multiple interpretations that include such irrelevancies as the researcher's hopes, dreams, and predilections. The consequence is that observations rarely result in definitive hypothesis tests. The final criticism follows from the many behavioral and cognitive inconsistencies between what scientists do in practice and what scientific norms prescribe they should do. Descriptions of scientists' behavior in laboratories reveal them as choosing to do particular experiments because they have an intuition about a relationship, or they are simply curious to see what happens, or they want to play with a new piece of equipment they happen to find lying around. Their impetus, therefore, is not a hypothesis carefully deduced from a theory that they then test by means of careful observation.

Although these critiques have some credibility, they are overgeneralized. Few experimenters believe that their work yields definitive results even after it has been subjected to professional review. Further, though these philosophical, historical, and social critiques complicate what a "fact" means for *any* scientific method, nonetheless many relationships have stubbornly recurred despite changes associated with the substantive theories, methods, and researcher biases that first generated them. Observations may never achieve the status of "facts," but many of them are so stubbornly replicable that they may be considered as though they were facts. For experimenters, the trick is to make sure that observations are not impregnated with just one theory, and this is done by building multiple theories into observations and by valuing independent replications, especially those of substantive critics—what we have elsewhere called **critical multiplism** (Cook, 1985; Shadish, 1989, 1994).

Although causal claims can never be definitively tested and proven, individual experiments still manage to probe such claims. For example, if a study produces negative results, it is often the case that program developers and other advocates then bring up methodological and substantive contingencies that might have changed the result. For instance, they might contend that a different outcome measure or population would have led to a different conclusion. Subsequent studies then probe these alternatives and, if they again prove negative, lead to yet another round of probes of whatever new explanatory possibilities have emerged. After a time, this process runs out of steam, so particularistic are the contingencies that remain to be examined. It is as though a consensus emerges: "The causal relationship was not obtained under many conditions. The conditions that remain to be examined are so circumscribed that the intervention will not be worth much even if it is effective under these conditions." We agree that this process is as much or more social than logical. But the reality of elastic theory does not mean that decisions about causal hypotheses are only social and devoid of all empirical and logical content.

The criticisms noted are especially useful in highlighting the limited value of individual studies relative to reviews of research programs. Such reviews are better because the greater diversity of study features makes it less likely that the same theoretical biases that inevitably impregnate any one study will reappear across all the studies under review. Still, a dialectic process of point, response, and counterpoint is needed even with reviews, again implying that no single review is definitive. For example, in response to Smith and Glass's (1977) meta-analytic claim that psychotherapy was effective, Eysenck (1977) and Presby (1977) pointed out methodological and substantive contingencies that challenged the original reviewers' results. They suggested that a different answer would have been achieved if Smith and Glass had not combined randomized and nonrandomized experiments or if they had used narrower categories in which to classify types of therapy. Subsequent studies probed these challenges to Smith and Glass or brought forth novel ones (e.g., Weisz et al., 1992). This process of challenging causal claims with specific alternatives has now slowed in reviews of psychotherapy as many major contingencies that might limit effectiveness have been explored. The current consensus from reviews of many experiments in many kinds of settings is that psychotherapy is effective; it is not just the product of a regression process (spontaneous remission) whereby those who are temporarily in need seek professional help and get better, as they would have even without the therapy.

Neglected Ancillary Questions

Our focus on causal questions within an experimental framework neglects many other questions that are relevant to causation. These include questions about how to decide on the importance or leverage of any single causal question. This could entail exploring whether a causal question is even warranted, as it often is not at the early stage of development of an issue. Or it could entail exploring what type of causal question is more important—one that fills an identified hole in some literature, or one that sets out to identify specific boundary conditions limiting a causal connection, or one that probes the validity of a central assumption held by all the theorists and researchers within a field, or one that reduces uncertainty about an important decision when formerly uncertainty was high. Our approach also neglects the reality that how one formulates a descriptive causal question usually entails meeting some stakeholders' interests in the social research more than those of others. Thus to ask about the effects of a national program meets the needs of Congressional staffs, the media, and policy wonks to learn about whether the program works. But it can fail to meet the needs of local practitioners who usually want to know about the effectiveness of microelements within the program so that they can use this knowledge to improve their daily practice. In more theoretical work, to ask how some intervention affects personal self-efficacy is likely to promote individuals' autonomy needs, whereas to ask about the effects of a persuasive communication designed to change attitudes could well cater to the needs of those who would limit or manipulate such autonomy. Our narrow technical approach to causation also neglected issues related to how such causal knowledge might be used and misused. It gave short shrift to a systematic analysis of the kinds of causal questions that can and cannot be answered through experiments. What about the effects of abortion, divorce, stable cohabitation, birth out of wedlock, and other possibly harmful events that we cannot ethically manipulate? What about the effects of class, race, and gender that are not amenable to experimentation? What about the effects of historical occurrences that can be studied only by using time-series methods on whatever variables might or might not be in the archives? Of what use, one might ask, is a method that cannot get at some of the most important phenomena that shape our social world, often over generations, as in the case of race, class, and gender?

Many statisticians now consider questions about things that cannot be manipulated as being beyond causal analysis, so closely do they link manipulation to causation. To them, the cause must be at least potentially manipulable, even if it is not actually manipulated in a given observational study. Thus they would not consider race a cause, though they would speak of the causal analysis of race in studies in which Black and White couples are, say, randomly assigned to visiting rental units in order to see if the refusal rates vary, or that entail chemically changing skin color to see how individuals are responded to differently as a function of pigmentation, or that systematically varied the racial mix of students in schools or classrooms in order to study teacher responses and student performance. Many critics do not like so tight a coupling of manipulation and causation. For example, those who do status attainment research consider it obvious that race causally influences how teachers treat individual minority students and thus affects how well these children do in school and therefore what jobs they get and what prospects their own children will subsequently have. So this coupling of cause to manipulation is a real limit of an experimental approach to causation. Although we like the coupling of causation and manipulation for purposes of defining experiments, we do not see it as necessary to all useful forms of cause.

VALIDITY

Objections to Internal Validity

There are several criticisms of Campbell's (1957) validity typology and its extensions (Gadenne, 1976; Kruglanski & Kroy, 1976; Hultsch & Hickey, 1978; Cronbach, 1982; Cronbach et al., 1980). We start first with two criticisms of internal validity raised by Cronbach (1982) and to a lesser extent by Kruglanski and Kroy (1976): (1) an atheoretically defined internal validity (A causes B) is trivial without reference to constructs; and (2) causation in single instances is impossible, including in single experiments.

Internal Validity Is Trivial

Cronbach (1982) writes:

> I consider it pointless to speak of causes when all that can be validly meant by refer-
> ence to a cause in a particular instance is that, on one trial of a partially specified ma-
> nipulation under conditions A, B, and C, along with other conditions not named, phe-
> nomenon P was observed. To introduce the word cause seems pointless. Campbell's
> writings make internal validity a property of trivial, past-tense, and local statements.
> (p. 137)

Hence, "causal language is superfluous" (p. 140). Cronbach does not retain a specific role for causal inference in his validity typology at all. Kruglanski and Kroy
(1976) criticize internal validity similarly, saying:

> The concrete events which constitute the treatment within a specific research are
> meaningful only as members of a general conceptual category. . . . Thus, it is simply
> impossible to draw strictly specific conclusions from an experiment: our concepts are
> general and each presupposes an implicit general theory about resemblance between
> different concrete cases. (p. 167)

All these authors suggest collapsing internal with construct validity in different
ways.

Of course, we agree that researchers conceptualize and discuss treatments and
outcomes in conceptual terms. As we said in Chapter 3, constructs are so basic to
language and thought that it is impossible to conceptualize scientific work without them. Indeed, in many important respects, the constructs we use constrain
what we experience, a point agreed to by theorists ranging from Quine (1951,
1969) to the postmodernists (Conner, 1989; Tester, 1993). So when we say that
internal validity concerns an atheoretical local molar causal inference, we do not
mean that the researcher should conceptualize experiments or report a causal
claim as "Something made a difference," to use Cronbach's (1982, p. 130) exaggerated characterization.

Still, it is both sensible and useful to differentiate internal from construct validity. The task of sorting out constructs is demanding enough to warrant separate
attention from the task of sorting out causes. After all, operations are concept
laden, and it is very rare for researchers to know fully what those concepts are. In
fact, the researcher almost certainly cannot know them fully because paradigmatic
concepts are so implicitly and universally imbued that those concepts and their assumptions are sometimes entirely unrecognized by research communities for
years. Indeed, the history of science is replete with examples of famous series of
experiments in which a causal relationship was demonstrated early, but it took
years for the cause (or effect) to be consensually and stably named. For instance,
in psychology and linguistics many causal relationships originally emanated from
a behaviorist paradigm but were later relabeled in cognitive terms; in the early
Hawthorne study, illumination effects were later relabeled as effects of obtrusive
observers; and some cognitive dissonance effects have been reinterpreted as

attribution effects. In the history of a discipline, relationships that are correctly identified as causal can be important even when the cause and effect constructs are incorrectly labeled. Such examples exist because the reasoning used to draw causal inferences (e.g., requiring evidence that treatment preceded outcome) differs from the reasoning used to generalize (e.g., matching operations to prototypical characteristics of constructs). Without understanding what is meant by descriptive causation, we have no means of telling whether a claim to have established such causation is justified.

Cronbach's (1982) prose makes clear that he understands the importance of causal logic; but in the end, his sporadically expressed craft knowledge does not add up to a coherent theory of judging the validity of descriptive causal inferences. His equation of internal validity as part of reproducibility (under replication) misses the point that one can replicate incorrect causal conclusions. His solution to such questions is simply that "the force of each question can be reduced by suitable controls" (1982, p. 233). This is inadequate, for a complete analysis of the problem of descriptive causal inference requires concepts we can use to recognize suitable controls. If a suitable control is one that reduces the plausibility of, say, history or maturation, as Cronbach (1982, p. 233) suggests, this is little more than internal validity as we have formulated it. If one needs the concepts enough to use them, then they should be part of a validity typology for cause-probing methods.

For completeness, we might add that a similar boundary question arises between construct validity and external validity and between construct validity and statistical conclusion validity. In the former case, no scientist ever frames an external validity question without couching the question in the language of constructs. In the latter case, researchers never conceptualize or discuss their results solely in terms of statistics. Constructs are ubiquitous in the process of doing research because they are essential for conceptualizing and reporting operations. But again, the answer to this objection is the same. The strategies for making inferences about a construct are not the same as strategies for making inferences about whether a causal relationship holds over variation in persons, settings, treatments, and outcomes in external validity or for drawing valid statistical conclusions in the case of statistical conclusion validity. Construct validity requires a theoretical argument and an assessment of the correspondence between samples and constructs. External validity requires analyzing whether causal relationships hold over variations in persons, settings, treatments, and outcomes. Statistical conclusion validity requires close examination of the statistical procedures and assumptions used. And again, one can be wrong about construct labels while being right about external or statistical conclusion validity.

Objections to Causation in Single Experiments

A second criticism of internal validity denies the possibility of inferring causation in a single experiment. Cronbach (1982) says that the important feature of causation is the "progressive localization of a cause" (Mackie, 1974, p. 73) over multiple experiments in a program of research in which the uncertainties about the essential features of the cause are reduced to the point at which one can characterize exactly what the cause is and is not. Indeed, much philosophy of causation asserts that we only recognize causes through observing multiple instances of a putative causal relationship, although philosophers differ as to whether the mechanism for recognition involves logical laws or empirical regularities (Beauchamp, 1974; P. White, 1990).

However, some philosophers do defend the position that causes can be inferred in single instances (e.g., Davidson, 1967; Ducasse, 1951; Madden & Humber, 1971). A good example is causation in the law (e.g., Hart & Honore, 1985), by which we judge whether or not one person, say, caused the death of another despite the fact that the defendant may never before have been on trial for a crime. The verdict requires a plausible case that (among other things) the defendant's actions preceded the death of the victim, that those actions were related to the death, that other potential causes of the death are implausible, and that the death would not have occurred had the defendant not taken those actions—the very logic of causal relationships and counterfactuals that we outlined in Chapter 1. In fact, the defendant's criminal history will often be specifically excluded from consideration in judging guilt during the trial. The lesson is clear. Although we may learn more about causation from multiple than from single experiments, we *can* infer cause in single experiments. Indeed, experimenters will do so whether we tell them to or not. Providing them with conceptual help in doing so is a virtue, not a vice; failing to do so is a major flaw in a theory of cause-probing methods.

Of course, individual experiments virtually always use prior concepts from other experiments. However, such prior conceptualizations are entirely consistent with the claim that internal validity is about causal claims in single experiments. If it were not (at least partly) about single experiments, there would be no point to doing the experiment, for the prior conceptualization would successfully predict what will be observed. The possibility that the data will not support the prior conceptualization makes internal validity essential. Further, prior conceptualizations are not logically necessary; we can experiment to discover effects that we have no prior conceptual structure to expect: "The physicist George Darwin used to say that once in a while one should do a completely crazy experiment, like blowing the trumpet to the tulips every morning for a month. Probably nothing will happen, but if something did happen, that would be a stupendous discovery" (Hacking, 1983, p. 154). But we would still need internal validity to guide us in judging if the trumpets had an effect.

Objections to Descriptive Causation

A few authors object to the very notion of descriptive causation. Typically, however, such objections are made about a caricature of descriptive causation that has not been used in philosophy or in science for many years—for example, a billiard ball model that requires a commitment to deterministic causation or that excludes reciprocal causation. In contrast, most who write about experimentation today espouse theories of probabilistic causation in which the many difficulties associated with identifying dependable causal relationships are humbly acknowledged. Even more important, these critics inevitably use causal-sounding language themselves, for example, replacing "cause" with "mutual simultaneous shaping" (Lincoln & Guba, 1985, p. 151). These replacements seem to us to avoid the word but keep the concept, and for good reason. As we said at the end of Chapter 1, if we wiped the slate clean and constructed our knowledge of the world anew, we believe we would end up reinventing the notion of descriptive causation all over again, so greatly does knowledge of causes help us to survive in the world.

Objections Concerning the Discrimination Between Construct Validity and External Validity

Although we traced the history of the present validity system briefly in Chapter 2, readers may want additional historical perspective on why we made the changes we made in the present book regarding construct and external validity. Both Campbell (1957) and Campbell and Stanley (1963) only used the phrase external validity, which they defined as inferring to what populations, settings, treatment variables, and measurement variables an effect can be generalized. They did not refer at all to construct validity. However, from his subsequent writings (Campbell, 1986), it is clear Campbell thought of construct validity as being part of external validity. In Campbell and Stanley, therefore, external validity subsumed generalizing from research operations about persons, settings, causes, and effects for the purposes of labeling these particulars in more abstract terms, and also generalizing by identifying sources of variation in causal relationships that are attributable to person, setting, cause, and effect factors. All subsequent conceptualizations also share the same generic strategy based on sampling instances of persons, settings, causes, and effects and then evaluating them for their presumed correspondence to targets of inference.

In Campbell and Stanley's formulation, person, setting, cause, and effect categories share two basic similarities despite their surface differences—to wit, all of them have both ostensive qualities and construct representations. Populations of persons or settings are composed of units that are obviously individually ostensive. This capacity to point to individual persons and settings, especially when they are known to belong in a referent category, permits them to be readily enumerated and selected for study in the formal ways that sampling statisticians prefer. By contrast, although individual measures (e.g., the Beck Depression Inventory) and treatments (e.g., a syringe full of a vaccine) are also ostensive, efforts to enumerate all existing ways of measuring or manipulating such measures and treatments are much more rare (e.g., Bloom, 1956; Ciarlo et al., 1986; Steiner & Gingrich, 2000). The reason is that researchers prefer to use substantive theory to determine which attributes a treatment or outcome measure should contain in any given study, recognizing that scholars often disagree about the relevant attributes of the higher order entity and of the supposed best operations to represent them. None of this negates the reality that populations of persons or settings are also defined in part by the theoretical constructs used to refer to them, just like treatments and outcomes; they also have multiple attributes that can be legitimately contested. What, for instance, is the American population? While a legal definition surely exists, it is not inviolate. The German conception of nationality allows that the great grandchildren of a German are Germans even if their parents and grandparents have not claimed German nationality. This is not possible for Americans. And why privilege a legal definition? A cultural conception might admit as American all those illegal immigrants who have been in the United States for decades and it might exclude those American adults with passports who have never lived in the United States. Given that persons, settings, treatments, and outcomes all have both construct and ostensive qualities, it is no surprise that Campbell and Stanley did not distinguish between construct and external validity.

Cook and Campbell, however, did distinguish between the two. Their unstated rationale for the distinction was mostly pragmatic—to facilitate memory for the very long list of threats that, with the additions they made, would have had to fit under Campbell and Stanley's umbrella conception of external validity. In their theoretical discussion, Cook and Campbell associated construct validity with generalizing to causes and effects, and external validity with generalizing to and across persons, settings, and times. Their choice of terms explicitly referenced Cronbach and Meehl (1955) who used construct and construct validity in measurement theory to justify inferences "about higher-order constructs from research operations" (Cook & Campbell, 1979, p. 38). Likewise, Cook and Campbell associated the terms *population* and *external validity* with sampling theory and the formal and purposive ways in which researchers select instances of persons and settings. But to complicate matters, Cook and Campbell also briefly acknowledged that "all aspects of the research require naming samples in generalizable terms, including samples of peoples and settings as well as samples of measures or manipulations" (p. 59). And in listing their external validity threats as statistical interactions between a treatment and population, they linked external validity more to generalizing across populations than to generalizing to them. Also, their construct validity threats were listed in ways that emphasized generalizing to cause and effect constructs. Generalizing across different causes and effects was listed as external validity because this task does not involve attributing meaning to a particular measure or manipulation. To read the threats in Cook and Campbell, external validity is about generalizing across populations of persons and settings and across different cause and effect constructs, while construct validity is about generalizing to causes and effects. Where, then, is generalizing from samples of persons or settings to their referent populations? The text discusses this as a matter of external validity, but this classification is not apparent in the list of validity threats. A system is needed that can improve on Cook and Campbell's partial confounding between objects of generalization (causes and effects versus persons and settings) and functions of generalization (generalizing to higher-order constructs from research operations versus inferring the degree of replication across different constructs and populations).

This book uses such a functional approach to differentiate construct validity from external validity. It equates construct validity with labeling research operations, and external validity with sources of variation in causal relationships. This new formulation subsumes all of the old. Thus, Cook and Campbell's understanding of construct validity as generalizing from manipulations and measures to cause and effect constructs is retained. So is external validity understood as generalizing across samples of persons, settings, and times. And generalizing across different cause or effect constructs is now even more clearly classified as part of external validity. Also highlighted is the need to label samples of persons and settings in abstract terms, just as measures and manipulations need to be labeled. Such labeling would seem to be a matter of construct validity, given that construct validity is functionally defined in terms of labeling. However, labeling human samples might have been read as being a matter of external validity in Cook and Campbell, given that their referents were human populations and their validity types were organized more around referents than functions. So, although the new formulation in this book is definitely more systematic than its predecessors, we are unsure whether that systematization will ultimately result in greater terminological clarity or confusion. To keep the latter to a minimum, the following discussion reflects issues pertinent to the demarcation of construct and external validity that have emerged either in deliberations between the first two authors or in classes that we have taught using pre-publication versions of this book.

Is Construct Validity a Prerequisite for External Validity?

In this book, we equate external validity with variation in causal relationships and construct validity with labeling research operations. Some readers might see this as suggesting that successful generalization of a causal relationship requires the accurate labeling of each population of persons and each type of setting to which generalization is sought, even though we can never be certain that anything is labeled with perfect accuracy. The relevant task is to achieve the most accurate assessment available under the circumstances. Technically, we can test generalization across entities that are already known to be confounded and thus not labeled well—e.g., when causal data are broken out by gender but the females in the sample are, on average, more intelligent than the males and therefore score higher on everything else correlated with intelligence. This example illustrates how dangerous it is to rely on measured surface similarity alone (i.e., gender differences) for determining how a sample should be labeled in population terms. We might more accurately label gender differences if we had a random sample of each gender taken from the same population. But this is not often found in experimental work, and even this is not perfect because gender is known to be confounded with other attributes (e.g., income, work status) even in the population, and those other attributes may be pertinent labels for some of the inferences being made. Hence, we usually have to rely on the assumption that, because gender samples come from the same physical setting, they are comparable on all background characteristics that might be correlated with the outcome. Because this assumption cannot be fully tested and is anyway often false—as in the hypothetical example above—this means that we could and should measure all the potential confounds within the limits of our theoretical knowledge to suggest them, and that we should also use these measures in the analysis to reduce confounding.

Even with acknowledged confounding, sample-specific differences in effect sizes may still allow us to conclude that a causal relationship varies by something associated with gender. This is a useful conclusion for preventing premature over-generalization. With more breakdowns, confounded or not, one can even get a sense of the percentage of contrasts across which a causal relationship does and does not hold. But without further work, the populations across which the relationship varies are incompletely identified. The value of identifying them better is particularly salient when some effect sizes cannot be distinguished from zero. Although this clearly identifies a nonuniversal causal relationship, it does not advance theory or practice by specifying the labeled boundary conditions over which a causal relationship fails to hold. Knowledge gains are also modest from generalization strategies that do not explicitly contrast effect sizes. Thus, when different populations are lumped together in a single hypothesis test, researchers can learn how large a causal relationship is despite the many unexamined sources of variation built into the analysis. But they cannot accurately identify which constructs do and do not co-determine the relationship's size. Construct validity adds useful specificity to external validity concerns, but it is not a necessary condition for external validity. We can generalize across entities known to be confounded, albeit less usefully than across accurately labeled entities.

This last point is similar to the one raised earlier to counter the assertion of Gadenne (1976) and Kruglanski and Kroy (1976) that internal validity requires the high construct validity of both cause and effect. They assert that all science is about constructs, and so it has no value to conclude that "something caused something else"—the result that would follow if we did a technically exemplary randomized experiment with correspondingly high internal validity, but the cause and effect were not labeled. Nonetheless, a causal relationship is demonstrably entailed, and the finding that "something reliably caused something else" might lead to further research to refine whatever clues are available about the cause and effect constructs. A similar argument holds for the relationship of construct to external validity. Labels with high construct validity are not necessary for internal or for external validity, but they are useful for both.

Researchers necessarily use the language of constructs (including human and setting population ones) to frame their research questions and select their representations of constructs in the samples and measures chosen. If they have designed their work well and have had some luck, the constructs they begin and end with will be the same, though critics can challenge any claims they make. However, the samples and constructs might not match well, and then the task is to examine the samples and ascertain what they might alternatively stand for. As critics like Gadenne, Kruglanski, and Kroy have pointed out, such reliance on the operational level seems to legitimize operations as having a life independent of constructs. This is not the case, though, for operations are intimately dependent on interpretations at all stages of research. Still, every operation fits some interpretations, however tentative that referent may be due to poor research planning or to nature turning out to be more complex than the researcher's initial theory.

How Does Variation Across Different Operational Representations of the Same Intended Cause or Effect Relate to Construct and External Validity?

In Chapter 3 we emphasized how the valid labeling of a cause or effect benefits from multiple operational instances, and also that these various instances can be fruitfully analyzed to examine how a causal relationship varies with the definition used. If each operational instance is indeed of the same underlying construct, then the same causal relationship should result regardless of how the cause or effect is operationally defined. Yet data analysis sometimes reveals that a causal relationship varies by operational instance. This means that the operations are not in fact equivalent, so that they presumably tap both into different constructs and into different causal relationships. Either the same causal construct is differently related to what now must be seen as two distinct outcomes, or the same effect construct is differently related to two or more unique causal agents. So the intention to promote the construct validity of causes and effects by using multiple operations has now facilitated conclusions about the external validity of causes or effects; that is, when the external validity of the cause and effect are in play, the data analysis has revealed that more than one causal relationship needs to be invoked.

Fortunately, when we find that a causal relationship varies over different causes or different effects, the research and its context often provide clues as to how the causal elements in each relationship might be (re)labeled. For example, the researcher will generally examine closely how the operations differ in their particulars, and will also study which unique meanings have been attached to variants like these in the existing literature. While the meanings that are achieved might be less successful because they have been devised post hoc to fit novel findings, they may in some circumstances still attain an acceptable level of accuracy, and will certainly prompt continued discussion to account for the findings. Thus, we come full circle. We began with multiple operational representations of the same cause or effect when testing a single causal relationship; then the data forced us to invoke more than one relationship; and finally the pattern of the outcomes and their relationship to the existing literature can help improve the labeling of the new relationships achieved. A construct validity exercise begets an external validity conclusion that prompts the need for relabeling constructs. Demonstrating effect size variation across operations presumed to represent the same cause or effect can enhance external validity by showing that more constructs and causal relationships are involved than was originally envisaged; and in that case, it can eventually increase construct validity by preventing any mislabeling of the cause or effect inherent in the original choice of measures and by providing clues from details of the causal relationships about how the elements in each relationship should be labeled. We see here analytic tasks that flow smoothly between construct and external validity concerns, involving each.

Should Generalizing from a Single Sample of Persons or Settings Be Classified as External or Construct Validity?

If a study has a single sample of persons or settings, this sample must represent a population. How this sample should be labeled is an issue. Given that construct validity is about labeling, is labeling the sample an issue of construct validity? After all, external validity hardly seems relevant since with a single sample it is not immediately obvious what comparison of variation in causal relationships would be involved. So if generalizing from a sample of persons or settings is treated as a matter of construct validity analogous to generalizing from treatment and outcome operations, two problems arise. First, this highlights a potential conflict in usage in the general social science community, some parts of which say that generalizations from a sample of people to its population are a matter of external validity, even when other parts say that labeling people is a matter of construct validity. Second, this does not fit with the discussion in Cook and Campbell that treats generalizing from individual samples of persons and settings as an external validity matter, though their list of external validity threats does not explicitly deal with this and only mentions interactions between the treatment and attributes of the setting and person.

The issue is most acute when the sample was randomly selected from the population. Consider why sampling statisticians are so keen to promote random sampling for representing a well-designated universe. Such sampling ensures that the sample and population distributions are identical on all measured and unmeasured variables within the limits of sampling error. Notice that this includes the population label (whether more or less accurate), which random sampling guarantees also applies to the sample. Key to the usefulness of random sampling is having a well bounded population from which to sample, a requirement in sampling theory and something often obvious in practice. Given that many well bounded populations are also well labeled, random sampling then guarantees that a valid population label can equally validly be applied to the sample. For instance, the population of telephone prefixes used in the city of Chicago is known and is obviously correctly labeled. Hence, it would be difficult to use random digit dialing from that list of Chicago prefixes and then mislabel the resulting sample as representing telephone owners in Detroit or only in the Edgewater section of Chicago. Given a clearly bounded population and random sampling, the sample label is the population label, which is why sampling statisticians believe that no method is superior to random selection for labeling samples when the population label is known.

With purposive sample selection, this elegant rationale cannot be used, whether or not the population label is known. Thus, if respondents were selected haphazardly from shopping malls all over Chicago, many of the people studied would belong in the likely population of interest—residents of Chicago. But many would not because some Chicago residents do not go to malls at the hours interviewing takes place, and because many persons in these malls are not from Chicago. Lacking random sampling, we could not even confidently call this sample "people walking in Chicago malls," for other constructs such as volunteering to be interviewed may be systematically confounded with sample membership. So, mere membership in the sample is not sufficient for accurately representing a population, and by the rationale in the previous paragraph, it is also not sufficient for accurately labeling the sample. All this leads to two conclusions worth elaborating: (1) that random sampling can sometimes promote construct validity, and (2) that external validity is in play when inferring that a single causal relationship from a sample would hold in a population, whether from a random sample or not.

On the first point, the conditions under which random sampling can sometimes promote the construct validity of single samples are straightforward. Given a well bounded universe, sampling statisticians have justified random sampling as a way of clearly representing in the sample all population attributes. This must include the population label, and so random sampling results in labeling the sample in the same terms that apply to the population. Random sampling does not, of course, tell us whether the population label is itself reasonably accurate; random sampling will also replicate in the sample any mistakes that are made in labeling the population. However, given that many populations are already reasonably well-labeled based on past research and theory and that such situations are often intuitively obvious for researchers experienced in an area, random sampling can, under these circumstances, be counted on to promote construct validity. However, when random selection has not occurred or when the population label is itself in doubt, this book has explicated other principles and methods that can be used for labeling study operations, including labeling the samples of persons and settings in a study.

On the second point, when the question concerns the validity of generalizing from a causal relationship in a single sample to its population, the reader may also wonder how external validity can be in play at all. After all, we have framed external validity as being about whether the causal relationship holds over *variation* in persons, settings, treatment variables, and measurement variables. If there is only one random sample from a population, where is the variation over which to examine that causal relationship? The answer is simple: the variation is between sampled and unsampled persons in that population. As we said in Chapter 2 (and as was true in our predecessor books), external validity questions can be about whether a causal relationship holds (a) over variations in persons, settings, treatments, and outcomes that *were* in the experiment, and (b) for persons, settings, treatments, and outcomes that *were not* in the experiment. Those persons in a population who were not randomly sampled fall into the latter category. Nothing about external validity, either in the present book or in its predecessors, requires that all possible variations of external validity interest actually be observed in the study—indeed, it would be impossible to do so, and we provided several arguments in Chapter 2 about why it would not be wise to limit external validity questions only to variations actually observed in a study. Of course, in most cases external validity generalizations to things that were not studied are difficult, having to rely on the concepts and methods we outlined in our grounded theory of generalized causal inference in Chapters 11 through 13. But it is the great beauty of random sampling that it guarantees that this generalization will hold over both sampled and unsampled persons. So it is indeed an external validity question whether a causal relationship that has been observed in a single random sample would hold for those units that were in the population but not in the random sample.

In the end, this book treats the labeling of a single sample of persons or settings as a matter of construct validity, whether or not random sampling is used. It also treats the generalization of causal relationships from a single sample to unobserved instances as a matter of external validity—again, whether or not random sampling was used. The fact that random sampling (which is associated with external validity in this book) sometimes happens to facilitate the construct labeling of a sample is incidental to the fact that the population label is already known. Though many population labels are indeed well-known, many more are still matters of debate, as reflected in the examples we gave in Chapter 3 of whether persons should be labeled schizophrenic or settings labeled as hostile work environments. In these latter cases, random sampling makes no contribution to resolving debates about the applicability of those labels. Instead, the principles and methods we outlined in Chapters 11 through 13 will have to be brought to bear. And when random sampling has not been used, those principles and methods will also have to be brought to bear on the external validity problem of generalizing causal relationships from single samples to unobserved instances.

Objections About the Completeness of the Typology

The first objection of this kind is that our lists of particular threats to validity are incomplete. Bracht and Glass (1968), for example, added new external validity threats that they thought were overlooked by Campbell and Stanley (1963); and more recently Aiken and West (1991) pointed to new reactivity threats. These challenges are important because the key to the most confident causal conclusions in our theory of validity is the ability to construct a persuasive argument that every plausible and identified threat to validity has been identified and ruled out. However, there is no guarantee that all relevant threats to validity have been identified. Our lists are not divinely ordained, as can be observed from the changes in the threats from Campbell (1957) to Campbell and Stanley (1963) to Cook and

Campbell (1979) to this book. Threats are better identified from insider knowledge than from abstract and nonlocal lists of threats.

A second objection is that we may have left out particular validity types or organized them suboptimally. Perhaps the best illustration that this is true is Sackett's (1979) treatment of bias in case-control studies. Case-control studies do not commonly fall under the rubric of experimental or quasi-experimental designs; but they are cause-probing designs, and in that sense a general interest in generalized causal inference is at least partly shared. Yet Sackett created a different typology. He organized his list around seven stages of research at which bias can occur: (1) in reading about the field, (2) in sample specification and selection, (3) in defining the experimental exposure, (4) in measuring exposure and outcome, (5) in data analysis, (6) in interpretation of analyses, and (7) in publishing results. Each of these could generate a validity type, some of which would overlap considerably with our validity types. For example, his concept of biases "in executing the experimental manoeuvre" (p. 62) is quite similar to our internal validity, whereas his withdrawal bias mirrors our attrition. However, his list also suggests new validity types, such as biases in reading the literature, and biases he lists at each stage are partly orthogonal to our lists. For example, biases in reading include biases of rhetoric in which "any of several techniques are used to convince the reader without appealing to reason" (p. 60).

In the end, then, our claim is only that the present typology is reasonably well informed by knowledge of the nature of generalized causal inference and of some of the problems that are frequently salient about those inferences in field experimentation. It can and hopefully will continue to be improved both by addition of threats to existing validity types and by thoughtful exploration of new validity types that might pertain to the problem of generalized causal inference that is our main concern.[1]

---

1. We are acutely aware of, and modestly dismayed at, the many different usages of these validity labels that have developed over the years and of the risk that poses for terminological confusion—even though we are responsible for many of these variations ourselves. After all, the understandings of validity in this book differ from those in Campbell and Stanley (1963), whose only distinction was between internal and external validity. They also differ from Cook and Campbell (1979), in which external validity was concerned with generalizing to and across populations of persons and settings, whereas all issues of generalizing from the cause and effect operations constituted the domain of construct validity. Further, Campbell (1986) himself relabeled internal validity and external validity as local molar causal validity and the principle of proximal similarity, respectively. Stepping outside Campbell's tradition, Cronbach (1982) used these labels with yet other meanings. He said internal validity is the problem of generalizing from samples to the domain about which the question is asked, which sounds much like our construct validity except that he specifically denied any distinction between construct validity and external validity, using the latter term to refer to generalizing results to unstudied populations, an issue of extrapolation beyond the data at hand. Our understanding of external validity includes such extrapolations as one case, but it is not limited to that because it also has to do with empirically identifying sources of variation in an effect size when existing data allow doing so. Finally, many other authors have casually used all these labels in completely different ways (Goetz & LeCompte, 1984; Kleinbaum, Kupper, & Morgenstern, 1982; Menard, 1991). So in view of all these variations, we urge that these labels be used only with descriptions that make their intended understandings clear.

Objections Concerning the Nature of Validity

We defined validity as the approximate truth of an inference. Others define it differently. Here are some alternatives and our reasons for not using them.

Validity in the New Test Theory Tradition

Test theorists discussed validity (e.g., Cronbach, 1946; Guilford, 1946) well before Campbell (1957) invented his typology. We can only begin to touch on the many issues pertinent to validity that abound in that tradition. Here we outline a few key points that help differentiate our approach from that of test theory. The early emphasis in test theory was mostly on inferences about what a test measured, with a pinnacle being reached in the notion of construct validity. Cronbach (1989) credits Cook and Campbell for giving "proper breadth to the notion of constructs" (p. 152) in construct validity through their claim that construct validity is not just limited to inferences about outcomes but also about causes and about other features of experiments. In addition, early test theory tied validity to the truth of such inferences: "The literature on validation has concentrated on the truthfulness of test interpretation" (Cronbach, 1988, p. 5).

However, the years have brought change to this early understanding. In one particularly influential definition of validity in test theory, Messick (1989) said, "Validity is an integrated evaluative judgment of the degree to which empirical evidence and theoretical rationales support the adequacy and appropriateness of inferences and actions based on test scores or other modes of assessment" (p. 13); and later he says that "Validity is broadly defined as nothing less than an evaluative summary of both the evidence for and the actual—as well as potential—consequences of score interpretation and use" (1995, p. 742). Whereas our understanding of validity is that *inferences* are the subject of validation, this definition suggests that *actions* are also subject to validation and that validation is actually evaluation. These extentions are far from our view.

A little history will help here. Tests are designed for practical use. Commercial test developers hope to profit from sales to those who use tests; employers hope to use tests to select better personnel; and test takers hope that tests will tell them something useful about themselves. These practical applications generated concern in the American Psychological Association (APA) to identify the characteristics of better and worse tests. APA appointed a committee chaired by Cronbach to address the problem. The committee produced the first in a continuing series of test standards (APA, 1954); and this work also led to Cronbach and Meehl's (1955) classic article on construct validity. The test standards have been frequently revised, most recently cosponsored by other professional associations (American Educational Research Association, American Psychological Association, and National Council on Measurement in Education, 1985, 1999). Requirements to adhere to the standards became part of professional ethical codes. The standards were also influential in legal and regulatory proceedings and have been cited, for example, in U.S. Supreme Court cases about alleged misuses of testing practices (e.g., Albermarle Paper Co. v. Moody, 1975; Washington v. Davis, 1976) and have influenced the "Uniform Guidelines" for personnel selection by the Equal Employment Opportunity Commission (EEOC) et al. (1978). Various validity standards were particularly salient in these uses.

Because of this legal, professional, and regulatory concern with the use of testing, the research community concerned with measurement validity began to use the word *validity* more expansively, for example, "as one way to justify the use of a test" (Cronbach, 1989, p. 149). It is only a short distance from validating use to validating action, because most of the relevant uses were actions such as hiring or firing someone or labeling someone retarded. Actions, in turn, have consequences—some positive, such as efficiency in hiring and accurate diagnosis that allows better tailoring of treatment, and some negative, such as loss of income and stigmatization. So Messick (1989, 1995) proposed that validation also evaluate those consequences, especially the social justice of consequences. Thus evaluating the consequences of test use became a key feature of validity in test theory. The net result was a blurring of the line between validity-as-truth and validity-as-evaluation, to the point where Cronbach (1988) said "Validation of a test or test use is evaluation" (p. 4).

We strongly endorse the legitimacy of questions about the use of both tests and experiments. Although scientists have frequently avoided value questions in the mistaken belief that they cannot be studied scientifically or that science is value free, we cannot avoid values even if we try. The conduct of experiments involves values at every step, from question selection through the interpretation and reporting of results. Concerns about the uses to which experiments and their results are put and the value of the consequences of those uses are all important (e.g., Shadish et al., 1991), as we illustrated in Chapter 9 in discussing ethical concerns with experiments.

However, if validity is to retain its primary association with the truth of knowledge claims, then it is fundamentally impossible to validate an action because actions are not knowledge claims. Actions are more properly evaluated, not validated. Suppose an employer administers a test, intending to use it in hiring decisions. Suppose the action is that a person is hired. The action is not itself a knowledge claim and therefore cannot be either true or false. Suppose that person then physically assaults a subordinate. That consequence is also not a knowledge claim and so also cannot be true or false. The action and the consequences merely exist; they are ontological entities, not epistemological ones. Perhaps Messick (1989) really meant to ask whether *inferences* about actions and consequences are true or false. If so, the inclusion of action in his (1989) definition of validity is entirely superfluous, for validity-as-truth is already about evidence in support of inferences, including those about action or consequences.[2]

---

2. Perhaps partly in recognition of this, the most recent version of the test standards (American Educational Research Association, American Psychological Association, and National Council on Measurement in Education, 1999) helps resolve some of the problems outlined herein by removing reference to validating action from the definition of validity: "Validity refers to the degree to which evidence and theory support the interpretations of test scores entailed by proposed uses of tests" (p. 9).

Alternatively, perhaps Messick (1989, 1995) meant his definition to instruct test validators to *evaluate* the action or its consequences, as intimated in: "Validity is broadly defined as nothing less than an evaluative summary of both the evidence for and the actual—as well as potential—consequences of score interpretation and use" (1995, p. 742). Validity-as-truth certainly plays a role in evaluating tests and experiments. But we must be clear about what that role is and is not. Philosophers (e.g., Scriven, 1980; Rescher, 1969) tell us that a judgment about the value of something requires that we (1) select criteria of merit on which the thing being evaluated would have to perform well, (2) set standards of performance for how well the thing must do on each criterion to be judged positively, (3) gather pertinent data about the thing's performance on the criteria, and then (4) integrate the results into one or more evaluative conclusions. Validity-as-truth is one (but only one) criterion of merit in evaluation; that is, it is good if inferences about a test are true, just as it is good for the causal inference made from an experiment to be true. However, validation is not isomorphic with evaluation. First, criteria of merit for tests (or experiments) are not limited to validity-as-truth. For example, a good test meets other criteria, such as having a test manual that reports norms, being affordable for the contexts of application, and protecting confidentiality as appropriate. Second, the theory of validity Messick proposed gives no help in accomplishing some of the other steps in the four-step evaluation process outlined previously. To evaluate a test, we need to know something about how much validity the inference should have to be judged good; and we need to know how to integrate results from all the other criteria of merit along with validity into an overall evaluation. It is not a flaw in validity theory that these other steps are not addressed, for they are the domain of evaluation theory. The latter tells us something about how to execute these steps (e.g., Scriven, 1980, 1991) and also about other matters to be taken into account in the evaluation. Validation is not evaluation; truth is not value.

Of course, the definition of terms is partly arbitrary. So one might respond that one should be able to conflate validity-as-truth and validity-as-evaluation if one so chooses. However:

> The very fact that terms must be supplied with arbitrary meanings requires that words be used with a great sense of responsibility. This responsibility is twofold: first, to established usage; second, to the limitations that the definitions selected impose on the user. (Goldschmidt, 1982, p. 642)

We need the distinction between truth and value because true inferences can be about bad things (the fact that smoking causes cancer does not make smoking or cancer good); and false inferences can lead to good things (the astrologer's advice to Pisces to "avoid alienating your coworkers today" may have nothing to do with heavenly bodies, but may still be good advice). Conflating truth and value can be actively harmful. Messick (1995) makes clear that the social consequences of testing are to be judged in terms of "bias, fairness, and distributive justice" (p. 745). We agree with this statement, but this is test evaluation, not test validity. Messick notes that his intention is not to open the door to the social policing of truth (i.e., a test is valid if its social consequences are good), but ambiguity on this issue has nonetheless opened this very door. For example, Kirkhart (1995) cites Messick as justification for judging the validity of evaluations by their social consequences: "Consequential validity refers here to the soundness of change exerted on systems by evaluation and the extent to which those changes are just" (p. 4). This notion is risky because the most powerful arbiter of the soundness and justice of social consequences is the sociopolitical system in which we live. Depending on the forces in power in that system at any given time, we may find that what counts as valid is effectively determined by the political preferences of those with power.

Validity in the Qualitative Traditions

One of the most important developments in recent social research is the expanded use of qualitative methods such as ethnography, ethnology, participant observation, unstructured interviewing, and case study methodology (e.g., Denzin & Lincoln, 2000). These methods have unrivaled strengths for the elucidation of meanings, the in-depth description of cases, the discovery of new hypotheses, and the description of how treatment interventions are implemented or of possible causal explanations. Even for those purposes for which other methods are usually preferable, such as for making the kinds of descriptive causal inferences that are the topic of this book, qualitative methods can often contribute helpful knowledge and on rare occasions can be sufficient (Campbell, 1975; Scriven, 1976). Whenever resources allow, field experiments will benefit from including qualitative methods both for the primary benefits they are capable of generating and also for the assistance they provide to the descriptive causal task itself. For example, they can uncover important site-specific threats to validity and also contribute to explaining experimental results in general and perplexing outcome patterns in particular.

However, the flowering of qualitative methods has often been accompanied by theoretical and philosophical controversy, often referred to as the qualitative-quantitative debates. These debates concern not just methods but roles and rewards within science, ethics and morality, and epistemologies and ontologies. As part of the latter, the concept of validity has received considerable attention (e.g., Eisenhart & Howe, 1992; Goetz & LeCompte, 1984; Kirk & Miller, 1986; Kvale, 1989; J. Maxwell, 1992; J. Maxwell & Lincoln, 1990; Mishler, 1990; Phillips, 1987; Wolcott, 1990). Notions of validity that are different from ours have occasionally resulted from qualitative work, and sometimes validity is rejected entirely. However, before we review those differences we prefer to emphasize the commonalities that we think dominate on all sides of the debates.

Commonalities.　As we read it, the predominant view among qualitative theorists is that validity is a concept that is and should be applicable to their work. We start with examples of discussions of validity by qualitative theorists that illustrate these similarities because they are surprisingly more common than some portrayals in the qualitative-quantitative debates suggest and because they demonstrate an underlying unity of interest in producing valid knowledge that we believe is widely shared by most social scientists. For example, Maxwell (1990) says, "qualitative researchers are just as concerned as quantitative ones about 'getting it wrong,' and validity broadly defined simply refers to the possible ways one's account might be wrong, and how these 'validity threats' can be addressed" (p. 505). Even those qualitative theorists who say they reject the word *validity* will admit that they "go to considerable pains not to get it all wrong" (Wolcott, 1990, p. 127). Kvale (1989) ties validity directly to truth, saying "concepts of validity are rooted in more comprehensive epistemological assumptions of the nature of true knowledge" (p. 11); and later that validity "refers to the truth and correctness of a statement" (p. 73). Kirk and Miller (1986) say "the technical use of the term 'valid' is as a properly hedged weak synonym for 'true' " (p. 19). Maxwell (1992) says "Validity, in a broad sense, pertains to this relationship between an account and something outside that account" (p. 283). All these seem quite compatible with our understanding of validity.

Maxwell's (1992) account points to other similarities. He claims that validity is always relative to "the kinds of understandings that accounts can embody" (p. 284) and that different communities of inquirers are interested in different kinds of understandings. He notes that qualitative researchers are interested in five kinds of understandings about: (1) the descriptions of what was seen and heard, (2) the meaning of what was seen and heard, (3) theoretical constructions that characterize what was seen and heard at higher levels of abstraction, (4) generalization of accounts to other persons, times, or settings than originally studied, and (5) evaluations of the objects of study (Maxwell, 1992; he says that the last two understandings are of interest relatively rarely in qualitative work). He then proposes a five-part validity typology for qualitative researchers, one for each of the five understandings. We agree that validity is relative to understanding, though we usually refer to inference rather than understanding. And we agree that different communities of inquirers tend to be interested in different kinds of understandings, though common interests are illustrated by the apparently shared concerns that both experimenters and qualitative researchers have in how best to characterize what was seen and heard in a study (Maxwell's theoretical validity and our construct validity). Our extended discussion of internal validity reflects the interest of the community of experimenters in understanding descriptive causes, proportionately more so than is relevant to qualitative researchers, even when their reports are necessarily replete with the language of causation. This observation is not a criticism of qualitative researchers, nor is it a criticism of experimenters as being less interested than qualitative researchers in thick description of an individual case.

On the other hand, we should not let differences in prototypical tendencies across research communities blind us to the fact that when a particular understanding *is* of interest, the pertinent validity concerns are the same no matter what the methodology used to develop the knowledge claim. It would be wrong for a qualitative researcher to claim that internal validity is irrelevant to qualitative methods. Validity is not a property of methods but of inferences and knowledge claims. On those infrequent occasions in which a qualitative researcher has a strong interest in a local molar causal inference, the concerns we have outlined under internal validity pertain. This argument cuts both ways, of course. An experimenter who wonders what the experiment means to participants could learn a lot from the concerns that Maxwell outlines under interpretive validity.

Maxwell (1992) also points out that his validity typology suggests threats to validity about which qualitative researchers seek "evidence that would allow them to be ruled-out . . . using a logic similar to that of quasi-experimental researchers such as Cook and Campbell" (p. 296). He does not outline such threats himself, but his description allows one to guess what some might look like. To judge from Maxwell's prose, threats to descriptive validity include errors of commission (describing something that did not occur), errors of omission (failing to describe something that did occur), errors of frequency (misstating how often something occurred), and interrater disagreement about description. Threats to the validity of knowledge claims have also been invoked by qualitative theorists other than Maxwell—for example, by Becker (1979), Denzin (1989), and Goetz and LeCompte (1984). Our only significant disagreement with Maxwell's discussion of threats is his claim that qualitative researchers are less able to use "design features" (p. 296) to deal with threats to validity. For instance, his preferred use of multiple observers *is* a qualitative design feature that helps to reduce errors of omission, commission, and frequency. The repertoire of design features that qualitative researchers use will usually be quite different from those used by researchers in other traditions, but they are design features (methods) all the same.

Differences.   These agreements notwithstanding, many qualitative theorists approach validity in ways that differ from our treatment. A few of these differences are based on arguments that are simply erroneous (Heap, 1995; Shadish, 1995a). But many are thoughtful and deserve more attention than our space constraints allow. Following is a sample.

Some qualitative theorists either mix together evaluative and social theories of truth (Eisner, 1979, 1983) or propose to substitute the social for the evaluative. So Jensen (1989) says that validity refers to whether a knowledge claim is "meaningful and relevant" (p. 107) to a particular language community; and Guba and Lincoln (1982) say that truth can be reduced to whether an account is credible to those who read it. Although we agree that social and evaluative theories complement each other and are both helpful, replacing the evaluative with the social is misguided. These social alternatives allow for devastating counterexamples (Phillips, 1987): the swindler's story is coherent but fraudulent; cults convince members of beliefs that have little or no apparent basis otherwise; and an account of an interaction between teacher and student might be true even if neither found it to be credible. Bunge (1992) shows how one cannot define the basic idea of error using social theories of truth. Kirk and Miller (1986) capture the need for an evaluative theory of truth in qualitative methods:

> In response to the propensity of so many nonqualitative research traditions to use such hidden positivist assumptions, some social scientists have tended to overreact by stressing the possibility of alternative interpretations of everything to the exclusion of any effort to choose among them. This extreme relativism ignores the other side of objectivity—that there is an external world at all. It ignores the distinction between knowledge and opinion, and results in everyone having a separate insight that cannot be reconciled with anyone else's. (p. 15)

A second difference refers to equating the validity of knowledge claims with their evaluation, as we discussed earlier with test theory (e.g., Eisenhart & Howe, 1992). This is most explicit in Salner (1989), who suggested that much of validity in qualitative methodology concerns the criteria "that are useful for evaluating competing claims" (p. 51); and she urges researchers to expose the moral and value implications of research, much as Messick (1989) said in reference to test theory. Our response is the same as for test theory. We endorse the need to evaluate knowledge claims broadly, including their moral implications; but this is not the same as saying that the claim is true. Truth is just one criterion of merit for a good knowledge claim.

A third difference makes validity a result of the process by which truth emerges. For instance, emphasizing the dialectic process that gives rise to truth, Salner (1989) says: "Valid knowledge claims emerge . . . from the conflict and differences between the contexts themselves as these differences are communicated and negotiated among people who share decisions and actions" (p. 61). Miles and Huberman (1984) speak of the problem of validity in qualitative methods being an insufficiency of "analysis procedures for qualitative data" (p. 230). Guba and Lincoln (1989) argue that trustworthiness emerges from communication with other colleagues and stakeholders. The problem with all these positions is the error of thinking that validity is a property of methods. Any procedure for generating knowledge can generate invalid knowledge, so in the end it is the knowledge claim itself that must be judged. As Maxwell (1992) says, "The validity of an account is inherent, not in the procedures used to produce and validate it, but in its relationship to those things it is intended to be an account of" (p. 281).

A fourth difference suggests that traditional approaches to validity must be reformulated for qualitative methods because validity "historically arose in the context of experimental research" (Eisenhart & Howe, 1992, p. 644). Others reject validity for similar reasons except that they say that validity arose in test theory (e.g., Wolcott, 1990). Both are incorrect, for validity concerns probably first arose systematically in philosophy, preceding test theory and experimental science by hundreds or thousands of years. Validity is pertinent to any discussion of the warrant for believing knowledge and is not specific to particular methods.

A fifth difference concerns the claim that there is no ontological reality at all, so there is no truth to correspond to it. The problems with this perspective are enormous (Schmitt, 1995). First, even if it were true, it would apply only to correspondence theories of truth; coherence and pragmatist theories would be unaffected. Second, the claim contradicts our experience. As Kirk and Miller (1986) put it:

> There is a world of empirical reality out there. The way we perceive and understand that world is largely up to us, but the world does not tolerate all understandings of it equally (so that the individual who believes he or she can halt a speeding train with his or her bare hands may be punished by the world for acting on that understanding). (p. 11)

Third, the claim ignores evidence about the problems with people's constructions. Maxwell notes that "one of the fundamental insights of the social sciences is that people's constructions are often systematic distortions of their actual situation" (p. 506). Finally, the claim is self-contradictory because it implies that the claim itself cannot be true.

A sixth difference is the claim that it makes no sense to speak of truth because there are many different realities, with multiple truths to match each (Filstead, 1979; Guba & Lincoln, 1982; Lincoln & Guba, 1985). Lincoln (1990), for example, says that "a realist philosophical stance requires, indeed demands, a singular reality, and therefore a singular truth" (p. 502), which she juxtaposes against her own assumption of multiple realities with multiple truths. Whatever the merits of the underlying ontological arguments, this is not an argument against validity. Ontological realism (a commitment that "something" does exist) does not require a singular reality, but merely a commitment that there be at least one reality. To take just one example, physicists have speculated that there may be circumstances under which multiple physical realities could exist in parallel, as in the case of Schrodinger's cat (Davies, 1984; Davies & Brown, 1986). Such circumstances would in no way constitute an objection to pursuing valid characterizations of those multiple realities. Nor for that matter would the existence of multiple realities require multiple truths; physicists use the same principles to account for the multiple realities that might be experienced by Schrodinger's cat. Epistemological realism (a commitment that our knowledge reflects ontological reality) does not require only one true account of that world(s), but only that there not be two contradictory accounts that are both true of the same ontological referent.[3] How many realities there might be, and how many truths it takes to account for them, should not be decided by fiat.

A seventh difference objects to the belief in a monolithic or absolute Truth (with capital T). Wolcott (1990) says, "What I seek is something else, a quality that points more to identifying critical elements and wringing plausible interpretations from them, something one can pursue without becoming obsessed with

---

3. The fact that different people might have different beliefs about the same referent is sometimes cited as violating this maxim, but it need not do so. For example, if the knowledge claim being validated is "John views the program as effective but Mary views it as ineffective," the claim can be true even though the views of John and Mary are contradictory.

finding the right or ultimate answer, the correct version, the Truth" (p. 146). He describes "the critical point of departure between quantities-oriented and qualities-oriented research [as being that] we cannot 'know' with the former's satisfying levels of certainty" (p. 147). Mishler (1990) objects that traditional approaches to validation are portrayed "as universal, abstract guarantors of truth" (p. 420). Lincoln (1990) thinks that "the realist position demands absolute truth" (p. 502). However, it is misguided to attribute beliefs in certainty or absolute truth to approaches to validity such as that in this book. We hope we have made clear by now that there are no guarantors of valid inferences. Indeed, the more experience that most experimenters gain, the more they appreciate the ambiguity of their results. Albert Einstein once said, "An experiment is something everybody believes except the person who made it" (Holton, 1986, p. 13). Like Wolcott, most experimenters seek only to wring plausible interpretations from their work, believing that "prudence sat poised between skepticism and credulity" (Shapin, 1994, p. xxix). We need not, should not, and frequently cannot decide that one account is absolutely true and the other completely false. To the contrary, tolerance for multiple knowledge constructions is a virtual necessity (Lakatos, 1978) because evidence is frequently inadequate to distinguish between two well-supported accounts (is light a particle or wave?), and sometimes accounts that appear to be unsupported by evidence for many years turn out to be true (do germs cause ulcers?).

An eighth difference claims that traditional understandings of validity have moral shortcomings. The arguments here are many, for example, that it "forces issues of politics, values (social and scientific), and ethics to be submerged" (Lincoln, 1990, p. 503) and implicitly empowers "social science 'experts' . . . whose class preoccupations (primarily White, male, and middle-class) ensure status for some voices while marginalizing . . . those of women, persons of color, or minority group members" (Lincoln, 1990, p. 502). Although these arguments may be overstated, they contain important cautions. Recall the example in Chapter 3 that "Even the rats were white males" in health research. No doubt this bias was partly due to the dominance of White males in the design and execution of health research. None of the methods discussed in this book are intended to redress this problem or are capable of it. The purpose of experimental design is to elucidate causal inferences more than moral inferences. What is less clear is that this problem requires abandoning notions of validity or truth. The claim that traditional approaches to truth forcibly submerge political and ethical issues is simply wrong. To the extent that morality is reflected in the questions asked, the assumptions made, and the outcomes examined, experimenters can go a long way by ensuring a broad representation of stakeholder voices in study design. Further, moral social science requires commitment to truth. Moral righteousness without truthful analysis is the stuff of totalitarianism. Moral diversity helps prevent totalitarianism, but without the discipline provided by truth-seeking, diversity offers no means to identify those options that are good for the human condition, which is, after all, the essence of morality. In order to have a moral social science, we must have both the capacity to elucidate personal constructions and the capacity to see how those constructions reflect and distort reality (Maxwell, 1992). We embrace the moral aspirations of scholars such as Lincoln, but giving voice to those aspirations simply does not require us to abandon such notions as validity and truth.

QUASI-EXPERIMENTATION

Criteria for Ruling Out Threats: The Centrality of Fuzzy Plausibility

In a randomized experiment in which all groups are treated in the same way except for treatment assignment, very few assumptions need to be made about sources of bias. And those that are made are clear and can be easily tested, particularly as concerns the fidelity of the original assignment process and its subsequent maintenance. Not surprisingly, statisticians prefer methods in which the assumptions are few, transparent, and testable. Quasi-experiments, however, rely heavily on researcher judgments about assumptions, especially on the fuzzy but indispensable concept of plausibility. Judgments about plausibility are needed for deciding which of the many threats to validity are relevant in a given study, for deciding whether a particular design element is capable of ruling out a given threat, for estimating by how much the bias might have been reduced, and for assessing whether multiple threats that might have been only partially adjusted for might add up to a total bias greater than the effect size the researcher is inclined to claim. With quasi-experiments, the relevant assumptions are numerous, their plausibility is less evident, and their single and joint effects are less easily modeled. We acknowledge the fuzzy way in which particular internal validity threats are often ruled out, and it is because of this that we too prefer randomized experiments (and regression discontinuity designs) over most of their quasi-experimental alternatives.

But quasi-experiments vary among themselves with respect to the number, transparency, and testability of assumptions. Indeed, we deliberately ordered the chapters on quasi-experiments to reflect the increase in inferential power that comes from moving from designs without a pretest or without a comparison group to those with both, to those based on an interrupted time series, and from there to regression discontinuity and random assignment. Within most of these chapters we also illustrated how inferences can be improved by adding design elements—more pretest observation points, better stable matching, replication and systematic removal of the treatment, multiple control groups, and nonequivalent dependent variables. In a sense, the plan of the four chapters on quasi-experiments reflects two purposes. One is to show how the number, transparency, and testability of assumptions varies by type of quasi-experimental design so that, in the best of quasi-experiments, internal validity is not much worse than with the randomized experiment. The other is to get students of quasi-experiments to be more sparing with the use of this overly general label, for it threatens to tar all quasi-experiments with the same negative brush. As scholars who have contributed to the institutionalization of the term *quasi-experiment,* we feel a lot of ambivalence about our role. Scholars need to think critically about alternatives to the randomized experiment, and from this need arises the need for the quasi-experimental label. But all instances of quasi-experimental design should not be brought under the same unduly broad quasi-experimental umbrella if attributes of the best studies do not closely match the weaker attributes of the field writ large.

Statisticians seek to make their assumptions transparent through the use of formal models laid out as formulae. For the most part, we have resisted this strategy because it backfires with so many readers, alienating them from the very conceptual issues the formulae are designed to make evident. We have used words instead. There is a cost to this, and not just in the distaste of statistical cognoscenti, particularly those whose own research has emphasized statistical models. The main cost is that our narrative approach makes it more difficult to formally demonstrate how much fewer and more evident and more testable the alternative interpretations became as we moved from the weaker to the stronger quasi-experiments, both within the relevant quasi-experimental chapters and across the set of them. We regret this, but do not apologize for the accessibility we tried to create by minimizing the use of Greek symbols and Roman subscripts. Fortunately, this deficit is not absolute, as both we and others have worked to develop methods that can be used to measure the size of particular threats, both in particular studies (e.g., Gastwirth et al., 1994; Shadish et al., 1998; Shadish, 2000) and in sets of studies (e.g., Kazdin & Bass, 1989; Miller, Turner, Tindale, Posavac, & Dugoni, 1991; Rosenthal & Rubin, 1978; Willson & Putnam, 1982). Further, our narrative approach has a significant advantage over a more narrowly statistical emphasis—it allows us to address a broader array of qualitatively different threats to validity, threats for which no statistical measure is yet available and that therefore might otherwise be overlooked with too strict an emphasis on quantification. Better to have imprecise attention to plausibility than to have no attention at all paid to many important threats just because they cannot be well measured.

Pattern Matching as a Problematic Criterion

This book is more explicit than its predecessors about the desirability of imbuing a causal hypothesis with multiple testable implications in the data, provided that they serve to reduce the viability of alternative causal explanations. In a sense, we have sought to substitute a pattern-matching methodology for the usual assessment of whether a few means, often only two, reliably differ. We do this not because complexity itself is a desideratum in science. To the contrary, simplicity in the number of questions asked and methods used is highly prized in science. The simplicity of randomized experiments for descriptive causal inference illustrates this well. However, the same simple circumstance does not hold with quasi-experiments. With them, we have asserted that causal inference is improved the more specific, the more numerous, and the more varied are the causal implications of a treatment. Thus, in interrupted time-series work, much depends on an effect occurring at a specified time point and on the time intervals being briefer rather than longer. In work with a single treatment group and no control, much depends on theory predicting different results for different but conceptually related outcomes and on obtaining effects that covary with the introduction and removal of the treatment. Modifications to the frequently used nonequivalent control group design with pretests and posttests can involve adding a staggered replication component if the treatment can be later introduced to the original controls. In all these cases a multivariate pattern of relationships is expected, and the data are examined for their fit to the specific pattern predicted. Thus, in one of the preceding cases, the predicted pattern is a change in mean or slope at a preordained point in a time series; in another, the expectation is of differential effects across outcome measures plus covariation with whether a treatment is present or not; and in the third case, the predicted pattern is of an initial group difference that subsequently decreases.

The logic of pattern matching promotes ruling out specific identified alternative causal claims. There is no virtue to a pattern matching that does not achieve this. But pattern matching is no panacea that permits confident claims of no bias such as random assignment permits when it is successfully implemented. The major difficulties with pattern matching are more practical. One has to do with the specificity of the theory generating the patterned prediction. In the interrupted time-series case, what happens when the effect appears to be delayed and no prior theory specifies the expected lag? What happens in the single-group case if the two nonequivalent dependent variables act in similar ways for at least one time segment? And what happens in the usual nonequivalent control group case if the expected replication fails to appear or does so only weakly? In retrospect, advocates for the causal hypothesis under test can always invent a rationale for why part of the pattern deviates from what was predicted. A second, related difficulty has to do with chance. Because most social science fields are characterized by stochastic processes, it is inevitable that failures to corroborate the expected causal pattern are more likely the more complex the prediction is in form, especially when corroboration is made to depend on all the data points being in the predicted direction—and reliably so. Given a pattern-matching logic, statistical analyses are required that test the overall fit and not just the difference between adjacent means. But such tests are not as well developed as those for testing the difference among a small number of means.

The Excuse Not to Do a Randomized Experiment

A major problem with quasi-experiments is that they can undermine the likelihood of doing even better studies. In our experience, they are frequently invoked as adequate causal tests when a better test would have been feasible. It is disheartening to read study after study that blithely pronounces itself to be a good cause-testing study just because a quasi-experimental design is being used. No cognizance is taken of the fact that some quasi-experimental designs are much stronger than others. Thus we have even seen studies in which the poorest designs without pretests or control groups have been extolled as adequate, even though these were the designs that Cook and Campbell (1979) pronounced to be "generally inadequate." It is as though some researchers think: if such and such a quasi-experiment is in "the book," then its mere presence there is a sufficient justification for using it. Obviously, each study calls for the strongest possible design, not the design of least resistance.

In many cases the strongest feasible design might entail a randomized experiment or a regression-discontinuity study rather than even a superior form of quasi-experiment. But the incidental costs of a randomized study can be high. It can take more work to put in place; it can involve some difficult negotiations to get the permissions required; it can inconvenience respondents more; it can require greater vigilance in the treatment assignment process and in order to reduce attrition; it can raise ethical issues that need not arise with other designs; and it can limit the range of persons, settings, treatments, and outcomes over which a causal effect can be generalized. One must be convinced of its inferential benefits over quasi-experimental alternatives in order to incur the costs required. Random assignment has to be fought for (Gueron, 1999); quasi-experiments usually less so.

The role of disciplinary culture is also crucial. Random assignment in the health sciences is institutionally supported by funding agencies, publishing outlets, graduate training programs, and a tradition of clinical trials. The culture in agriculture also favors such experiments, even in schools (St. Pierre, Cook, & Straw, 1981; Connell, Turner, & Mason, 1985), as does the culture in marketing and in research on surveys (e.g., Bradburn, 1983). Steps toward this same culture are emerging in preschool education given (1) congressional mandates to assign randomly to Early Head Start and to the Comprehensive Child Care Program; (2) the high political and scholarly visibility of experiments on the Perry Preschool Program (Schweinhart, Barnes, & Weikart, 1993), the Abacadarian project (Campbell & Ramey, 1995), and the home visiting nurse program (Olds et al., 1997); and (3) the involvement of researchers trained in fields that value experiments, such as psychology, human development, medicine, and microeconomics.

In other areas, the culture is more favorable toward quasi-experiments and even qualitative causal studies, and the press to go beyond quasi-experiments is minimal. For example, reports from the Office of Educational Research and Improvement (OERI) aim to identify effective school practices, but no particular privilege is accorded to random assignment (Vinovskis, 1998). A recent report on bilingual education repeated old saws about the impossibility of doing randomized studies and claimed that alternative quasi-experimental designs are as good. At a recent foundation meeting on teaching and learning attended by one of us (Cook), the representative of a reform-minded state governor spoke about a list of best practices that was being disseminated to all schools. He did not care, and he believed that no governors care, about the technical quality of the research generating these lists. The main concern was to have a consensus of education researchers endorsing each practice; and he guessed that the number of these best practices that depended on randomized experiments would be zero. Several nationally known educational researchers were present, agreed that such assignment probably played no role in generating the list, and felt no distress at this. So long as the belief is widespread that quasi-experiments constitute the summit of what is needed to support causal conclusions, the support for experimentation that is currently found in health, agriculture, or health in schools is unlikely to occur. Yet randomization is possible in many educational contexts within schools if the will exists to carry it out (Cook et al., 1999; Cook et al., in press). An unfortunate and inadvertent side effect of serious discussion of quasi-experiments may sometimes be the practical neglect of randomized experiments. That is a pity.

RANDOMIZED EXPERIMENTS

This section lists objections that have been raised to doing randomized experiments, and our analysis of the more and less legitimate issues that these objections raise.

Experiments Cannot Be Successfully Implemented

Even a little exposure to large-scale social experimentation shows that treatments are often improperly or incompletely implemented and that differential attrition often occurs. Organizational obstacles to experiments are many. They include the reality that different actors vary in the priority they attribute to random assignment, that some interventions seem disruptive at all levels of the organization, and that those at the point of service delivery often find the treatment requirements a nuisance addition to their already overburdened daily routine. Then there are sometimes treatment crossovers, as units in the control condition adopt or adapt components from the treatment or as those in a treatment group are exposed to some but not all of these same components. These criticisms suggest that the correct comparison is not between the randomized experiment and better quasi-experiments when each is implemented perfectly but rather between the randomized experiment as it is often imperfectly implemented and better quasi-experiments. Indeed, implementation can sometimes be better in the quasi-experiment if the decision not to randomize is based on fears of treatment degradation. This argument cannot be addressed well because it depends on specifying the nature and degree of degradation and the kind of quasi-experimental alternative. But taken to its extreme it suggests that randomized experiments have no special warrant in field settings because there is no evidence that they are stronger than other designs *in practice* (only in theory).

But the situation is probably not so bleak. Methods for preventing and coping with treatment degradation are improving rapidly (see Chapter 10, this volume; Boruch, 1997; Gueron, 1999; Orr, 1999). More important, random assignment may still create a superior counterfactual to its alternatives even with the flaws mentioned herein. For example, Shadish and Ragsdale (1996) found that, compared with randomized experiments without attrition, randomized experiments with attrition still yielded better effect size estimates than did nonrandomized experiments. Sometimes, of course, an alternative to severely degraded randomization will be best, such as a strong interrupted time series with a control. But routine rejection of degraded randomized experiments is a poor rule to follow; it takes careful study and judgment to decide. Further, many alternatives to experimentation are themselves subject to treatment implementation flaws that threaten the validity of inferences from them. Attrition and treatment crossovers also occur in them. We also suspect that implementation flaws are salient in experimentation because experiments have been around so long and experimenters are so critical of each other's work. By contrast, criteria for assessing the quality of implementation and results from other methods are far more recent (e.g., Datta, 1997), and they may therefore be less well developed conceptually, less subjected to peer criticism, and less improved by the lessons of experience.

Experimentation Needs Strong Theory and Standardized Treatment Implementation

Many critics claim that experimentation is more fruitful when an intervention is based on strong substantive theory, when implementation of treatment details is faithful to that theory, when the research setting is well managed, and when implementation does not vary much between units. In many field experiments, these conditions are not met. For example, schools are large, complex, social organizations with multiple programs, disputatious politics, and conflicting stakeholder goals. Many programs are implemented variably across school districts, as well as across schools, classrooms, and students. There can be no presumption of standard implementation or fidelity to program theory (Berman & McLaughlin, 1977).

But these criticisms are, in fact, misplaced. Experiments do not require well-specified program theories, good program management, standard implementation, or treatments that are totally faithful to theory. Experiments make a contribution when they simply probe whether an intervention-as-implemented makes a marginal improvement beyond other background variability. Still, the preceding factors can reduce statistical power and so cloud causal inference. This suggests that in settings in which more of these conditions hold, experiments should: (1) use large samples to detect effects; (2) take pains to reduce the influence of extraneous variation either by design or through measurement and statistical manipulation; and (3) study implementation quality both as a variable worth studying in its own right in order to ascertain which settings and providers implement the intervention better and as a mediator to see how implementation carries treatment effects to outcome.

Indeed, for many purposes the lack of standardization may aid in understanding how effective an intervention will be under normal conditions of implementation. In the social world, few treatments are introduced in a standard and theory-faithful way. Local adaptations and partial implementation are the norm. If this is the case, then some experiments should reflect this variation and ask whether the treatment can continue to be effective despite all the variation within groups that we would expect to find if the treatment were policy. Program developers and social theorists may want standardization at high levels of implementation, but policy analysts should not welcome this if it makes the research conditions different from the practice conditions to which they would like to generalize. Of course, it is most desirable to be able to answer both sets of questions—about policy-relevant effects of treatments that are variably implemented and also about the more theory-relevant effects of optimal exposure to the intervention. In this regard, one might recall recent efforts to analyze the effects of the original intent to treat through traditional means but also of the effects of the actual treatment through using random assignment as an instrumental variable (Angrist et al., 1996a).

Experiments Entail Tradeoffs Not Worth Making

The choice to experiment involves a number of tradeoffs that some researchers believe are not worth making (Cronbach, 1982). Experimentation prioritizes on unbiased answers to descriptive causal questions. But, given finite resources, some researchers prefer to invest what they have not into marginal improvements in internal validity but into promoting higher construct and external validity. They might be content with a greater degree of uncertainty about the quality of a causal connection in order to purposively sample a greater range of populations of people or settings or, when a particular population is central to the research, in order to generate a formally representative sample. They might even use the resources to improve treatment fidelity or to include multiple measures of a very important outcome construct. If a consequence of this preference for construct and external validity is to conduct a quasi-experiment or even a nonexperiment rather than a randomized experiment, then so be it. Similar preferences make other critics look askance when advocates of experimentation counsel restricting a study to volunteers in order to increase the chances of being able to implement and maintain random assignment or when these same advocates advise close monitoring of the treatment to ensure its fidelity, thereby creating a situation of greater obtrusiveness than would pertain if the same treatment were part of some ongoing social policy (e.g., Heckman, 1992). In the language of Campbell and Stanley (1963), the claim was that experimentation traded off external validity in favor of internal validity. In the parlance of this book and of Cook and Campbell (1979), it is that experimentation trades off both external and construct validity for internal validity, to its detriment.

Critics also claim that experiments overemphasize conservative standards of scientific rigor. These include (1) using a conservative criterion to protect against wrongly concluding a treatment is effective ($p < .05$) at the risk of failing to detect true treatment effects; (2) recommending intent-to-treat analyses that include as part of the treatment those units that have never received treatment; (3) denigrating inferences that result from exploring unplanned treatment interactions with characteristics of units, observations, settings, or times; and (4) rigidly pursuing a priori experimental questions when other interesting questions emerge during a study. Most laypersons use a more liberal risk calculus to decide about causal inferences in their own lives, as when they consider taking up some potentially lifesaving therapy. Should not science do the same, be less conservative? Should it not at least sometimes make different tradeoffs between protection against incorrect inferences and the failure to detect true effects?

Critics further object that experiments prioritize descriptive over explanatory causation. The critics in question would tolerate more uncertainty about whether the intervention works in order to learn more about any explanatory processes that have the potential to generalize across units, settings, observations, and times. Further, some critics prefer to pursue this explanatory knowledge using qualitative methods similar to those of the historian, journalist, and ethnographer than by means of, say, structural equation modeling that seems much more opaque than the narrative reports of these other fields.

Critics also dislike the priority that experiments give to providing policymakers with often belated answers about what works instead of providing real-time help to service providers in local settings. These providers are rarely interested in a long-delayed summary of what a program has achieved. They often prefer receiving continuous feedback about their work and especially about those elements of practice that they can change without undue complication. A recent letter to the *New York Times* captured this preference:

> Alan Krueger . . . claims to eschew value judgments and wants to approach issues (about educational reform) empirically. Yet his insistence on postponing changes in education policy until studies by researchers approach certainty is itself a value judgment in favor of the status quo. In view of the tragic state of affairs in parts of public education, his judgment is a most questionable one. (Petersen, 1999)

We agree with many of these criticisms. Among all possible research questions, causal questions constitute only a subset. And of all possible causal methods, experimentation is not relevant to all types of questions and all types of circumstance. One need only read the list of options and contingencies outlined in Chapters 9 and 10 to appreciate how foolhardy it is to advocate experimentation on a routine basis as a causal "gold standard" that will invariably result in clearly interpretable effect sizes. However, many of the criticisms about tradeoffs are based on artificial dichotomies, correctable problems, and even oversimplifications. Experiments can and should examine reasons for variable implementation, and they should search to uncover mediating processes. They need not use stringent alpha rates; only statistical tradition argues for the .05 level. Nor need one restrict data analyses only to the intent-to-treat, though that should definitely be one analysis. Experimenters can also explore statistical interactions to the extent that substantive theory and statistical power allow, guarding against profligate error rates and couching their conclusions cautiously. Interim results from experiments can be published. There can and should also be nonexperimental analyses of the representativeness of samples and the construct validity of assessments of persons, settings, treatments, and outcomes. There can and should be qualitative data collection aimed at discovering unintended outcomes and mediating processes. And as much information as possible about causal generalization should be generated using the methods outlined in this book. All these procedures require resources, but sometimes few of them (e.g., adding measures of mediating variables). Experiments need not be as rigid as some texts suggest, and the goal of ever-finer marginal improvements in internal validity is often a poor one.

In the latter regard, some critics have claimed that more useful information will be learned from programs of research that consist mostly or even entirely of quasi-experimental and nonexperimental studies than from programs emphasizing the stronger experimental methods (e.g., Cronbach et al., 1980; Cronbach, 1982). Although we are generally sympathetic to this point, some bounds cannot be crossed without compromising the integrity of key inferences. Unless threats to internal validity are clearly implausible on logical or evidential grounds, to have *no* strong experimental studies on the effects of an intervention is to risk drawing broad general conclusions about a causal connection that is undependable. This happens all too often, alas. It is now 30 years since school vouchers were proposed, and we still have no clear answers about their effects. It is 15 years since Henry Levin began accelerated schools, and we have no experiments and no answers. It is 30 years since James Comer began the School Development Program, and almost the same situation holds. Although premature experimentation is a real danger, such decade-long time lines without clear answers are probably even more problematic, particularly for those legislators and their staffs who want to promote effectiveness-based social policies. Finding out what works is too important to suggest that experiments require tradeoffs that are *never* worth making.

By contrast, we are impressed with the capacity of programs of experimental research to address both construct and external validity issues modestly well. Granted, individual experiments have limited reach in addressing both these issues, but as we see most clearly in meta-analysis, the capacity to address both construct and external validity issues over multiple experiments greatly exceeds what past critics have suggested. Of course, as we made clear in Chapter 2, we are not calling for any routine primacy of internal validity over construct or external validity (every validity type must have its time in the spotlight). Rather, we are calling attention to the inferential weaknesses that history suggests have emerged in programs of research that deemphasize internal validity too much and to the surprisingly broad inferential reach of programs in which internal validity plays a much more prominent role.

Experiments Assume an Invalid Model of Research Utilization

To some critics, experiments recreate a naïve rational choice model of decision making. That is, one first lays out the alternatives to choose among (the treatments); then one decides on criteria of merit (the outcomes); then one collects information on each criterion for each treatment (the data collection), and finally one makes a decision about the superior alternative. Unfortunately, empirical work on the use of social science data shows that use is not so simple as the rational choice model suggests (C. Weiss & Bucuvalas, 1980; C. Weiss, 1988).

First, even when cause and effect questions are asked in decision contexts, experimental results are still used along with other forms of information—from existing theories, personal testimony, extrapolations from surveys, consensus of a field, claims from experts with interests to defend, and ideas that have recently become trendy. Decisions are shaped partly by ideology, interests, politics, personality, windows of opportunity, and values; and they are as much made by a policy-shaping community (Cronbach et al., 1980) as by an individual or committee. Further, many decisions are not so much made as accreted over time as earlier decisions constrain later ones, leaving the final decision maker with few options (Weiss, 1980). Indeed, by the time experimental results are available, new decision makers and issues may have replaced old ones.

Second, experiments often yield contested rather than unanimous verdicts that therefore have uncertain implications for decisions. Disputes arise about whether the causal questions were correctly framed, whether results are valid, whether relevant outcomes were assessed, and whether the results entail a specific decision. For example, reexaminations of the Milwaukee educational voucher study offered different conclusions about whether and where effects occurred (H. Fuller, 2000; Greene, Peterson, & Du, 1999; Witte, 1998, 1999, 2000). Similarly, different effect sizes were generated from the Tennessee class size experiment (Finn & Achilles, 1990; Hanushek, 1999; Mosteller, Light, & Sachs, 1996). Sometimes, scholarly disagreements are at issue, but at other times the disputes reflect deeply conflicted stakeholder interests.

Third, short-term instrumental use of experimental data is more likely when the intervention is a minor variant on existing practice. For example, it is easier to change textbooks in a classroom or pills given to patients or eligibility criteria for program entry than it is to relocate hospitals to underserved locations or to open day-care centers for welfare recipients throughout an entire state. Because the more feasible changes are so modest in scope, they are less likely to dramatically affect the problem they address. So critics note that prioritizing on short-term instrumental change tends to preserve most of the status quo and is unlikely to solve trenchant social problems. Of course, there are some experiments that truly twist the lion's tail and involve bold initiatives. Thus moving families from densely poor inner-city locations to the suburbs involved a change of three standard deviations in the poverty level of the sending and receiving communities, much greater than what happens when poor families spontaneously move. Whether such a dramatic change could ever be used as a model for cleaning out the inner cities of those who want to move is a moot issue. Many would judge such a policy to be unlikely. Truly bold experiments have many important rationales; but creating new policies that look like the treatment soon after the experiment is not one of them.

Fourth, the most frequent use of research may be conceptual rather than instrumental, changing how users think about basic assumptions, how they understand contexts, and how they organize or label ideas. Some conceptual uses are intentional, as when a person deliberately reads a book on a current problem; for example, Murray's (1984) book on social policy had such a conceptual impact in the 1980s, creating a new social policy agenda. But other conceptual uses occur in passing, as when a person reads a newspaper story referring to social research. Such uses can have great long-run impact as new ways of thinking move through the system, but they rarely change particular short-term decisions.

These arguments against a naïve rational decision-making model of experimental usefulness are compelling. That model is rightly rejected. However, most of the objections are true not just of experiments but of all social science methods. Consider controversies over the accuracy of the U.S. Census, the entirely descriptive results of which enter into a decision-making process about the apportionment of resources that is complex and highly politically charged. No method offers a direct road to short-term instrumental use. Moreover, the objections are exaggerated. In settings such as the U.S. Congress, decision making is *sometimes* influenced instrumentally by social science information (Chelimsky, 1998), and experiments frequently contribute to that use as part of a research review on effectiveness questions. Similarly, policy initiatives get recycled, as happened with school vouchers, so that social science data that were not used in past years are used later when they become instrumentally relevant to a current issue (Polsby, 1984; Quirk, 1986). In addition, data about effectiveness influence many stakeholders' thinking even when they do not use the information quickly or instrumentally. Indeed, research suggests that high-quality experiments can confer extra credibility among policymakers and decision makers (C. Weiss & Bucuvalas, 1980), as happened with the Tennessee class size study. We should also not forget that the conceptual use of experiments occurs when the texts used to train professionals in a given field contain results of past studies about successful practice (Leviton & Cook, 1983). And using social science data to produce incremental change is not always trivial. Small changes can yield benefits of hundreds of millions of dollars (Fienberg, Singer, & Tanur, 1985). Sociologist Carol Weiss, an advocate of doing research for enlightenment's sake, says that 3 decades of experience and her studies of the use of social science data leave her "impressed with the utility of evaluation findings in stimulating incremental increases in knowledge and in program effectiveness. Over time, cumulative increments are not such small potatoes after all" (Weiss, 1998, p. 319). Finally, the usefulness of experiments can be increased by the actions outlined earlier in this chapter that involve complementing basic experimental design with adjuncts such as measures of implementation and mediation or qualitative methods—anything that will help clarify program process and implementation problems. In summary, invalid models of the usefulness of experimental results seem to us to be no more nor less common than invalid models of the use of any other social science methods. We have learned much in the last several decades about use, and experimenters who want their work to be useful can take advantages of those lessons (Shadish et al., 1991).

The Conditions of Experimentation Differ from the Conditions of Policy Implementation

Experiments are often done on a smaller scale than would pertain if services were implemented state- or nationwide, and so they cannot mimic all the details relevant to full policy implementation. Hence policy implementation of an intervention may yield different outcomes than the experiment (Elmore, 1996). For example, based partly on research about the benefits of reducing class size, Tennessee and California implemented statewide policies to have more classes with fewer students in each. This required many new teachers and new classrooms. However, because of a national teacher shortage, some of those new teachers may have been less qualified than those in the experiment; and a shortage of classrooms led to more use of trailers and dilapidated buildings that may have harmed effectiveness further.

Sometimes an experimental treatment is an innovation that generates enthusiastic efforts to implement it well. This is particularly frequent when the experiment is done by a charismatic innovator whose tacit knowledge may exceed that of those who would be expected to implement the program in ordinary practice and whose charisma may induce high-quality implementation. These factors may generate more successful outcomes than will be seen when the intervention is implemented as routine policy.

Policy implementation may also yield different results when experimental treatments are implemented in a fashion that differs from or conflicts with practices in real-world application. For example, experiments studying psychotherapy outcome often standardize treatment with a manual and sometimes observe and correct the therapist for deviating from the manual (Shadish et al., 2000); but these practices are rare in clinical practice. If manualized treatment is more effective (Chambless & Hollon, 1998; Kendall, 1998), experimental results might transfer poorly to practice settings.

Random assignment may also change the program from the intended policy implementation (Heckman, 1992). For example, those willing to be randomized may differ from those for whom the treatment is intended; randomization may change people's psychological or social response to treatment compared with those who self-select treatment; and randomization may disrupt administration and implementation by forcing the program to cope with a different mix of clients.

Heckman claims this kind of problem with the Job Training Partnership Act (JTPA) evaluation "calls into question the validity of the experimental estimates as a statement about the JTPA system as a whole" (Heckman, 1992, p. 221).

In many respects, we agree with these criticisms, though it is worth noting several responses to them. First, they *assume* a lack of generalizability from experiment to policy, but that is an *empirical* question. Some data suggest that generalization may be high despite differences between lab and field (C. Anderson, Lindsay, & Bushman, 1999) or between research and practice (Shadish et al., 2000). Second, it can help to implement treatment under conditions that are more characteristic of practice if it does not unduly compromise other research priorities. A little forethought can improve the surface similarity of units, treatments, observations, settings, or times to their intended targets. Third, some of these criticisms are true of *any* research methodology conducted in a limited context, such as locally conducted case studies or quasi-experiments, because local implementation issues always differ from large-scale issues. Fourth, the potentially disruptive nature of experimentally manipulated interventions is shared by many locally invented novel programs, *even when they are not studied by any research methodology at all*. Innovation inherently disrupts, and substantive literatures are rife with examples of innovations that encountered policy implementation impediments (Shadish, 1984).

However, the essential problem remains that large-scale policy implementation is a singular event, the effects of which cannot be fully known except by doing the full implementation. A single experiment, or even a small series of similar ones, cannot provide complete answers about what will happen if the intervention is adopted as policy. However, Heckman's criticism needs reframing. He fails to distinguish among validity types (statistical conclusion, internal, construct, external). Doing so makes it clear that his claim that such criticism "calls into question the validity of the experimental estimates as a statement about the JTPA system as a whole" (Heckman, 1992, p. 221) is really about external validity and construct validity, not statistical conclusion or internal validity. Except in the narrow econometrics tradition that he understandably cites (Haavelmo, 1944; Marschak, 1953; Tinbergen, 1956), few social experimenters ever claimed that experiments could describe the "system as a whole"—even Fisher (1935) acknowledged this trade-off. Further, the econometric solutions that Heckman suggests cannot avoid the same tradeoffs between internal and external validity. For example, surveys and certain quasi-experiments can avoid some problems by observing existing interventions that have already been widely implemented, but the validity of their estimates of program effects are suspect and may themselves change if the program were imposed even more widely as policy.

Addressing these criticisms requires multiple lines of evidence—randomized experiments of efficacy and effectiveness, nonrandomized experiments that observe existing interventions, nonexperimental surveys to yield estimates of representativeness, statistical analyses that bracket effects under diverse assumptions, qualitative observation to discover potential incompatibilities between the intervention and its context of likely implementation, historical study of the fates of similar interventions when they were implemented as policy, policy analyses by those with expertise in the type of intervention at issue, and the methods for causal generalization in this book. The conditions of policy implementation will be different from the conditions characteristic of *any* research study of it, so predicting generalization to policy will always be one of the toughest problems.

Imposing Treatments Is Fundamentally Flawed Compared with Encouraging the Growth of Local Solutions to Problems

Experiments impose treatments on recipients. Yet some late 20th-century thought suggests that imposed solutions may be inferior to solutions that are locally generated by those who have the problem. Partly, this view is premised on research findings of few effects for the Great Society social programs of the 1960s in the United States (Murray, 1984; Rossi, 1987), with the presumption that a portion of the failure was due to the federally imposed nature of the programs. Partly, the view reflects the success of late 20th-century free market economics and conservative political ideologies compared with centrally controlled economies and more liberal political beliefs. Experimentally imposed treatments are seen in some quarters as being inconsistent with such thinking.

Ironically, the first objection is based on results of experiments—if it is true that imposed programs do not work, experiments provided the evidence. Moreover, these no-effect findings may have been partly due to methodological failures of experiments as they were implemented at that time. Much progress in solving practical experimental problems occurred after, and partly in response to, those experiments. If so, it is premature to assume these experiments definitively demonstrated no effect, especially given our increased ability to detect small effects today (D. Greenberg & Shroder, 1997; Lipsey, 1992; Lipsey & Wilson, 1993).

We must also distinguish between political-economic currency and the effects of interventions. We know of no comparisons of, say, the effects of locally generated versus imposed solutions. Indeed, the methodological problems in doing such comparisons are daunting, especially accurately categorizing interventions into the two categories and unconfounding the categories with correlated method differences. Barring an unexpected solution to the seemingly intractable problems of causal inference in nonrandomized designs, answering questions about the effects of locally generated solutions may require exactly the kind of high-quality experimentation being criticized. Though it is likely that locally generated solutions may indeed have significant advantages, it also is likely that some of those solutions will have to be experimentally evaluated.

CAUSAL GENERALIZATION: AN OVERLY COMPLICATED THEORY?

Internal validity is best promoted via random assignment, an omnibus mechanism that ensures that we do not have many assumptions to worry about when causal inference is our goal. By contrast, quasi-experiments require us to make explicit many assumptions—the threats to internal validity—that we then have to rule out by fiat, by design, or by measurement. The latter is a more complex and assumption-riddled process that is clearly inferior to random assignment. Something similar holds for causal generalization, in which random selection is the most parsimonious and theoretically justified method, requiring the fewest assumptions when causal generalization is our goal. But because random selection is so rarely feasible, one instead has to construct an acceptable theory of generalization out of purposive sampling, a much more difficult process. We have tried to do this with our five principles of generalized causal inference. These, we contend, are the keys to generalized inference that lie behind random sampling and that have to be identified, explicated, and assessed if we are to make better general inferences, even if they are not perfect ones. But these principles are much more complex to implement than is random sampling.

Let us briefly illustrate this with the category called American adult women. We could represent this category by random selection from a critically appraised register of all women who live in the United States and who are at least 21 years of age. Within the limits of sampling error, we could formally generalize any characteristics we measured on this sample to the population on that register. Of course, we cannot select this way because no such register exists. Instead, one does one's experiment with an opportunistic sample of women. On inspection they all turn out to be between 19 and 30 years of age, to be higher than average in achievement and ability, and to be attending school—that is, we have used a group of college women. Surface similarity suggests that each is an instance of the category *woman*. But it is obvious that the modal American woman is clearly not a college student. Such students constitute an overly homogeneous sample with respect to educational abilities and achievement, socioeconomic status, occupation, and all observable and unobservable correlates thereof, including health status, current employment, and educational and occupational aspirations and expectations. To remedy this bias, we could use a more complex purposive sampling design that selects women heterogeneously on all these characteristics. But purposive sampling for heterogeneous instances can never do this as well as random selection can, and it is certainly more complex to conceive and execute. We could go on and illustrate how the other principles facilitate generalization. The point is that any theory of generalization from purposive samples is bound to be more complicated than the simplicity of random selection.

But because random selection is rarely possible when testing causal relationships within an experimental framework, we need these purposive alternatives.

Yet most experimental work probably still relies on the weakest of these alternatives, surface similarity. We seek to improve on such uncritical practice. Unfortunately, though, there is often restricted freedom for the more careful selection of instances of units, treatments, outcomes, and settings, even when the selection is done purposively. It requires resources to sample irrelevancies so that they are heterogeneous on many attributes, to measure several related constructs that can be discriminated from each other conceptually, and to measure a variety of possible explanatory processes. This is partly why we expect more progress on causal generalization from a review context rather than from single studies. Thus, if one researcher can work with college women, another can work with female schoolteachers, and another with female retirees, this creates an opportunity to see if these sources of irrelevant homogeneity make a difference to a causal relationship or whether it holds over all these different types of women.

Ultimately, causal generalization will always be more complicated than assessing the likelihood that a relationship is causal. The theory is more diffuse, more recent, and less well tested in the crucible of research experience. And in some quarters there is disdain for the issue, given the belief and practice that relationships that replicate once should be considered as general until proven otherwise, not to speak of the belief that little progress and prestige can be achieved by designing the next experiment to be some minor variant on past studies. There is no point in pretending that causal generalization is as institutionalized procedurally as other methods in the social sciences. We have tried to set the theoretical agenda in a systematic way. But we do not expect to have the last word. There is still no explication of causal generalization equivalent to the empirically produced list of threats to internal validity and the quasi-experimental designs that have evolved over 40 years to rule out these threats. The agenda is set but not complete.

NONEXPERIMENTAL ALTERNATIVES

Though this book is about experimental methods for answering questions about causal hypotheses, it is a mistake to believe that only experimental approaches are used for this purpose. In the following, we briefly consider several other approaches, indicating the major reasons why we have not dwelt on them in detail. Basically, the reason is that we believe that, whatever their merits for some research purposes, they generate less clear causal conclusions than randomized experiments or even the best quasi-experiments such as regression-discontinuity or interrupted time series.

The nonexperimental alternatives we examine are the major ones to emerge in various academic disciplines. In education and parts of anthropology and sociology, one alternative is intensive qualitative case studies. In these same fields, and also in developmental psychology, there is an emerging interest in theory-based causal studies based on causal modeling practices. Across the social sciences other than economics and statistics, the word *quasi-experiment* is routinely used to justify causal inferences, even though designs so referred to are so primitive in structure that causal conclusions are often problematic. We have to challenge such advocacy of low-grade quasi-experiments as a valid alternative to the quality of studies we have been calling for in this book. And finally, in parts of statistics and epidemiology, and overwhelmingly in econometrics and those parts of sociology and political science that draw from econometrics, the emphasis is more on control through statistical manipulation than on experimental design. When descriptive causal inferences are the primary concern, all of these alternatives will usually be inferior to experiments.

Intensive Qualitative Case Studies

The call to generate causal conclusions from intensive case studies comes from several sources. One is from quantitative researchers in education who became disenchanted with the tools of their trade and subsequently came to prefer the qualitative methods of the historian and journalist and especially of the ethnographer (e.g., Guba, 1981, 1990; and more tentatively, Cronbach, 1986). Another is from those researchers originally trained in primary disciplines such as qualitative anthropology (e.g., Fetterman, 1984) or sociology (Patton, 1980).

The enthusiasm for case study methods arises for several different reasons. One is that qualitative methods often reduce enough uncertainty about causation to meet stakeholder needs. Most advocates point out that journalists, historians, ethnographers, and lay persons regularly make valid causal inferences using a qualitative process that combines reasoning, observation, and falsificationist procedures in order to rule out threats to internal validity—even if that kind of language is not explicitly used (e.g., Becker, 1958; Cronbach, 1982). A small minority of qualitative theorists go even further to claim that case studies can routinely replace experiments for nearly any causal-sounding question they can conceive (e.g., Lincoln & Guba, 1985). A second reason is the belief that such methods can also engage a broad view of causation that permits getting at the many forces in the world and human minds that together influence behavior in much more complex ways than any experiment will uncover. And the third reason is the belief that case studies are broader than experiments in the types of information they yield. For example, they can inform readers about such useful and diverse matters as how pertinent problems were formulated by stakeholders, what the substantive theories of the intervention are, how well implemented the intervention components were, what distal, as well as proximal, effects have come about in respondents' lives, what unanticipated side effects there have been, and what processes explain the pattern of obtained results. The claim is that intensive case study methods allow probes of an A to B connection, of a broad range of factors conditioning this relationship, and of a range of intervention-relevant questions that is broader than the experiment allows.

Although we agree that qualitative evidence can reduce some uncertainty about cause—sometimes substantially—the conditions under which this occurs are usually rare (Campbell, 1975). In particular, qualitative methods usually produce unclear knowledge about the counterfactual of greatest importance, how those who received treatment would have changed without treatment. Adding design features to case studies, such as comparison groups and pretreatment observations, clearly improves causal inference. But it does so by melding case-study data collection methods with experimental design. Although we consider this as a valuable addition to ways of thinking about case studies, many advocates of the method would no longer recognize it as still being a case study. To our way of thinking, case studies are very relevant when causation is at most a minor issue; but in most other cases when substantial uncertainty reduction about causation is required, we value qualitative methods within experiments rather than as alternatives to them, in ways similar to those we outlined in Chapter 12.

Theory-Based Evaluations

This approach has been formulated relatively recently and is described in various books or special journal issues (Chen & Rossi, 1992; Connell, Kubisch, Schorr, & Weiss, 1995; Rogers, Hacsi, Petrosino, & Huebner, 2000). Its origins are in path analysis and causal modeling traditions that are much older. Although advocates have some differences with each other, basically they all contend that it is useful: (1) to explicate the theory of a treatment by detailing the expected relationships among inputs, mediating processes, and short- and long-term outcomes; (2) to measure all the constructs specified in the theory; and (3) to analyze the data to assess the extent to which the postulated relationships actually occurred. For shorter time periods, the available data may address only the first part of a postulated causal chain; but over longer periods the complete model could be involved. Thus, the priority is on highly specific substantive theory, high-quality measurement, and valid analysis of multivariate explanatory processes as they unfold in time (Chen & Rossi, 1987, 1992).

Such theoretical exploration is important. It can clarify general issues with treatments of a particular type, suggest specific research questions, describe how the intervention functions, spell out mediating processes, locate opportunities to remedy implementation failures, and provide lively anecdotes for reporting results (Weiss, 1998). All these serve to increase the knowledge yield, even when such theoretical analysis is done within an experimental framework. There is nothing about the approach that makes it an alternative to experiments. It can clearly be a very important adjunct to such studies, and in this role we heartily endorse the approach (Cook, 2000).

However, some authors (e.g., Chen & Rossi, 1987, 1992; Connell et al., 1995) have advocated theory-based evaluation as an attractive alternative to experiments when it comes to testing causal hypotheses. It is attractive for several reasons. First, it requires only a treatment group, not a comparison group whose agreement to be in the study might be problematic and whose participation increases research costs. Second, demonstrating a match between theory and data suggests the validity of the causal theory without having to go through a laborious process of explicitly considering alternative explanations. Third, it is often impractical to measure distant end points in a presumed causal chain. So confirmation of attaining proximal end points through theory-specified processes can be used in the interim to inform program staff about effectiveness to date, to argue for more program resources if the program seems to be on theoretical track, to justify claims that the program might be effective in the future on the as-yet-not-assessed distant criteria, and to defend against premature summative evaluations that claim that an intervention is ineffective before it has been demonstrated that the processes necessary for the effect have actually occurred.

However, major problems exist with this approach for high-quality descriptive causal inference (Cook, 2000). First, our experience in writing about the theory of a program with its developer (Anson et al., 1991) has shown that the theory is not always clear and could be clarified in diverse ways. Second, many theories are linear in their flow, omitting reciprocal feedback or external contingencies that might moderate the entire flow. Third, few theories specify how long it takes for a given process to affect an indicator, making it unclear if null results disconfirm a link or suggest that the next step did not yet occur. Fourth, failure to corroborate a model could stem from partially invalid measures as opposed to invalidity of the theory. Fifth, many different models can fit a data set (Glymour et al., 1987; Stelzl, 1986), so our confidence in any given model may be small. Such problems are often fatal to an approach that relies on theory to make strong causal claims. Though some of these problems are present in experiments (e.g., failure to incorporate reciprocal causation, poor measures), they are of far less import because experiments do not require a well-specified theory in constructing causal knowledge. Experimental causal knowledge is less ambitious than theory-based knowledge, but the more limited ambition is attainable.

Weaker Quasi-Experiments

For some researchers, random assignment is undesirable for practical or ethical reasons, so they prefer quasi-experiments. Clearly, we support thoughtful use of quasi-experimentation to study descriptive causal questions. Both interrupted time series and regression discontinuity often yield excellent effect estimates. Slightly weaker quasi-experiments can also yield defensible estimates, especially when they involve control groups with careful matching on stable pretest attributes combined with other design features that have been thoughtfully chosen to address contextually plausible threats to validity. However, when a researcher can choose, randomized designs are usually superior to nonrandomized designs.

This is especially true of nonrandomized designs in which little thought is given to such matters as the quality of the match when creating control groups, including multiple hypothesis tests rather than a single one, generating data from several pretreatment time points rather than one, or having several comparison groups to create controls that bracket performance in the treatment groups. Indeed, when results from typical quasi-experiments are compared with those from randomized experiments on the same topic, several findings emerge. Quasi-experiments frequently misestimate effects (Heinsman & Shadish, 1996; Shadish & Ragsdale, 1996). These biases are often large and plausibly due to selection biases such as the self-selection of more distressed clients into psychotherapy treatment conditions (Shadish et al., 2000) or of patients with a poorer prognosis into controls in medical experiments (Kunz & Oxman, 1998). These biases are especially prevalent in quasi-experiments that use poor quality control groups and have higher attrition (Heinsman & Shadish, 1996; Shadish & Ragsdale, 1996). So, if the answers obtained from randomized experiments are more credible than those from quasi-experiments on theoretical grounds and are more accurate empirically, then the arguments for randomized experiments are even stronger whenever a high degree of uncertainty reduction is required about a descriptive causal claim.

Because all quasi-experiments are not equal in their ability to reduce uncertainty about cause, we want to draw attention again to a common but unfortunate practice in many social sciences—to say that a quasi-experiment is being done in order to provide justification that the resulting inference will be valid. Then a quasi-experimental design is described that is so deficient in the desirable structural features noted previously, which promote better inference, that it is probably not worth doing. Indeed, over the years we have repeatedly noted the term *quasi-experiment* being used to justify designs that fell into the class that Campbell and Stanley (1963) labeled as uninterpretable and that Cook and Campbell (1979) labeled as generally uninterpretable. These are the simplest forms of the designs discussed in Chapters 4 and 5. Quasi-experiments cannot be an alternative to randomized experiments when the latter are feasible, and poor quasi-experiments can never be a substitute for stronger quasi-experiments when the latter are also feasible. Just as Gueron (1999) has reminded us about randomized experiments, good quasi-experiments have to be fought for, too. They are rarely handed out as though on a silver plate.

Statistical Controls

In this book, we have advocated that statistical adjustments for group nonequivalence are best used *after* design controls have already been used to the maximum in order to reduce nonequivalence to a minimum. So we are not opponents of statistical adjustment techniques such as those advocated by the statisticians and econometricians described in the appendix to Chapter 5. Rather, we want to use them as the last resort. The position we do not like is the assumption that statistical controls are so well developed that they can be used to obtain confident results in nonexperimental and weak quasi-experimental contexts. As we saw in Chapter 5, research in the past 2 decades has not much supported the notion that a control group can be constructed through matching from some national or state registry when the treatment group comes from a more circumscribed and local setting. Nor has research much supported the use of statistical adjustments in longitudinal national surveys in which individuals with different experiences are explicitly contrasted in order to estimate the effects of this experience difference. Undermatching is a chronic problem here, as are consequences of unreliability in the selection variables, not to speak of specification errors due to incomplete knowledge of the selection process. In particular, endogeneity problems are a real concern. We are heartened that more recent work on statistical adjustments seems to be moving toward the position we represent, with greater emphasis being placed on internal controls, on stable matching within such internal controls, on the desirability of seeking cohort controls through the use of siblings, on the use of pretests collected on the same measures as the posttest, on the utility of such pretest measures collected at several different times, and on the desirability of studying interventions that are clearly exogenous shocks to some ongoing system. We are also heartened by the progress being made in the statistical domain because it includes progress on design considerations, as well as on analysis per se (e.g., Rosenbaum, 1999a). We are agnostic at this time as to the virtues of the propensity score and instrumental variable approaches that predominate in discussions of statistical adjustment. Time will tell how well they pan out relative to the results from randomized experiments. We have surely not heard the last word on this topic.

CONCLUSION

We cannot point to one new development that has revolutionized field experimentation in the past few decades, yet we have seen a very large number of incremental improvements. As a whole, these improvements allow us to create far better field experiments than we could do 40 years ago when Campbell and Stanley (1963) first wrote. In this sense, we are very optimistic about the future. We believe that we will continue to see steady, incremental growth in our knowledge about how to do better field experiments. The cost of this growth, however, is that field experimentation has become a more specialized topic, both in terms of knowledge development and of the opportunity to put that knowledge into practice in the conduct of field experiments. As a result, nonspecialists who wish to do a field experiment may greatly benefit by consulting with those with the expertise, especially for large experiments, for experiments in which implementation problems may be high, or for cases in which methodological vulnerabilities will greatly reduce credibility. The same is true, of course, for many other methods. Case-study methods, for example, have become highly enough developed that most researchers would do an amateurish job of using them without specialized training or supervised practice. Such Balkanization of methodology is, perhaps, inevitable, though none the less regrettable. We can ease the regret somewhat by recognizing that with specialization may come faster progress in solving the problems of field experimentation.

Glossary

Alternative Hypothesis: Whatever alternative to the null hypothesis is being considered. (See also *Null Hypothesis, Null Hypothesis Significance Testing*)

Analogue Experiment: An experiment that manipulates a cause that is similar to another cause of interest in order to learn about the latter cause.

Assignment Variable: A variable or variables used to assign units to conditions.

Attrition: Loss of units; in randomized experiments, refers to loss that occurs after random assignment has taken place (also called *Mortality*).

Autocorrelation: The correlation of consecutive observations over time.

Balanced Sample: A purposive sample whose mean on a characteristic matches the population mean for that characteristic.

Bandwidth: The capacity of a method to provide data about many different kinds of questions, often at the cost of reduced precision in the answers.

Batch Randomization: Many or all units are available to be assigned to conditions at one time.

Between-Participants Design: Different units are studied in different conditions. (See also *Within-Participants Design*)

Bias: Systematic error in an estimate or an inference.

Blocking: The process of dividing units into groups with similar scores on a blocking variable, each group having the same number of units as the number of conditions. (See also *Matching, Stratifying*)

Carryover Effects: The effects of one treatment do not end prior to the administration of a second treatment, so that the effects observed in the second treatment include residual effects from the first.

Case-Control Study: A study that contrasts units with an outcome of interest to those without the outcome to identify retrospectively the predictors or causes of the outcome (also called *Case-Referent Study*).

Case-Referent Study: See *Case-Control Study*

Causal Description: Identifying that a causal relationship exists between A and B.

Causal Explanation: Explaining how A causes B.

Causal Generalization: Inferences that describe how well a causal relationship extends across or beyond the conditions that were studied.

Causal Model: A model of causal relationships, usually with mediators; sometimes refers to efforts to identify causes and effects in nonexperimental studies.

Cause: A variable that produces an effect or result.

Ceiling Effect: Responses on a variable closely approach the maximum possible response so that further increases are difficult to obtain. (See also *Floor Effect*)

Coherence Theory of Truth: An epistemological theory that says a claim is true if it belongs to a coherent set of claims.

Comparison Group: In an experiment, a group that is compared with a treatment group and that may receive either an alternate intervention or no intervention. (See also *Control Group, Placebo, Treatment Group*)

Compound Path: A path consisting of two or more direct paths connected together.

Confirmation: The strategy of showing that a hypothesis is correct or is supported by evidence.

Confound: An extraneous variable that covaries with the variable of interest.

Construct: A concept, model, or schematic idea.

Construct Validity: The degree to which inferences are warranted from the observed persons, settings, and cause-and-effect operations sampled within a study to the constructs that these samples represent.

Control Group: In an experiment, this term typically refers to a comparison group that does not receive a treatment but that may be assigned to a no-treatment condition, to a wait list for treatment, or sometimes to a placebo intervention group. (See also *Comparison Group, Placebo, Treatment Group*)

Convergent Validity: The idea that two measures of the same thing should correlate with each other. (See also *Discriminant Validity*)

Correlation: A measure of the strength of relationship between two variables.

Correlational Study: A study that observes relationships between variables. (See also *Nonexperimental Study, Observational Study, Quasi-Experiment*)

Correspondence Theory of Truth: An epistemological theory that says a knowledge claim is true if it corresponds to the world.

Counterbalancing: In within-participants designs, arranging the order of conditions to vary over units so that some units are given Treatment A first but others are given Treatment B first.

Counterfactual: The state of affairs that would have happened in the absence of the cause.

Critical Multiplism: The claim that no single method is bias free, so that the strategy should be to use multiple methods, each of which has a different bias.

Cross-Lagged Panel Design: A design in which a cause and an effect are both measured at Times 1 and 2 and the researcher looks to see if the relationship between the cause at Time 1 and the effect at Time 2 is stronger than the relationship between the effect at Time 1 and the cause at Time 2.

Crossed Designs: Designs in which all units are exposed to all conditions.

Debriefing: The process of informing research participants about a study after it is over.

Deflationism: An epistemological theory that says truth is a trivial linguistic device for assenting to propositions expressed by sentences too numerous, lengthy, or cumbersome to utter.

Dependent Variable: Often synonymous with *effect* or *outcome*, a variable with a value that varies in response to the independent variable.

Design Element: Something an experimenter can manipulate or control in an experiment to help address a threat to validity.

Direct Path: A causal path that directly connects two variables.

Discriminant Validity: The notion that a measure of A can be discriminated from a measure of B, when B is thought to be different from A; discriminant validity correlations should be lower than convergent validity correlations. (See also *Convergent Validity*)

Dismantling Study: A study that breaks down a treatment into its component parts to test the effectiveness of the parts.

Double-Blind Study: An experiment in which both the treatment provider and treatment recipient are unaware of which treatment or control condition is being administered, primarily used in medical clinical trials.

Effect Size: A measure of the magnitude of a relationship, specific instances of which include the standardized mean difference statistic, the odds ratio, the correlation coefficient, the rate difference, and the rate ratio.

Effectiveness: How well an intervention works when it is implemented under conditions of actual application. (See also *Efficacy*)

Efficacy: How well an intervention works when implemented under ideal conditions. (See also *Effectiveness*)

Endogenous Variable: A variable that is caused by other variables within the model.

Epistemology: Philosophy of the justifications for knowledge claims.

Ethnography: Unstructured exploratory investigation, usually of a small number of cases, of the meaning and functions of human action, reported primarily in narrative form.

Exogenous Variable: A variable that is not caused by other variables in the model.

Expectation: The mean of a statistic based on repeated samplings. (See also *Sampling Error*)

Experiment: To explore the effects of manipulating a variable.

External Validity: The validity of inferences about whether the causal relationship holds over variations in persons, settings, treatment variables, and measurement variables.

Falsification: To show that data are inconsistent with a theory or hypothesis.

Fatigue Effects: Participants tire over time, causing performance to deteriorate in later conditions or later assessments. (See also *Practice Effects*, *Testing Effects*)

Fidelity: The capacity of a method to provide precise answers about a narrow question, often at the cost of high bandwidth.

File Drawer Problem: The hypothesis that studies that were rejected because of reviewer prejudice against null findings are never published and so remain unavailable to future literature reviews, resulting in a systematic bias in the results of the review. (See also *Publication Bias*)

Floor Effect: Responses on a variable approach the minimum possible score so that further decreases are difficult to obtain. (See also *Ceiling Effect*)

Functional Form: The characteristics of the true relationship among variables, represented graphically by the shape of the relationship (e.g., is it a curve?) and represented statistically by a model that may include nonlinear terms (e.g., powers and interactions) or other transformations.

Heterogeneity of Irrelevancies: Identifying things that are irrelevant to the inference at issue and then making those irrelevancies heterogeneous so inferences are not confounded with the same irrelevancy or with different irrelevancies whose direction of bias is presumptively in the same direction.

Hidden Bias: Unobserved variables that may cause bias in treatment effect estimates. (See also *Omitted Variables*)

Implementation: The activities, both intended and unintended, that did and did not occur as part of the treatment conditions. (See also *Process Model*)

Independent Variable: Often synonymous with *cause* or *treatment*, a variable that purports to be independent of other influences. Some authors advocate a more limited usage whereby a variable is independent only if the methodology isolates the variable from other influences. (See also *Dependent Variable*)

Indirect Path: A path between two variables that requires going through a third variable to make the connection.

Informed Consent: The process of giving research participants the information they need to make an informed choice about whether to participate in a study given its risks and benefits.

Instrumental Variable: A variable or set of variables (or more generally, an estimation technique) that is correlated with outcome only through an effect on other variables.

Intent-to-Treat Analysis: An analysis of a randomized experiment in which units are analyzed in the condition to which they were assigned, regardless of whether they actually received the treatment in that condition.

Interaction: In experiments, when the effects of treatment vary over levels of another variable. (See also *Moderator*)

Internal Validity: The validity of inferences about whether the relationship between two variables is causal.

Interrupted Time-Series Design: A design in which a string of consecutive observations is interrupted by the imposition of a treatment to see if the slope or intercept of the series changes as a result of the intervention.

Inus Condition: From philosopher J. L. Mackie (1984), the idea that a cause is an *i*nsufficient but *n*on-redundant part of an *u*nnecessary but *s*ufficient condition for bringing about an effect.

Latent Variable: A variable that is not directly observed but is inferred or estimated from observed variables. (See also *Observed Variable*)

Local Molar Causal Validity: Alternative phrase for internal validity suggested by Donald Campbell (1986) as more clearly indicating the nature of internal validity.

Logic of Causation: To infer a causal relationship, the requirements that cause precedes effect, that cause covaries with effect, that alternative explanations can be ruled out, and that knowledge is available of what would have happened in the absence of the cause. (See also *Counterfactual*)

Lowess Smoother: A *lo*cally *we*ighted *s*catterplot *s*moother in which the result is a regression-fitted value for a local regression on a sample of observations in the vicinity of a selected horizontal axis point, done for many such points.

Matching: Sometimes synonymous with blocking, sometimes more specific to imply blocks in which units are exactly equal (rather than just similar) on a matching variable. (See also *Blocking, Stratifying*)

Measurement Attrition: Failure to obtain measures on units (whether or not they are treated).

Mediator: A third variable that comes between a cause and effect and that transmits the causal influence from the cause to the effect. (See also *Molecular Causation*)

Meta-Analysis: A set of quantitative methods for synthesizing research studies on the same topic (also called *Research Synthesis*).

Moderator: In an experiment, a variable that influences the effects of treatment. (See also *Interaction*)

Modus Operandi (M.O.): A method for inferring the cause of an observed effect by matching the pattern of observed effects to the patterns usually left by known causes (analogous to detective work investigating whether clues left at a crime match the modus operandi of known criminals).

Molar Causation: An interest in the overall causal relationship between a treatment package and its effects, in which both may consist of multiple parts.

Molecular Causation: An interest in knowing which parts of a treatment package are more or less responsible for which parts of the effects through which mediational processes. (See also *Mediator*)

Mortality: See *Attrition*

Multiple Operationalism: The notion that all the operations used to index a construct are relevant to the construct of interest but that, across the set of operations, there will be heterogeneity in conceptually irrelevant features.

Natural Experiment: Investigates the effects of a naturally occurring event, sometimes limited to events that are not manipulable, such as earthquakes, and sometimes used more generally.

Nested Designs: Designs in which units are exposed to some but not all conditions. (See also *Nesting, Unit of Analysis Problem*)

Nesting: When some units (e.g., students) are grouped together into aggregate units (e.g., classrooms), units are said to be nested within aggregates. (See also *Nested Designs, Unit of Analysis Problem*)

Nonequivalent Dependent Variable: A dependent variable that is predicted *not* to change because of the treatment but is expected to respond to some or all of the contextually important internal validity threats in the same way as the target outcome.

Nonexperimental Study: Any study that is not an experiment. (See also *Correlational Study, Observational Study*)

Nonrecursive Model: In the structural equation modeling literature, a model that allows reciprocal causation, although some literatures use the term differently. (See also *Reciprocal Causation, Recursive Model*)

Null Hypothesis: The hypothesis being tested, traditionally that there is no relationship between variables. (See also *Alternative Hypothesis, Null Hypothesis Significance Testing*)

Null Hypothesis Significance Testing: The practice of testing the hypothesis that there is no effect [the nil hypothesis] at $\alpha = .05$ and then declaring that an effect exists only if $p < .05$. (See also *Alternative Hypothesis, Null Hypothesis*)

Observational Study: A study in which variables are observed rather than manipulated; used in some literatures to include quasi-experiments (see also *Correlational Study, Nonexperimental Study, Quasi-Experiment*)

Observed Variable: A variable that is directly measured in a study.

Odds Ratio: An effect size measure for the difference between groups on a dichotomous outcome.

Omitted Variables: Variables that are not in a model or an analysis that influence both the cause and the effect and so may cause bias. (See also *Hidden Bias*)

Ontology: Philosophy of the nature of reality.

Operationalization: Usually synonymous with operations but sometimes used in a restricted sense to imply the methods used to represent a construct. (See also *Operations*)

Operations: The actions actually done in a study to represent units, treatments, observations, settings, and times. (See also *Operationalization*)

Order Effects: The outcome of a study is affected by the order in which the treatments were presented.

Participant Observation: A form of observation in which the researcher takes on an established participant role in the context being studied.

Path Coefficient: A measure of the strength of relationship between two variables connected by a direct path.

Pattern Matching: The general concept of matching a pattern of evidence to the pattern predicted by theory or past research.

Placebo: An intervention that does not include the presumed active ingredients of treatment. (See also *Control Group, Treatment Group*)

Power: The probability of correctly rejecting a false null hypothesis; in an experiment, usually interpreted as the probability of finding an effect when an effect exists. (See also *Type II error*)

Practice Effects: Participants become better at something the more often they do it, a potential problem in within-participants designs in which repeated tests are given to the same participants. (See also *Fatigue Effects, Testing Effects*)

Pragmatic Theory of Truth: An epistemological theory that says a claim is true if it is useful to believe that claim.

Process Model: A model that portrays the sequence of events that occur in an intervention. (See also *Implementation*)

Propensity Score: A predicted probability of group membership based on observed predictors, usually obtained from a logistic regression.

Publication Bias: A prejudice on the part of manuscript reviewers against publishing studies that fail to reject the null hypothesis. (See also *File Drawer Problem*)

Purposive Sample: A method by which units are selected to be in a sample by a deliberate method that is not random. (See also *Balanced Sample*)

Purposive Sampling of Heterogeneous Instances: Selecting features of a study (units, treatments, observations, settings, times) that are heterogeneous on characteristics that might make a difference to the inference.

Purposive Sampling of Typical Instances: Selecting features of a study (units, treatments, observations, settings, times) that are similar to typical units in the population of interest, where *typical* may be defined as the mean, median, or mode of that population, determined either impressionistically or based on data about the population.

Quasi-Experiment: An experiment in which units are not randomly assigned to conditions. (See also *Correlational Study, Nonexperimental Study, Observational Study*)

Random Assignment: In an experiment, any procedure for assigning units to conditions based on chance, with every unit having a nonzero probability of being assigned to each condition. (See also *Randomized Experiment*)

Random Measurement Error: Chance factors that influence observed scores so that those scores do not measure the true variable of interest.

Random Sampling: Any procedure for selecting a sample of units from a larger group based on chance, frequently used in survey research to facilitate generalization from sample to population.

Random Selection: More general term that is sometimes used synonymously with either random sampling or random assignment in different contexts.

Randomized Experiment: An experiment in which units are randomly assigned to conditions. (See also *Random Assignment*)

Reciprocal Causation: When two variables cause each other. (See also *Nonrecursive Model, Recursive Model*)

Recursive Model: In the structural equation modeling literature, a model that does not allow reciprocal causation, although some literatures use the term differently. (See also *Nonrecursive Model, Reciprocal Causation*)

Regression Discontinuity: The regression line for a treatment group is discontinuous from the regression line for the control group.

Regression Discontinuity Design: An experiment in which units are assigned to conditions based on exceeding a cutoff on an assignment variable.

Reliability: Consistency.

Research Synthesis: See *Meta-Analysis*

Response Burden: The costs of adding additional measurement to a study in terms of respondent time, energy, and goodwill.

Risk Analysis: An analysis of the likely risks and benefits from a study, including the size of the risks, the likelihood of the risks, and who will suffer them.

Sampling Error: That part of the difference between a population parameter and its sample estimate that is due to the fact that only a sample of observations from the population are observed. (See also *Expectation*)

Secondary Analysis: Reanalysis of primary study data after the study is completed, usually done by someone other than the original authors.

Selection: (1) The process by which units are assigned to conditions. (2) A threat to internal validity in which systematic differences over conditions in respondent characteristics could also cause the observed effect.

Selection Bias: When selection results in differences in unit characteristics between conditions that may be related to outcome differences.

Selection Bias Model: A statistical model that attempts to adjust effect estimates for selection bias.

Self-Selection: When units decide the condition they will enter.

Simple Random Assignment: Random assignment with equal probability of assignment to each condition, without use of ancillary methods such as blocking, matching, or stratification.

Single-Case Designs: A time series done on one person, common in clinical research.

Specification Error: An incorrect specification of the model presumed to have given rise to the data.

Stakeholder: Persons or groups with a stake in a treatment or the study of that treatment.

Standardized Mean Difference Statistic: An effect size measure for continuous variables, computed as the difference between two means divided by the variability of that difference.

Statistical Conclusion Validity: The validity of inferences about covariation between two variables.

Stratifying: The process of creating homogeneous groups of units in which each group has more units than there are experimental conditions. (See also *Blocking, Matching*)

Step Function: A functional relationship between two variables in which the value of one variable suddenly and completely moves from one level to another.

Testing Effects: Effects due to repeated testing of participants over time. (See also *Fatigue Effects, Practice Effects*)

Threats to Validity: Reasons why an inference might be incorrect.

Treatment Adherence: Whether the participant uses the treatment as instructed.

Treatment Attrition: Failure of units to receive treatment (whether or not they are measured).

Treatment Delivery: Whether the treatment is provided by the experimenter to the participant.

Treatment Group: In an experiment, the group that receives the intervention of interest. (See also *Comparison Group, Control Group, Placebo*)

Treatment Receipt: Whether the participant actually receives the treatment that was provided.

Trickle Process Assignment: Units to be assigned are available slowly over time.

Type I Error: Incorrectly rejecting a true null hypothesis; in an experiment, this usually implies concluding that there is an effect when there really is no effect.

Type II Error: Failing to reject a false null hypothesis; in an experiment, this usually implies concluding that there is no effect when there really is an effect. (See also *Power*)

Unit: An opportunity to apply or withhold the treatment.

Unit of Analysis Problem: Units are nested within aggregates in a way that may violate the independence assumption of many statistics. (See also *Nested Designs, Nesting*)

Unreliability: See *Reliability*

utos: An acronym to indicate the study operations that were actually done, where u = units, t = treatment, o = observations, s = setting (from Cronbach, 1982).

UTOS (Pronounced "capital utos"): An acronym to indicate generalizing to the "domain about which [the] question is asked" (Cronbach, 1982, p. 79).

*UTOS (Pronounced "star utos"): An acronym to indicate generalizing to "units, treatments, variables, and settings not directly observed" (Cronbach, 1982, p. 83).

Validity: The truth of, correctness of, or degree of support for an inference.

Within-Participants Designs: The same units are studied in different conditions. (See also *Between-Participants Design*)

References

Abadzi, H. (1984). Ability grouping effects on academic achievement and self-esteem in a southwestern school district. *Journal of Educational Research, 77,* 287–292.

Abadzi, H. (1985). Ability grouping effects on academic achievement and self-esteem: Who performs in the long run as expected? *Journal of Educational Research, 79,* 36–39.

Abelson, R. P. (1995). *Statistics as principled argument.* Hillsdale, NJ: Erlbaum.

Abelson, R. P. (1996). Vulnerability of contrast tests to simpler interpretations: An addendum to Rosnow and Rosenthal. *Psychological Science, 7,* 242–246.

Abelson, R. P. (1997). On the surprising longevity of flogged horses: Why there is a case for the significance test. *Psychological Science, 8,* 12–15.

Achen, C. H. (1986). *The statistical analysis of quasi-experiments.* Berkeley: University of California Press.

Adair, J. G. (1973). The Hawthorne effect: A reconsideration of a methodological artifact. *Journal of Applied Psychology, 69,* 334–345.

Ahlbom, A., & Norell, S. (1990). *Introduction to modern epidemiology.* Chestnut Hill, MA: Epidemiology Resources.

Ahn, C.-K. (1983). A Monte Carlo comparison of statistical methods for estimating treatment effects in regression discontinuity design (Doctoral dissertation, Washington State University, 1983). *Dissertation Abstracts International, 44*(03), 733A.

Aigner, D. J., & Hausman, J. A. (1980). Correcting for truncation bias in the analysis of experiments in time-of-day pricing of electricity. *Bell Journal, 35,* 405.

Aiken, L. S., & West, S. G. (1990). Invalidity of true experiments: Self-report pretest biases. *Evaluation Review, 14,* 374–390.

Aiken, L. S., & West, S. G. (1991). *Testing and interpreting interactions in multiple regression.* Newbury Park, CA: Sage.

Aiken, L. S., West, S. G., Schwalm, D. E., Carroll, J. L., & Hsiung, S. (1998). Comparison of a randomized and two quasi-experimental designs in a single outcome evaluation: Efficacy of a university-level remedial writing program. *Evaluation Review, 22,* 207–244.

Albermarle Paper Co. v. Moody, 442 U.S. 435 (1975).

Alexander, R. A., Barrett, G. V., Alliger, G. M., & Carson, K. P. (1986). Towards a general model of non-random sampling and the impact on population correlations: Generalization of Berkson's Fallacy and restriction of range. *British Journal of Mathematical and Statistical Psychology, 39,* 90–115.

Allen, J. P., Philliber, S., Herrling, S., & Kuperminc, G. P. (1997). Preventing teen pregnancy and academic failure: Experimental evaluation of a developmentally based approach. *Child Development, 64,* 729–742.

Allison, D. B. (1995). When is it worth measuring a covariate in a randomized trial? *Journal of Consulting and Clinical Psychology, 63,* 339–343.

Allison, D. B., Allison, R. L., Faith, M. S., Paultre, F., & Pi-Sunyer, F. X. (1997). Power and money: Designing statistically powerful studies while minimizing financial costs. *Psychological Methods, 2,* 20–33.

Allison, D. B., & Gorman, B. S. (1993). Calculating effect sizes for meta-analysis: The case of the single case. *Behavior Research and Therapy, 31,* 621–631.

Allison, P. D. (1987). Estimation of linear models with incomplete data. In C. Clogg (Ed.), *Sociological methodology* (pp. 71–103). San Francisco: Jossey-Bass.

Allison, P. D., & Hauser, R. M. (1991). Reducing bias in estimates of linear models by re-measurement of a random subsample. *Sociological Methods and Research, 19,* 466–492.

Alwin, D. F., & Tessler, R. C. (1985). Causal models, unobserved variables, and experimental data. In H. M. Blalock (Ed.), *Causal models in panel and experimental designs* (pp. 55–88). New York: Aldine.

Amato, P. R., & Keith, B. (1991). Parental divorce and the well-being of children: A meta-analysis. *Psychological Bulletin, 110,* 26–46.

American Educational Research Association, American Psychological Association, and National Council on Measurement in Education. (1985). *Standards for educational and psychological testing.* Washington, DC: American Psychological Association.

American Educational Research Association, American Psychological Association, and National Council on Measurement in Education. (1999). *Standards for educational and psychological testing.* Washington, DC: American Educational Research Association.

American Evaluation Association. (1995). Guiding principles for evaluators. In W. R. Shadish, D. L. Newman, M. A. Scheirer, & C. Wye (Eds.), *Guiding principles for evaluators* (pp. 19–26). San Francisco: Jossey-Bass.

American Psychiatric Association. (1994). *Diagnostic and statistical manual of mental disorders* (4th ed.). Washington, DC: Author.

American Psychiatric Association. (2000). *Handbook of psychiatric measures.* Washington, DC: Author.

American Psychological Association (1954). Technical recommendations for psychological tests and diagnostic techniques. *Psychological Bulletin, 51* (Supplement).

American Psychological Association. (1992). Ethical principles of psychologists and code of conduct. *American Psychologist, 47,* 1597–1611.

American Psychological Association. (1994). *Publication manual of the American Psychological Association* (4th ed.). Washington DC: Author.

Anastasi, A. (1968). *Psychological testing* (3rd ed.). New York: Macmillan.

Anderman, C., Cheadle, A., Curry, S., Diehr, P., Shultz, L., & Wagner, E. (1995). Selection bias related to parental consent in school-based survey research. *Evaluation Review, 19,* 663–674.

Anderson, C. A., Lindsay, J. J., & Bushman, B. J. (1999). Research in the psychological laboratory: Truth or triviality? *Current Directions in Psychological Science, 8,* 3–10.

Anderson, J. G. (1987). Structural equation models in the social and behavioral sciences: Model building. *Child Development, 58,* 49–64.

Anderson, V. L., & McLean, R. A. (1984). *Applied factorial and fractional designs.* New York: Dekker.

Angrist, J. D., & Imbens, G. W. (1995). Two-stage least squares estimation of average causal effects in models with variable treatment intensity. *Journal of the American Statistical Association, 90,* 431–442.

Angrist, J. D., Imbens, G. W., & Rubin, D. B. (1996a). Identification of causal effects using instrumental variables. *Journal of the American Statistical Association, 91,* 444–455.

Angrist, J. D., Imbens, G. W., & Rubin, D. B. (1996b). Rejoinder. *Journal of the American Statistical Association, 91,* 468–472.

Anson, A., Cook, T. D., Habib, F., Grady, M. K., Haynes, N. & Comer, J. P. (1991). The Comer School Development Program: A theoretical analysis. *Journal of Urban Education, 26,* 56–82.

Arbuckle, J. J. (1997). *Amos users' guide, version 3.6.* Chicago: Small Waters Corporation.

Armitage, P. (1999). Data and safety monitoring in the Concorde and Alpha trials. *Controlled Clinical Trials, 20,* 207–228.

Aronson, D. (1998). Using sibling data to estimate the impact of neighborhoods on children's educational outcomes. *Journal of Human Resources, 33,* 915–956.

Ashenfelter, O. (1978). Estimating the effects of training programs on earnings. *Review of Economics and Statistics, 60,* 47–57.

Ashenfelter, O., & Card, D. (1985). Using the longitudinal structure of earnings to estimate the effect of training programs. *Review of Economics and Statistics, 67,* 648–660.

Ashenfelter, O., & Krueger, A. B. (1994). Estimates of the economic returns to schooling from a new sample of twins. *American Economic Review, 84,* 1157–1173.

Atkinson, A. C. (1985). An introduction to the optimum design of experiments. In A. C. Atkinson & S. E. Fienberg (Eds.), *A celebration of statistics: The ISI centenary volume* (pp. 465–473). New York: Springer-Verlag.

Atkinson, A. C., & Donev, A. N. (1992). *Optimum experimental designs.* Oxford, England: Clarendon Press.

Atkinson, D. R., Furlong, M. J., & Wampold, B. E. (1982). Statistical significance, reviewer evaluations, and the scientific process: Is there a (statistically) significant relationship? *Journal of Counseling Psychology, 29,* 189–194.

Atkinson, R. C. (1968). Computerized instruction and the learning process. *American Psychologist, 23,* 225–239.

Atwood, J. R., & Taylor, W. (1991). Regression discontinuity design: Alternative for nursing research. *Nursing Research, 40,* 312–315.

Babcock, J. L. (1998). Retrospective pretests: Conceptual and methodological issues (Doctoral dissertation, University of Arizona, 1997). *Dissertation Abstracts International, 58*(08), 4513B.

Bagozzi, R. P., & Warshaw, P. R. (1992). An examination of the etiology of the attitude-behavior relation for goal-directed behaviors. *Multivariate Behavioral Research, 27,* 601–634.

Baker, F., & Curbow, B. (1991). The case-control study in health program evaluation. *Evaluation and Program Planning, 14,* 263–272.

Baker, S. H., & Rodriguez, O. (1979). Random time quote selection: An alternative to random selection in experimental evaluation. In L. Sechrest, S. G. West, M. A. Phillips, R.

Redner, & W. Yeaton (Eds.), *Evaluation studies review annual* (Vol. 4, pp. 185–196). Beverly Hills, CA: Sage.

Balke, A., & Pearl, J. (1997). Bounds on treatment effects from studies with imperfect compliance. *Journal of the American Statistical Association, 92*, 1171–1176.

Ball, S., & Bogatz, G. A. (1970). *The first year of Sesame Street: An evaluation.* Princeton, NJ: Educational Testing Service.

Ballart, X., & Riba, C. (1995). Impact of legislation requiring moped and motorbike riders to wear helmets. *Evaluation and Program Planning, 18*, 311–320.

Barlow, D. H., & Hersen, M. (1984). *Single case experimental designs: Strategies for studying behavior change* (2nd ed.). New York: Pergamon Press.

Barnard, J., Du, J., Hill, J. L., & Rubin, D. R. (1998). A broader template for analyzing broken randomized experiments. *Sociological Methods and Research, 27*, 285–317.

Barnes, B. (1974). *Scientific knowledge and sociological theory.* London: Routledge & Kegan Paul.

Barnow, B. S. (1987). The impact of CETA programs on earnings: A review of the literature. *Journal of Human Resources, 22*, 157–193.

Barnow, B. S., Cain, G. G., & Goldberger, A. S. (1980). Issues in the analysis of selectivity bias. In E. W. Stromsdorfer & G. Farkas (Eds.), *Evaluation studies review annual* (Vol. 5, pp. 43–59). Beverly Hills, CA: Sage.

Baron, R. M., & Kenny, D. A. (1986). The moderator-mediator variable distinction in social psychological research: Conceptual, strategic, and statistical considerations. *Journal of Personality and Social Psychology, 51*, 1173–1182.

Beach, M. L., & Meier, P. (1989). Choosing covariates in the analysis of clinical trials. *Controlled Clinical Trials, 10*, 161S–175S.

Beauchamp, T. L. (Ed.). (1974). *Philosophical problems of causation.* Encino, CA: Dickenson.

Bechtel, W. (1988). *Philosophy of science: An overview for cognitive science.* Hillsdale, NJ: Erlbaum.

Beck, A. T., Ward, C. H., Mendelsohn, M., Mock, J., & Erbaugh, J. (1961). An inventory for measuring depression. *Archives of General Psychiatry, 4*, 561–571.

Becker, B. J. (1988). Synthesizing standardized mean-change measures. *British Journal of Mathematical and Statistical Psychology, 41*, 257–278.

Becker, B. J. (1992). Models of science achievement: Forces affecting male and female performance in school science. In T. D. Cook, H. M. Cooper, D. S. Cordray, H. Hartmann, L. V. Hedges, R. J. Light, T. A. Louis, & F. Mosteller (Eds.), *Meta-analysis for explanation: A casebook* (pp. 209–281). New York: Russell Sage Foundation.

Becker, B. J. (1994). Combining significance levels. In H. Cooper & L. V. Hedges (Eds.), *The handbook of research synthesis* (pp. 215–230). New York: Russell Sage Foundation.

Becker, B. J., & Schram, C. M. (1994). Examining explanatory models through research synthesis. In H. Cooper & L. V. Hedges (Eds.), *The handbook of research synthesis* (pp. 357–381). New York: Russell Sage Foundation.

Becker, H. S. (1958). Problems of inference and proof in participant observation. *American Sociological Review, 23*, 652–660.

Becker, H. S. (1979). Do photographs tell the truth? In T. D. Cook & C. S. Reichardt (Eds.), *Qualitative and quantitative methods in evaluation research* (pp. 99–117). London: Sage.

Becker, M. H. (1992). Theoretical models of adherence and strategies for improving adherence. In S. A. Shumaker, E. B. Schron, & J. K. Onkene (Eds.), *The handbook of health behavior change* (pp. 5–43). New York: Springer.

Beecher, H. (1955). The powerful placebo. *Journal of the American Medical Association, 159,* 1602–1606.

Beecher, H. (1966). Ethics and clinical research. *New England Journal of Medicine, 274,* 1354–1360.

Begg, C., Cho, M., Eastwood, S., Horton, R., Moher, D., Olkin, I., Pitkin, R., Rennie, D., Schulz, K. F., Simel, D., & Stroup, D. F. (1996). Improving the quality of reporting of randomized controlled trials. *Journal of the American Medical Association, 276,* 637–639.

Begg, C. B. (1990). Suspended judgment: Significance tests of covariate imbalance in clinical trials. *Controlled Clinical Trials, 11,* 223–225.

Begg, C. B. (1994). Publication bias. In H. Cooper & L. V. Hedges (Eds.), *The handbook of research synthesis* (pp. 399–409). New York: Russell Sage Foundation.

Begg, C. B. (2000). Ruminations on the intent-to-treat principle. *Controlled Clinical Trials, 21,* 241–243.

Bell, S. H., Orr, L. L., Blomquist, J. D., & Cain, G. G. (1995). *Program applicants as a comparison group in evaluating training programs.* Kalamazoo, MI: Upjohn Institute for Employment Research.

Bentler, P. M. (1987). Drug use and personality in adolescence and young adulthood: Structural models with nonnormal variables. *Child Development, 58,* 65–79.

Bentler, P. M. (1993). *EQS/Windows user's guide.* (Available from BMDP Statistical Software, Inc., 1440 Sepulveda Blvd., Suite 316, Los Angeles, CA 90025)

Bentler, P. M. (1995). *EQS: Structural equations program manual.* Encino, CA: *Multivariate Software.*

Bentler, P. M,. & Bonett, D. G. (1980). Significance tests and goodness of fit in the analysis of covariance structures. *Psychological Bulletin, 88,* 588–606.

Bentler, P. M., & Chou, C.-P. (1988). Practical issues in structural modeling. In J. S. Long (Ed.), *Common problems/proper solutions: Avoiding error in quantitative research* (pp. 161–192). Newbury Park, CA: Sage.

Bentler, P. M., & Chou, C.-P. (1990). Model search with TETRAD II and EQS. *Sociological Methods and Research, 19,* 67–79.

Bentler, P. M., & Speckart, G. (1981). Attitudes "cause" behaviors: A structural equation analysis. *Journal of Personality and Social Psychology, 40,* 226–238.

Bentler, P. M., & Woodward, J. A. (1978). A Head Start reevaluation: Positive effects are not yet demonstrable. *Evaluation Quarterly, 2,* 493–510.

Bentler, P. M., & Wu, E. J. C. (1995). *EQS/Windows user's guide.* (Available from Multivariate Software, Inc., 4924 Balboa Blvd., #368, Encino, CA 91316)

Berg, A. T., & Vickrey, B. G. (1994). Outcomes research. *Science, 264,* 757–758.

Berg, B. L. (1989). *Qualitative research methods for the social sciences.* Boston: Allyn & Bacon.

Berger, V. W., & Exner, D. V. (1999). Detecting selection bias in randomized clinical trials. *Controlled Clinical Trials, 20,* 319–327.

Bergner, R. M. (1974). The development and evaluation of a training videotape for the resolution of marital conflict. *Dissertation Abstracts International, 34,* 3485B. (University Microfilms No. 73-32510).

Bergstralh, E., Kosanke, J., & Jocobsen, S. (1996). Software for optimal matching in observational studies. *Epidemiology, 7,* 331–332.

Berk, R. A., & DeLeeuw, J. (1999). An evaluation of California's inmate classification system using a generalized regression discontinuity design. *Journal of the American Statistical Association, 94,* 1045–1052.

Berk, R. A., Lenihan, K. J., & Rossi, P. H. (1980). Crime and poverty: Some experimental evidence from ex-offenders. *American Sociological Review, 45,* 766–786.

Berk, R. A., & Rauma, D. (1983). Capitalizing on nonrandom assignment to treatment: A regression discontinuity evaluation of a crime control program. *Journal of the American Statistical Association, 78,* 21–27.

Berk, R. A., Smyth, G. K., & Sherman, L. W. (1988). When random assignment fails: Some lessons from the Minneapolis Spouse Abuse Experiment. *Journal of Quantitative Criminology, 4,* 209–223.

Berman, J. S., & Norton, N. C. (1985). Does professional training make a therapist more effective? *Psychological Bulletin, 98,* 401–407.

Berman, P., & McLaughlin, M. W. (1977). *Federal programs supporting educational change: Vol. 8. Factors affecting implementation and continuation.* Santa Monica, CA: RAND.

Besadur, M., Graen, G. B., & Scandura, T. A. (1986). Training effects on attitudes toward divergent thinking among manufacturing engineers. *Journal of Applied Psychology, 71,* 612–617.

Beutler, L. E., & Crago, M. (Eds.). (1991). *Psychotherapy research: An international review of programmatic studies.* Washington, DC: American Psychological Association.

Bhaskar, R. (1975). *A realist theory of science.* Leeds, England: Leeds.

Bickman, L. (1985). Randomized field experiments in education: Implementation lessons. In R. F. Boruch & W. Wothke (Eds.), *Randomization and field experimentation* (pp. 39–53). San Francisco: Jossey-Bass.

Biglan, A., Hood, D., Brozovsky, P., Ochs, L., Ary, D., & Black, C. (1991). Subject attrition in prevention research. In C. G. Leukfeld & W. Bukowski (Eds.), *Drug use prevention intervention research: Methodological issues* (NIDA Research Monograph 107, DHHS Publication No. 91-1761, pp. 213–228). Rockville, MD: U.S. Government Printing Office.

Biglan, A., Metzler, C. W., & Ary, D. V. (1994). Increasing the prevalence of successful children: The case for community intervention research. *Behavior Analyst, 17,* 335–351.

Birnbaum, A. (1961). Confidence curves: An omnibus technique for estimation and testing statistical hypotheses. *Journal of the American Statistical Association, 56,* 246-249.

Bishop, R. C., & Hill, J. W. (1971). Effects of job enlargement and job change on contiguous but non-manipulated jobs as a function of worker's status. *Journal of Applied Psychology, 55,* 175–181.

Blackburn, H., Luepker, R., Kline, F. G., Bracht, N., Carlaw, R., Jacos, D., Mittelmark, M., Stauffer, L., & Taylor, H. L. (1984). The Minnesota Heart Health Program: A research and demonstration project in cardiovascular disease prevention. In J. D. Matarazzo, S. Weiss, J. A. Herd, N. E. Miller, & S. M. Weiss (Eds.), *Behavioral health* (pp. 1171–1178). New York: Wiley.

Bloom, B. S. (Ed.). (1956). *Taxonomy of educational objectives: Handbook I. The cognitive domain.* New York: McKay.

Bloom, H. S. (1984a). Accounting for no-shows in experimental evaluation designs. *Evaluation Review, 8,* 225–246.

Bloom, H. S. (1984b). Estimating the effect of job-training programs, using longitudinal data: Ashenfelter's findings reconsidered. *Journal of Human Resources, 19,* 544–556.

Bloom, H. S. (1990). *Back to work: Testing reemployment services for displaced workers.* Kalamazoo, MI: Upjohn Institute.

Bloom, H. S., & Ladd, H. F. (1982). Property tax revaluation and tax levy growth. *Journal of Urban Economics, 11,* 73–84.

Bloor, D. (1976). *Knowledge and social imagery.* London: Routledge & Kegan Paul.

Bloor, D. (1997). Remember the strong program? *Science, Technology, and Human Values, 22,* 373–385.

Bock, R. D. (Ed.). (1989). *Multilevel analysis of educational data.* San Diego, CA: Academic Press.

Boissel, J. P., Blanchard, J., Panak, E., Peyrieux, J. C., & Sacks, H. (1989). Considerations for the meta-analysis of randomized clinical trials. *Controlled Clinical Trials, 10,* 254–281.

Bollen, K. A. (1989). *Structural equations with latent variables.* New York: Wiley.

Bollen, K. A. (1990). Outlier screening and a distribution-free test for vanishing tetrads. *Sociological Methods and Research, 19,* 80–92.

Boomsma, A. (1987). The robustness of maximum likelihood estimation in structural equation models. In P. Cuttance & R. Ecob (Eds.), *Structural modeling by example: Applications in educational, sociological, and behavioral research* (pp. 160–188). Cambridge, England: Cambridge University Press.

Borenstein, M., & Cohen, J. (1988). *Statistical power analysis: A computer program.* Hillsdale, New Jersey: Lawrence Erlbaum Associates.

Borenstein, M., Cohen, J., & Rothstein, H. (in press). *Confidence intervals, effect size, and power* [Computer program]. Hillsdale, NJ: Erlbaum.

Borenstein, M., & Rothstein, H. (1999). *Comprehensive meta-analysis.* Englewood, NJ: Biostat.

Borkovec, T. D., & Nau, S. D. (1972). Credibility of analogue therapy rationales. *Journal of Behavior Therapy and Experimental Psychiatry, 3,* 257–260.

Boruch, R. F. (1975). Coupling randomized experiments and approximations to experiments in social program evaluation. *Sociological Methods and Research, 4,* 31–53.

Boruch, R. F. (1982). Experimental tests in education: Recommendations from the Holtzman Report. *American Statistician, 36,* 1–8.

Boruch, R. F. (1997). *Randomized field experiments for planning and evaluation: A practical guide*. Thousand Oaks, CA: Sage.

Boruch, R. F., & Cecil, J. S. (1979). *Assuring the confidentiality of social research data*. Philadelphia: University of Pennsylvania Press.

Boruch, R. F., Dennis, M., & Carter-Greer, K. (1988). Lessons from the Rockefeller Foundation's experiments on the Minority Female Single Parent program. *Evaluation Review, 12*, 396–426.

Boruch, R. F., & Foley, E. (2000). The honestly experimental society: Sites and other entities as the units of allocation and analysis in randomized trials. In L. Bickman (Ed.), *Validity and social experimentation: Donald Campbell's legacy* (Vol. 1, pp. 193–238). Thousand Oaks, CA: Sage.

Boruch, R. F., & Gomez, H. (1977). Sensitivity, bias, and theory in impact evaluations. *Professional Psychology, 8*, 411–434.

Boruch, R. F., & Wothke, W. (1985). Seven kinds of randomization plans for designing field experiments. In R. F. Boruch & W. Wothke (Eds.), *Randomization and field experimentation* (pp. 95–118). San Francisco: Jossey-Bass.

Bos, H., Huston, A., Granger, R., Duncan, G., Brock, T., & McLoyd, V. (1999, April). *New hope for people with low incomes: Two-year results of a program to reduce poverty and reform welfare*. New York: Manpower Research Development.

Box, G. E. P., & Draper, N. R. (1987). *Empirical model-building and response surfaces*. New York: Wiley.

Box, G. E. P., Hunter, W. G., & Hunter, J. S. (1978). *Statistics for experimenters: An introduction to design, data analysis, and model building*. New York: Wiley.

Box, G. E. P., & Jenkins, G. M. (1970). *Time series analysis: Forecasting and control*. San Francisco: Holden-Day.

Box, G. E. P., Jenkins, G. M., & Reinsel, G. C. (1994). *Time series analysis: Forecasting and control* (3rd ed.). Englewood Cliffs, NJ: Prentice-Hall.

Bracht, G. H., & Glass, G. V. (1968). The external validity of experiments. *American Educational Research Journal, 5*, 437–474.

Bradburn, N. M. (1983). Response effects. In P. H. Rossi, J. D. Wright, & A. B. Anderson (Eds.), *Handbook of survey research* (pp. 289–328). San Diego, CA: Academic Press.

Braden, J. P., & Bryant, T. J. (1990). Regression discontinuity designs: Applications for school psychologists. *School Psychology Review, 19*, 232–239.

Bramel, D., & Friend, R. (1981). Hawthorne, the myth of the docile worker, and class bias in psychology. *American Psychologist, 36*, 867–878.

Braught, G. N., & Reichardt, C. S. (1993). A computerized approach to trickle-process, random assignment. *Evaluation Review, 17*, 79–90.

Braunholtz, D. A. (1999). A note on Zelen randomization: Attitudes of parents participating in a neonatal clinical trial. *Controlled Clinical Trials, 20*, 569–571.

Braver, M. C. W., & Braver, S. L. (1988). Statistical treatment of the Solomon Four-Group design: A meta-analytic approach. *Psychological Bulletin, 104*, 150–154.

Braver, S. L., & Smith, M. C. (1996). Maximizing both external *and* internal validity in longitudinal true experiments with voluntary treatments: The "combined modified" design. *Evaluation and Program Planning, 19*, 287–300.

Breger, M. J. (1983). Randomized social experiments and the law. In R. F. Boruch & J. S. Cecil (Eds.), *Solutions to ethical and legal problems in social research* (pp. 97–144). New York: Academic Press.

Breslau, D. (1997). Contract shop epistemology: Credibility and problem construction in applied social science. *Social Studies of Science, 27,* 363–394.

Brockwell, P. J., & Davis, R. A. (1991). *Time series: Theory and methods* (2nd ed.). New York: Springer-Verlag.

Bronfenbrenner, U. (1979). *The ecology of human development: Experiments by nature and design.* Cambridge, Massachusetts: Harvard University Press.

Brook, J. S., Cohen, P., & Gordon, A. S. (1983). Longitudinal study of adolescent drug use. *Psychological Reports, 53,* 375–378.

Brown, R. (1986). *Social psychology: The second edition.* New York: Free Press.

Brown, H. I. (1977). *Perception, theory and commitment: The new philosophy of science.* Chicago: University of Chicago Press.

Brown, H. I. (1989). Toward a cognitive psychology of *What? Social Epistemology, 3,* 129–138.

Brunette, D. (1995). Natural disasters and commercial real estate returns. *Real Estate Finance, 11,* 67–72.

Brunswik, E. (1956). *Perception and the representative design of psychological experiments* (2nd ed.). Berkeley: University of California Press.

Bryk, A. S., & Raudenbush, S. W. (1992). *Hierarchical linear models: Applications and data analysis methods.* Newbury Park, CA: Sage.

Bryk, A. S., Raudenbush, S. W., & Congdon, R. T. (1996). *HLM: Hierarchical linear modeling with the HLM/2L and HLM/3L programs.* (Available from Scientific Software International, 1525 E. 53rd Street, Suite 530, Chicago IL 60615)

Bunge, M. (1959). *Causality and modern science* (3rd ed.). New York: Dover.

Bunge, M. (1992). A critical examination of the new sociology of science (Part 2). *Philosophy of the Social Sciences, 22,* 46–76.

Burger, T. (in press). Ideal type: Understandings in the social sciences. In N. Smelser & P. Baltes (Eds.), *Encyclopedia of the behavioral and social sciences.* Amsterdam: Elsevier.

Burtless, G. (1995). The case for randomized field trials in economic and policy research. *Journal of Economic Perspectives, 9,* 63–84.

Byrne, B. (1989). *A primer of LISREL.* New York: Springer-Verlag.

Byrne, B. (1994). *Structural equation modeling with EQS and EQS/Windows: Basic concepts, applications, and programming.* Newbury Park, CA: Sage.

Cahan, S., & Davis, D. (1987). A between-grade-levels approach to the investigation of the absolute effects of schooling on achievement. *American Educational Research Journal, 24,* 1–12.

Cahan, S., Linchevski, L., Ygra, N., & Danziger, I. (1996). The cumulative effect of ability grouping on mathematical achievement: A longitudinal perspective. *Studies in Educational Evaluation, 22,* 29–40.

Cain, G. G. (1975). Regression and selection models to improve nonexperimental comparisons. In C. A. Bennett & A. A. Lumsdaine (Eds)., *Evaluation and experiment: Some critical issues in assessing social programs* (pp. 297–317). New York: Academic Press.

Caines, P. E. (1988). *Linear stochastic systems.* New York: Wiley.

Campbell, D. T. (1956). *Leadership and its effects on groups* (Ohio Studies in Personnel, Bureau of Business Research Monograph No. 83). Columbus: Ohio State University.

Campbell, D. T. (1957). Factors relevant to the validity of experiments in social settings. *Psychological Bulletin, 54,* 297–312.

Campbell, D. T. (1963). From description to experimentation: Interpreting trends as quasi-experiments. In C. W. Harris (Ed.), *Problems in measuring change* (pp. 212–243). Madison: University of Wisconsin Press.

Campbell, D. T. (1966a). Pattern matching as an essential in distal knowing. In K. R. Hammond (Ed.), *The psychology of Egon Brunswik.* New York: Holt, Rinehart, & Winston.

Campbell, D. T. (1966b). *The principle of proximal similarity in the application of science.* Unpublished manuscript, Northwestern University.

Campbell, D. T. (1969a). Prospective: Artifact and control. In R. Rosenthal & R. L. Rosnow (Eds.), *Artifact in behavioral research* (pp. 351–382). New York: Academic Press.

Campbell, D. T. (1975). "Degrees of freedom" and the case study. *Comparative Political Studies, 8,* 178–193.

Campbell, D. T. (1976). Focal local indicators for social program evaluation. *Social Indicators Research, 3,* 237–256.

Campbell, D. T. (1978). Qualitative knowing in action research. In M. Brenner & P. Marsh (Eds.), *The social contexts of method* (pp. 184–209). London: Croom Helm.

Campbell, D. T. (1982). Experiments as arguments. In E. R. House (Ed.), *Evaluation studies review annual* (Volume 7, pp. 117–127). Newbury Park, CA: Sage.

Campbell, D. T. (1984). Foreword. In W. M. K. Trochim, *Research design for program evaluation: The regression discontinuity approach* (pp. 15–43). Beverly Hills, CA: Sage.

Campbell, D. T. (1986). Relabeling internal and external validity for applied social scientists. In W. M. K. Trochim (Ed.), *Advances in quasi-experimental design and analysis* (pp. 67–77). San Francisco: Jossey-Bass.

Campbell, D. T. (1988). *Methodology and epistemology for social science: Selected papers* (E. S. Overman, Ed.). Chicago: University of Chicago Press.

Campbell, D. T., & Boruch, R. F. (1975). Making the case for randomized assignment to treatments by considering the alternatives: Six ways in which quasi-experimental evaluations in compensatory education tend to underestimate effects. In C. A. Bennett & A. A. Lumsdaine (Eds.), *Evaluation and experiments: Some critical issues in assessing social programs* (pp. 195–296). New York: Academic Press.

Campbell, D. T., & Erlebacher, A. E. (1970). How regression artifacts can mistakenly make compensatory education programs look harmful. In J. Hellmuth (Ed.), *The Disadvantaged Child: Vol. 3, Compensatory education: A national debate* (pp. 185–210). New York: Brunner/Mazel.

Campbell, D. T., & Fiske, D. W. (1959). Convergent and discriminant validation by the multitrait-multimethod matrix. *Psychological Bulletin, 56,* 81–105.

Campbell, D. T., & Kenny, D. A. (1999). *A primer on regression artifacts.* New York: Guilford Press.

Campbell, D. T., & Russo, M. J. (1999). *Social experimentation.* Thousand Oaks, CA: Sage.

Campbell, D. T., & Stanley, J. C. (1963). *Experimental and quasi-experimental designs for research*. Chicago: RandMcNally.

Campbell, F. A., & Ramey, C. T. (1995). Cognitive and school outcomes for high-risk African American students at middle adolescence: Positive effects of early intervention. *American Educational Research Journal, 32*, 743–772.

Camstra, A., & Boomsma, A. (1992). Cross-validation in regression and covariance structure analysis. *Sociological Methods and Research, 21*, 89–115.

Canner, P. (1984). How much data should be collected in a clinical trial? *Statistics in Medicine, 3*, 423–432.

Canner, P. (1991). Covariate adjustment of treatment effects in clinical trials. *Controlled Clinical Trials, 12*, 359–366.

Capaldi, D., & Patterson, G. R. (1987). An approach to the problem of recruitment and retention rates for longitudinal research. *Behavioral Assessment, 9*, 169–177.

Cappelleri, J. C. (1991). *Cutoff-based designs in comparison and combination with randomized clinical trials*. Unpublished doctoral dissertation, Cornell University, Ithaca, New York.

Cappelleri, J. C., Darlington, R. B., & Trochim, W. M. K. (1994). Power analysis of cutoff-based randomized clinical trials. *Evaluation Review, 18*, 141–152.

Cappelleri, J. C., Ioannidis, J. P. A., Schmid, C. H., deFerranti, S. D., Aubert, M., Chalmers, T. C., & Lau, J. (1996). Large trials vs meta-analysis of smaller trials: How do their results compare? *Journal of the American Medical Association, 276*, 1332–1338.

Cappelleri, J. C., & Trochim, W. M. K. (1992, May). *An illustrative statistical analysis of cutoff-based randomized clinical trials*. Paper presented at the annual meeting of the Society for Clinical Trials, Philadelphia, PA.

Cappelleri, J. C., & Trochim, W. M. K. (1994). An illustrative statistical analysis of cutoff-based randomized clinical trials. *Journal of Clinical Epidemiology, 47*, 261–270.

Cappelleri, J. C., & Trochim, W. M. K. (1995). Ethical and scientific features of cutoff-based designs of clinical trials. *Medical Decision Making, 15*, 387–394.

Cappelleri, J. C., Trochim, W. M. K., Stanley, T. D., & Reichardt, C. S. (1991). Random measurement error does not bias the treatment effect estimate in the regression-discontinuity design: I. The case of no interaction. *Evaluation Review, 15*, 395–419.

Carbonari, J. P., Wirtz, P. W., Muenz, L. R., & Stout, R. L. (1994). Alternative analytical methods for detecting matching effects in treatment outcomes. *Journal of Studies on Alcohol* (Suppl. 12), 83–90.

Card, D. (1990). The impact of the Mariel Boatlift on the Miami labor market. *Industrial and Labor Relations Review, 43*, 245–257.

Carrington, P. J., & Moyer, S. (1994). Gun availability and suicide in Canada: Testing the displacement hypothesis. *Studies on Crime and Crime Prevention, 3*, 168–178.

Carter, G. M., Winkler, J. D., & Biddle, A. K. (1987). *An evaluation of the NIH research career development award*. Santa Monica, CA: RAND.

Casella, G., & Schwartz, S.P. (2000). Comment. *Journal of the American Statistical Association, 95*, 425-428.

Catalano, R., & Serxner, S. (1987). Time series designs of potential interest to epidemiologists. *American Journal of Epidemiology, 126*, 724–731.

Cecil, J. S., & Boruch, R. F. (1988). Compelled disclosure of research data: An early warning and suggestions for psychologists. *Law and Human Behavior, 12*, 181–189.

Chaffee, S. H., Roser, C., & Flora, J. (1989). Estimating the magnitude of threats to validity of information campaign effects. In C. G. Salmon (Ed.), *Annual review of communication research* (Vol. 18). Newbury Park, CA: Sage.

Chalmers, I., Enkin, M., & Keirse, M. J. (Eds.). (1989). *Effective care in pregnancy and childbirth*. New York: Oxford University Press.

Chalmers, T. C. (1968). Prophylactic treatment of Wilson's disease. *New England Journal of Medicine, 278*, 910–911.

Chalmers, T. C., Berrier, J., Hewitt, P., Berlin, J., Reitman, D., Nagalingam, R., & Sacks, H. (1988). Meta-analysis of randomized controlled trials as a method of estimating rare complications of non-steroidal anti-inflammatory drug therapy. *Alimentary and Pharmacological Therapy, 2–5*, 9–26.

Chalmers, T. C., Celano, P., Sacks, H. S., & Smith, H. (1983). Bias in treatment assignment in controlled clinical trials. *New England Journal of Medicine, 309*, 1358–1361.

Chambless, D. L., & Hollon, S. D. (1998). Defining empirically supported therapies. *Journal of Consulting and Clinical Psychology, 66*, 7–18.

Chan, K.-C., & Tumin, J. R. (1997). Evaluating the U.S. nuclear triad. In E. Chelimsky & W. R. Shadish (Eds.), *Evaluation for the 21st century: A handbook* (pp. 284–298). Thousand Oaks, CA: Sage.

Chaplin, W. F. (1991). The next generation of moderator research in personality psychology. *Journal of Personality, 59*, 143–178.

Chaplin, W. F. (1997). Personality, interactive relations, and applied psychology. In S. R. Briggs, R. Hogan., & W. H. Jones (Eds.), *Handbook of personality psychology* (pp. 873–890). Orlando, FL: Academic Press.

Chapman, L. J., & Chapman, J. P. (1969). Illusory correlation as an obstacle to the use of valid psychodiagnostic signs. *Journal of Abnormal Psychology, 74*, 271–280.

Chelimsky, E. (1998). The role of experience in formulating theories of evaluation practice. *American Journal of Evaluation, 19*, 35–55.

Chen, H., & Rossi, P. H. (1987). The theory-driven approach to validity. *Evaluation and Program Planning, 10*, 95–103.

Chen, H.-T., & Rossi, P. H. (Eds.). (1992). *Using theory to improve program and policy evaluations*. New York: Greenwood Press.

Choi, S. C., & Pepple, P. A. (1989). Monitoring clinical trials based on predictive probability of significance. *Biometrics, 45*, 317–323.

Choi, S. C., Smith, P. J., & Becker, D. P. (1985). Early decision in clinical trials when treatment differences are small: Experience of a controlled trial in head trauma. *Controlled Clinical Trials, 6*, 280–288.

Ciarlo, J. A., Brown, T. R., Edwards, D. W., Kiresuk, T. J., & Newman, F. L. (1986). *Assessing mental health treatment outcome measurement techniques* (DHHS Publication No. ADM 86-1301). Washington, DC: U.S. Government Printing Office.

Cicirelli, V. G., and Associates. (1969). *The impact of Head Start: An evaluation of the effects of Head Start on children's cognitive and affective development: Vols. 1–2*. Athens: Ohio University and Westinghouse Learning Corporation.

Clark, P. I., & Leaverton, P. E. (1994). Scientific and ethical issues in the use of placebo controls in clinical trials. *Annual Review of Public Health, 15,* 19–38.

Clarridge, B. R., Sheehy, L. L., & Hauser, T. S. (1977). Tracing members of a panel: A 17-year follow-up. In K. F. Schuessler (Ed.), *Sociological methodology* (pp. 185–203). San Francisco: Jossey-Bass.

Cochran, W. G. (1965). The planning of observational studies in human populations. *Journal of the Royal Statistical Society (Series A), 128,* 134–155.

Cochran, W. G. (1968). The effectiveness of adjustment by subclassification in removing bias in observational studies. *Biometrics, 24,* 295–313.

Cochran, W. G. (1977). *Sampling techniques* (3rd ed.). New York: Wiley.

Cochran, W. G. (1983). *Planning and analysis of observational studies.* New York: Wiley.

Cochran, W. G., & Cox, G. M. (1957). *Experimental designs* (2nd ed.). New York: Wiley.

Cochran, W. G., & Rubin, D. B. (1973). Controlling bias in observational studies: A review. *Sankhyā, 35,* 417–446.

Cohen, E., Mowbray, C. T., Bybee, D., Yeich, S., Ribisl, K., & Freddolino, P. P. (1993). Tracking and follow-up methods for research on homelessness. *Evaluation Review, 17,* 331–352.

Cohen, J. (1988). *Statistical power analysis for the behavioral sciences* (2nd ed.). Hillsdale NJ: Lawrence Erlbaum Associates.

Cohen, J. (1994). The earth is round ($p<.05$). *American Psychologist, 49,* 997–1003.

Cohen, J., & Cohen, P. (1983). *Applied multiple regression/correlation analysis for the behavioral sciences* (2nd ed.). Hillsdale, NJ: Erlbaum.

Cohen, P., Cohen, J., Teresi, J., Marchi, M., & Velez, C. N. (1990). Problems in the measurement of latent variables in structural equation causal models. *Applied Psychological Measurement, 14,* 183–196.

Colditz, G. A., Miller, J. N., & Mosteller, F. (1988). The effect of study design on gain in evaluation of new treatments in medicine and surgery. *Drug Information Journal, 22,* 343–352.

Collins, H. M. (1981). Stages in the empirical programme of relativism. *Social Studies of Science, 11,* 3–10.

Collins, J. F., & Elkin, I. (1985). Randomization in the NIMH Treatment of Depression Collaborative Research Program. In R. F. Boruch & W. Wothke (Eds.), *Randomization and field experimentation* (pp. 27–37). San Francisco: Jossey-Bass.

Comer, J. P. (1988). Educating poor minority children. *Scientific American, 259,* 42–48.

Connell, D. B., Turner, R. R., & Mason, E. F. (1985). Summary of findings of the school health education evaluation: Health promotion effectiveness, implementation and costs. *Journal of School Health, 55,* 316–321.

Connell, J. P., Kubisch, A. C., Schorr, L. B., & Weiss, C. H. (Eds.). (1995). *New approaches to evaluating community initiatives: Concepts, methods and contexts.* Washington, DC: Aspen Institute.

Conner, R. F. (1977). Selecting a control group: An analysis of the randomization process in twelve social reform programs. *Evaluation Quarterly, 1,* 195–244.

Connor, S. (1989). *Postmodernist culture: An introduction to theories of the contemporary.* Oxford, England: Basil Blackwell.

Connors, A. F., Speroff, T., Dawson, N. V., Thomas, C., Harrell, F. E., Wagner, D., Desbiens, N., Goldman, L., Wu, A. W., Califf, R. M., Fulkerson, W. J ., Vidaillet, H., Broste, S., Bellamy, P., Lynn, J., & Knaus, W. A. (1996). The effectiveness of right heart catheterization in the initial care of critically ill patients. *Journal of the American Medical Association, 276,* 889–897.

Conrad, K. J. (Ed.). (1994). *Critically evaluating the role of experiments.* San Francisco: Jossey-Bass.

Conrad, K. J., & Conrad, K. M. (1994). Reassessing validity threats in experiments: Focus on construct validity. In K. J. Conrad (Ed.), *Critically evaluating the role of experiments* (pp. 5–25). San Francisco: Jossey-Bass.

Cook, R. D., & Weisberg, S. (1994). *An introduction to regression graphics.* New York: Wiley.

Cook, T. D. (1984). What have black children gained academically from school integration? Examination of the meta-analytic evidence. In T. D. Cook, D. Armor, R. Crain, N. Miller, W. Stephan, H. Walberg, & P. Wortman (Eds.), *School desegregation and black achievement* (pp. 6–67). Washington, DC: National Institute of Education. (ERIC Document Reproduction Service No. ED 241 671)

Cook, T. D. (1985). Postpositivist critical multiplism. In L. Shotland & M. M. Mark (Eds.), *Social science and social policy* (pp. 21–62). Newbury Park, CA: Sage.

Cook, T. D. (1990). The generalization of causal connections: Multiple theories in search of clear practice. In L. Sechrest, E. Perrin, & J. Bunker (Eds.), *Research methodology: Strengthening causal interpretations of nonexperimental data* (DHHS Publication No. PHS 90-3454, pp. 9–31). Rockville, MD: Department of Health and Human Services.

Cook, T. D. (1991). Clarifying the warrant for generalized causal inferences in quasi-experimentation. In M. W. McLaughlin & D. C. Phillips (Eds.), *Evaluation and education: At quarter-century* (pp. 115–144). Chicago: National Society for the Study of Education.

Cook, T. D. (2000). The false choice between theory-based evaluation and experimentation. In P. J. Rogers, T. A. Hasci, A. Petrosino, & T. A. Huebner (Eds.), *Program theory in evaluation: Challenges and opportunities* (pp. 27–34). San Francisco, CA: Jossey-Bass.

Cook, T. D., Appleton, H., Conner, R. F., Shaffer, A., Tamkin, G., & Weber, S. J. (1975). *"Sesame Street" revisited.* New York: Russell Sage Foundation.

Cook, T. D., Calder, B. J., & Wharton, J. D. (1978). *How the introduction of television affected a variety of social indicators* (Vols. 1–4). Arlington, VA: National Science Foundation.

Cook, T. D., & Campbell, D. T. (1979). *Quasi-experimentation: Design and analysis issues for field settings.* Chicago: Rand-McNally.

Cook, T. D., Cooper, H., Cordray, D. S., Hartmann, H., Hedges, L. V., Light, R. J., Louis, T. A., & Mosteller, F. (Eds.). (1992). *Meta-analysis for explanation: A casebook.* New York: Russell Sage Foundation.

Cook, T. D., Gruder, C. L., Hennigan, K. M., & Flay, B. R. (1979). History of the sleeper effect: Some logical pitfalls in accepting the null hypothesis. *Psychological Bulletin, 86,* 662–679.

Cook, T. D., Habib, F. N., Phillips, M., Settersten, R. A., Shagle, S. C., & Degirmencioglu, S. M. (1999). Comer's School Development Program in Prince George's County, Maryland: A theory-based evaluation. *American Educational Research Journal, 36,* 543–597.

Cook, T. D., Hunt, H. D., & Murphy R. F. (2000). Comer's School Development Program in Chicago: A theory-based evaluation. *American Educational Research Journal, 37,* 535–597.

Cook, T. D., & Shadish, W. R. (1994). Social experiments: Some developments over the past 15 years. *Annual Review of Psychology, 45,* 545–580.

Cook, T. D., Shagle, S. C., & Degirmencioglu, S. M. (1997). Capturing social process for testing mediational models of neighborhood effects. In J. Brooks-Gunn, G. J. Duncan, & J. L. Aber (Eds.), *Neighborhood poverty: Context and consequences for children* (Vol. 2). New York: Russell Sage Foundation.

Cooper, H. (1998). *Synthesizing research: A guide for literature reviews* (3rd ed.). Thousand Oaks, CA: Sage.

Cooper, H., & Hedges, L. V. (Eds.). (1994a). *The handbook of research synthesis.* New York: Russell Sage Foundation.

Cooper, H., & Hedges, L. V. (1994b). Research synthesis as a scientific enterprise. In H. Cooper & L. V. Hedges (Eds.), *The handbook of research synthesis* (pp. 3–14). New York: Russell Sage Foundation.

Cooper, W. H., & Richardson, A. J. (1986). Unfair comparisons. *Journal of Applied Psychology, 71,* 179–184.

Coover, J. E., & Angell, F. (1907). General practice effect of special exercise. *American Journal of Psychology, 18,* 328–340.

Copas, J., & Li, H. (1997). Inference for non-random samples (with discussion). *Journal of the Royal Statistical Society* (Series B), *59,* 55–95.

Cordray, D. S. (1986). Quasi-experimental analysis: A mixture of methods and judgment. In W. M. K. Trochim (Ed.), *Advances in quasi-experimental design and analysis* (pp. 9–27). San Francisco: Jossey-Bass.

Corrin, W. J., & Cook, T. D. (1998). Design elements of quasi-experimentation. *Advances in Educational Productivity, 7,* 35–57.

Cosgrove, N., Borhani, N. O., Bailey, G., Borhani, P., Levin, J., Hoffmeier, M., Krieger, S., Lovato, L. C., Petrovitch, H., Vogt, T., Wilson, A. C., Breeson, V., Probstfield, J. L., and the Systolic Hypertension in the Elderly Program (SHEP) Cooperative Research Group. (1999). Mass mailing and staff experience in a total recruitment program for a clinical trial: The SHEP experience. *Controlled Clinical Trials, 19,* 133–148.

Costanza, M. C. (1995). Matching. *Preventive Medicine, 24,* 425–433.

Cowles, M. (1989). *Statistics in psychology: An historical perspective.* Hillsdale, NJ: Erlbaum.

Cox, D. R. (1958). *Planning of experiments.* New York: Wiley.

Coyle, S. L., Boruch, R. F., & Turner, C. F. (Eds.). (1991). *Evaluating AIDS prevention programs* (Expanded ed.). Washington, DC: National Academy Press.

Cramer, D. (1990). Self-esteem and close relationships: A statistical refinement. *British Journal of Social Psychology, 29,* 189–191.

Cramer, J. A., & Spilker, B. (Eds.). (1991). *Patient compliance in medical practice and clinical trials.* New York: Raven Press.

Crano, W. D., & Mendoza, J. L. (1987). Maternal factors that influence children's positive behavior: Demonstration of a structural equation analysis of selected data from the Berkeley Growth Study. *Child Development, 58,* 38–48.

Critelli, J. W., & Neumann, K. F. (1984). The placebo: Conceptual analysis of a construct in transition. *American Psychologist, 39,* 32–39.

Crocker, J. (1981). Judgment of covariation by social perceivers. *Psychological Bulletin, 90,* 272–292.

Cromwell, J. B., Hannan, M. J., Labys, W. C., & Terraza, M. (1994). *Multivariate tests for time series models.* Thousand Oaks, CA: Sage.

Cromwell, J. B., Labys, W. C., & Terraza, M. (1994). *Univariate tests for time series models.* Thousand Oaks, CA: Sage.

Cronbach, L. J. (1946). Response sets and test validity. *Educational and Psychological Measurement, 6,* 475–494.

Cronbach, L. J. (1982). *Designing evaluations of educational and social programs.* San Francisco: Jossey-Bass.

Cronbach, L. J. (1986). Social inquiry by and for earthlings. In D. W. Fiske & R. A. Shweder (Eds.), *Metatheory in social science* (pp. 83–107). Chicago: University of Chicago Press.

Cronbach, L. J. (1988). Five perspectives on validity argument. In H. Wainer & H. Braun (Eds.), *Test validity* (pp. 3–17). Hillsdale, NJ: Erlbaum.

Cronbach, L. J. (1989). Construct validation after thirty years. In R. L. Linn (Ed.), *Intelligence: Measurement, theory and public policy* (pp. 147–171). Urbana: University of Illinois Press.

Cronbach, L. J., Ambron, S. R., Dornbusch, S. M., Hess, R. D., Hornik, R. C., Phillips, D. C., Walker, D. F., & Weiner, S. S. (1980). *Toward reform of program evaluation.* San Francisco: Jossey-Bass.

Cronbach, L. J., Gleser, G. C., Nanda, H., & Rajaratnam, N. (1972). *The dependability of behavioral measurements: Theory of generalizability for scores and profiles.* New York: Wiley.

Cronbach, L. J., & Meehl, P. E. (1955). Construct validity in psychological tests. *Psychological Bulletin, 52,* 281–302.

Cronbach, L. J., Rajaratnam, N., & Gleser, G. C. (1967). *The dependability of behavioral measurements: Multifacet studies of generalizability.* Stanford, CA: Stanford University Press.

Cronbach, L. J., Rogosa, D. R., Floden, R. E., & Price, G. G. (1977). *Analysis of covariance in nonrandomized experiments: Parameters affecting bias* (Occasional Paper). Palo Alto, CA: Stanford University, Stanford Evaluation Consortium.

Cronbach, L. J., & Snow, R. E. (1977). *Aptitudes and instructional methods: A handbook for research on interactions.* New York: Irvington.

Crosbie, J. (1993). Interrupted time-series analysis with brief single-subject data. *Journal of Consulting and Clinical Psychology, 61,* 966–974.

Cullen, K. W., Koehly, L. M., Anderson, C., Baranowski, T., Prokhorov, A., Basen-Engquist, K., Wetter, D., & Hergenroeder, A. (1999). Gender differences in chronic disease risk behaviors through the transition out of high school. *American Journal of Preventive Medicine, 17,* 1–7.

Cunningham, W. R. (1991). Issues in factorial invariance. In L. M. Collins & J. L. Horn (Eds.), *Best methods for the analysis of change: Recent advances, unanswered questions, future directions* (pp. 106–113). Washington, DC: American Psychological Association.

Currie, J., & Duncan, T. (1995). Does Head Start make a difference? *American Economic Review, 85,* 341–364.

Currie, J., & Duncan, T. (1999). Does Head Start help Hispanic children? *Journal of Public Economics, 74,* 235–262.

D'Agostino, R. B., & Kwan, H. (1995). Measuring effectiveness: What to expect without a randomized control group. *Medical Care, 33* (Suppl.), AS95–AS105.

D'Agostino, R. B., & Rubin, D. B. (2000). Estimating and using propensity scores with partially missing data. *Journal of the American Statistical Association, 95,* 749–759.

Dallmayr, F. R., & McCarthy, T. A. (Eds.). (1977). *Understanding and social inquiry.* Notre Dame, IN: University of Notre Dame Press.

Danziger, K. (1990). *Constructing the subject: Historical origins of psychological research.* Cambridge, England: Cambridge University Press.

Datta, L.-E. (1997). Multimethod evaluations: Using case studies together with other methods. In E. Chelimsky & W. R. Shadish (Eds.), *Evaluation for the 21st century: A handbook* (pp. 344–359). Thousand Oaks, CA: Sage.

Davidson, D. (1967). Causal relations. *Journal of Philosophy, 64,* 691–703.

Davies, P. (1984). *Superforce: The search for a grand unified theory of nature.* New York: Simon and Schuster.

Davies, P. C. W., & Brown, J. R. (Eds.). (1986). *The ghost in the atom? A discussion of the mysteries of quantum physics.* Cambridge, England: Cambridge University Press.

Davis, C. E. (1994). Generalizing from clinical trials. *Controlled Clinical Trials, 15,* 11–14.

Dawid, A. P. (2000). Causal inference without counterfactuals. *Journal of the American Statistical Association, 95,* 407–448.

Day, N. A., Dunt, D. R., & Day, S. (1995). Maximizing response to surveys in health program evaluation at minimum cost using multiple methods: Mail, telephone, and visit. *Evaluation Review, 19,* 436–450.

Dehejia, R. H., & Wahba, S. (1999). Causal effects in nonexperimental studies: Reevaluating the evaluation of training programs. *Journal of the American Statistical Association, 94,* 1053–1062.

Dehue, T. (2000). From deception trials to control reagents: The introduction of the control group about a century ago. *American Psychologist, 55,* 264–268.

DeLeeuw, J., & Kreft, I. (1986). Random coefficient models for multilevel analysis. *Journal of Educational Statistics, 11,* 57–85.

Della-Piana, G. M. (1981). Film criticism. In N. L. Smith (Ed.), *New techniques for evaluation* (pp. 274–286). Newbury Park, CA: Sage.

Delucchi, K. L. (1994). Methods for the analysis of binary outcome results in the presence of missing data. *Journal of Consulting and Clinical Psychology, 62,* 569–575.

Delucchi, K. L., & Bostrom, A. (1999). Small sample longitudinal clinical trials with missing data: A comparison of analytic methods. *Psychological Methods, 4,* 158–172.

Deluse, S. R. (1999). Mandatory divorce education: A program evaluation using a "quasi-random" regression discontinuity design (Doctoral dissertation, Arizona State University, 1999). *Dissertation Abstracts International, 60*(03), 1349B.

Dennis, M. L. (1988). *Implementing randomized field experiments: An analysis of criminal and civil justice research*. Unpublished doctoral dissertation, Northwestern University.

Dennis, M. L., Lennox, R. D., & Foss, M. A. (1997). Practical power analysis for substance abuse health services research. In K. L. Bryant, M. Windell, & S. G. West (Eds.), *The science of prevention: Methodological advances from alcohol and substance abuse research* (pp. 367–404). Washington, DC: American Psychological Association.

Denton, F. T. (1985). Data mining as an industry. *Review of Economics and Statistics, 67,* 124–127.

Denton, T. (1994). Kinship, marriage and the family: Eight time series, 35000 B.C. to 2000 A.D. *International Journal of Comparative Sociology, 35,* 240–251.

Denzin, N. (1989). *The research act: A theoretical introduction to sociological methods*. Englewood Cliffs, NJ: Prentice-Hall.

Denzin, N. K., & Lincoln, Y. S. (2000). *Handbook of qualitative research* (2nd ed.). Newbury Park, CA: Sage.

Devine, E. C. (1992). Effects of psychoeducational care with adult surgical patients: A theory-probing meta-analysis of intervention studies. In T. Cook, H. Cooper, D. Cordray, H. Hartmann, L. Hedges, R. Light, T. Louis, & F. Mosteller (Eds.), *Meta-analysis for explanation: A casebook* (pp. 35–82). New York: Russell Sage Foundation.

Devine, E. C., & Cook, T. D. (1983). A meta-analytic analysis of effects of psychoeducational interventions on length of post-surgical hospital stay. *Nursing Research, 32,* 267–274.

Devine, E. C., & Cook, T. D. (1986). Clinical and cost-saving effects of psychoeducational interventions with surgical patients: A meta-analysis. *Research in Nursing and Health, 9,* 89–105.

Devine, E. C., O'Connor, F. W., Cook, T. D., Wenk, V. A., & Curtin, T. R. (1988). Clinical and financial effects of psychoeducational care provided by staff nurses to adult surgical patients in the post-DRG environment. *American Journal of Public Health, 78,* 1293–1297.

Devlin, B. (Ed.). (1997). *Intelligence and success. Is it all in the genes?: Scientists respond to The Bell Curve*. New York: Springer-Verlag.

Diament, C., & Colletti, G. (1978). Evaluation of behavioral group counseling for parents of learning-disabled children. *Journal of Abnormal Child Psychology, 6,* 385–400.

Diaz-Guerrero, R., & Holtzman, W. H. (1974). Learning by televised "Plaza Sesamo" in Mexico. *Journal of Educational Psychology, 66,* 632–643.

Dickerson, K. (1994). Research registers. In H. Cooper & L. V. Hedges (Eds.), *The handbook of research synthesis* (pp. 71–83). New York: Russell Sage Foundation.

Dickerson, K., Higgins, K., & Meinert, C. L. (1990). Identification of meta-analyses: The need for standard terminology. *Controlled Clinical Trials, 11,* 52–66.

Diehr, P., Martin, D. C., Koepsell, T., & Cheadle, A. (1995). Breaking the matches in a paired *t*-test for community interventions when the number of pairs is small. *Statistics in Medicine, 14,* 1491–1504.

DiRaddo, J. D. (1996). The investigation and amelioration of a staff turnover problem. *Dissertation Abstracts International, 59* (04), 1133A (University Microfilms No. 316379).

Director, S. M. (1979). Underadjustment bias in the evaluation of manpower training. *Evaluation Review, 3,* 190–218.

Dixon, D. O., & Lagakos, S. W. (2000). Should data and safety monitoring boards share confidential interim data? *Controlled Clinical Trials, 21,* 1–6.

Dohrenwend, B. P., Shrout, P. E., Egri, G., & Mendelsohn, F. S. (1980). Nonspecific psychological distress and other dimensions of psychopathology. *Archives of General Psychiatry, 37,* 1229–1236.

Donner, A. (1992). Sample size requirements for stratified cluster randomization designs. *Statistics in Medicine, 11,* 743–750.

Donner, A., & Klar, N. (1994). Cluster randomization trials in epidemiology: Theory and application. *Journal of Statistical Planning and Inference, 42,* 37–56.

Donner, A., & Klar, N. (2000). *Design and analysis of cluster randomization trials in health research.* London: Arnold.

Drake, C. (1993). Effects of misspecification of the propensity score on estimators of treatment effects. *Biometrics, 49,* 1231–1236.

Drake, C., & Fisher, L. (1995). Prognostic models and the propensity score. *International Journal of Epidemiology, 24,* 183–187.

Drake, S. (1981). *Cause, experiment, and science.* Chicago: University of Chicago Press.

Draper, D. (1995). Inference and hierarchical modeling in social sciences. *Journal of Educational and Behavioral Statistics, 20,* 115–147.

Droitcour, J. A. (1997). Cross-design synthesis: Concepts and applications. In E. Chelimsky & W. R. Shadish (Eds.), *Evaluation for the 21st century: A handbook* (pp. 360–372). Thousand Oaks, CA: Sage.

Ducasse, C. J. (1951). *Nature, mind and death.* La Salle, IL: Open Court.

Duckart, J. P. (1998). An evaluation of the Baltimore Community Lead Education and Reduction Corps (CLEARCorps) Program. *Evaluation Review, 22,* 373–402.

Dukes, R. L., Ullman, J. B., & Stein, J. A. (1995). An evaluation of D.A.R.E. (Drug Abuse Resistance Education), using a Solomon Four-Group design with latent variables. *Evaluation Review, 19,* 409–435.

Duncan, G. J., Yeung, W. J., Brooks-Gunn, J., & Smith, J. R. (1998). How much does childhood poverty affect the life chances of children? *American Sociological Review, 63,* 406–423.

Dunford, F. W. (1990). Random assignment: Practical considerations from field experiments. *Evaluation and Program Planning, 13,* 125–132.

Durlak, J. A., & Lipsey, M. W. (1991). A practitioner's guide to meta-analysis. *American Journal of Community Psychology, 19,* 291–332.

Duval, S., & Tweedie, R. (2000). A nonparametric "trim and fill" method of accounting for publication bias in meta-analysis. *Journal of the American Statistical Association, 95,* 89–98.

Dwyer, J. H., & Flesch-Janys, D. (1995). Agent Orange in Vietnam. *American Journal of Public Health, 85,* 476–478.

Edgington, E. S. (1987). Randomized single-subject experiments and statistical tests. *Journal of Counseling Psychology, 34,* 437–442.

Edgington, E. S. (1992). Nonparametric tests for single-case experiments. In T. R. Kratochwill & J. R. Levin (Eds.), *Single-case research design and analysis* (pp. 133–157). Hillsdale, NJ: Erlbaum.

Edwards, J. R., & Bagozzi, R. P. (2000). On the nature and direction of relationships between constructs and measures. *Psychological Methods, 5,* 155–174.

Eells, E. (1991). *Probabilistic causality.* New York: Cambridge University Press.

Efron, B. (1971). Forcing a sequential experiment to be balanced. *Biometrika, 58,* 403–417.

Efron, B., & Feldman, D. (1991). Compliance as an explanatory variable in clinical trials. *Journal of the American Statistical Association, 86,* 9–26.

Efron, B., & Tibshirani, R. J. (1993). *An introduction to the bootstrap.* New York: Chapman & Hall.

Eggan, F. (1954). Social anthropology and the method of controlled comparison. *American Anthropologist, 56,* 743–763.

Einstein, A. (1949). Reply to criticisms. In P. A. Schilpp (Ed.), *Albert Einstein: Philosopher-scientist* (pp. 665–688) . Evanston, IL: Library of Living Philosophers.

Eisenhart, M., & Howe, K. (1992). Validity in educational research. In M. D. LeCompte, W. L. Millroy, & J. Preissle (Eds.), *The handbook of qualitative research in education* (pp. 643–680). San Diego: Academic Press.

Eisner, E. (1979). *The educational imagination.* New York: Macmillan.

Eisner, E. (1983). Anastasia might still be alive, but the monarchy is dead. *Educational Researcher, 12,* 5.

Elbourne, D., Garcia, J., & Snowdon, C. (1999). Reply. *Controlled Clinical Trials, 20,* 571–572.

Elkin, I., Parloff, M. B., Hadley, S. W., & Autry, J. H. (1985). NIMH Treatment of Depression Collaborative Research Program: Background and research plan. *Archives of General Psychiatry, 42,* 305–316.

Elkin, I., Shea, T., Watkins, J. T., Imber, S. D., Sotsky, S. M., Collins, J. F., Glass, D. R., Pilkonis, P. A., Leber, W. R., Docherty, J. P., Fiester, S. J., & Parloff, M. B. (1989). National Institute of Mental Health Treatment of Depression Collaborative Research Program: General effectiveness of treatments. *Archives of General Psychiatry, 46,* 971–982.

Ellenberg, J. H. (1994). Cohort studies: Selection bias in observational and experimental studies. *Statistics in Medicine, 13,* 557–567.

Ellenberg, S. S., Finkelstein, D. M., & Schoenfeld, D. A. (1992). Statistical issues arising in AIDS clinical trials. *Journal of the American Statistical Association, 87,* 562–569.

Elmore, R. F. (1996). Getting to scale with good educational practice. *Harvard Educational Review, 66,* 1–26.

Emanuel, E. J., Wendler, D., & Grady, C. (2000). What makes clinical research ethical? *Journal of the American Medical Association, 283,* 2701–2711.

Embretson, S. (1983). Construct validity: Construct representation versus nomothetic span. *American Psychologist, 93,* 179–197.

Emerson, R. M. (1981). Observational field work. *Annual Review of Sociology, 7,* 351–378.

Emerson, S. S. (1996). Statistical packages for group sequential methods. *American Statistician, 50,* 183–192.

Epperson, D. L., Bushway, D. J., & Warman, R. E. (1983). Client self-termination after one counseling session: Effects of problem recognition, counselor gender, and counselor experience. *Journal of Counseling Psychology, 30,* 307–315.

Equal Employment Opportunity Commission, Department of Labor, Department of Justice, and the Civil Service Commission. (1978, August). Adoption by four agencies of uniform guidelines on employee selection procedures. 34 Fed. Reg. 38290–38315.

Erbland, M. L., Deupree, R. H., & Niewoehner, D. E. (1999). Systemic corticosteroids in chronic obstructive pulmonary disease exacerbations (SCCOPE): Rationale and design of an equivalence trial. *Controlled Clinical Trials, 19,* 404–417.

Erez, E. (1986). Randomized experiments in correctional context: Legal, ethical, and practical concerns. *Journal of Criminal Justice, 14,* 389–400.

Esbensen, F.-A., Deschenes, E. P., Vogel, R. E., West, J., Arboit, K., & Harris, L. (1996). Active parental consent in school-based research: An examination of ethical and methodological issues. *Evaluation Review, 20,* 737–753.

Estes, W. K. (1997). Significance testing in psychological research: Some persisting issues. *Psychological Science, 8,* 18–20.

Estroff, S. E. (1981). *Making it crazy: An ethnography of psychiatric clients in an American community.* Berkeley: University of California Press.

Etzioni, R. D., & Kadane, J. B. (1995). Bayesian statistical methods in public health and medicine. *Annual Review of Public Health, 16,* 23–41.

Everitt, D. E., Soumerai, S. B., Avorn, J., Klapholz, H., & Wessels, M. (1990). Changing surgical antimicrobial prophylaxis practices through education targeted at senior department leaders. *Infectious Control and Hospital Epidemiology, 11,* 578–583.

Expanded availability of investigational new drugs through a parallel track mechanism for people with AIDS and HIV-related diseases, 55 Fed. Reg. 20856–20860 (1990).

Eyberg, S. M., & Johnson, S. M. (1974). Multiple assessment of behavior modification with families: Effects of contingency contracting and order of treated problems. *Journal of Consulting and Clinical Psychology, 42,* 594–606.

Eysenck, H. J. (1978). An exercise in mega-silliness. *American Psychologist, 33,* 517.

Eysenck, H. J., & Eysenck, M. (1983). *Mindwatching: Why people behave the way they do.* Garden City, NY: Anchor Press.

Fagan, J. A. (1990). Natural experiments in criminal justice. In K. L. Kempf (Ed.), *Measurement issues in criminology* (pp. 108–137). New York: Springer-Verlag.

Fagerstrom, D. O. (1978). Measuring degree of physical dependence to tobacco smoking with reference to individualization of treatment. *Addictive Behaviors, 3,* 235–241.

Fairweather, G. W., & Tornatsky, L. G. (1977). *Experimental methods for social policy research.* New York: Pergamon Press.

Faith, M. S., Allison, D. B., & Gorman, B. S. (1997). Meta-analysis of single-case research. In R. D. Franklin, D. B. Allison, & B. S. Gorman (Eds.), *Design and analysis of single-case research* (pp. 245–277). Hillsdale, NJ: Erlbaum.

Family Support Act, Pub. L. N. 100–485, Section 203, 102 Stat. 2380 (1988).

Farquhar, J. W., Fortmann, S. P., Flora, J. A., Taylor, C. B., Haskell, W. L., Williams, P. T., MacCoby, N., & Wood, P. D. (1990). The Stanford five-city project: Effects of community-wide education on cardiovascular disease risk factors. *Journal of the American Medical Association, 26,* 359–365.

Faust, D. (1984). *The limits of scientific reasoning.* Minneapolis: University of Minnesota Press.

Federal Judicial Center. (1981). *Experimentation in the law: Report of the Federal Judicial Center Advisory Committee on Experimentation in the Law.* Washington, DC: U.S. Government Printing Office.

Feinauer, D. M., & Havlovic, S. J. (1993). Drug testing as a strategy to reduce occupational accidents: A longitudinal analysis. *Journal of Safety Research, 24,* 1–7.

Feinberg, S. E. (1971). Randomization and social affairs: The 1970 draft lottery. *Science, 171,* 255–261.

Feinberg, S. E., Singer, B., & Tanur, J. M. (1985). Large-scale social experimentation in the United States. In A. C. Atkinson & S. E. Feinberg (Eds.), *A celebration of statistics: The ISI centenary volume* (pp. 287–326). New York: Springer-Verlag.

Feldman, H. A., & McKinlay, S. M. (1994). Cohort versus cross-sectional design in large field trials: Precision, sample size, and a unifying model. *Statistics in Medicine, 13,* 61–78.

Feldman, H. A., McKinlay, S. M., & Niknian, M. (1996). Batch sampling to improve power in a community trial: Experience from the Pawtucket Heart Health Program. *Evaluation Review, 20,* 244–274.

Feldman, R. (1968). Response to compatriot and foreigner who seek assistance. *Journal of Personality and Social Psychology, 10,* 202–214.

Festinger, L. (1953). Laboratory experiments. In L. Festinger & D. Katz (Eds.), *Research methods in the behavioral sciences* (pp. 136–172). New York: Holt, Rinehart & Winston.

Fetterman, D. M. (1982). Ibsen's baths: Reactivity and insensitivity. *Educational Evaluation and Policy Analysis, 4,* 261–279.

Fetterman, D. M. (Ed.). (1984). *Ethnography in educational evaluation.* Beverly Hills, CA: Sage.

Feyerabend, P. (1975). *Against method: Outline of an anarchisitic theory of knowledge.* Atlantic Highlands, NJ: Humanities Press.

Feyerabend, P. (1978). *Science in a free society.* London: New Left Books.

Filstead, W. (1979). Qualitative methods: A needed perspective in evaluation research. In T. Cook & C. Reichardt (Eds.), *Qualitative and quantitative methods in evaluation research* (pp. 33–48). Newbury Park, CA: Sage.

Fink, A. (1998). *Conducting research literature reviews.* Thousand Oaks, CA: Sage.

Finkelstein, M. O., Levin, B., & Robbins, H. (1996a). Clinical and prophylactic trials with assured new treatment for those at greater risk: I. A design proposal. *American Journal of Public Health, 86,* 691–695.

Finkelstein, M. O., Levin, B., & Robbins, H. (1996b). Clinical and prophylactic trials with assured new treatment for those at greater risk: II. Examples. *American Journal of Public Health, 86,* 696–705.

Finn, J. D., & Achilles, C. M. (1990). Answers and questions about class size: A statewide experiment. *American Educational Research Journal, 27,* 557–577.

Fischer, R. (1994). Control construct design in evaluating campaigns. *Public Relations Review, 21,* 45–58.

Fischer-Lapp, K., & Goetghebeur, E. (1999). Practical properties of some structural mean analyses of the effect of compliance in randomized trials. *Controlled Clinical Trials, 20,* 531–546.

Fischhoff, B. (1975). Hindsight/foresight: The effect of outcome knowledge on judgment under uncertainty. *Journal of Experimental Psychology: Human Perception and Performance, 1,* 288–299.

Fisher, L. D. (1999). Advances in clinical trials in the twentieth century. *Annual Review of Public Health, 20,* 109–124.

Fisher, R. A. (1925). *Statistical methods for research workers.* Edinburgh: Oliver & Boyd.

Fisher, R. A. (1926). The arrangement of field experiments. *Journal of the Ministry of Agriculture of Great Britain, 33,* 505–513.

Fisher, R. A. (1932). *Statistical methods for research workers* (4th ed.). London: Oliver & Boyd.

Fisher, R. A. (1935). *The design of experiments.* Edinburgh: Oliver & Boyd.

Fisher, R. A., & Yates, F. (1953). *Statistical tables for biological, agricultural, and medical research* (4th ed.). Edinburgh: Oliver & Boyd.

Fleiss, J. L. (1981). *Statistical methods for rates and proportions* (2nd ed.). New York: Wiley.

Fleiss, J. L. (1986). *The design and analysis of clinical experiments.* New York: Wiley.

Fleiss, J. L. (1994). Measures of effect size for categorical data. In H. Cooper & L. V. Hedges (Eds.), *The handbook of research synthesis* (pp. 245–260). New York: Russell Sage Foundation.

Flournoy, N., & Rosenberger, W. F. (Eds.). (1995). *Adaptive designs.* Hayward, CA: IMS.

Folkman, J. (1996). Fighting cancer by attacking its blood supply. *Scientific American, 275,* 150–154.

Fortin, F., & Kirouac, S. (1976). A randomized controlled trial of preoperative patient education. *International Journal of Nursing Studies, 13,* 11–24.

Foster, E. M., & Bickman, L. (1996). An evaluator's guide to detecting attrition problems. *Evaluation Review, 20,* 695–723.

Foster, E. M., & McLanahan, S. (1996). An illustration of the use of instrumental variables: Do neighborhood conditions affect a young person's chance of finishing high school? *Psychological Methods, 1,* 249–261.

Fowler, R. L. (1985). Testing for substantive significance in applied research by specifying nonzero effect null hypotheses. *Journal of Applied Psychology, 70,* 215–218.

Fraker, T., & Maynard, R. (1986, October). *The adequacy of comparison group designs for evaluations of employment-related programs.* (Available from Mathematica Policy Research, P.O. Box 2393, Princeton, NJ 08543-2393)

Fraker, T., & Maynard, R. (1987). Evaluating comparison group designs with employment-related programs. *Journal of Human Resources, 22,* 194–227.

Frangakis, C. E., & Rubin, D. B. (1999) Addressing complications of intention-to-treat analysis in the combined presence of all-or-none treatment-noncompliance and subsequent missing outcomes. *Biometrika, 86,* 366–379.

Frankel, M. (1983). Sampling theory. In P. H. Rossi, J. D. Wright, & A. B. Anderson (Eds.), *Handbook of survey research* (pp. 21–67). San Diego: Academic Press.

Franklin, C., Grant, D., Corcoran, J., Miller, P. O., & Bultman, L. (1997). Effectiveness of prevention programs for adolescent pregnancy: A meta-analysis. *Journal of Marriage and the Family, 59,* 551–567.

Franklin, R. D., Allison, D. B., & Gorman, B. S. (Eds.). (1997). *Design and analysis of single-case research*. Mahwah, NJ: Erlbaum.

Freedman, D. A. (1987). As others see us: A case study in path analysis. *Journal of Educational Statistics, 12,* 101–128.

Freedman, L. S., & White, S. J. (1976). On the use of Pocock and Simon's method for balancing treatment numbers over prognostic variables in the controlled clinical trial. *Biometrics, 32,* 691–694.

Freiman, J. A., Chalmers, T. C., Smith, H., & Kuebler, R. R. (1978). The importance of beta, the Type II error, and sample size in the design and interpretation of the randomized control trial. *New England Journal of Medicine, 299,* 690–694.

Frick, R. W. (1995). Accepting the null hypothesis. *Memory & Cognition, 23,* 132–138.

Frick, R. W. (1996). The appropriate use of null hypothesis testing. *Psychological Methods, 1,* 379–390.

Friedlander, D., & Robins, P. K. (1995). Evaluating program evaluations: New evidence on commonly used nonexperimental methods. *American Economic Review, 85,* 923–937.

Friedman, J., & Weinberg, D. H. (Eds.). (1983). *Urban affairs annual review: Volume 24, The great housing experiment*. Thousand Oaks, CA: Sage.

Fuller, H. (2000). Evidence supports the expansion of the Milwaukee parental choice program. *Phi Delta Kappan, 81,* 390–391.

Fuller, W. A. (1995). *Introduction to statistical time series* (2nd ed.). New York: Wiley.

Furby, L. (1973). Interpreting regression toward the mean in development research. *Developmental Psychology, 8,* 172–179.

Furlong, M. J., Casas, J. M., Corrall, C., & Gordon, M. (1997). Changes in substance use patterns associated with the development of a community partnership project. *Evaluation and Program Planning, 20,* 299–305.

Furlong, M. J., & Wampold, B. E. (1981). Visual analysis of single-subject studies by school psychologists. *Psychology in the Schools, 18,* 80–86.

Gadenne, V. (1976). *Die Gultigkeit psychologischer Unterscuchungen*. Stuttgart, Germany: Kohlhammer.

Gail, M. H., Byar, D. P., Pechacek, T. F., & Corle, D. K. (1992). Aspects of statistical design for the Community Intervention Trial for Smoking Cessation (COMMIT). *Controlled Clinical Trials, 13,* 6–21.

Gail, M. H., Mark, S. D., Carroll, R. J., Green, S. B., & Pee, D. (1996). On design considerations and randomization-based inference for community intervention trials. *Statistics in Medicine, 15,* 1069–1092.

Gallini, J. K., & Bell, M. E. (1983). Formulation of a structural equation model for the evaluation of curriculum. *Educational Evaluation and Policy Analysis, 5,* 319–326.

Galton, F. (1872). Statistical inquiries into the efficacy of prayer. *Fortnightly Review, 12,* 124–135.

Galton, F. (1886). Regression towards mediocrity in hereditary stature. *Journal of the Anthropological Institute, 15,* 246–263.

Garber, J., & Hollon, S. D. (1991). What can specificity designs say about causality in psychopathology research? *Psychological Bulletin, 110,* 129–136.

Garfinkel, I., Manski, C. F., & Michalopoulos, C. (1992). Micro experiments and macro effects. In C. F. Manski & I. Garfinkel (Eds.), *Evaluating welfare and training programs* (pp. 253–273). Cambridge, MA: Harvard University Press.

Garner, J., Fagen, J., & Maxwell, C. (1995). Published findings from the Spouse Assault Replication Program: A critical review. *Journal of Quantitative Criminology, 11,* 3–28.

Gastwirth, J. (1992). Method for assessing the sensitivity of statistical comparisons used in Title VII cases to omitted variables. *Jurimetrics, 33,* 19–34.

Gastwirth, J., Krieger, A., & Rosenbaum, P. (1994). How a court accepted an impossible explanation. *American Statistician, 48,* 313–315.

Geertz, C. (1973). Thick description: Toward an interpretative theory of culture. In C. Geertz (Ed.), *The interpretation of culture* (pp. 3–30). New York: Basic Books.

Gephart, W. J. (1981). Watercolor painting. In N. L. Smith (Ed.), *New techniques for evaluation* (pp. 286–298). Newbury Park, CA: Sage.

Gergen, K. J. (1973). Social psychology as history. *Journal of Personality and Social Psychology, 26,* 309–320.

Geronimus, A. T., & Korenman, S. (1992). The socioeconomic consequences of teen childbearing reconsidered. *Quarterly Journal of Economics, 107,* 1187–1214.

Gholson, B., & Houts, A. C. (1989). Toward a cognitive psychology of science. *Social Epistemology, 3,* 107–127.

Gholson, B. G., Shadish, W. R., Neimeyer, R. A., & Houts, A. C. (Eds.). (1989). *Psychology of science: Contributions to metascience.* Cambridge, England: Cambridge University Press.

Gibbons, R. D., Hedeker, D. R., & Davis, J. M. (1993). Estimation of effect size from a series of experiments involving paired comparisons. *Journal of Educational Statistics, 18,* 271–279.

Gigerenzer, G. (1996). On narrow norms and vague heuristics: A reply to Kahneman and Tversky. *Psychological Review, 103,* 592–596.

Gilbert, J. P., McPeek, B., & Mosteller, F. (1977a). Progress in surgery and anesthesia: Benefits and risks of innovative therapy. In J. P. Bunker, B. A. Barnes, & F. Mosteller (Eds.), *Costs, risks, and benefits of surgery* (pp. 124–169). New York: Oxford University Press.

Gilbert, J. P., McPeek, B., & Mosteller, F. (1977b). Statistics and ethics in surgery and anesthesia. *Science, 198,* 684–689.

Gillespie, R. (1988). The Hawthorne experiments and the politics of experimentation. In J. Morawski (Ed.), *The rise of experimentation in American psychology* (pp. 114–137). New Haven, CT: Yale University Press.

Gilovich, T. (1991). *How we know what isn't so: The fallibility of human reasoning in everyday life.* New York: Free Press.

Glaser, B. G., & Strauss, A. L. (1967). *The discovery of grounded theory: Strategies for qualitative research.* New York: Aldine.

Glasgow, R. E., Vogt, T. M., & Boles, S. M. (1999). Evaluating the public health impact of health promotion interventions: The RE-AIM framework. *American Journal of Public Health, 89,* 1322–1327.

Glass, G. V. (1976). Primary, secondary, and meta-analysis. *Educational Researcher, 5,* 3–8.

Glass, G. V., & Smith, M. L. (1979). Meta-analysis of research on the relationship of class-size and achievement. *Educational Evaluation and Policy Analysis, 1,* 2–16.

Gleser, L. J., & Olkin, I. (1994). Stochastically dependent effect sizes. In H. Cooper & L. V. Hedges (Eds.), *The handbook of research synthesis* (pp. 339–355). New York: Russell Sage Foundation.

Glymour, C., Scheines, R., Spirtes, P., & Kelly, K. (1987). *Discovering causal structure: Artificial intelligence, philosophy of science, and statistical modeling.* San Diego, CA: Academic Press.

Goetghebeur, E., & Molenberghs, G. (1996). Causal inference in a placebo-controlled clinical trial with binary outcome and ordered compliance. *Journal of the American Statistical Association, 91,* 928–934.

Goetghebeur, E., & Shapiro, S. H. (1996). Analyzing non-compliance in clinical trials: Ethical imperative or mission impossible? *Statistics in Medicine, 15,* 2813–2826.

Goetz, J. P., & LeCompte, M. D. (1984). *Ethnography and qualitative design in educational research.* San Diego, CA: Academic Press.

Goldberg, H. B. (1997, February). Prospective payment in action: The National Home Health Agency demonstration. *CARING, 17*(2), 14–27.

Goldberger, A. S. (1972a). *Selection bias in evaluating treatment effects: Some formal illustrations* (Discussion Paper No. 123). Madison: University of Wisconsin, Institute for Research on Poverty.

Goldberger, A. S. (1972b). *Selection bias in evaluating treatment effects: The case of interaction* (Discussion paper). Madison: University of Wisconsin, Institute for Research on Poverty.

Goldman, J. (1977). A randomization procedure for "trickle-process" evaluations. *Evaluation Quarterly, 1,* 493–498.

Goldschmidt, W. (1982). [Letter to the editor]. *American Anthropologist, 84,* 641–643.

Goldstein, H. (1987). *Multilevel models in educational and social research.* London: Oxford University Press.

Goldstein, H., Yang, M., Omar, R., Turner, R., & Thompson, S. (2000). Meta-analysis using multilevel models with an application to the study of class size effects. *Applied Statistics, 49,* 399–412.

Goldstein, J. P. (1986). The effect of motorcycle helmet use on the probability of fatality and the severity of head and neck injuries. *Evaluation Review, 10,* 355–375.

Gooding, D., Pinch, T., & Schaffer, S. (1989b). Preface. In D. Gooding, T. Pinch, & S. Schaffer (Eds.), *The uses of experiment: Studies in the natural sciences* (pp. xiii–xvii). Cambridge, England: Cambridge University Press.

Goodman, J. S., & Blum, T. C. (1996). Assessing the non-random sampling effects of subject attrition in longitudinal research. *Journal of Management, 22,* 627–652.

Goodson, B. D., Layzer, J. I., St. Pierre, R. G., Bernstein, L. S. & Lopez, M. (2000). Effectiveness of a comprehensive five-year family support program on low-income children and their families: Findings from the Comprehensive Child Development Program. *Early Childhood Research Quarterly, 15,* 5–39.

Gorman, B. S., & Allison, D. B. (1997). Statistical alternatives for single-case designs. In R. D. Franklin, D. B. Allison, & B. S. Gorman (Eds.), *Design and analysis of single-case research* (pp. 159–214). Hillsdale, NJ: Erlbaum.

Gorman, M. E. (1994). Toward an experimental social psychology of science: Preliminary results and reflexive observations. In W. R. Shadish & S. Fuller (Eds.), *The social psychology of science* (pp. 181–196). New York: Guilford Press.

Gosnell, H. F. (1927). *Getting out the vote.* Chicago: University of Chicago Press.

Graham, J. W., & Donaldson, S. I. (1993). Evaluating interventions with differential attrition: The importance of nonresponse mechanisms and use of follow-up data. *Journal of Applied Psychology, 78,* 119–128.

Grandy, J. (1987). *Characteristics of examinees who leave questions unanswered on the GRE general test under rights-only scoring* (GRE Board Professional Rep. No. 83-16P; ETS Research Rep. No. 87-38). Princeton, NJ: Educational Testing Service.

Granger, C. W. J. (1969). Investigating causal relations by econometric models and cross-spectral methods. *Econometrica, 37,* 424–438.

Green, S. B., Corle, D. K., Gail, M. H., Mark, S. D., Pee, D., Freedman, L. S., Graubard, B. I., & Lynn, W. R. (1995). Interplay between design and analysis for behavioral intervention trials with community as the unit of randomization. *American Journal of Epidemiology, 142,* 587–593.

Greenberg, D., & Shroder, M. (1997). *The digest of social experiments* (2nd ed.). Washington, DC: Urban Institute Press.

Greenberg, J., & Folger, R. (1988). *Controversial issues in social research methods.* New York: Springer-Verlag.

Greenberg, R. P., Bornstein, R. F., Greenberg, M.D., & Fisher, S. (1992). A meta-analysis of antidepressant outcome under "blinder" conditions. *Journal of Consulting and Clinical Psychology, 60,* 664–669.

Greene, C. N., & Podsakoff, P. M. (1978). Effects of removal of a pay incentive: A field experiment. *Proceedings of the Academy of Management, 38,* 206–210.

Greene, J. P., Peterson, P. E., & Du, J. (1999). Effectiveness of school choice: The Milwaukee experiment. *Education and Urban Society, 31,* 190–213.

Greene, W. H. (1985). LIMDEP: An econometric modeling program for the IBM PC. *American Statistician, 39,* 210.

Greene, W. H. (1999). *Econometric analysis.* Upper Saddle River, NJ: Prentice-Hall.

Greenhouse, J. B., & Iyengar, S. (1994). Sensitivity analysis and diagnostics. In H. Cooper & L. V. Hedges (Eds.), *The handbook of research synthesis* (pp. 383–398). New York: Russell Sage Foundation.

Greenhouse, S. W. (1982). Jerome Cornfield's contributions to epidemiology. *Biometrics, 28* (Suppl.), 33–45.

Greenland, S., & Robins, J. M. (1986). Identifiability, exchangeability, and epidemiological confounding. *International Journal of Epidemiology, 15,* 413–419.

Greenwald, A. G. (1975). Consequences of prejudice against the null hypothesis. *Psychological Bulletin, 82,* 1–20.

Greenwald, A. G., Gonzalez, R., Harris, R. J., & Guthrie, D. (1996). Effect sizes and *p* values: What should be reported and what should be replicated? *Psychophysiology, 33,* 175–183.

Greenwald, P., & Cullen, J. W. (1984). The scientific approach to cancer control. *CA-A Cancer Journal for Clinicians, 34,* 328–332.

Greenwood, J. D. (1989). *Explanation and experiment in social psychological science: Realism and the social constitution of action.* New York: Springer-Verlag.

Griffin, L., & Ragin, C. C. (Eds.). (1994). Formal methods of qualitative analysis [Special issue]. *Sociological Methods and Research, 23*(1).

Grilli, R., Freemantle, N., Minozzi, S., Domenighetti, G., & Finer, D. (2000). Mass media interventions: Effects on health services utilization (Cochrane Review). *The Cochrane Library,* Issue 3. Oxford, England: Update Software.

Gross, A. J. (1993). Does exposure to second-hand smoke increase lung cancer risk? *Chance: New Directions for Statistics and Computing, 6,* 11–14.

Grossarth-Maticek, R., & Eysenck, H. J. (1989). Is media information that smoking causes illness a self-fulfilling prophecy? *Psychological Reports, 65,* 177–178.

Grossman, J., & Tierney, J. P. (1993). The fallibility of comparison groups. *Evaluation Review, 17,* 556–571.

Groves, R. M. (1989). *Survey errors and survey costs.* New York: Wiley.

Gu, X. S., & Rosenbaum, P. R. (1993). Comparison of multivariate matching methods: Structures, distances, and algorithms. *Journal of Computational and Graphical Statistics, 2,* 405–420.

Guba, E., & Lincoln, Y. (1982). *Effective evaluation.* San Francisco: Jossey-Bass.

Guba, E., & Lincoln, Y. (1989). *Fourth generation evaluation.* Newbury Park, CA: Sage.

Guba, E. G. (1981). Investigative journalism. In N. L. Smith (Ed.), *New techniques for evaluation* (pp. 167–262). Newbury Park, CA: Sage.

Guba, E. G. (Ed.). (1990). *The paradigm dialog.* Newbury Park, CA: Sage.

Gueron, J. M. (1985). The demonstration of state work/welfare initiatives. In R. F. Boruch & W. Wothke (Eds.), *Randomization and field experimentation* (pp. 5–13). San Francisco: Jossey-Bass.

Gueron, J. M. (1999, May). *The politics of random assignment: Implementing studies and impacting policy.* Paper presented at the conference on Evaluation and Social Policy in Education of the American Academy of Arts and Sciences, Cambridge, MA.

Guilford, J. P. (1946). New standards for test evaluation. *Educational and Psychological Measurement, 6,* 427–439.

Gunn, W. J., Iverson, D. C., & Katz, M. (1985). Design of school health education evaluation. *Journal of School Health, 55,* 301–304.

Gurman, A. S., & Kniskern, D. P. (1978). Research on marital and family therapy: Progress, perspective, and prospect. In S. L. Garfield & A. E. Bergin (Eds.), *Handbook of psychotherapy and behavior change: An empirical analysis* (2nd ed., pp. 817–901). New York: Wiley.

Gwadz, M., & Rotheram-Borus, M. J. (1992, Fall). Tracking high-risk adolescents longitudinally. *AIDS Education and Prevention* (Suppl.), 69–82.

Haavelmo, T. (1944, July). The probability approach in econometrics. *Econometrica, 12* (Suppl.).

Hacking, I. (1983). *Representing and intervening: Introductory topics in the philosophy of natural science.* Cambridge, England: Cambridge University Press.

Hacking, I. (1988). Telepathy: Origins of randomization in experimental design. *Isis, 79,* 427–451.

Hackman, J. R., Pearce, J. L., & Wolfe, J. C. (1978). Effects of changes in job characteristics on work attitudes and behaviors: A naturally occurring quasi-experiment. *Organizational Behavior and Human Performance, 21,* 289–304.

Haddock, C. K., Rindskopf, D., & Shadish, W. R. (1998). Using odds ratios as effect sizes for meta-analysis of dichotomous data: A primer on methods and issues. *Psychological Methods, 3,* 339–353.

Haddock, C. K., Shadish, W. R., Klesges, R. C., & Stein, R. J. (1994). Treatments for childhood and adolescent obesity: A meta-analysis. *Annals of Behavioral Medicine, 16,* 235–244.

Hahn, G. J. (1984). Experimental design in the complex world. *Technometrics, 26,* 19–31.

Halvorsen, K. T. (1994). The reporting format. In H. Cooper & L. V. Hedges (Eds.), *The handbook of research synthesis* (pp. 425–437). New York: Russell Sage Foundation.

Hambleton, R. K., Swaminathan, H., & Rogers, H. J. (1991). *Fundamentals of item response theory.* Thousand Oaks, CA:: Sage.

Hamilton, J. D. (1994). *Time series analysis.* Princeton, NJ: Princeton University Press.

Hand, H. H., & Slocum, J. W., Jr. (1972). A longitudinal study of the effects of a human relations training program on managerial effectiveness. *Journal of Applied Psychology, 56,* 412–417.

Hankin, J. R., Sloan, J. J., Firestone, I. J., Ager, J. W., Sokol, R. J., & Martier, S. S. (1993). A time series analysis of the impact of the alcohol warning label on antenatal drinking. *Alcoholism: Clinical and Experimental Research, 17,* 284–289.

Hannan, E. G., & Deistler, M. (1988). *The statistical theory of linear systems.* New York: Wiley.

Hannan, P. J., & Murray, D. M. (1996). Gauss or Bernoulli? A Monte Carlo comparison of the performance of the linear mixed-model and the logistic mixed-model analyses in simulated community trials with a dichotomous outcome variable at the individual level. *Evaluation Review, 20,* 338–352.

Hansen, M. H., & Hurwitz, W. N. (1996, March). The problem of non-response in sample surveys. *Amstat News,* 25–26.

Hansen, M. H., Hurwitz, W. N., & Madow, W. G. (1993). *Sample survey methods and theory* (Vols. 1–2). Somerset, NJ: Wiley.

Hansen, W. B., Tobler, N. S., & Graham, J. W. (1990). Attrition in substance abuse prevention research: A meta-analysis of 85 longitudinally followed cohorts. *Evaluation Review, 14,* 677–685.

Hanson, N. R. (1958). *Patterns of discovery: An inquiry into the conceptual foundations of science.* Cambridge, England: Cambridge University Press.

Hanushek, E. A. (1999). The evidence on class size. In S. E. Mayer & P. E. Peterson (Eds.) *Earning and learning: How schools matter* (pp. 131–168). Washington, DC: Brookings.

Harlow, L. L., Mulaik, S. A., & Steiger, J. H. (Eds.). (1997). *What if there were no significance tests?* Hillsdale, NJ: Erlbaum.

Harré, R. (1981). *Great scientific experiments.* Oxford, England: Phaidon Press.

Harris, M. J., & Rosenthal, R. (1985). Mediation of interpersonal expectancy effects: 31 meta-analyses. *Psychological Bulletin, 97,* 363–386.

Harris, R. J. (1997). Significance tests have their place. *Psychological Science, 8,* 8–11.

Harrop, J. W., & Velicer, W. F. (1990a). Computer programs for interrupted time series analysis: I. A qualitative evaluation. *Multivariate Behavioral Research, 25,* 219–231.

Harrop, J. W., & Velicer, W. F. (1990b). Computer programs for interrupted time series analysis: II. A quantitative evaluation. *Multivariate Behavioral Research, 25,* 233–248.

Hart, H. L. A., & Honore, T. (1985). *Causation in the law.* Oxford, England: Clarendon Press.

Hartman, R. S. (1991). A Monte Carlo analysis of alternative estimators in models involving selectivity. *Journal of Business and Economic Statistics, 9,* 41–49.

Hartmann, D. P., & Hall, R. V. (1976). The changing criterion design. *Journal of Applied Behavior Analysis, 9,* 527–532.

Hartmann, G. W. (1936). A field experiment on the comparative effectiveness of "emotional" and "rational" political leaflets in determining election results. *Journal of Abnormal and Social Psychology, 31,* 99–114.

Harvey, A. (1990). *The econometric analysis of time series* (2nd ed.). Cambridge, MA: MIT Press.

Harwell, M. (1997). An empirical study of Hedges's homogeneity test. *Psychological Methods, 2,* 219–231.

Hathaway, S. R., & McKinley, J. C. (1989). *MMPI-2: Manual for Administration and Scoring.* Minneapolis: University of Minnesota Press.

Hauk, W. W., & Anderson, S. (1986). A proposal for interpreting and reporting negative studies. *Statistics in Medicine, 5,* 203–209.

Hausman, J. A., & Wise, D. A. (Eds.). (1985). *Social experimentation.* Chicago: University of Chicago Press.

Havassey, B. (1988). *Efficacy of cocaine treatments: A collaborative study* (NIDA Grant Number DA05582). San Francisco: University of California.

Haveman, R. H. (1987). *Poverty policy and poverty research: The Great Society and the social sciences.* Madison: University of Wisconsin Press.

Hayduk, L. A. (1987). *Structural equation modeling with LISREL.* Baltimore: Johns Hopkins University Press.

Haynes, R. B., Taylor, D. W., & Sackett, D. L. (Eds.). (1979). *Compliance in health care.* Baltimore: Johns Hopkins University Press.

Heap, J. L. (1995). Constructionism in the rhetoric and practice of Fourth Generation Evaluation. *Evaluation and Program Planning, 18,* 51–61.

Hearst, N., Newman, T., & Hulley, S. (1986). Delayed effects of the military draft on mortality: A randomized natural experiment. *New England Journal of Medicine, 314,* 620–634.

Heckman, J. J. (1979). Sample selection bias as a specification error. *Econometrica, 47,* 153–161.

Heckman, J. J. (1992). Randomization and social policy evaluation. In C. F. Manski & I. Garfinkel (Eds.), *Evaluating welfare and training programs* (pp. 201–230). Cambridge, MA: Harvard University Press.

Heckman, J. J. (1996). Comment. *Journal of the American Statistical Association, 91,* 459–462.

Heckman, J. J., & Hotz, V. J. (1989a). Choosing among alternative nonexperimental methods for estimating the impact of social programs: The case of manpower training. *Journal of the American Statistical Association, 84,* 862–874.

Heckman, J. J., & Hotz, V. J. (1989b). Rejoinder. *Journal of the American Statistical Association, 84,* 878–880.

Heckman, J. J., Hotz, V. J., & Dabos, M. (1987). Do we need experimental data to evaluate the impact of manpower training on earnings? *Evaluation Review, 11,* 395–427.

Heckman, J. J., Ichimura, H., & Todd, P. E. (1997). Matching as an econometric evaluation estimator: Evidence from evaluating a job training programme. *Review of Economic Studies, 64,* 605–654.

Heckman, J. J., LaLonde, R. J., & Smith, J. A. (1999). The economics and econometrics of active labor market programs. In A. Ashenfelter & D. Card (Eds.), *Handbook of labor economics* (Vol. 3, pp. 1–160). Amsterdam: Elsevier Science.

Heckman, J. J., & Robb, R. (1985). Alternative methods for evaluating the impact of interventions. In J. J. Heckman & B. Singer (Eds.), *Longitudinal analysis of labor market data* (pp. 156–245). Cambridge, England: Cambridge University Press.

Heckman, J. J., & Robb, R. (1986a). Alternative methods for solving the problem of selection bias in evaluating the impact of treatments on outcomes. In H. Wainer (Ed.), *Drawing inferences from self-selected samples* (pp. 63–107). New York: Springer-Verlag.

Heckman, J. J., & Robb, R. (1986b). Postscript: A rejoinder to Tukey. In H. Wainer (Ed.), *Drawing inferences from self-selected samples* (pp. 111–113). New York: Springer-Verlag.

Heckman, J. J., & Roselius, R. L. (1994, August). *Evaluating the impact of training on the earnings and labor force status of young women: Better data help a lot.* (Available from the Department of Economics, University of Chicago)

Heckman, J. J., & Roselius, R. L. (1995, August). *Non-experimental evaluation of job training programs for young men.* (Available from the Department of Economics, University of Chicago)

Heckman, J. J., & Todd, P. E. (1996, December). *Assessing the performance of alternative estimators of program impacts: A study of adult men and women in JTPA.* (Available from the Department of Economics, University of Chicago)

Hedeker, D., & Gibbons, R. D. (1994). A random-effects ordinal regression model for multilevel data. *Biometrics, 50,* 933–944.

Hedges, L. V. (1984). Estimation of effect size under nonrandom sampling: The effects of censoring studies yielding statistically insignificant mean differences. *Journal of Educational Statistics, 9,* 61–85.

Hedges, L. V. (1992). Modeling publication selection effects in meta-analysis. *Statistical Science, 7,* 246–255.

Hedges, L. V. (1994). Fixed effects models. In H. Cooper & L. V. Hedges (Eds.), *The handbook of research synthesis* (pp. 285–299). New York: Russell Sage Foundation.

Hedges, L. V. (1997a). The promise of replication in labour economics. *Labour Economics, 4,* 111–114.

Hedges, L. V. (1997b). The role of construct validity in causal generalization: The concept of total causal inference error. In V. R. McKim & S. P. Turner (Eds.), *Causality in crisis? Statistical methods and the search for causal knowledge in the social sciences* (pp. 325–341). Notre Dame, IN: University of Notre Dame Press.

Hedges, L. V., & Olkin, I. (1985). *Statistical methods for meta-analysis.* Orlando, FL: Academic Press.

Hedges, L. V., & Olkin, I. (in press). *Statistical methods for meta-analysis in the medical and social sciences.* Orlando, FL: Academic Press.

Hedges, L. V., & Vevea, J. L. (1996). Estimating effect size under publication bias: Small sample properties and robustness of a random effects selection model. *Journal of Educational and Behavioral Statistics, 21,* 299–332.

Hedges, L. V., & Vevea, J. L. (1998). Fixed- and random-effects models in meta-analysis. *Psychological Methods, 4,* 486–504.

Heider, F. (1944). Social perception and phenomenal causality. *Psychological Review, 51,* 358–374.

Heinsman, D. T., & Shadish, W. R. (1996). Assignment methods in experimentation: When do nonrandomized experiments approximate the answers from randomized experiments? *Psychological Methods, 1,* 154–169.

Heitjan, D. F. (1999). Causal inference in a clinical trial: A comparative example. *Controlled Clinical Trials, 20,* 309–318.

Hennigan, K. M., Del Rosario, M. L., Heath, L., Cook, T. D., Wharton, J. D., & Calder, B. J. (1982). Impact of the introduction of television on crime in the United States: Empirical findings and theoretical implications. *Journal of Personality and Social Psychology, 55,* 239–247.

Henry, G. T., & McMillan, J. H. (1993). Performance data: Three comparison methods. *Evaluation Review, 17,* 643–652.

Herbst, A., Ulfelder, H., & Poskanzer, D. (1971). Adenocarcinoma of the vagina: Association of maternal stilbestrol therapy with tumor appearance in young women. *New England Journal of Medicine, 284,* 878–881.

Herrnstein, R. J., & Murray, C. (1994). *The bell curve.* New York: The Free Press.

Hill, C. E., O'Grady, K. E., & Elkin, I. (1992). Applying the Collaborative Study Psychotherapy Rating Scale to rate therapist adherence in cognitive-behavior therapy, interpersonal therapy, and clinical management. *Journal of Consulting and Clinical Psychology, 60,* 73–79.

Hill, J. L., Rubin, D. B., & Thomas, N. (2000). The design of the New York School Choice Scholarship program evaluation. In L. Bickman (Ed.), *Validity and social experimentation: Donald Campbell's legacy* (Vol. 1, pp. 155–180). Thousand Oaks, CA: Sage.

Hillis, A., Rajab, M. H., Baisden, C. E., Villamaria, F. J., Ashley, P., & Cummings, C. (1998). Three years of experience with prospective randomized effectiveness studies. *Controlled Clinical Trials, 19,* 419–426.

Hillis, J. W., & Wortman, C. B. (1976). Some determinants of public acceptance of randomized control group experimental designs. *Sociometry, 39,* 91–96.

Hintze, J. L. (1996). *PASS User's Guide: PASS 6.0 Power Analysis and Sample Size for Windows.* (Available from Number Cruncher Statistical Systems, 329 North 1000 East, Kaysville, Utah 84037)

Hogg, R. V., & Tanis, E. A. (1988). *Probability and statistical inference* (3rd ed.). New York: Macmillan.

Hohmann, A. A., & Parron, D. L. (1996). How the new NIH guidelines on inclusion of women and minorities apply: Efficacy trials, effectiveness trials, and validity. *Journal of Consulting and Clinical Psychology, 64,* 851–855.

Holder, H. D., & Wagenaar, A. C. (1994). Mandated server training and reduced alcohol-involved traffic crashes: A time series analysis of the Oregon experience. *Accident Analysis and Prevention, 26,* 89–97.

Holland, P. W. (1986). Statistics and causal inference. *Journal of the American Statistical Association, 81,* 945–970.

Holland, P. W. (1988). Causal inference, path analysis, and recursive structural equation models. In C. C. Clogg (Ed.), *Sociological methodology* (pp. 449–493). Washington, DC: American Sociological Association.

Holland, P. W. (1989). Comment: It's very clear. *Journal of the American Statistical Association, 84,* 875–877.

Holland, P. W. (1994). Probabilistic causation without probability. In P. Humphreys (Ed.), *Pattrick Suppes: Scientific philosopher* (Vol. 1, pp. 257–292). Dordrecht, Netherlands: Kluwer.

Holland, P. W., & Rubin, D. B. (1983). On Lord's paradox. In H. Wainer & S. Messick (Eds.), *Principles of modern psychological measurement* (pp. 3–25). Hillsdale, NJ: Erlbaum.

Holland, P. W., & Rubin, D. B. (1988). Causal inference in retrospective studies. *Evaluation Review, 12,* 203–231.

Hollister, R. G., & Hill, J. (1995). Problems in the evaluation of community-wide initiatives. In J. P. Connell, A. C. Kubisch, L. B. Schorr, & C. H. Weiss (Eds.), *New approaches to evaluating community initiatives: Concepts, methods, and contexts* (pp. 127–172). Washington, DC: Aspen Institute.

Holton, G. (1986). *The advancement of science, and its burdens.* Cambridge, England: Cambridge University Press.

Hopson, R. K. (Ed.). (2000). *How and why language matters in evaluation.* San Francisco: Jossey-Bass.

Horn, J. L. (1991). Comments on "Issues in factorial invariance." In L. M. Collins & J. L. Horn (Eds.), *Best methods for the analysis of change: Recent advances, unanswered questions, future directions* (pp. 114–125). Washington, DC: American Psychological Association.

Horowich, P. (1990). *Truth.* Worcester, England: Basil Blackwell.

Houts, A., & Gholson, B. (1989). Brownian notions: One historicist philosopher's resistance to psychology of science via three truisms and ecological validity. *Social Epistemology, 3,* 139–146.

Howard, G. S., Maxwell, S. E., & Fleming, K. J. (2000). The proof of the pudding: An illustration of the relative strengths of null hypothesis, meta-analysis, and Bayesian analysis. *Psychological Methods, 5,* 315–332.

Howard, G. S., Millham, J., Slaten, S., & O'Donnell, L. (1981). The effect of subject response style factors on retrospective measures. *Applied Psychological Measurement, 5,* 89–100.

Howard, G. S., Ralph, K. M., Gulanick, N. A., Maxwell, S. E., Nance, D. W., & Gerber, S. K. (1979). Internal invalidity in pretest–posttest self-reports and a re-evaluation of retrospective pretests. *Applied Psychological Measurement, 3,* 1–23.

Howard, K. I., Cox, W. M., & Saunders, S. M. (1988). Attrition in substance abuse comparative treatment research: The illusion of randomization. In L. S. Onken & J. D. Blaine (Eds.), *Psychotherapy and counseling in the treatment of drug abuse* (pp. 66–79). Rockville, MD: National Institute on Drug Abuse.

Howard, K. I., Kopta, S. M., Krause, M. S., & Orlinsky, D. E. (1986). The dose-effect relationship in psychotherapy. *American Psychologist, 41,* 159–164.

Howard, K. I., Krause, M. S., & Orlinsky, D. E. (1986). The attrition dilemma: Toward a new strategy for psychotherapy research. *Journal of Consulting and Clinical Psychology, 54,* 106–110.

Hox, J. J. (1995). AMOS, EQS, and LISREL for Windows: A comparative review. *Structural Equation Modeling, 2,* 79–91.

Hrobjartsson, A., Gotzche, P. C., & Gluud, C. (1998). The controlled clinical trial turns 100: Fibieger's trial of serum treatment of diptheria. *British Medical Journal, 317,* 1243–1245.

Hsiao, C. (1986). *Analysis of panel data.* New York: Cambridge University Press.

Hsiao, C., Lahiri, K., Lee, L.-F., & Pesaran, M. H. (Eds.). (1999). *Analysis of panels and limited dependent variable models: In honour of G. S. Maddala.* Cambridge, England: Cambridge University Press.

Huitema, B. E. (1980). *The analysis of covariance and alternatives.* New York: Wiley.

Hultsch, D. F., & Hickey, T. (1978). External validity in the study of human development: Theoretical and methodological issues. *Human Development, 21,* 76–91.

Humphreys, P. (Ed.). (1986a). Causality in the social sciences [Special issue]. *Synthese, 68*(1).

Humphreys, P. (1989). *The chances of explanation: Causal explanation in the social, medical, and physical sciences.* Princeton, NJ: Princeton University Press.

Hunter, J. E. (1997). Needed: A ban on significance tests. *Psychological Science, 8,* 3–7.

Hunter, J. E., & Schmidt, F. L. (1990). *Methods of meta-analysis: Correcting error and bias in research findings.* Newbury Park CA: Sage.

Hunter, J. E., & Schmidt, F. L. (1994). Correcting for sources of artificial variation across studies. In H. Cooper & L. V. Hedges (Eds.), *The handbook of research synthesis* (pp. 323–336). New York: Russell Sage Foundation.

Imbens, G. W., & Rubin, D. B. (1997a). Bayesian inference for causal effects in randomized experiments with non-compliance. *Annals of Statistics, 25,* 305–327.

Imbens, G. W., & Rubin, D. B. (1997b). Estimating outcome distributions for compliers in instrumental variables models. *Review of Economic Studies, 64,* 555–574.

Imber, S. D., Pilkonis, P. A., Sotsky, S. M., Elkin, I., Watkins, J. T., Collins, J. F., Shea, M. T., Leber, W. R., & Glass, D. R. (1990). Mode-specific effects among three treatments for depression. *Journal of Consulting and Clinical Psychology, 58,* 352–359.

Innes, J. M. (1979). Attitudes towards randomized control group experimental designs in the field of community welfare. *Psychological Reports, 44,* 1207–1213.

International Conference on Harmonization. (1999, May 7). *Draft consensus guideline: Choice of control group in clinical trials* [On-line]. Available: *http://www.ifpma.org/ich1.html,* or from ICH Secretariat, c/o IFPMA, 30 rue de St-Jean, P.O. Box 9, 1211 Geneva 18, Switzerland.

Ioannidis, J. P. A., Dixon, D. O., McIntosh, M., Albert, J. M., Bozzette, S. A., & Schnittman, S. M. (1999). Relationship between event rates and treatment effects in clinical site differences within multicenter trials: An example from primary Pneumocystic carinii prophylaxis. *Controlled Clinical Trials, 20,* 253–266.

Isserman, A., & Rephann, T. (1995). The economic effects of the Appalachian Regional Commission: An empirical assessment of 26 years of regional development planning. *Journal of the American Planning Association, 61,* 345–364.

Iyengar, S., & Greenhouse, J. B. (1988). Selection models and the file-drawer problem [with discussion]. *Statistical Science, 3,* 109–135.

Jacobson, N. S., & Baucom, D. H. (1977). Design and assessment of nonspecific control groups in behavior modification research. *Behavior Therapy, 8,* 709–719.

Jacobson, N. S., Follette, W. C., & Revenstorf, D. (1984). Psychotherapy outcome research: Methods for reporting variability and evaluating clinical significance. *Behavior Therapy, 15,* 336–352.

Jacobson, N. S., Schmaling, K. B., & Holtzworth-Munroe, A. (1987). Component analysis of behavioral marital therapy: Two-year follow-up and prediction of relapse. *Journal of Marital and Family Therapy, 13,* 187–195.

Jadad, A. R., Moore, A., Carroll, D., Jenkinson, C., Reynolds, D. J. M., Gavaghan, D. J., & McQuay, H. J. (1996). Assessing the quality of reports of randomized clinical trials: Is blinding necessary? *Controlled Clinical Trials, 17,* 1–12.

James, L. R., & Brett, J. M. (1984). Mediators, moderators, and tests for mediation. *Journal of Applied Psychology, 69,* 307–321.

Jason, L. A., McCoy, K., Blanco, D., & Zolik, E. S. (1981). Decreasing dog litter: Behavioral consultation to help a community group. In H. E. Freeman & M. A. Solomon (Eds.), *Evaluation studies review annual* (Vol. 6, pp. 660–674). Thousand Oaks, CA: Sage.

Jennrich, R. I., & Schlucter, M. D. (1986). Unbalanced repeated measures models with structured covariance matrices. *Biometrics, 42,* 805–820.

Jensen, K. B. (1989). Discourses of interviewing: Validating qualitative research findings through textual analysis. In S. Kvale (Ed.), *Issues of validity in qualitative research* (pp. 93–108). Lund, Sweden: Studentliteratur.

Johnson, B. T. (1989). *DSTAT: Software for the meta-analytic review of research literatures.* Hillsdale NJ: Erlbaum.

Johnson, B. T. (1993). *DSTAT 1.10: Software for the meta-analytic review of research literatures* [Upgrade documentation]. Hillsdale NJ: Erlbaum.

Johnson, M., Yazdi, K., & Gelb, B. D. (1993). Attorney advertising and changes in the demand for wills. *Journal of Advertising, 22,* 35–45.

Jones, B. J., & Meiners, M. R. (1986, August). *Nursing home discharges: The results of an incentive reimbursement experiment* (Long-Term Care Studies Program Research Report; DHHS Publication No. PHS 86-3399). Rockville, MD: U.S. Department of Health and Human Services, Public Health Service, National Center for Health Services Research and Health Care Technology Assessment.

Jones, E. E. (1985). Major developments in social psychology during the past five decades. In G. Lindzey & E. Aronson (Eds.), *Handbook of social psychology* (Vol. 1, pp. 47–107). New York: Random House.

Jones, E. E., & Sigall, H. (1971). The bogus pipeline: A new paradigm for measuring affect and attitude. *Psychological Bulletin, 76,* 349–364.

Jones, J. H. (1981). *Bad blood: The Tuskegee syphilis experiment.* New York: Free Press.

Jones, K. (1991). The application of time series methods to moderate span longitudinal data. In L. M. Collins & J. L. Horn (Eds.), *Best methods for the analysis of change: Recent advances, unanswered questions, future directions* (pp. 75–87). Washington, DC: American Psychological Association.

Jones, W. T. (1969a). *A history of Western philosophy: Vol. 1. The classical mind* (2nd ed.). New York: Harcourt, Brace, & World.

Jones, W. T. (1969b). *A history of Western philosophy: Vol. 3. Hobbes to Hume* (2nd ed.). New York: Harcourt, Brace, & World.

Joreskog, K. G., & Sorbom, D. (1988). *LISREL 7: A Guide to the Program and Applications.* (Available from SPSS, Inc., 444 N. Michigan Ave., Chicago, IL)

Joreskog, K. G., & Sorbom, D. (1990). Model search with TETRAD II and LISREL. *Sociological Methods and Research, 19,* 93–106.

Joreskog, K. G., & Sorbom, D. (1993). *LISREL 8: Structural equation modeling with the SIMPLIS command language.* (Available from Scientific Software International, Inc., 1525 East 53rd Street, Suite 906, Chicago IL)

Judd, C. M., & Kenny, D. A. (1981a). *Estimating the effects of social interventions.* Cambridge, England: Cambridge University Press.

Judd, C. M., & Kenny, D. A. (1981b). Process analysis: Estimating mediation in treatment evaluations. *Evaluation Review, 5,* 602–619.

Judd, C. M., McClelland, G. H., & Culhane, S. E. (1995). Data analysis: Continuing issues in the everyday analysis of psychological data. *Annual Review of Psychology, 46,* 433–465.

Judge, G., Hill, C., Griffiths, W., & Lee, T. (1985). *The theory and practice of econometrics.* New York: Wiley.

Kadane, J. B. (Ed.). (1996). *Bayesian methods and ethics in clinical trial design.* New York: Wiley.

Kalaian, H. A., & Raudenbush, S. W. (1996). A multivariate mixed linear model for meta-analysis. *Psychological Methods, 1,* 227–235.

Kalish, L. A., & Begg, C. B. (1985). Treatment allocation methods in clinical trials: A review. *Statistics in Medicine, 4,* 129–144.

Karlin, S. (1987). Path analysis in genetic epidemiology and alternatives. *Journal of Educational Statistics, 12,* 165–177.

Katz, L. F., Kling, J., & Liebman, J. (1997, November). *Moving to opportunity in Boston: Early impacts of a housing mobility program.* Unpublished manuscript, Kennedy School of Government, Harvard University.

Kazdin, A. E. (1992). *Research design in clinical psychology* (2nd ed.). Boston: Allyn & Bacon.

Kazdin, A. E. (1996). Dropping out of child psychotherapy: Issues for research and implications for practice. *Clinical Child Psychology and Psychiatry, 1,* 133–156.

Kazdin, A. E., & Bass, D. (1989). Power to detect differences between alternative treatments in comparative psychotherapy outcome research. *Journal of Consulting and Clinical Psychology, 57,* 138–147.

Kazdin, A. E., Mazurick, J. L., & Bass, D. (1993). Risk for attrition in treatment of antisocial children and families. *Journal of Clinical Child Psychology, 22,* 2–16.

Kazdin, A. E., & Wilcoxon, L. A. (1976). Systematic desensitization and non-specific treatment effects: A methodological evaluation. *Psychological Bulletin, 83,* 729–758.

Keller, R. T., & Holland, W. E. (1981). Job change: A naturally occurring field experiment. *Human Relations, 134,* 1053–1067.

Kelling, G. L., Pate, T., Dieckman, D., & Brown, C. E. (1976). The Kansas City Preventive Patrol Experiment: A summary report. In G. V. Glass (Ed.), *Evaluation studies review annual* (Vol. 1, pp. 605–657). Beverly Hills, CA: Sage.

Kelly, J. A., Murphy, D. A., Sikkema, K. J., McAuliffe, T. L., Roffman, R. A., Solomon, L. J., Winett, R. A., Kalichman, S. C., & The Community HIV Prevention Research Collaborative. (1997). Randomised, controlled, community-level HIV-prevention intervention for sexual-risk behaviour among homosexual men in US cities. *Lancet, 350,* 1500–1505.

Kendall, M., & Ord, J. K. (1990). *Time series* (3rd ed.). London: Arnold.

Kendall, P. C. (1998). Empirically supported psychological therapies. *Journal of Consulting and Clinical Psychology, 66,* 3–6.

Kenny, D. A. (1979). *Correlation and causality.* New York: Wiley.

Kenny, D. A., & Harackiewicz, J. M. (1979). Cross-lagged panel correlation: Practice and promise. *Journal of Applied Psychology, 64,* 372–379.

Kenny, D. A., & Judd, C. M. (1984). Estimating the nonlinear and interactive effects of latent variables. *Psychological Bulletin, 96,* 201–210.

Keppel, G. (1991). *Design and analysis: A researcher's handbook* (3rd ed.). Englewood Cliffs, NJ: Prentice-Hall.

Kershaw, D., & Fair, J. (1976). *The New Jersey income-maintenance experiment: Vol. 1. Operations, surveys, and administration.* New York: Academic Press.

Kershaw, D., & Fair, J. (1977). *The New Jersey income-maintenance experiment: Vol. 3. Expenditures, health, and social behavior.* New York: Academic Press.

Kiecolt, K. J., & Nathan, L. E. (1990). *Secondary analysis of survey data.* Thousand Oaks, CA: Sage.

Kim, J., & Trivedi, P. K. (1994). Econometric time series analysis software: A review. *American Statistician, 48,* 336–346.

Kirk, J., & Miller, M. L. (1986). *Reliability and validity in qualitative research.* Thousand Oaks, CA: Sage.

Kirk, R. E. (1982). *Experimental design: Procedures for the behavioral sciences* (2nd ed.). Belmont, CA: Brooks/Cole.

Kirk, R. E. (1996). Practical significance: A concept whose time has come. *Educational and Psychological Measurement, 56,* 746–759.

Kirkhart, K. E. (1995). Seeking multicultural validity: A postcard from the road. *Evaluation Practice, 16,* 1–12.

Kirsch, I. (1996). Hypnotic enhancement of cognitive-behavioral weight loss treatments: Another meta-reanalysis. *Journal of Consulting and Clinical Psychology, 64,* 517–519.

Kish, L. (1987). *Statistical design for research.* New York: Wiley.

Kisker, E. E., & Love, J. M. (1999, December). *Leading the way: Characteristics and early experiences of selected Early Head Start programs.* Washington, DC: U.S. Department of Health and Human Services, Administration on Children, Youth, and Families.

Kitzman, H., Olds, D. L., Henderson, C. R., Hanks, C., Cole, R., Tatelbaum, R., McConnochie, K. M., Sidora, K., Luckey, D. W., Shaver, D., Engelhardt, K., James, D., & Barnard, K. (1997). Effect of prenatal and infancy home visitation by nurses on pregnancy outcomes, childhood injuries, and repeated childbearing. A randomized controlled trial. *Journal of the American Medical Association, 278,* 644–652.

Klein, L. R. (1992). Self-concept, enhancement, computer education and remediation: A study of the relationship between a multifaceted intervention program and academic achievement. *Dissertation Abstracts International, 53* (05), 1471A. (University Microfilms No. 9227700)

Kleinbaum, D. G., Kupper, L. L., & Morgenstern, H. (1982). *Epidemiologic research: Principles and quantitative methods.* New York: Van Nostrand Reinhold.

Klesges, R. C., Brown, K., Pascale, R. W., Murphy, M., Williams, E., & Cigrang, J. A. (1988). Factors associated with participation, attrition, and outcome in a smoking cessation program at the workplace. *Health Psychology, 7,* 575–589.

Klesges, R. C., Haddock, C. K., Lando, H., & Talcott, G. W. (1999). Efficacy of a forced smoking cessation and an adjunctive behavioral treatment on long-term smoking rates. *Journal of Consulting and Clinical Psychology, 67,* 952–958.

Klesges, R. C., Vasey, M. M., & Glasgow, R. E. (1986). A worksite smoking modification competition: Potential for public health impact. *American Journal of Public Health, 76,* 198–200.

Kline, R. B., Canter, W. A., & Robin, A. (1987). Parameters of teenage alcohol abuse: A path analytic conceptual model. *Journal of Consulting and Clinical Psychology, 55,* 521–528.

Knatterud, G. L., Rockhold, F. W., George, S. L., Barton, F. B., Davis, C. E., Fairweather, W. R., Honohan, T., Mowery, R., & O'Neill, R. (1998). Guidelines for quality assurance in multicenter trials: A position paper. *Controlled Clinical Trials, 19,* 477–493.

Knight, G. P., Fabes, R. A., & Higgins, D. A. (1996). Concerns about drawing causal inferences from meta-analyses: An example in the study of gender differences in aggression. *Psychological Bulletin, 119,* 410–421.

Knorr-Cetina, K.D. (1981). *The manufacture of knowledge: An essay on the constructivist and contextual nature of science.* Oxford, England: Pergamon.

Koehler, M. J., & Levin, J. R. (1998). Regulated randomization: A potentially sharper analytical tool for the multiple baseline design. *Psychological Methods, 3,* 206–217.

Koepke, D., & Flay, B. R. (1989). Levels of analysis. In M. T. Braverman (Ed.), *Evaluating health promotion programs* (pp. 75–87). San Francisco: Jossey-Bass.

Koepsell, T. D., Martin, D. C., Diehr, P. H., Psaty, B. M., Wagner, E. G., Perrin, E. B., & Cheadle, A. (1991). Data analysis and sample size issues in evaluations of community-based health promotion and disease prevention programs: A mixed-model analysis of variance approach. *Journal of Clinical Epidemiology, 44,* 701–713.

Kollins, S. H., Newland, M. C., & Critchfield, T. S. (1999). Quantitative integration of single-subject studies: Methods and misinterpretations. *Behavior Analyst, 22,* 149–157.

Kopta, S. M., Howard, K. I., Lowry, J. L., & Beutler, L. E. (1994). Patterns of symptomatic recovery in psychotherapy. *Journal of Consulting and Clinical Psychology, 62,* 1009–1016.

Korfmacher, J., O'Brien, R., Hiatt, S., & Olds, D. (1999). Differences in program implementation between nurses and paraprofessionals providing home visits during pregnancy and infancy: A randomized trial. *American Journal of Public Health, 89*, 1847–1851.

Koricheva, J., Larsson, S., & Haukioja, E. (1998). Insect performance on experimentally stressed woody plants: A meta-analysis. *Annual Review of Entomology, 43*, 195–216.

Kraemer, H. C., Gardner, C., Brooks, J. L., & Yesavage, J. A. (1998). Advantages of excluding underpowered studies in meta-analysis: Inclusionist versus exclusionist viewpoints. *Psychological Methods, 3*, 23–31.

Kraemer, H. C., & Thiemann, S. (1989). A strategy to use soft data effectively in randomized controlled clinical trials. *Journal of Consulting and Clinical Psychology, 57*, 148–154.

Krantz, D. H. (1999). The null hypothesis testing controversy in psychology. *Journal of the American Statistical Association, 94*, 1372–1381.

Kratochwill, T. R., & Levin, J. R. (1992). *Single-case research design and analysis: New directions for psychology and education.* Hillsdale, NJ: Erlbaum.

Kromrey, J. D., & Foster-Johnson, L. (1996). Determining the efficacy of intervention: The use of effect sizes for data analysis in single-subject research. *Journal of Experimental Education, 65*, 73–93.

Kruglanski, A. W., & Kroy, M. (1976). Outcome validity in experimental research: A reconceptualization. *Journal of Representative Research in Social Psychology, 7*, 168–178.

Krull, J. L., & MacKinnon, D. P. (1999). Multilevel mediation modeling in group-based intervention studies. *Evaluation Review, 23*, 418–444.

Kruse, A. Y., Kjaergard, L. L., Krogsgaard, K., Gluud, C., Mortensen, E. L., Gottschau, A., Bjerg, A., and the INFO Trial Group. (2000). A randomized trial assessing the impact of written information on outpatients' knowledge about and attitude toward randomized clinical trials. *Controlled Clinical Trials, 21*, 223–240.

Kruskal, W., & Mosteller, F. (1979a). Representative sampling: I. Non-scientific literature. *International Statistical Review, 47*, 13–24.

Kruskal, W., & Mosteller, F. (1979b). Representative sampling: II. Scientific literature, excluding statistics. *International Statistical Review, 47*, 111–127.

Kruskal, W., & Mosteller, F. (1979c). Representative sampling: III. The current statistical literature. *International Statistical Review, 47*, 245–265.

Kuhn, T. S. (1962). *The structure of scientific revolutions.* Chicago: University of Chicago Press.

Kunz, R., & Oxman, D. (1998). The unpredictability paradox: Review of empirical comparisons of randomised and non-randomised clinical trials. *British Medical Journal, 317*, 1185–1190.

Kvale, S. (Ed.). (1989). *Issues of validity in qualitative research.* Lund, Sweden: Studentlitteratur.

Lachin, J. M. (1988). Statistical properties of randomization in clinical trials. *Controlled Clinical Trials, 9*, 289–311.

Lachin, J. M. (2000). Statistical considerations in the intent-to-treat principle. *Controlled Clinical Trials, 21*, 167–189.

Lachin, J. M., Matts, J. P., & Wei, L. J. (1988). Randomization in clinical trials: Conclusions and recommendations. *Statistics in Medicine, 9,* 365–374.

Lakatos, I. (1978). *The methodology of scientific research programmes.* Cambridge, England: Cambridge University Press.

Lakoff, G. (1985). *Women, fire, and dangerous things.* Chicago: University of Chicago Press.

LaLonde, R. (1986). Evaluating the econometric evaluations of training programs with experimental data. *American Economic Review, 76,* 604–620.

LaLonde, R., & Maynard, R. (1987). How precise are evaluations of employment and training experiments: Evidence from a field experiment. *Evaluation Review, 11,* 428–451.

Lam, J. A., Hartwell, S. W., & Jekel, J. F. (1994). "I prayed real hard, so I know I'll get in": Living with randomization. In K. J. Conrad (Ed.), *Critically evaluating the role of experiments* (pp. 55–66). San Francisco: Jossey-Bass.

Lana, R. C. (1969). Pretest sensitization. In R. Rosenthal & R. L. Rosnow (Eds.), *Artifact in behavioral research* (pp. 119–141). New York: Academic Press.

Larson, R. C. (1976). What happened to patrol operations in Kansas City? *Evaluation, 3,* 117–123.

Latané, B., & Darley, J. M. (1970). *The unresponsive bystander: Why doesn't he help?* New York: Appleton-Century-Crofts.

Latané, B., & Nida, S. (1981). Ten years of research on group size and helping. *Psychological Bulletin, 89,* 308–324.

Latour, B. (1987). *Science in action.* Cambridge, MA: Harvard University Press.

Latour, B., & Woolgar, S. (1979). *Laboratory life: The social construction of scientific facts.* Beverly Hills, CA: Sage.

Lavori, P. W. (1992). Clinical trials in psychiatry: Should protocol deviation censor patient data? *Neuropsychopharmacology, 6,* 39–48.

Lavori, P. W., Louis, T. A., Bailar, J. C., & Polansky, H. (1986). Designs for experiments: Parallel comparisons of treatment. In J. C. Bailar & F. Mosteller (Eds.), *Medical uses of statistics* (pp. 61–82). Waltham, MA: New England Journal of Medicine.

Lazar, I., & Darlington, R. (1982). Lasting effects of early education. *Monographs of the Society for Research in Child Development, 47* (2–3, Serial No. 195).

Lazarsfeld, P. F. (1947). *The mutual effects of statistical variables.* Unpublished manuscript, Columbia University, Bureau of Applied Social Research.

Lazarsfeld, P. F. (1948). The use of panels in social research. *Proceedings of the American Philosophical Society, 92,* 405–410.

Leaf, R. C., DiGiuseppe, R., Mass, R., & Alington, D. E. (1993). Statistical methods for analyses of incomplete service records: Concurrent use of longitudinal and cross-sectional data. *Journal of Consulting and Clinical Psychology, 61,* 495–505.

Lee, S., & Hershberger, S. (1990). A simple rule for generating equivalent models in covariance structure modeling. *Multivariate Behavioral Research, 25,* 313–334.

Lee, Y., Ellenberg, J., Hirtz, D., & Nelson, K. (1991). Analysis of clinical trials by treatment actually received: Is it really an option? *Statistics in Medicine, 10,* 1595–1605.

Lehman, D. R., Lempert, R. O., & Nisbett, R. E. (1988). The effects of graduate training on reasoning: Formal discipline and thinking about everyday-life events. *American Psychologist, 43,* 431–442.

LeLorier, J., Gregoire, G., Benhaddad, A., Lapierre, J., & Derderian, F. (1997). Discrepancies between meta-analyses and subsequent large randomized, controlled trials. *New England Journal of Medicine, 337,* 536–542.

Leviton, L. C., & Cook, T. D. (1983). Evaluation findings in education and social work textbooks. *Evaluation Review, 7,* 497–518.

Leviton, L. C., Finnegan, J. R., Zapka, J. G., Meischke, H., Estabrook, B., Gilliland, J., Linares, A., Weitzman, E. R., Raczynski, J., & Stone, E. (1999). Formative research methods to understand patient and provider responses to heart attack symptoms. *Evaluation and Program Planning, 22,* 385–397.

Levy, A. S., Mathews, O., Stephenson, M., Tenney, J. E., & Schucker, R. E. (1985). The impact of a nutrition information program on food purchases. *Journal of Public Policy and Marketing, 4,* 1–13.

Lewin, K. (1935). *A dynamic theory of personality: Selected papers.* New York: McGraw-Hill.

Lewis, D. (1973). Causation. *Journal of Philosophy, 70,* 556–567.

Lewontin, R. (1997, January 9). Billions and billions of demons. *New York Review of Books, 64*(1), 28–32.

Li, Z., & Begg, C. B. (1994). Random effects models for combining results from controlled and uncontrolled studies in a meta-analysis. *Journal of the American Statistical Association, 89,* 1523–1527.

Lichstein, K. L. (1988). *Clinical relaxation strategies.* New York: Wiley.

Lichstein, K. L., Riedel, B. W., & Grieve, R. (1994). Fair tests of clinical trials: A treatment implementation model. *Advances in Behavior Research and Therapy, 16,* 1–29.

Lichtenstein, E. L., Glasgow, R. E., & Abrams, D. B. (1986). Social support in smoking cessation: In search of effective interventions. *Behavior Therapy, 17,* 607–619.

Lichtenstein, L. M. (1993). Allergy and the immune system. *Scientific American, 269,* 117–124.

Lieberman, S. (1956). The effects of changes in roles on the attitudes of role occupants. *Human Relations, 9,* 385–402.

Lieberson, S. (1985). *Making it count: The improvement of social research and theory.* Berkeley: University of California Press.

Liebman, B. (1996). Vitamin E and fat: Anatomy of a flip-flop. *Nutrition Action Newsletter, 23,* 10–11.

Light, R. J., Singer, J. D., & Willett, J. B. (1990). *By design: Planning research in higher education.* Cambridge, MA: Harvard University Press.

Light, R. J., Singer, J. D., & Willett, J. B. (1994). The visual presentation and interpretation of meta-analysis. In H. Cooper & L. V. Hedges (Eds.), *The handbook of research synthesis* (pp. 439–453). New York: Russell Sage Foundation.

Lincoln, Y. S. (1990). Campbell's retrospective and a constructivist's perspective. *Harvard Educational Review, 60,* 501–504.

Lincoln, Y. S., & Guba, E. G. (1985). *Naturalistic inquiry.* Newbury Park, CA: Sage.

Lind, E. A. (1985). Randomized experiments in the Federal courts. In R. F. Boruch & W. Wothke (Eds.), *Randomization and field experimentation* (pp. 73–80). San Francisco: Jossey-Bass.

Lind, J. (1753). *A treatise of the scurvy. Of three parts containing an inquiry into the nature, causes and cure of that disease.* Edinburgh: Sands, Murray, & Cochran.

Lipsey, M. W. (1990). *Design sensitivity: Statistical power for experimental research.* Thousand Oaks, CA: Sage.

Lipsey, M. W. (1992). Juvenile delinquency treatment: A meta-analytic inquiry into the variability of effects. In T. D. Cook, H. M. Cooper, D. S. Cordray, H. Hartmann, L. V. Hedges, R. J. Light, T. A. Louis, & F. Mosteller (Eds.), *Meta-analysis for explanation: A casebook* (pp. 83–127). New York: Russell Sage Foundation.

Lipsey, M. W., Cordray, D. S., & Berger, D. E. (1981). Evaluation of a juvenile diversion program. *Evaluation Review, 5,* 283–306.

Lipsey, M. W., & Wilson, D. B. (1993). The efficacy of psychological, educational, and behavioral treatment: Confirmation from meta-analysis. *American Psychologist, 48,* 1181–1209.

Lipsey, M. W., & Wilson, D. B. (2000). *Practical meta-analysis.* Newbury Park, CA: Sage.

Little, R. J. (1985). A note about models for selectivity bias. *Econometrica, 53,* 1469–1474.

Little, R. J. (1995). Modeling the drop-out mechanism in repeated-measures studies. *Journal of the American Statistical Association, 90,* 1112–1121.

Little, R. J., & Rubin, D. B. (1987). *Statistical analysis with missing data.* New York: Wiley.

Little, R. J., & Rubin, D. B. (1999). Comment. *Journal of the American Statistical Association, 94,* 1130–1132.

Little, R. J., & Schenker, N. (1995). Missing data. In G. Arminger, C. C. Clogg, & M. E. Sobel (Eds.), *Handbook of statistical modeling for the social and behavioral sciences* (pp. 39–75). New York: Plenum Press.

Little, R. J., & Yau, L. (1996). Intent-to-treat analysis for longitudinal studies with dropouts. *Biometrics, 52,* 1324–1333.

Little, R. J., & Yau, L. (1998). Statistical techniques for analyzing data from prevention trials: Treatment of no-shows using Rubin's causal model. *Psychological Methods, 3,* 147–159.

Locke, E. A. (1986). *Generalizing from laboratory to field settings.* Lexington, MA: Lexington Books.

Locke, H. J., & Wallace, K. M. (1959). Short-term marital adjustment and prediction tests: Their reliability and validity. *Journal of Marriage and Family Living, 21,* 251–255.

Locke, J. (1975). *An essay concerning human understanding.* Oxford, England: Clarendon Press. (Original work published in 1690)

Lockhart, D. C. (Ed.). (1984). *Making effective use of mailed questionnaires.* San Francisco: Jossey-Bass.

Loehlin, J. C. (1992, January). *Latent variable models: An introduction to factor, path, and structural analysis* (2nd ed.). Hillsdale, NJ: Erlbaum.

Lohr, B. W. (1972). *An historical view of the research on the factors related to the utilization of health services.* Unpublished manuscript. Rockville, MD: Bureau for Health Services Research and Evaluation, Social and Economic Analysis Division.

Looney, M. A., Feltz, C. J., & Van Vleet, C. N. (1994). The reporting and analysis of research findings for within-subject designs: Methodological issues for meta-analysis. *Research Quarterly for Exercise & Sport, 65,* 363–366.

Lord, F. M. (1963). Elementary models for measuring change. In C. W. Harris (Ed.), *Problems in measuring change* (pp. 21–38). Madison: University of Wisconsin Press.

Lord, F. M. (1967). A paradox in the interpretation of group comparisons. *Psychological Bulletin, 68,* 304–305.

Lord, F. M. (1980). *Applications of item response theory to practical testing problems.* Hillsdale, NJ: Erlbaum.

Lord, F. M., & Novick, M. R. (1968). *Statistical theories of mental test scores.* Reading, MA: Addison-Wesley.

Louis, T. A., Fineberg, H. V., & Mosteller, F. (1985). Findings for public health from meta-analyses. *Annual Review of Public Health, 6,* 1–20.

Louis, T. A., & Zelterman, D. (1994). Bayesian approaches to research synthesis. In H. Cooper & L. V. Hedges (Eds.), *The handbook of research synthesis* (pp. 411–422). New York: Russell Sage Foundation.

Ludwig, J., Duncan, G. J., & Hirschfield, P. (1998, September). *Urban poverty and juvenile crime: Evidence from a randomized housing-mobility experiment.* (Available from author, Ludwig, Georgetown Public Policy Institute, 3600 N Street NW, Suite 200, Washington, DC 20007)

Luft, H. S. (1990). The applicability of the regression discontinuity design in health services research. In L. Sechrest, E. Perrin, & J. Bunker (Eds.), *Research methodology: Strengthening causal interpretations of nonexperimental data* (pp. 141–143). Rockville, MD: Public Health Service, Agency for Health Care Policy and Research.

Lund, E. (1989). The validity of different control groups in a case-control study: Oral contraceptive use and breast cancer in young women. *Journal of Clinical Epidemiology, 42,* 987–993.

MacCallum, R. C. (1986). Specification searches in covariance structure modeling. *Psychological Bulletin, 100,* 107–120.

MacCallum, R. C., Browne, M. W., & Sugawara, H. M. (1996). Power analysis and determination of sample size for covariance structure modeling. *Psychological Methods, 1,* 130–149.

MacCallum, R. C., Wegener, D. T., Uchino, B. N., & Fabrigar, L. R. (1993). The problem of equivalent models in applications of covariance structure analysis. *Psychological Bulletin, 114,* 185–199.

MacCready, R. A. (1974). Admissions of phenylketonuric patients to residential institutions before and after screening programs of the newborn infant. *Journal of Pediatrics, 85,* 383–385.

MacIntyre, A. (1981). *After virtue.* Notre Dame, IN: University of Notre Dame Press.

MacKenzie, A., Funderburk, F. R., Allen, R. P., & Stefan, R. L. (1987). The characteristics of alcoholics frequently lost to follow-up. *Journal of Studies on Alcohol, 48,* 119–123.

Mackie, J. L. (1974). *The cement of the universe: A study of causation.* Oxford, England: Oxford University Press.

MacKinnon, D. P., Johnson, C. A., Pentz, M. A., Dwyer, J. H., Hansen, W. B., Flay, B. R., & Wang, E.Y.-I. (1991). Mediating mechanisms in a school-based drug prevention program: First-year effects of the Midwestern Prevention Project. *Health Psychology, 10,* 164–172.

MacKinnon, D. P., Warsi, G., & Dwyer, J. H. (1995). A simulation study of mediated effect measures. *Multivariate Behavioral Research, 30,* 41–62.

Madden, E. H., & Humber, J. (1971). Nomological necessity and C. J. Ducasse. *Ratio, 13,* 119–138.

Madaus, G. F., & Greaney, V. (1985). The Irish Experience in competency testing: Implications for American education. *American Journal of Education, 93,* 268–294.

Magidson, J. (1977). Toward a causal model approach for adjusting for preexisting differences in the nonequivalent control group situation. *Evaluation Quarterly, 1,* 399–420.

Magidson, J. (1978). Reply to Bentler and Woodward: The .05 significance level is not all-powerful. *Evaluation Quarterly, 2,* 511–520.

Magidson, J. (2000). On models used to adjust for preexisting differences. In L. Bickman (Ed.), *Research design: Donald Campbell's legacy* (Vol. 2, pp. 181–194). Thousand Oaks, CA: Sage.

Magnusson, D. (2000). The individual as the organizing principle in psychological inquiry: A holistic approach. In L. R. Bergman, R. B. Cairns, L. Nilsson, & L. Nystedt (Eds.), *Developmental science and the holistic approach* (pp. 33–47). Mahwah, NJ: Erlbaum.

Makuch, R., & Simon, R. (1978). Sample size requirements for evaluating a conservative therapy. *Cancer Treatment Reports, 62,* 1037–1040.

Mallams, J. H., Godley, M. D., Hall, G. M., & Meyers, R. J. (1982). A social systems approach to resocializing alcoholics in the community. *Journal of Studies on Alcohol, 43,* 1115–1123.

Maltz, M. D., Gordon, A. C., McDowall, D., & McCleary, R. (1980). An artifact in pretest-posttest designs: How it can mistakenly make delinquency programs look effective. *Evaluation Review, 4,* 225–240.

Mann, C. (1994). Can meta-analysis make policy? *Science, 266,* 960–962.

Mann, T. (1994). Informed consent for psychological research: Do subjects comprehend consent forms and understand their legal rights? *Psychological Science, 5,* 140–143.

Manski, C. F. (1990). Nonparametric bounds on treatment effects. *American Economic Review Papers and Proceedings, 80,* 319–323.

Manski, C. F., & Garfinkel, I. (1992). Introduction. In C. F. Manski & I. Garfinkel (Eds.), *Evaluating welfare and training programs* (pp. 1–22). Cambridge, MA: Harvard University Press.

Manski, C. F., & Nagin, D. S. (1998). Bounding disagreements about treatment effects: A case study of sentencing and recidivism. In A. Raftery (Ed.), *Sociological methodology* (pp. 99–137). Cambridge, MA: Blackwell.

Manski, C. F., Sandefur, G. D., McLanahan, S., & Powers, D. (1992). Alternative estimates of the effect of family structure during adolescence on high school graduation. *Journal of the American Statistical Association, 87,* 25–37.

Marascuilo, L. A., & Busk, P. L. (1988). Combining statistics for multiple-baseline AB and replicated ABAB designs across subjects. *Behavioral Assessment, 10,* 1–28.

Marcantonio, R. J. (1998). *ESTIMATE: Statistical software to estimate the impact of missing data* [Computer software]. Lake in the Hills, IL: Statistical Research Associates.

Marcus, S. M. (1997a). Assessing non-consent bias with parallel randomized and nonrandomized clinical trials. *Journal of Clinical Epidemiology, 50,* 823–828.

Marcus, S. M. (1997b). Using omitted variable bias to assess uncertainty in the estimation of an AIDS education treatment effect. *Journal of Educational and Behavioral Statistics, 22,* 193–201.

Marcus, S. M. (2001). A sensitivity analysis for subverting randomization in controlled trials. *Statistics in Medicine, 20,* 545–555.

Margraf, J., Ehlers, A., Roth, W. T., Clark, D. B., Sheikh, J., Agras, W. S., & Taylor, C. B. (1991). How "blind" are double-blind studies? *Journal of Consulting and Clinical Psychology, 59,* 184–187.

Marin, G., Marin, B. V., Perez-Stable, E. J., Sabogal, F., & Ostero-Sabogal, R. (1990). Changes in information as a function of a culturally appropriate smoking cessation community intervention for Hispanics. *American Journal of Community Psychology, 18,* 847–864.

Mark, M. M. (1986). Validity typologies and the logic and practice of quasi-experimentaton. In W. M. K. Trochim (Ed.), *Advances in quasi-experimental design and analysis* (pp. 47–66). San Francisco: Jossey-Bass.

Mark, M. M. (2000). Realism, validity, and the experimenting society. In L. Bickman (Ed.), *Validity and social experimentation: Donald Campbell's legacy* (Vol. 1, pp. 141–166). Thousand Oaks, CA: Sage.

Mark, M. M., & Mellor, S. (1991). Effect of self-relevance of an event on hindsight bias: The foreseeability of a layoff. *Journal of Applied Psychology, 76,* 569–577.

Marquis, D. (1983). Leaving therapy to chance. *Hastings Center Report, 13,* 40–47.

Marriott, F. H. C. (1990). *A dictionary of statistical terms* (5th ed.). Essex, England: Longman Scientific and Technical.

Marschak, J. (1953). Economic measurements for policy and prediction. In W. C. Hood & T. C. Koopmans (Ed.), *Studies in econometric method* (Cowles Commission Monograph No. 13). New York: Wiley.

Marsh, H. W. (1998). Simulation study of non-equivalent group-matching and regression-discontinuity designs: Evaluation of gifted and talented programs. *Journal of Experimental Education, 66,* 163–192.

Marshall, E. (1989). Quick release of AIDS drugs. *Science, 245,* 345, 347.

Martin, D. C., Diehr, P., Perrin, E. B., & Koepsell, T. D. (1993). The effect of matching on the power of randomized community intervention studies. *Statistics in Medicine, 12,* 329–338.

Martin, S. E., Annan, S., & Forst, B. (1993). The special deterrent effects of a jail sanction on first-time drunk drivers: A quasi-experimental study. *Accident Analysis and Prevention, 25,* 561–568.

Marx, J. L. (1989). Drug availability is an issue for cancer patients, too. *Science, 245,* 346–347.

Mase, B. F. (1971). *Changes in self-actualization as a result of two types of residential group experience.* Unpublished doctoral dissertation, Northwestern University, Evanston, IL.

Mastroianni, A. C., Faden, R., & Federman, D. (Eds.). (1994). *Women and health research* (Vols. 1–2). Washington, DC: National Academy Press.

Matt, G. E. (1989). Decision rules for selecting effect sizes in meta-analysis: A review and reanalysis of psychotherapy outcome studies. *Psychological Bulletin, 105,* 106–115.

Matt, G. E., & Cook, T. D. (1994). Threats to the validity of research syntheses. In H. Cooper & L. V. Hedges (Eds.), *The handbook of research synthesis* (pp. 503–520). New York: Russell Sage Foundation.

Matt, G. E., Cook, T. D., & Shadish, W. R. (2000). *Generalizing about causal inferences.* Manuscript in preparation.

Mauro, R. (1990). Understanding L.O.V.E. (Left Out Variables Error): A method for examining the effects of omitted variables. *Psychological Bulletin, 108,* 314–329.

Maxwell, J. A. (1990). Response to "Campbell's retrospective and a constructivist's perspective." *Harvard Educational Review, 60,* 504–508.

Maxwell, J. A. (1992). Understanding and validity in qualitative research. *Harvard Educational Review, 62,* 279–300.

Maxwell, J. A., Bashook, P. G., & Sandlow, L. J. (1986). Combining ethnographic and experimental methods in educational evaluation: A case study. In D. M. Fetterman & M. A. Pittman (Eds.), *Educational evaluation: Ethnography in theory, practice, and politics* (pp. 121–143). Newbury Park, CA: Sage.

Maxwell, J. A., & Lincoln, Y. S. (1990). Methodology and epistemology: A dialogue. *Harvard Educational Review, 60,* 497–512.

Maxwell, S. E. (1993). Covariate imbalance and conditional size: Dependence on model-based adjustments. *Statistics in Medicine, 12,* 101–109.

Maxwell, S. E. (1994). Optimal allocation of assessment time in randomized pretest-posttest designs. *Psychological Bulletin, 115,* 142–152.

Maxwell, S. E. (1998). Longitudinal designs in randomized group comparisons: When will intermediate observations increase statistical power? *Psychological Methods, 3,* 275–290.

Maxwell, S. E., Cole, D. A., Arvey, R. D., & Salas, E. (1991). A comparison of methods for increasing power in randomized between-subjects designs. *Psychological Bulletin, 110,* 328–337.

Maxwell, S. E., & Delaney, H. D. (1990). *Designing experiments and analyzing data: A model comparison approach.* Pacific Grove, CA: Brooks/Cole.

Maxwell, S. E., Delaney, H. D., & Dill, C. A. (1984). Another look at ANCOVA versus blocking. *Psychological Bulletin, 95,* 136–147.

Mayer, L. S. (1986). Statistical inferences for cross-lagged panel models without the assumption of normal errors. *Social Science Research, 15,* 28–42.

McAweeney, M. J., & Klockars, A. J. (1998). Maximizing power in skewed distributions: Analysis and assignment. *Psychological Methods, 3,* 117–122.

McCall, W. A. (1923). *How to experiment in education.* New York: MacMillan.

McCardel, J. B. (1972). Interpersonal effects of structured and unstructured human relations groups. *Dissertation Abstracts International, 33,* 4518–4519. (University Microfilms No. 73-5828)

McClannahan, L. E., McGee, G. G., MacDuff, G. S., & Krantz, P. J. (1990). Assessing and improving child care: A personal appearance index for children with autism. *Journal of Applied Behavior Analysis, 23,* 469–482.

McCleary, R. D. (2000). The evolution of the time series experiment. In L. Bickman (Ed.), *Research design: Donald Campbell's legacy* (Vol. 2, pp. 215–234). Thousand Oaks, CA: Sage.

McCleary, R. D., & Welsh, W. N. (1992). Philosophical and statistical foundations of time-series experiments. In T. R. Kratochwill & J. R. Levin (Eds.), *Single-case research design and analysis* (pp. 41–91). Hillsdale, NJ: Erlbaum.

McClelland, G. H. (1997). Optimal design in psychological research. *Psychological Methods, 2,* 3–19.

McClelland, G. H. (2000). Increasing statistical power without increasing sample size. *American Psychologist, 55,* 963–964.

McClelland, G. H., & Judd, C. M. (1993). Statistical difficulties of detecting interactions and moderator effects. *Psychological Bulletin, 114,* 376–390.

McCord, J. (1978). A thirty-year followup of treatment effects. *American Psychologist, 33,* 284–289.

McCord, W., & McCord, J. (1959). *Origins of crime.* New York: Columbia University Press.

McCoy, H. V., & Nurco, D. M. (1991). Locating subjects by traditional techniques. In D. M. Nurco (Ed.), *Follow-up fieldwork: AIDS outreach and IV drug abuse* (DHHS Publication No. ADM 91-1736, pp. 31–73). Rockville, MD: National Institute on Drug Abuse.

McCullough, B. D., & Wilson, B. (1999). On the accuracy of statistical procedure in Microsoft Excel 97. *Computational Statistics and Data Analysis, 31,* 27–37.

McDonald, R. P. (1994). The bilevel reticular action model for path analysis with latent variables. *Sociological Methods and Research, 22,* 399–413.

McDowall, D., McCleary, R., Meidinger, E. E., & Hay, R. A. (1980). *Interrupted time series analysis.* Newbury Park CA: Sage.

McFadden, E. (1998). *Management of data in clinical trials.* New York: Wiley.

McGuire, W. J. (1984). A contextualist theory of knowledge: Its implications for innovation and return in psychological research. In L. Berkowitz (Ed.), *Advances in experimental social psychology* (pp. 1–47). New York: Academic Press.

McGuire, W. J. (1997). Creative hypothesis generating in psychology: Some useful heuristics. *Annual Review of Psychology, 48,* 1–30.

McKay, H., Sinisterra, L., McKay, A., Gomez, H., & Lloreda, P. (1978). Improving cognitive ability in chronically deprived children. *Science, 200,* 270–278.

McKillip, J. (1992). Research without control groups: A control construct design. In F. B. Bryant, J. Edwards, R. S. Tindale, E. J. Posavac, L. Heath, & E. Henderson (Eds.), *Methodological issues in applied psychology* (pp. 159–175). New York: Plenum.

McKillip, J., & Baldwin, K. (1990). Evaluation of an STD education media campaign: A control construct design. *Evaluation Review, 14,* 331–346.

McLeod, R. S., Taylor, D. W., Cohen, A., & Cullen, J. B. (1986, March 29). Single patient randomized clinical trial: Its use in determining optimal treatment for patient with inflammation of a Kock continent ileostomy reservoir. *Lancet, 1,* 726–728.

McNees, P., Gilliam, S. W., Schnelle, J. F., & Risley, T. (1979). Controlling employee theft through time and product identification. *Journal of Organizational Behavior Management, 2,* 113–119.

McSweeny, A. J. (1978). The effects of response cost on the behavior of a million persons: Charging for directory assistance in Cincinnati. *Journal of Applied Behavioral Analysis, 11,* 47–51.

Mead, R. (1988). *The design of experiments: Statistical principles for practical application.* Cambridge, England: Cambridge University Press.

Medin, D. L. (1989). Concepts and conceptual structures. *American Psychologist, 44,* 1469–1481.

Meehl, P. E. (1967). Theory testing in psychology and physics: A methodological paradox. *Philosophy of Science, 34,* 103–115.

Meehl, P. E. (1978). Theoretical risks and tabular asterisks: Sir Karl, Sir Ronald, and the slow progress of soft psychology. *Journal of Consulting and Clinical Psychology, 46,* 806–834.

Meier, P. (1972). The biggest public health experiment ever: The 1954 field trial of the Salk poliomyelitis vaccine. In J. M. Tanur, F. Mosteller, W. H. Kruskal, R. F. Link, R. S. Pieters, & G. R. Rising (Eds.), *Statistics: A guide to the unknown* (pp. 120–129). San Francisco: Holden-Day.

Meinert, C. L., Gilpin, A. K., Unalp, A., & Dawson, C. (2000). Gender representation in trials. *Controlled Clinical Trials, 21,* 462–475.

Menard, S. (1991). *Longitudinal research.* Thousand Oaks, CA: Sage.

Mennicke, S. A., Lent, R. W., & Burgoyne, K. L. (1988). Premature termination from university counseling centers: A review. *Journal of Counseling and Development, 66,* 458–464.

Messick, S. (1989). Validity. In R. L. Linn (Ed.), *Educational measurement* (3rd ed.), (pp. 13–103). New York: Macmillan.

Messick, S. (1995). Validity of psychological assessment: Validation of inferences from persons' responses and performances as scientific inquiry into score meaning. *American Psychologist, 50,* 741–749.

Meyer, B. D. (1995). Natural and quasi-experiments in economics. *Journal of Business and Economic Statistics, 13,* 151–161.

Meyer, D. L. (1991). Misinterpretation of interaction effects: A reply to Rosnow and Rosenthal. *Psychological Bulletin, 110,* 571–573.

Meyer, T. J., & Mark, M. M. (1995). Effects of psychosocial interventions with adult cancer patients: A meta-analysis of randomized experiments. *Health Psychology, 14,* 101–108.

Miettinen, O. S. (1985). The "case-control" study: Valid selection of subjects. *Journal of Chronic Diseases, 38,* 543–548.

Miké, V. (1989). Philosophers assess randomized clinical trials: The need for dialogue. *Controlled Clinical Trials, 10,* 244–253.

Miké, V. (1990). Suspended judgment: Ethics, evidence, and uncertainty. *Controlled Clinical Trials, 11,* 153–156.

Miles, M. B., & Huberman, A. M. (1984). *Qualitative data analysis: A sourcebook of new methods.* Newbury Park, CA: Sage.

Miller, N., Pedersen, W. C., & Pollock, V. E. (2000). Discriminative validity. In L. Bickman (Ed.), *Validity and social experimentation: Donald Campbell's legacy* (Vol. 1, pp. 65–99). Thousand Oaks, CA: Sage.

Miller, T. Q., Turner, C. W., Tindale, R. S., Posavac, E. J., & Dugoni, B. L. (1991). Reasons for the trend toward null findings in research on Type A behavior. *Psychological Bulletin, 110,* 469–485.

Millsap, M. A., Goodson, B., Chase, A., & Gamse, B. (1997, December). *Evaluation of "Spreading the Comer School Development Program and Philosophy."* Report submitted to the Rockefeller Foundation, 420 Fifth Avenue, New York, NY 10018 by Abt Associates Inc., 55 Wheeler Street, Cambridge MA 02138.

Minton, J. H. (1975). The impact of "Sesame Street" on reading readiness of kindergarten children. *Sociology of Education, 48,* 141–151.

Mishler, E. G. (1990). Validation in inquiry-guided research: The role of exemplars in narrative studies. *Harvard Educational Review, 60,* 415–442.

Mitroff, I. I., & Fitzgerald, I. (1977). On the psychology of the Apollo moon scientists: A chapter in the psychology of science. *Human Relations, 30,* 657–674.

Moberg, D. P., Piper, D. L., Wu, J., & Serlin, R. C. (1993). When total randomization is impossible: Nested random assignment. *Evaluation Review, 17,* 271–291.

Moerbeek, M., van Breukelen, G. J. P., & Berger, M. P. F. (2000). Design issues for experiments in multilevel populations. *Journal of Educational and Behavioral Statistics, 25,* 271–284.

Moffitt, R. A. (1989). Comment. *Journal of the American Statistical Association, 84,* 877–878.

Moffitt, R. A. (1991). Program evaluation with nonexperimental data. *Evaluation Review, 15,* 291–314.

Moffitt, R. A. (1996). Comment. *Journal of the American Statistical Association, 91,* 462–465.

Moher, D., Jadad, A. R., Nichol, G., Penman, M., Tugwell, P., & Walsh, S. (1995). Assessing the quality of randomized controlled trials: An annotated bibliography of scales and checklists. *Controlled Clinical Trials, 16,* 62–73.

Moher, D., & Olkin, I. (1995). Meta-analysis of randomized controlled trials: A concern for standards. *Journal of the American Medical Association, 274,* 1962–1963.

Mohr, L. B. (1988). *Impact analysis for program evaluation.* Chicago: Dorsey Press.

Mohr, L. B. (1995). *Impact analysis for program evaluation* (2nd ed.). Thousand Oaks, CA: Sage.

Moos, R. H. (1997). *Evaluating treatment environments: The quality of psychiatric and substance abuse programs* (2nd ed.). New Brunswick, NJ: Transaction.

Morales, A. (2000, November). *Investigating rules and principles for combining qualitative and quantitative data.* Paper presented at the annual conference of the American Evaluation Association, Honolulu, Hawaii.

Morawski, J. G. (1988). *The rise of experimentation in American psychology.* New Haven, CT: Yale University Press.

Mosteller, F. (1990). Improving research methodology: An overview. In L. Sechrest, E. Perrin, & J. Bunker (Eds.), *Research methodology: Strengthening causal interpretations of nonexperimental data* (pp. 221–230). Rockville, MD: U.S. Public Health Service, Agency for Health Care Policy and Research.

Mosteller, F., Gilbert, J. P., & McPeek, B. (1980). Reporting standards and research strategies for controlled trials: Agenda for the editor. *Controlled Clinical Trials, 1,* 37–58.

Mosteller, F., Light, R. J., & Sachs, J. A. (1996). Sustained inquiry in education: Lessons from skill grouping and class size. *Harvard Educational Review, 66,* 797–842.

Mulford, H. A., Ledolter, J., & Fitzgerald, J. L. (1992). Alcohol availability and consumption: Iowa sales data revisited. *Journal of Studies on Alcohol, 53,* 487–494.

Mulkay, M. (1979). *Science and the sociology of knowledge.* London: Allen & Unwin.

Mullin, B. (1993). *Advanced BASIC meta-analysis.* Hillsdale, NJ: Erlbaum.

Mumford, E., Schlesinger, H. J., Glass, G. V., Patrick, C., & Cuerdon, T. (1984). A new look at evidence about reduced cost of medical utilization following mental health treatment. *American Journal of Psychiatry, 141,* 1145–1158.

Murdoch, J. C., Singh, H., & Thayer, M. (1993). The impact of natural hazards on housing values: The Loma Prieta earthquake. *Journal of the American Real Estate and Urban Economics Association, 21,* 167–184.

Murnane, R. J., Newstead, S., & Olsen, R. J. (1985). Comparing public and private schools: The puzzling role of selectivity bias. *Journal of Business and Economic Statistics, 3,* 23–35.

Murray, C. (1984). *Losing ground: American social policy, 1950–1980.* New York: Basic Books.

Murray, D. M. (1998). *Design and analysis of group-randomized trials.* New York: Oxford University Press.

Murray, D. M., & Hannan, P. J. (1990). Planning for the appropriate analysis in school-based drug-use prevention studies. *Journal of Consulting and Clinical Psychology, 58,* 458–468.

Murray, D. M., Hannan, P. J., & Baker, W. L. (1996). A Monte Carlo study of alternative responses to intraclass correlation in community trials: Is it ever possible to avoid Cornfield's penalties? *Evaluation Review, 20,* 313–337.

Murray, D. M., McKinlay, S. M., Martin, D., Donner, A. P., Dwyer, J. H., Raudenbush, S. W., & Graubard, B. I. (1994). Design and analysis issues in community trials. *Evaluation Review, 18,* 493–514.

Murray, D. M., Moskowitz, J. M., & Dent, C. W. (1996). Design and analysis issues in community-based drug abuse prevention. *American Behavioral Scientist, 39,* 853–867.

Muthen, B. O. (1994). Multilevel covariance structure analysis. *Sociological Methods and Research, 22,* 376–398.

Muthen, B. O., Kaplan, D., & Hollis, M. (1987). On structural equation modeling with data that are not missing completely at random. *Psychometrika, 52,* 431–462.

Narayanan, V. K., & Nath, R. (1982). A field test of some attitudinal and behavioral consequences of flexitime. *Journal of Applied Psychology, 67,* 214–218.

National Commission for the Protection of Human Subjects of Biomedical and Behavioral Research. (1979). *The Belmont report: Ethical principles and guidelines for the protection of human subjects of research* (OPRR Report; FR Doc. No. 79-12065). Washington, DC: U.S. Government Printing Office.

National Institutes of Health. (1994). *NIH guidelines on the inclusion of women and minorities as subjects in clinical research, 59* Del. Reg. 14, 508 (Document No. 94-5435).

Naylor, R. H. (1989). Galileo's experimental discourse. In D. Gooding, T. Pinch, & S. Schaffer (Eds.), *The uses of experiment: Studies in the natural sciences* (pp. 117–134). Cambridge, England: Cambridge University Press.

Neal-Schuman Publishers. (Eds.). (1980). *National Directory of Mental Health*. New York: Wiley.

Nesselroade, J. R., Stigler, S. M., & Baltes, P. B. (1980). Regression to the mean and the study of change. *Psychological Bulletin, 88,* 622–637.

Neter, J., Wasserman, W., & Kutner, M. H. (1983). *Applied linear regression models*. New York: Gardner Press.

Neustrom, M. W., & Norton, W. M. (1993). The impact of drunk driving legislation in Louisiana. *Journal of Safety Research, 24,* 107–121.

Newbold, P., Agiakloglou, C., & Miller, J. (1994). Adventures with ARIMA software. *International Journal of Forecasting, 10,* 573–581.

Newhouse, J. P. (1993). *Free for all? Lessons from the RAND Health Insurance Experiment*. Cambridge, MA: Harvard University Press.

Newhouse, J. P., & McClellan, M. (1998). Econometrics in outcomes research: The use of instrumental variables. *Annual Review of Public Health, 19,* 17–34.

Nicholson, R. A., & Berman, J. S. (1983). Is follow-up necessary in evaluating psychotherapy? *Psychological Bulletin, 93,* 261–278.

Nickerson, R. S. (2000). Null hypothesis significance testing: A review of an old and continuing controversy. *Psychological Methods, 5,* 241–301.

Nietzel, M. T., Russell, R. L., Hemmings, K. A., & Gretter, M. L. (1987). Clinical significance of psychotherapy for unipolar depression: A meta-analytic approach to social comparison. *Journal of Consulting and Clinical Psychology, 55,* 156–161.

Notz, W. W., Staw, B. M., & Cook, T. D. (1971). Attitude toward troop withdrawal from Indochina as a function of draft number: Dissonance or self-interest? *Journal of Personality and Social Psychology, 20,* 118–126.

Nunnally, J. C., & Bernstein, I. H. (1994). *Psychometric theory* (3rd ed.). New York: McGraw-Hill.

Nurco, D. N., Robins, L. N., & O'Donnel, J. A. (1977). Locating respondents. In L. D. Johnston, D. N. Nurco, & L. N. Robins (Eds.), *Conducting follow-up research on drug treatment programs* (NIDA Treatment Program Monograph Series, No. 2, pp. 71–84). Rockville, MD: National Institute on Drug Abuse.

Nuremberg Code. (1949). *Trials of war criminals before the Nuremberg Military Tribunals under Control Council Law No. 10* (Vol. 2). Washington, DC: U.S. Government Printing Office.

Oakes, D., Moss, A. J., Fleiss, J. L., Bigger, J. T., Jr., Therneau, T., Eberly, S. W., McDermott, M. P., Manatunga, A., Carleen, E., Benhorn, J., and The Multicenter Diltiazem Post-Infarction Trial Research Group. (1993). Use of compliance measures in an analysis of the effect of Diltiazem on mortality and reinfarction after myocardial infarction. *Journal of the American Statistical Association, 88,* 44–49.

O'Carroll, P. W., Loftin, C., Waller, J. B., McDowall, D., Bukoff, A., Scott, R. O., Mercy, J. A., & Wiersema, B. (1991). Preventing homicide: An evaluation of the efficacy of a Detroit gun ordinance. *American Journal of Public Health, 81,* 576–581.

O'Connor, F. R., Devine, E. C., Cook, T. D. & Curtin, T. R. (1990). Enhancing surgical nurses' patient education. *Patient Education and Counseling, 16,* 7–20.

Okene, J. (Ed.). (1990). *Adoption and maintenance of behaviors for optimal health.* New York: Academic Press.

Oldroyd, D. (1986). *The arch of knowledge: An introductory study of the history of the philosophy and methodology of science.* New York: Methuen.

Olds, D. L., Eckenrode, D., Henderson, C. R., Kitzman, H., Powers, J., Cole, R., Sidora, K., Morris, P., Pettitt, L. M., & Luckey, D. (1997). Long-term effects of home visitation on maternal life course and child abuse and neglect. *Journal of the American Medical Association, 278,* 637–643.

Olds, D. L, Henderson, C. R., Cole, R., Eckenrode, J., Kitzman, H., Luckey, D., Pettitt, L. M., Sidora, K., Morris, P., & Powers, J. (1998). Long-term effects of nurse home visitation on children's criminal and antisocial behavior: 15-year follow-up of a randomized controlled trial. *Journal of the American Medical Association, 280,* 1238–1244.

Olds, D., Henderson, C. R., Kitzman, H., & Cole, R. (1995). Effects of prenatal and infancy nurse home visitation on surveillance of child maltreatment. *Pediatrics, 95,* 365–372.

O'Leary, K. D., Becker, W. C., Evans, M. B., & Saudargas, R. A. (1969). A token reinforcement program in a public school: A replication and systematic analysis. *Journal of Applied Behavior Analysis, 3,* 3–13.

O'Leary, K. D., & Borkovec, T. D. (1978). Conceptual, methodological, and ethical problems of placebo groups in psychotherapy research. *American Psychologist, 33,* 821–830.

Ones, D. S., Viswesvaran, C., & Schmidt, F. L. (1993). Comprehensive meta-analysis of integrity test validities: Findings and implications for personnel selection and theories of job performance [Monograph]. *Journal of Applied Psychology, 78,* 679–703.

Orne, M. T. (1959). The nature of hypnosis: Artifact and essence. *Journal of Abnormal and Social Psychology, 58,* 277–299.

Orne, M. T. (1962). On the social psychology of the psychological experiment. *American Psychologist, 17,* 776–783.

Orne, M. T. (1969). Demand characteristics and the concept of quasi-controls. In R. Rosenthal & R. L. Rosnow (Eds.), *Artifact in behavioral research* (pp. 143–179). New York: Academic Press.

Orr, L. L. (1999). *Social experiments: Evaluating public programs with experimental methods.* Thousand Oaks, CA: Sage.

Orr, L. L., Johnston, T., Montgomery, M., & Hojnacki, M. (1989). *Design of the Washington Self-Employment and Enterprise Development (SEED) Demonstration.* Bethesda, MD: Abt/Battell Memorial Institute.

Orwin, R. G. (1983). A fail-safe N for effect size in meta-analysis. *Journal of Educational Statistics, 8,* 157–159.

Orwin, R. G. (1984). Evaluating the life cycle of a product warning: Saccharin and diet soft drinks. *Evaluation Review, 8,* 801–822.

Orwin, R. G. (1994). Evaluating coding decisions. In H. Cooper & L. V. Hedges (Eds.), *The handbook of research synthesis* (pp. 140–162). New York: Russell Sage Foundation.

Orwin, R. G., & Cordray, D. S. (1985). Effects of deficient reporting on meta-analysis: A conceptual framework and reanalysis. *Psychological Bulletin, 85,* 185–193.

Orwin, R. G., Cordray, D. S., & Huebner, R. B. (1994). Judicious application of randomized designs. In K. J. Conrad (Ed.), *Critically evaluating the role of experiments* (pp. 73–86). San Francisco: Jossey-Bass.

Ostrom, C. W. (1990). *Time series analysis: Regression techniques* (2nd ed.). Thousand Oaks, CA: Sage.

Ottenbacher, K. J. (1986). Reliability and accuracy of visually analyzing graphed data from single-subject designs. *American Journal of Occupational Therapy, 40,* 464–469.

Overall, J. E., & Woodward, J. A. (1977). Nonrandom assignment and the analysis of covariance. *Psychological Bulletin, 84,* 588–594.

Overton, R. C. (1998). A comparison of fixed-effects and mixed (random-effects) models for meta-analysis tests of moderator variable effects. *Psychological Methods, 3,* 354–379.

Ozminkowski, R. J., Wortman, P. M., & Roloff, D. W. (1989). Inborn/outborn status and neonatal survival: A meta-analysis of non-randomized studies. *Statistics in Medicine, 7,* 1207–1221.

Page, E. B. (1958). Teacher comments and student performance: A seventy-four classroom experiment in school motivation. *Journal of Educational Psychology, 49,* 173–181.

Palmer, C. R., & Rosenberger, W. F. (1999). Ethics and practice: Alternative designs for Phase III randomized clinical trials. *Controlled Clinical Trials, 20,* 172–186.

Patterson, G. R. (1986). Performance models for antisocial boys. *American Psychologist, 41,* 432–444.

Patton, M. Q. (1980). *Qualitative evaluation methods.* Beverly Hills, CA: Sage Publications.

Paulos, J. A. (1988). *Innumeracy: Mathematical illiteracy and its consequences.* New York: Hill & Wang.

Pearl, J. (2000). *Causality: Models, reasoning, and inference.* Cambridge, England: Cambridge University Press.

Pearlman, S., Zweben, A., & Li, S. (1989). The comparability of solicited versus clinic subjects in alcohol treatment research. *British Journal of Addictions, 84,* 523–532.

Pearson, K. (1904). Report on certain entiric fever inoculation statistics. *British Medical Journal, 2,* 1243–1246.

Peirce, C. S., & Jastrow, J. (1884). On small differences of sensation. *Memoirs of the National Academy of Sciences, 3,* 75–83.

Pelz, D. C., & Andrews, F. M. (1964). Detecting causal priorities in panel study data. *American Sociological Review, 29,* 836–848.

Permutt, T. (1990). Testing for imbalance of covariates in controlled experiments. *Statistics in Medicine, 12,* 1455–1462.

Perng, S. S. (1985). Accounts receivable treatments study. In R. F. Boruch & W. Wothke (Eds.), *Randomization and field experimentation* (pp. 55–62). San Francisco: Jossey-Bass.

Petersen, W. M. (1999, April 20). Economic status quo [Letter to the editor]. *New York Times,* p. A18.

Petty, R. E., Fabrigar, L. R., Wegener, D. T., & Priester, J. R. (1996). Understanding data when interactions are present or hypothesized. *Psychological Science, 7,* 247–252.

Pfungst, O. (1911). *Clever Hans (The horse of Mr. Von Osten)*. New York: Henry Holt.

Phillips, D. C. (1987). Validity in qualitative research: Why the worry about warrant will not wane. *Education and Urban Society, 20,* 9–24.

Phillips, D. C. (1990). Postpositivistic science: Myths and realities. In E. G. Guba (Ed.), *The paradigm dialog* (pp. 31–45). Newbury Park, CA: Sage.

Pigott, T. D. (1994). Methods for handling missing data in research syntheses. In H. Cooper & L. V. Hedges (Eds.), *The handbook of research synthesis* (pp. 163–175). New York: Russell Sage Foundation.

Pinch, T. (1986). *Confronting nature*. Dordrecht, Holland: Reidel.

Pirie, P. L., Thomson, M. A., Mann, S. L., Peterson, A. V., Murray, D. M., Flay, B. R., & Best, J. A. (1989). Tracking and attrition in longitudinal school-based smoking prevention research. *Preventive Medicine, 18,* 249–256.

Platt, J. R. (1964). Strong inference. *Science, 146,* 347–353.

Plomin, R., & Daniels, D. (1987). Why are children from the same family so different from one another? *Behavioral and Brain Sciences, 10,* 1–60.

Pocock, S. J. (1983). *Clinical trials: A practical approach*. Chichester, England: Wiley.

Pocock, S. J., & Simon, R. (1975). Sequential treatment assignment with balancing for prognostic factors in the controlled clinical trial. *Biometrics, 31,* 103–115.

Polanyi, M. (1958). *Personal knowledge: Toward a post-critical philosophy*. London: Routledge & Kegan Paul.

Polsby, N. W. (1984). *Political innovation in America: The politics of policy initiation*. New Haven, CT: Yale University Press.

Popper, K. R. (1959). *The logic of scientific discovery*. New York: Basic Books.

Population Council. (1986). *An experimental study of the efficiency and effectiveness of an IUD insertion and back-up component* (English summary; Report No. PC PES86). Lima, Peru: Author.

Potvin, L., & Campbell, D. T. (1996). *Exposure opportunity, the experimental paradigm and the case-control study*. Unpublished manuscript.

Pound, C. R., Partin, A. W., Eisenberger, M. A., Chan, D. W., Pearson, J. D., & Walsh, P. C. (1999). Natural history of progression after PSA elevation following radical prostatectomy. *Journal of the American Medical Association, 281,* 1591–1597.

Powers, K. I., & Anglin, M. D. (1993). Cumulative versus stabilizing effects of methadone maintenance: A quasi-experimental study using longitudinal self-report data. *Evaluation Review, 17,* 243–270.

Powers, E., & Witmer, H. (1951). *An experiment in the prevention of delinquency*. New York: Columbia University Press.

Premack, S. L., & Hunter, J. E. (1988). Individual unionization decisions. *Psychological Bulletin, 103,* 223–234.

Prentice, D. A., & Miller, D. T. (1992). When small effects are impressive. *Psychological Bulletin, 112,* 160–164.

Presby, S. (1978). Overly broad categories obscure important differences between therapies. *American Psychologist, 33,* 514–515.

Pressman, J. L., & Wildavsky, A. (1984). *Implementation* (3rd ed.). Berkeley: University of California Press.

Project MATCH Research Group (1993). Project MATCH: Rationale and methods for a multisite clinical trial matching patients to alcoholism treatment. *Alcoholism: Clinical and Experimental Research, 17,* 1130–1145.

Protection of Human Subjects, Title 45 C.F.R. Part 46, Subparts A–D (Revised 1991).

Psaty, B. M., Koepsell, T. D., Lin, D., Weiss, N. S., Siscovick, D. S., Rosendaal, F. R., Pahor, M., & Furberg, C. D. (1999). Assessment and control for confounding by indication in observational studies. *Journal of the American Geriatric Society, 47,* 749–754.

Puma, M. J., Burstein, N. R., Merrell, K., & Silverstein, G. (1990). *Evaluation of the Food Stamp Employment and Training Program. Final report: Volume I.* Bethesda, MD: Abt.

Quine, W. V. (1951). Two dogmas of empiricism. *Philosophical Review, 60,* 20–43.

Quine, W. V. (1969). *Ontological relativity and other essays.* New York: Columbia University Press.

Quirk, P. J. (1986). Public policy [Review of *Political Innovation in America* and *Agendas, Alternatives, and Public Policies*]. *Journal of Policy Analysis and Management, 6,* 607–613.

Ralston, D. A., Anthony, W. P., & Gustafson, D. J. (1985). Employees may love flextime, but what does it do to the organization's productivity? *Journal of Applied Psychology, 70,* 272–279.

Ranstam, J., Buyse, M., George, S. L., Evans, S., Geller, N. L., Scherrer, B., Lasaffre, E., Murray, G., Edler, L., Hutton, J. L., Colton, T., & Lachenbruch, P. (2000). Fraud in medical research: An international survey of biostatisticians. *Controlled Clinical Trials, 21,* 415–427.

Raudenbush, S. W. (1994). Random effects models. In H. Cooper & L. V. Hedges (Eds.), *The handbook of research synthesis* (pp. 301–321). New York: Russell Sage Foundation.

Raudenbush, S. W. (1997). Statistical analysis and optimal design for cluster randomized design. *Psychological Methods, 2,* 173–185.

Raudenbush, S. W., Becker, B. J., & Kalaian, H. (1988). Modeling multivariate effect sizes. *Psychological Bulletin, 103,* 111–120.

Raudenbush, S. W., & Liu, X. (2000). Statistical power and optimal design for multisite randomized trials. *Psychological Methods, 5,* 199–213.

Raudenbush, S. W., & Willms, J. D. (Eds.). (1991). *Schools, classrooms, and pupils: International studies of schooling from a multilevel perspective.* San Diego, CA: Academic Press.

Raudenbush, S. W., & Willms, J. D. (1995). The estimation of school effects. *Journal of Educational and Behavioral Statistics, 20,* 307–335.

Rauma, D., & Berk, R. A. (1987). Remuneration and recidivism: The long-term impact of unemployment compensation on ex-offenders. *Journal of Quantitative Criminology, 3,* 3–27.

Ray, J. W., & Shadish, W. R. (1996). How interchangeable are different estimators of effect size? *Journal of Consulting and Clinical Psychology, 64,* 1316–1325. (See also "Correction to Ray and Shadish (1996)," *Journal of Consulting and Clinical Psychology, 66,* 532, 1998)

Reding, G. R., & Raphelson, M. (1995). Around-the-clock mobile psychiatric crisis intervention: Another effective alternative to psychiatric hospitalization. *Community Mental Health Journal, 31,* 179–187.

Reed, J. G., & Baxter, P. M. (1994). Using reference databases. In H. Cooper & L. V. Hedges (Eds.), *The handbook of research synthesis* (pp. 57–70). New York: Russell Sage Foundation.

Rees, A. (1974). The graduated work incentive experiment: An overview of the labor-supply results. *Journal of Human Resources, 9,* 158–180.

Reichardt, C. S. (1985). Reinterpreting Seaver's (1973) study of teacher expectancies as a regression artifact. *Journal of Educational Psychology, 77,* 231–236.

Reichardt, C. S. (1991). Comments on "The application of time series methods to moderate span longitudinal data." In L. M. Collins & J. L. Horn (Eds.), *Best methods for the analysis of change: Recent advances, unanswered questions, future directions* (pp. 88–91). Washington, DC: American Psychological Association.

Reichardt, C. S. (2000). A typology of strategies for ruling out threats to validity. In L. Bickman (Ed.), *Research design: Donald Campbell's legacy* (Vol. 2, pp. 89–115). Thousand Oaks, CA: Sage.

Reichardt, C. S., & Gollob, H. F. (1986). Satisfying the constraints of causal modeling. In W. M. K. Trochim (Ed.), *Advances in quasi-experimental design and analysis* (pp. 91–107). San Francisco: Jossey-Bass.

Reichardt, C. S., & Gollob, H. F. (1987, October). *Setting limits on the bias due to omitted variables.* Paper presented at the meeting of the Society of Multivariate Experimental Psychology, Denver, CO.

Reichardt, C. S., & Gollob, H. F. (1997). When confidence intervals should be used instead of statistical tests, and vice versa. In L. L. Harlow, S. A. Mulaik, & J. H. Steiger (Eds.), *What if there were no significance tests?* (pp. 259–284). Hillsdale, NJ: Erlbaum.

Reichardt, C. S., & Rallis, S. F. (Eds.). (1994). *The qualitative-quantitative debate: New perspectives.* San Francisco: Jossey-Bass.

Reichardt, C. S., Trochim, W. M. K., & Cappelleri, J. C. (1995). Reports of the death of the regression-discontinuity design are greatly exaggerated. *Evaluation Review, 19,* 39–63.

Reicken, H. W., Boruch, R. F., Campbell, D. T., Caplan, N., Glennan, T. K., Pratt, J. W., Rees, A., & Williams, W. (1974). *Social experimentation: A method for planning and evaluating social intervention.* New York: Academic Press.

Reinsel, G. (1993). *Elements of multivariate time series analysis.* New York: Springer-Verlag.

Rescher, N. (1969). *Introduction to value theory.* Englewood Cliffs, NJ: Prentice-Hall.

Revelle, W., Humphreys, M. S., Simon, L., & Gilliland, K. (1980). The interactive effect of personality, time of day, and caffeine: A test of the arousal model. *Journal of Experimental Psychology: General, 109,* 1–31.

Reynolds, A. J., & Temple, J. A. (1995). Quasi-experimental estimates of the effects of a preschool intervention: Psychometric and econometric comparisons. *Evaluation Review, 19,* 347–373.

Reynolds, K. D., & West, S. G. (1987). A multiplist strategy for strengthening nonequivalent control group designs. *Evaluation Review, 11,* 691–714.

Rezmovic, E. L., Cook, T. J., & Dobson, L. D. (1981). Beyond random assignment: Factors affecting evaluation integrity. *Evaluation Review, 5,* 51–67.

Ribisl, K. M., Walton, M. A., Mowbray, C. T., Luke, D. A., Davidson, W. S., & Bootsmiller, B. J. (1996). Minimizing participant attrition in panel studies through the use of effective retention and tracking strategies: Review and recommendations. *Evaluation and Program Planning, 19,* 1–25.

Richet, C. (1884). La suggestion mentale et le calcul des probabilites. *Revue Philosophique de la France et de l'Etranger, 18,* 609–674.

Rindskopf, D. (1986). New developments in selection modeling for quasi-experimentation. In W. M. K. Trochim (Ed.), *Advances in quasi-experimental design and analysis* (pp. 79–89). San Francisco: Jossey-Bass.

Rindskopf, D. (2000). Plausible rival hypotheses in measurement, design, and scientific theory. In L. Bickman (Ed.), *Research design: Donald Campbell's legacy* (Vol. 1, pp. 1–12). Thousand Oaks, CA: Sage.

Rindskopf, D. M. (1981). Structural equation models in analysis of nonexperimental data. In R. F. Boruch, P. M. Wortman, & D. S. Cordray (Eds.), *Reanalyzing program evaluations* (pp. 163–193). San Francisco: Jossey-Bass.

Rivlin, A. M., & Timpane, P. M. (1975). (Eds.). *Planned variation in education.* Washington, DC: Brookings.

Robbins, H., & Zhang, C.-H. (1988). Estimating a treatment effect under biased sampling. *Proceedings of the National Academy of Science, USA, 85,* 3670–3672.

Robbins, H., & Zhang, C.-H. (1989). Estimating the superiority of a drug to a placebo when all and only those patients at risk are treated with the drug. *Proceedings of the National Academy of Science, USA, 86,* 3003–3005.

Robbins, H., & Zhang, C.-H. (1990). *Estimating a treatment effect under biased allocation.* (Working paper.) New Brunswick, NJ: Rutgers University, Institute of Biostatistics and Department of Statistics.

Roberts, J. V., & Gebotys, R. J. (1992). Reforming rape laws: Effects of legislative change in Canada. *Law and Human Behavior, 16,* 555–573.

Robertson, T. S., & Rossiter, J. R. (1976). Short-run advertising effects on children: A field study. *Journal of Marketing Research, 8,* 68–70.

Robins, J. M. (1998). Correction for non-compliance in equivalence trials. *Statistics in Medicine, 17,* 269–302.

Robins, J. M. (2000). Marginal structural models versus structural nested models as tools for causal inference. In M. E. Halloran & D. Berry (Eds.), *Statistical models in epidemiology, the environment, and clinical trials* (pp. 95–133). New York: Springer-Verlag.

Robins, J. M., & Greenland, S. (1992). Identifiability and exchangeability for direct and indirect effects. *Epidemiology, 3,* 143–155.

Robins, J. M., & Greenland, S. (1996). Comment. *Journal of the American Statistical Association, 91,* 456–458.

Robins, J. M., Greenland, S., & Hu, F.-C. (1999). Estimation of the causal effect of a time-varying exposure on the marginal mean of a repeated binary outcome (with discussion). *Journal of the American Statistical Association, 94,* 687–712.

Robinson, A., Bradley, R. D., & Stanley, T. D. (1990). Opportunity to achieve: Identifying and serving mathematically talented black students. *Contemporary Educational Psychology, 15,* 1–12.

Robinson, A., & Stanley, T. D. (1989). Teaching to talent: Evaluating an enriched and accelerated mathematics program. *Journal of the Education of the Gifted, 12,* 253–267.

Robinson, L. A., Berman, J. S., & Neimeyer, R. A. (1990). Psychotherapy for the treatment of depression: A comprehensive review of controlled outcome research. *Psychological Bulletin, 108,* 30–49.

Rockette, H. E. (1993). What evidence is needed to link lung cancer to second-hand smoke? *Chance: New Directions for Statistics and Computing, 6,* 15–18.

Roese, N. J., & Jamieson, D. W. (1993). Twenty years of bogus pipeline research: A critical review and meta-analysis. *Psychological Bulletin, 114,* 363–375.

Roethlisberger, F. S., & Dickson, W. J. (1939). *Management and the worker.* Cambridge, MA: Harvard University Press.

Rogers, J. L., Howard, K. I., & Vessey, J. T. (1993). Using significance tests to evaluate equivalence between two experimental groups. *Psychological Bulletin, 113,* 553–565.

Rogers, P. J., Hacsi, T. A., Petrosino, A., & Huebner, T. A. (Eds.). (2000). *Program theory in evaluation: Challenges and opportunities.* San Francisco: Jossey-Bass.

Rogosa, D. (1980). A critique of cross-lagged correlation. *Psychological Bulletin, 88,* 245–258.

Rogosa, D. (1988). Myths about longitudinal research. In K. W. Schaie, R. T. Campbell, W. Meredith, & S. C. Rawlings (Eds.), *Methodological issues in aging research* (pp. 171–210). New York: Springer.

Rosch, E. H. (1978). Principles of categorization. In E. Rosch & B. B. Lloyd (Eds.), *Cognition and categorization* (pp. 27–48). Hillsdale, NJ: Erlbaum.

Rosenbaum, P. R. (1984). From association to causation in observational studies: The role of tests of strongly ignorable treatment assumptions. *Journal of the American Statistical Association, 79,* 41–48.

Rosenbaum, P. R. (1986). Dropping out of high school in the United States: An observational study. *Journal of Educational Statistics, 11,* 207–224.

Rosenbaum, P. R. (1987). Sensitivity analysis for certain permutation tests in matched observational studies. *Biometrika, 74,* 13–26.

Rosenbaum, P. R. (1988). Sensitivity analysis for matching with multiple controls. *Biometrika, 75,* 577–581.

Rosenbaum, P. R. (1989). Sensitivity analysis for matched observational studies with many ordered treatments. *Scandinavian Journal of Statistics, 16,* 227–236.

Rosenbaum, P. R. (1991a). Discussing hidden bias in observational studies. *Annals of Internal Medicine, 115,* 901–905.

Rosenbaum, P. R. (1991b). Sensitivity analysis for matched case-control studies. *Biometrics, 47,* 87–100.

Rosenbaum, P. R. (1993). Hodges-Lehmann point estimates of treatment effect in observational studies. *Journal of the American Statistical Association, 88,* 1250–1253.

Rosenbaum, P. R. (1995a). *Observational studies.* New York: Springer-Verlag.

Rosenbaum, P. R. (1995b). Quantiles in nonrandom samples and observational studies. *Journal of the American Statistical Association, 90,* 1424–1431.

Rosenbaum, P. R. (1996a). Comment. *Journal of the American Statistical Association, 91,* 465–468.

Rosenbaum, P. R. (1996b). Observational studies and nonrandomized experiments. In S. Ghosh & C. R. Rao (Eds.), *Handbook of statistics* (Vol. 13, pp. 181–197). Amsterdam: Elsevier Science.

Rosenbaum, P. R. (1998). Multivariate matching methods. In S. Kotz, N. L. Johnson, L. Norman, & C. B. Read (Eds.), *Encyclopedia of statistical sciences* (Update Volume 2, pp. 435–438). New York: Wiley.

Rosenbaum, P. R. (1999a). Choice as an alternative to control in observational studies. *Statistical Science, 14,* 259–304.

Rosenbaum, P. R. (1999b). Using quantile averages in matched observational studies. *Applied Statistics, 48,* 63–78.

Rosenbaum, P. R. (in press). Observational studies. In N. J. Smelser & P. B. Baltes (Eds.), *International encyclopedia of social and behavioral sciences.* Oxford, England: Elsevier Science.

Rosenbaum, P. R., & Krieger, A. (1990). Sensitivity analysis for matched case-control studies. *Journal of the American Statistical Association, 85,* 493–498.

Rosenbaum, P. R., & Rubin, D. (1984). Reducing bias in observational studies using subclassification on the propensity score. *Journal of the American Statistical Association, 79,* 516–524.

Rosenberg, M., Adams, D. C., & Gurevitch, J. (1997). *MetaWin: Statistical software for meta-analysis with resampling tests.* (Available from Sinauer Associates, Inc., P.O. Box 407, Sunderland, MA 01375-0407)

Rosenberg, M. J. (1969). The conditions and consequences of evaluation apprehension. In R. Rosenthal & R. L. Rosnow (Eds.), *Artifact in behavioral research* (pp. 279–349). New York: Academic Press.

Rosenberger, W. F. (1999). Randomized play-the-winner clinical trials: Review and recommendations. *Controlled Clinical Trials, 20,* 328–342.

Rosenthal, M. C. (1994). The fugitive literature. In H. Cooper & L. V. Hedges (Eds.), *The handbook of research synthesis* (pp. 85–94). New York: Russell Sage Foundation.

Rosenthal, R. (1956). *An attempt at the experimental induction of the defense mechanism of projection.* Unpublished doctoral dissertation, University of California, Los Angeles.

Rosenthal, R. (1966). *Experimenter effects in behavioral research.* New York: Appleton-Century-Crofts.

Rosenthal, R. (1973a). The mediation of Pygmalion effects: A four-factor theory. *Papua New Guinea Journal of Education, 9,* 1–12.

Rosenthal, R. (1973b). *On the social psychology of the self-fulfilling prophecy: Further evidence for Pygmalion effects and their mediating mechanisms.* New York: MSS Modular Publication, Module 53.

Rosenthal, R. (1979). The "file drawer problem" and tolerance for null results. *Psychological Bulletin, 86,* 638–641.

Rosenthal, R. (1986). Meta-analytic procedures and the nature of replication: The ganzfeld debate. *Journal of Parapsychology, 50,* 315–336.

Rosenthal, R. (1994). Parametric measures of effect size. In H. Cooper & L. V. Hedges (Eds.), *The handbook of research synthesis* (pp. 231–244). New York: Russell Sage Foundation.

Rosenthal, R., & Rosnow, R. L. (1991). *Essentials of behavioral research: Methods and data analysis.* New York: McGraw-Hill.

Rosenthal, R., & Rubin, D. B. (1978). Interpersonal expectancy effects: The first 345 studies. *Behavioral and Brain Sciences, 3,* 377–386.

Rosenthal, R., & Rubin, D. B. (1986). Meta-analytic procedures for combining studies with multiple effect sizes. *Psychological Bulletin, 99,* 400–406.

Rosenthal, R., & Rubin, D. B. (1994). The counternull value of an effect size: A new statistic. *Psychological Science, 5,* 329–334.

Rosenzweig, S. (1933). The experimental situation as a psychological problem. *Psychological Review, 40,* 337–354.

Rosnow, R. L., & Rosenthal, R. (1989). Definition and interpretation of interaction effects. *Psychological Bulletin, 105,* 143–146.

Rosnow, R. L., & Rosenthal, R. (1996). Contrasts and interaction effects redux: Five easy pieces. *Psychological Science, 7,* 253–257.

Rosnow, R. L., & Rosenthal, R. (1997). *People studying people: Artifacts and ethics in behavioral research.* New York: Freeman.

Ross, A. S., & Lacey, B. (1983). A regression discontinuity analysis of a remedial education programme. *Canadian Journal of Higher Education, 13,* 1–15.

Ross, H. L. (1973). Law, science and accidents: The British Road Safety Act of 1967. *Journal of Legal Studies, 2,* 1–75.

Ross, H. L., Campbell, D. T., & Glass, G. V. (1970). Determining the social effects of a legal reform: The British "breathalyser" crackdown of 1967. *American Behavioral Scientist, 13,* 493–509.

Rossi, P. H. (1987). The iron law of evaluation and other metallic rules. In J. Miller & M. Lewis (Eds.), *Research in social problems and public policy* (Vol. 4, pp. 3–20). Greenwich, CT: JAI Press.

Rossi, P. H. (1995). Doing good and getting it right. In W. R. Shadish, D. L.Newman, M. A. Scheirer, & C. Wye (Eds.), *Guiding principles for evaluators* (pp. 55–59). San Francisco: Jossey-Bass.

Rossi, P. H., Berk, R. A., & Lenihan, K. J. (1980). *Money, work and crime: Some experimental findings.* New York: Academic Press.

Rossi, P. H., & Freeman, H. E. (1989). *Evaluation: A systematic approach* (4th ed). Thousand Oaks, CA: Sage.

Rossi, P. H., Freeman, H. E., & Lipsey, M. W. (1999). *Evaluation: A systematic approach* (6th ed.). Thousand Oaks, CA: Sage.

Rossi, P. H., & Lyall, K. C. (1976). *Reforming public welfare.* New York: Russell Sage.

Rossi, P. H., & Lyall, K. C. (1978). An overview evaluation of the NIT Experiment. In T. D. Cook, M. L. DelRosario, K. M. Hennigan, M. M. Mark, & W. M. K. Trochim (Eds.), *Evaluation studies review annual* (Volume 3, pp. 412–428). Newbury Park, CA: Sage.

Rossi, P. H., & Wright, J. D. (1984). Evaluation research: An assessment. *Annual Review of Sociology, 10,* 331–352.

Rossi, P. H., Wright, J. D., & Anderson, A. B. (Eds.). (1983). *Handbook of survey research.* San Diego, CA: Academic Press.

Rothman, K. (1986). *Modern epidemiology.* Boston: Little Brown.

Rouanet, H. (1996). Bayesian methods for assessing importance of effects. *Psychological Bulletin, 119,* 149–158.

Rouse, C. E. (1998). Private school vouchers and student achievement: An evaluation of the Milwaukee Parental Choice Program. *Quarterly Journal of Economics, 113,* 553–602.

Rowe, P. M. (1999). What is all the hullabaloo about endostatin? *Lancet, 353,* 732.

Rozeboom, W. W. (1960). The fallacy of the null hypothesis significance test. *Psychological Bulletin, 57,* 416–428.

Rubin, D. B. (1974). Estimating causal effects of treatments in randomized and nonrandomized studies. *Journal of Educational Psychology, 66,* 688–701.

Rubin, D. B. (1977). Assignment to treatment group on the basis of a covariate. *Journal of Educational Statistics, 2,* 1–26.

Rubin, D. B. (1978). Bayesian inference for causal effects: The role of randomization. *Annals of Statistics, 6,* 34–58.

Rubin, D. B. (1986). Comment: Which ifs have causal answers. *Journal of the American Statistical Association, 81,* 961–962.

Rubin, D. B. (1987). *Multiple imputation for nonresponse in surveys.* New York: Wiley.

Rubin, D. B. (1990). A new perspective. In K. W. Wachter & M. L. Straf (Eds.), *The future of meta-analysis* (pp. 155–165). New York: Russell Sage Foundation.

Rubin, D. B. (1991). Practical implications of modes of statistical inference for causal effects and the critical role of the assignment mechanism. *Biometrics, 47,* 1213–1234.

Rubin, D. B. (1992a). Clinical trials in psychiatry: Should protocol deviation censor patient data? A comment. *Neuropsychopharmacology, 6,* 59–60.

Rubin, D. B. (1992b). Meta-analysis: Literature synthesis or effect-size surface estimation? *Journal of Educational Statistics, 17,* 363–374.

Rubin, D. B. (1997). Estimating causal effects from large data sets using propensity scores. *Annals of Internal Medicine, 127,* 757–763.

Rubin, D. B., & Thomas, N. (1996). Matching using estimated propensity scores: Relating theory to practice. *Biometrics, 52,* 249–264.

Rubin, D. B., & Thomas, N. (2000). Combining propensity score matching with additional adjustments for prognostic covariates. *Journal of the American Statistical Association, 95,* 573–585.

Rubins, H. B. (1994). From clinical trials to clinical practice: Generalizing from participant to patient. *Controlled Clinical Trials, 15,* 7–10.

Rudd, P., Ahmed, S., Zachary, V., Barton, C., & Bonduelle, D. (1990). Improved compliance measures: Applications in an ambulatory hypertensive drug trial. *Clinical Pharmacological Therapy, 48,* 676–685.

Ryle, G. (1971). *Collected papers* (Vol. 2). London: Hutchinson.

Sackett, D. L. (1979). Bias in analytic research. *Journal of Chronic Diseases, 32,* 51–63.

Sackett, D. L. (2000). Why randomized controlled trials fail but needn't: 1. Failure to gain "coal-face" commitment and to use the uncertainty principle. *Canadian Medical Association Journal, 162,* 1311–1314.

Sackett, D. L., & Haynes, R. B. (1976). *Compliance with therapeutic regimens.* Baltimore: Johns Hopkins University Press.

Sackett, D. L., & Hoey, J. (2000). Why randomized controlled trials fail but needn't: A new series is launched. *Canadian Medical Association Journal, 162,* 1301–1302.

Sacks, H. S., Chalmers, T. C., & Smith, H. (1982). Randomized versus historical controls for clinical trials. *American Journal of Medicine, 72,* 233–240.

Sacks, H. S., Chalmers, T. C., & Smith, H. (1983). Sensitivity and specificity of clinical trials: Randomized v historical controls. *Archives of Internal Medicine, 143*, 753–755.

St. Pierre, R. G., Cook, T. D., & Straw, R. B. (1981). An evaluation of the Nutrition Education and Training Program: Findings from Nebraska. *Evaluation and Program Planning, 4*, 335–344.

St. Pierre, R. G., Ricciuti, A., & Creps, C. (1998). *Summary of state and local Even Start evaluations*. Cambridge, MA: Abt.

Sales, B. D., & Folkman, S. (Eds.). (2000). *Ethics in research with human participants*. Washington, DC: American Psychological Association.

Salmon, W. C. (1984). *Scientific explanation and the causal structure of the world*. Princeton, NJ: Princeton University Press.

Salmon, W. C. (1989). *Four decades of scientific explanation*. Minneapolis: University of Minnesota Press.

Salner, M. (1989). Validity in human science research. In S. Kvale (Ed.), *Issues of validity in qualitative research* (pp. 47–71). Lund, Sweden: Studentlitteratur.

Sampson, R. J., Raudenbush, S. W., & Earls, F. (1997). Neighborhoods and violent crime: A multilevel study of collective efficacy. *Science, 277*, 918–924.

Sanchez-Meca, J., & Marin-Martinez, F. (1998). Weighting by inverse variance or by sample size in meta-analysis: A simulation study. *Educational and Psychological Measurement, 58*, 211–220.

Sarason, S. B. (1978). The nature of problem solving in social action. *American Psychologist, 33*, 370–380.

Saretsky, G. (1972). The OEO PC experiment and the John Henry effect. *Phi Delta Kappan, 53*, 579–581.

Sargent, D. J., Sloan, J. A., & Cha, S. S. (1999). Sample size and design considerations for Phase II clinical trials with correlated observations. *Controlled Clinical Trials, 19*, 242–252.

Saunders, L. D., Irwig, L. M., Gear, J. S., & Ramushu, D. L. (1991). A randomized controlled trial of compliance improving strategies in Soweto hypertensives. *Medical Care, 29*, 669–678.

Sayrs, L. W. (1989). *Pooled time series analysis*. Thousand Oaks, CA: Sage.

Scarr, S. (1997). Rules of evidence: A larger context for statistical debate. *Psychological Science, 8*, 16–17.

Schaffer, S. (1989). Glass works: Newton's prisms and the uses of experiment. In D. Gooding, T. Pinch, & S. Schaffer (Eds.), *The uses of experiment: Studies in the natural sciences* (pp. 105–114). Cambridge, England: Cambridge University Press.

Schaffner, K. F. (Ed.). (1986). Ethical issues in the use of clinical controls. *Journal of Medical Philosophy, 11*, 297–404.

Scharfstein, D. O., Rotnitzky, A., & Robins, J. M. (1999). Adjusting for nonignorable drop-out using semiparametric nonresponse models. *Journal of the American Statistical Association, 94*, 1096–1120.

Schlesselman, J. J. (1982). *Case-control studies: Design, conduct, analysis*. New York: Oxford University Press.

Schmidt, D., & Leppik, I. E. (Eds.). (1988). *Compliance in epilepsy.* Amsterdam: Elsevier.

Schmidt, F. L. (1996). Statistical significance testing and cumulative knowledge in psychology: Implications for training of researchers. *Psychological Methods, 1,* 115–129.

Schmidt, F. L., & Hunter, J. E. (1977). Development of a general solution to the problem of validity generalization. *Journal of Applied Psychology, 62,* 529–540.

Schmitt, F. F. (1995). *Truth: A primer.* Boulder, CO: Westview Press.

Schoenberg, R. (1989). Covariance structure models. *Annual Review of Sociology, 15,* 425–440.

Schonemann, P. H. (1991). In praise of randomness. *Behavioral and Brain Sciences, 14,* 162–163.

Schulz, K. F. (1995). Subverting randomization in controlled trials. *Journal of the American Medical Association, 274,* 1456–1458.

Schulz, K. F., Chalmers, I., Hayes, R. J., & Altman, D. G. (1995). Empirical evidence of bias: Dimensions of methodological quality associated with estimates of treatment effects in controlled trials. *Journal of the American Medical Association, 273,* 408–412.

Schumacher, J. E., Milby, J. B., Raczynski, J. M., Engle, M., Caldwell, E. S., & Carr, J. A. (1994). Demoralization and threats to validity in Birmingham's Homeless Project. In K. J. Conrad (Ed.), *Critically evaluating the role of experiments* (pp. 41–44). San Francisco: Jossey-Bass.

Schweinhart, L. J., Barnes, H. V., & Weikart, D. P. (1993). *Significant benefits: The High/Scope Perry Preschool study through age 27.* (Available from High/Scope Foundation, 600 North River Street, Ypsilanti, MI 48198)

Scientists quibble on calling discovery "planets." (2000, October 6). *The Memphis Commercial Appeal,* p. A5.

Scott, A. G., & Sechrest, L. (1989). Strength of theory and theory of strength. *Evaluation and Program Planning, 12,* 329–336.

Scriven, M. (1976). Maximizing the power of causal investigation: The Modus Operandi method. In G. V. Glass (Ed.), *Evaluation studies review annual* (Vol. 1, pp. 101–118). Newbury Park, CA: Sage.

Scriven, M. (1980). *The logic of evaluation.* Inverness, CA: Edgepress.

Scriven, M. (1991). *Evaluation thesaurus* (4th ed.). Thousand Oaks, CA: Sage.

Seamon, F., & Feiock, R. C. (1995). Political participation and city/county consolidation: Jacksonville-Duval County. *International Journal of Public Administration, 18,* 1741–1752.

Seaver, W. B. (1973). Effects of naturally induced teacher expectancies. *Journal of Personality and Social Psychology, 28,* 333–342.

Seaver, W. B., & Quarton, R. J. (1976). Regression-discontinuity analysis of dean's list effects. *Journal of Educational Psychology, 66,* 459–465.

Sechrest, L., West, S. G., Phillips, M. A., Redner, R., & Yeaton, W. (1979). Some neglected problems in evaluation research: Strength and integrity of research. In L. Sechrest, S. G. West, M. A. Phillips, R. Redner, & W. Yeaton (Eds.), *Evaluation studies review annual* (Vol. 4, pp. 15–35). Beverly Hills, CA: Sage.

Sedlmeier, P., & Gigerenzer, G. (1989). Do studies of statistical power have an effect on the power of studies? *Psychological Bulletin, 105,* 309–316.

Seligman, M. E. P. (1969). Control group and conditioning: A comment on operationalism. *Psychological Review, 76,* 484–491.

SenGupta, S. (1995). A similarity-based single study approach to construct and external validity. *Dissertation Abstracts International, 55*(11), 3458A. (University Microfilms No. 9509453)

Serlin, R. A., & Lapsley, D. K. (1993). Rational appraisal of psychological research and the good-enough principle. In G. Keren & C. Lewis (Eds.), *A handbook for data analysis in the behavioral sciences: Methodological issues* (pp. 199–228). Hillsdale, NJ: Erlbaum.

Shadish, W. R. (1984). Policy research: Lessons from the implementation of deinstitutionalization. *American Psychologist, 39,* 725–738.

Shadish, W. R. (1989). Critical multiplism: A research strategy and its attendant tactics. In L. Sechrest, H. Freeman, & A. Mulley (Eds.), *Health services research methodology: A focus on AIDS* (DHHS Publication No. PHS 89-3439, pp. 5–28). Rockville, MD: U.S. Department of Health and Human Services, Public Health Service, National Center for Health Services Research and Health Care Technology Assessment.

Shadish, W. R. (1992a). Do family and marital psychotherapies change what people do? A meta-analysis of behavioral outcomes. In T. D. Cook, H. M. Cooper, D. S. Cordray, H. Hartmann, L. V. Hedges, R. J. Light, T. A. Louis, & F. Mosteller (Eds.), *Meta-analysis for explanation: A casebook* (pp. 129–208). New York: Russell Sage Foundation.

Shadish, W. R. (1992b, August). *Mediators and moderators in psychotherapy meta-analysis.* Paper presented at the annual convention of the American Psychological Association, Washington, DC.

Shadish, W. R. (1994). Critical multiplism: A research strategy and its attendant tactics. In L. B. Sechrest & A. J. Figueredo (Eds.), *New directions for program evaluation* (pp. 13–57). San Francisco: Jossey-Bass.

Shadish, W. R. (1995a). Philosophy of science and the quantitative-qualitative debates: Thirteen common errors. *Evaluation and Program Planning, 18,* 63–75.

Shadish, W. R. (1995b). The logic of generalization: Five principles common to experiments and ethnographies. *American Journal of Community Psychology, 23,* 419–428.

Shadish, W. R. (1996). Meta-analysis and the exploration of causal mediating processes: A primer of examples, methods, and issues. *Psychological Methods, 1,* 47–65.

Shadish, W. R. (2000). The empirical program of quasi-experimentation. In L. Bickman (Ed.), *Validity and social experimentation: Donald Campbell's legacy* (pp. 13–35). Thousand Oaks, CA: Sage.

Shadish, W. R., & Cook, T. D. (1999). Design rules: More steps towards a complete theory of quasi-experimentation. *Statistical Science, 14,* 294–300.

Shadish, W. R., Cook, T. D., & Houts, A. C. (1986). Quasi-experimentation in a critical multiplist mode. In W. M. K. Trochim (Ed.), *Advances in quasi-experimental design and analysis* (pp. 29–46). San Francisco: Jossey-Bass.

Shadish, W. R., Cook, T. D., & Leviton, L. C. (1991). *Foundations of program evaluation: Theories of practice.* Newbury Park, CA: Sage.

Shadish, W. R., Doherty, M., & Montgomery, L. M. (1989). How many studies are in the file drawer? An estimate from the family/marital psychotherapy literature. *Clinical Psychology Review, 9,* 589–603.

Shadish, W. R., & Fuller, S. (Eds.). (1994). *The social psychology of science.* New York: Guilford Press.

Shadish, W. R., Fuller, S., Gorman, M. E., Amabile, T. M., Kruglanski, A. W., Rosenthal, R., & Rosenwein, R. E. (1994). Social psychology of science: A conceptual and research program. In W. R. Shadish & S. Fuller (Eds.), *Social psychology of science* (pp. 3–123). New York: Guilford Press.

Shadish, W. R., & Haddock, C. K. (1994). Combining estimates of effect size. In H. M. Cooper & L. V. Hedges (Eds.), *The handbook of research synthesis* (pp. 261–281). New York: Russell Sage Foundation.

Shadish, W. R., & Heinsman, D. T. (1997). Experiments versus quasi-experiments: Do you get the same answer? In W. J. Bukoski (Ed.), *Meta-analysis of drug abuse prevention programs* (NIDA Research Monograph, DHHS Publication No. ADM 97-170, pp. 147–164). Washington, DC: Superintendent of Documents.

Shadish, W. R., Hu, X., Glaser, R. R., Kownacki, R. J., & Wong, T. (1998). A method for exploring the effects of attrition in randomized experiments with dichotomous outcomes. *Psychological Methods, 3,* 3–22.

Shadish, W. R., Matt, G. E., Navarro, A. M., & Phillips, G. (2000). The effects of psychological therapies under clinically representative conditions: A meta-analysis, *Psychological Bulletin, 126,* 512–529.

Shadish, W. R., Matt, G., Navarro, A., Siegle, G., Crits-Christoph, P., Hazelrigg, M., Jorm, A., Lyons, L. S., Nietzel, M. T., Prout, H. T., Robinson, L., Smith, M. L., Svartberg, M., & Weiss, B. (1997). Evidence that therapy works in clinically representative conditions. *Journal of Consulting and Clinical Psychology, 65,* 355–365.

Shadish, W. R., Montgomery, L. M., Wilson, P., Wilson, M. R., Bright, I., & Okwumabua, T. (1993). The effects of family and marital psychotherapies: A meta-analysis. *Journal of Consulting and Clinical Psychology, 61,* 992–1002.

Shadish, W. R., Newman, D. L., Scheirer, M. A., & Wye, C. (1995). Developing the guiding principles. In W. R. Shadish, D. L. Newman, M. A. Scheirer, & C. Wye (Eds.), *Guiding principles for evaluators* (pp. 3–18). San Francisco: Jossey-Bass.

Shadish, W. R., & Ragsdale, K. (1996). Random versus nonrandom assignment in psychotherapy experiments: Do you get the same answer? *Journal of Consulting and Clinical Psychology, 64,* 1290–1305.

Shadish, W. R., & Reis, J. (1984). A review of studies of the effectiveness of programs to improve pregnancy outcome. *Evaluation Review, 8,* 747–776.

Shadish, W. R., Robinson, L., & Lu, C. (1999). *ES: A computer program and manual for effect size calculation.* St. Paul, MN: Assessment Systems Corporation.

Shadish, W. R., Silber, B., Orwin, R. G., & Bootzin, R. R. (1985). The subjective well-being of mental patients in nursing homes. *Evaluation and Program Planning, 8,* 239–250.

Shadish, W. R., Straw, R. B., McSweeny, A. J., Koller, D. L., & Bootzin, R. R.(1981). Nursing home care for mental patients: Descriptive data and some propositions. *American Journal of Community Psychology, 9,* 617–633.

Shadish, W. R., & Sweeney, R. (1991). Mediators and moderators in meta-analysis: There's a reason we don't let dodo birds tell us which psychotherapies should have prizes. *Journal of Consulting and Clinical Psychology, 59,* 883–893.

Shapin, S. (1994). *A social history of truth: Civility and science in seventeenth-century England*. Chicago: University of Chicago Press.

Shapiro, A. K., & Shapiro, E. (1997). *The powerful placebo*. Baltimore: Johns Hopkins University Press.

Shapiro, J. Z. (1984). The social costs of methodological rigor: A note on the problem of massive attrition. *Evaluation Review, 8*, 705–712.

Sharpe, T. R., & Wetherbee, H. (1980). *Final report: Evaluation of the Improved Pregnancy Outcome Program*. Tupelo, MS: Mississippi State Board of Health, Three Rivers District Health Department.

Shaw, R. A., Rosati, M. J., Salzman, P., Coles, C. R., & McGeary, C. (1997). Effects on adolescent ATOD behaviors and attitudes of a 5-year community partnership. *Evaluation and Program Planning, 20*, 307–313.

Sherif, J., Harvey, O. J., White, B. J., Hood, W. R., & Sherif, C. W. (1961). *Intergroup conflict and cooperation: The Robbers Cave Experiment*. Norman: University of Oklahoma Book Exchange.

Sherman, L. W., & Berk, R. A. (1985). The randomization of arrest. In R. F. Boruch & W. Wothke (Eds.), *Randomization and field experimentation* (pp. 15–25). San Francisco: Jossey-Bass.

Shih, W. J., & Quan, H. (1997). Testing for treatment differences with dropouts present in clinical trials: A composite approach. *Statistics in Medicine, 16*, 1225–1239.

Shoham-Salomon, V., & Rosenthal, R. (1987). Paradoxical interventions: A meta-analysis. *Journal of Consulting and Clinical Psychology, 55*, 22–28.

Shönemann, P. H. (1991). In praise of randomness. *Behavioral and Brain Sciences, 14*, 162–163.

Shonkoff, J. P., & Phillips, D. A. (Eds.). (2000). *From neurons to neighborhoods: The science of early childhood development*. Washington, DC: National Academy Press.

Shrout, P. E. (1997). Should significance tests be banned? Introduction to a special section exploring the pros and cons. *Psychological Science, 8*, 1–2.

Shumaker, S. A., & Rejeski, W. J. (Eds.). (2000). Adherence to behavioral and pharmacological interventions in clinical research in older adults [Special issue]. *Controlled Clinical Trials, 21*(5S).

Shumway, R. H. (1988). *Applied statistical time series analysis*. Englewood Cliffs, NJ: Prentice-Hall.

Sidman, M. (1960). *Tactics of scientific research: Evaluating experimental data in psychology*. Boston: Authors Cooperative.

Sieber, J. E. (1992). *Planning ethically responsible research: A guide for students and internal review boards*. Newbury Park, CA: Sage.

Siegel, A. E., & Siegel, S. (1957). Reference groups, membership groups, and attitude change. *Journal of Abnormal and Social Psychology, 55*, 360–364.

Siemiatycki, J. (1989). Friendly control bias. *Journal of Clinical Epidemiology, 42*, 687–688.

Siemiatycki, J., Colle, S., Campbell, S., Dewar, R., & Belmonte, M. M. (1989). Case-control study of insulin dependent (type I) diabetes mellitus. *Diabetes Care, 12*, 209–216.

Silka, L. (1989). *Intuitive judgments of change*. New York: Springer-Verlag.

Silliman, N. P. (1997). Hierarchical selection models with applications in meta-analysis. *Journal of the American Statistical Association, 92*, 926–936.

Silverman, W. A. (1977). The lesson of retrolental fibroplasia. *Scientific American, 236*, 100–107.

Simes, R. J. (1987). Confronting publication bias: A cohort design for meta-analysis. *Statistics in Medicine, 6*, 11–29.

Simon, H. A. (1976). *Administrative behavior*. New York: Free Press.

Simpson, J. M., Klar, N., & Donner, A. (1995). Accounting for cluster randomization: A review of primary prevention trials, 1990 through 1993. *American Journal of Public Health, 85*, 1378–1383.

Skinner, B. F. (1961). *Cumulative record*. New York: Appleton-Century-Crofts.

Slavin, R. E. (1986). Best-evidence synthesis: An alternative to meta-analysis and traditional reviews. *Educational Researchers, 15*, 5–11.

Smith, B., & Sechrest, L. (1991). Treatment of aptitude × treatment interactions. *Journal of Consulting and Clinical Psychology, 59*, 233–244.

Smith, E. E., & Medin, D. L. (1981). *Categories and concepts*. Cambridge, MA: Harvard University Press.

Smith, E. R. (1992). Beliefs, attributions, and evaluations: Nonhierarchical models of mediation in social cognition. *Journal of Personality and Social Psychology, 43*, 248–259.

Smith, G. (1997). Do statistics test scores regress toward the mean? *Chance, 10*, 42–45.

Smith, H. (1997). Matching with multiple controls to estimate treatment effects in observational studies. *Sociological Methodology, 27*, 325–353.

Smith, M. L. (1980). Publication bias and meta-analysis. *Evaluation in Education, 4*, 22–24.

Smith, M. L., & Glass, G. V. (1977). Meta-analysis of psychotherapy outcome studies. *American Psychologist, 32*, 752–760.

Smith, M. L., Glass, G. V., & Miller, T. I. (1980). *The benefits of psychotherapy*. Baltimore: Johns Hopkins University Press.

Smith, N. L. (Ed.). (1992). *Varieties of investigative journalism*. San Francisco: Jossey-Bass.

Smoot, S. L. (1989). Meta-analysis of single subject research in education: A comparison of four metrics (Doctoral dissertation, Georgia State University). *Dissertation Abstracts International, 50*(07), 1928A.

Snow, R. E. (1991). Aptitude-treatment interactions as a framework for research on individual differences in psychotherapy. *Journal of Consulting and Clinical Psychology, 59*, 205–216.

Snowdon, C., Elbourne, D., & Garcia, J. (1999). Zelen randomization: Attitudes of parents participating in a neonatal clinical trial. *Controlled Clinical Trials, 20*, 149–171.

Snijders, T. A. B., & Bosker, R. J. (1999). *Multilevel analysis: An introduction to basic and advanced multilevel modeling*. London: Sage.

Snyder, D. K., & Wills, R. M. (1989). Behavioral versus insight-oriented marital therapy: Effects on individual and interspousal functioning. *Journal of Consulting and Clinical Psychology, 57*, 39–46.

Snyder, D. K., Wills, R. M., & Grady-Fletcher, A. (1991). Long-term effectiveness of behavioral versus insight-oriented marital therapy: A 4-year follow-up study. *Journal of Consulting and Clinical Psychology, 59,* 138–141.

Sobel, M. E. (1993). Causal inference in the social and behavioral sciences. In G. Arminger, C. C. Clogg, & M. E. Sobel (Eds.), *Handbook for statistical modeling in the social and behavioral sciences* (pp. 1–38). New York: Plenum.

Sobel, M. E. (2000). Causal inference in the social sciences. *Journal of the American Statistical Association, 95,* 647–650.

Solomon, R. L. (1949). An extension of control group design. *Psychological Bulletin, 46,* 137–150.

Sommer, A., & Zeger, S. L. (1991). On estimating efficacy from clinical trials. *Statistics in Medicine, 10,* 45–52.

Sommer, B. (1987). The file drawer effect and publication rates in menstrual cycle research. *Psychology of Women Quarterly, 11,* 233–242.

Sorensen, G., Emmons, K., Hunt, M., & Johnston, D. (1998). Implications of the results of community trials. *Annual Review of Public Health, 19,* 379–416.

Speer, D. C. (1994). Can treatment research inform decision makers? Nonexperimental method issues and examples among older outpatients. *Journal of Consulting and Clinical Psychology, 62,* 560–568.

Speer, D. C., & Swindle, R. (1982). The "monitoring model" and the mortality × treatment interaction threat to validity in mental health outcome evaluation. *American Journal of Community Psychology, 10,* 541–552.

Spiegelhalter, D. J., Freedman, L. S., & Blackburn, P. R. (1986). Monitoring clinical trials: Conditional or predictive power? *Controlled Clinical Trials, 7,* 8–17.

Spirtes, P., Glymour, C., & Scheines, R. (2000). *Causation, prediction and search* (2nd ed.). Cambridge, MA: MIT Press.

Spirtes, P., Scheines, R., & Glymour, C. (1990a). Reply to comments. *Sociological Methods and Research, 19,* 107–121.

Spirtes, P., Scheines, R., & Glymour, C. (1990b). Simulation studies of the reliability of computer-aided model specification using the TETRAD II, EQS, and LISREL programs. *Sociological Methods and Research, 19,* 3–66.

Spitz, H. H. (1993). Were children randomly assigned in the Perry Preschool Project? *American Psychologist, 48,* 915.

Stadthaus, A. M. (1972). A comparison of the subsequent academic achievement of marginal selectees and rejectees for the Cincinnati public schools special college preparatory program: An application of Campbell's regression discontinuity design (Doctoral dissertation, University of Cincinnati, 1972). *Dissertation Abstracts International, 33*(06), 2825A.

Staines, G. L., McKendrick, K., Perlis, T., Sacks, S., & DeLeon, G. (1999). Sequential assignment and treatment-as-usual: Alternatives to standard experimental designs in field studies of treatment efficacy. *Evaluation Review, 23,* 47–76.

Stake, R. E., & Trumbull, D. J. (1982). Naturalistic generalizations. *Review Journal of Philosophy and Social Science, 7,* 1–12.

Stanley, B., & Sieber, J. E. (Eds.). (1992). *Social research on children and adolescents: Ethical issues*. Newbury Park, CA: Sage.

Stanley, T. D. (1991). "Regression-discontinuity design" by any other name might be less problematic. *Evaluation Review, 15*, 605–624.

Stanley, T. D., & Robinson, A. (1990). Sifting statistical significance from the artifact of regression-discontinuity design. *Evaluation Review, 14*, 166–181.

Stanley, W. D. (1987). Economic migrants or refugees from violence? A time series analysis of Salvadoran migration to the United States. *Latin American Law Review, 12*, 132–154.

Stanton, M. D., & Shadish, W. R. (1997). Outcome, attrition and family-couples treatment for drug abuse: A meta-analysis and review of the controlled, comparative studies. *Psychological Bulletin, 122*, 170–191.

Starfield, B. (1977). Efficacy and effectiveness of primary medical care for children. In *Harvard Child Health Project, Children's medical care needs and treatment: Report of the Harvard Child Health Project*. Cambridge, MA: Ballinger.

Statistical Solutions. (1998). *SOLAS for Missing Data Analysis 1.0* [Computer software]. (Available from Statistical Solutions, 8 South Bank, Crosse's Green, Cork, Ireland)

Steering Committee of the Physicians' Health Study Research Group. (1988). Preliminary report: Findings from the aspirin component of the ongoing physicians' health study. *New England Journal of Medicine, 318*, 271–295.

Stein, M. A., & Test, L. I. (1980). Alternative to mental hospital treatment: I. Conceptual model, treatment program, clinical evaluation. *Archives of General Psychiatry, 37*, 392–397.

Steiner, M. S., & Gingrich, J. R. (2000). Gene therapy for prostate cancer: Where are we now? *Journal of Urology, 164*, 1121–1136.

Stelzl, I. (1986). Changing a causal hypothesis without changing the fit: Some rules for generating equivalent path models. *Multivariate Behavioral Research, 21*, 309–331.

Stevens, S. J. (1994). Common implementation issues in three large-scale social experiments. In K. J. Conrad (Ed.), *Critically evaluating the role of experiments* (pp. 45–53). San Francisco: Jossey-Bass.

Stewart, A. L., Sherbourne, C. D., Wells, K. B., Burnam, M. A., Rogers, W. H., Hays, R. D., & Ware, J. E. (1993). Do depressed patients in different treatment settings have different levels of well-being and functioning? *Journal of Consulting and Clinical Psychology, 61*, 849–857.

Stigler, S. M. (1986). *The history of statistics: The measurement of uncertainty before 1900*. Cambridge, MA, and London, England: Harvard University/Belnap Press.

Stock, W. A. (1994). Systematic coding for research synthesis. In H. Cooper & L. V. Hedges (Eds.), *The handbook of research synthesis* (pp. 126–138). New York: Russell Sage Foundation.

Stolzenberg, R., & Relles, D. (1990). Theory testing in a world of constrained research design: The significance of Heckman's censored sampling bias correction for nonexperimental research. *Sociological Methods and Research, 18*, 395–415.

Stone, R. A., Obrosky, D. S., Singer, D. E., Kapoor, W. N., Fine, M. J., & The Pneumonia Patient Outcomes Research Team (PORT) Investigators. (1995). Propensity score adjustment for pretreatment differences between hospitalized and ambulatory patients with community-acquired pneumonia. *Medical Care, 33* (Suppl.), AS56–AS66.

Stout, R. L., Brown, P. J., Longabaugh, R., & Noel, N. (1996). Determinants of research follow-up participation in an alcohol treatment outcome trial. *Journal of Consulting and Clinical Psychology, 64,* 614–618.

Stromsdorfer, E. W., & Farkas, G. (Eds.). (1980). *Evaluation studies review annual* (Vol. 5). Beverly Hills, CA: Sage.

Stroup, D. F., Berlin, J. A., Morton, S. C., Olkin, I., Williamson, G. D., Rennie, D., Moher, D., Becker, B. J., Sipe, T. A., Thacker, S. B., for the Meta-Analysis of Observational Studies in Epidemiology (MOOSE) Group. (2000). Meta-analysis of observational studies in epidemiology: A proposal for reporting. *Journal of the American Medical Association, 283,* 2008–2012.

Sullivan, C. M., Rumptz, M. H., Campbell, R., Eby, K. K., & Davidson, W. S. (1996). Retaining participants in longitudinal community research: A comprehensive protocol. *Journal of Applied Behavioral Science, 32,* 262–276.

Swanson, H. L., & Sachselee, C. (2000). A meta-analysis of single-subject-design intervention research for students with LD. *Journal of Learning Disabilities, 33,* 114–136.

Tallmadge, G. K., & Horst, D. P. (1976). *A procedural guide for validating achievement gains in educational projects.* (Evaluation in Education Monograph No. 2). Washington, DC: U.S. Department of Health, Education, and Welfare.

Tallmadge, G. K., & Wood, C. T. (1978). *User's guide: ESEA Title I evaluation and reporting system.* Mountain View, CA: RMC Research.

Tamura, R. N., Faries, D. E., Andersen, J. S., & Heiligenstein, J. H. (1994). A case study of an adaptive clinical trial in the treatment of out-patients with depressive disorder. *Journal of the American Statistical Association, 89,* 768–776.

Tan, M., & Xiong, X. (1996). Continuous and group sequential conditional probability ratio tests for Phase II clinical trials. *Statistics in Medicine, 15,* 2037–2051.

Tanaka, J. S., & Huba, G. J. (1984). Confirmatory hierarchical factor analysis of psychological distress measures. *Journal of Personality and Social Psychology, 46,* 621–635.

Tanaka, J. S., Panter, A. T., Winborne, W. C., & Huba, G. J. (1990). Theory testing in personality and social psychology with structural equation models: A primer in 20 questions. In C. Hendrick & M. S. Clark (Eds.), *Research methods in personality and social psychology* (pp. 217–242). Newbury Park, CA: Sage.

Taylor, S. J., & Bogdan, R. (1984). *Introduction to qualitative research methods: The search for meanings.* New York: Wiley.

Taylor, G. J., Rubin, R., Tucker, M., Greene, H. L., Rudikoff, M. D., & Weisfeldt, M. L. (1978). External cardiac compression: A randomized comparison of mechanical and manual techniques. *Journal of the American Medical Association, 240,* 644–646.

Teague, M. L., Bernardo, D. J., & Mapp, H. P. (1995). Farm-level economic analysis incorporating stochastic environmental risk assessment. *American Journal of Agricultural Economics, 77,* 8–19.

Tebes, J. K., Snow, D. L., & Arthur, M. W. (1992). Panel attrition and external validity in the short-term follow-up study of adolescent substance use. *Evaluation Review, 16,* 151–170.

Tesoriero, J. M., Sorin, M. D., Burrows, K. A., & LaChance-McCullough, M. L. (1995). Harnessing the heightened public awareness of celebrity HIV disclosures: "Magic" and "Cookie" Johnson and HIV testing. *AIDS Education and Prevention, 7,* 232–250.

Test, M. A., & Burke, S. S. (1985). Random assignment of chronically mentally ill persons to hospital or community treatment. In R. F. Boruch & W. Wothke (Eds.), *Randomization and field experimentation* (pp. 81–93). San Francisco: Jossey-Bass.

Test, M. A., & Stein, L. I. (1980). Alternative to mental hospital treatment: III. Social cost. *Archives of Geneal Psychiatry, 37,* 409–412.

Tester, K. (1993). *The life and times of post-modernity.* London: Routledge.

Thistlewaite, D. L., & Campbell, D. T. (1960). Regression-discontinuity analysis: An alternative to the ex post facto experiment. *Journal of Educational Psychology, 51,* 309–317.

Thomas, A., Spiegelhalter, D. J., & Gilks, W. R. (1992). BUGS: A program to perform Bayesian inference using Gibbs sampling. In J. M. Bernardo, J. O. Berger, A. P. Dawid, & A. F. M. Smith (Eds.), *Bayesian statistics 4.* Oxford, England: Clarendon Press.

Thomas, G. B. (1997). A program evaluation of the remedial and developmental studies program at Tennessee State University (Doctoral dissertation, Vanderbilt University, 1997). *Dissertation Abstracts International, 58*(08), 3042A.

Thomas, L., & Krebs, C. J. (1997). A review of statistical power analysis software. *Bulletin of the Ecological Society of America, 78,* 128–139.

Thompson, B. (1993). Statistical significance testing in contemporary practice: Some proposed alternatives with comments from journal editors [Special issue]. *Journal of Experimental Education, 61*(4).

Thompson, D. C., Rivara, F. P., & Thompson, R. (2000). Helmets for preventing head and facial injuries in bicyclists (Cochrane Review). *The Cochrane Library,* Issue 3. Oxford, England: Update Software.

Thompson, S. K. (1992). *Sampling.* New York: Wiley.

Tilden, V. P., & Shepherd, P. (1987). Increasing the rate of identification of battered women in an emergency department: Use of a nursing protocol. *Research in Nursing and Health, 10,* 209–215.

Time series database of U.S. and international statistics ready for manipulation. (1992). *Database Searcher, 8,* 27–29.

Tinbergen, J. (1956). *Economic policy principles and design.* Amsterdam: North-Holland.

Tong, H. (1990). *Non-linear time series: A dynamical system approach.* New York: Oxford University Press.

Toulmin, S. E. (1961). *Foresight and understanding: An inquiry into the aims of science.* Bloomington: Indiana University Press.

Tracey, T. J., Sherry, P., & Keitel, M. (1986). Distress and help-seeking as a function of person-environment fit and self-efficacy: A causal model. *American Journal of Community Psychology, 14,* 657–676.

Trend, M. G. (1979). On the reconciliation of qualitative and quantitative analyses: A case study. In T. D. Cook & C. S. Reichardt (Eds.), *Qualitative and quantitative methods in evaluation research* (pp. 68–86). Newbury Park, CA: Sage.

Triplett, N. (1898). The dynamogenic factors in pacemaking and competition. *American Journal of Psychology, 9,* 507–533.

Trochim, W. M. K. (1980). *The regression-discontinuity design in Title I evaluation: Implementation, analysis, and variations.* Unpublished doctoral dissertation, Northwestern University, Evanston, IL.

Trochim, W. M. K. (1984). *Research design for program evaluation: The regression-discontinuity approach.* Newbury Park, CA: Sage.

Trochim, W. M. K. (1985). Pattern matching, validity, and conceptualization in program evaluation. *Evaluation Review, 9,* 575–604.

Trochim, W. M. K. (1990). The regression discontinuity design. In L. Sechrest, E. Perrin, & J. Bunker (Eds.), *Research methodology: Strengthening causal interpretations of nonexperimental data* (pp. 119–140). Rockville, MD: Public Health Service, Agency for Health Care Policy and Research.

Trochim, W. M. K., & Campbell, D. T. (1996). *The regression point displacement design for evaluating community-based pilot programs and demonstration projects.* Unpublished manuscript. (Available from the Department of Policy Analysis and Management, Cornell University, Room N136C, MVR Hall, Ithaca, NY 14853)

Trochim, W. M. K., & Cappelleri, J. C. (1992). Cutoff assignment strategies for enhancing randomized clinical trials. *Controlled Clinical Trials, 13,* 190–212.

Trochim, W. M. K., Cappelleri, J. C., & Reichardt, C. S. (1991). Random measurement error does not bias the treatment effect estimate in the regression-discontinuity design: II. When an interaction effect is present. *Evaluation Review, 15,* 571–604.

Tufte, E. R. (1983). *The visual display of quantitative information.* Cheshire, CT: Graphics Press.

Tufte, E. R. (1990). *Envisioning information.* Cheshire, CT: Graphics Press.

Tukey, J. W. (1991). The philosophy of multiple comparisons. *Statistical Science, 6,* 100–116.

Turpin, R. S., & Sinacore, J. M. (Eds.). (1991). *Multisite evaluations.* San Francisco: Jossey-Bass.

Tversky, A., & Kahneman, D. (1974). Judgment under uncertainty: Heuristics and biases. *Science, 185,* 1124–1131.

Uebel, T. E. (1992). *Overcoming logical positivism from within: The emergence of Neurath's naturalism in the Vienna Circle's protocol sentence debate.* Amsterdam and Atlanta, GA: Editions Rodopi B.V.

Valins, S., & Baum, A. (1973). Residential group size, social interaction, and crowding. *Environment and Behavior, 5,* 421–439.

Varnell, S., Murray, D. M., & Baker, W. L. (in press). An evaluation of analysis options for the one group per condition design: Can any of the alternatives overcome the problems inherent in this design? *Evaluation Review.*

Veatch, R., & Sollitto, S. (1973). Human experimentation: The ethical questions persist. *Hastings Center Report, 3,* 1–3.

Velicer, W. F. (1994). Time series models of individual substance abusers. In L. M. Collins & L. A. Seitz (Eds.), *Advances in data analysis for prevention intervention research* (NIDA Research Monograph No. 142, pp. 264–299). Rockville MD: National Institute on Drug Abuse.

Velicer, W. F., & Harrop, J. (1983). The reliability and accuracy of time series model identification. *Evaluation Review, 7,* 551–560.

Veney, J. E. (1993). Evaluation applications of regression analysis with time-series data. *Evaluation Practice, 14,* 259–274.

Verbeek, M., & Nijman, T. (1992). Testing for selectivity bias in panel data models. *International Economic Review, 33,* 681–703.

Vinokur, A. D., Price, R. H., & Caplan, R. D. (1991). From field experiments to program implementation: Assessing the potential outcomes of an experimental intervention program for unemployed persons. *American Journal of Community Psychology, 19,* 543–562.

Vinovskis, M. A. (1998). *Changing federal strategies for supporting educational research, development and statistics.* Unpublished manuscript, National Educational Research Policy and Priorities Board, U.S. Department of Education.

Virdin, L. M. (1993). *A test of the robustness of estimators that model selection in the nonequivalent control group design.* Unpublished doctoral dissertation, Arizona State University, Tempe.

Vessey, M. P. (1979). Comment. *Journal of Chronic Diseases, 32,* 64–66.

Visser, R. A., & deLeeuw, J. (1984). Maximum likelihood analysis for a generalized regression-discontinuity design. *Journal of Educational Statistics, 9,* 45–60.

Viswesvaran, C., & Schmidt, F. L. (1992). A meta-analytic comparison of the effectiveness of smoking cessation methods. *Journal of Applied Psychology, 77,* 554–561.

Vosniadou, S., & Ortony, A. (1989). Similarity and analogical reasoning: A synthesis. In S. Vosniadou & A. Ortony (Eds.), *Similarity and analogical reasoning* (pp. 1–17). New York: Cambridge University Press.

Wagenaar, A. C., & Holder, H. D. (1991). A change from public to private sale of wine: Results from natural experiments in Iowa and West Virginia. *Journal of Studies on Alcohol, 52,* 162–173.

Wagoner, J. L. (1992). The contribution of group therapy to the successful completion of probation for adult substance abusers. *Dissertation Abstracts International, 53*(03), 724A. (University Microfilms No. AAC92-20873)

Wainer, H. (Ed.). (1986). *Drawing inferences from self-selected samples.* New York: Springer-Verlag.

Wallace, L. W. (1987). *The Community Penalties Act of 1983: An evaluation of the law, its implementation, and its impact in North Carolina.* Unpublished doctoral dissertation, University of Nebraska.

Wallace, P., Cutler, S., & Haines, A. (1988). Randomised controlled trial of general practitioner intervention in patients with excessive alcohol consumption. *British Medical Journal, 297,* 663–668.

Walther, B. J., & Ross, A. S. (1982). The effect on behavior of being in a control group. *Basic and Applied Social Psychology, 3,* 259–266.

Wampler, K. S., & Serovich, J. M. (1996). Meta-analysis in family therapy research. In D. H. Sprenkle & S. M. Moon (Eds.), *Research methods in family therapy* (pp. 286–303). New York: Guilford Press.

Wampold, B. E. (1992). The intensive examination of social interactions. In T. R. Kratochwill & J. R. Levin (Eds.), *Single-case research design and analysis* (pp. 93–131). Hillsdale, NJ: Erlbaum.

Wampold, B. E., & Furlong, M. J. (1981). The heuristics of visual inspection. *Behavioral Assessment, 3,* 79–92.

Wampold, B. E., Mondin, G. W., Moody, M., Stich, F., Benson, K., & Ahn, H. (1997). A meta-analysis of outcome studies comparing bona fide psychotherapies: Empirically, "All must have prizes." *Psychological Bulletin, 122,* 203–215.

Wampold, B. E., & Worsham, N. L. (1986). Randomization tests for multiple-baseline designs. *Behavioral Assessment, 8,* 135–143.

Wang, M. C., & Bushman, B. J. (1998). Using the normal quantile plot to explore meta-analytic data sets. *Psychological Methods, 3,* 46–54.

Wang, M. C., & Bushman, B. J. (1999). *Integrating results through meta-analytic review using SAS software.* Cary, NC: SAS Institute.

Washington v. Davis, 426 U.S. 229 (1976).

Watts, H., & Rees, A.W. (1976). *The New Jersey income-maintenance experiment: Vol. 2. Labor-supply responses.* New York: Academic Press.

Webb, E. J., Campbell, D. T., Schwartz, R. D., & Sechrest, L. (1966). *Unobtrusive measures.* Skokie, IL: Rand McNally.

Webb, E. J., Campbell, D. T., Schwartz, R. D., Sechrest, L., & Grove, J.B. (1981). *Nonreactive measures in the social sciences* (2nd ed.). Boston, MA: Houghton Mifflin.

Webb, J. F., Khazen, R. S., Hanley, W. B., Partington, M. S., Percy, W. J. L., & Rathburn, J. C. (1973). PKU screening: Is it worth it? *Canadian Medical Association Journal, 108,* 328–329.

Weber, S. J., Cook, T. D., & Campbell, D. T. (1971). *The effects of school integration on the academic self-concept of public-school children.* Paper presented at the annual meeting of the Midwestern Psychological Association, Detroit, MI.

Wei, L. J. (1978). An application of an urn model to the design of sequential controlled trials. *Journal of the American Statistical Association, 73,* 559–563.

Wei, W. W. S. (1990). *Time series analysis: Univariate and multivariate methods.* Redwood City, CA: Addison-Wesley.

Weiss, B., Williams, J. H., Margen, S., Abrams, B., Caan, B., Citron, L. J., Cox, C., McKibben, J., Ogar, D., & Schultz, S. (1980). Behavioral responses to artificial food colors. *Science, 207,* 1487–1489.

Weiss, C. H. (1980). Knowledge creep and decision accretion. *Knowledge: Creation, Diffusion, Utilization, 1,* 381–404.

Weiss, C. H. (1988). Evaluation for decisions: Is anybody there? Does anybody care? *Evaluation Practice, 9,* 5–20.

Weiss, C. H. (1998). *Evaluation* (2nd ed.). Upper Saddle River, NJ: Prentice-Hall.

Weiss, C. H., & Bucuvalas, M. J. (1980). *Social science research and decision-making.* New York: Columbia University Press.

Weisz, J. R., Weiss, B., & Donenberg, G. R. (1992). The lab versus the clinic: Effects of child and adolescent psychotherapy. *American Psychologist, 47,* 1578–1585.

Weisz, J. R., Weiss, B., & Langmeyer, D. B. (1987). Giving up on child psychotherapy: Who drops out? *Journal of Consulting and Clinical Psychology, 55,* 916–918.

Welch, W. P., Frank, R. G., & Costello, A. J. (1983). Missing data in psychiatric research: A solution. *Psychological Bulletin, 94,* 177–180.

West, S. G., Aiken, L. S., & Todd, M. (1993). Probing the effects of individual components in multiple component prevention programs. *American Journal of Community Psychology, 21,* 571–605.

West, S. G., Biesanz, J., & Pitts, S. C. (2000). Causal inference and generalization in field settings: Experimental and quasi-experimental designs. In H. T. Reis & C. M. Judd

(Eds.), *Handbook of research methods in social psychology* (pp. 40–84). New York: Cambridge University Press.

West, S. G., Finch, J. F., & Curran, P. J. (1995). Structural equation models with nonnormal variables: Problems and remedies. In R. Hoyle (Ed.), *Structural equation modeling: Issues and applications* (pp. 56–75). Thousand Oaks, CA: Sage.

West, S. G., & Hepworth, J. T. (1991). Statistical issues in the study of temporal data: Daily experiences. *Journal of Personality, 59,* 609–662.

West, S. G., Hepworth, J. T., McCall, M. A., & Reich, J. W. (1989). An evaluation of Arizona's July 1982 drunk driving law: Effects on the City of Phoenix. *Journal of Applied Social Psychology, 19,* 1212–1237.

West, S. G., & Sagarin, B. (2000). Subject selection and loss in randomized experiments. In L. Bickman (Ed.), *Research design: Donald Campell's legacy* (Vol. 2, pp. 117–154). Thousand Oaks, CA: Sage.

Westlake, W. J. (1988). Bioavailability and bioequivalence of pharmaceutical formulations. In K. E. Peace (Ed.), *Biopharmaceutical statistics for drug development* (pp. 329–352). New York: Dekker.

Westmeyer, H. (in press). Explanation in the social sciences. In N. J. Smelser & P. B. Baltes (Eds.), *International encyclopedia of the social and behavioral sciences.* Oxford, England: Elsevier.

White, D. M., Rusch, F. R., Kazdin, A. E., & Hartmann, D. P. (1989). Applications of meta-analysis in individual-subject research. *Behavioral Assessment, 11,* 281–296.

White, H. (1981). Consequences and detection of misspecified nonlinear regression models. *Journal of the American Statistical Association, 76,* 419–433.

White, H. D. (1994). Scientific communication and literature retrieval. In H. Cooper & L. V. Hedges (Eds.), *The handbook of research synthesis* (pp. 41–55). New York: Russell Sage Foundation.

White, L., Tursky, B., & Schwartz, G. E. (Eds.). (1985). *Placebo: Theory, research, and mechanisms.* New York: Guilford Press.

White, P. A. (1990). Ideas about causation in philosophy and psychology. *Psychological Bulletin, 108,* 3–18.

Whittier, J.G. (1989). *The works of John Greenleaf Whittier* (Vol. 1). New York: Houghton Mifflin.

Widom, C. S., Weiler, B. L., & Cottler, L. B. (1999). Childhood victimization and drug abuse: A comparison of prospective and retrospective findings. *Journal of Consulting and Clinical Psychology, 67,* 867–880.

Wilcox, R. R. (1995). ANOVA: A paradigm for low power and misleading measures of effect size? *Review of Educational Research, 65,* 51–77.

Wilcox, R. R. (1996). *Statistics for the social sciences.* New York: Academic Press.

Wilder, C. S. (1972, July). *Physician visits, volume, and interval since last visit, U.S., 1969* (Series 10, No. 75; DHEW Pub. No. HSM 72-1064). Rockville, MD: National Center for Health Statistics.

Wilkinson, L., & the Task Force on Statistical Inference. (1999). Statistical methods in psychology journals: Guidelines and explanations. *American Psychologist, 54,* 594–604.

Willett, J. B. (1988). Questions and answers in the measurement of change. *Review of Research in Education, 15,* 345–422.

Willett, J. B., & Singer, J. D. (1991). From whether to when: New methods for studying student dropout and teacher attrition. *Review of Educational Research, 61,* 407–450.

Williams, S. V. (1990). Regression-discontinuity design in health evaluation. In L. Sechrest, B. Perrin, & J. Bunker (Eds.), *Health services research methodology: Strengthening causal interpretations of nonexperimental data* (DHHS Publication No. PHS 90–3454, pp. 145–149). Rockville, MD: U.S. Department of Health and Human Services.

Willms, J. D. (1992). *Monitoring school performance: A guide for educators.* Washington, DC: The Falmer Press.

Willner, P. (1991). Methods for assessing the validity of animal models of human psychopathology. In A. A. Boulton, G. B. Baker, & M. T. Martin-Iverson (eds.), *Neuromethods* (Vol. 18, pp. 1–23). Clifton, NJ: Humana Press.

Willson, V. L., & Putnam, R. R. (1982). A meta-analysis of pretest sensitization effects in experimental design. *American Educational Research Journal, 19,* 249–258.

Wilson, E. B. (1952). *An introduction to scientific research.* New York: McGraw-Hill.

Wilson, M. C., Hayward, R. S. A., Tunis, S. R., Bass, E. B. & Guyatt, G. (1995). Users' guides to the medical literature: Part 8. How to use clinical practice guidelines. B. What are the recommendations and will they help you in caring for your patients? *Journal of the American Medical Association, 274,* 1630–1632.

Winer, B. J., Brown, D. R., & Michels, K. M. (1991). *Statistical principles in experimental design* (3rd ed.). New York: McGraw-Hill.

Winship, C., & Mare, R. D. (1992). Models for sample selection bias. *Annual Review of Sociology, 18,* 327–350.

Winship, C., & Morgan, S. L. (1999). The estimation of causal effects from observational data. *Annual Review of Sociology, 25,* 659–707.

Winston, A. S. (1990). Robert Sessions Woodworth and the "Columbia Bible": How the psychological experiment was redefined. *American Journal of Psychology, 103,* 391–401.

Winston, A. S., & Blais, D. J. (1996). What counts as an experiment? A transdisciplinary analysis of textbooks, 1930–1970. *American Journal of Psychology, 109,* 599–616.

Winston, P. H., & Horn, B. K. P. (1989). *LISP* (3rd ed.). Reading, MA: Addison-Wesley.

Witte, J. F. (1998). The Milwaukee voucher experiment. *Educational Evaluation and Policy Analysis, 20,* 229–251.

Witte, J. F. (1999). The Milwaukee voucher experiment: The good, the bad, and the ugly. *Phi Delta Kappan, 81,* 59–64.

Witte, J. F. (2000). Selective reading is hardly evidence. *Phi Delta Kappan, 81,* 391.

Wolchik, S. A., West, S. G., Westover, S., Sandler, I. N., Martin, A., Lustig, J., Tein, J.-Y., & Fisher, J. (1993). The Children of Divorce Parenting Intervention: Outcome evaluation of an empirically based program. *American Journal of Community Psychology, 21,* 293–331.

Wolcott, H. F. (1990). On seeking—and rejecting—validity in qualitative research. In E. W. Eisner & A. Peshkin (Eds.), *Qualitative inquiry in education: The continuing debate* (pp. 121–152). New York: Teachers College Press.

Wolf, F. M. (1986). *Meta-analysis: Quantitative methods for research synthesis*. Thousand Oaks, CA: Sage.

Wood, G. (1978). The knew-it-all-along effect. *Journal of Experimental Psychology: Human Perception and Performance, 4*, 345–353.

Woodworth, G. (1994). Managing meta-analytic data bases. In H. Cooper & L. V. Hedges (Eds.), *The handbook of research synthesis* (pp. 177–189). New York: Russell Sage Foundation.

World Medical Association. (2000). Declaration of Helsink: Ethical principles for medical research involving human subjects. *Journal of the American Medical Association, 284*, 3043–3045.

Wortman, C. B., & Rabinowitz, V. C. (1979). Random assignment: The fairest of them all. In L. Sechrest, S. G. West, M. A. Phillips, R. Redner, & W. Yeaton (Eds.), *Evaluation studies review annual* (Vol. 4, pp. 177–184). Beverly Hills, CA: Sage.

Wortman, P. M. (1992). Lessons from the meta-analysis of quasi-experiments. In F. B. Bryant, J. Edwards, R. S. Tindale, E. J. Posavac, L. Heath, E. Henderson, & Y. Suarez-Balcazar (Eds.), *Methodological issues in applied social psychology* (pp. 65–81). New York: Plenum Press.

Wortman, P. M. (1994). Judging research quality. In H. Cooper & L. V. Hedges (Eds.), *The handbook of research synthesis* (pp. 97–109). New York: Russell Sage Foundation.

Wortman, P. M., Reichardt, C. S., & St. Pierre, R. G. (1978). The first year of the education voucher demonstration. *Evaluation Quarterly, 2*, 193–214.

Wortman, P. M., Smyth, J. M., Langenbrunner, J. C., & Yeaton, W. H. (1998). Consensus among experts and research synthesis. *International Journal of Technology Assessment in Health Care, 14*, 109–122.

Wright, S. (1921). Correlation and causation. *Journal of Agricultural Research, 20*, 557–585.

Wright, S. (1934). The method of path coefficients. *Annals of Mathematical Statistics, 5*, 161–215.

Yaremko, R. M., Harari, H., Harrison, R. C., & Lynn, E. (1986). *Handbook of research and quantitative methods in psychology for students and professionals*. Hillsdale, NJ: Erlbaum.

Yeaton, W. H., & Sechrest, L. (1981). Critical dimensions in the choice and maintenance of successful treatments: Strength, integrity, and effectiveness. *Journal of Consulting and Clinical Psychology, 49*, 156–167.

Yeaton, W. H., & Sechrest, L. (1986). Use and misuse of no-difference findings in eliminating threats to validity. *Evaluation Review, 10*, 836–852.

Yeaton, W. H., & Wortman, P. M. (1993). On the reliability of meta-analytic reviews. *Evaluation Review, 17*, 292–309.

Yeaton, W. H., Wortman, P. M., & Langberg, N. (1983). Differential attrition: Estimating the effect of crossovers on the evaluation of a medical technology. *Evaluation Review, 7*, 831–840.

Yinger, J. (1995). *Closed doors, opportunities lost*. New York: Russell Sage Foundation.

Yu, J., & Cooper, H. (1983). A quantitative review of research design effects on response rates to questionnaires. *Journal of Marketing Research, 20*, 36–44.

Zabin, L. S., Hirsch, M. B., & Emerson, M. R. (1989). When urban adolescents choose abortion: Effects on education, psychological status, and subsequent pregnancy. *Family Planning Perspectives, 21,* 248–255.

Zadeh, L. A. (1987). *Fuzzy sets and applications.* New York: Wiley.

Zajonc, R. B., & Markus, H. (1975). Birth order and intellectual development. *Psychological Review, 82,* 74–88.

Zeisel, H. (1973). Reflections on experimental technique in the law. *Journal of Legal Studies, 2,* 107–124.

Zelen, M. (1974). The randomization and stratification of patients to clinical trials. *Journal of Chronic Diseases, 27,* 365–375.

Zelen, M. (1979). A new design for randomized clinical trials? *New England Journal of Medicine, 300,* 1242–1245.

Zelen, M. (1990). Randomized consent designs for clinical trials: An update. *Statistics in Medicine, 9,* 645–656.

Zhu, S. (1999). A method to obtain a randomized control group where it seems impossible. *Evaluation Review, 23,* 363–377.

Zigler, E., & Weikart, D. P. (1993). Reply to Spitz's comments. *American Psychologist, 48,* 915–916.

Zigulich, J. A. (1977). *A comparison of elementary school environments: Magnet schools versus traditional schools.* Unpublished doctoral dissertation, Northwestern University, Evanston, IL.

Zucker, D. M., Lakatos, E., Webber, L. S., Murray, D. M., McKinlay, S. M., Feldman, H. A., Kelder, S. H., & Nader, P. R. (1995). Statistical design of the child and adolescent trial for cardiovascular health (CATCH): Implications of cluster randomization. *Controlled Clinical Trials, 16,* 96–118.

Name Index

Subject Index

D

Data
  analyzing, from designs with nonequivalent groups, 161–70
  imputing values for missing, 337
Debriefing, 325, 506
Deep similarity, 368
Definitional operationalism, 68
Deflationism, 35*n*, 506
Delayed causation, 197–98
Delayed effects, 173, 178
Demand outstripping supply, 269–70
Dependent variables, 13, 507
  nonequivalent, 184–88
Description, causal, 9–12
Descriptive causation, 10, 98
  objections to, 465–66
Desideratum, 97
Design elements, 18, 507
Designs without control groups, 106–15
  improving, by constructing contrasts other than with independent control groups, 125–28
Directed programs of experiments, 420–21
Direct measurement, 150–51
  of threats to validity, 148
Direct paths, 396, 507
Disaggregated groups, lack of statistical power for studying, 455
Discontinuity, defined, 207
Discontinuous effect, 173
Discriminant validity, 350, 364, 507
Discrimination
  making, 25, 353–54
    construct validity and, 364–65
    external validity and, 365–66
    meta-analysis and, 440–42
    purposive sampling and, 382–83

objections concerning, between construct validity and external validity, 466–73
Dismantling study, 262, 507
Disordinal interactions, 265*n*
Disruption effects as threat to construct validity, 79
Disturbances, 399
Domain of intended application, 81
Dose-response designs, 285
Dose-response relationship, 285, 352
Double-blind study, 190, 441, 507
Double pretest, 145–46
  improving one-group pretest-posttest design with, 110
  untreated control group with, and independent and dependent samples, 154–56
Dropouts, replacing, 334

E

Ecological validity, 37*n*
Effect(s), 5–6
  defined, 4
  delayed, 178
  describing types of, 172–73
  formal sampling of, 344–46
  weak, 178
Effectiveness, 319, 507
Effectiveness studies, treatment implementation in, 319
Effect sizes, 507
  bias in computing, 449
  failure to test for heterogeneity in, 455
  failure to weight study level, proportional to their precision, 449–50
  lack of statistical independence among, 449
Efficacy studies, 507
  treatment implementation in, 319
Endogenous variables, 394, 507

Enhancement models, 415
Epistemological criticisms of experiments, 459–61
Epistemological relativism, 28
Epistemology, 456, 507
  implications for, 29–31
Equivalent-time-samples design, 270–71
Error rate problem, fishing and, 48–49
Errors
  measurement, 401–2, 412
  random, 58
  sampling, 34
  specification, 251, 402–2, 412
  Type I, 42, 43, 48, 108
    rates of, 45–46, 49
  Type II, 42, 48
    rates of, 46
ESTIMATE, 336, 337
Ethics
  codes and principles in, 281–82
  defined, 279
  discontinuing experiments for reasons of, 289–90
  of experimentation, 281–83
  of random assignment, 286–89
  of withholding potentially effective treatment, 283–86
Ethnography, 390, 507
Evaluative theories of truth, 36
Even Start Literacy Program, 104
Excel, 296, 313
Exogenous variable, 394, 504, 507
Expectation, 164, 507
  equating groups on, 250–51
Experiment(s), 2, 507. *See also* Quasi-experiment(s); Randomized experiment(s)
  analogue, 8
  causation and, 3–12, 457–62